The Belvedere: 300 Years a Venue for Art

The Belvedere

300 Years a Venue for Art

belvedere

DE GRUYTER

Editors:
Stella Rollig and Christian Huemer

With contributions from:
Johanna Aufreiter, Björn Blauensteiner, Brigitte Borchhardt-Birbaumer, Thomas DaCosta Kaufmann, Christiane Erharter, Nora Fischer, Anna Frasca-Rath, Antoinette Friedenthal, Martin Fritz, Thomas W. Gaehtgens, Sabine Grabner, Katinka Gratzer-Baumgärtner, Cäcilia Henrichs, Alice Hoppe-Harnoncourt, Christian Huemer, Georg Lechner, Stefan Lehner, Gernot Mayer, Monika Mayer, Sabine Plakolm-Forsthuber, Georg Plattner, Matthew Rampley, Luise Reitstätter, Stella Rollig, Claudia Slanar, Franz Smola, Nora Sternfeld, Silvia Tammaro, Wolfgang Ullrich, Leonhard Weidinger, Christian Witt-Dörring, Luisa Ziaja, Christoph Zuschlag

Contents

Chapter I
Prince Eugene of Savoy
as an Impresario of Art
1697–1736

Chapter II
The Imperial Collections in the Belvedere
1776–1891

Chapter III
From the Modern Gallery to the Austrian Gallery
1903–1938

Chapter IV
The Museum during the Nazi Period 1938–1945

Chapter V
Changes and Continuities
After 1945

Perspectives
2023

Appendices

STELLA ROLLIG —
Foreword

"Work for life," Aleksandr Rodchenko told artists in his *Slogans* in 1920, "not for palaces, cathedrals, cemeteries, and museums." Similarly, albeit coming from the opposite political spectrum, the *Futurist Manifesto* proclaimed: "We intend to destroy museums."

To this day, museums are battling to escape the accusation that they are elitist, exclusive, and hopelessly old-fashioned, tombs to the past. During the course of the twentieth century, they therefore evolved into venues for the presentation and ultimately the production of contemporary art, offering not only the space but also the means for fostering the sustained development of new art, from performance to installations and participative projects. They designed accessible exhibitions, education programs, children's activities, discussion forums, and neighborhood groups, and organized concerts and parties. This is true of the Belvedere and of hundreds, if not thousands, of art museums worldwide. They are vibrant and full of life.

What distinguishes the Belvedere from most of the others is the length of its existence: three hundred years. In 2023 we celebrate the anniversary of the completion of the Upper Belvedere—an art venue from the outset thanks to its founder Prince Eugene of Savoy. In 1777, under Empress Maria Theresa, it became one of the first publicly accessible museums in Europe. (The Uffizi in Florence, for example, had opened to the public only a few years earlier, in 1769.) As a result of this legacy, the Belvedere not only offers a magnificent historical setting, but also provides a museum environment that works—one might even say has a duty to work—in the awareness of this impressive three-hundred-year tradition. Against the background of epochal developments and events, its activities have been continually influenced by the museological discourse and perceptions of its time. From a historical perspective, all of the changes it has undergone have been evolutionary and rarely radical. The collection, conservation, investigation, and communication of artworks has always been at the heart of its identity and mission. Its core domains of "art, research, education" were recently confirmed in an internal process.

However, this does not mean that the museum is simply treading water. We are constantly developing all manner of new ideas and concepts. Innovative exhibition formats are being devised, and the history of the collection, including the museum's responsibility and complicity during the Nazi period, continues to be uncovered. A public program encourages *Joint Ventures* (as the compelling title suggests). The new ICOM (International Council of Museums) museum definition, arrived at in 2022 after long and contentious discussions, makes inclusion, accessibility, diversity, and sustainability non-negotiable characteristics of a museum. This is nothing new for the Belvedere team. The COVID-19 pandemic, whose outbreak in 2020 sent a shockwave of health, social, and not least financial devastation through the museum world—the extent of which we will no doubt find difficult to imagine in a few years time—the alarming climate crisis, wars, civil unrest, economic upheavals, and the intrusion of tech giants and the digital industry into all areas of life, with the enormous psychological impact this has… all of this has left its mark and is changing the work of museums. At its core, however, this work still has a permanence and a duty not only to the cultural heritage in its care, but also to the most human need for an existence rooted in the past in order to conceive a viable future. This idea is reflected in the logo for the anniversary year, designed by Belvedere art director Paul Mayer, which adds roots to the palace and turns it dynamically on its head (→ p. 398). An interim review of what has been achieved in the first three hundred years could be summed up with the words of the Prince of Salina in *The Leopard* by Guiseppe Tomasi di Lampedusa: "If we want things to stay as they are, things will have to change."

The anniversary year provides us with an occasion and also an incentive to organize unusual exhibitions and events, make infrastructural changes, and, not least, to produce this book. We are declaring a "Golden Spring," a radiant year of optimism, commonality, and enjoyment. People still celebrate even in challenging times so as to gain strength to overcome the difficulties. We are celebrating the artists: For a whole year, the Belvedere 21 will be communicating the visions and energy of contemporary art made in Austria. The Lower Belvedere is devoting an exhibition on a scale hitherto unseen in Europe to the bold, profoundly existential, stirringly beautiful life's work of Louise Bourgeois, one of the greatest artists of the twentieth century, starting with her early paintings. A completely new interpretation of Gustav Klimt places him in the stylistic history of international Modernism, thereby revising the entrenched art-historical profiling of him as a solitarily Viennese phenomenon. The result can be seen in an exhibition entitled *Klimt: Inspired by Van Gogh, Rodin, Matisse…* In the Orangery, *The Belvedere: 300 Years a Venue for Art* presents works from the museum's holdings and archive, offering an insight into the eventful history of the museum and its art collections (→ p. 310).

And, as if that were not enough, our exuberance in this anniversary year has inspired us to initiate two major projects. The first is an exhibition of contemporary sculptures and installations throughout the entire grounds of the Belvedere, from the Privy Garden next to the Lower Belvedere to the gardens of the Belvedere 21. *Public Matters*, a deliberately ambiguous title, brings together some thirty works by international artists in the Baroque garden of the Upper Belvedere and as far as the modern setting of the Schweizergarten with Karl Schwanzer's pavilion. The exhibition features items from the collection, loaned objects, and commissioned works, creating a diverse narrative about the location and its history—outdoors and free of charge. For the Upper Belvedere, the entire curatorial team has worked together on a complete redisplay of the collection. Here, too, it is the artists who are the focus. How does an era shape its art? How do artists respond to upheavals and crises while themselves being part of social developments? A chronological tour of some four hundred works, many being shown for the first time, takes visitors through eight hundred years of artistic production, from Romanesque art to the 1970s.

How can we make this magnificent Baroque building—designed to overwhelm and demonstrate political power and artistic refinement—more comfortable for today's visitors? Where can our visitors rest their weary legs, browse a catalogue, send a WhatsApp message? We have commissioned the artist Sascha Reichstein to design a lounge on the ground floor. We have repainted, repaired chipped edges and corners, and refreshed the gilt ornamentation across three floors. We are also becoming more "green." Since 2021, we have been holders of the Austrian eco-label. The ongoing replacement of all windows in the Upper Belvedere will help us save energy in the long term. A solar energy installation is planned for the flat roof of the Belvedere 21.

Digital communication is being continuously improved. Strategic decisions have been taken and implemented with respect to open science, knowledge sharing, und open content. The rapid development of Web 3.0, mixed reality applications, and the metaverse are major themes for the museum, in which analogue and digital experience will very soon be merging as a matter of course.

Three hundred years and so much future to feel excited about! I am eternally grateful to all of my predecessors who have headed this incomparably beautiful and rich museum (→ pp. 369–73) for making the Belvedere into a beacon in the European cultural landscape that radiates out into the world. My heartfelt thanks go also to the entire Belvedere team for their enthusiasm and the inexhaustible and infectious energy they invest into the museum, not only in this anniversary year. I should also like to mention just one colleague by name: Christian Huemer, head of the Belvedere Research Center, who designed and co-published this book with me.

So much will change in order for things to stay as they are.

Acknowledgments

A comprehensive and complex publication such as this one cannot be realized without the expertise and dedication of a large number of contributors. The concept arose from a cooperative process in which the authors of the longer texts did not simply deliver a commissioned piece of work, but over the course of three workshops engaged in an intensive exchange of ideas.

We would especially like to thank the following for their time and inspiring contributions to the discussions: Brigitte Borchhardt-Birbaumer, Nora Fischer, Antoinette Friedenthal, Martin Fritz, Thomas W. Gaehtgens, Sabine Grabner, Cäcilia Henrichs, Alice Hoppe-Harnoncourt, Georg Lechner, Gernot Mayer, Monika Mayer, Matthew Rampley, Nora Sternfeld, Silvia Tammaro, Luisa Ziaja, and Christoph Zuschlag. Advice and support were also provided at the outset by Gudrun Swoboda and Beatrice von Bismarck. We would also like to thank all the other authors for their contributions: Johanna Aufreiter, Björn Blauensteiner, Thomas DaCosta Kaufmann, Christiane Erharter, Anna Frasca-Rath, Katinka Gratzer-Baumgärtner, Stefan Lehner, Sabine Plakolm-Forsthuber, Georg Plattner, Luise Reitstätter, Claudia Slanar, Franz Smola, Wolfgang Ullrich, Leonhard Weidinger, and Christian Witt-Dörring. Maximilian Kaiser created the visualizations of the collection contents in the appendix. Although the anniversary exhibition and the anniversary publication were conceived separately, the simple fact of overlaps in personnel resulted in creative sparks in both directions. We therefore wish to acknowledge Alexander Klee, the one colleague from the exhibition curatorial team who has not yet been mentioned.

Our thanks also go to all our colleagues at the Belvedere and other institutions for their assistance in sourcing literature, documents, and images: Anna Blau, Bettina Bosin, Delphine Burghgraeve, Nikolaus Domes, Gianmaria Gava, Nicole Gyürü, Michael Huey, Alice Hundsdorfer-Zhou, Adolf Krischanitz, Sarah Kronschläger, Stefan Mach, Thomas Matyk, Ouriel Morgensztern, Carmen Müller, Gerald Piffl, Lorenz Seidler, Johannes Stoll, Wolfgang Thaler, Alexandra Travnicek-Grünvald, Natascha Unkart, Katharina Wallerits, Caroline Wedam, Eva Würdinger. Particularly painstaking was the work involved in researching and selecting the visitor comments through the ages, which was completed by Cäcilia Henrichs, Silvia Tammaro, Monika Mayer, Caroline Wedam,

Katinka Gratzer-Baumgärtner, and Georg Lechner. Franz Gschwandtner assisted us in rediscovering Prince Eugene's library cabinets in the Theresianum.

The complex editorial process involved in producing this book in two languages also required a large team, whose efforts need to be expressly acknowledged. First and foremost, Monika Mayer deserves special mention, who, as our institutional memory, commented on, corrected, and added to many of the texts. For individual chapters this task was completed by the curators Georg Lechner, Sabine Grabner, Luisa Ziaja in addition to Anna-Marie Kroupová and Stefan Lehner from the Research Center. We thank Betti Moser for the precise and conscientious copy-editing of the English edition, and Katharina Sacken for copy-editing the German edition and for compiling the comprehensive bibliography. Jutta Mühlenberg gave great support by preparing a detailed index of persons for both language editions. The professional translations were provided by Rebecca Law, Wilfried Prantner, Nick Somers, Sarah Swift, and Jessica West. The sophisticated and engaging graphic design was created by Marie Artaker; Kevin Mitrega was responsible for the accurate typesetting and microtypography. Dominik Strzelec helped to adapt the architectural drawings for the embossed cover. Manfred Kostal from Pixelstorm did a wonderful job preparing the images for printing, including a great deal of retouching. We were able to consult Reinhard Gugler on a number of specialist questions concerning embossing, paper selection, index tab cutting, foldouts, and much more besides. Katharina Holas from the publishers supervised the project with great enthusiasm. We would like to thank everyone for their patience and professional assistance.

All these threads came together under the expert eye of Eva Lahnsteiner, who coordinated the smooth production of the book with skill, care, and nerves of steel, while also contributing significantly with editorial refinements to the content. The success of this publication is fundamentally down to her. She was supported by Beba Pikall-Kotyza. Many thanks to everybody involved!

Stella Rollig, Christian Huemer

CHRISTIAN HUEMER — Introduction

The concept of a museum and its role in society is subject to constant reappraisal. After a worldwide museum boom lasting decades, ICOM (International Council of Museums) adopted a new museum definition in Prague on August 24, 2022, the outcome of an intense discussion process. For a long time, museums were regarded essentially as not-for-profit institutions that collected, conserved, researched, communicated, and exhibited the tangible and intangible heritage of mankind and its environment. By contrast, the new ICOM interpretation emphasizes their sociopolitical function and urges them to see themselves as democratizing, inclusive, and multifaceted spaces for critical dialogue about the past and future: "Open to the public, accessible and inclusive, museums foster diversity and sustainability. They operate and communicate ethically, professionally and with the participation of communities, offering varied experiences for education, enjoyment, reflection and knowledge sharing."[1] All of these values are also to be found in the Belvedere mission statement "A museum that matters."

The Belvedere in Vienna provides a good illustration of the change in the perception of museums in Europe over the past three centuries. The garden palace completed in 1723 was not originally intended as a museum. Prince Eugene of Savoy commissioned the architect Johann Lucas von Hildebrand to design a palace that would reflect his prestige as a prince. Yet the "suitability of the building" for art-historical presentation was quickly recognized by Christian von Mechel, as one of its earliest curators: "This pleasure palace, built originally by the immortal Eugene simply for his enjoyment and as a summer residence, [...] proved so convenient for this purpose through its internal room arrangement and high ceilings that one might be led to believe the hero may have had the intention from the outset to build a temple to art."[2] Prince Eugene commissioned Italian star painters, such as Francesco Solimena, Carlo Innocenzo Carlone, and Giacomo del Pò, to design the interior of this unique ensemble. The painting collection, most of which was transferred to Turin after Eugene's death (→ pp. 62–63), was one of the most impressive in Vienna. Its drawings

1 https://icom.museum/en/resources/standards-guidelines/museum-definition/ (accessed on March 31, 2023).

2 Mechel 1783, p. IX.

and prints now form an important part of the Albertina's holdings (→ p. 71), and the treasures of the Bibliotheca Eugeniana adorn the center oval of the State Hall in the Austrian National Library.

The birth of the public art museum was not a result of the French Revolution, as is often assumed. In chronological terms alone, the Louvre, which did not open until 1793, lagged behind other museums internationally. The idea of the independent artist, unattached to a guild, and of an art museum open to the public was in fact the result of considerations at court. In Vienna, Maria Theresa took the decision in 1776 to transfer the Imperial Picture Gallery from the Hofburg to the Upper Belvedere and to make it accessible to the general public. The rational arrangement by schools devised by Mechel (→ p. 82), who was commissioned for the reorganization by Emperor Joseph II, had a clear educational purpose that was not only adopted by many museums in other countries but also had a significant influence on the early development of art history as an academic discipline. Furthermore, it has been convincingly argued that the sequence of rooms in Baroque palaces like the Belvedere ultimately continued to inform the historical narrative right up to the era of Modernism. Instead of new, purpose-built edifices, castles and palaces were used as museums throughout Europe, and the state-run Modern Gallery in the Belvedere, originally a temporary solution, became permanent (→ p. 153).

Although the imperial collection also contained works by living artists, the Modern Gallery was established in the Lower Belvedere in 1903 at the instigation of the Secessionists and with support from Emperor Franz Joseph I. The museumification of the avant-garde was the order of the day. The presentation of Austrian art in an international context, as the founding mission stated, still guides the Belvedere's agenda today. In this book we address the museum's involvement in Nazi cultural policy and also the halting attempts after World War II to reconnect with the international avant-garde. Recent decades have been marked by the contrasting objectives of democratization on the one hand and commercialization of museum operations on the other, of critical questioning of the present versus meeting tourist expectations.

Narrating the 300-year history of the Belvedere in 300 pages and exhibiting it in an area of 300 square meters proved so much of a challenge that the current exhibition in the Orangery in fact occupies 354 square meters (→ p. 310) and this book has grown to 398 pages. Even so, the art of deciding what to omit had to be employed—which is why historical events for which the Belvedere merely provided a decorative backdrop are mentioned only in passing. For example, the grandiose masked ball at the Belvedere on April 17, 1770, to celebrate the marriage of Marie Antoinette and the future king of France Louis XVI, the use of the Upper Belvedere as a residence by heir apparent Archduke Franz Ferdinand and his family (1898–1914), or even an event of such significance for Austria's identity as the signing of the State Treaty in the Marble Hall on October 15, 1955, are listed only in the appendix (→ pp. 368–73).

Here is not the place to even touch on the literature, which has grown exponentially in the past five decades, about the museum as an institution. Apart from the numerous specialized studies of individual museums or particular aspects, research in recent years has also produced several comparative surveys, including Bénédicte Savoy, *Tempel der Kunst: Die Geburt des öffentlichen Museums in Deutschland 1701–1815* (2006), Carole Paul, *The First Modern Museums of Art: The Birth of an Institution in 18th- and Early 19th-Century Europe* (2012), or Matthew Rampley, *The Museum Age in Austria-Hungary: Art and Empire in the Long Nineteenth Century* (2020).[3] There have also been two books devoted specifically to the history of the Belvedere. *Das Belvedere: Genese eines Museums* (2011) describes its development up to 1900 (the planned second volume was never published), while *Das Museum: Spiegel und Motor kulturpolitischer Visionen* (2003) contains conference proceedings and was published to mark the centenary of the Modern Gallery's existence.[4]

This publication is not a Festschrift like the one published by the Städel Museum to mark its 200th anniversary in 2015. Nor did we want to write our history in-house. Instead, we sought a critical perspective from the outside by involving external experts. The idea of presenting a history of the collection, as was done to mark the bicentenary of the Museo del Prado (2019) or the 150th anniversary of the Metropolitan Museum of Art (2020), was rejected because the history of the museum's holdings goes back only to the early days of the Modern Gallery in the late nineteenth century.[5] In its place, there are a number of visualizations of the current collection contents in the appendix (→ pp. 374–77). It quickly became apparent to us that the focus should be not so much on the works as on the museum's visitors. The approach developed by Jürgen Habermas in his theory on the structural transformation of the public sphere (representational—bourgeois—digital), although initially promising, turned out to be too restrictive to work with. Ultimately, the content, structure, and methodology of the book were arrived at in three workshops with the active involvement of the authors of the lengthier contributions. This format enabled us to identify common issues and to avoid thematic overlaps to a large extent. The idea was to present individual narrative strands and lines of discussion that would clearly transcend different eras, even though the book eventually ended up containing contributions from a total of thirty-three authors. While it was never really our aim to produce a large unbroken narrative as if written by one person, we wanted to offer more than a collection of unconnected essays, but create a book that was deliberately collage-like, fragmentary, and multifaceted.

3 Paul 2012; Savoy 2006; Rampley/Prokopovych/Veszprémi 2020. For a discussion of European collection culture around 1800, see also the seminal publication by Swoboda 2013a.

4 Husslein-Arco/Schoeller 2011; Frodl/Kräutler 2004.

5 Städel Museum 2015; Portús 2019; Bayer/Corey 2020.

The concept was devised in the workshops, and the four central terms—collecting, arranging, showing, opening—have been strikingly conveyed by Marie Artaker in the design of the book. The structure of the publication in five chapters is immediately visible from the book exterior, not least as each chapter starts with a foldout page in "Timid Grey," containing thumbnails of the chapter's illustrations arranged in rows in the style of St. Petersburg or salon hanging and numbered in large print—a graphic element that museum visitors will recognize from exhibition guides showing the location of works. Often facing views of the different rooms in the Belvedere and printed in a large font, visitor comments over the years draw the reader's attention to these short and incisive statements as they browse through the book. Text boxes are positioned as stand-alone elements in the layout, liberally arranged within chapters and on pages that are shorter than the rest of the book. They thus evoke the sensation of discovering an interesting document in an archive. All articles contain numerous cross-references, inviting the reader to seek out further information, as if following hyperlinks. The collage-like concept and multiple perspectives are also reflected in the variety of typefaces and font sizes, from curly initial capitals to sans-serif lettering, all inspired by Salomon Kleiner's engravings. Even the palace's Baroque architecture is reflected in the design: the color scheme is based on the pastel tones of one of the ceiling paintings in the Lower Belvedere.

We hope you will enjoy browsing this book and will gain new insights while reading it.

Chapter I

Prince Eugene of Savoy as an Impresario of Art

1697–1736

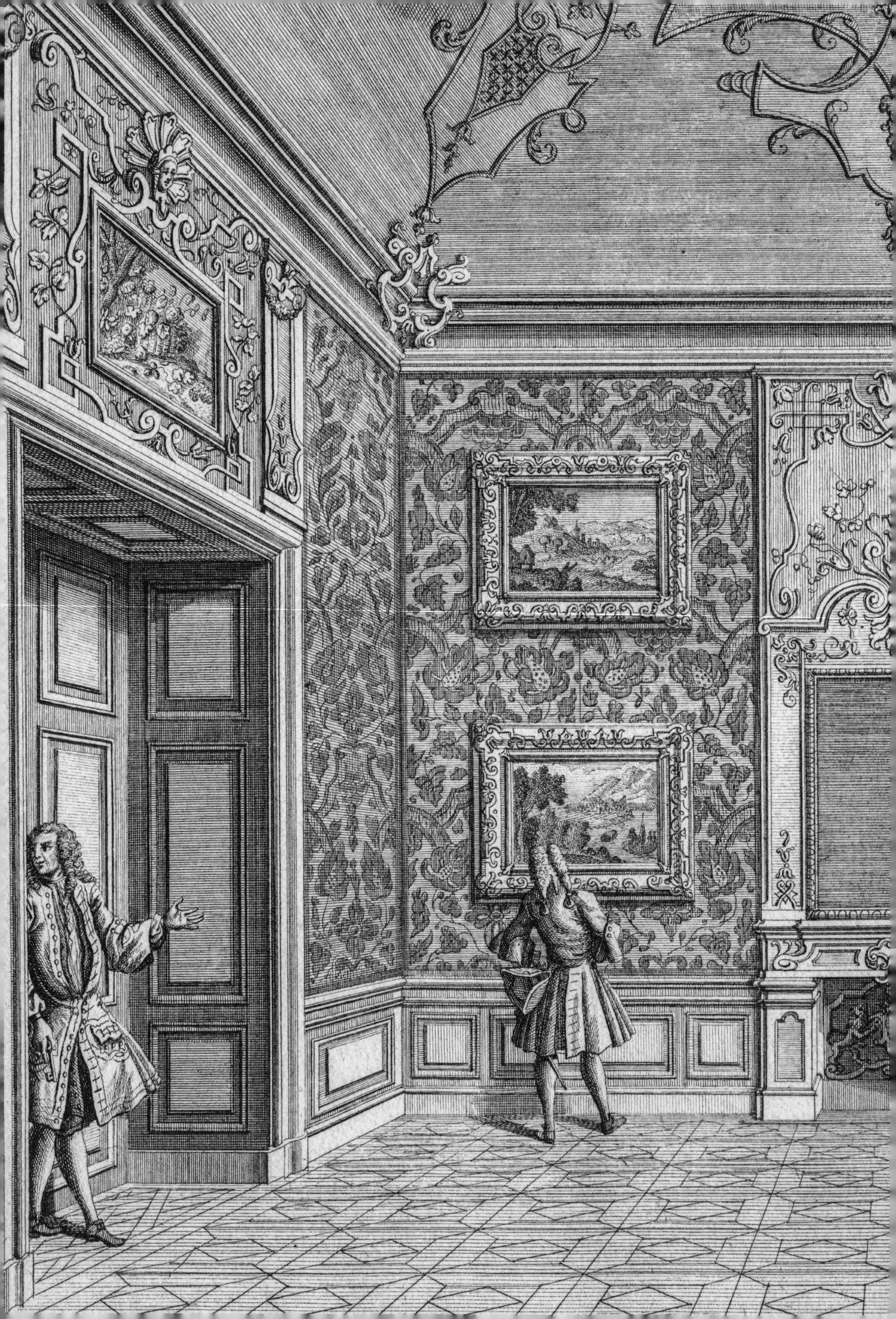

Chapter I
Prince Eugene of Savoy
as an Impresario of Art

1697–1736

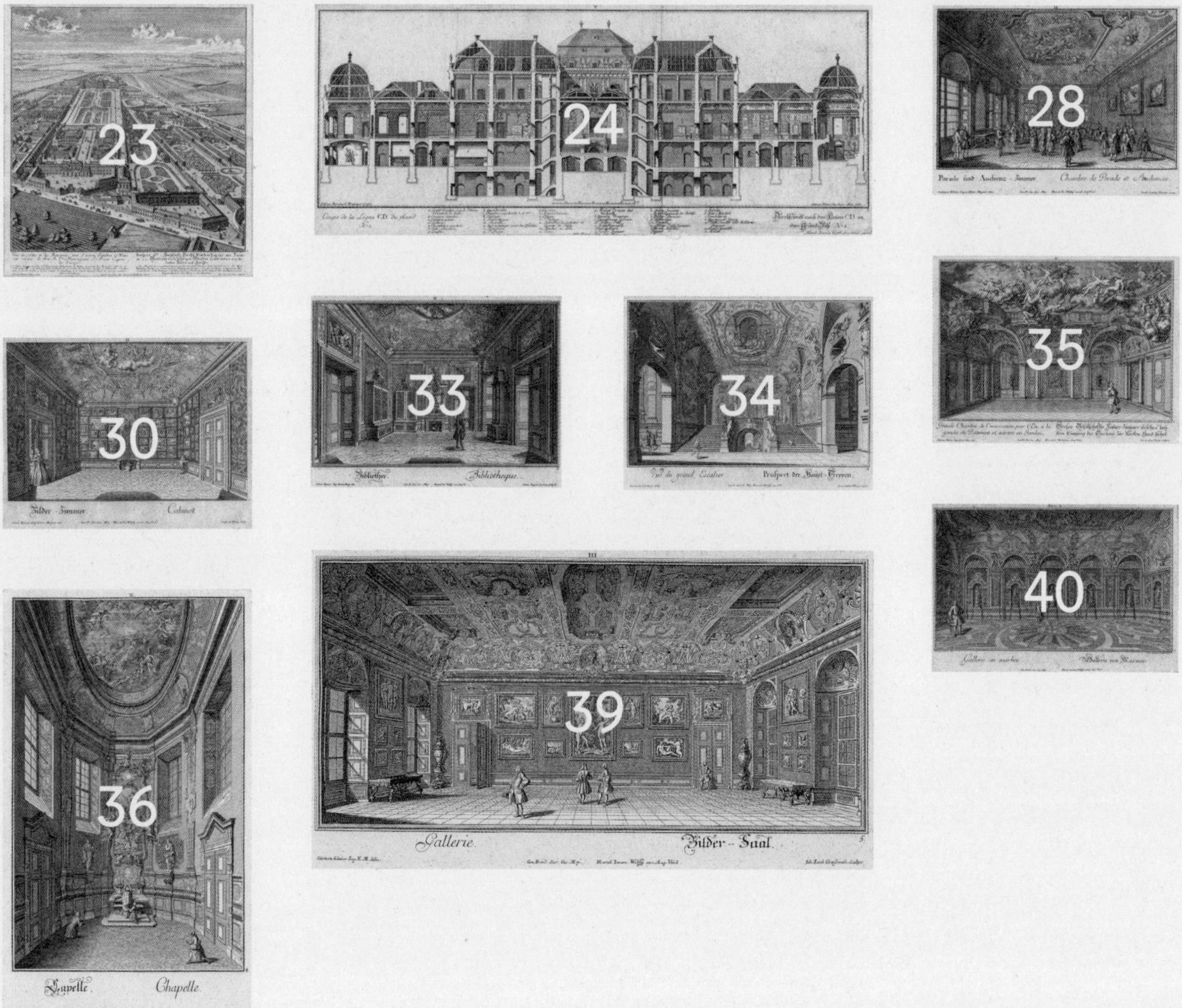

←
Johann August Corvinus after Salomon Kleiner, *Picture Cabinet in the Lower Belvedere* (detail), 1740, Belvedere Library, Vienna

The Palaces of the Suburbs are infinitely more grand than those of the City, and they have both Court-yards and Gardens. The most noble are the Palaces of Trautsheim, Rofrano, Schwartzenberg, Altheim, and Eugene of Savoy. This last especially is a superb Structure with magnificent Gardens, a fine Orangery, and a Menagery stor'd with the most uncommon Creatures that the four Parts of the World can furnish. 'Tis in this fine great House that Prince Eugene passes the beautiful Season of the Year. There is not so fine a Sight as an Assembly at this Prince's House, for not only the outer Court, in which there's a fine Piece of Water, but the Gardens are illuminated by an infinite Number of Lanthorns made in form of a Bowl of extraordinary white Glass, which cast a very great Light and make a glorious appearance.

—— Carl Ludwig von Pöllnitz, *The Memoirs of Charles-Lewis, Baron de Pollnitz. Being the Observations he made in his late Travels from Prussia thro' Germany, Italy, France, Flanders, Holland, England, etc. in Letters to his Friend* (London, 1739), p. 237.

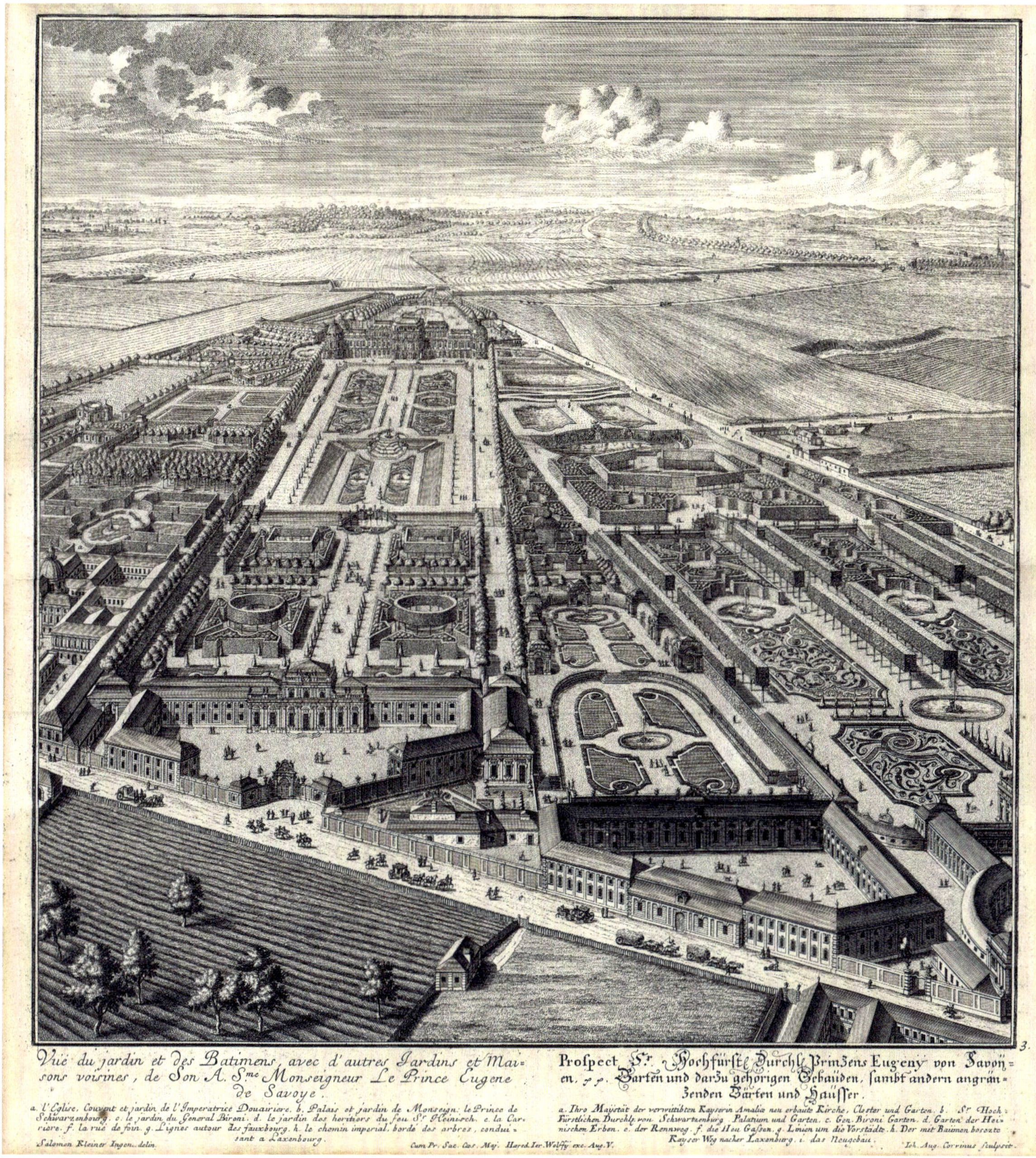

Prospect of Prince Eugene's Gardens and the Adjoining Gardens of the Salesian Convent and Palais Schwarzenberg (so-called Bird's-Eye View), 1731

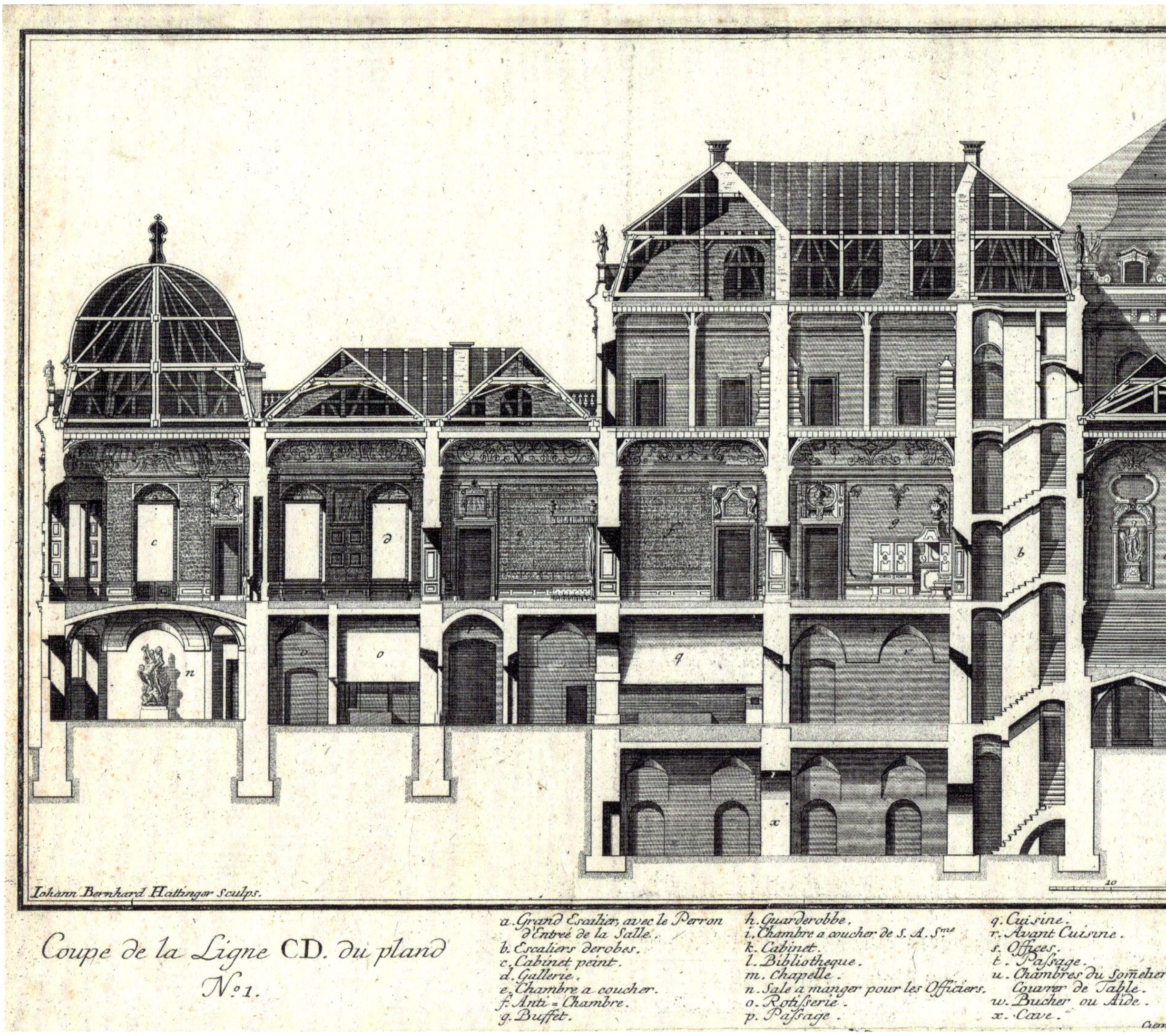

Longitudinal Section of the Upper Belvedere Viewed from the Cour d'Honneur, 1736

1

The Belvedere: Construction and Interiors

Georg Lechner

In 1697, Prince Eugene of Savoy started acquiring plots of land on Rennweg and initially commissioned extensive groundworks. Dominique Girard was subsequently placed in charge of designing the gardens, while the two palaces and their annexes were created by Johann Lucas von Hildebrandt (→ p. 23). Based on his plans, the Lower Belvedere was built between 1712 and 1717, followed by construction of the Upper Belvedere from 1717 to 1723. After Prince Eugene's death, the entire estate was inherited by his niece, Princess Victoria of Savoy. In 1752 she sold the Belvedere and the Winter Palace on Himmelpfortgasse (→ p. 49, ④) to the monarch, Maria Theresa. Thus it became imperial and, eventually, public property.

Both the gardens and the palaces were lavishly furnished and decorated to reflect the interests of their owner (→ p. 24). The orangeries next to the Lower Belvedere housed a multitude of exotic plants, which were greatly admired. Prince Eugene devoted particular attention to the construction of his aviary and menagerie, which he filled with birds and animals often acquired with the help of international connections the successful general had gained during his military career. Some of the garden sculptures, as well as the upper and lower cascade—which originally had its own separate water main—have survived to this day.

At the heart of the Lower Belvedere is the *corps de logis* with its central Marble Hall, preserved in all its original splendor. The hall is adorned with a ceiling fresco by Martino Altomonte, depicting Apollo in his sun chariot as the leader of the Muses, an allusion to Prince Eugene's art-loving side (→ p. 51, fig. 2). Further state rooms are located in the palace's west wing: the Hall of Grotesques, the Marble Gallery, and, finally, the Gold Cabinet, the sumptuous décor of which was added later, under Maria Theresa.

Originally entered from the mezzanine floor to the south, several rooms in the Upper Belvedere have also been passed down to us in their initial design. On the bel étage, we again encounter a breathtaking Marble Hall with a ceiling fresco by Carlo Innocenzo Carlone, exalting the eternal glory of Prince Eugene accompanied by the princely virtues. Carlone also painted the frescoes in the hall named after him that adjoins the Sala Terrena (→ p. 35), as well as in the Palace Chapel. The latter has been preserved in its original appearance, complete with an altarpiece by Francesco Solimena depicting the Resurrection of Christ, a masterpiece of Neapolitan Baroque painting (→ p. 36).

2

The Set of Engravings *Residences Memorables*

Silvia Tammaro

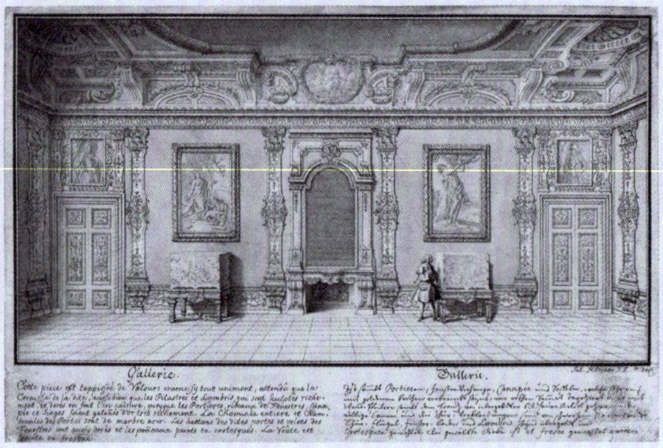

1

From 1720, Salomon Kleiner resided in Vienna, where he worked on a commission for the Augsburg-based art publishers Johann Andreas Pfeffel and Jeremias Wolff. He had been asked to draw the city's greatest squares, palaces, churches, and secular buildings for the later publication of a set of engravings showing views of Vienna. In the ensuing years, the artist also produced drawings of palaces for the Elector and Prince-Bishop Lothar Franz von Schönborn as well as for his nephew, Imperial Vice-Chancellor Friedrich Karl von Schönborn, which were also later engraved. Probably inspired by the Schönborn family's patronage, Prince Eugene commissioned Salomon Kleiner to create a set of engravings depicting his garden palace on Rennweg.

The realization of Prince Eugene's engravings was presumably similar to the production of the prints for the Schönborn family: The patron paid for the drawings, while publication costs were borne by the publisher. Eugene thus secured a prestigious suite of prints depicting his palaces, which, at the same time, was a profitable product for the publisher, catering to an international audience of collectors, bibliophiles, and art lovers. The series of engravings showing Prince Eugene's garden palace was published from 1731 through to 1741 in ten independent instalments. The 114 plates show the interior and the collection as documented by Salomon Kleiner in 1729/30 (→ pp. 23–43). Original plans envisaged depicting the prince's city palace, too, as some of Kleiner's surviving preliminary drawings document (→ p. 70, fig. 1). However, in the end, this part of the series was never published, whereas thirteen plates were devoted to depictions of the prince's menagerie of exotic animals.

To create his drawings, Salomon Kleiner made use of a camera obscura. This apparatus—a box with a small hole through which light falls—produces inverted, reversed projections of reality. The artist merely needed to transfer the outlines onto paper. With this optical aid, Kleiner was able to capture all the details from the interior of Eugene's residence—fittings, decoration, furniture, and the art collection—in the correct proportions and foreshortening. Indeed, paintings on the walls and ceilings are depicted in the engravings with such precision as to allow clear identification of the pictures' subjects.

Fig. 1
Salomon Kleiner, *Gallery in Prince Eugene's City Palace on Himmelpfortgasse*, before 1730, Wien Museum

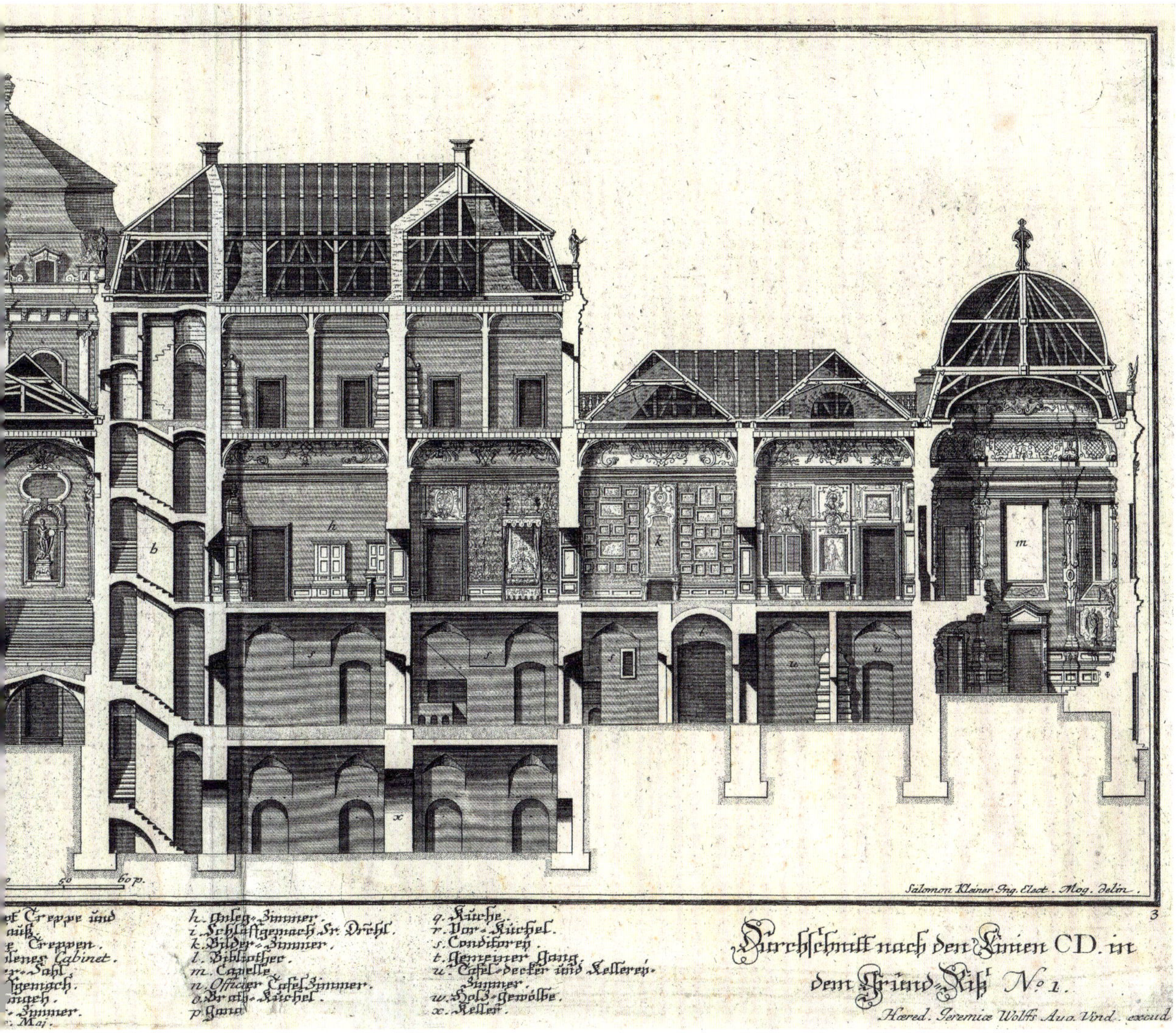
Salomon Kleiner Ing. Elect. Mog. delin.
h. Anleg-Zimmer.
i. Schlaffgemach Sr. Dchl.
k. Bilder-Zimmer.
l. Bibliothec.
m. Capelle.
n. Officier Tafel Zimmer.
o. Brath-Küchel.
p. Gang.
q. Küche.
r. Vor-Küchel.
s. Conditorey.
t. Gemeiner Gang.
u. Tafel-decker und Kellerey-Zimmer.
w. Holz-gewölbe.
x. Keller.
Durchschnitt nach den Linien CD. in dem Grund-Riß No 1.
Hæred. Jeremiæ Wolffs Aug. Vind. excud.

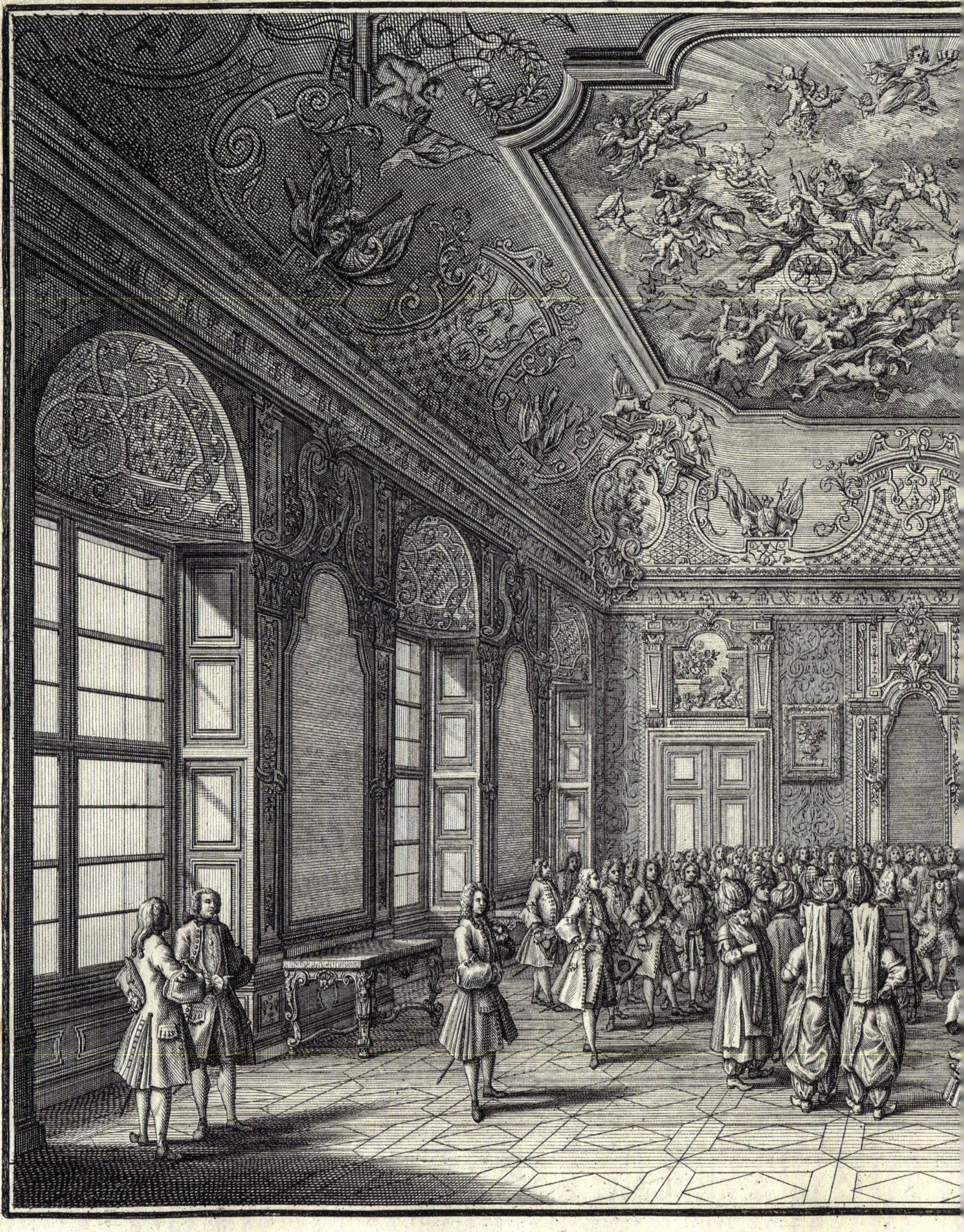

Parade und Audienz - Zimmer.

Salomon Kleiner Ingen. Elect. Mogunt. delin.

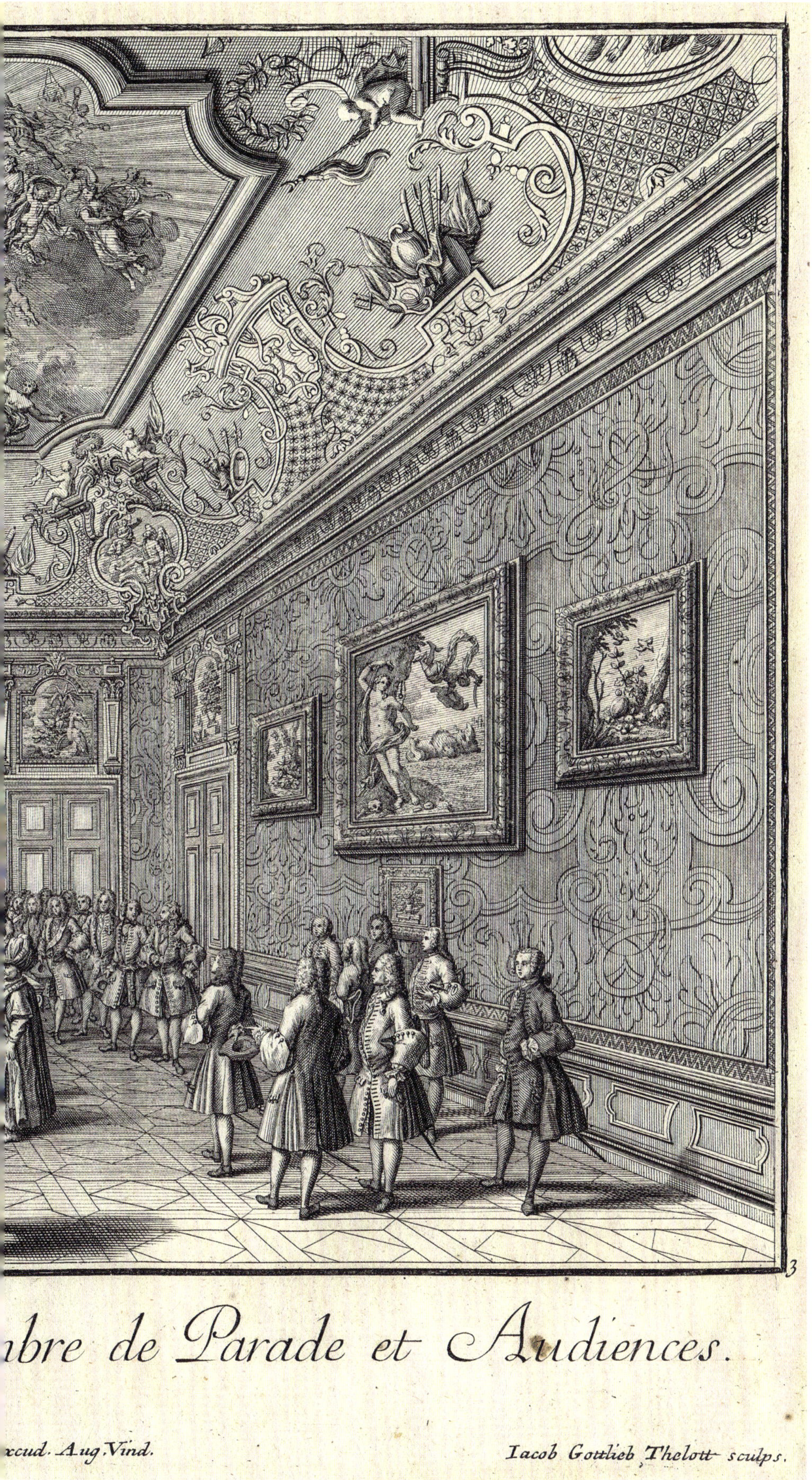

Audience Room in the Upper Belvedere, 1731

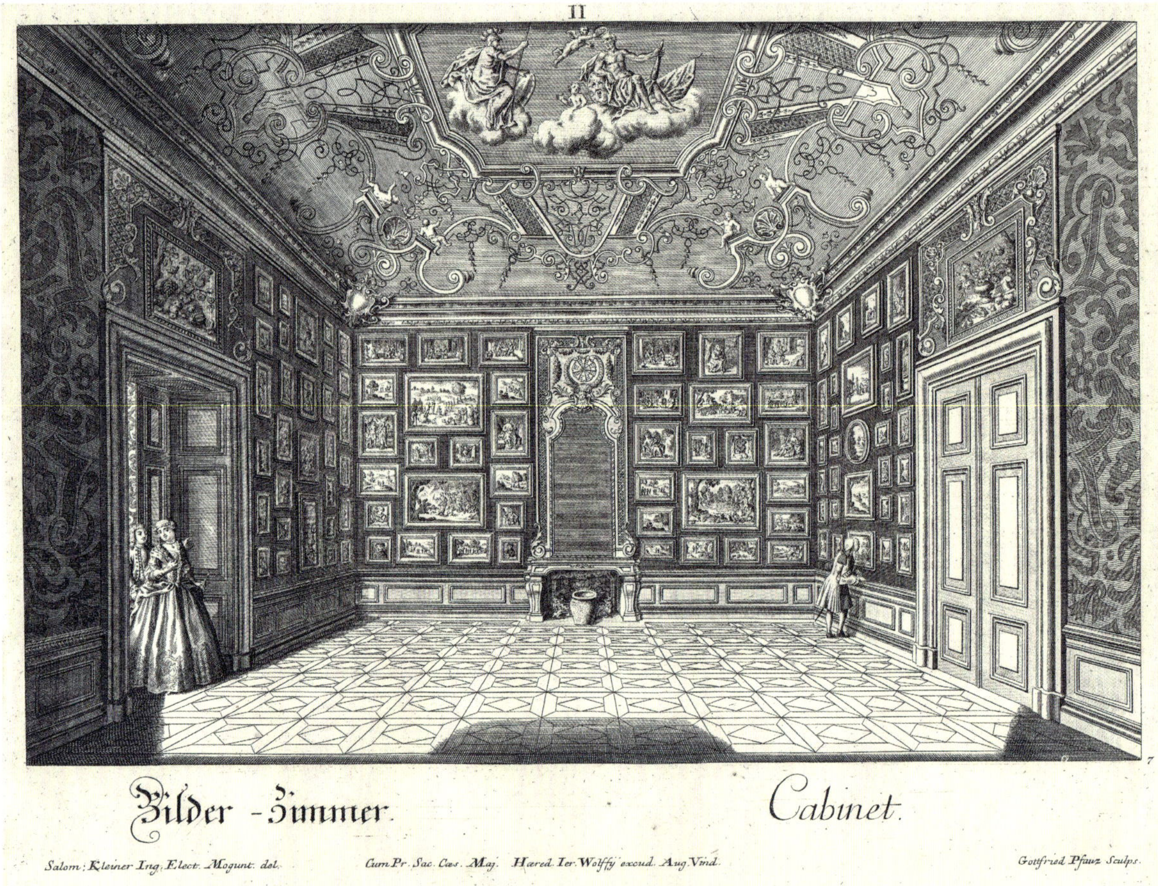

Picture Cabinet in the Upper Belvedere, 1733

In the room adjoining to the prince's bedchamber are several exquisite pieces of small paintings, and in the next chamber is a very precious chandelier of rock crystal, valued at twenty thousand guldens. Here is also a Dutch piece of painting, which cost thirteen thousand guldens, representing an old woman on her death-bed, with her daughter on her knee taking her leave of her, while her maid is administering a medicine in a spoon, and the physician looking at the urine.

—— Translation adapted from Johann Georg Keyssler, *Travels through Germany, Bohemia, Hungary, Switzerland, Italy, and Lorrain* (London, 1757), vol. 4, p. 19.

Prince Eugene was so polite as to shew me his library yesterday; we found him attended by Rousseau, and his favourite count Bonneval, who is a man of wit, and is here thought a very bold and enterprizing spirit. The library, though not very ample, is well chosen; but as the prince will admit into it no editions but what are beautiful and pleasing to the eye, and there are nevertheless numbers of excellent books that are but indifferently printed, this finikin and foppish taste makes many disagreeable chasms in this collection. The books are pompously bound in Turkey leather; and two of the most famous bookbinders of Paris were expressly sent for to do this work.

— *Letters of Lady Mary Wortley Montague Written during Her Travels in Europe, Asia, and Africa* (Paris, 1822), p. 228.

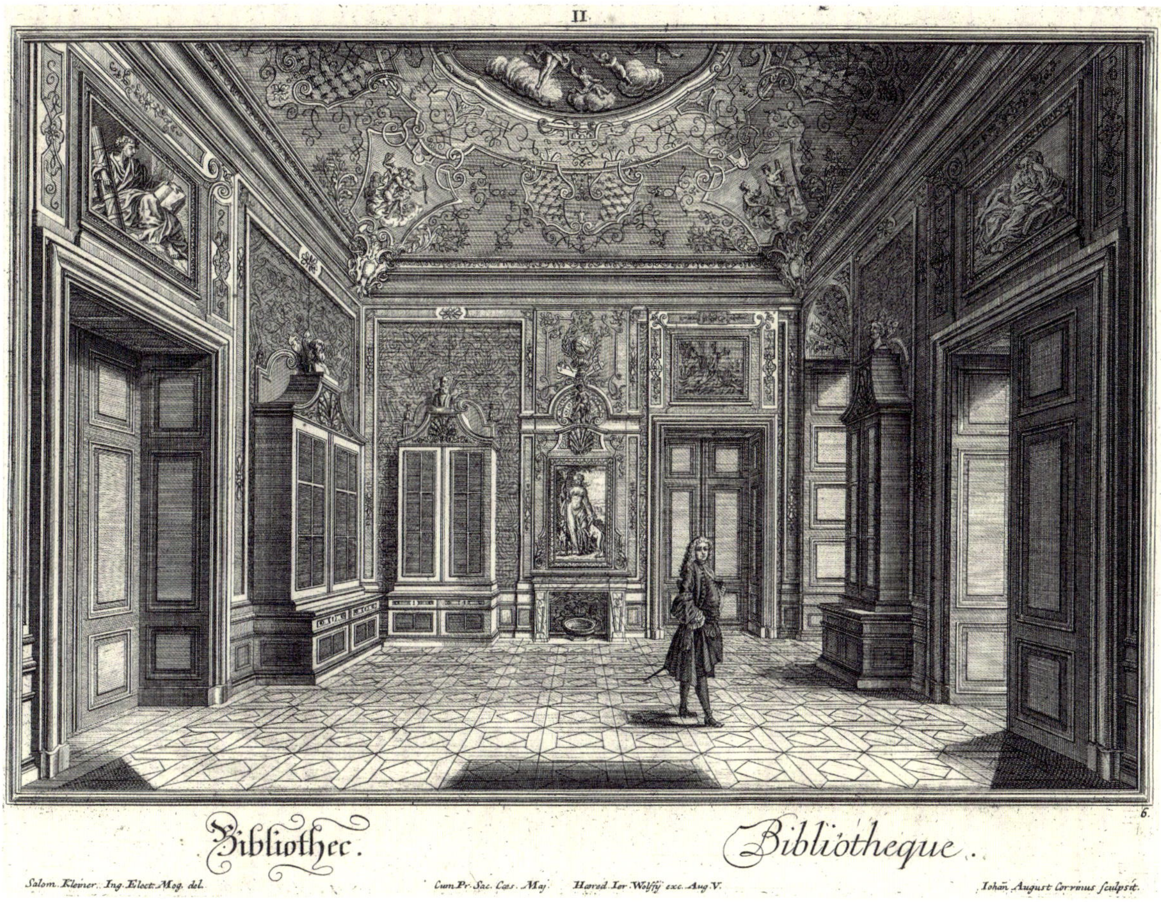

Library in the Upper Belvedere, 1733

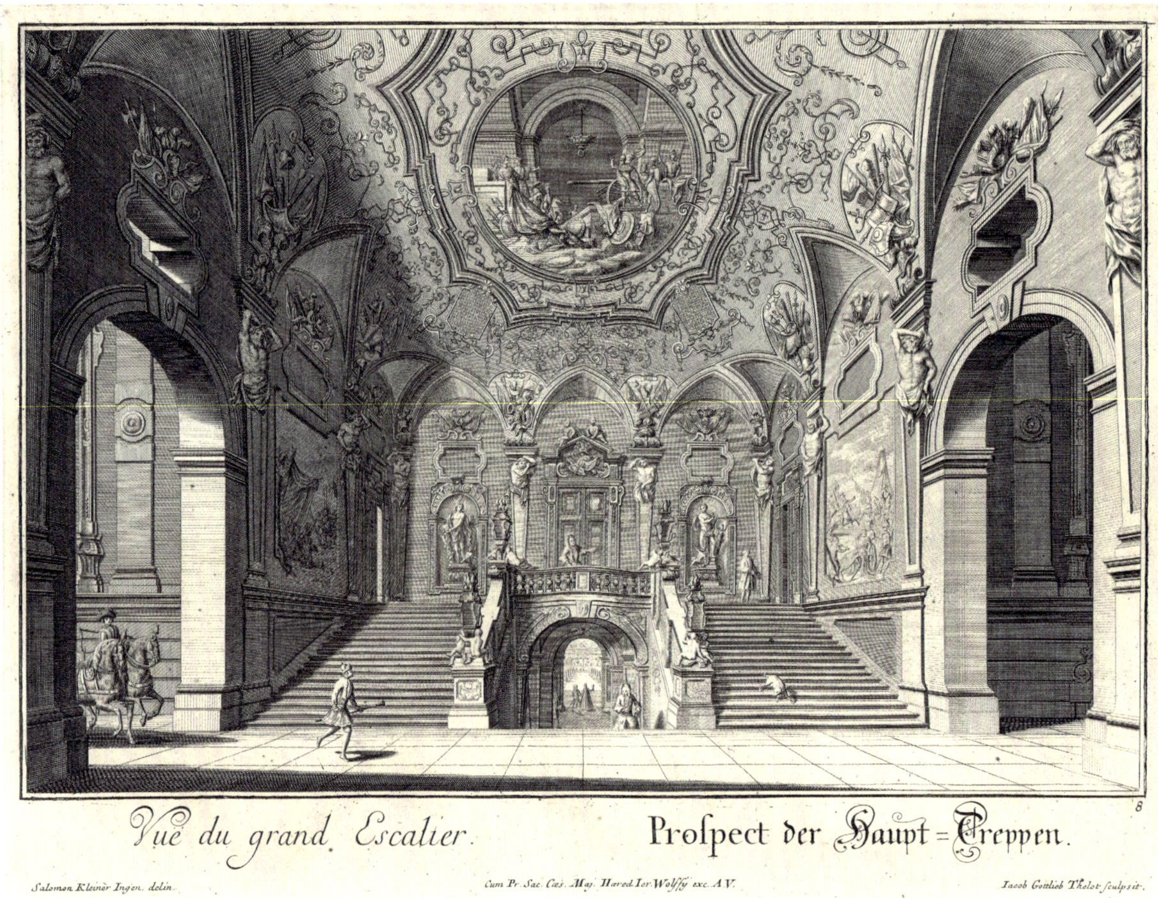

Grand Staircase in the Upper Belvedere, 1731

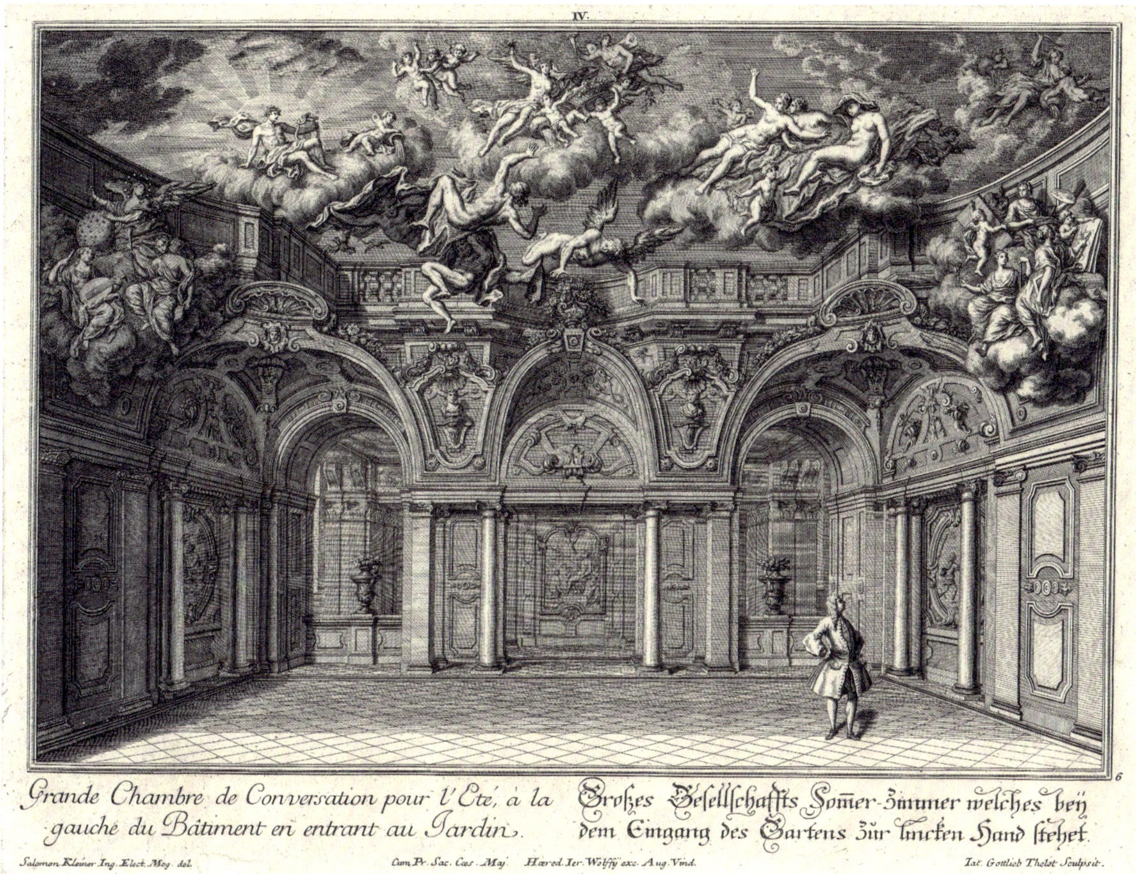

Grande Chambre de Conversation in the West Wing on the Ground Floor of the Upper Belvedere, 1735

II.

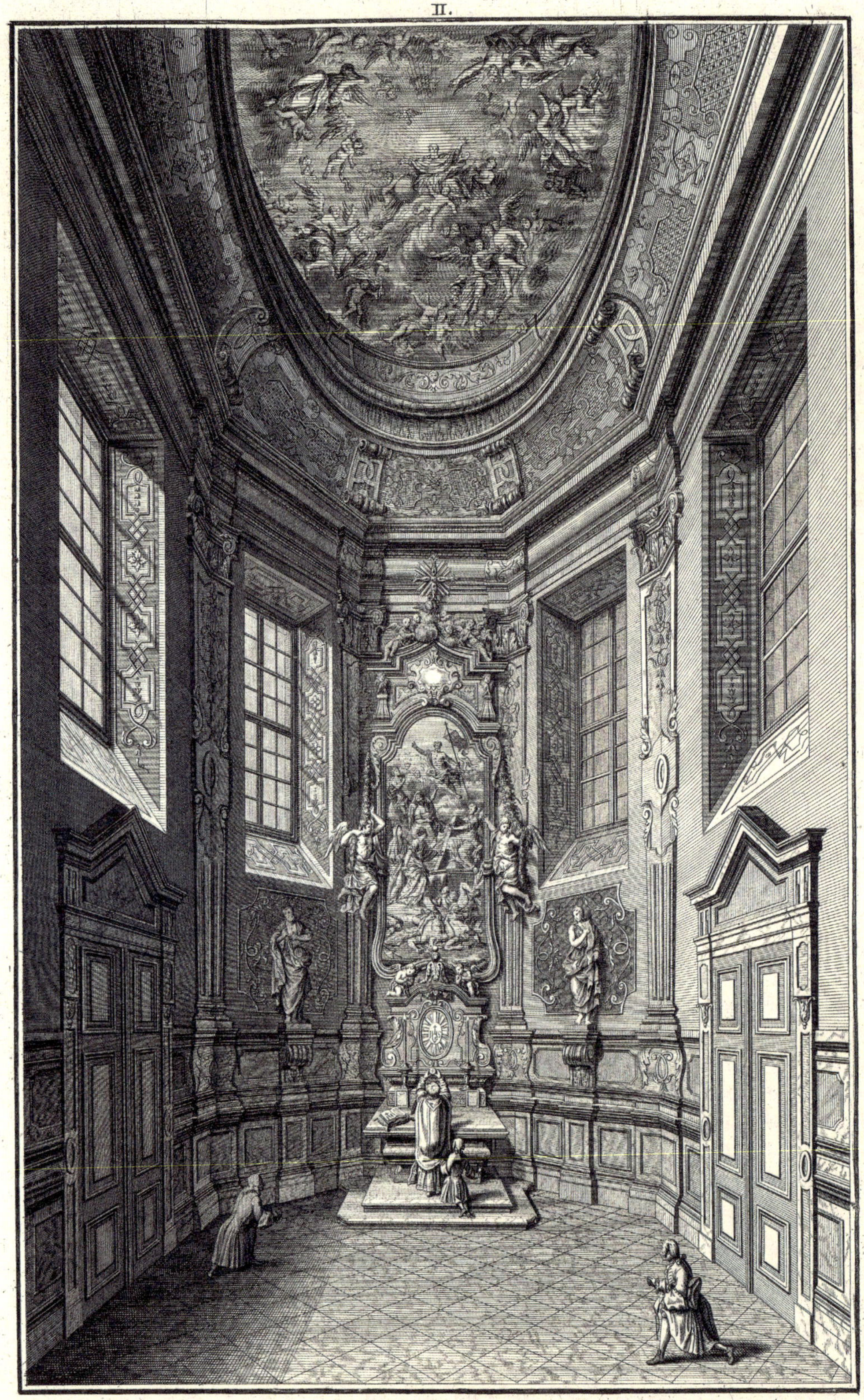

4.

Capelle. Chapelle.

Salomon Kleiner Ing. Elect. Mogunt. del. C. Pr. Sac. Cæs. Maj. Hæred. Ier. Wolffij exc. A.V. Iacob Gottlieb Thelott Sculpsit.

This is followed by the chapel, which is located in the low tower on the first right-hand corner facing east. Although not too large, it is still very beautiful, clad throughout with brown marble and gilded. On the altar is the fine painting depicting the Resurrection of Christ, and after this, the large and richly gilded festoons are particularly noteworthy.

—— Johann Basilius Küchelbecker, *Allerneueste Nachricht vom Römisch-Käyserl. Hofe* (Hannover, 1730), p. 786.

← *Palace Chapel in the Upper Belvedere*, 1733

Among the excellent paintings in the other apartments are a life-sized Adam and Eve, which is said to have cost fifty thousand guldens; a woman embracing a youth in a bath, valued at thirty thousand, and the hunter Endymion with Diana worth twelve thousand guldens. Here is also a copy of Rubens's three graces, which is very much esteemed.

—— Translation adapted from Johann Georg Keyssler, *Travels through Germany, Bohemia, Hungary, Switzerland, Italy, and Lorrain* (London, 1757), vol. 4, p. 19.

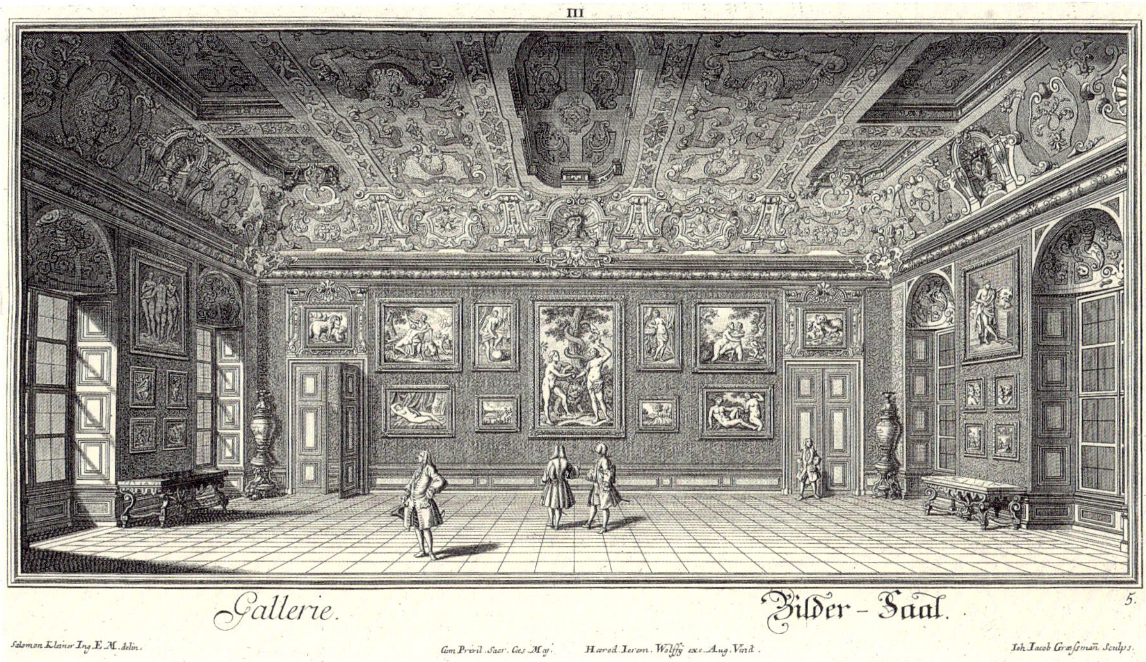

↑
Gallery in the Upper Belvedere, 1734

→ p. 40
Marble Gallery in the Lower Belvedere, 1740

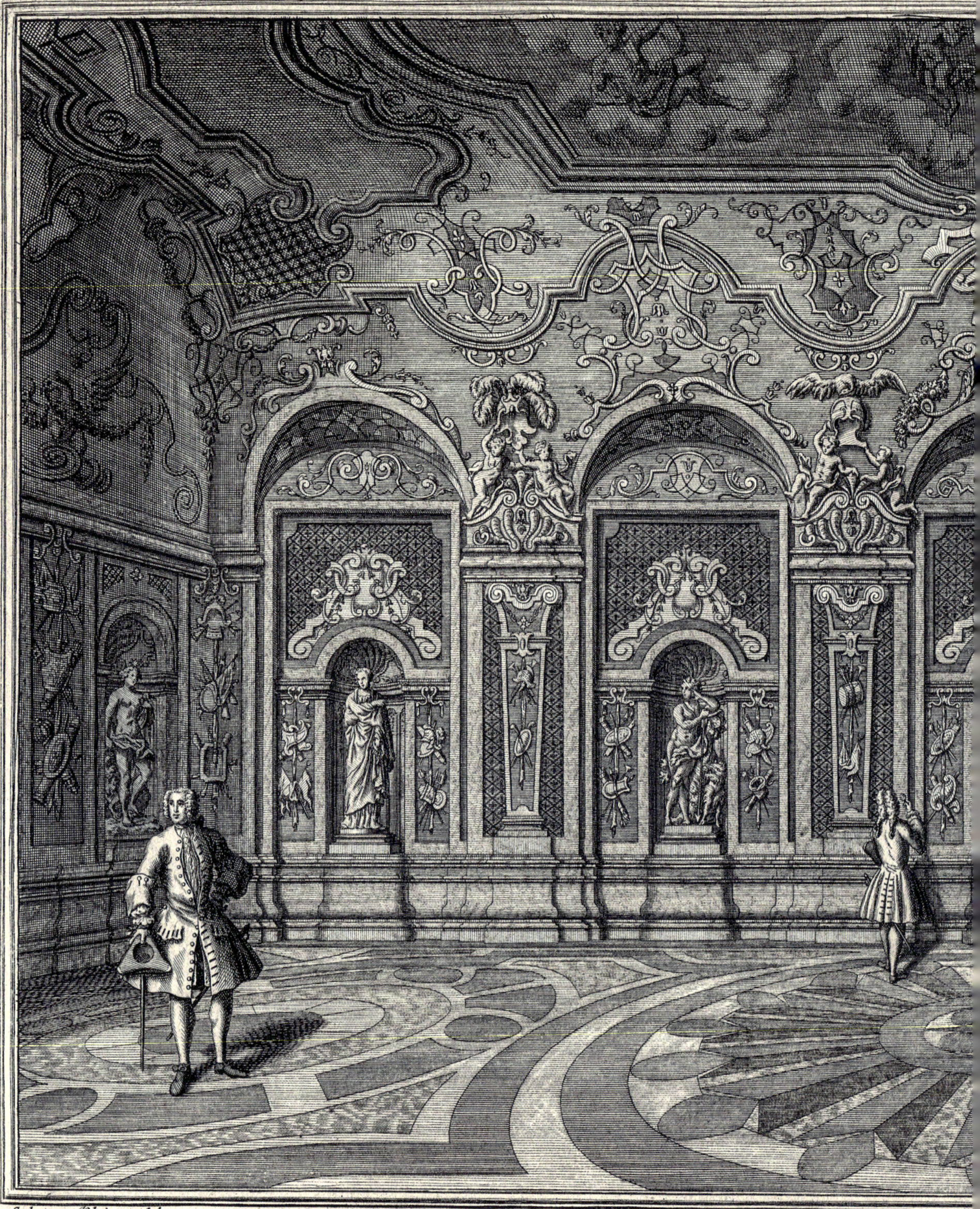

Salomon Kleiner del.

Gallerie en marbre .

Cum Privil. Sac. Cæs. Maj.

3

The Marble Gallery Sculptures

Silvia Tammaro

One of Prince Eugene of Savoy's collections was devoted to antiquities and sculptures. These works were exhibited in the gardens and in the Marble Gallery of the lower garden palace (→ p. 40). This gallery, still in existence today, owes its name to the material with which it is clad, evidently a tribute to the marble statues displayed in the hall. The floor is adorned with a pattern of reddish-brown, white, and ocher marble, continuing on the walls in marble and imitation marble. The white stuccowork on the ceiling, attributed to Santino Bussi, originally incorporated gold highlights that are now lost. At the center, the stucco relief depicts the Apotheosis of Prince Eugene as a warrior hero, while war trophies on the walls allude to his military victories. Two mirrors at either end of the gallery give the impression of the space extending into infinity. The garden-facing wall has windows and a door with steps leading outside, the interior thus seamlessly connects to the palace's exterior space. In a sequence of niches across the entire opposite wall, "modern" and "classical" statues were originally juxtaposed. Prince Eugene owned the most precious antiquities in all of Vienna: three Roman statues known as the *Herculaneum Women*, now in the Dresden State Art Collections (fig. 1). These draped female figures came from excavations at Ercolano and had arrived in Vienna in 1713, an illustrious gift from Emmanuel-Maurice de Lorraine, Prince D'Elbeuf, who had been serving Emperor Charles VI in Naples since 1707.[1] Such full-figure statues, modeled on a lost Greek sculpture, were unusual and extremely precious, owing to their size and completeness, and the prince presented them to his guests as

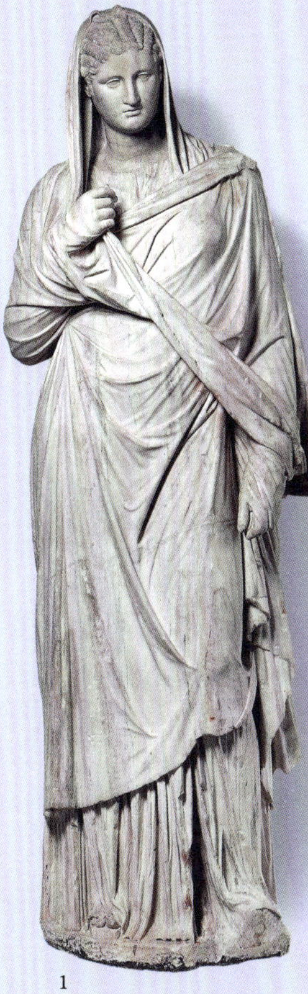

1

Fig. 1
Large Herculaneum Woman, middle of the 1st cent. CE, Dresden State Art Collections, Sculpture Collection

prestigious showpieces. The "modern" statues in the Marble Gallery's other niches were Baroque sculptures executed by Francesco Biggi after designs by Domenico Parodi.[2] These Genoese artists delivered to the prince nine statues of mythological figures, including *Ariadne*, *Adonis*, and *Diana* (fig. 2). They were probably given the commission after being recommended by the architect Johann Lucas von Hildebrandt. Also a native of Genoa, Hildebrandt was the creative genius behind Prince Eugene's entire garden palace, including the design of the Marble Gallery.

1 Daehner 2007, pp. 1–17.
2 Comoglio 2022, pp. 83–92.

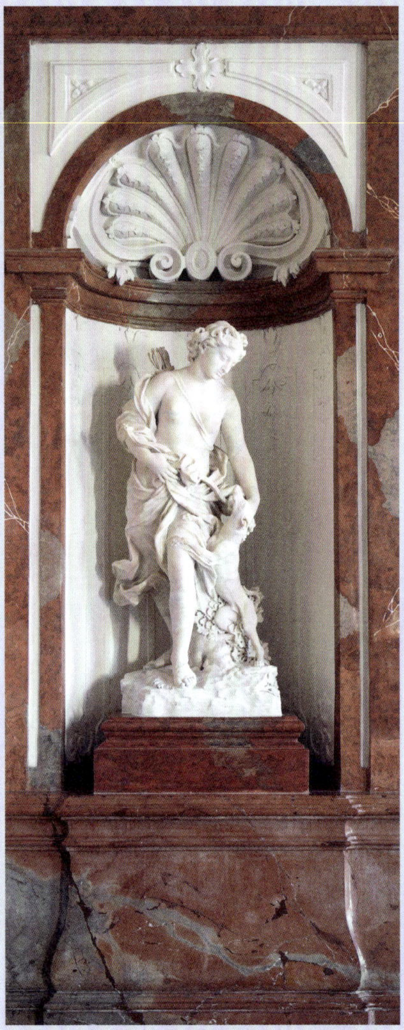

2

Fig. 2
Francesco Biggi after designs by Domenico Parodi, *Diana*, Belvedere, Vienna

X.

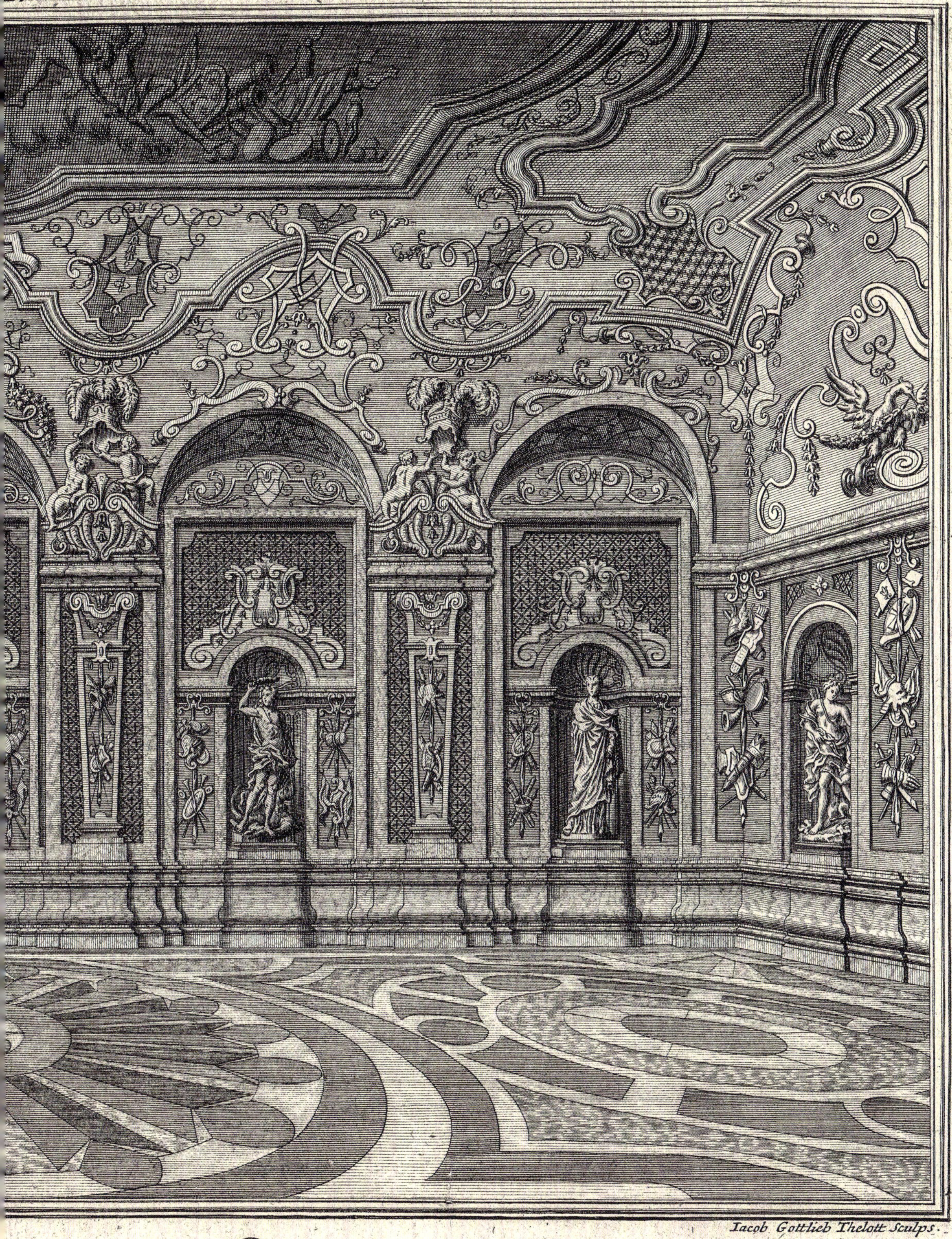

7

Iacob Gottlieb Thelott Sculps.

Gallerie von Marmor.

Hæred. Ieremiæ Wolffÿ excud. Aug. Vind.

P. 44

THOMAS DACOSTA KAUFMANN —
Patronage and Collecting in the Habsburg Empire c. 1700

The stage was set in Europe c. 1700 for a theater of magnificence. From Portugal to St. Petersburg and from Sicily to Stockholm, grand palaces and churches were erected, gardens were laid out, and monuments put up. Paintings, sculpture, and elaborate interior decoration adorned new constructions.[1] At this time, Vienna became arguably the major European venue for artists, architects, designers, and craftsmen. And Prince Eugene of Savoy (fig. 1) was one of the protagonists of its imperial theater, as he was in the military dramas that accompanied it.[2] A look at his patronage and collecting in relation to his career illuminates both his activity and the general situation.

In 1683, Turkish armies were routed at the walls of Vienna. In the following four decades the Habsburgs succeeded in pushing the Ottomans out of the Hungarian crown lands and northern Serbia. At the same time, they countered the French threat to the west. While the Habsburgs had died out in Spain, triggering the War of the Spanish Succession, the treaty of Rastatt that ended it in 1714 gave the Austrian Habsburgs control over Sicily, Sardinia, Lombardy, the Southern Netherlands, and Freiburg im Breisgau.[3] Even though Emperor Charles VI (r. 1711–1740) regretted not being able to hold on to the Spanish throne, his realms represented their largest expansion in ancien régime Europe.

Habsburg successes created the circumstances, means, and atmosphere for a construction boom in and around Vienna. Territorial gains and resulting income supported new urban constructions and the rebuilding of the ravaged Viennese suburbs, as in central Hungary. The waning of the Turkish threat allowed Vienna to expand outside its inner walls, now traced by the Ringstrasse. A new confidence and competitive

1 For general overviews and the term see DaCosta Kaufmann 1998, pp. 315–78, and DaCosta Kaufmann 1999.
2 Still useful summaries are provided in McKay 1977; Gutkas 1985; (more popular) Egghardt 2007; exh. cat. Vienna 2010a; and exh. cat. Vienna 2010a.
3 A useful brief introduction to these complicated events is available in Schnettger 2014.

spirit, internally among abbeys and aristocrats and externally with other courts, especially with Louis XIV, sparked extensive patronage of decoration and collecting as well as of building.

Vienna succeeded Italy and more precisely Rome as epicenter of the arts. Like Rome, it became a focus or magnet, to which artists, artisans, and architects were attracted from many parts of Europe. Visitors moreover noticed how much Italian they heard in the imperial city. Other aspects of Italian culture, for example, its music, were also highly favored. Italian paintings and painters were preferred by collectors, and Italian sculptors like Lorenzo Mattielli came north. Artists who had been active in Rome, notably Johann Bernard Fischer von Erlach,[4] who had been in Gianlorenzo Bernini's workshop and worked with one of his collaborators, became prominent in Vienna. Even though contemporary voices like Wagner von Wagenfels proudly announced the accomplishments of local genius said to surpass France, the standard of comparison remained Italy.

Although Versailles was a point for competition, it does not always serve well for comparison. Significant differences should be kept in mind when one tries to assess the role of the Habsburgs in the creation of what was famously called a *Reichsstil* but to whom a now paradigmatic corrective has attributed little importance until the reign of Charles VI.[5] While both courts had their own rituals of power, the Bourbon and Habsburg theaters were structured differently. Whereas Louis XIV was king of France, Habsburg rulers during Prince Eugene's lifetime (Leopold I, Joseph I, and Charles VI) were not only officially Holy Roman Emperors but had actual empires in which they ruled over separate and widely strewn territories. They were, for instance, kings of Bohemia and Hungary.

However, titles do not necessarily bring along with them great means: an ongoing problem for the Habsburgs remained the funding of military and cultural ventures from often intractable subjects. The history of Hungary from this time demonstrates some of the difficulties: while central Hungary was eventually freed from the Turks, divergent interests of the Habsburgs and Magyar nobles and estates incited repeated revolts from the 1660s onwards, leading ultimately to the Rakoczi rebellion (or first Hungarian war of independence) 1703–1711. Not until the Habsburgs achieved peace in Hungary could their claims on sources of income there be secured.[6]

Furthermore, as the urban residence of the ruler, Vienna is better matched with Paris, not with Versailles. And the Louvre is better compared with Vienna's Hofburg than is Versailles. Leopold I and Louis XIV planned and built simultaneously major wings in their respective palaces (the Leopoldine Tract and Perrault's façade): these exemplify visions of grandeur in employing respectively giant orders of pilasters or columns

4 See Karner/Schütze/Telesko 2022.

5 Cf. Sedlmayr 1938, pp. 126–40. Hellmut Lorenz has repeatedly countered this thesis and established what is now effectively a paradigm, here questioned: Lorenz 1985a; Lorenz 1985b, p. 235; Lorenz 1993; Lorenz 1994, pp. 32–36; Lorenz 1999, pp. 220, 224.

6 Sugar 1994, pp. 100–20 provides an accessible introduction in English.

on high rusticated basements. At the same time, aristocrats had their own palaces not only in Vienna but also in Paris. Indeed, Louis XIV aggrandized Versailles and made it his seat of power to control them.

Prince Eugene was a key player in many important events connected with these developments. His military career bookends the turn of the century. He arrived from France just in time to participate in the successful relief of Vienna. He led armies in Hungary and the Balkans where he won victories at Zenta (1697) and Petrowardein and took Buda and Belgrade. Along with the Duke of Marlborough, he defeated French armies at the battles of Blenheim, Oudenarde, and Malplaquet, and on his own raised the siege of Turin. He served as an adviser, viceroy, and stateholder, and was the Habsburgs' principal negotiator at Rastatt.

Eugene distinguished himself in *arte et marte*, modes used to describe him, or as an enlightened Apollo (fig. 2) and heroic Hercules, as he styled himself. He has been called the most "grandiose and influential private patron in Europe.[7]" Though of princely stock, he came to Vienna as a penniless outcast from Versailles. Having quickly begun a successful career, as soon as his fortunes allowed, in 1695, he followed what was *standesgemäss* and, like many a prince from Bohemia (Lobkovic) or Hungary (Batthyány), had a city palace built on Himmelpfortgasse (→ p. 49, fig. 1). In this, and in his subsequent patronage, he might thus seem to support the interpretation that nobles took the lead. The construction and decoration of his suburban garden palace (the Belvedere) followed other aristocratic precedents (Trautson and Althan), as did the expansion of a country residence (Schloss Hof) and its gardens. Yet it should be recalled that most of Eugene's good fortune depended on imperial favor. Gifts, positions, and their income allowed him to patronize on a grand scale. The Belvedere, with its vista and structures staggered over the hillside (→ p. 23), may be viewed not only as the culmination of Eugene's (and aristocratic) patronage but also as a realization of Fischer's first unrealized plan for the imperial palace at Schönbrunn.

Eugene's collecting (really inextricable from patronage) can also be considered in this context. Nobles from various parts of the empire, such as Ferdinand Bonaventura von Harrach and Johann Adam von Liechtenstein, housed their outstanding collections in new palaces in Vienna (fig. 3). Elsewhere, as in Bohemia, aristocratic families (Černín and Nostic[8]) also assembled important collections. Prince Eugene did much the same in his collecting as well as his patronage of Italian art, particularly from Bologna and Naples.[9] Even Eugene's menagerie was probably inspired by that of the Starhembergs. While Eugene's French upbringing may account for some of his taste in gardens, boiserie, and mirrors, the Netherlandish elements in his collecting taste (both for the so-called "primitives" and the Rubens circle) also have precedents: in

7 Haskell 1963, p. 201.
8 Slavíček 1993b; Slavíček 1993c.
9 As first pointed out by Haskell 1963, p. 201.

Vienna, art dealers like Guillaume Forchondt were catering to this taste by the mid-century.[10]

It would, however, be a mistake to see the development of collections c. 1700 and beyond in Central Europe as a *novum* or as independent of imperial precedents. The mid-seventeenth-century presence of dealers in Vienna parallels the accumulation of major collections in the region by the Liechtensteins and Prince-Bishop Liechtenstein-Castelcorno.[11] By this time, parts of Rudolf II's collections of paintings, drawings, and objets d'art had also been absorbed into the imperial collections in Vienna, and, in 1656, Leopold Wilhelm brought his outstanding collection of paintings there (fig. 4). Leopold I inherited the archduke's holdings in 1662. The imperial holdings not only far surpassed any aristocratic collections but also continued to provide a paragon for collecting.[12]

To be sure, Eugene gathered an outstanding collection of books, drawings (including Rembrandt), and prints, the latter bound into volumes, as was contemporary custom (→ p. 71).[13] Significantly, however, these entered the imperial library after his death. The Belvedere, too, passed into imperial hands, where it would lead a new life as a museum under the Habsburgs (and later the Austrian Republic). Eugene's patronage and collecting have thus continued to be linked with imperial Vienna.

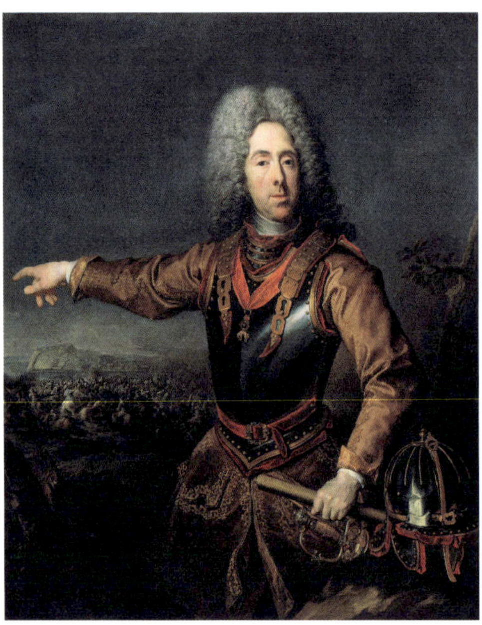

1

10 Slavíček 1993a.
11 For an overview of the collections see exh. cat. Bern 2016; Jakubec 2019; Švacha/Potůčková/Kroupa 2019, pp. 283–378
12 Lhotsky 1941–45, pp. 355–409, remains important for details on the period. See, more recently, Schreiber 2004; exh. cat. Vienna 2010b.
13 See exh. cat. Vienna 1986; Friedenthal 2022.

④

The Winter Palace

Georg Lechner

When Prince Eugene of Savoy arrived in Vienna in 1683, he did not have sufficient wealth to finance his own residence. However, he gradually established his position in the imperial army and, moreover, in 1688, was made lay abbot of two abbeys in Piedmont, securing him an income befitting his social status. By 1694 he was able to purchase a building on Himmelpfortgasse, which was by no means a prime location in the city at the time. In 1697, construction began on a seven-bay town palace after plans by Johann Bernhard Fischer von Erlach. Despite limited space, the architect designed a residence that met his patron's aspirations to grandeur and display. Expanding the palace had probably been envisaged from the outset. And indeed, following the purchase of adjacent plots, the building was extended between 1708 and 1711, and again from 1723 to 1725, by five bays on each side (fig. 1). Most of these new rooms served to house the collections of books (→ p. 73, fig. 1) and paintings, which the prince had amassed with great zeal. Interestingly, he had decided to change architects before extending the palace, entrusting this to Johann Lucas von Hildebrandt.

After Prince Eugene of Savoy's death, the Winter Palace formed part of the estate inherited by his niece Princess Victoria of Savoy, who, in 1752, sold it—together with the Belvedere—to Maria Theresa. Under the monarch, the building, which had already lost most of its movables, was adapted for use by the mining agency. Since 1848 it has been the seat of the Ministry of Finance. Under the Nazis, plans were made to create a museum about Prince Eugene in the Winter Palace. Collecting for this had already begun, but the project floundered as the war progressed. In the end, the Winter Palace was only open to the public from 2013 until 2017, when, as an additional venue of the Österreichische Galerie Belvedere (Austrian Gallery Belvedere), special exhibitions were staged in its state rooms.

The Grand Staircase with its four impressive atlantes (fig. 2), an outstanding achievement by Johann Bernhard Fischer von Erlach, as well as several ceiling frescoes and paintings have been preserved from the

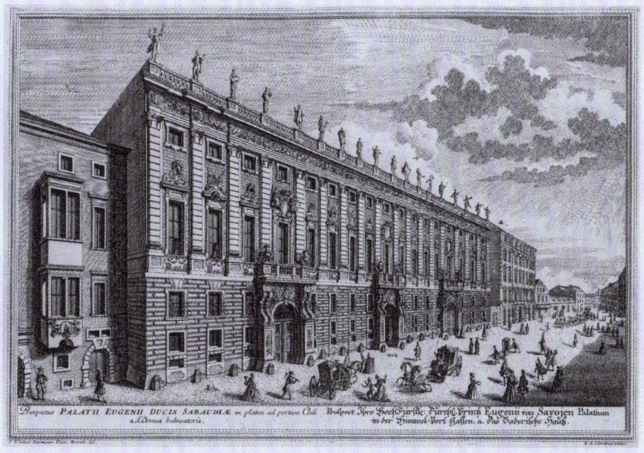

1

Fig. 1
Johann August Corvinus after Salomon Kleiner, *The Façade of the Winter Palace*, 1725, Austrian National Library, Vienna

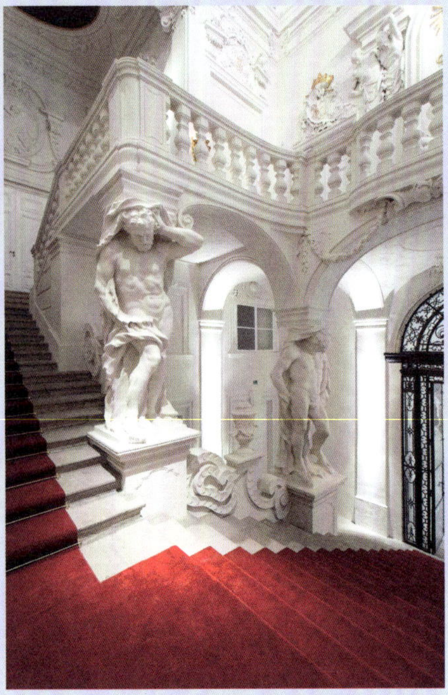

2

original building. In several rooms on the bel étage, however, the original visual impression was irrevocably lost when additional partition walls and false ceilings were installed. Ignace Jacques Parrocel's large battle paintings, which illustrate Prince Eugene's most illustrious military victories and were originally hung in the Great Hall, were later displayed in a room designed especially for this purpose. Happily, between 2007 and 2013, a conservation project was able to retrieve the painted grotesques in the Sala Terrena on the ground floor by removing later additions and overpaintings (fig. 3). Meanwhile, it emerged that one of the rooms on the bel étage had been frescoed when the palace was remodeled after 1752. So far, only a sample section has been exposed, but this suggests the work of an artist associated with the Vienna Academy, possibly Franz Anton Maulbertsch.

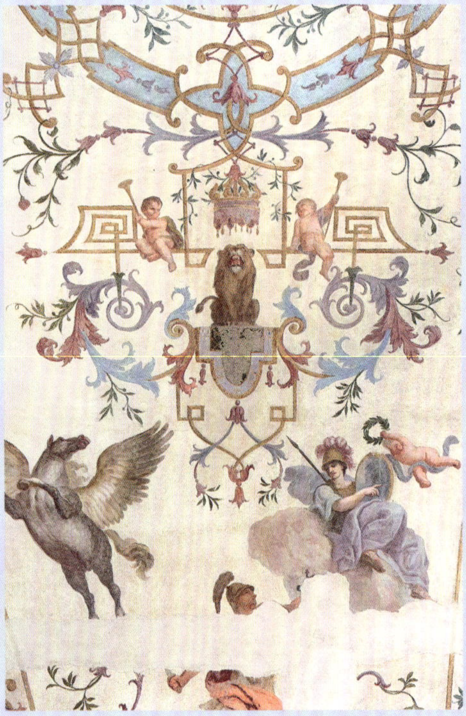

3

Fig. 2
Grand Staircase in the Winter Palace

Fig. 3
Grotesques in the Sala Terrena at the Winter Palace, c. 1700

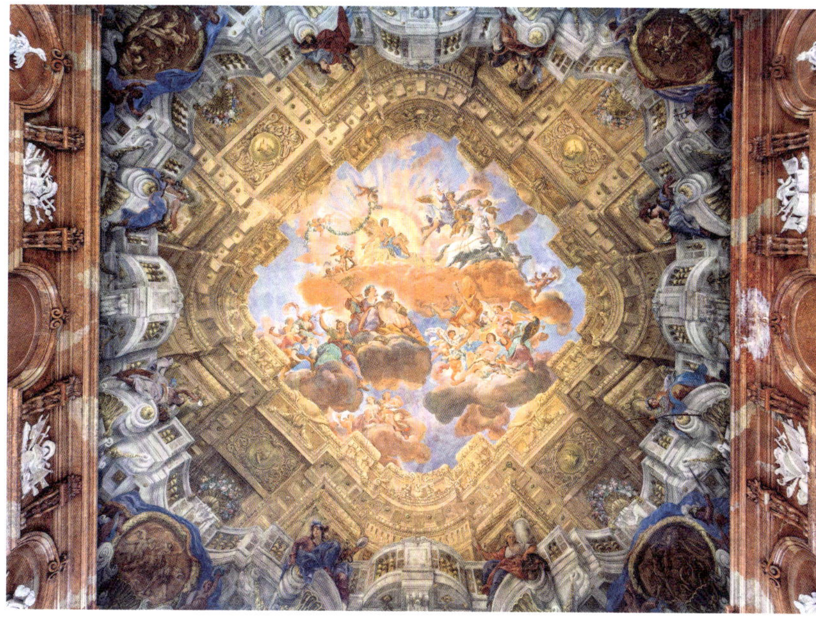

2

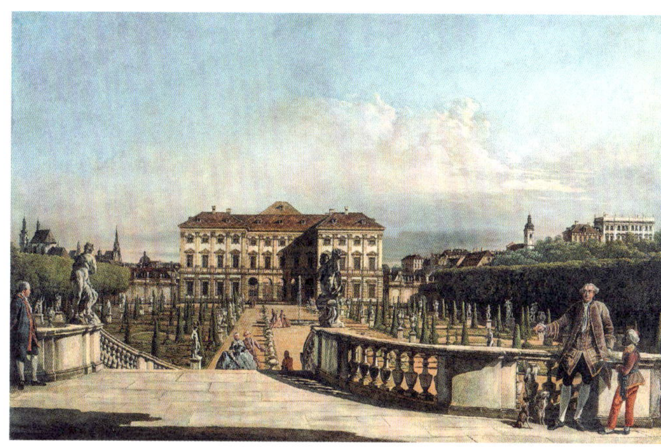

3

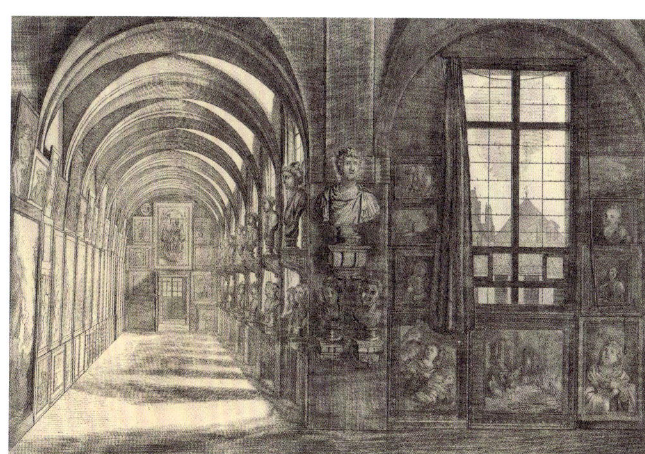

4

Fig. 1
Jacob van Schuppen, *Prince Eugene of Savoy after the Battle of Belgrade on August 16, 1717*, 1718, Belvedere, Vienna, loan from the Rijksmuseum Amsterdam

Fig. 2
Martino Altomonte, ceiling painting in the Marble Hall of the Lower Belvedere with a depiction of the sun god Apollo and the Muses, 1717, Belvedere, Vienna

Fig. 3
Bernardo Bellotto, *The Liechtenstein Garden Palace in Vienna Seen from the Belvedere*, 1759/60, Liechtenstein. The Princely Collections, Vaduz—Vienna

Fig. 4
Frans van der Steen after Nikolaus van Hoy, *A View of Archduke Leopold Wilhelm's Picture Gallery in the Stallburg*, 1654–60, British Museum, London

P. 52 SILVIA TAMMARO — Prestige and Passion: Prince Eugene of Savoy's Picture Collection at His Garden Palace

Kneeling in front of a painting, discovering a delightful detail and discussing this with other art connoisseurs—this is how Pieter van den Berge depicts Eugene of Savoy in a sketch documenting the prince's visit to the art dealer Jan Pieterszoon Zomer in Amsterdam (fig. 1).[1] Eugene's passion for the fine arts was well known, and he owned one of the most impressive collections of paintings in his day. Amassed in only a few years, this was displayed in the magnificent rooms of his city palace and at his summer residences (→ p. 28). When the prince acquired his first plot of land on Rennweg in 1697 and started planning his garden palace, his aim was not only to create a grand residence but also a place of art.[2] It took until 1723 for these buildings, now known as the Belvedere Palace, to be completed. The project reflected Prince Eugene's wish to secure his place in courtly society, which in this period built their summer residences in Vienna's suburbs, following the example of the imperial family's Favorita.

The tradition of the garden palace had evolved from the Italian *villa suburbana*, established during the Renaissance: a residence outside the city, close to nature, where the owner and his guests were able to spend the summer months dividing their time between *otium* (refined, cultivated leisure) and *negotium* (work and business). Eugene's garden palace, too, provided both a place of retreat and a magnificent setting for affairs of state. After the prince's appointment in 1716 as governor of the Austrian Netherlands, plans for the upper garden palace were altered and more sumptuously decorated state rooms were added to accommodate audiences with all due court ceremonial.[3] The lower garden palace had already been completed in 1717, a ground-level *maison de plaisance* with a more private character.

1 On this drawing, see Friedenthal 2022.
2 For further discussion about the creation and construction of the Belvedere garden palace, see Seeger 2004.
3 Seeger 2004, pp. 173–77, 406.

The entire garden palace was also designed to showcase Prince Eugene's valuable art collection. This demonstrates not only the prince's passionate interest in the arts but also the outstanding importance of such a collection in the early modern period, when it served both as a means of self-representation and as a reflection of status and prestige at court.

Eugene's collection[4] comprised some three hundred paintings, as well as artworks that were part of the palace interior, such as overdoor and ceiling paintings, and paintings forming part of the wall décor that the prince had commissioned from artists in both Italy and Vienna. Thanks to his friendship with Count Wirich Philipp Lorenz von Daun, the Austrian Viceroy of Naples, Eugene had the opportunity to order three works from the most sought-after painter of his day: the Neapolitan artist Francesco Solimena. Solimena was tasked with creating two altarpieces (→ p. 36) and a ceiling painting for the garden palace, although the prince grew impatient when it took the artist a long time to execute these works.[5] In addition to being concerned to have the interior decoration of his palace completed, the prince also wanted his commission to take precedence, much to the infuriation of the painter's other aristocratic clients.

In Naples, Eugene ordered three further ceiling paintings for his new garden palace from Giacomo del Pò.[6] These commissions were organized on the prince's behalf by Gabriele Montani, an engineer and military officer. Montani was the contact person and in charge of settling accounts as well as checking the completed work. Indeed, before the ceiling paintings were sent to Vienna, he ordered several amendments to the colors and even checked the accuracy of perspective and proportions by having the canvases mounted to the ceiling of the Viceroy of Naple's palace, which was a similar height to those at the garden palace in Vienna. Prince Eugene was very pleased with the result and entrusted further commissions to his agent.[7] Artworks, books, and some lemon trees for his greenhouse were all ordered from southern Italy as a result.

For his acquisitions of paintings and other artworks, Prince Eugene could rely on the support of a solid network that made purchases on his behalf in Italy and throughout Europe.[8] This comprised the usual art dealers and artists as well as envoys and diplomats with whom the prince shared a passion for the arts. Eugene had his trusted agents in every major Italian city—Milan, Turin, Venice, Bologna, Naples, etc.—and thus received advance notification about artworks for sale and upcoming liquidations of famous collections. The prince also made numerous purchases in Brussels, Paris, and in the Netherlands, including paintings, drawings, engravings, etchings, and many lavish editions of books, for Eugene also maintained an extensive library known as the Bibliotheca Eugeniana, as well as an impressive collection of graphic art (→ pp. 70–1).

4 The collection is known today from the so-called Robinson catalogue. This is a copy of the original inventory sent to London by Sir Thomas Robinson, British ambassador in Vienna, probably intended for the art collector Robert Walpole: see Auer/Black 1985. No known example exists of the printed inventory that Eugene's heiress, Victoria of Savoy, published for the auction of the collection. For a reconstruction of the collection, see Baudi di Vesme 1886; Diekamp 2005; Diekamp 2010; Diekamp 2012.

5 The altarpiece depicting *The Resurrection of Christ* is still in the Belvedere Palace Chapel. The second altarpiece, a *Deposition from the Cross*, is now exhibited at the Kunsthistorisches Museum Vienna (inv. no. 3507). The ceiling painting, however, was destroyed in a fire in 1950; see Seeger 2004, p. 404. For further discussion of Solimena's work for Prince Eugene, see Braubach 1963–65, V, p. 33; Wolfang Prohaska in exh. cat. Vienna/Naples 1993, pp. 246–47; Prohaska 2001, pp. 146–52; Tammaro 2018, pp. 91–93.

6 Tammaro 2018.

7 See Tammaro 2018.

8 Concerning Eugene's purchases and commissions in Italy, see e.g. Heinz 1963; Comoglio 2012; Swoboda 2013b; Seeger 2002; Tammaro 2018.

The prince's collecting cannot be considered separately from the interior of his palaces, as the function of the various rooms played a decisive role in the selection of paintings. Conversely, the valuable paintings in the collection influenced the design of new rooms in his garden palace, as the décor was matched to the pictures' themes (fig. 2).

The highest-ranking room in the upper garden palace was the Audience Room (→ p. 28), where ambassadors, diplomats, and delegations were received. Only a few paintings were exhibited here, but these were all the more important and were part of a thematic program. At the center of the main wall was a large-scale image of *Perseus and Andromeda* (fig. 4),[9] a subject that allowed for a variety of allegorical and political interpretations. For, not only had Eugene of Savoy played a key role in the liberation of Vienna from the Turkish siege (1683), he had also repelled the Ottoman army at the fortress in Peterwardein (1716), thus averting the danger of its advance into the heart of Europe, akin to Perseus fighting and vanquishing the monster on the canvas. Diagonally opposite was a battle painting by Jacques Courtois, showing a skirmish between Hungarian and Ottoman soldiers.[10] The ceiling painting by Giacomo del Pò, too, was a tribute to the general's military successes, depicting *Prince Eugene's Admission into Olympus*.[11] The other pictures in the room had more "neutral" motifs, comprising delicately painted and richly detailed flower pieces and still lifes by the Dutch artist Cornelis de Heem and by Abraham Mignon. The overdoors, showing depictions of birds and flowers by Franz Werner Tamm, were similarly restrained in character.

The collection's most valuable works, displayed in prime position in a bespoke gallery at the upper garden palace (→ p. 39), were large-scale Old Master paintings from the Italian school, predominantly by Bolognese and Venetian artists from the sixteenth and seventeenth centuries. This selection of artists not only reflected Eugene's personal taste, but was also in line with the zeitgeist of the time and with contemporary art theory, such as the writings of Roger de Piles, for example.[12] In the eighteenth century, the debate about aesthetic theory had been reignited, harking back to the juxtaposition of different schools of painting and ranking artists according to categories such as composition, color, expression, and quality of drawing. The prince's preference for painters from Bologna continued into the great hall with illusionistic architecture frescoed onto the ceiling by Gaetano Fanti.[13]

The gallery was located at the end of the *appartement de société* and was an oblong room, full of light, ideal for ambling while perusing the pictures. Its design had been entrusted to the French architect and designer Claude Le Fort du Plessy (→ p. 39). Paintings were hung on the walls, rather than being integrated in the paneling, as was the case, for exam-

9 The picture is listed in the catalogue as a work by Titian, see Auer/Black 1985, p. 337. Maria Antonietta Terzoli recently identified the picture and attributed it to Artemisia Gentileschi; Terzoli 2021, pp. 319–21.
10 This picture is now at the Galleria Sabauda in Turin, inv. no. 500.
11 This ceiling painting was destroyed in a fire.
12 Piles 1708.
13 The illusionistic painting is no longer extant.

ple, with the imperial collection at the Stallburg (→ p. 51, fig. 4), redesigned at the same time and by the same architect. This free arrangement was common in many picture galleries in France and Italy, and allowed for greater flexibility when it came to redisplaying the collection.

The hang of the pictures, all in carved gold frames, was in a strictly symmetrical arrangement and followed a so-called "pendant system," which paired works according to motifs, formats, or schools. At the center of the main wall, Guido Reni's *Adam and Eve* dominated the space (→ p. 39, fig. 3), while to its right and left was a juxtaposition of *Venus and Adonis*, attributed to Titian, and *Hermaphroditus and the Nymph Salmacis* by Francesco Albani (fig. 5). The subjects of these latter paintings were from Ovid's *Metamorphoses*, but the paintings represented two different schools and periods, their pairing thus inspiring direct comparison. Furthermore, these pictures also fitted thematically with a garden palace, where a preference for mythological depictions and landscapes was the norm. By contrast, the picture gallery in the prince's city palace contained paintings with historical and religious subject matter (→ p. 26, fig. 1), as, in the hierarchy of residences, this space surpassed all the others. Since the palace on Himmelpfortgasse was more important, it followed that it should be more lavishly designed and decorated. The paintings at his picture gallery there, also hung in a dense, symmetrical arrangement, showed saints, portraits of historical personalities and heroes, as well as Eugene's ancestors, such as the then renowned Prince Tomaso of Savoy-Carignan. The other large-scale paintings were supreme works by Guido Reni, Peter Paul Rubens, and Anthony van Dyck.

The prince owned several pictures by van Dyck, for example *Amaryllis and Mirtillo* (fig. 6), probably purchased from the art dealer Zomer in Amsterdam.[14] The subject of this picture, now known in different versions, was from *Il pastor fido* by Giovanni Battista Guarini, a work that belonged to the then extremely popular genre of pastoral literature, and was, moreover, a most suitable motif for a country residence. *Amaryllis and Mirtillo* was exhibited in the gallery at the upper garden palace, where Padovanino's *Sleeping Venus* and *David with the Head of Goliath*, attributed to Guido Reni, were also on display. Not all of the paintings were actually originals, as demand for pictures exceeded supply on the art market. As a result, workshop paintings—pictures following the master's idea but executed by his students—or copies were also collected and valued, to demonstrate the collector's grasp of art theory as well as to achieve completeness in terms of themes or schools.

Prince Eugene's personal taste showed through in the numerous battle and landscape paintings by Flemish and Dutch artists, displayed both in the gallery between the Italian Old Masters and in the other rooms of the palace. Eugene of Savoy particularly appreciated, for in-

14 Gelder 1978, p. 237.

stance, battle scenes by Philips Wouwerman, of which he owned several. He also commissioned paintings of his own victories to adorn rooms in his city palace and at Schloss Hof: Series of large-scale works by Jan van Huchtenburgh and Ignace Jacques Parrocel created a carefully articulated artistic program of self-fashioning. These images not only depicted impressive battle scenes, but the viewer could also identify their exact location, and thus follow the field marshal's military strategy.

The most admired room, however, was the picture cabinet in the upper garden palace (→ p. 30). Here, ninety-eight small-scale paintings by Dutch and Flemish masters were on display.[15] This cabinet, its walls lined with blue damask, was first used as the wardrobe room in the prince's private apartment, and only later became a picture cabinet.[16] It is likely that the prince acquired these paintings *en bloc* from an existing collection and had the room repurposed as a result. In the middle of the room, a chimney piece with a mirror emulating the French example (*cheminée à la royale*), provided a vertical, central axis for the display. The paintings were hung in up to seven tiers reaching all the way to the ceiling and positioned very close together—almost frame to frame—as was customary for a picture cabinet. Finer, more expensive paintings were placed very visibly in the lower tiers. Pictures in the upper rows, on the other hand, were hard to decipher, and the fact that some could hardly be seen at all appears to have been of little concern, for the aim was to design a room that left visitors awestruck. One of the most prominent places was assigned to the painting *The Dropsical Woman* by Gerrit Dou (fig. 7), given to Eugene in 1690 by Elector Palatine Philip William on his diplomatic visit to Vienna.[17] This exquisite painting was even kept inside a black box, its doors adorned with a still life, to protect it from light and pollution. Structures like this, as well as curtains, were commonplace in picture galleries, not only to protect the finest paintings and to surprise visitors when these were revealed, but also to conceal certain subjects that might cause offense, as a way of respecting guests' prudery or sensitivities.

The picture gallery also included several other paintings by Gerrit Dou and his students and successors, known as *fijnschilder* ("fine painters") for their meticulous technique and realistic representation. Further paintings on display included works by Rembrandt, Jan Brueghel the Elder, and Hans Holbein the Younger, who not only enjoyed great international acclaim but were also highly sought-after for other collections in Vienna, such as those of the Liechtenstein and Schönborn families. Rembrandt's *The Visitation* (fig. 8), a work particularly cherished by Eugene, held a special magic, for the artist had kept this painting in his studio until his death.

A further picture room was located in the lower garden palace. This was a space for socializing; guests would congregate here at the

15 See the copy of the inventory in Auer/Black 1985, pp. 338–42.
16 Seeger 2004, p. 387.
17 See Braubach 1965, p. 40.

prince's receptions, drifting between dining room and great hall, and pausing to admire the artworks (fig. 9). Twenty landscapes[18] were on display in this room, with a particular emphasis on works by the Dutch painter Jan Griffier the Elder (fig. 10). Eugene may have acquired these paintings in 1712 on a diplomatic journey to London, where the painter lived until his death.[19] It therefore seems fair to assume[20] that Prince Eugene purchased these pictures specifically for this room, a theory supported by his choice of landscape paintings, as these were lowest in the hierarchy of Baroque genres and would have been well-suited to a small cabinet, while mythological themes were among the highest-ranking subjects and were mostly exhibited in a gallery.

Even then, the prince's palaces were already open for selected visitors, as was the case with many other noble residences. Not only Prince Eugene's guests[21] but also travelers of noble descent were allowed to visit the rooms, usually when the owner was not present. Hence the palace regularly featured in the city guides and travel accounts of the time. Keyssler's *Travels through Germany, Bohemia, Hungary, Switzerland, Italy, and Lorrain* states, for example: "Of all the buildings at Vienna, the palace of Prince Eugene, in the suburbs, is undoubtedly the finest."[22] The numerous contemporary reports and travel guides document how the prince's garden palace was praised and admired, not only for its innovative architecture and elaborate garden design but especially for its magnificent décor and rich art collection. It emerges from many descriptions that the extensive collection contained pictures by the most important painters, reflecting the connoisseur's eye of the owner. The accounts not only discuss the artists and the subjects of the paintings, but the exorbitant prices paid for each of these works also drew visitors' attention.

Shortly after completion of his garden palace, Prince Eugene launched his most ambitious project of media self-fashioning. He commissioned the Augsburg-born artist Salomon Kleiner to create a set of engravings depicting the prince's palaces. The aim of the *Residences Memorables*[23] was to illustrate every room in the garden palace, complete with artworks, furniture, and décor, and to publicize this to a broader international audience (→ p. 26, ②). This was to secure the prince's *aeterna memoria*, or eternal memory, and honor Eugene of Savoy as a patron and art collector.

This set of engravings also provided a final glimpse of the collection and the garden palace before all of the prince's property and possessions were sold and dispersed. After Eugene's death, the picture collection was sold in 1741 by his heiress, Princess Victoria of Savoy, to her cousin, Charles Emanuel III, king of Sardinia, who brought the paintings to Turin.[24]

18 See the copy of the inventory in Auer/Black 1985, pp. 342–43.
19 See Seeger 2004, p. 327.
20 Seeger 2004, p. 327.
21 Norbert Elias writes that festivities and receptions in courtly society helped the nobility's career, and hence every courtier was obliged to open his house to guests; Elias 1969, p. 83.
22 Keyssler 1741.
23 Kleiner 1731–40; Aurenhammer 1969.
24 See Baudi di Vesme 1886; Spantigati 1982, pp. 17–51; Diekamp 2005; Spantigati in exh. cat. Vienna 2010, pp. 275–83; Spantigati in exh. cat. Turin 2012, pp. 35–49.

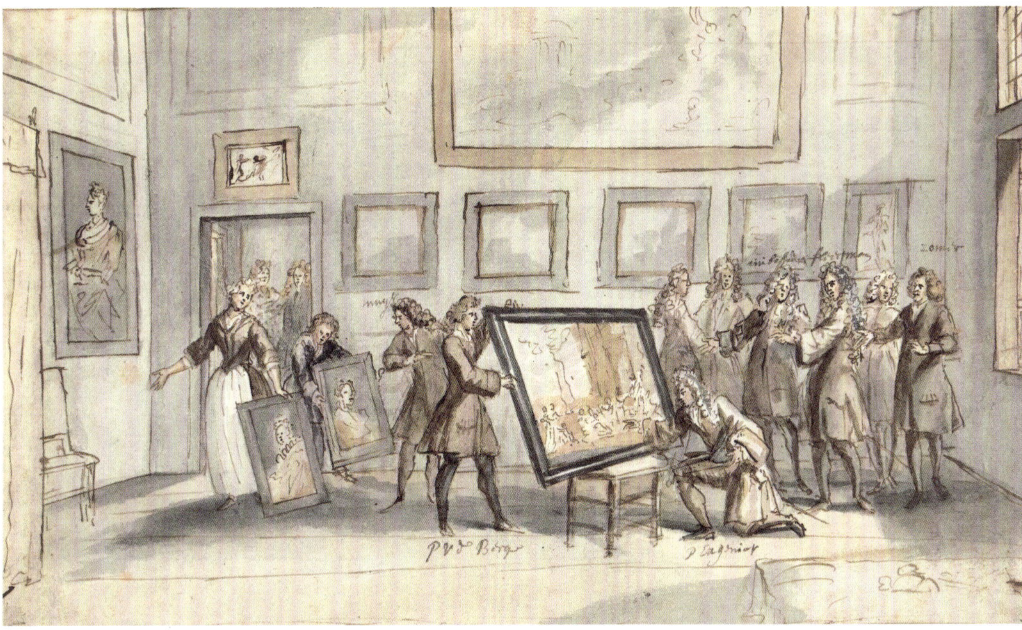

1

Fig. 1
Pieter van den Berge,
Prince Eugene of Savoy Visiting the Art Dealer Zomer,
1709–10, Rijksmuseum Amsterdam

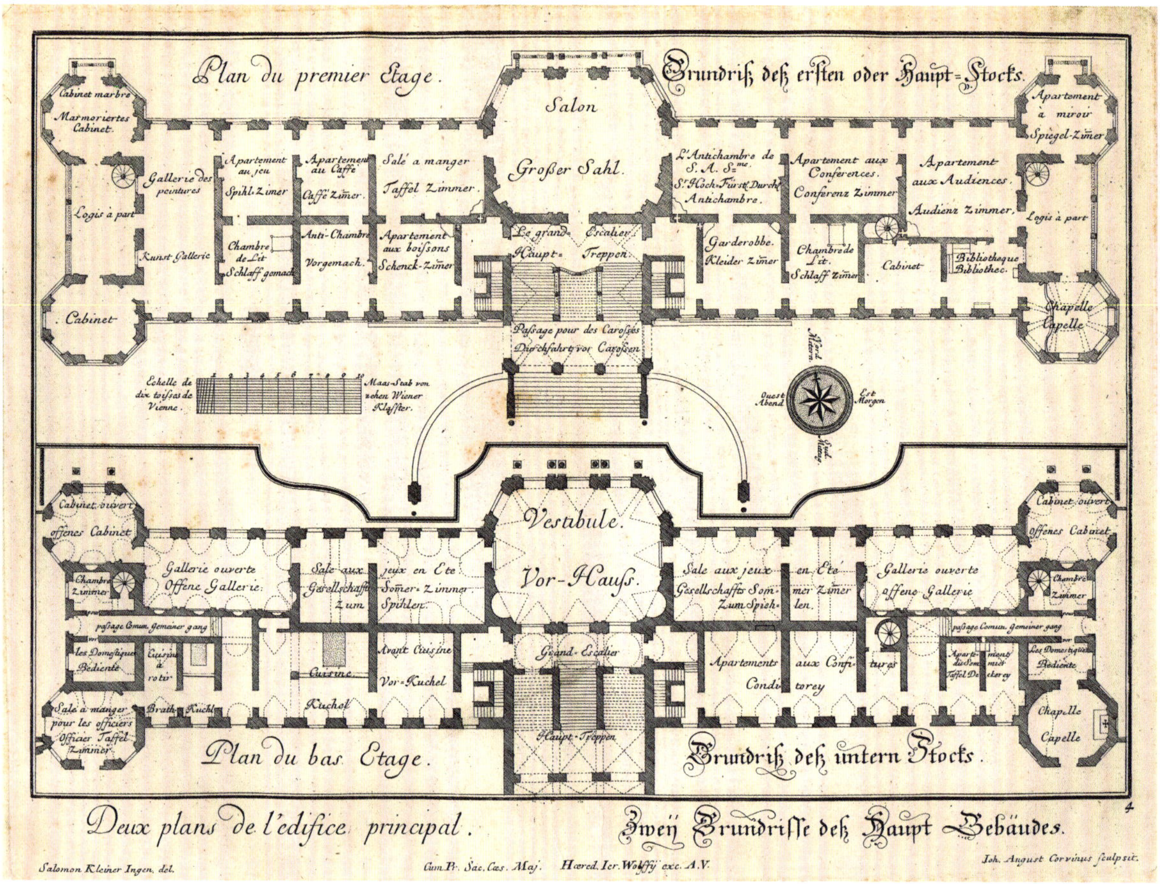

2

Fig. 2
Johann August Corvinus after Salomon Kleiner, *Floor Plan of the Upper Belvedere's Ground Floor and Bel Étage*, 1731, Belvedere Library, Vienna

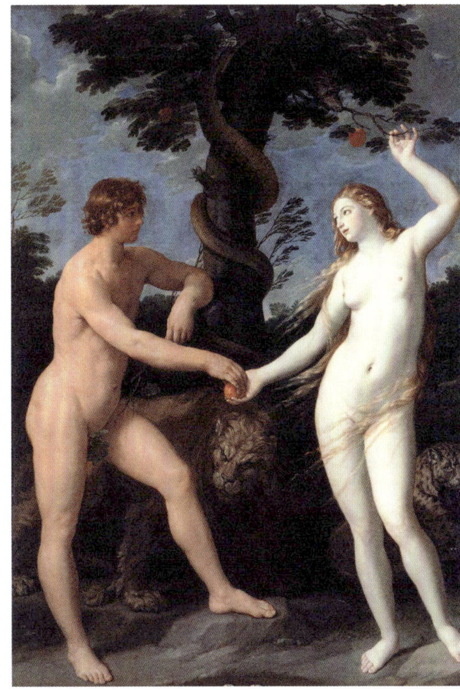

3

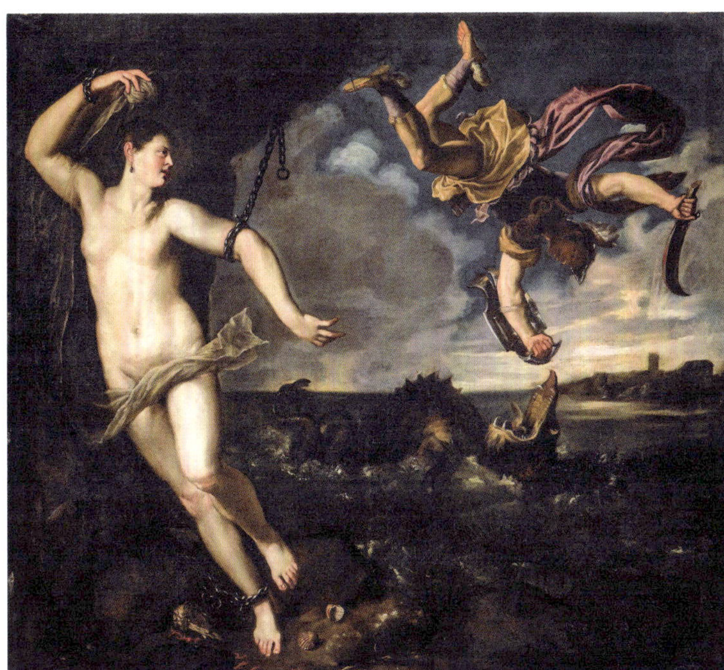

4

Fig. 3
Guido Reni, *Adam and Eve in Paradise*, c. 1620, Musée des Beaux-Arts de Dijon

Fig. 4
Copy after Titian, *Perseus and Andromeda*, 1630–40, private collection

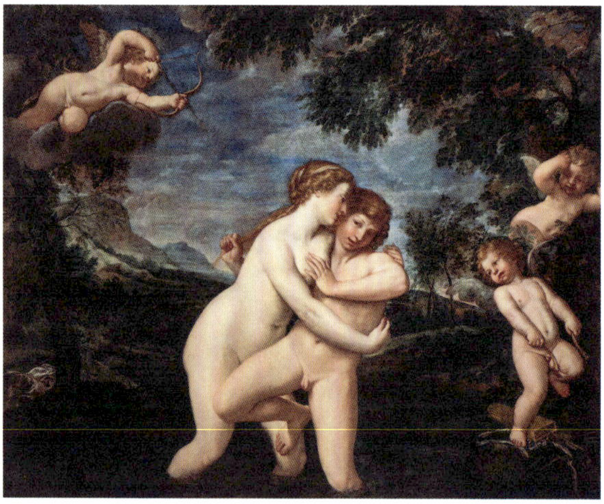

5

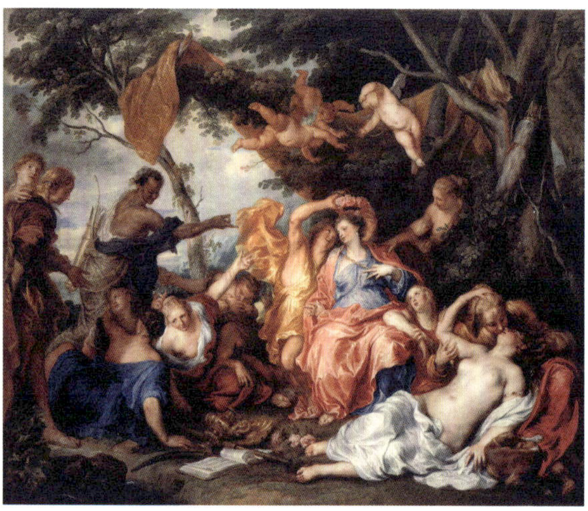

6

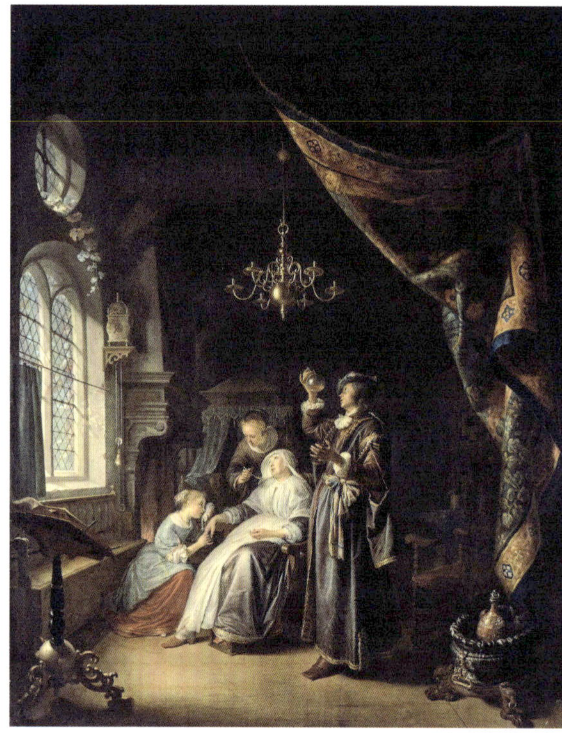

7

Fig. 5
Francesco Albani, *Hermaphroditus and the Nymph Salmacis*, 1633–35, Musei Reali Torino, Galleria Sabauda

Fig. 6
Anthony van Dyck, *Amaryllis and Mirtillo*, 1631/32, Musei Reali Torino, Galleria Sabauda

Fig. 7
Gerrit Dou, *The Dropsical Woman*, 1663, Musée du Louvre, Paris

Fig. 8
Rembrandt van Rijn, *The Visitation*, 1640, Detroit Institute of Arts, City of Detroit Purchase

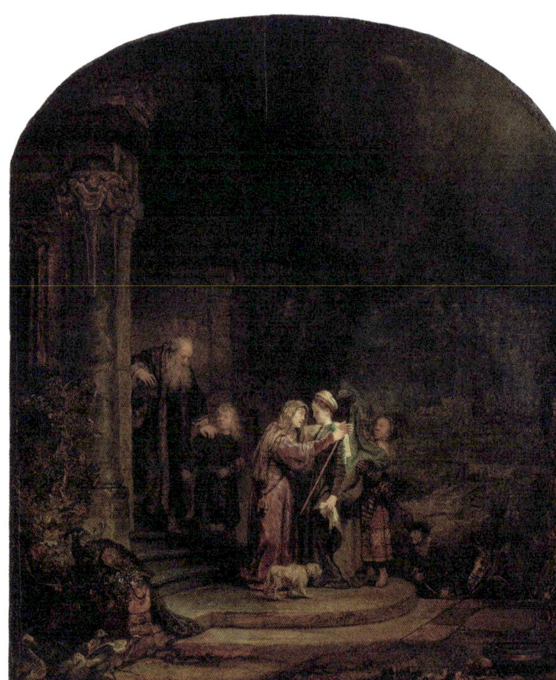

8

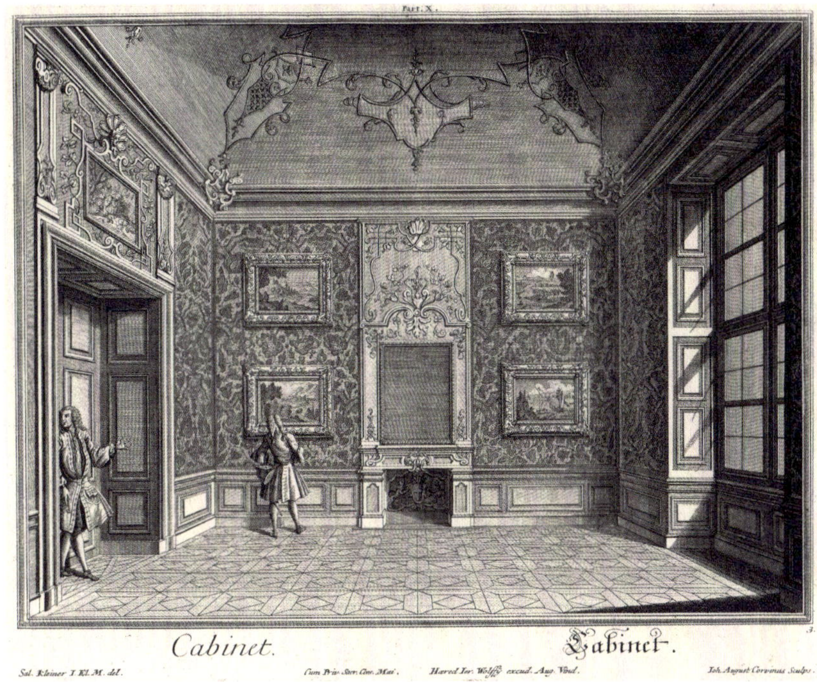

9

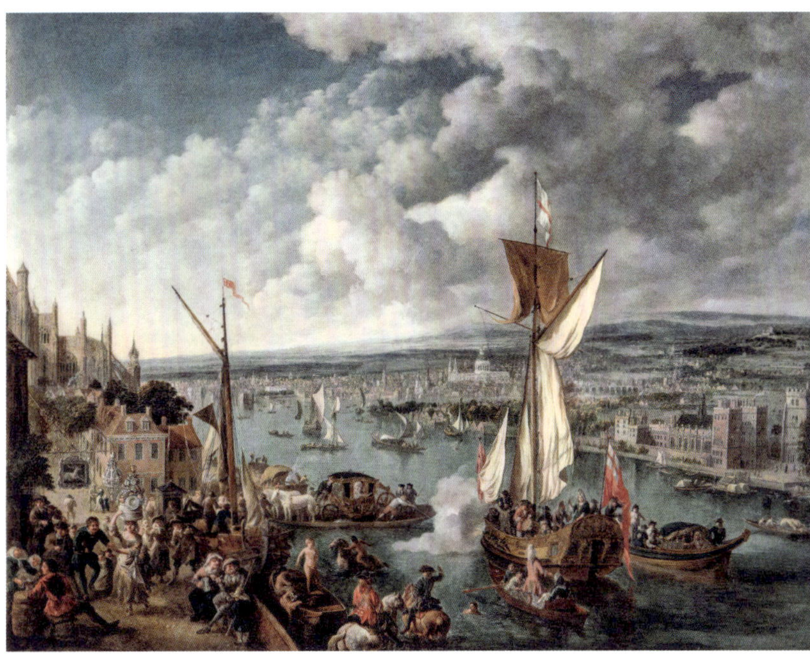

10

Fig. 9
Johann August Corvinus after Salomon Kleiner, *Picture Room in the Lower Belvedere*, 1740, Belvedere Library, Vienna

Fig. 10
Jan Griffier the Elder, *View of London from Horseferry Pier*, 1710–18, Musei Reali Torino, Galleria Sabauda

P. 64

ANTOINETTE FRIEDENTHAL —
Collect, Collate, Catalogue: Prince Eugene of Savoy and the Beauty of Classification

On August 24, 1718, a young man from Paris had the privilege of attending Prince Eugene's *levée* in Vienna (fig. 1). Eugene had been ill—in itself a newsworthy event in Europe at the time—but appeared now to have fully recovered. The best indication of the prince's good health is the subject of his conversation with Pierre Jean Mariette, his visitor and house guest: They were discussing art, more specifically, prints. And it was also prints that were to be brought to the prince's *jardin*—presumably the Belvedere gardens—on that same day.[1]

This is just one of several episodes bearing witness to the prince's keen interest in his collections. Mariette, who was part of Prince Eugene's household from October 1717 to mid-December 1718, was the scion of a book and print selling family, and as such stayed in the palace on Himmelpfortgasse in Vienna in order to assemble, classify, and catalogue prints and drawings for the prince. In letters home to his father in Paris he reported on his activities, writing about the prince's ardent zeal for learning about prints and his excitement as he awaited further deliveries from Paris.[2] Father and son alike were impressed by the intensity and seriousness of Eugene's efforts to become fully versed in the subject. The prince even declared his intention to visit Pierre Jean Mariette at work, prompting the young man to move his workplace from his room to the library.[3] Eugene's curiosity is evident in a drawing from 1709/10 (→ p. 59, fig. 1), which might be characterized as a press photo *avant la lettre*. It shows him in animated mood, paying a possibly spontaneous visit to Jan Pietersz. Zomer's commercial gallery in Amsterdam. Prince Eugene clearly had no qualms about getting personally involved in visiting art dealers, even kneeling down to examine the works close up.[4]

The prince acquired a huge number of works on paper (or similar supports, such as parchment), which he assigned to his library.[5] The hand-

1 Pierre Jean Mariette to his father Jean Mariette, Vienna, August 24, 1718; see Friedenthal 2023b, no. 56. For Prince Eugene's illness, see Braubach 1963–65, vol. 3, p. 379, and vol. 4, p. 56. For Salomon Kleiner's drawing, see Heinz 1967; Lorenz 1987. For Prince Eugene's sleeping quarters in the state and residential apartments, see, esp., Seeger 2004, pp. 47–53, 71–72. The name "Belvedere" for the estate outside the gates of the city was not used until the mid-eighteenth century; see Ginhart 1948, p. 118.

2 Pierre Jean Mariette to Jean Mariette, Vienna, March 26, 1718 ("S. A. S. qui se jette à corps perdu dans la connoissance des estampes"); see Friedenthal 2023b, no. 32.

3 Pierre Jean Mariette to Jean Mariette, date illegible [October 29, 1717 (?)]; see Friedenthal 2023b, no. 14.

4 For the drawing, see, most recently, Friedenthal 2022, pp. 457–58.

5 No account can be taken here of already bound art, such as illustrations in printed works and manuscripts (see the essays by Helmut Nader and Dagmar Thoss in exh. cat. Vienna 1986). Nor can this essay consider the diverse natural history drawings in the Eugeniana (see Friedenthal 2023c, with secondary literature). For the library in the city palace before the extension, see Lorenz 1987, pp. 228, 227; cf. Seeger 2004, p. 121 and n. 369. The library was later installed in the dedicated wing added from 1723 (see below).

written Eugeniana library catalogue lists these works as *Imaginum Collectio* (image collection).[6] These are mostly prints, but there is also a sizeable number of drawings.[7] Their provenance is diverse and only partly documented.[8] How and according to what criteria did Jean Mariette in Paris and his son Pierre Jean Mariette in Vienna (re)classify all these artworks? And why were different means of organization and storage used—not only portfolios (*portefeuilles*) but above all boxes and albums? Then there is also the question of making the collection accessible by way of indexes in French—handwritten like the library catalogue—complementing the images with texts in varying degrees of detail. Some of these indexes are veritable collection catalogues, while others are more like simple lists.

Boxes for portraits

Prince Eugene's collection of portrait prints is today in the Picture Archives of the Austrian National Library in Vienna. Time has left its mark, but the original condition of the collection can be reconstructed relatively well.[9] The portraits were originally stored in 217 boxes, arranged by state or country and then hierarchically by estate or profession.[10] The surviving folio-format boxes (fig. 2), which are no longer used for the collection, are covered in red morocco leather, embossed in gold with the prince's coat-of-arms and mirror monogram, ornamentation, and lettering. On the inside they are lined with colored marble paper. In addition to the portrait prints, which were mounted on backing paper, title sheets and tables of contents were also originally included.[11] The handwritten title sheets (fig. 3) were adorned with printed frames etched by Rochefort after Claude Gillot, which were also used for many of the Eugeniana albums.[12] The boxes were indexed by means of detailed tables of contents (fig. 4) listing the names of each sitter, the original artist, and the engraver.

The portrait collection was classified by Pierre Jean Mariette. When the work was brought to a temporary close at the end of 1718, he had identified and organized 25,248 portraits in 179 portfolios and also listed the entire collection in a separate catalogue.[13] The boxes were presumably produced afterwards, but the decision to store the prints in this loose form must have been made earlier. It enabled the portraits to be flexibly arranged in any desired manner. New acquisitions could be integrated quite easily into the existing system—an appreciable advantage, considering the anticipated further additions to the collection.[14] Having returned to Paris, Mariette appears not to have given the matter his full attention, however. In July 1724, Prince Eugene felt prompted to remind Mariette of his duties in a letter revealing his personal desire to put together the most complete portrait collection possible.[15]

6 Two multi-volume copies of the library catalogue exist: *Catalogus Librorum Bibliothecæ Ser.mi Principis Eugenii è Sabaudia [...] Tom. III* (ÖNB, Sig. Cod. 13965), s. p., pp. 1549–98; and *Catalogus Librorum Bibliothecæ Serenissimi Principis Eugenii è Sabaudiâ [...] Tomus III* (ÖNB, Sig. Cod. 14378), s. p., pp. 1353–76, 1401–02.

7 For the latter, see Friedenthal 2023c.

8 For discussion of provenance, see Krasa 1986; Gauna 2011, pp. 185–89; Smentek 2014, pp. 45, 51 and *passim*; Friedenthal 2017, pp. 54–59; Friedenthal 2022; Friedenthal 2023a; Friedenthal 2023b.

9 Wieser 1986; Poch 2018, ch. 7.5 and annex I; Friedenthal 2018; Friedenthal 2023b.

10 For the number of boxes, see *Catalogus Librorum* (ÖNB, Sig. 13965), pp. 1595–96; Van Swieten 1787 (annex III to Wieser 1968, p. 321); Ilg 1889, p. 24; Lugt 1921, p. 222; Poch 2018, p. 234 (indirectly citing Adam von Bartsch). Bartsch 1854, p. IV; Strebl 1968, p. 210; and Wieser 1986, p. 273 speak of 215 "portrait cartons," i. e., boxes, however.

11 In many cases there were also interleaves on which the titles of the subcategories within a box were written in calligraphy within printed cartouches.

12 The fact that the etching by Pierre de Massart, who signed as "De Rochefort," was based on a design by (Claude) Gillot can be inferred from a letter by Pierre Jean Mariette of September 16, 1718, to his father; see Friedenthal 2023b, no. 60. For a different frame used for the title pages, see note 17.

13 Held in the British Museum, London, Department of Prints and Drawings, inv. no. 1845,1223.1; see Griffiths 1994, p. 48; Friedenthal 2018; Poch 2018, p. 213.

14 For a general discussion of the "open order" and "loose-leaf collection," see Brakensiek 2009. For the organization of print portrait collections, see Bracht 2016; Poch 2018.

15 "[...] la collection des portraits la plus completee [sic] qu'il sera possible"; Prince Eugene to Pierre Jean Mariette, July 22, 1724 (draft), ÖStA/HHStA, GK Fasc. 98b-11, fol. 78r; see Müntz 1884, p. 177; Krasa 1986, no. 182; Poch 2018, p. 214.

Albums for artists' œuvres

Most of Eugene's collection now in the Albertina is arranged topographically by artistic region. It starts with the Italian schools, namely Florence (including Siena), Rome, Venice, Lombardy, Bologna, and finally Genoa and Naples. This is followed by the various Northern schools—i. e., German and Netherlandish masters, including Flemish artists, with no further geographical breakdown—and, as a third and final category, the French school. Within each individual school, the arrangement is more or less chronological by artist—among them also a few women. The result is a uniquely comprehensive collection of art on paper, extending from the beginnings of printing technology in the fifteenth century to the immediate present of the early eighteenth century. It is effectively a history of art consisting of thousands of prints glued into large-format albums (fig. 5).

The collection is characterized by prints reproducing paintings as well as prints conceived as such from the start—corresponding to the contemporary perception of an "œuvre."[16] A smaller number of prints depict sculpture and architecture. The individual artists' œuvres (fig. 6) are arranged iconographically,[17] starting, where possible, with a portrait of the artist concerned. Prince Eugene attached particular importance to this not uncommon practice of linking artists' portraits with their œuvre.[18] The catalogues (fig. 7), handwritten lists of contents produced at Eugene's insistence, concluded the albums.[19] In the more in-depth entries in these catalogues, which, as mentioned, vary in detail, the Mariettes pay tribute to the unique features of each print—notwithstanding the fact that the medium allows for multiple copies. They discuss their quality and condition and invite comparison—an instruction that corresponds with the arrangement of the prints within each œuvre. Some of the albums include(d) not only prints but also drawings. This was the case, for example, with the now dismantled Rembrandt œuvre.[20] Apart from the albums classified by artist, making up the majority of the collection, there were also albums organized by subject matter or technique.[21]

Art public in the Age of Reason

The aristocratic courtly society of the early modern era made no distinction between public and private sphere, as we understand it today.[22] This is apparent both in the institution of the *levée* mentioned earlier and in the fact that aristocratic and princely residences were not only used for ceremonial functions but were also open to visitors, as long as they were able to pay a gratuity and wore suitable attire.[23] The prince's library, too, was open to this kind of public during his lifetime. Beyond these general remarks, the contemporary perception of his collection requires a more nuanced examination.

16 See definitions in Furetière 1690, vol. 2, s. p.; *Dictionnaire* 1694, vol. 2, p. 144.

17 The printed frame with palm and laurel motifs shown here was a frequent theme used for the title pages. The Mariettes used a plate by Robert Nanteuil for this purpose; see Friedenthal 2017, pp. 50–52.

18 See Friedenthal 2023a; Lehner 2021.

19 Friedenthal 2017, pp. 50, 66–70 and *passim*; Friedenthal 2023b, nos. 1 and 12 (among others); for a general discussion of print collections in the era of Louis XIV and their catalogues, see Meyer 2015.

20 See Friedenthal 2022; Friedenthal 2023c.

21 Although there has been intensified research on the Mariettes and Prince Eugene recently, a systematic study of the Eugeniana, its art collections and their later fate is still a *desideratum*.

22 See Elias 1969/2002, pp. 91–94, 96–98, 142–46 (for Louis XIV's *levées*), p. 86, n. 15 (for nudity in a social setting).

23 For a general discussion of the subject, see Völkel 2007.

First of all, there is Prince Eugene and his circle, who, in 1718 for instance, would be contemplating Raphael's œuvre while listening to the young Mariette reading extracts from the catalogue before both were bound and covered in red morocco leather.[24] While this early and exclusive appreciation of the artworks is described in the correspondence between Mariette and his father, later visitors to the prince's city palace published travel reports with more or less detailed descriptions of the collection[25]—which by then was already housed in Johann Lucas von Hildebrandt's new library wing (→ p. 73, fig. 1), a westward extension of the palace, begun in 1723. There it was installed in the piano nobile's first room with five street-facing windows. One visitor was impressed by the "books" mostly bound in red saffian (morocco leather) with gilded titles and ornamentation, standing in boxwood "repositoria" fitted "on all shelves with green cloth" as protection against dust.[26] Prints and drawings were placed on the lower shelves.[27] Furthermore, there were three tables in the room "with drawers underneath."[28] As early as 1728, a how-to guide was published advising on the collection of portraits of "famous and scholarly men" (fig. 8); its author may well have had the prince's collection in mind.[29] Undoubtedly, the collection functioned as a model for other patrons, who sometimes had only heard of but not seen it for themselves, among them King John V of Portugal.[30] Thus, within just a few years, Prince Eugene's collection—shaped by a (military) love of order and protoscientific classification "furor," and compiled by way of two distinct systems in boxes and albums—became a benchmark for collecting in Europe.

The library's purchase by Charles VI after Prince Eugene's death and its installation in the state room of the imperial court library initiated a new chapter in its history, a history full of turns, at least for the prints and drawings and their reception. The latter included in-depth contemplation of artworks by way of copying, as practiced by the budding artist Johann Daniel Laurentz, who in the 1750s made etchings after drawings by Rembrandt and his school that were part of Prince Eugene's estate (fig. 9).[31] Moreover, the collection also started to become a point of reference in a more general debate. In 1768, as part of the ongoing and often heated argument as to whether it was better to collect the complete œuvre of an artist or just a selection, William Gilpin expressed sharp criticism of Prince Eugene, citing him as a typical example of the collector who misguidedly aims for completeness, an ambition that, according to Gilpin, is also financially unwise.[32]

Other participants in the debate, meanwhile, were more appreciative of Prince Eugene's objective. In 1778, for example, Carl Heinrich von Heineken, former director of the print room in Dresden, mentioned the prince's celebrated collection, then in the court library, in the first volume of his *Dictionnaire des artistes, dont nous avons des estampes*. Although

24 Friedenthal 2017, pp. 66–70. The Frenchman Etienne Boyet (also Boyer) was a bookbinder in the service of Prince Eugene; his father, Luc Antoine Boyet (Boyer), bookbinder to Louis XIV, sent animal hides and marble paper from Paris. Stamps with the prince's coat-of-arms and the paper on which the prints and drawings were to be mounted were also sent from Paris; see Friedenthal 2023b. For a general discussion of another place where contemporaries contemplated art, i. e., the picture gallery as a space for conversation and reading, see Penzel 2007.

25 See Küchelbecker 1730, pp. 628–30, 688–89; Pöllnitz 1735, pp. 228–29; anon. 1739, pp. 1130–40; Keyßler 1741b, pp. 936–37. A testimony from Prince Eugene's immediate circle can be found in the eulogy by Passionei 1737, here pp. 74–83.

26 Anon. 1739 (describing the situation in 1736), p. 1130. The surviving library cabinets from the Eugeniana in the library of the Theresianum (Vienna) were largely ignored in the literature (see Seeger 2004, p. 136 and n. 434) until their first close examination at the author's initiative in November 2022; see the essay by Christian Witt-Dörring in this volume, pp. 73–74.

27 Anon. 1739, p. 1131.

28 Anon. 1739, p. 1132. There follows a description of the second library room facing the courtyard, whose appearance is also captured in a drawing by Salomon Kleiner, p. 73.

29 Apin 1728.

30 Mandroux-França/Préaud 2003; see also Cohn 1992 (the "Spencer albums").

31 See Friedenthal 2022.

32 Gilpin 1768, pp. 231–32.

hesitant, for various reasons, to lavish unqualified praise on the Eugeniana albums and catalogues, he advised that an apparently planned publication of the catalogues in Vienna—in order to do justice to the "illustrious amateur"—should be entrusted to an expert in the matter.[33]

The planned undertaking alluded to by Heineken is not traceable in any of the known sources.[34] His information might have been correct, however, not least considering that, since 1777, the court library had a new director in the well-known music lover and patron Gottfried van Swieten.[35] It was under his aegis that the *Josephinischer Katalog*—sometimes said to be the first index-card catalogue in the history of libraries—was developed.[36] It is also possible that the engraver and print expert Adam Bartsch, who joined the court library in early 1777, was involved in the project mentioned by Heineken.[37] The catalogues raisonnés published by Bartsch from 1795 onward may well have their roots in this project, especially since they are proven to have been based on Eugene's collection catalogues compiled by the Mariettes. This also applies to Bartsch's most important work, the *Peintre Graveur* (1803–21), which is still consulted today.[38] Towards the end of the Age of Reason, public opinion increasingly demanded access to the contents of the court library, even if only in the form of manuscript editions.[39]

With the establishment of the Imperial Picture Gallery in the Upper Belvedere in 1781, the premises and collection were to be transformed into a "visible history of art." Setting forth this intention, Christian von Mechel, who directed the hanging, drew the analogy with a "rich library [...] in which those thirsty for knowledge enjoy to encounter works of all types and eras, not just pleasant or perfect works, but also a succession of contrasts that, through observation and comparison (the only way to acquire knowledge), will enable the visitor to become a connoisseur of art."[40]

Mechel's approach has given rise to controversy, not only among his contemporaries but also among scholars today. The arrangement of the paintings in the Upper Belvedere was celebrated as a pioneering achievement in museum display. It was seen as an updated implementation of older concepts in art theory, qualified as the conclusion of a project essentially based on the work of a predecessor. Not least, it was subsumed under the epochal phenomenon of scientific classification, on a par with the taxonomies adopted in natural history—and this by no means covers the full spectrum of interpretations.[41] Regardless of which of them is the most convincing, those involved in setting up the Picture Gallery must have been familiar with the Eugeniana. In view of its significance for the history of art and science and its renown, it would be surprising if it was not a defining source in one way or another for the Picture Gallery in the Upper Belvedere. This is especially likely to per-

33 Heineken 1778, pp. XV–XVII. For the portrait collection, see Heineken 1771, pp. 505–06.
34 See Smentek 2014, p. 250.
35 Heineken states that he was in Vienna in 1769 and in contact with van Swieten, whom he thanks for his assistance; see Heineken 1786, pp. 198–99 (citing a letter to him from van Swieten in 1785).
36 See Krajewski 2017, pp. 52–57; Rieger 2014, pp. 23–24; both with older literature.
37 For the beginnings of Bartsch's appointment, see Rieger 2014, p. 23.
38 Bartsch 1803–21; see also Gauna 2012, p. 90; Smentek 2014, pp. 2, 42, 250. For case studies, see Friedenthal 2008; Friedenthal 2017.
39 See anonymous claims in late 1781 in the *Realzeitung*; Wieser 1968, p. 292 and annex II.
40 Mechel 1783, pp. 11–12.
41 From the extensive literature, see e.g., Wüthrich 1956, pp. 151, 153; Meijers 1995a (original ed. 1991); Meijers 1995b; Trautwein 1997, p. 1991; Sheehan 2002, p. 69; Penzel 2007, pp. 42–46 and *passim*; Fischer 2013a; Mayer 2021, ch. 5.

tain to the albums sorted by artistic regions and then chronologically by artists.[42] As a matter of fact, the concept of a history of art exemplified by the objects themselves dates back much further: it continues a particular and important line of tradition that leads from Paris art dealers to Prince Eugene's library in Vienna, from where its influence spread far and wide.

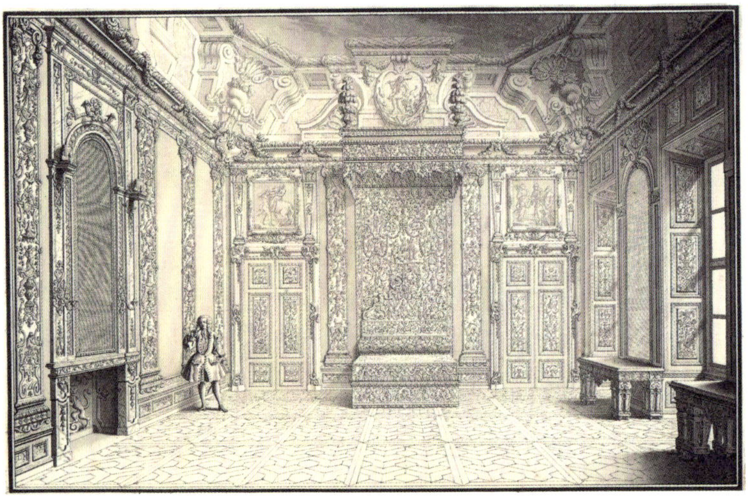

1

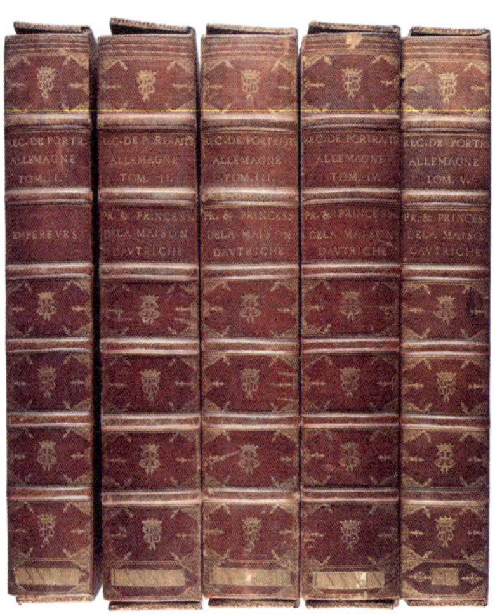

2

42 Bickendorf 2007, pp. 51–52 and *passim*, mentions the fundamental relevance of print collection concepts for the picture arrangements in the Upper Belvedere, albeit incorrectly assuming that Mariette worked at the same time for Prince Eugene and on the *Recueil Crozat* (1729 and 1742). Fischer 2013a, pp. 56–58, states that the *Recueil Crozat* had a model function for Mechel's gallery arrangement and mentions Pierre Jean Mariette in this context, whom Mechel is said to have visited in Paris. No mention is made, however, of the importance of the Eugeniana albums for Mechel's project, although note 139 briefly points out that Mariette was involved from 1717 to 1718 in the development of Prince Eugene's print collections. For the albums as an important prerequisite for the *Recueil Crozat*, see Gauna 2012, p. 97; Friedenthal 2017, p. 73.

Fig. 1
Salomon Kleiner, *State Bedroom in Prince Eugene's City Palace*, c. 1730 or earlier, Wien Museum

Fig. 2
Empereurs & Princes et Princesses de la maison d'Autriche, boxes from Prince Eugene's portrait collection, nos. 86–90, c. 1719, Austrian National Library, Vienna, Picture Archives

Fig. 3
Title sheet of *Empereurs*, box no. 86, c. 1719, Austrian National Library, Vienna, Picture Archives

Fig. 4
First page of the table of contents of *Empereurs*, box no. 86, c. 1719, Austrian National Library, Vienna, Picture Archives

Fig. 5
The album *Œuvres de Louis Carache*, 1718 or soon after, Albertina, Vienna

Fig. 6
Title page of the album *Œuvres de Louis Carache*, 1718, Albertina, Vienna

Fig. 7
First page of the catalogue of the album *Œuvres de Louis Carache*, 1718, Albertina, Vienna

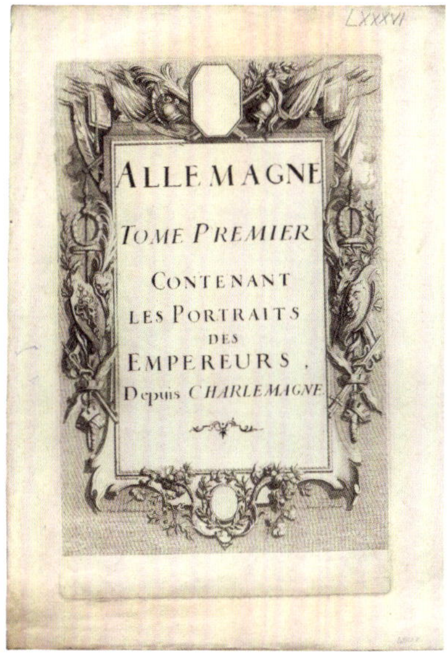

3

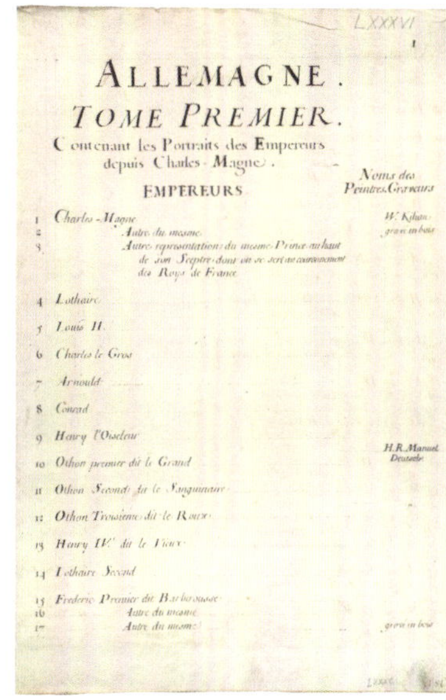

4

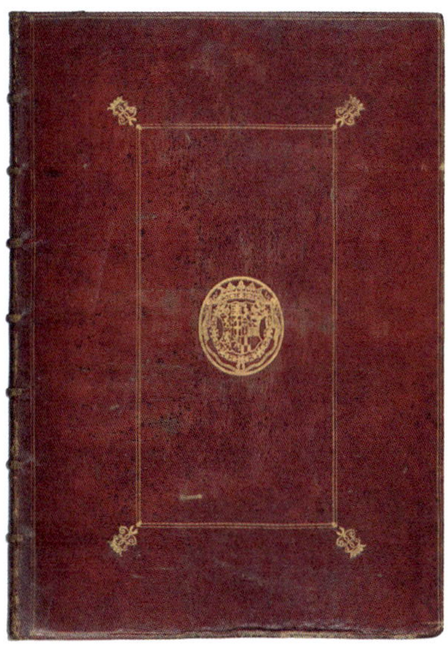

5

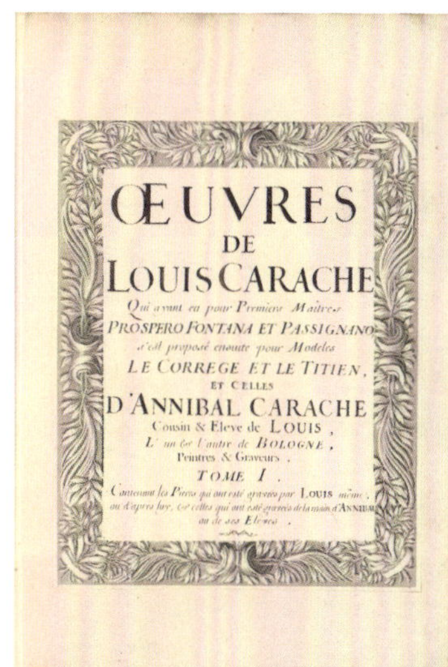

6

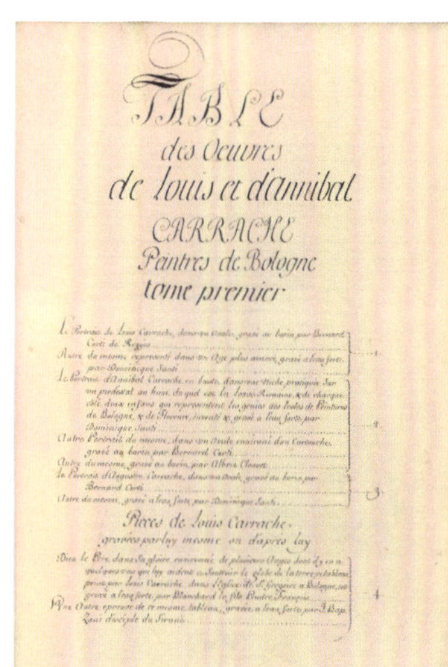

7

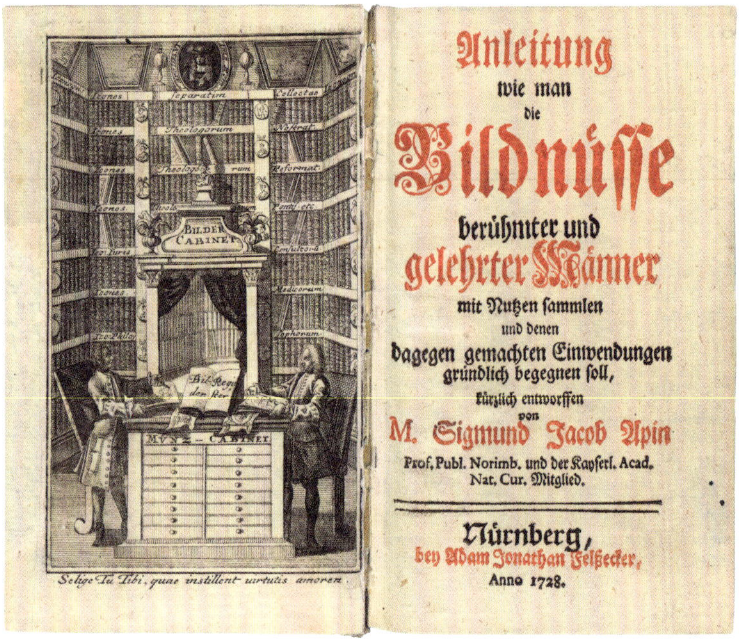

Anleitung
wie man
die
Bildnüsse
berühmter und
gelehrter Männer
mit Nutzen sammlen
und denen
dagegen gemachten Einwendungen
gründlich begegnen soll,
kürzlich entworffen
von
M. Sigmund Jacob Apin
Prof. Publ. Norimb. und der Kayserl. Acad.
Nat. Cur. Mitglied.

Nürnberg,
bey Adam Jonathan Felßecker,
Anno 1728.

8

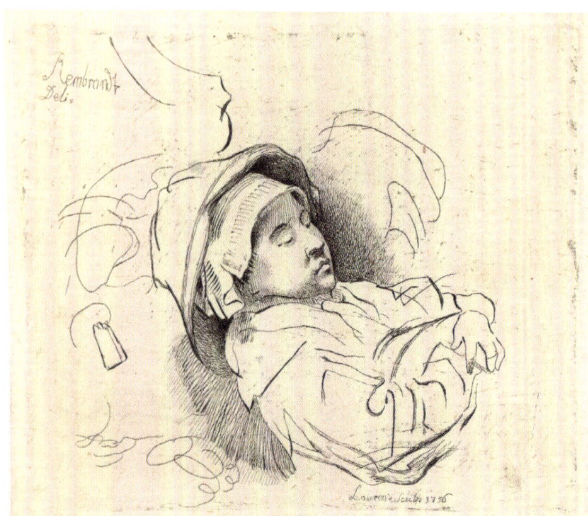

9

Fig. 8
Frontispiece and title page of Sigmund Jacob Apin, *Anleitung wie man die Bildnüsse berühmter und gelehrter Männer mit Nutzen sammlen und denen dagegen gemachten Einwendungen gründlich begegnen soll*, 1728, Austrian National Library, Vienna

Fig. 9
Johann Daniel Laurentz after Rembrandt, *Sleeping Child*, 1756, Albertina, Vienna

(5)

The Theresianum Library Cabinets from Prince Eugene's Winter Palace

Christian Witt-Dörring

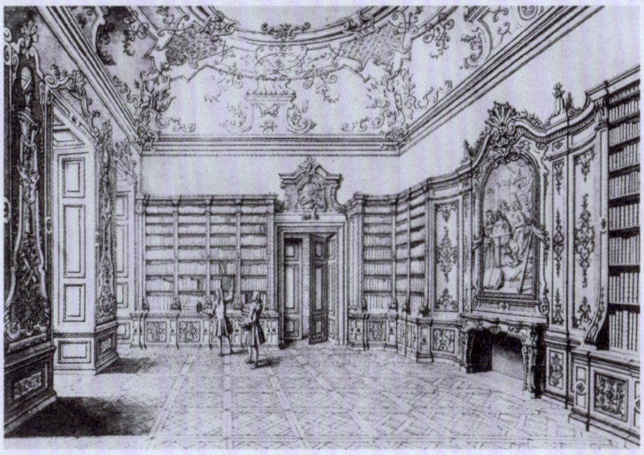

1

Fig. 1
Salomon Kleiner, *Middle Library Room in Prince Eugene's Winter Palace*, c. 1730, private collection

The centermost of the three library rooms in Prince Eugene's Winter Palace was captured in a drawing by Salomon Kleiner (fig. 1). Thanks to this drawing and a 1739 description,[1] elements of the wall-mounted furnishings in the library of the Theresianum have been identified as possibly originating from that room.

In 1737, only a year after Prince Eugene's death, Emperor Charles VI acquired the prince's collection of books and art prints from his heiress. The library wing in Prince Eugene's city palace, installed in 1723, thus no longer functioned as such and was repurposed as a rental property.[2] It was presumably then—or some time later—that the wall-mounted library cabinets were also removed.

In 1746, Empress Maria Theresa decided to establish a school for children of the nobility in the Favorita, which was to become today's Theresianum Academy. On July 31, 1748, she also ordered the books from the Garellian Library to be transferred there,[3] and two rooms were refurbished for that purpose. On August 4, 1749, the empress visited the "new library and museum mathematicum" for the first time.[4] According to a description in 1780 by the librarian Michael Denis, "fifteen narrow cabinets containing [books on] linguistics" were installed in the second, smaller room. "They have not been newly made, but were purchased from the estate of the great Prince Eugene, together with an outstanding painting by Jos. Heinze [sic], also installed here, showing an aged philosopher explaining the globe to an attentive boy. One of the cabinets has a cleverly hidden door leading to the librarian's living quarters."[5]

The room today bears little resemblance to this description from 1780. The large painting by Heinitz is no longer there, and the original, aesthetically uniform arrangement of the cabi-

1 Anon. 1739, pp. 1134–35: "On entering, one sees on the right-hand side, opposite the windows, a beautiful marble fireplace, next to which are the portraits of Diana and Apollo in white marble. Above the fireplace is a painting by the celebrated Heinitz showing an aged philosopher measuring a globe on which a woman, possibly symbolizing geography, is pointing out places to him; […] directly opposite, above the door to the third room, is a young person, also by the same brush, browsing a book."
2 Seeger 2004, p. 11, n. 5.
3 Denis 1780, p. 7.
4 Guglia 1912, p. 33.
5 Denis 1780, p. 11.

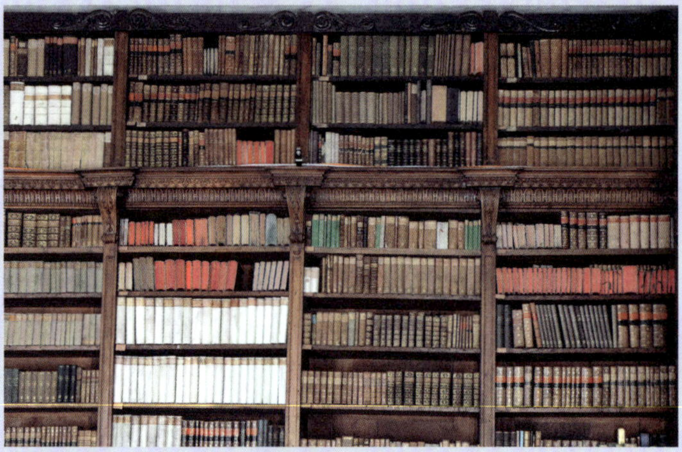

2

Fig. 2
Parts of the cabinets from the middle library room in Prince Eugene's Winter Palace in their present-day location in the Theresianum library, Vienna

Fig. 3
Detail of the side of the cabinets from the middle library room, Vienna

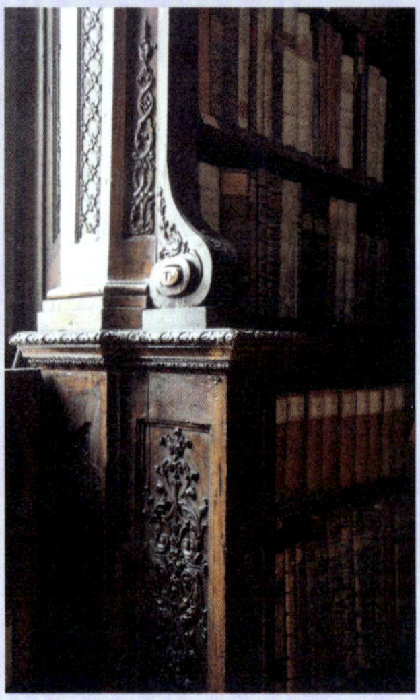

3

nets (shelves) reflecting the proportions of Eugene's wall-mounted furnishings has also given way to a storeroom-like set-up that makes maximum use of the available wall space (fig. 2). It incorporates part of the cornice and the base—minus its original carved paneling—and the narrow vertical pilasters on volutes bordering the individual cabinets from the library on Himmelpfortgasse (fig. 3). The cabinets are thought to have been designed by Claude Le Fort du Plessy, an upholsterer (and thereby also interior decorator) from Paris, who designed all of Prince Eugene's interiors.[6] He used a system of decoration developed in Paris around 1710, similar to the décor systems by Robert de Cotte, Louis XIV's first architect.[7] When the Winter Palace was dismantled, its library furnishings were no longer deemed fashionable and hence not suitable for the demonstration of courtly or aristocratic status.[8]

It is not known when and for what reason the original furniture arrangement, evidently still taken into account at the time the library was installed in the Theresianum, was abandoned in favor of a more space-efficient, purely practical arrangement. It is possible that it became necessary in the second half of the nineteenth century, by which time the library had grown to contain over 80,000 books.

6 Schmidt 1933, p. 118, n. 48.
7 Fossier 1997, dossier 409.
8 Witt-Dörring 2006, p. 89.

Chapter II

The Imperial Collections in the Belvedere

1776–1891

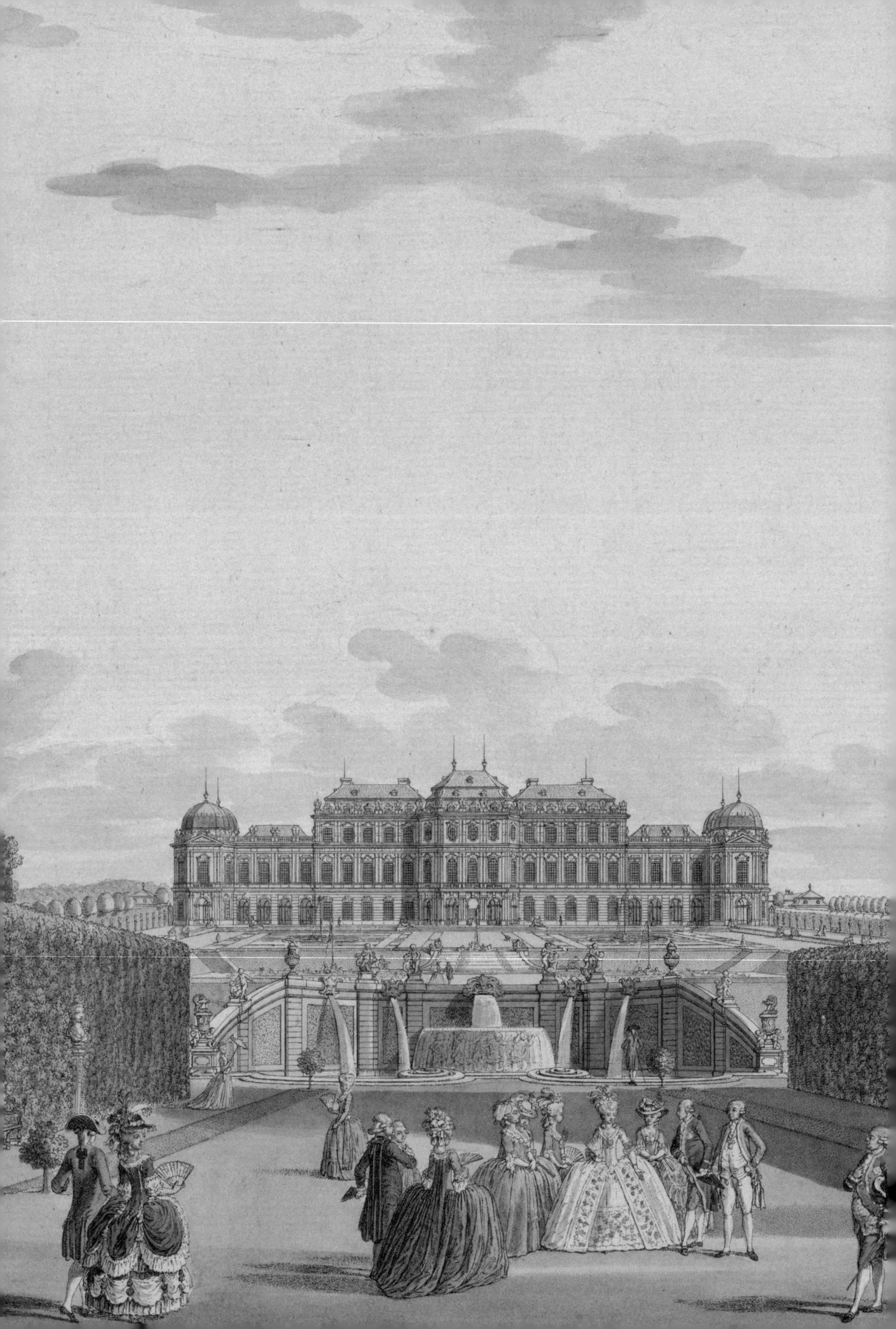

Chapter II
The Imperial Collections
in the Belvedere

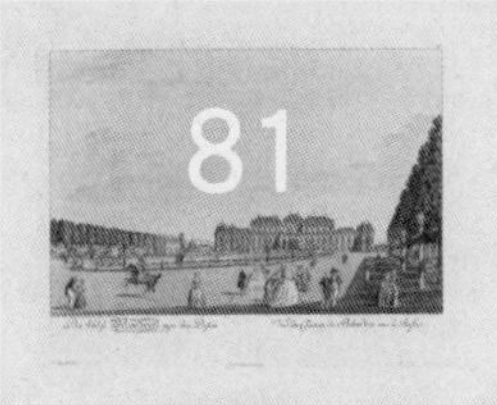
81

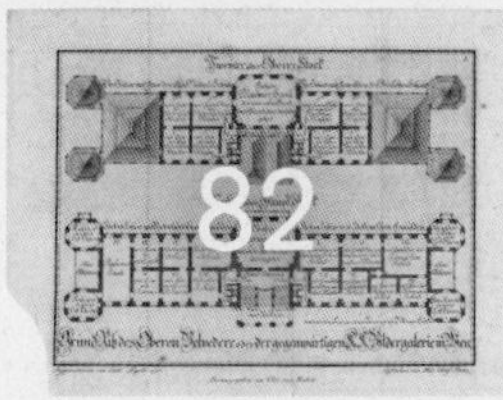
82

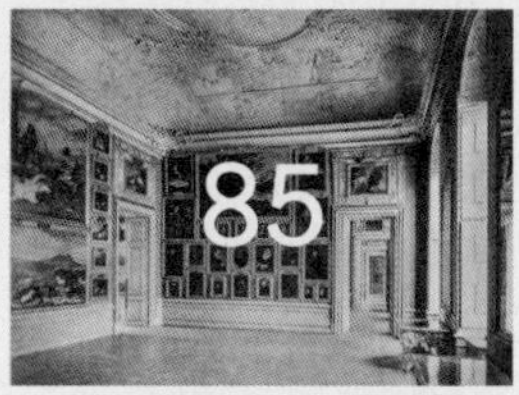
85

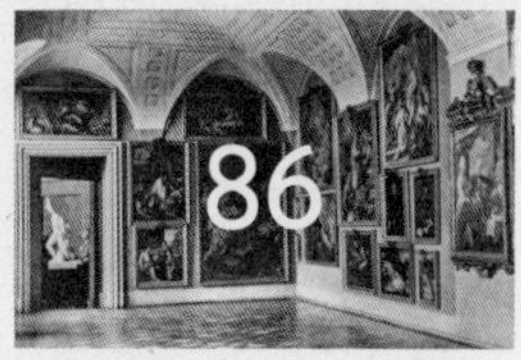
86

89

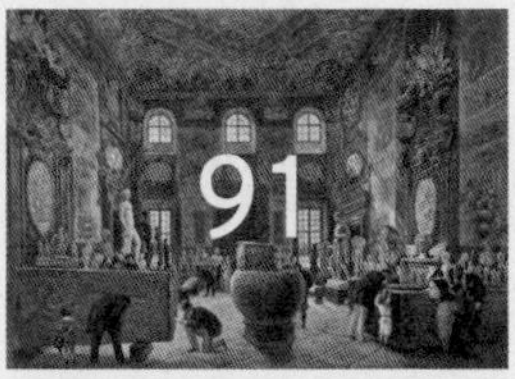
91

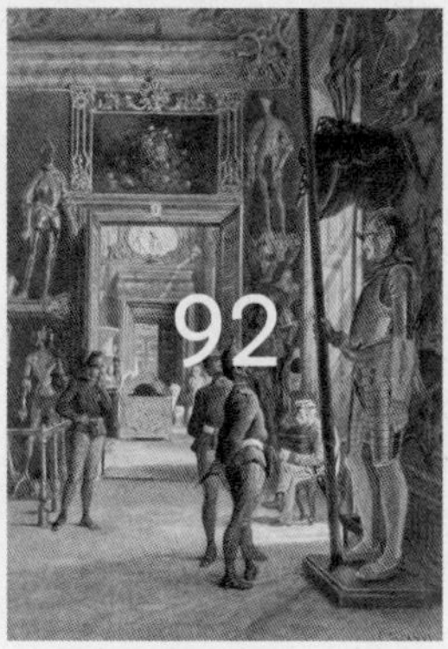
92

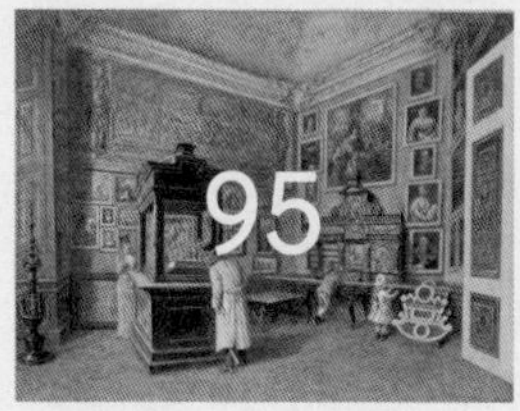
95

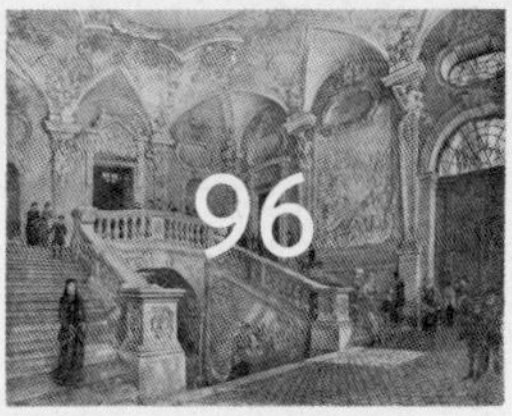
96

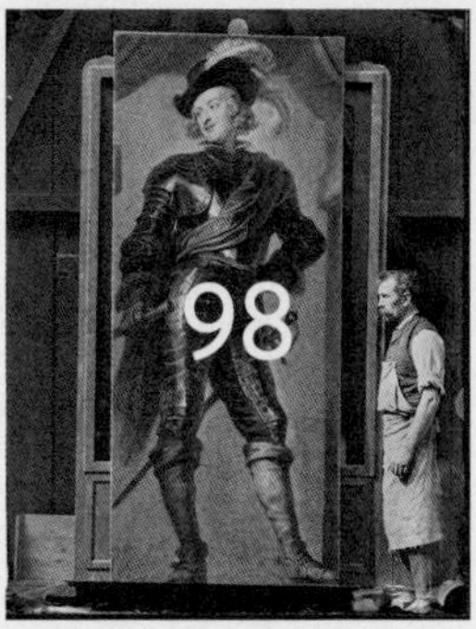
98

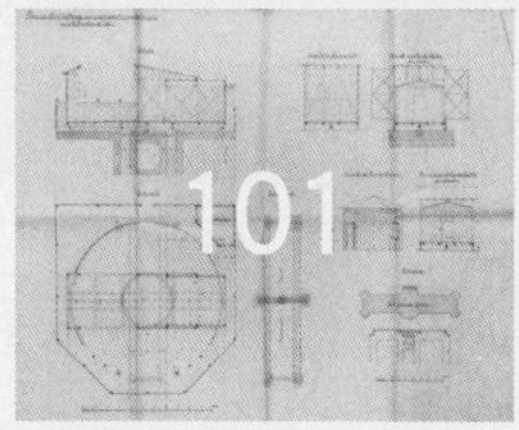
101

←
Carl Schütz, *View of the Grounds of Belvedere Palace* (detail), 1785, Wien Museum

The gallery is open to everyone on Mondays, Wednesdays, and Fridays. [...] Here we must point out that it is forbidden to enter the gallery with a stick, since various meddlesome individuals have been touching the paintings with one of those. This ban is very moderate—many impudent visitors should be told, if this were possible, to leave their fingers by the door, too.

—— Joseph von Kurzböck, *Neueste Beschreibung aller Merkwürdigkeiten Wiens*, Vienna 1779, p. 56

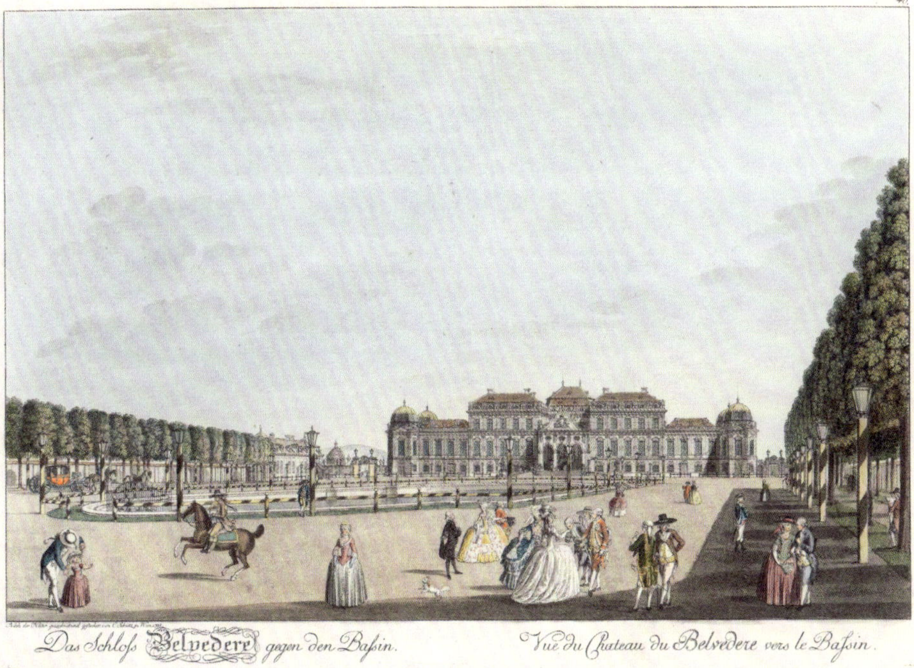

Carl Schütz, *View of the Pond of Belvedere Palace*, c. 1805

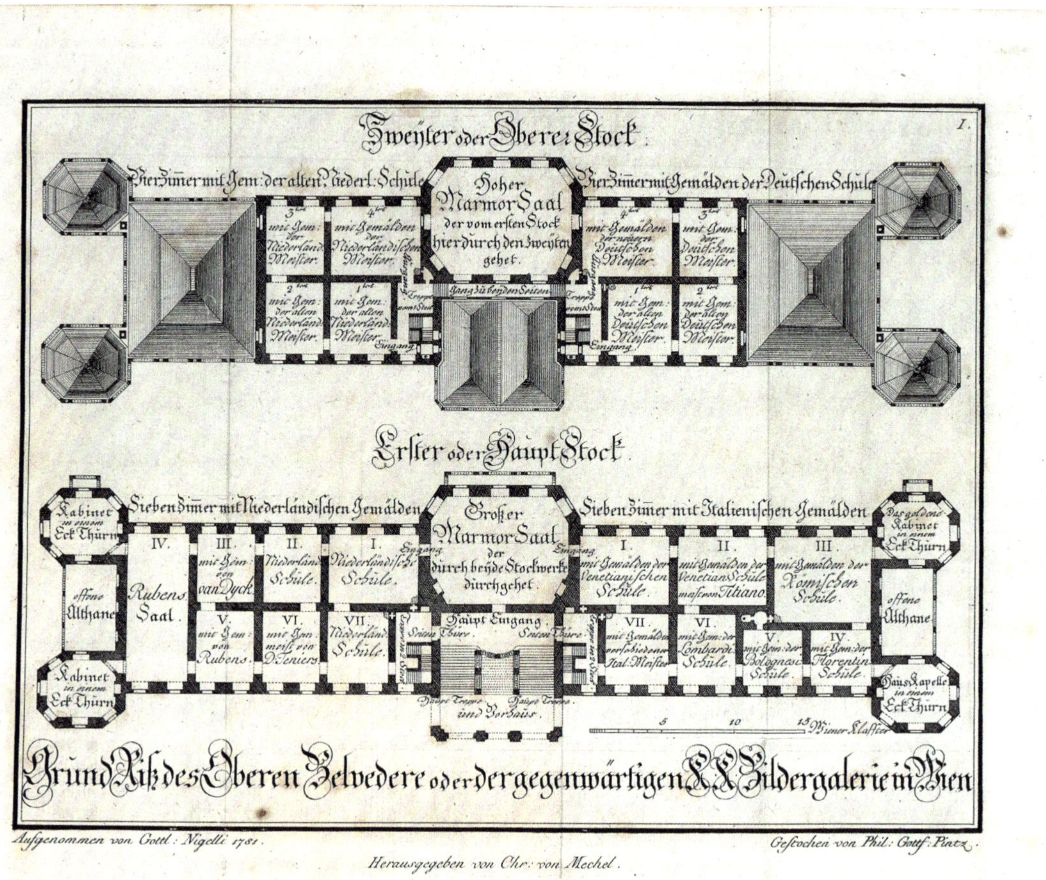

Philipp Gottfried Pintz after Gottlieb Nigelli, *Floor Plan of the Upper Belvedere in Vienna*, 1781

I was very pleased to see the works from the various schools and artists together, and not mixed up, as is the case in some other painting galleries. Students can explore the style and distinctive character of the different schools and masters much more easily if they can view them in an uninterrupted sequence, without being befuddled by such distracting variation, where contrast follows contrast, confusing and benumbing the imagination.

—— August Klingemann, in *Zeitung für die elegante Welt*, no. 104, June 1, 1820, p. 828

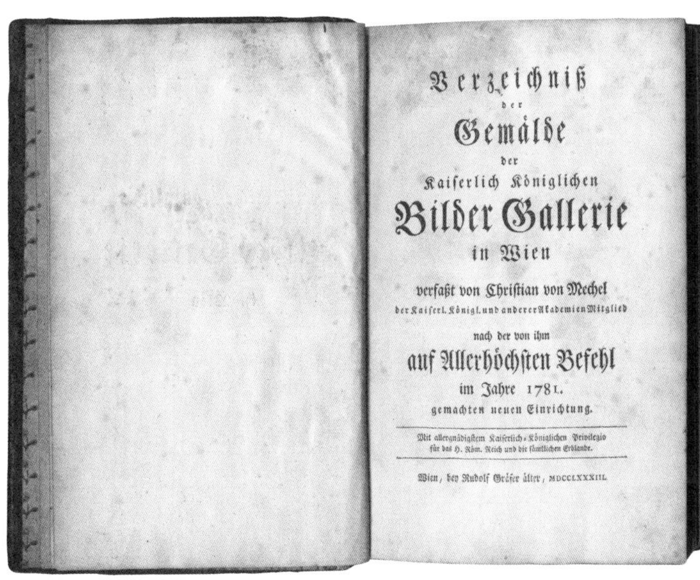
Verzeichniß
der
Gemälde
der
Kaiserlich Königlichen
Bilder Gallerie
in Wien
verfaßt von Christian von Mechel
der Kaiserl. Königl. und anderer Akademien Mitglied
nach der von ihm
auf Allerhöchsten Befehl
im Jahre 1781.
gemachten neuen Einrichtung.
Mit allergnädigstem Kaiserlich-Königlichen Privilegio
für das H. Röm. Reich und die sämtlichen Erblande.
Wien, bey Rudolf Gräfer älter, MDCCLXXXIII.

Christian von Mechel, *Verzeichniß der Gemälde der Kaiserlich Königlichen Bilder Gallerie in Wien*, Vienna 1783, Belvedere Library, Vienna

As it was not easy, without a special recommendation, to gain access to some of the noteworthy painting galleries in Vienna, including, in particular, the collections of the Prince of Liechtenstein and the Counts von Fries and von Lamberg—besides the fact that some of their owners were absent—I contented myself with the imperial collection in the Belvedere, a former summer residence of the celebrated Eugene of Savoy, which had been arranged very usefully by Mechel and Rosa according to the different schools, occupying all the rooms in the large building on Rennweg.

—— Georg v. Martens, *Reise nach Venedig: Erster Theil*, Ulm 1824, p. 142

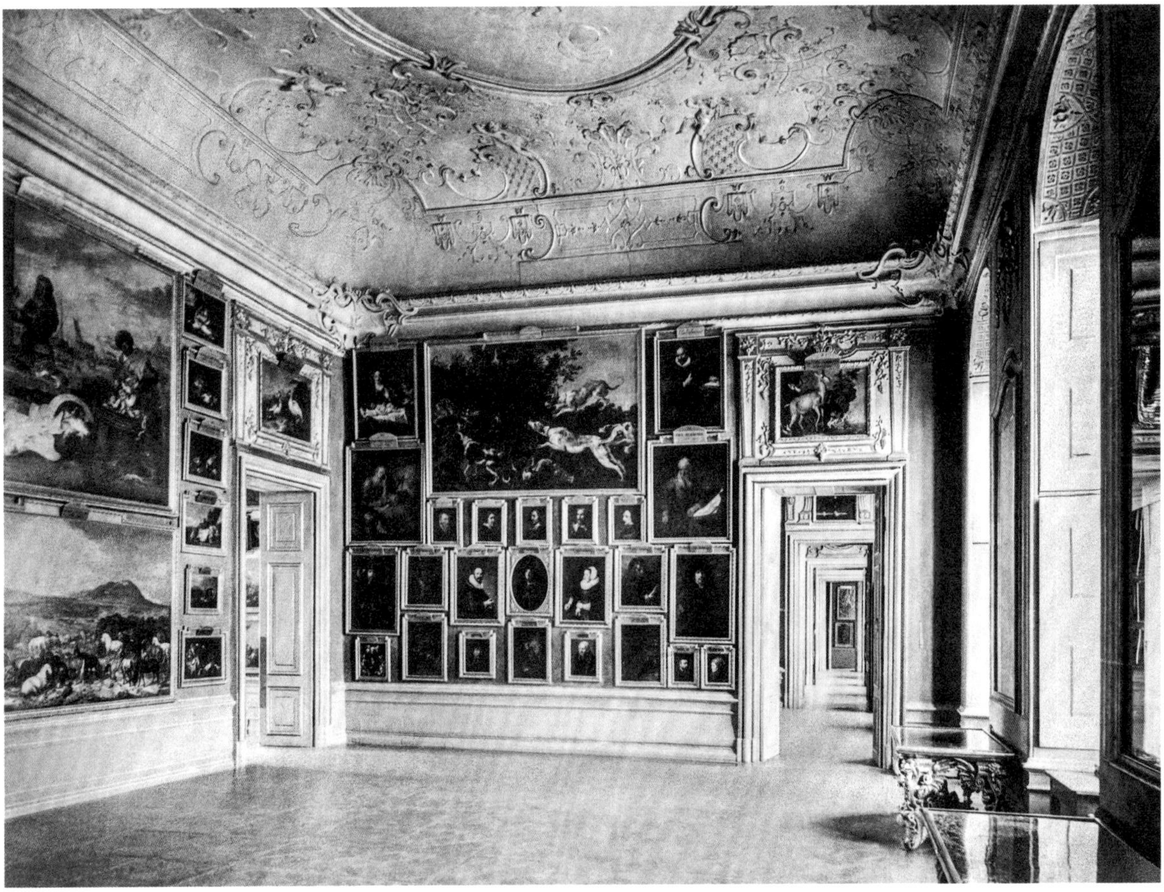

First room of the Netherlandish school in the Imperial Picture Gallery on the bel étage of the Upper Belvedere, c. 1880

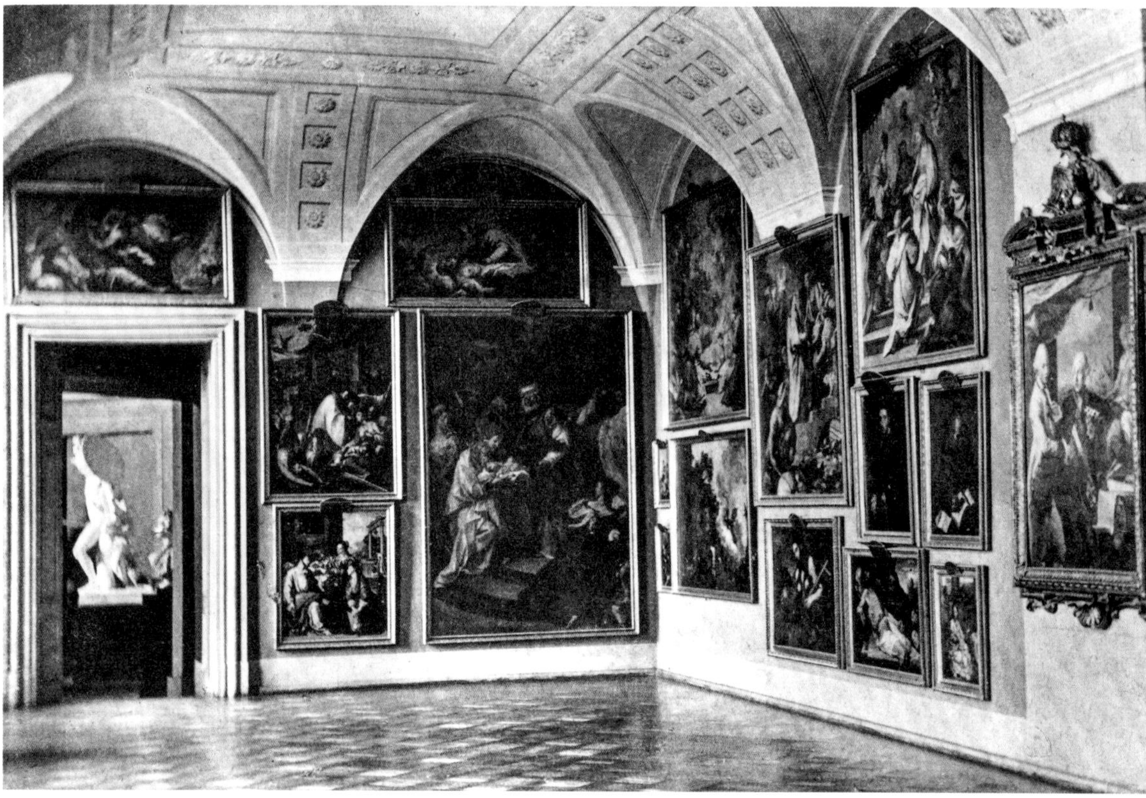

Imperial Picture Gallery on the ground floor of the Upper Belvedere, c. 1880

For the pictures from the most important and richest periods, the names of their authors are always provided insofar as they could be determined or were known from reliable sources. At any event, this consistent labeling is a valuable addition, all the more so as it partially takes the place of a catalogue. In some other galleries, it occasionally happens that one or other of the numbers comes off, and the visitor with the catalogue has to hunt them down, like a fugitive in hiding; a nuisance that is carefully avoided in the Belvedere.

— *Wiener Zeitschrift für Kunst, Literatur, Theater und Mode*, December 5, 1837, p. 1160

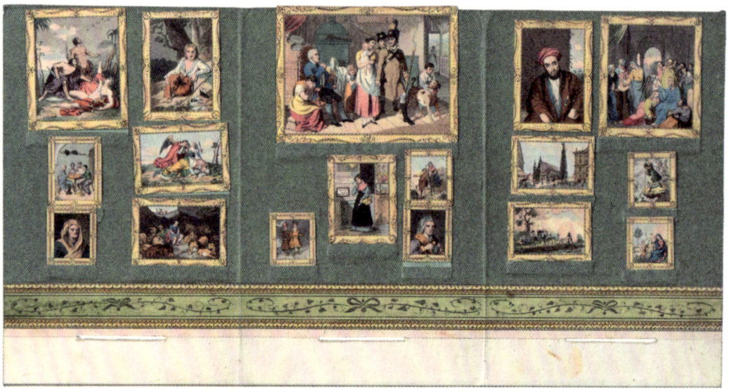

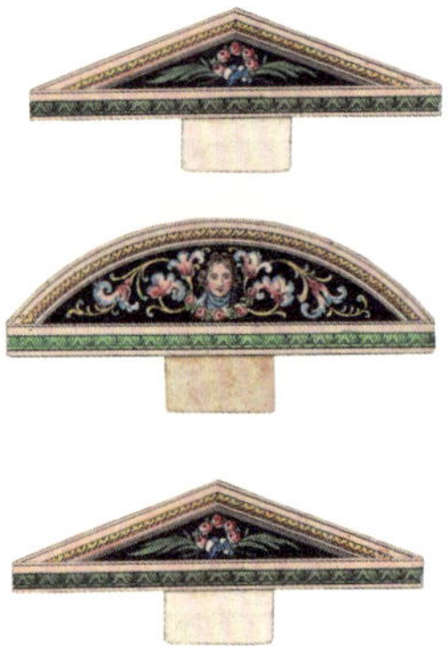

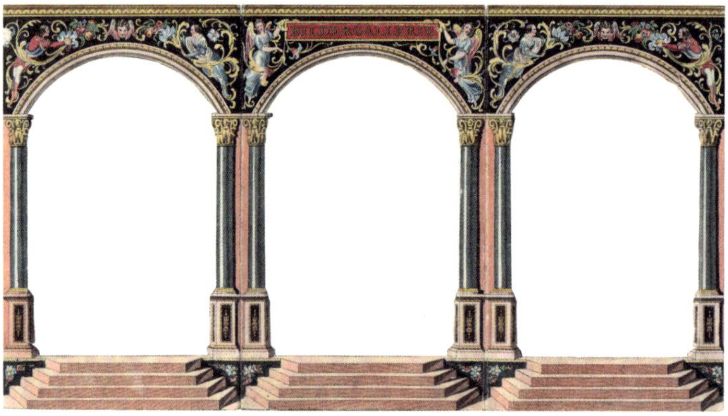

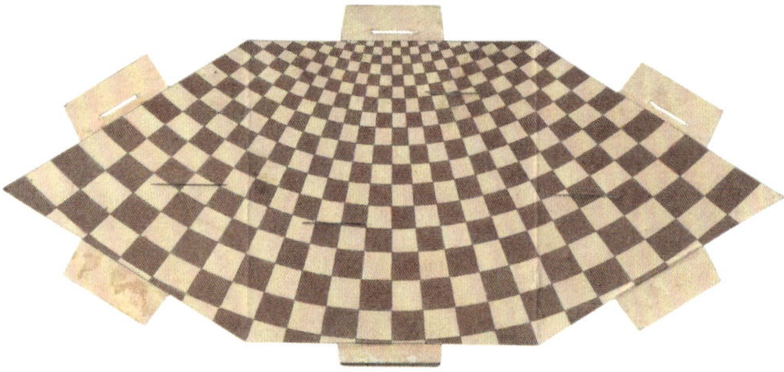

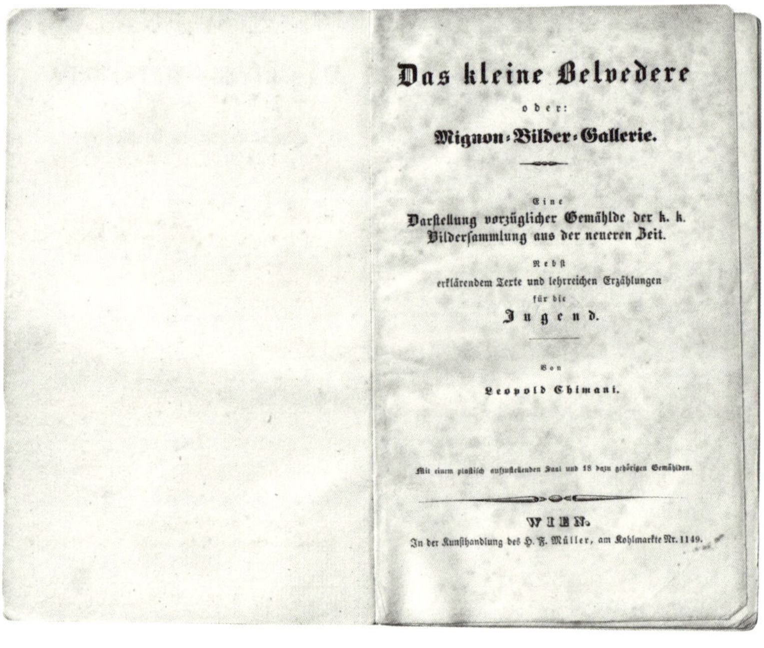

Das kleine Belvedere

oder:

Mignon-Bilder-Gallerie.

Eine

Darstellung vorzüglicher Gemählde der k. k. Bildersammlung aus der neueren Zeit.

Nebst

erklärendem Texte und lehrreichen Erzählungen

für die

Jugend.

Von

Leopold Chimani.

Mit einem plastisch aufzustellenden Saal und 18 dazu gehörigen Gemählden.

WIEN.

In der Kunsthandlung des H. F. Müller, am Kohlmarkte Nr. 1149.

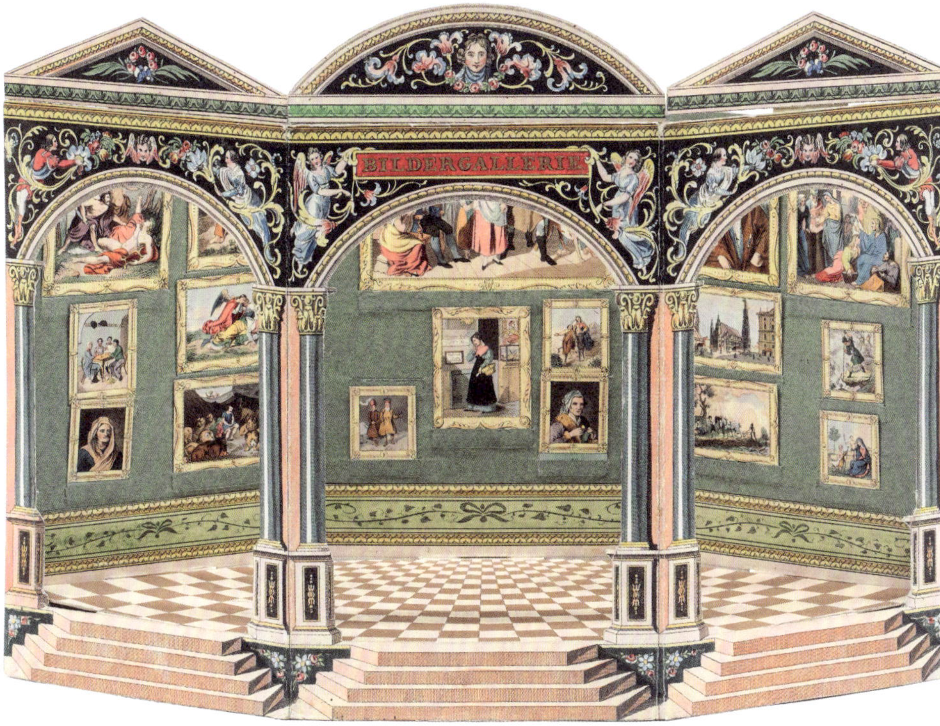

Leopold Chimani, *Das kleine Belvedere oder Mignon-Bilder-Gallerie*, Vienna 1840

Leopold Chimani's *Mignon-Bilder-Gallerie* was aimed at children, introducing them to art with the help of the most recent works in the Belvedere. Its production may have been prompted by the redisplay of the Imperial Picture Gallery in 1836. *Das kleine Belvedere* was accompanied by a booklet with short descriptions of the works, and details of the public access to the Picture Gallery and its opening times.

Mondays are usually very crowded and busy. Plenty of folk from the lower classes, apprentices taking the Monday off, and even menial servant girls with children on their arms, enjoy spending an afternoon in the picture gallery. I would like this to change. Children are dangerous for the gallery: they touch the most precious pieces with their grubby fingers. Why would children come to a gallery at all? I believe it would be quite feasible, without incommoding visitors too much, to ban children and other base elements. After all, an art collection is not a puppet show, and it is clear that these people do not appreciate the pictures any more than if, out of boredom, they were to visit a Savoyard and his peepshow.

—— Johann Pezzl, *Skizze von Wien: Drittes Heft*, Vienna 1787, pp. 441–42.

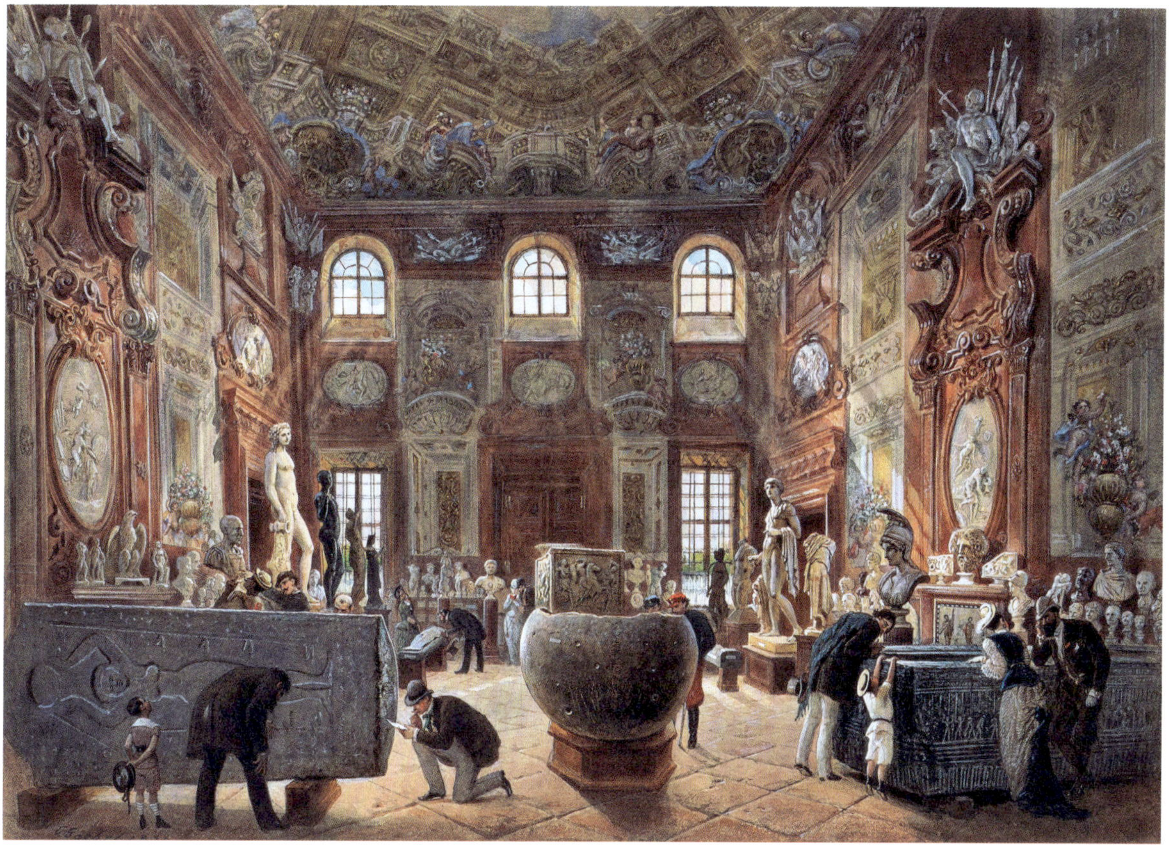

Carl Goebel the Younger, *The Marble Hall of the Lower Belvedere with Sculptures from the Antiquities Collection*, 1876

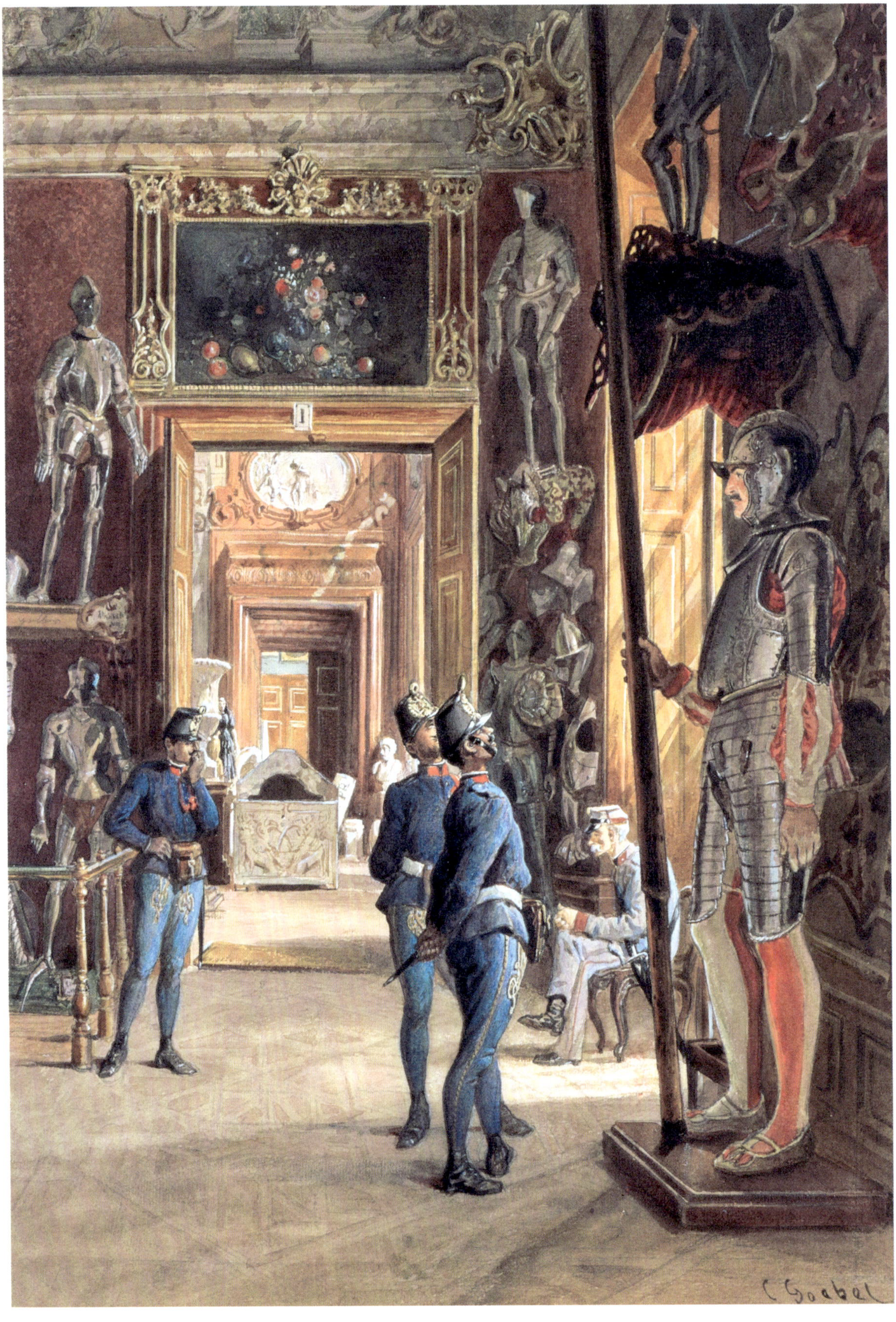

⑥

The Ambras Collection

Georg Lechner

The Ambras Collection was originally housed at Ambras Castle, nowadays within Innsbruck's city boundaries and part of the Kunsthistorisches Museum. Its founder was Archduke Ferdinand II of Tyrol, who amassed a rich array of objects for his *Kunst- und Wunderkammer* (cabinet of art and marvels), including armor, portraits, books, and artifacts. Built especially for these holdings, the lower castle is still used as a museum today, and continues to house parts of the collection.

During the Coalition Wars, the collection had to be moved to safety several times. With the Peace of Pressburg, signed on December 26, 1805, Tyrol and Vorarlberg were ceded to the new Kingdom of Bavaria, and the Ambras holdings were transferred to Vienna as a result. In 1811, Emperor Francis II/I decided to display the collection at the Lower Belvedere, but the political situation delayed implementation of this plan until the last objects had been evacuated in 1813. Moreover, to ensure their safe passage, the artifacts and curiosities were accompanied by their keeper Johann Baptist Primisser, who was responsible for Ambras Castle and its collection. His son Alois Primisser, who later became a numismatist and archaeologist, assisted him with the displays at the Lower Belvedere. Both were also very committed to the production of a catalogue, which was published in 1819.

A vivid impression of the abundance of objects exhibited at the Lower Belvedere is conveyed in the watercolors by Carl Goebel the Younger. From 1875 to 1889, he depicted the individual rooms, and these paintings are now in the Belvedere's collection (→ pp. 91–95). They show that the Marble Gallery contained display cases filled with a rich array of objects, while the frescoed walls of the Hall of Grotesques were entirely concealed by the House of Habsburg family tree and numerous portraits (fig. 1). The extensive holdings of classical Roman and ancient Egyptian material culture were exhibited in other rooms. Amidst the displays, we can also detect paintings from the Imperial Picture Gallery, for which there was no space in the Upper Belvedere.

The Ambras Collection was transferred from the Lower Belvedere to the newly built Kunsthistorisches Museum shortly before it opened in 1891. Until the early 1930s, some of the now empty rooms in the Lower Belvedere came to house objects excavated from Ephesus, which had been brought to Vienna between 1896 and 1906 (→ p. 207, ⑮).

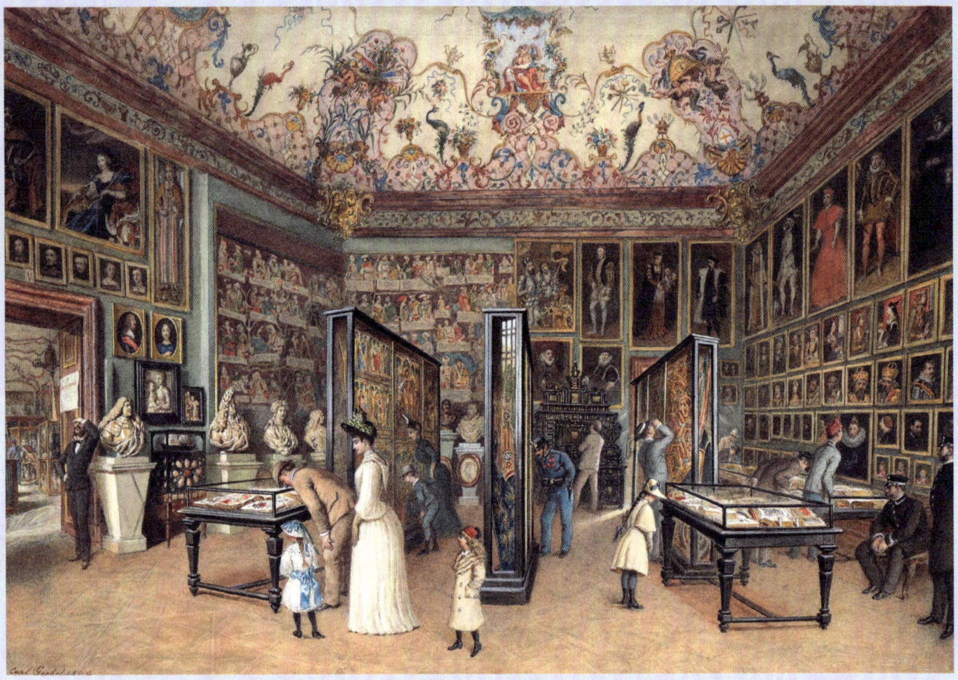

1

Fig. 1
Carl Goebel the Younger, *The Family Tree Hall*, 1888, Belvedere, Vienna

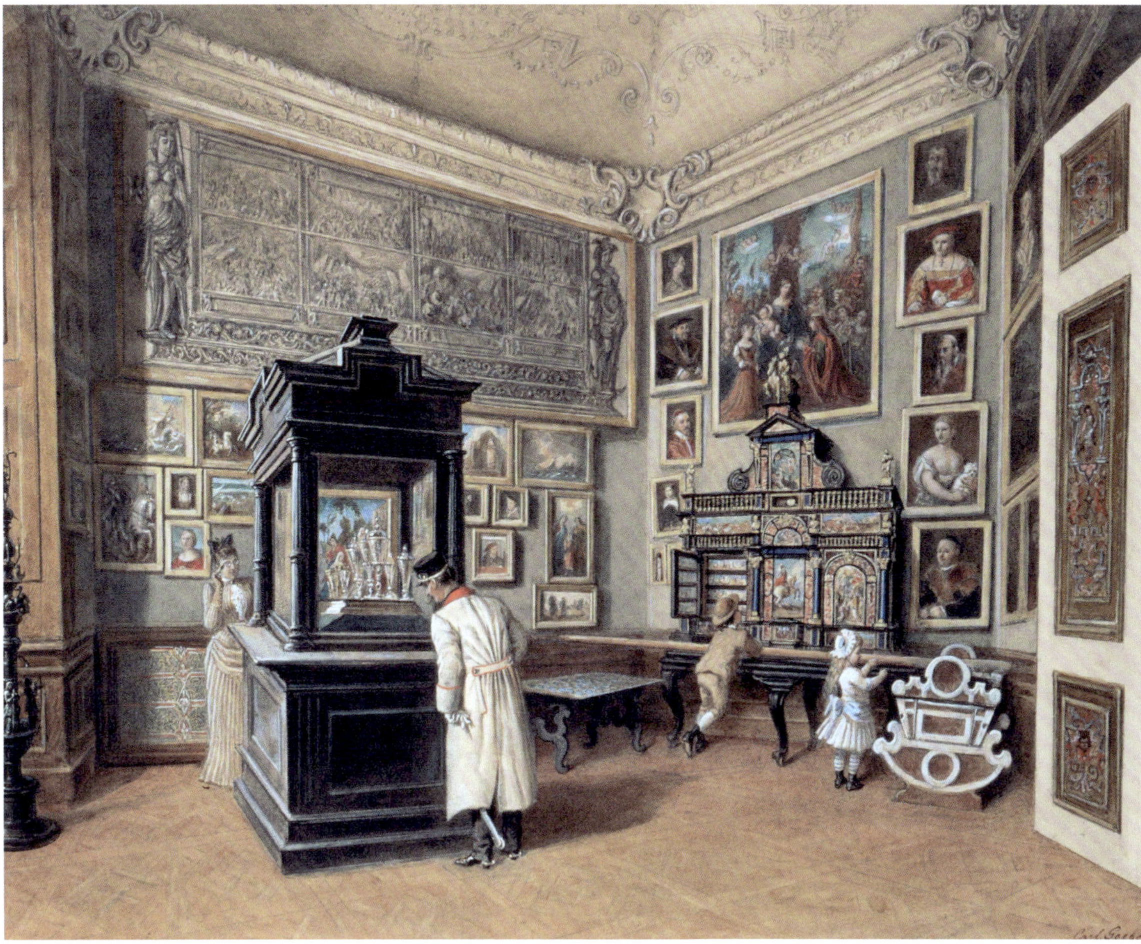

↑
Carl Goebel the Younger, *Last Cabinet of the Ambras Collection with Bohemian Glassware*, 1889

← p. 92
Carl Goebel the Younger, *Entrance to the First Armory Room*, 1875

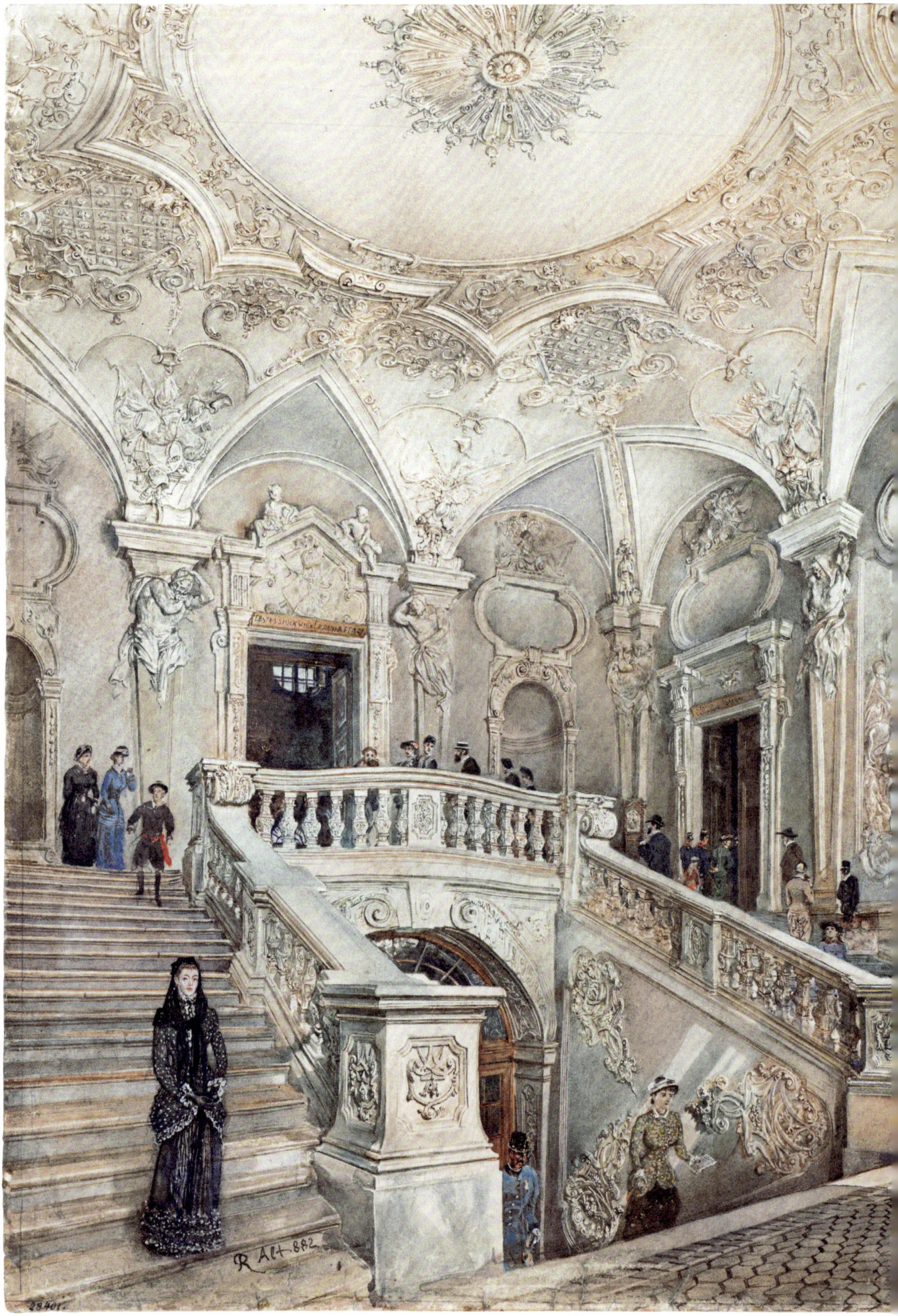
R Alt 882

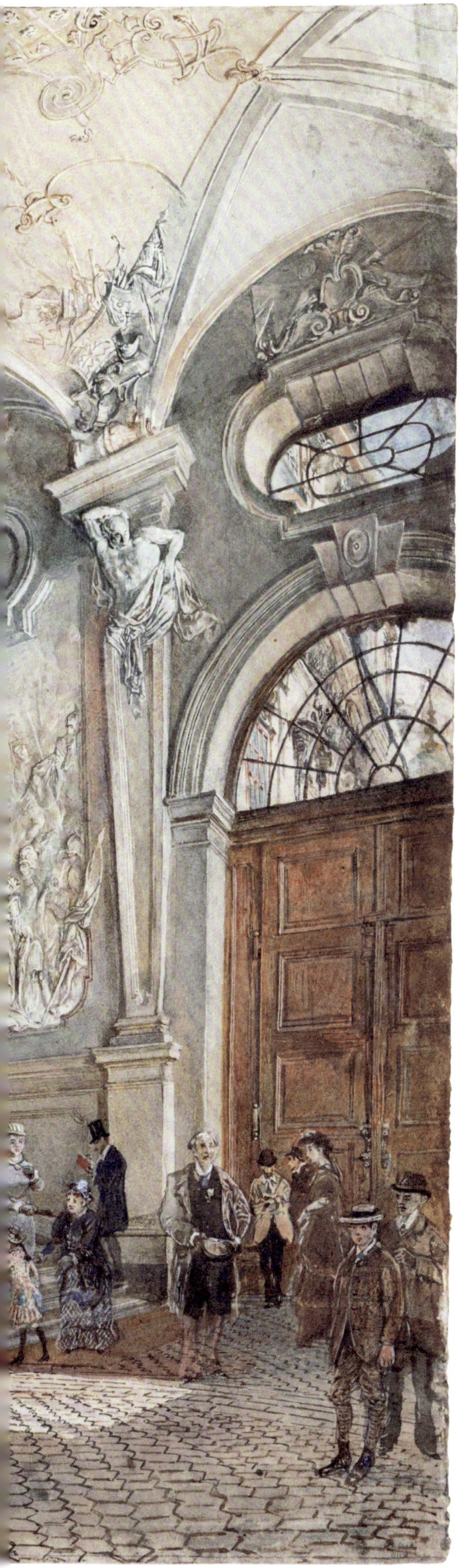

Rudolf von Alt,
The Upper Belvedere Staircase with Visitors to the Imperial Picture Gallery, 1882

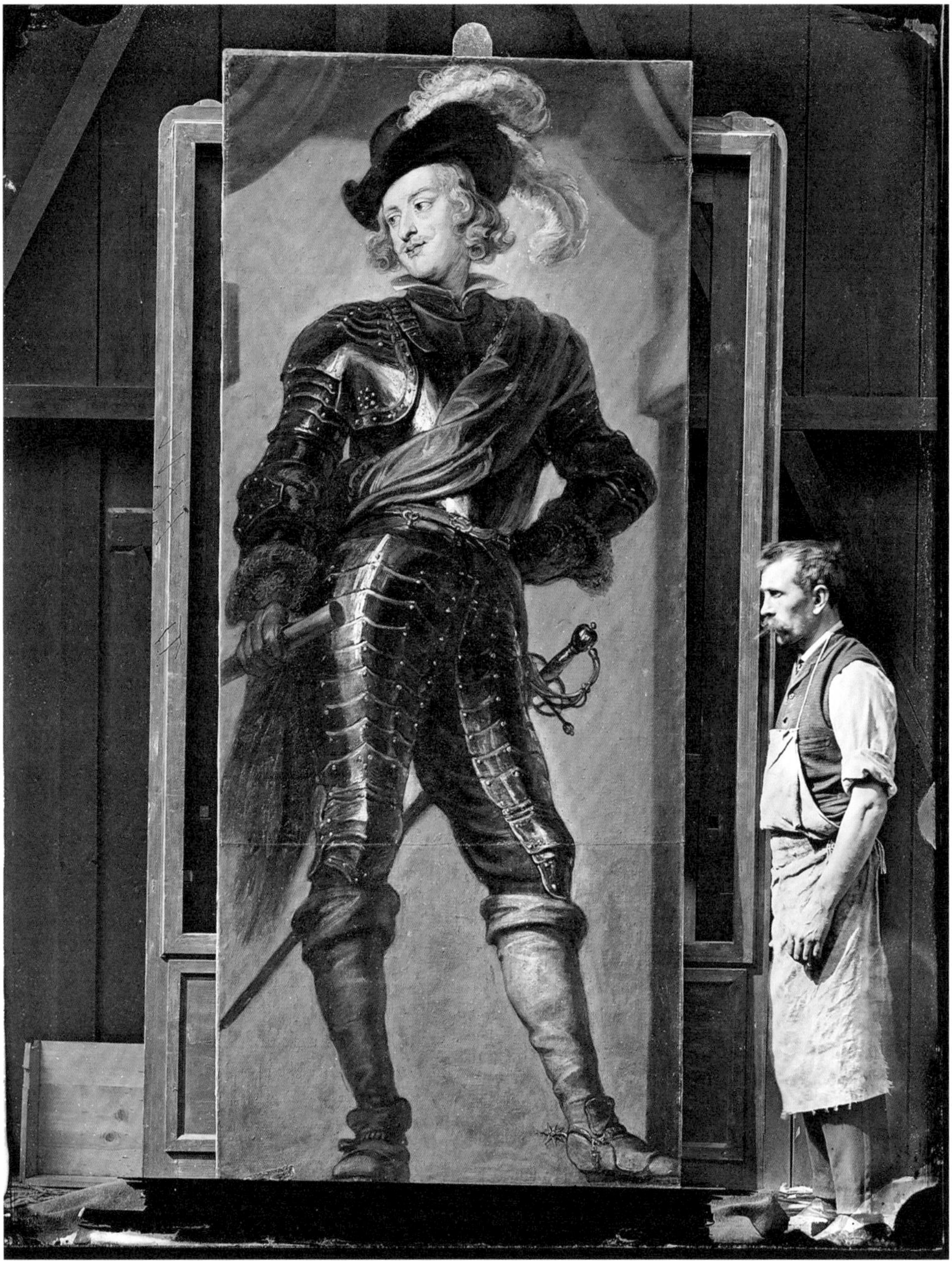

Josef Löwy, photograph of the painting *Cardinal-Infante Ferdinand* by Jan van den Hoecke (reworked by Peter Paul Rubens, c. 1634/35) in front of the Imperial Picture Gallery in the Upper Belvedere, August 22, 1889

This photo documents how photographic reproductions of the paintings were made in a wooden hut, which had been constructed in front of the Upper Belvedere and was equipped with a turntable and a darkroom.

⑦

The First Restoration Studio

Alice Hoppe-Harnoncourt

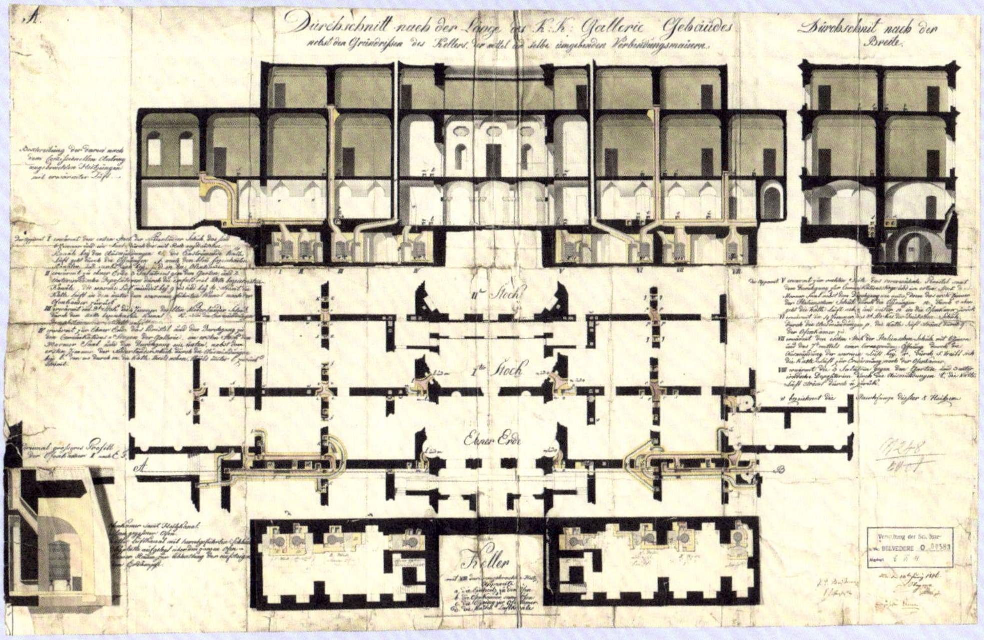

1

Like the palace interior itself, the paintings in the Imperial Picture Gallery had suffered considerable damage during the Napoleonic Wars (→ p. 133, ⑨). Joseph Rebell, the newly appointed director, consequently devised a restoration concept that, for the first time, included a systematic program of conservation measures. Stage one involved setting up a laboratory for "mechanical operations" such as cleaning and relining, and from 1826 also cradling (the supports were thinned and then strengthened using glued-on wood battens and flexible sliding bars). Furthermore, in order to stabilize the environment of the gallery building, structural modifications were made in 1826, such as adding glass doors to seal off the entrance hall. A hot-air heating system was also installed to keep the gallery rooms at a more constant temperature, replacing the individual wood-burning stoves with a flow of warm air heated in the basement (fig. 1). Although this succeeded as intended in drying out the building, it turned out to have serious repercussions for the panel paintings, as director Peter Krafft observed in 1829: "Since Your Excellency ordered that [...] the panel paintings of the German and Netherlandish schools should be cradled in the course of this summer to avoid the danger of warping and cracking due to the Meissner heating system at the Imperial-Royal Gallery," he requested a raise in the budget. He gave assurance that "with these preventative measures, the heating system will cause no further harm."[1]

In 1843, for the first time in the gallery's history, a restoration expert, Erasmus von Engert, was appointed as curator. In 1856 he went on to become gallery director. As the dry air continued to cause problems, he followed the advice of Gustav Friedrich Waagen, director of the Berlin Picture Gallery, and had receptacles of water installed above the openings in the walls to act as humidifiers, regularly taking measurements to check their efficacy. In 1868, Engert—anticipating the upcoming work in preparation for the pictures being transferred to the new Kunsthistorisches Museum—set up a school of restoration with its own designated rooms (fig. 2). This school soon became a department in its own right with a permanent staff. From 1874, records were kept about all paintings entering and leaving the department, with a brief description of any treatments carried out.[2]

1 See Hoppe-Harnoncourt 2001, pp. 177–87; Urban/Rechberger 2011, pp. 140–41; Hoppe-Harnoncourt 2012, paras. 9–17.

2 Oberthaler 1996, pp. 30–31; Urban/Rechberger 2011, p. 143.

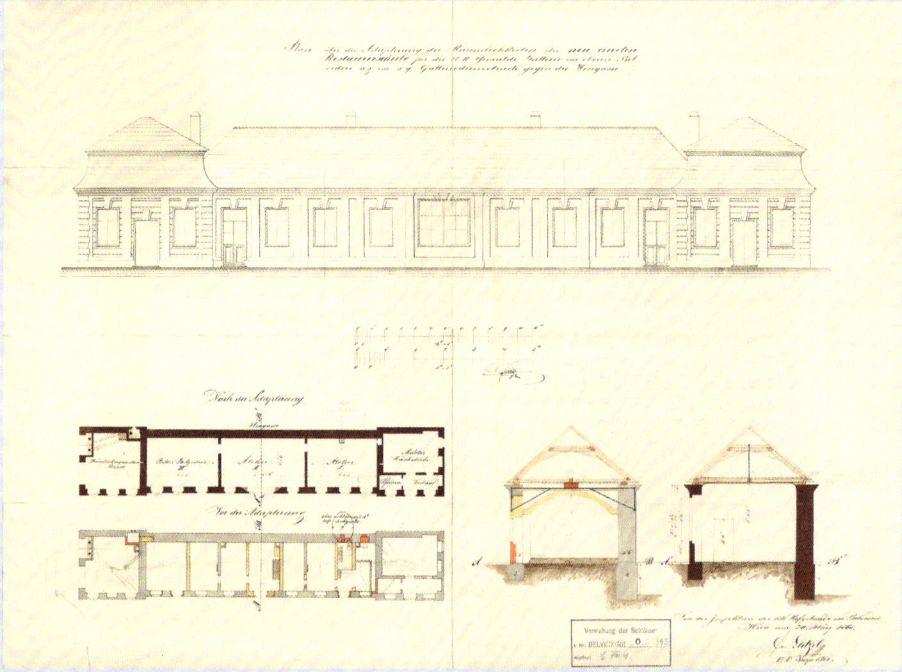

2

Fig. 1
Paul Traugott Meissner and Johann Aman, *Cross Section of the Imperial Picture Gallery*, 1826, Austrian State Archives, Haus-, Hof- und Staatsarchiv, PAB, C, VI, 11, O-00583

Fig. 2
Conrad Latzel the Elder, *Plan for the Adaptation of the Rooms for the New School of Restoration*, 1868, Burghauptmannschaft Österreich, Vienna, Plan Archive, inv. no. C, VIII, 4, O-00365

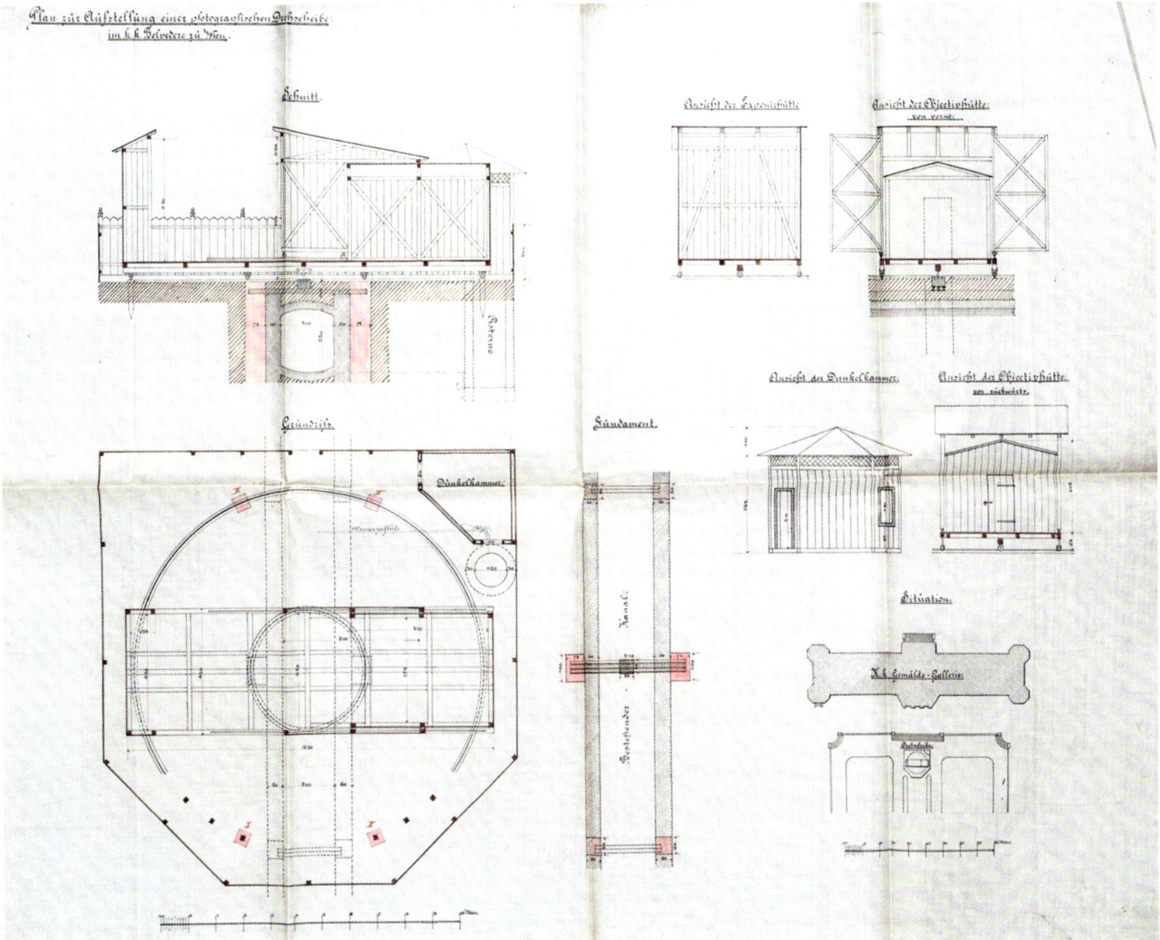

Josef Löwy, *Plan to Set Up a Photography Turntable at the Imperial-Royal Belvedere in Vienna*, before 1888

Located on the north side of the Upper Belvedere, the photography studio, with turntable, darkroom, and two separate huts—one for the photographic equipment and one for the artworks—was set up to make reproductions of the paintings in the collection.

P. 102

THOMAS W. GAEHTGENS — The Emergence of the Art Museum in the Eighteenth Century

In the Enlightenment era, European aristocrats began reorganizing the collections they had accumulated in their palaces over the centuries. Two reasons lay behind this laborious endeavor. On the one hand, the artworks and curiosities were no longer seen merely as precious marvels, acquired to be adored, they were now perceived as objects that inspired aesthetic sensibilities and whose study could reveal scientific insights. On the other hand, an audience emerged in the eighteenth century that increasingly expressed the desire—and eventually the demand—to participate in the contemplation and exploration of these collections. It was in the context of this social, cultural, and educational process that the institution of the museum was born.

While experts worked on developing criteria for their display, it was necessary to find locations suitable for housing the collections that were also accessible for a growing audience. As a result of the completion of monumental museum buildings during the nineteenth century, the emergence of museums is often attributed to this period. In reality, however, the museum, from initial experiments to successful models such as the Belvedere in Vienna, is the intellectual product of the Enlightenment of the eighteenth century.

In the early history of this institution, a variety of ideas were being discussed at the princely courts, which, thanks to their international connections, spread rapidly. Usually, the principal aim was to consolidate and redistribute the collections that were scattered across various palaces. Some early new buildings also emerged, for instance in Düsseldorf, Potsdam, and Kassel. At the Académie d'architecture in Paris students drew up the first fanciful, often somewhat megalomaniacal designs for museum buildings.

Several courts with especially important collections served as templates. In most cases, the decision was made to separate libraries, cabinets of curiosities, natural history collections, and picture-rich galleries. Only occasionally, where size permitted, the concept of a universalist museum, combining several areas of the collection, persevered. The separation required the development of suitable criteria for the reorganization of each area.[1]

Galleries of antiques and paintings had already been separated out from the former *cabinets de curiosités* for some time. These galleries, arranged according to decorative and presentational criteria, were the precursors to the art museum as it evolved in Düsseldorf, Dresden, Braunschweig, Potsdam, London, Vienna, Florence, Rome, Paris, Munich, and Berlin.

A vivid illustration of this culturally and academically significant development is a list produced by Augustus the Strong himself at around 1718, documenting the reorganization of his rich collections (fig. 1).[2] In this project, he envisaged their systematic presentation in the Green Vault at Dresden Castle. Interestingly, his list also includes the paintings. However, under his successor Augustus III, in 1747, they were removed from the galleries within the castle and presented in their own dedicated building in the Johanneum on Dresden's Neumarkt, a much more public location.

Even earlier, between 1709 and 1714, Johann Wilhelm, Elector Palatine, and his Florentine spouse, Anna Maria Luisa de' Medici, had added a gallery to their residence in Düsseldorf. It comprised three wings and was, effectively, already an independent museum building, on account of being accessible via the courtyard to visitors from the city. However, a side wing retained the connection to the palace, thereby still preserving the tradition of the princely gallery of paintings (fig. 2).

The prince elector, owner of one of the most comprehensive collections in Europe (today housed in the Alte Pinakothek, Munich), commissioned an engraving of the gallery display from the Basel-born copperplate engraver and art connoisseur Christian von Mechel (→ p. 116, fig. 3), published in an opulent volume in 1778 (fig. 3). It presented not only the high quality of the Flemish, Dutch, and Italian paintings, but also the collection's arrangement by schools.

In 1755, Frederick the Great commissioned a building in Potsdam dedicated to the finest paintings from his collection, nearby yet outside his private residence Sanssouci. In a few steps, the monarch could take guests to his picture gallery, which could also be accessed from the garden by outside visitors on prior arrangement. To look after his treasured art, Frederick summoned the "gallery inspector" Matthias Oesterreich from Dresden, who, in 1757, published a catalogue of the collection that could be purchased by visitors (fig. 4). In the Potsdam gallery, too, Dutch

1 Fischer 2021.
2 Gaehtgens 2012, pp. 210–13.

and Flemish works were housed in the first part of the long building, separate from the Italian works in the second.

The most sophisticated system, however, was that of the Imperial Picture Collection at the Belvedere in Vienna, as it was to be arranged not only by school but also chronologically within each school. In 1778, Emperor Joseph II entrusted this task to Mechel, who had already proven himself in Düsseldorf. Mechel's work has been the subject of extensive research and analysis. In his catalogue, which was published in French and German (→ p. 83), Mechel laid down the fundamental principles of his vision, that "the installation as a whole, as well as in its parts, should be instructive and, insofar as possible, a visible history of art."[3]

With this conceptual orientation, art gained an educational mission alongside its decorative and presentational function. Unlike princely galleries, the museum represented an educational institution, enabling the study of the history of art. The writings of the founder of archeology as an academic discipline, Johann Joachim Winckelmann, whom Mechel had met in Italy in 1766, were not without influence on the classification system based on schools, to which Mechel, motivated by patriotic sentiments, alongside those of Italy, France, and the Netherlands, added a German school spanning several rooms (→ p. 117, fig. 7).[4]

Arrangements by schools and chronology were to remain the most important criteria in the presentation of artworks in a museum to this day. Nevertheless, after the opening of the Belvedere, this system came under heavy criticism. In 1782, there was even talk of "gallery assassination." Mechel, it was claimed, had reduced the imperial collection to "a sample card."[5] In 1785, the protests became even louder. Granted, in the case of large collections, the arrangement created a certain clarity, so the argument went, but the aesthetic perception of art was being undermined: "The fine arts must be allowed to go straight to the heart; that is their purpose and everything else must be removed."[6] This rejection of art museums organized according to academic principles was to remain prominent throughout the following eras, even up to the present day.

While the imperial paintings were being transferred to the Belvedere and displayed in their new arrangement, the Grand Duke of Tuscany Pietro Leopoldo, Joseph II's brother, commissioned a redesign of the Uffizi in Florence. Under Giuseppe Pelli Bencivenni and Luigi Lanzi, Italian painting was presented chronologically here, too. Their family ties, as well as the two monarchs' personal commitment to reform and to opening up their collections to the public, led to close cooperation between Florence and Vienna, and even to the project of exchanging paintings to mutually complete the chronological displays in each city (→ p. 125, ⑧).

The new arrangement in the Belvedere continued to set the standard for European museums, even as further refinements were made. With

3 Mechel 1783, p. XI. For more on the reorganization of the picture collections in Vienna, see, in particular, Meijers 1995; likewise Fischer 2013a. For a general overview of the topic discussed here, see Savoy 2015 with additional literature.
4 Mayer G. 2021b.
5 Schryen 2015, p. 459.
6 Rittershausen 1785, p. 23; Schryen 2015, p. 460.

the establishment of the Louvre in 1793 during the French Revolution, the Viennese model was followed, not without eliciting criticism here as well. The decision to present the royal collections—and later also the paintings looted from conquered countries—by school and chronology faced fierce opposition, for instance from the art dealer Le Brun, who regretted that the "simple pictorial variety engendered by the viewer's own curiosity and personal perception" would not receive sufficient emphasis.[7]

A unique overview of the history of European painting, which was enthusiastically received by its visitors, was offered by the Musée Napoléon, to be visited in the Louvre between 1803 and 1815. It not only comprised the royal collections but was expanded under Napoleon through acquisitions, though most of all through art lootings by revolutionary troops. Its director, Dominique-Vivant Denon, stole from conquered countries using pre-prepared lists, with the aim of providing the best and most complete survey of art history. Not least, he was after German paintings by Dürer, Cranach, Altdorfer, and Baldung, as these were poorly represented in the French collections. A further contribution by Denon was the integration of previously neglected periods into the museum tour, such as early Italian painting, then known as *primitifs*. He also created a sophisticated art-historical arrangement in the Musée Napoléon, comparing, for instance, Raphael's works with those of his teacher Perugino, in order to showcase the artistic development and exceptional mastery of the Renaissance artist (fig. 5). Denon's staging of early Italian and German painting, and his emphasis on Raphael as the greatest genius with ongoing contemporary relevance, was later to resonate widely with the Romantic movement, not least thanks to Friedrich Schlegel's observations.

The fall of Napoleon and the return of the stolen artworks led in some countries to a renewed, patriotically motivated call for the public presentation of art in museums.[8] The museum buildings by Leo von Klenze in Munich and the Altes Museum by Karl Friedrich Schinkel, completed in 1830 opposite the Berlin Palace, were constructed in this historical context. The function of the Berlin museum, however, which was under the directorship of the distinguished art historian Gustav Waagen, continued to be debated. The criticism of the Belvedere arrangement found its continuation here, whereby Schinkel's motto that the museum should "first delight, then instruct" contradicted the inscription on the frieze stating that it should serve the "study of all kinds of antiquity and the liberal arts."

In the Romantic period, the two approaches to art, academic study and individual perception, clashed once again. Wilhelm Heinrich Wackenroder elevated the museum into a temple, where art was not to be perused like goods at a fair, but where the appreciation of the artworks was to be experienced as prayer. In this sense, the early Nazarenes, who formed in Vienna in 1809, were particularly inspired by the paintings

7 Le Brun 1992, p. 93.
8 Sheehan 2002.

of the Early German school. After the return of the stolen pictures from Paris, an arrangement following more aesthetic lines and a more liberal mixing of schools prevailed at the Belvedere, whereby in the nineteenth century the Neoclassicist concept of the museum of the Enlightenment eventually had to give way to a new approach.[9]

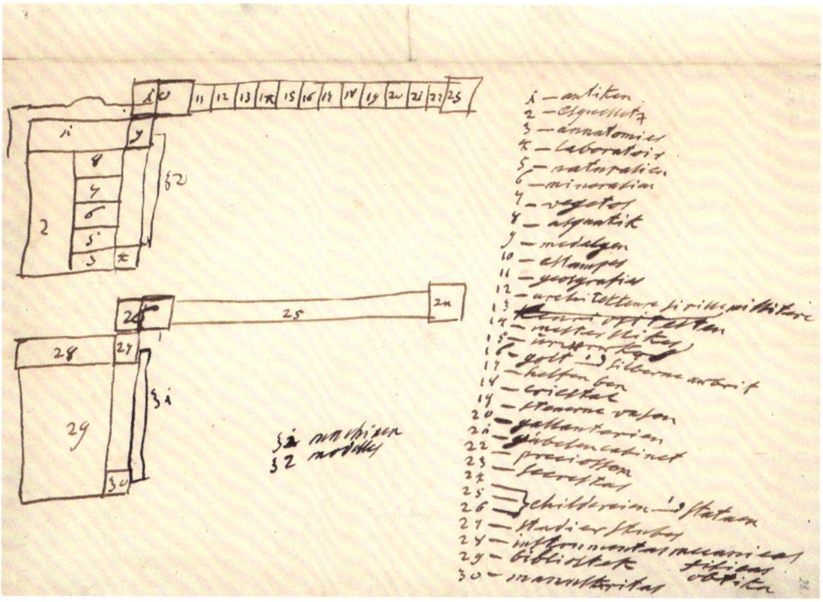

1

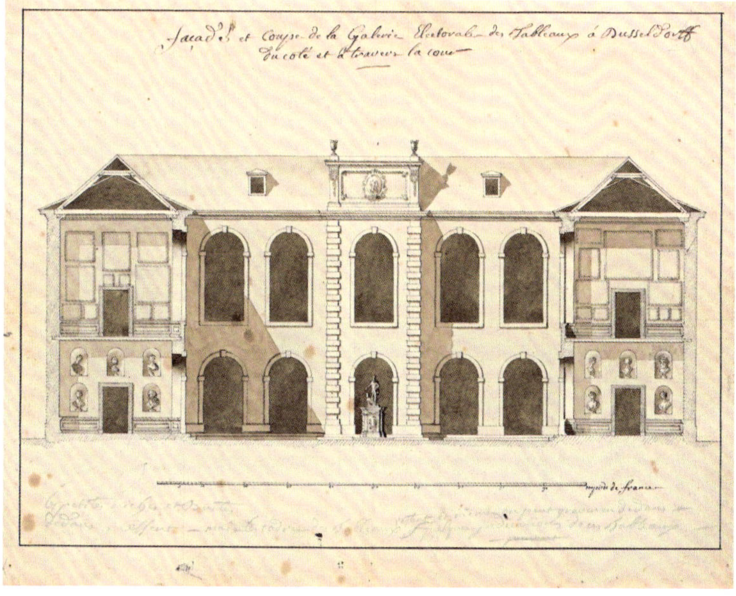

2

Fig. 1
Augustus II the Strong, design for the re-organization of the collections in Dresden Castle, c. 1718/19, Saxon State Archives, Main State Archive, Dresden, 10026 Geheimes Kabinett, Loc. 02079/33, Bl. 28a

Fig. 2
Christian von Mechel et al., preliminary sketch for *La Galerie electorale de Dusseldorff*, c. 1768–78, The Getty Research Institute, Special Collections, Los Angeles

9 Hoppe-Harnoncourt 2013, pp. 90–114.

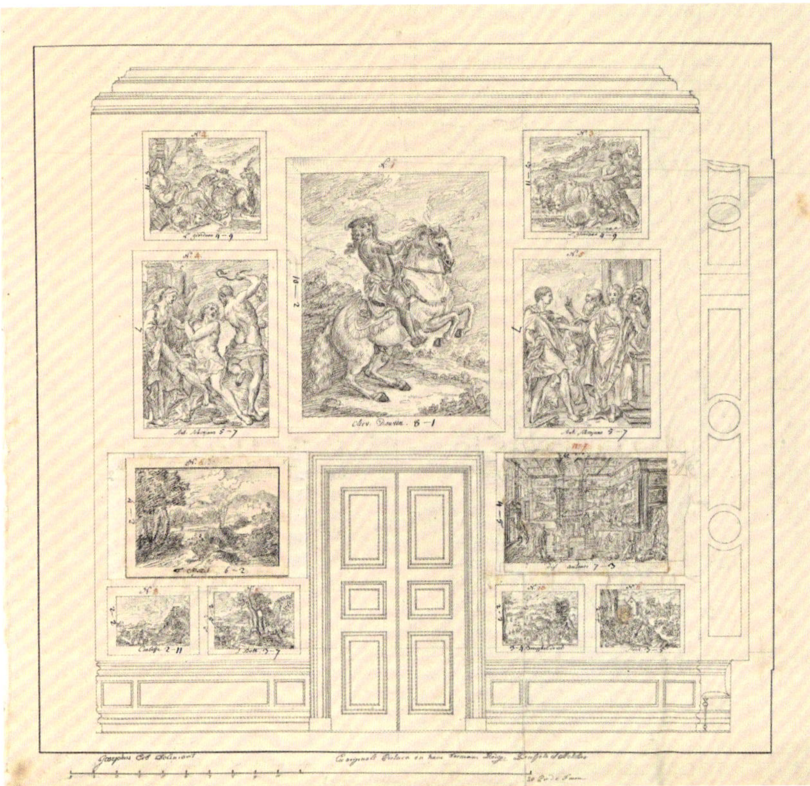

3

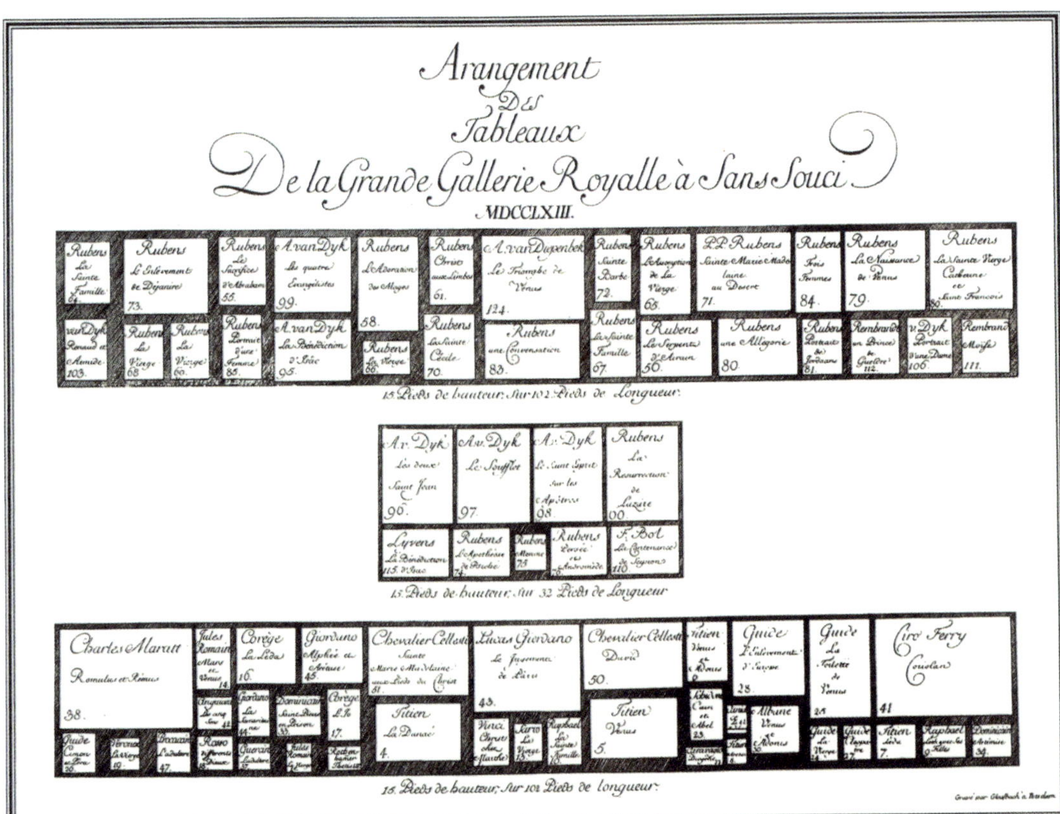
Arangement
Des
Tableaux
De la Grande Gallerie Royalle à Sans Souci
MDCCLXIII.
15. Pieds de hauteur, sur 102 Pieds de longueur.
15. Pieds de hauteur, sur 32 Pieds de Longueur
16. Pieds de hauteur, sur 102 Pieds de longueur.

4

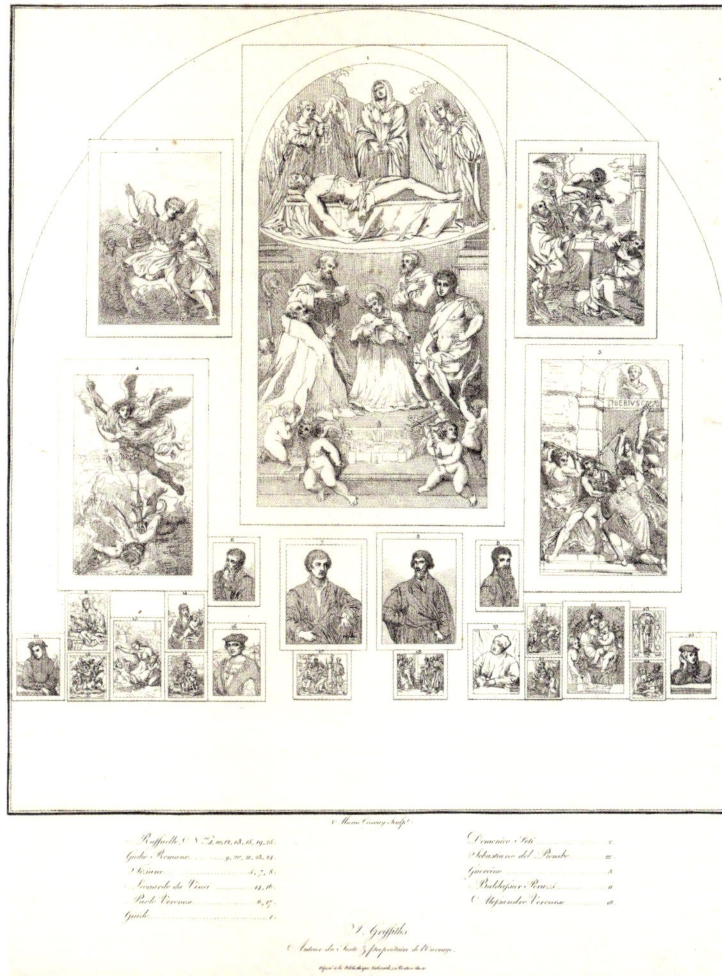

5

Fig. 3
Christian von Mechel et al., preliminary sketch for *La Galerie electorale de Dusseldorff*, c. 1768–78, The Getty Research Institute, Special Collections, Los Angeles

Fig. 4
Plan for the arrangement of the picture gallery at Sanssouci Palace, 1773, in Matthias Oesterreich, *Beschreibung aller Gemähide, Antiquitäten, und anderer kostbarer und merkwürdiger Sachen, so in denen beiden Schlössern von Sans-Souci*, Berlin 1773

Fig. 5
Maria Cosway, *La Galerie du Louvre*, arrangement of twenty-five paintings by Italian masters (including Guido Reni, Raphael, and Titian), 1802, British Museum, London

P.
110 GERNOT MAYER —

The Museumification of the Imperial Picture Gallery

Along with other properties from Prince Eugene of Savoy's estate—like Schloss Hof and the Winter Palace on Himmelpfortgasse, for example—the Belvedere, too, came into Habsburg ownership after the prince's death in 1736. To what purpose Empress Maria Theresa acquired the garden palace on Rennweg in 1752 is not known. In any event, the palace was rarely used and only once, in 1770, stood briefly at the center of court life, with a magnificent ball celebrating the nuptials of Archduchess Marie Antoinette.[1] Also dating from that year is a detailed description of the Upper Belvedere, revealing the palace's opulent interior of precious Oriental art, porcelain, and paintings. It included, for instance, the series of large-scale paintings by Martin van Meytens and his workshop, documenting the election of the king, his coronation, and the first marriage of Joseph II, as well as portraits of the Habsburg family and statues of several emperors. In addition to the ruling family, the décor also paid tribute to the builder of the palace, Prince Eugene of Savoy, in the form of battle paintings and Balthasar Permoser's allegorical marble effigy of the field marshal.[2]

While, at around 1770, the Belvedere was thus a site of dynastic display and memoria, the building was to assume an entirely different function and character only a few years later—namely that of a public museum.[3] In 1776, the Imperial Picture Gallery was transferred to the Upper Belvedere, where it was completely reorganized and made accessible to the general public at specific times (fig. 1).[4] But what led to this radical step? What motivated the transfer of this collection? And why was the Belvedere chosen to accommodate this new art museum?

Until then, the Imperial Picture Gallery was housed within the Hofburg. The majority of the pictures were concentrated in the Stall-

1 For the history of the Belvedere after Prince Eugene of Savoy, see Aurenhammer 1969; Schoeller 2011.

2 Fuhrmann 1770, pp. 27–38.

3 For more on the establishment of public museums in the eighteenth century, see Sheehan 2002; Savoy 2006 (for the Belvedere see Édouard Pommier, pp. 55–56.; Annette Schryen, pp. 279–307); Paul 2012 (for the Belvedere see Michael Yonan, pp. 167–89); Gaehtgens 2012; Swoboda 2013a.

4 For more on the reorganization of the Imperial Gallery in the Belvedere, see Meijers 1995; Lechner 2011; Fischer 2013a; Fischer 2021; Mayer 2021a.

burg, a multifunctional Renaissance building; a number of paintings were also hung in the two treasuries of the Hofburg. Between 1718 and 1728, the Stallburg gallery had been completely redesigned according to plans by Claude Le Fort du Plessy, who was also the interior designer for Prince Eugene of Savoy at the Belvedere.[5] The paintings were installed in a wall-filling display, mostly set within artfully designed wood paneling. The pictures' strictly symmetrical arrangement was predominantly along aesthetic lines, with many paintings cropped or extended to achieve the desired decorative effect. During the eighteenth century, this type of arrangement came under increasing criticism. The gallery now looked neglected; its late Baroque design had gone out of fashion and its formal aesthetic principle was no longer relevant.[6]

In 1772, the appointment of landscape painter Joseph Rosa as the gallery's director marked a new beginning at the Stallburg.[7] Rosa (fig. 2) completed a general survey (started by his colleague, the painter Anton von Maron) of all the art collections dotted throughout the Habsburg territories and selected new paintings for Vienna's Stallburg gallery.[8] Joseph II showed great interest in this development and is even said to have been scouring the Hofburg himself in search of valuable pictures.[9] Under Rosa's leadership, paintings were restored and reframed, several smaller picture cabinets were reorganized, and the sculptures, until then also kept in the gallery, were removed from the collection. However, the rigid arrangement of paintings set within wall paneling and the limited space at the Stallburg hindered Rosa's redesign plans significantly.

By 1775, the Stallburg's space limitations had become a major obstacle. At the time, Joseph Rosa had been sent to the Austrian Netherlands to look at pictures from the collection of the Jesuit order dissolved two years previously, with a view to acquiring some of them for the gallery in Vienna. The thirty-one paintings selected by Rosa included two by Peter Paul Rubens from the former altarpiece of the Jesuit church in Antwerp, depicting the miracles of St. Ignatius of Loyola (fig 4) and St. Francis Xavier. Detached from their sacred context, these pictures had lost their original function and were now lauded—reduced to their artistic merits—as masterpieces of Flemish painting. Rubens' visual rhetoric, with all its propagandistic power, was now placed in the service of the Enlightenment, as shown in an allegory of Joseph II's Patent of Toleration (1781), celebrating religious freedom as a modern miracle (fig. 5). At over five meters in height, Rubens's two altar paintings could not be accommodated in the Stallburg, and so the search for a new gallery location became imperative. Yet, the decision made by 1776 to move the entire Imperial Picture Gallery to the Upper Belvedere was motivated by more than the two altar paintings' enormous size.[10] The transfer of the gallery and the ensuing redesignation of the Belvedere as a public museum formed part

5 For more on the Stallburg gallery, see Haag/Swoboda 2010.

6 See, for example, "Auszug eines Briefes von Wien, den 12. Jun. 1763," in *Bibliothek der schönen Wissenschaften und der freyen Künste*, vol. 9, part 2, 1763, pp. 326–30.

7 For more on Rosa (or Roos) see Schütz 2009.

8 A comprehensive sourcebook on changes to the Imperial Gallery from 1772 is offered in Hassmann 2013; Hassmann 2015.

9 Thus reported by Wenzel Anton von Kaunitz from Vienna in 1772; see letters from Wenzel Anton von Kaunitz to Graf Karl von Firmian, October 5, 1772, Archivio di Stato di Milano, Studi, p. a., K. 4.

10 The chronology: In spring 1776, Rosa returned from the Netherlands; in April the same year, the first record relating to the planned transfer of the gallery appears; in summer, adaptations were made to the Upper Belvedere; from September the transport of pictures from the Stallburg began. For the relevant sources cf. Hassmann 2013, pp. 129–32.

of a wider cultural policy and also of a justification strategy. To better understand this, we must look again at the dissolution of the Jesuit order, which, following a Papal decree in 1773, also took place in the Habsburg lands. The expropriation and subsequent sale of Jesuit property occurred under the premise of the greater good, with all revenue allocated to the funding of education. Acquired funds thus went to schools and universities and former Jesuit libraries were now being made accessible to the public.

In logical conclusion, the former Jesuit paintings acquired by Rosa for the gallery in Vienna could not be "hidden away" in the Habsburgs' princely palaces as part of a private collection—they had to be brought to the public eye and made available for the education and edification of the people. This was the only way to legitimize the controversial dissolution of the Jesuit order, the profaning of sacred objects, and the removal of this cultural heritage from the Austrian Netherlands.[11] With their translocation from the Stallburg, the pictures left the realm of courtly aggrandization to be placed in the service of public instruction at the Belvedere, beyond the city walls. This line of thought was reflected not only in the introduction of regular opening times for the Belvedere, after its reorganization was completed in 1777,[12] but also in the presentation of the collection itself. While Rosa was still working on the new display, Friedrich Justus Riedel already reported that this new arrangement was "very systematic, much like how an insightful librarian would organize his library, according to age, school, master, and suite" and that one could "study intuitively the entire history of painting from one room to the next."[13] The presentation therefore followed an educational concept, which was a radical departure from the primarily aesthetic arrangement of the Stallburg gallery. How consistently this educational concept was implemented in the initial display is unknown. The innovative method of arrangement, reflecting chronology as well as schools and the oeuvres of individual artists, may have been familiar to Rosa from Dresden, where similar concepts had been discussed while he was working there as professor of landscape painting at the local art academy.[14] As Rosa himself later explained, the intention behind his didactic exhibition display was to establish the Belvedere as "an open school for artists and art connoisseurs."[15] Even his earlier interventions at the Stallburg, implemented concurrently with the reform of Vienna's Academy of Fine Arts, were motivated by the desire to give artists more opportunities to study the Old Masters.[16] For Rosa, the didactic potential of the Imperial Picture Gallery resided primarily in the education of future artists rather than of the public at large.[17]

A different objective was pursued by Christian von Mechel, who, only a few years later, would completely revise Rosa's arrangement. His "instructive" display was aimed at every "curious" and "attentive art lov-

11 This reasoning can be traced back to writings by Wenzel Anton von Kaunitz; as state chancellor he was also responsible for the administration of the Austrian Netherlands. For more on the significance of the paintings from the Jesuit estate to the discourse surrounding cultural heritage and its museumization, see Mayer 2021a, pp. 265–70.

12 The gallery was open on Mondays, Wednesdays, and Fridays; see Hassmann 2015, p. 119.

13 *Litterarische Monate*, October 1776, pp. 101–02, signed R.[iedel].

14 Cf. Spenlé 2004.

15 Rosa 1796a, p. 206.

16 For more on the reform of the Academy, cf. Mayer 2021a, pp. 169–208; for more on the close relationship between the Academy and the Imperial Picture Gallery, see Schütz 2011.

17 The function of a public gallery was also defined in this sense by Johann Georg Sulzer: "Galleries of this nature are to the illustrative arts what public libraries are to scholarship; treasures for the public use of artists. Thus they must remain open at all times to artists and lovers of art for study," Sulzer 1771 p. 415.

er," who, so he promised, by studying the paintings in the Upper Belvedere, would soon become a "connoisseur of art."[18]

The Basel-born copperplate engraver and publisher Christian von Mechel (fig. 3) arrived in Vienna in 1778, possibly to produce an illustrated catalogue of the Imperial Picture Gallery, similar to the one he had just created for the painting collection in Düsseldorf.[19] However, rather than simply documenting the contents of the Imperial Picture Gallery as it presented itself in the form of Rosa's arrangement, Mechel argued for a complete reorganization of the gallery, winning over Joseph II and State Chancellor Wenzel Anton von Kaunitz for his plans. The latter became a prominent patron of Mechel, supporting his projects with great personal investment, for which he was later honored with a memorial in the Gold Cabinet of the Upper Belvedere (fig. 6).[20] Work on the redisplay was to take three years, until 1781, as completion of the new arrangement was delayed several times by further new acquisitions and transfers. The end result, documented in a catalogue published in 1783, was a groundbreaking innovation and set new standards for the presentation of collections all over Europe (→ p. 83). Much more consistently than in Rosa's concept, the gallery was now seen as a center of knowledge for "public and communal benefit,"[21] as an educational institution designed to communicate a "visible history of art"[22] to its audience. One of the main changes in its arrangement was the establishment of a separate section for German painting on the second floor (fig. 7). For this patriotically motivated project, Mechel first had to practically "invent" an independent German school, along with its hitherto little-researched history. He experimented with academic research, incorporated previously neglected works of medieval art into the museum, made bold attributions, and was also the first to place the paintings in chronological order.[23] A detailed chronology was introduced for Early Netherlandish art, albeit not for Italian and more contemporary Dutch and Flemish painting. Although his audacious plans for a "periodo arrangement"[24] were thus only partially realized and the hanging was undoubtedly less revolutionary than Mechel's grandiose claims imply, the new presentation of the gallery in the Upper Belvedere must nevertheless be considered a milestone in European museum history. Its public character, educational mission, and scientific orientation, alongside its innovative communication strategy, facilitated by labeling of artworks and the publication of a pocket-sized catalogue, made this new Imperial Picture Gallery in the Belvedere a model museum, even by today's standards.[25]

The broad public appeal of this museum—consistently referred to as "gallery" by contemporaries—is well documented. Chancellor Kaunitz, for example, had called for the collection to be presented in a style aesthetically pleasing to all eyes, not just those of a handpicked group

18 Mechel 1783, pp. XIf.

19 For more on Mechel, see Wüthrich 1956; Meijers 2007.

20 For more on Prince Kaunitz's considerable influence on the new presentation, see Mayer 2021a, pp. 261–311.

21 Mechel 1783, p. XII.

22 Mechel 1783, p. XI.

23 The strength of the national and patriotic notions behind this undertaking is illustrated by the events surrounding the Karlstein pictures; cf. Hoppe-Harnoncourt 2013; Mayer 2021b.

24 Letter from Christian von Mechel, June 27, 1780, Central Library, Zürich, Ms Z II 392.25.

25 The ICOM *Code of Ethics for Museums* (2010) defines a museum as "a non-profit, permanent institution in the service of society and its development, open to the public, which acquires, conserves, researches, communicates, and exhibits the tangible and intangible heritage of humanity and its environment for the purposes of education, study, and enjoyment."

of art connoisseurs.[26] According to Mechel, the redesigned gallery provoked great public interest across all classes. He proudly reported that, after completion of the gallery in 1781, "among the frequent public visitors, many a good citizen, many a nobleman, little or great, would often ask for me and come to thank me, as an unknown, for the enjoyment I had bestowed on them with this new installation."[27]

What still remains to be examined is the reason the Upper Belvedere specifically was chosen in 1776 for this innovative undertaking. One reason is that the palace was awaiting a new use at the time; furthermore, its location outside of the city walls assisted the detachment of the collection from the courtly sphere of the imperial residence. Christian von Mechel gives additional reasons in his gallery catalogue of 1783. Above all, he praises the palace's idyllic location, suggesting that no other place offered such an effective union of art and nature.[28] More than this, however, the building's spatial arrangement provided the perfect framework for classifying and reorganizing the collection. According to Mechel, the Upper Belvedere was so perfectly suited to this function that one could be led to believe that Prince Eugene "may have had the intention from the outset to build a temple to art."[29] This idea also informs an allegory designed by Mechel and translated into an oil painting by Vinzenz Fischer (fig. 1). The poet Michael Denis in turn composed an epigram for this picture, celebrating the relocation of the Imperial Picture Gallery to the Belvedere as an act of directed wisdom, in other words, of enlightened policy.[30]

> *To Emperor Joseph II's Use of the Belvedere Palace for the Imperial-Royal Picture Gallery in Vienna*
> Emulator of creative Nature,
> Art seeks to gift Caesar her riches.
> He reflects and chooses: Where shall those riches go?
> Petitioning Minerva to guide his choice.
> Minerva speaks: Behold this temple!
> Built by a hero, Nature suffused it with charm.
> And remains the heroes' friend, Nature's beloved.
> Need Caesar hesitate any more?

26 Mayer 2021a, p. 277.
27 Letter from Christian von Mechel to Friedrich Dominikus Ring, January 7, 1781, University Library Freiburg, NL 10/IV B 359, fol 220f.
28 Mechel 1783, p. VIII.
29 Mechel 1783, p. IX.
30 For more on this painting and the poem, see Meijers 1995, p. 17.

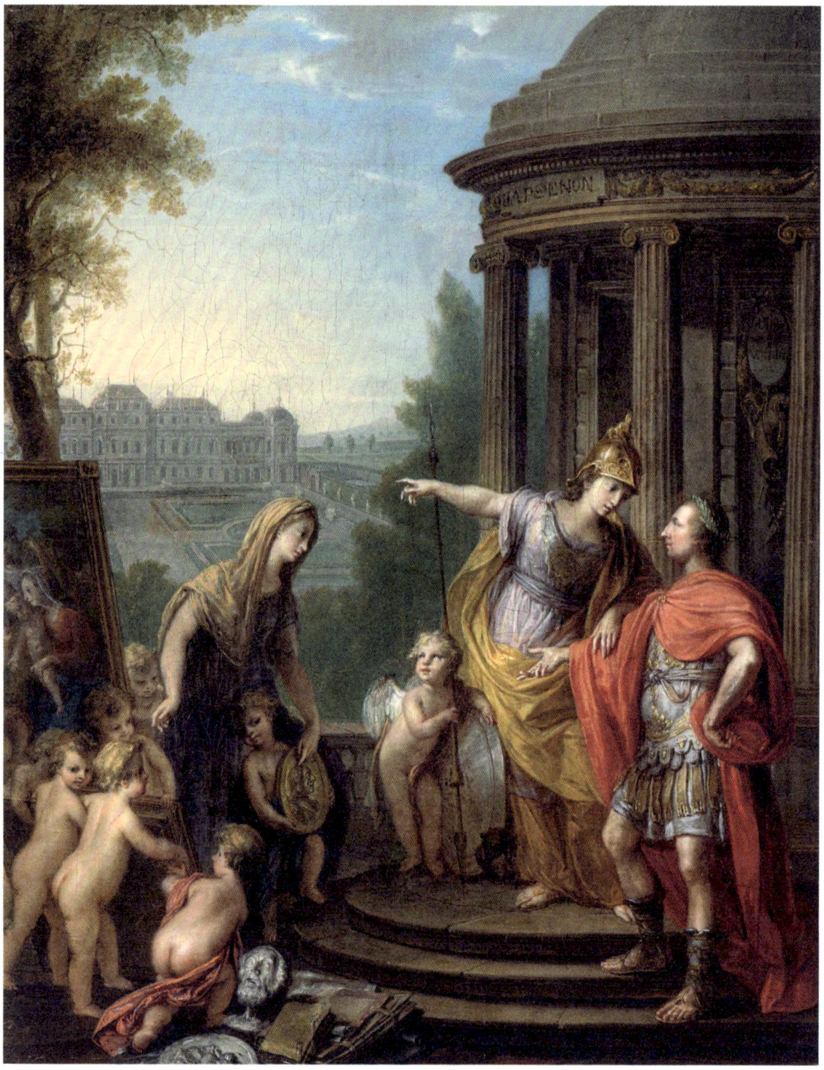

1

Fig. 1
Vinzenz Fischer, *Allegory of the Transferral of the Imperial Gallery to the Belvedere*, 1781, Belvedere, Vienna

The painting alludes to the search for a location for the imperial collection, which was transferred from the Stallburg to the Upper Belvedere in 1776. This move also marked the transition from a gallery in the service of courtly representation to a museum as an institution open to the wider public.

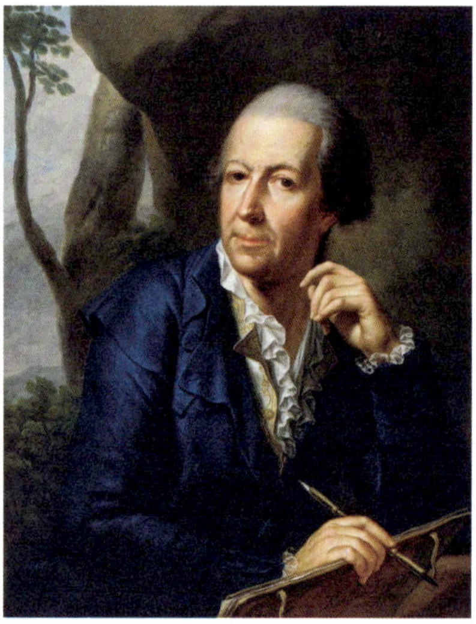

2

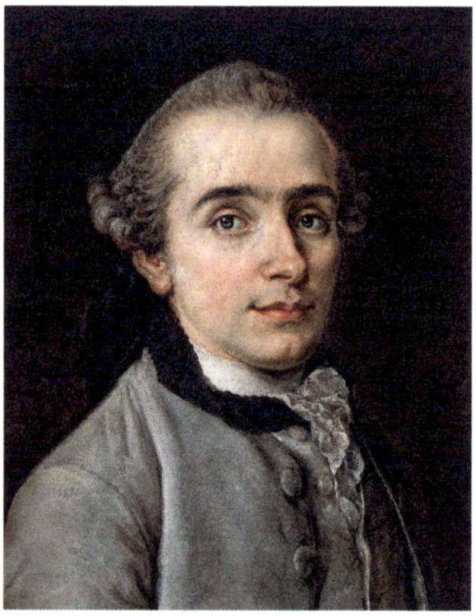

3

Fig. 2
Martin Knoller, *Joseph Rosa*, 1791, Belvedere, Vienna

Joseph Rosa was director of the Imperial Picture Gallery from 1769 to 1805.

Fig. 3
Johann Nikolaus Grooth, *Christian von Mechel*, c. 1765, Basel Historical Museum

Basel-born Christian von Mechel was summoned to Vienna in 1778, possibly at the request of Emperor Joseph II, to produce an inventory of the Imperial Picture Gallery. The opening of the Picture Gallery is thought to have taken place on October 13, 1781.

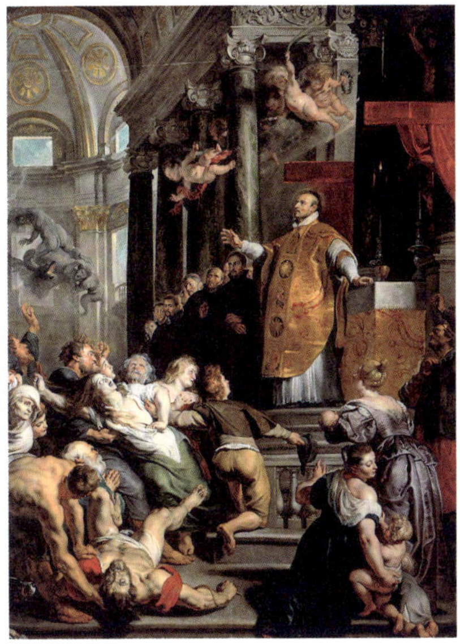

4

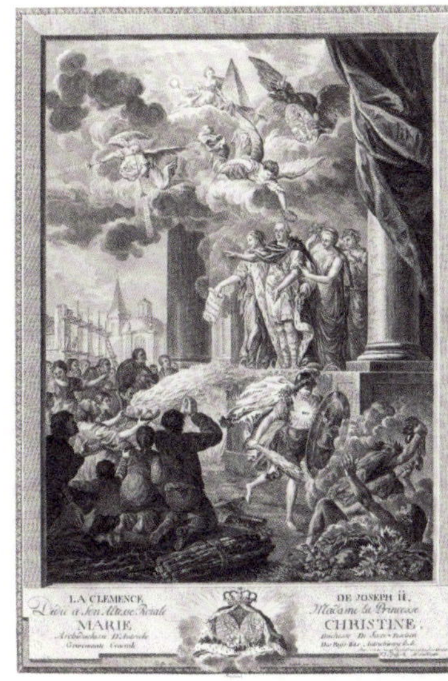

5

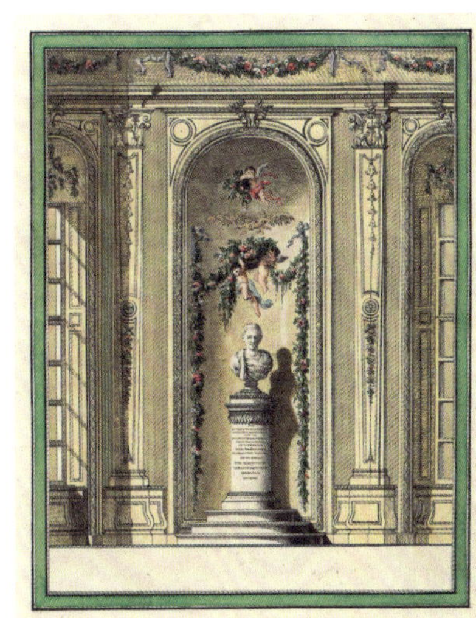

6

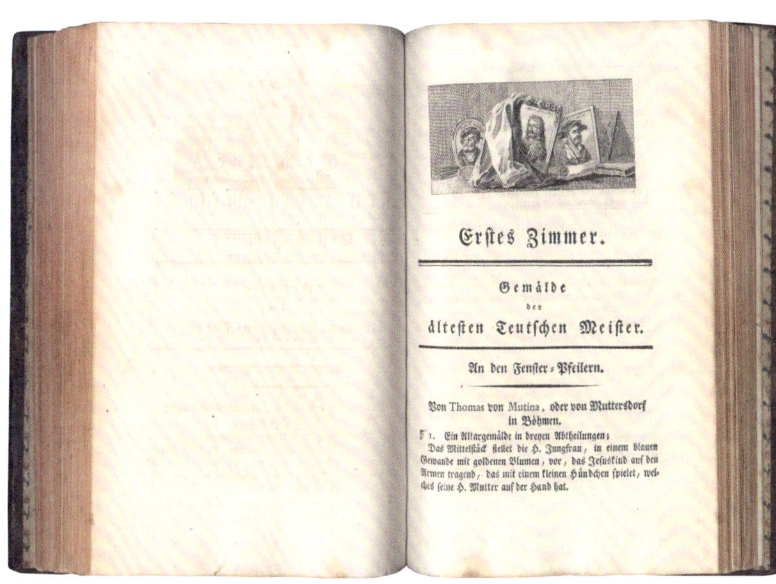

7

Fig. 4
Peter Paul Rubens, *The Wonder of St. Ignatius of Loyola*, c. 1617/18, Kunsthistorisches Museum Vienna, Picture Gallery

Fig. 5
Mathias de Sallieth after François Joseph Pfeiffer, *La Clemence de Joseph II*, 1783, Rijksmuseum Amsterdam

Fig. 6
Carl Schütz, *Memorial for Wenzel Anton von Kaunitz in the Gold Cabinet of the Upper Belvedere*, 1781, Wien Museum

Fig. 7
First page of "Gemälde der ältesten Teutschen Meister," in Christian von Mechel, *Verzeichniß der Gemälde der Kaiserlich Königlichen Bilder Gallerie in Wien*, Vienna 1783, Belvedere Library, Vienna

P. 118 NORA FISCHER —— Opening and Public Access in the Upper Belvedere around 1800

A brief announcement appeared on April 9, 1777, in the *Wienerisches Diarium*, barely noticeable among the general news about Vienna: "Following the establishment by supreme order of the Imperial Royal Picture Gallery in the Belvedere under the supervision of Imperial Royal Gallery Director Herr von Rosa in the most perfect order with a department for each art school," it states, the Picture Gallery was open to all "art lovers every Monday, Wednesday, and Friday during summer in the morning from 8 a.m. to noon and in the afternoon from 3 to 7 p.m. and during winter in the morning from 9 a.m. to noon, at the latest until 1 p.m."[1] However inconspicuous it may have been, in mentioning the transfer of the painting collection from the Stallburg to the Belvedere, its rearrangement by gallery director Joseph Rosa, and the opening of the gallery to the general public, this announcement established the three most important conditions for the transformation of the Imperial Picture Gallery from a court gallery into a museum in the modern sense. The Belvedere, as the site of this transformation, thus represents the place where significant museological events intersected, overlapped, and interacted. This essay looks at the various developments in the gallery's history in the context of its opening and the public access to the collection.[2]

Access in principle to the imperial painting collection is documented for as early as 1774,[3] but the move from the Stallburg to the Belvedere is likely to have enabled and significantly accelerated the opening of the Imperial Gallery to a wider public (fig. 1). The transfer of the gallery, as an institution of the Viennese court, did not merely change its location; it also signified its detachment from the imperial court, in other words from the architectural context of the Hofburg, and made for a more autonomous presentation of the collection. It had been difficult to direct the flow of

1 *Wienerisches Diarium*, no. 29, April 9, 1777, p. 7; *Preßburger Zeitung*, no. 30, April 12, 1777, p. 6.
2 In one of the many studies about the history of the imperial painting collection in the eighteenth century, Debora J. Meijers recently looked in particular at the accessibility of the court collections; Meijers 2021.
3 ÖStA/HHStA, HBA, box 6, 12th session, no. 7 ex 1774, fol. 296, 29.10.1774; Hassmann 2013, p. 128, doc. 18.

visitors in the former Stallburg gallery, as it was so closely linked to the other rooms used by the imperial court. A *Votum* from October 1774—the earliest document mentioning the Imperial Gallery being opened to the public—gives as the decisive factor for the smooth running of the gallery that "outsiders may be admitted only if they do not impede the most sovereign court."[4] There were probably several reasons for the transfer of the Imperial Gallery from the Stallburg: the lack of space for the growing collection of pictures, the incompatibility of the existing sequence of rooms with a "modern" art-historical concept of pictures organized according to schools, and, not least, the location of the gallery within the Hofburg complex, which ultimately proved unsuitable for accommodating larger numbers of visitors at fixed times without disrupting the life of the court. It was primarily to resolve these problems that the move of the Imperial Picture Gallery to the Belvedere was proposed.

The head chamberlain's office, which was behind the announcement in the *Wienerisches Diarium*, presumably did not anticipate much public interest in the collection, because the information about the visiting days and times was followed by the injunction that "those who wish to visit the said Imperial Royal Gallery should inform the gallery director von Rosa the day before, so that the necessary arrangements can be made in good time."[5] Evidently the announcement was intended solely for a limited circle of art lovers and connoisseurs, who would have to make a formal application to the gallery director, as had already been required of artists and art students wishing to copy pictures in the Stallburg gallery.

The opening of the Imperial Picture Gallery proved a great public success, but not in the way it had been expected. Not only connoisseurs and artists but also "folk from the lower classes" flocked in large numbers to the Belvedere. Johann Pezzl noted in his *Skizze von Wien* (Sketch of Vienna): "Mondays are usually very crowded and busy. Plenty of folk from the lower classes, apprentices taking the Monday off, and even menial servant girls with children on their arms, enjoy spending an afternoon in the picture gallery."[6] The crowds, particularly if they consisted of "folk from the lower classes" or children, were seen increasingly as a problem, and thus, towards the end of the eighteenth century, it was suggested that visits by the public be more strictly controlled. Pezzl continues: "I believe it would be quite feasible, without incommoding visitors too much, to ban children and people from the lowest classes. After all, an art collection is not a puppet show."[7] The Viennese court did not respond to this call for greater control of the public. It was not until April 1813, when Heinrich Friedrich Füger, the gallery director at the time, called for a reduction of opening hours from three days to two and the introduction of admission tickets, claiming that "art and academic collections are not suitable for the lowliest classes from the street,"[8] that this suggestion was taken up,

4 See note 3.
5 *Wienerisches Diarium*, no. 29, April 9, 1777, p. 7; *Preßburger Zeitung*, no. 30, April 12, 1777, p. 6.
6 Pezzl 1787, pp. 440–42. Translation from *Maria Theresa and the Arts*, exh. cat. Belvedere Vienna (Vienna, 2017), p. 7.
7 See note 6.
8 Lhotsky 1941–45, p. 488.

and then only five years later, in 1818. And even this was probably more a result of the complete closure of the gallery, after the collection had already been evacuated five times between 1799 and 1813, as a result of the Napoleonic Wars.[9] The fact that the gallery remained open to all social classes without restriction (at least until the end of the eighteenth century), despite the objections by its directors, suggests that the imperial household had other reasons for presenting the collection than its directors. While the "enlightened" imperial court was no doubt keen to ensure that the Imperial Gallery was generally visible and accessible, the directors were more concerned with conservation aspects, and their priority was to communicate the specific art-historical content of the collection.

The same divergence of interests, approaches, and strategies is also reflected in the reports on the Imperial Picture Gallery in international magazines and journals, which focused in particular on the repeated changes in the arrangement of the paintings. It should be mentioned that, after the collection had been moved, visitors to the Belvedere were confronted with a rapid succession of reshufflings and rehangings. Joseph Rosa's achievement in transferring the picture collection to the Belvedere and installing it there, soon faded into the background in the light of the new arrangement devised around 1780 by the Swiss engraver and publisher Christian von Mechel, who was unexpectedly tasked with reorganizing the collection (fig. 2). After Mechel's short intermezzo, Rosa was once again placed in charge of the gallery and promptly rearranged the pictures again (fig. 3).

Of the many articles devoted to Mechel's complete reorganization of the gallery, two interesting commentaries—one in favor and one against it—are cited here. They were published successively in the same magazine, *Deutsches Museum*. In contrast to the "feast for the eyes" offered by the Dresden gallery, states the critic, the Imperial Picture Gallery had been "deprived of its gallery character and reduced to a picture sample card." He even went as far as calling it a "gallery assassination."[10] The supporter of the new arrangement, on the other hand, writes that the gallery had "indisputably gained rather than lost the character of a gallery," thanks to the clear arrangement, which now offered "a vivid history of the human intellect."[11] The controversy as to whether the gallery should serve as a platform for developing artistic taste or as an educational institution to provide knowledge of art history in accordance with Johann Joachim Winckelmann's theories is indicative of the way in which the new arrangement reflected the individual protagonists' specific ideals, which were based on different collection traditions and schools of thought. But the discussions also reveal that the different arrangements were in fact aimed at different sections of the population: at connoisseurs and scholars on the one hand, and at artists and art students on the other.

9 Hoppe-Harnoncourt 2021, pp. 50–52.

10 Fortsetzung der Gedanken 1782, p. 254.

11 Wezel 1783.

It seems that it was only the Viennese court that considered the wider public, that is “folk from the lower classes,” in the presentation of the collection. This is suggested at least by the extraordinary fact that a few months before the new arrangement by Mechel was completed in 1781, State Chancellor Wenzel Anton von Kaunitz-Rietberg intervened personally, insisting, as he writes in a letter to Emperor Joseph II, that the arrangement should be more in line with the rules of symmetry. Remarkably, he explains that only a symmetrical display would be able to satisfy both the “scholarly and intelligent person” and the diverse public, which he refers to in his letter as “multitude.”[12]

One reason why Mechel’s work on the gallery received so much attention, perhaps even too much, was because his activities were publicized in magazines and journals—for example, by his friend, the Protestant theologian Carl Wilhelm Hilchenbach, who described himself as an “early witness” of the changes in the Picture Gallery.[13] But Mechel’s success—or, more precisely, the success of his picture arrangement—was also due to the exceptionally wide circulation of his catalogue, *Verzeichniß der Gemälde der Kaiserlich Königlichen Bilder Gallerie in Wien* and *Catalogue de Tableaux de la Galerie Impériale et Royale de Vienne* (→ p. 83), published in German and French in 1783 and 1784.[14] The fact that Mechel was commissioned as an outsider to produce the gallery catalogue was not unusual in itself, since other catalogues of the imperial collections were also produced by external specialists.[15] Much more unusual was the fact that, following the commission to produce the catalogue, Mechel was also appointed to reorganize the paintings. He had been summoned to Vienna initially merely to produce the catalogue, which he planned to publish in two volumes. The first volume would contain a “general list of all existing pictures,” while the second would be “confined to the most outstanding, attractive, and instructive pieces, to be described in the most precise historical and critical detail.”[16] In fact, only the *Verzeichniß/Catalogue* was published. The planned critical historical catalogue raisonné was never completed.

At first glance, the Mechel catalogue, with its small format and simple design, appears quite unremarkable. The addition of a list of artists (fig. 4) and the layout and vertical plan of the Upper and Lower Belvedere are the only unusual features (→ p. 82). One innovative element of the catalogue was the inclusion of a foreword describing the history of the collection and of the art of painting, whereby the German and French versions each had a slightly different focus. In the German version, the history of the collection was described with reference to the Habsburg collectors, while the French version focused on the history of painting, in particular the invention of oil painting by the Early German masters. It is unclear whether the divergent forewords were aimed specifically

12 Letter, Wenzel Anton Kaunitz-Rietberg to Emperor Joseph II, July 15, 1780, OeStA/AVA, Unterricht StHK, part 1 A 75.7, Academy of Fine Arts (“Kaunitz-Konvolut”), fol. 36–40; Gruber 2008, p. 199. For a discussion of the term “multitude,” see Kernbauer 2011 *passim*; Mayer 2021a, p. 277; see also the essay by Gernot Mayer in this volume, pp. 110–17.

13 Letter from Vienna 1782.

14 Mechel 1783; Mechel 1784.

15 Hassmann 2013, pp. 136–37.

16 Hilchenbach 1781, pp. 37–38.

at different German- and French-speaking readers, or whether the later French version was merely the result of further research by Mechel.

However unspectacular the Mechel catalogue might appear, it had an astonishing impact. It was distributed throughout Europe, even though it soon became outdated, following Mechel's replacement by Rosa and the latter's rearrangement of the pictures. In fact, Rosa himself published a two-volume catalogue in 1796, but this only featured the Italian painting schools and Netherlandish art on the first floor of the Belvedere (figs. 5, 6).[17]

Mechel's catalogue also had an influence on some key events in the history of the gallery. It played a major role in the acquisition of paintings and in the exchange between the Imperial Picture Gallery and the Uffizi in 1792 (→ p. 125, ⑧), but also in the art looting that took place during the Napoleonic Wars in 1809 (→ p. 133, ⑨).[18] In both cases, the protagonists—the directors Giuseppe Pelli Bencivenni (Uffizi) and Dominique-Vivant Denon (Napoleonic collections)—used the Mechel catalogue to select the most valuable paintings. In this way, the unusual publicity surrounding this small and unassuming catalogue established the international reputation of the imperial painting collection in the Belvedere.

17 Rosa 1796a; Rosa 1796b. A supplementary catalogue was published in 1804; Rosa 1804.

18 For a discussion on the exchange, see Fischer 2013a, pp. 68–77; for the looting during the Napoleonic Wars, see Savoy 2011, p. 135.

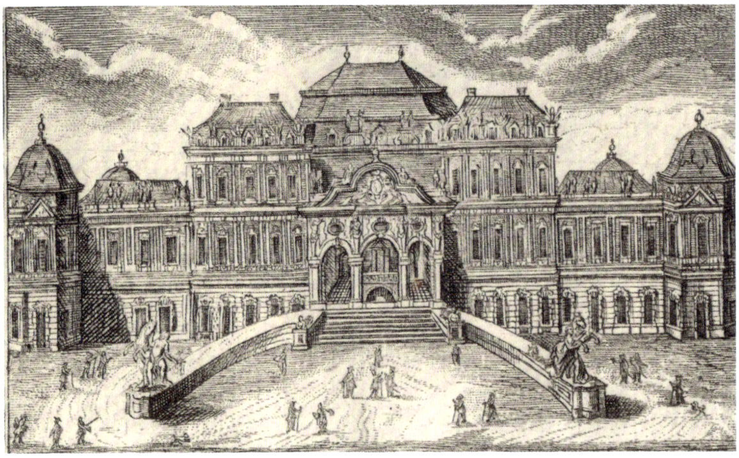

1

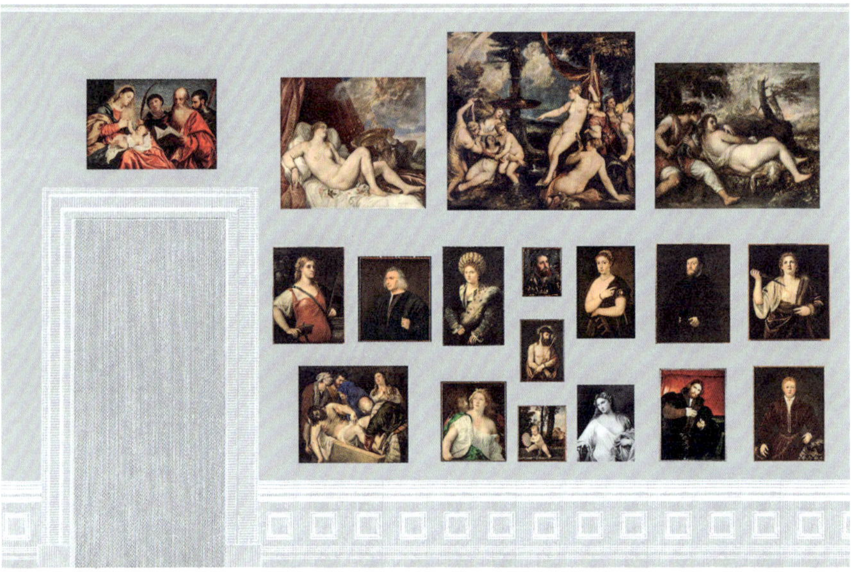

2

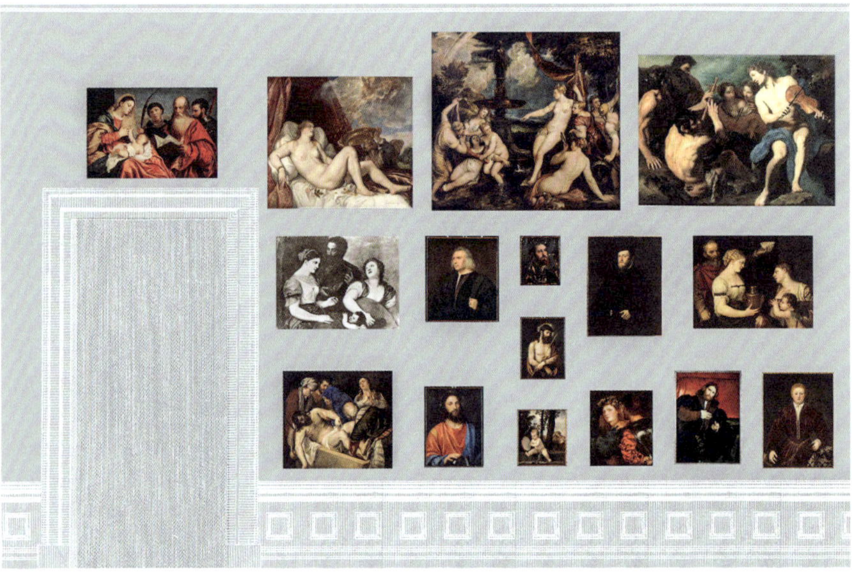

3

Fig. 1
The Upper Belvedere, in Joseph von Kurzböck, *Nouveau guide par Vienne: pour les etrangers et les nationales de l'an 1792; ou courte description de toutes les particularites de la ville de Vienne*, Vienna 1792, Vienna City Library

Fig. 2
Third wall in the second room of the Venetian school, with paintings by Titian, on the first floor of the Upper Belvedere, digital reconstruction after Mechel 1783, visualization: Nora Fischer

Fig. 3
Third wall in the second room of the Venetian school, with paintings by Titian, on the first floor of the Upper Belvedere, digital reconstruction after Rosa 1796a, visualization: Nora Fischer

8

The Exchange of Pictures between Florence and Vienna

Nora Fischer

The reorganization of the Imperial Picture Gallery by Christian von Mechel with a view to presenting a "visible history of art" (→ p. 82) was in line with the academic thinking of the time but presented a new set of problems. In view of the limited selection of works available, an arrangement illustrating the development of art since the early modern period in its entirety necessarily entailed some gaps. In an attempt to fully document the different schools of painting, copies or second-rate originals were placed between original masterpieces. This deficiency was particularly apparent in the room with paintings from the Florentine school, which were in short supply in the imperial collection.

The plan for the exchange of paintings, agreed in May 1792 between Emperor Francis II and his brother Grand Duke Ferdinand III of Tuscany, appeared at first glance to be an ingenious solution to the problem. The idea was to compensate for the deficiencies of one gallery with the profusion of paintings in the other and to enhance both in this way. Joseph Rosa (→ p. 116, fig. 2) wrote in his 1796 catalogue: "An exchange would appear to be the most suitable way of mutually enriching the Grand Ducal Gallery in Florence and the Imperial Gallery in Vienna with works of painting that were lacking in one or the other."[1] But this expectation was disappointed, as illustrated not least by the procedure by which the paintings were exchanged.

The project started with a list drawn up by Rosa, which he submitted to the Uffizi in May 1792. With a marked lack of enthusiasm, director Giuseppe Pelli Bencivenni put together an expert committee to select the pictures to be exchanged, justifying their choices and keeping losses to a minimum. In return, Pelli was allowed to submit his own list. Immediately after the arrival of the first shipment of paintings from Florence, the gallery in Vienna made ample use of the agreement by which pictures that failed to live up to expectations could be returned.[2] The first shipment from Vienna thus included pictures returned to the Uffizi on account of their inferior artistic quality, along with a new list. With the second shipment of replacement pictures from Florence, and the subsequent return shipment from Vienna in 1793, the exchange seemed to have been completed. Eighteen months later, however, Tommaso Puccini, the new director of the Uffizi, resumed negotiations, demanding a shipment that had allegedly not arrived and suggesting a new exchange. Eventually, he obtained approval from the emperor in 1795 for a final shipment from Vienna. In return for two rejected paintings, four others were promised. Although the two paintings (one of which was Titian's *Nymph and Shepherd*) were returned by the Uffizi in 1796, the shipment of the four pictures from Vienna (including Dürer's *Adoration of the Kings*) was postponed because of the war with Napoleon. It was not until 1821, with the third shipment from Vienna to Florence, that the exchange was finally completed.

In the process, some fifty paintings changed location (fig. 1). The paintings arriving in Vienna included in particular works by Florentine masters (among others, Bronzino's *Holy Family* and Fra Bartolomeo's *Presentation of Christ in the Temple*). Paintings by Flemish, German, and Venetian masters (including Bellini's *Allegory*, Titian's *Flora*, and Giorgione's *Gattamelata*) were sent from Vienna to Florence. Many of the exchanged pictures are still on prominent display in the Kunsthistorisches Museum, the Uffizi, and the Galleria Palatina.

1 Rosa 1796a, pp. XI–XII.

2 Note by gallery director Joseph Rosa of June 20, 1794, ÖStA/HHStA, OKäA, SR 38b, no. 74.

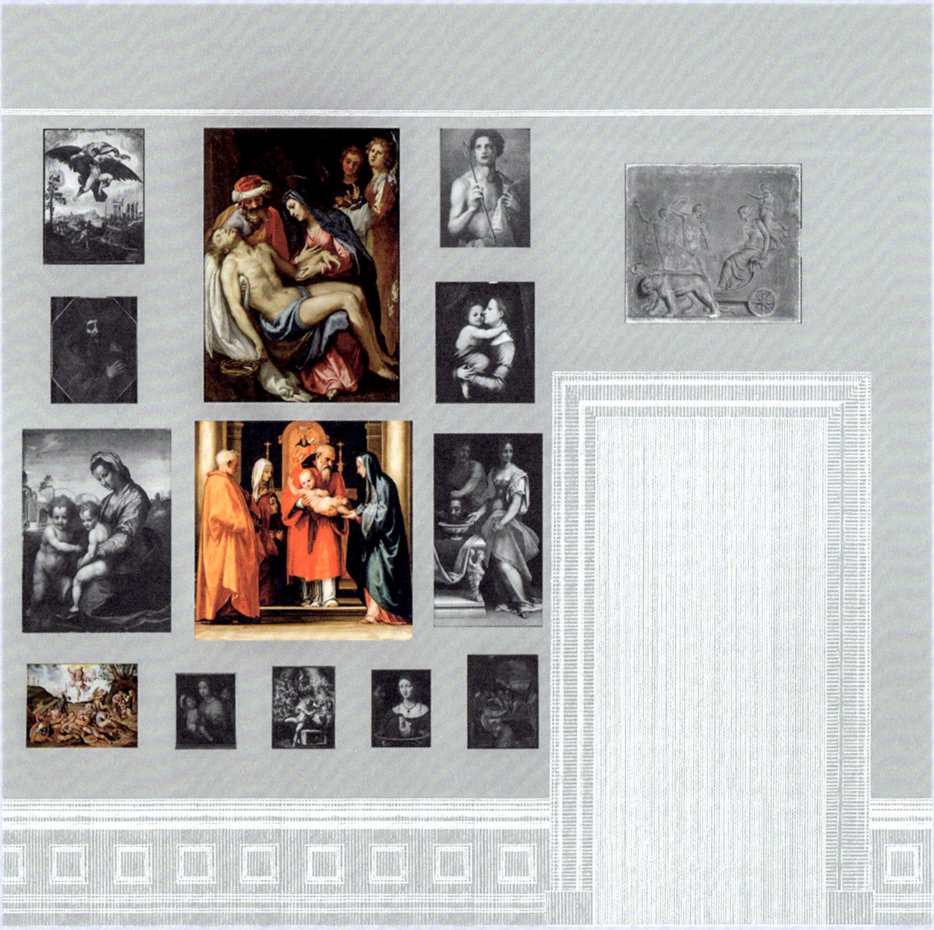

1

Fig. 1
First wall in the fourth room of the Florentine school on the first floor of the Upper Belvedere with paintings obtained through the exchanges with the Uffizi: Fra Bartolomeo, *Presentation of Christ in the Temple*, 1516; Ludovico Cardi da Cigoli, *Lamentation of Christ*, 1599; Florentine (anonymous), *Resurrection of Christ*, 1560, digital reconstruction after Rosa 1796a, visualization: Nora Fischer

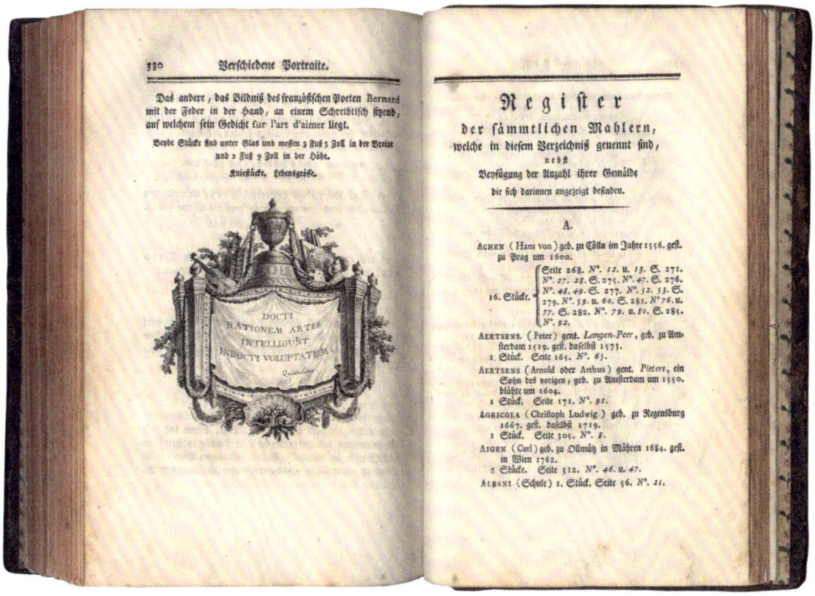

330 Verschiedene Portraite.

Das andere, das Bildniß des französischen Poeten Bernard mit der Feder in der Hand, an einem Schreibtisch sitzend, auf welchem sein Gedicht für l'art d'aimer liegt.

Beyde Stücke sind unter Glas und messen 3 Fuß 3 Zoll in der Breite und 2 Fuß 9 Zoll in der Höhe.

Kniestücke. Lebensgröße.

Register der sämmtlichen Mahlern, welche in diesem Verzeichniß genennt sind, nebst Beyfügung der Anzahl ihrer Gemälde die sich darinnen angezeigt befinden.

A.

ACHEN (Hans von) geb. zu Cölln im Jahre 1556. gest. zu Prag um 1600.
16. Stücke. Seite 268. N°. 12. u. 13. S. 271. N°. 27. 28. S. 275. N°. 47. S. 276. N°. 48. 49. S. 277. N°. 52. 53. S. 279. N°. 59. u. 60. S. 281. N° 76. u. 77. S. 282. N°. 79. u. 80. S. 285. N°. 92.

AERTSENS. (Peter) gent. *Langen-Peer*, geb. zu Amsterdam 1519. gest. daselbst 1573.
1. Stück. Seite 165. N°. 65.

AERTSENS (Arnold oder Arthus) gent. *Pieters*, ein Sohn des vorigen, geb. zu Amsterdam um 1550. blühte um 1604.
1 Stück. Seite 171. N°. 91.

AGRICOLA (Christoph Ludwig) geb. zu Regensburg 1667. gest. daselbst 1719.
1 Stück. Seite 305. N°. 8.

AIGEN (Carl) geb. zu Ollmütz in Mähren 1684. gest. in Wien 1762.
2 Stücke. Seite 312. N°. 46. u. 47.

ALBANI (Schule) 1. Stück. Seite 56. N°. 21.

4

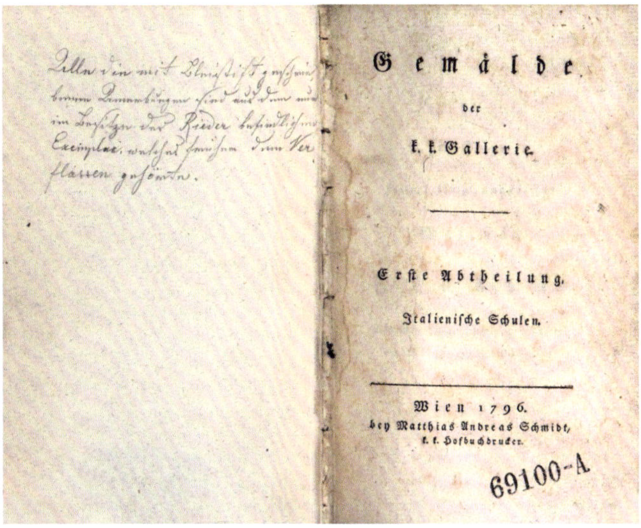

Gemälde der k. k. Gallerie.

Erste Abtheilung.

Italienische Schulen.

Wien 1796.
bey Matthias Andreas Schmidt, k. k. Hofbuchdrucker.

5

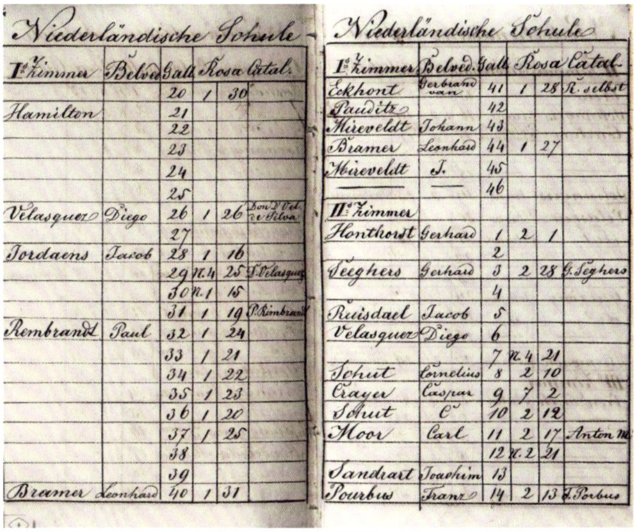

Niederländische Schule

I. Zimmer	Belved.	Gall.	Rosa	Catal.
		20	1	30
Hamilton		21		
		22		
		23		
		24		
		25		
Velasquez	Diego	26	1	26 Don D. Vel. de Silva
		27		
Jordaens	Jacob	28	1	16
		29	N. 4	25 S. Velasquez
		30	N. 1	15
		31	1	19 S. Rembrandt
Rembrandt	Paul	32	1	24
		33	1	21
		34	1	22
		35	1	23
		36	1	20
		37	1	25
		38		
		39		
Bramer	Leonhard	40	1	31

Niederländische Schule

I. Zimmer	Belved.	Gall.	Rosa	Catal.
Eckhont	Gerbrand van	41	1	28 R. selbst
Paudetz		42		
Mieveldt	Johann	43		
Bramer	Leonhard	44	1	27
Mieveldt	J.	45		
	—	46		
II. Zimmer				
Honthorst	Gerhard	1	2	1
		2		
Seeghers	Gerhard	3	2	28 G. Seghers
		4		
Ruisdael	Jacob	5		
Velasquez	Diego	6		
		7	N. 4	21
Schut	Cornelius	8	2	10
Crayer	Caspar	9	7	2
Schut	C.	10	2	12
Moor	Carl	11	2	17 Anton M.
		12	N. 2	21
Sandrart	Joachim	13		
Pourbus	Franz	14	2	13 F. Porbus

6

Fig. 4
Index of painters, in Christian von Mechel, *Verzeichniß der Gemälde der Kaiserlich Königlichen Bilder Gallerie in Wien*, Vienna 1783, Belvedere Library, Vienna

Fig. 5
Title page of Joseph Rosa's *Gemälde der k. k. Gallerie. Erste Abteilung. Italienische Schulen*, Vienna 1796, Austrian National Library, Vienna

Fig. 6
Handwritten index, supplement to Joseph Rosa's *Gemälde der k. k. Gallerie. Erste Abteilung. Italienische Schulen*, Austrian National Library, Vienna

P. 128

ALICE HOPPE-HARNONCOURT —
New Concepts for the Display of Painting Schools in the Early Nineteenth Century

Joseph Rosa (→ p. 116, fig. 2) had served as director of the Imperial Picture Gallery for over thirty years, when, suffering from poor health, he retired in 1805. Heinrich Friedrich Füger (→ p. 369, fig. 4), then director of the Academy of Fine Arts, had already submitted his application for the soon-to-be vacant post.[1] He was at the zenith of his career and now hoped for a less pressurized position in order to be able to devote more time to his own art.[2] To this end, when his appointment as gallery director and keeper of the Belvedere was officially agreed in June 1806, it came with the promise of allowing him to set up a studio in his director's apartment at the palace.[3]

Thanks to Rosa's 1796 catalogues, the arrangement of the gallery is well documented for the first floor (→ p. 127, fig. 5), with the Netherlandish school on the west side and Italian painting from the sixteenth to eighteenth centuries in the east wing.[4] In 1804, Rosa still managed to complete a third volume of his collection catalogues, comprising four new gallery rooms on the ground floor, in which works recently transferred from Italy were now exhibited.[5] The reorganization of the paintings on the second floor, showcasing the German and Early Netherlandish schools, however, did not take place under Rosa. This became the task of his successor, who thus introduced fresh ideas to the appearance of the gallery in the nineteenth century.

At the very beginning of Füger's tenure, the gallery was in a state of emergency. The paintings evacuated in 1805 had been returned, but repair work on the building prevented them from being unpacked.[6] In addition, the director had to accommodate deliveries of artworks from Ambras Castle and from Salzburg. While the Ambras Collection was allocated its own venue at the Lower Belvedere (→ p. 93, ⑥)—separate from the Imperial Picture Gallery—the wealth of pictures from the secularized Archbishopric of Salzburg significantly enriched the gallery's holdings of fifteenth-century paintings. These included the panels depicting the Passion by Rueland Frueauf the Elder, Conrad Laib's large Crucifixion, and two altarpieces by the Master of Grossgmain, then categorized as the so-called Early German school.[7] The ongoing active collecting of Emperor Francis II/I, moreover, resulted in the acquisition of further important works, such as Caravaggio's *Crowning with Thorns* from the Giustiniani Collection, Bernard van Orley's *Altarpiece of the Saints Thomas and Matthew*, and the *Adoration of the Kings* by Jan Brueghel the Elder.[8] The emperor also devoted equal attention to acquiring contemporary paintings, which were added to the collection even in its first decade. Lorenz Adolf Schönberger's large-format *The Bay of Baiae at Sunset*, acquired in July 1806, is one such example.[9]

Influenced by the ongoing changes to the collection's composition, Füger introduced his first new concept for reorganizing the paintings on the second floor as early as 1808. In March 1809, the displays would have

1 Hoppe-Harnoncourt 2001, p. 158.
2 Grabner 2013, p. 361; Keil 2009, pp. 20, 118.
3 Grabner 2018, pp. 35–43.
4 Rosa 1796a; Rosa 1796b; see Fischer 2013b, chapter 7.
5 These were paintings seized by Austrian troops in Italy, works that had previously been stolen by the French, for example from the Albani Collection in Rome; see Mayer/Swoboda 2018, esp. pp. 97 and 108; Rosa 1804; Hoppe-Harnoncourt 2001, pp. 152–53.
6 Hoppe-Harnoncourt 2001, pp. 158–59; Grabner 2013, p. 361.
7 Füger's diary entries 1806–07, in Frimmel 1909, pp. 95–96; Hoppe-Harnoncourt 2013, p. 100; Walderdorff 2008, p. 328.
8 Swoboda/Prohaska 2010, pp. 65–66; Füger's diary entries in February 1809, in Frimmel 1909, p. 99; coll. cat. Vienna 1886, pp. 300–01.
9 Grabner 2013, p. 361; Füger's diary entry in July 1806, in Frimmel 1909, p. 97.

been ready for the public, but the opening of the gallery was prevented by the War of the Fourth Coalition. Since Füger had not brought the gallery's recent acquisitions of early paintings to safety, the French seized some of the works, including the panels that had only just arrived from Salzburg, and sent them to France.[10] The Belvedere had suffered badly during the French occupation (→ p. 133, ⑨), and it was not until 1813 that any thoughts of reopening the gallery could be entertained—plans that were, once again, thwarted by the war. During the Congress of Vienna, a visit to the Picture Gallery was mainly reserved for high-ranking statesmen. Füger often took this opportunity to include his nearby studio in the gallery tour.[11]

In 1816, following the return of the paintings from France, Füger immediately started tackling the displays, in all likelihood based on his concept from 1808. Since a manuscript of his planned catalogue has survived, we know the arrangement of the gallery and can reconstruct his innovations:[12] In contrast to his predecessors, Füger, for the first time, allocated the west wing for recent and modern painting, and reserved the east wing for painting from the fourteenth to the seventeenth centuries. Here he brought together the already familiar Early German and Early Netherlandish works, and added, also for the first time, Early Italian paintings (fig. 2). He explained the objective behind this arrangement in his catalogue preface: The paintings from the early schools would show that they had "a simple imitation of the surrounding environment as their sole and ultimate goal," while the works on the first floor would prove that painting from the sixteenth and seventeenth centuries, under the influence of classical antiquity, had become the "arbiter of good taste" in the fine arts of the modern era.[13]

Füger's concept from 1808 reflects the theoretical considerations behind organizing the fine arts around 1800. As director of the Vienna Academy, Füger was a well-known exponent of Neoclassical art theory. At the same time, as an artist he was constantly searching for ways to adapt this ideal.[14] Therefore, alongside attempts to revive Neoclassicism, the emerging reorientation heralded by early Romanticism was surely not lost on him.[15] Friedrich Schlegel had just written his reports on Italian painting at the Paris Musée Napoléon, in which he shared his observations on the development of painting around 1500. Whereas Füger preferred the visual language influenced by antiquity, Schlegel found true art especially in the naturalistic painting from an earlier age, as, for him, this came much closer to the familiar Christian expression of emotion.[16] Füger's deliberations about reclassifying the early art schools coincided with Schlegel's theories first flourishing in Vienna among the younger artists around Franz Pforr and Friedrich Overbeck. Members of this group now looked at the early paintings in the Imperial Picture

10 Hoppe-Harnoncourt 2021, pp. 48–50.

11 Grabner 2018, pp. 47–48.

12 Füger's arrangement can be reconstructed from three inventories from the years 1816, 1817, and 1820. The well-known inventory of 1824 had already obscured this system; Hoppe-Harnoncourt 2021, chapter 2.

13 Preface to the catalogue of 1816, KHM, Archives of the Picture Gallery, transcribed after Nora Fischer in Hoppe-Harnoncourt 2021, pp. 112–13.

14 Keil 2009, pp. 66, 120–21.

15 Hoppe-Harnoncourt 2021, pp. 71–76.

16 See Schlegel's text "Vom Raphael," published in 1803, in Schlegel 1995, pp. 40–45; cf. Hoppe-Harnoncourt 2021, pp. 90–91.

Gallery with fresh eyes, ultimately causing them to turn their backs on the Vienna Academy in 1809 and to found their own community of artists that would later go down in the annals of nineteenth-century art history as the Nazarenes.[17] At the time, the Picture Gallery, as a pool of all manner of models, must have been a particularly valuable resource.

The gallery did not reopen to the general public until May 1818, but from then on was open twice a week.[18] In the end, Füger was unable to enjoy the normal operations of the gallery for long, as he died only a few months later, in November. He still managed to initiate the expansion of the gallery on the ground floor by adding one large room on each side, leaving the curator Joseph Rosa junior in charge of arranging the displays. As a result, a secondary gallery with Netherlandish and Italian paintings that could not be accommodated in the main gallery was available from as early as 1820.[19]

The long struggle to fill the position of gallery director reveals a certain indecisiveness about the intended future direction of the Imperial Picture Gallery. By now, Füger's arrangement was out of date and did not seem to meet the needs of its audience. The plan, first pursued in earnest around 1820, to appoint an art historian for the post, came to nothing and, consequently, starting with the appointment of Joseph Rebell (→ p. 369, fig. 5) in 1824, painters continued to hold the post of director for the entire duration of the nineteenth century.[20]

In the summer of 1825, two rooms of the Italian school had been tentatively rearranged and the manuscript of a catalogue presented as documentation.[21] Director Peter Krafft (→ p. 369, fig. 6), Rebell's successor in 1828, retained this concept, and thus the reorganization of the gallery occurred over the course of a decade during normal museum operations. This work was carried out alongside an unprecedented restoration campaign and extensive modifications to the palace, such as the installation of a new hot-air heating system, which explains why it took so long (→ p. 125, ⑧).[22]

The redisplay was completed in 1836, as documented in a new catalogue published in 1837 (the first in over fifty years that covered the entire gallery) (fig. 1).[23] Its form and the way the pictures were described was modeled on Christian von Mechel's catalogue (→ p. 82).[24] In the gallery itself, labels were added to the frames, giving the artists' names and their biographical dates. In keeping with Füger's concept, the early works of Netherlandish and German painting remained on the second floor. The west wing was now dedicated exclusively to the exhibition of modern artists. The secondary gallery on the ground floor remained and was extended by a fourth room on each side, although the Carlone Hall stayed empty and was used as a copying room.[25]

After all this work was completed, Krafft was particularly keen to ensure that this arrangement could not be changed on a whim. As a nega-

17 Pforr's account to his guardian about his visit to the Imperial Picture Gallery, published in Lehr 1924, p. 37.
18 Announcement in the *Wiener Zeitung*, May 6, 1818; Hoppe-Harnoncourt 2021, pp. 51–52.
19 Hoppe-Harnoncourt 2001, pp. 168–69. Count Lamberg-Sprinzenstein visited these rooms in 1821, as there were plans to exhibit his gift to the Academy at the Belvedere. He noted that the rooms were not open to the public due to staff shortages. Copy of a letter by Lamberg from October 21, 1821, regarding the deed of gift, UAAbKW, VA 43, 1822/3, fol. 382–85.
20 Grabner 2022c, pp. 141–43, 371–74; Hoppe-Harnoncourt 2021, pp. 58–59.
21 Joseph Rebell, *Musterheft des über die k. k. Bildergallerie im Belvedere zu verfassenden Cataloges*, manuscript, c. 1825, ÖNB (Austrian National Library), Picture Archives and Graphics, sign. 283920-C.
22 Grabner 2022c, pp. 145–51; Hoppe-Harnoncourt 2021, pp. 59–60.
23 Krafft 1837.
24 Mechel 1783.
25 Krafft 1837, pp. VII–XVI.

tive example he gave the fact that Christian von Mechel's "scientific classification" had been "unnecessarily" destroyed by director Rosa.[26] Krafft's appeal was heeded and the departments with the Old Masters remained largely in the same arrangement devised by Rebell and Krafft (→ pp. 85–6) until the works were moved in 1891.[27] The department of modern painting was different, of course, as its very nature was to change and grow with new acquisitions.[28]

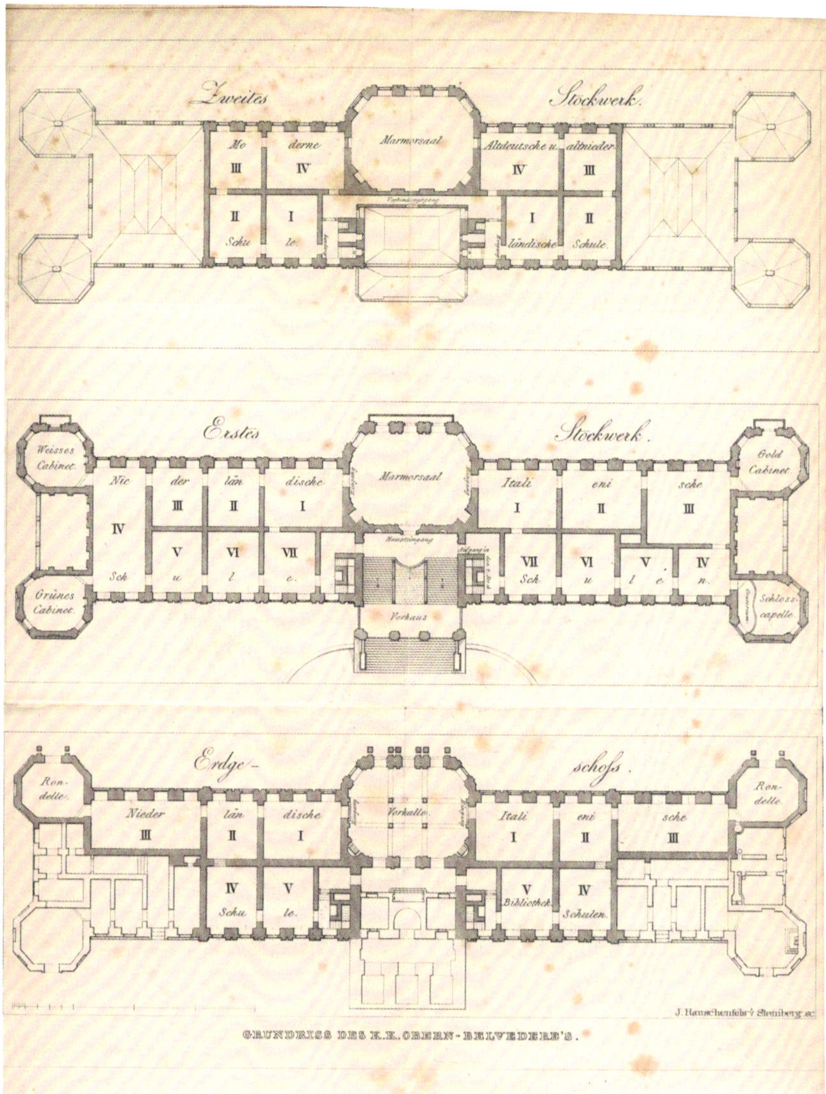

1

Fig. 1
Floor plans of the Imperial Picture Gallery, in Albrecht Krafft, *Verzeichniss der kais. kön. Gemälde-Gallerie im Belvedere zu Wien*, Vienna 1837, Belvedere Library, Vienna

26 Report by Peter Krafft from October 1836, quoted in Hoppe-Harnoncourt 2021, pp. 104–05.

27 The arrangement of the Old Masters is documented in pencil drawings; Wilhelm von Wartenegg, *Aufstellung der Kaiserlichen Gemäldegalerie im Belvedere: Aufgenommen im Jahre 1891 durch Wilhelm von Wartenegg*, manuscript, KHM, library, sign. 19283, (fig. 3).

28 Hoppe-Harnoncourt 2021, pp. 61–62; see the essay by Sabine Grabner in this volume, pp. 138–42.

⑨

Napoleonic Looting and Evacuation of Artworks

Alice Hoppe-Harnoncourt

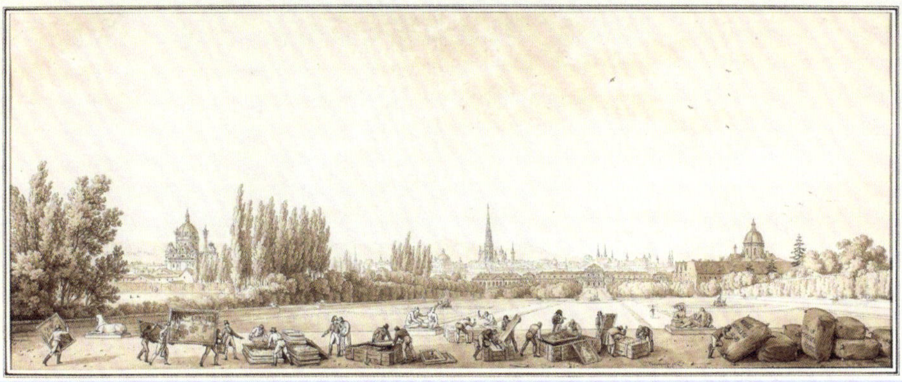

1

As early as 1797 and the turn of the century, gallery director Joseph Rosa arranged for some five hundred paintings to be packed in crates and transported eastward. Further art evacuations took place in 1805 and in 1809, the years in which Napoleon actually came to Vienna.

The second French occupation began in May 1809. A month later, director Heinrich Friedrich Füger was summoned to the governor-general Antoine-François Andréossy, who inquired about the remaining works of art in the Belvedere. Three days later, Dominique-Vivant Denon, director of the Musée Napoléon, arrived with written permission from the governor-general to select all the paintings he considered suitable (fig. 1). Among the works he chose were valuable items such as Rubens's *Assumption of the Virgin Mary* and a mosaic copy after Pompeo Batoni. Füger was forced to explain the losses in a letter to the emperor: "The aforementioned large picture of the Assumption of the Virgin Mary by Rubens (fig. 2) and the mosaic of Emperor Joseph and Leopold II had to be removed from the wall, lowered, and prepared for transport. All my remonstrations were in vain. In reply to my comment that this painting by Rubens had never been taken down on account of its size, weight, and fragility, Mr. Denon stated that he intended to separate it into three parts. Even my admonition that an operation so unusual for a painting would provide material for an anecdote in the history of art and was something I would not be prepared to be held responsible for had no effect. [...] Moreover, not only did Mr. Denon take this picture and the mosaic, along with many other pieces from storage, most of which were not of sufficient artistic value to be suitable for the Paris museum, but he also decided to take [...] Prince Eugene's large battle scenes from the Lower Belvedere." From July, convalescing soldiers were housed in the Upper Belvedere, and Füger was kept busy trying to prevent damage to the building and the remaining pictures and frames left in storage, until the

French left the city in November 1809. Füger's report did not exonerate him, as a personal note from Francis I shows: "I take note of this information, and in view of the great loss suffered by the gallery cannot reward director Füger."[1]

When the city was under threat again in 1813, Füger had all the remaining paintings in the gallery—1,235 in all—packed in crates and evacuated as a precautionary measure. All in all there were thus five evacuations and one transport to Paris. The constant removing and rehanging of the pictures finally came to an end when the restituted paintings were returned from France in November 1815.[2]

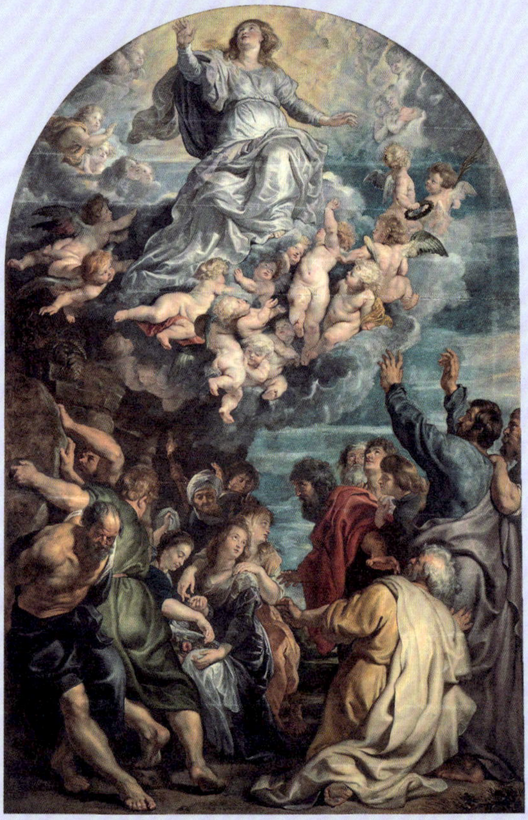

2

1 Füger's report to the office of the head chamberlain, November 22, 1809, and the handwritten note by Emperor Francis I of February 16, 1813, quoted by Lhotsky 1941–45, p. 514, and others.

2 Hoppe-Harnoncourt 2001, pp. 156–63; Pénot 2009; Gustavson 2012, pp. 49–66.

Fig. 1
Benjamin Zix and Constant Bourgeois, *Packing of Paintings in Front of the Upper Belvedere for Transport to France in June 1809*, 1810, private collection

Fig. 2
Peter Paul Rubens, *Assumption of the Virgin Mary*, c. 1611/14–21, Kunsthistorisches Museum Vienna, Picture Gallery

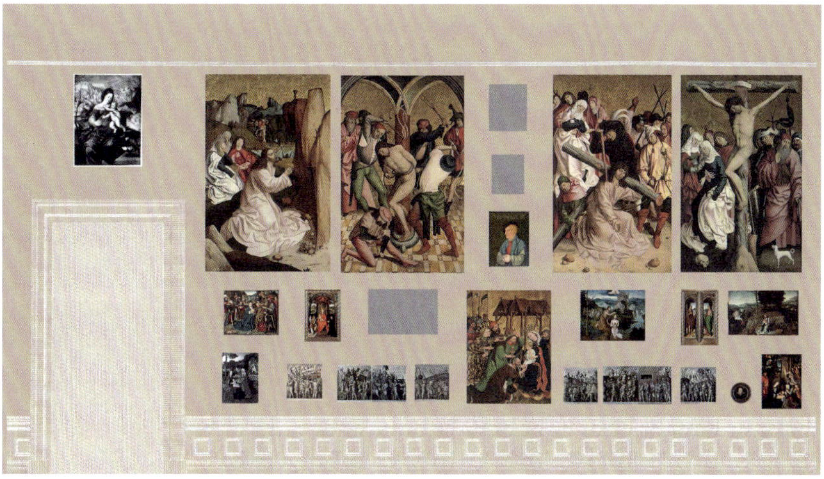

2

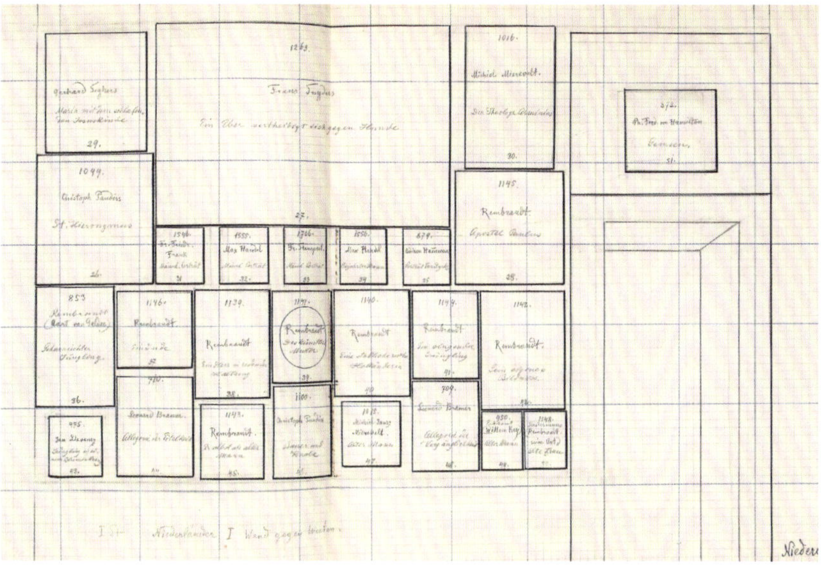

3

Fig. 2
First wall in the second room in the east wing of the second floor of the Upper Belvedere with paintings of the old German, old Netherlandish and old Italian schools; digital reconstruction after Heinrich Füger's inventory of 1816, visualization: Alice Hoppe-Harnoncourt

Füger enabled direct comparison of paintings around 1500 from different regional schools. On this wall, the large Passion panels by Rueland Frueauf the Elder were presented in comparison with Dutch paintings by Hans Memling and Joachim Patinir, as well as the grisaille series after Andrea Mantegna.

Fig. 3
Documentation of the first wall in the first room of the Dutch School on the second floor of the Upper Belvedere before their transfer to the Kunsthistorisches Museum. *Installation of the Imperial Picture Gallery in the Belvedere. Taken in 1891 by Wilhelm von Wartenegg*, manuscript, Kunsthistorisches Museum, Vienna, Library, fol. 26.

P. 136 SABINE GRABNER — The “Modern School” of the Imperial Picture Gallery

"I wish to dedicate the annual sum of three thousand guldens to the purchase of domestic works of art from every fine art discipline."[1] These words from Emperor Francis I on April 9, 1827, had a great impact on the future of the Imperial Picture Gallery. With this commitment, the monarch took the gallery's procurement policy in a new direction, since, for the rest of the century, the majority of acquisitions were of art by living and primarily Austrian artists. Francis I was keen to make the decisions on purchases himself, which is why he asked his art experts to keep him informed about the "most exceptional domestic works of art submitted for the [Academy] exhibition as well as their prices."[2] The first purchase made under this premise was in 1828.[3]

From its beginnings, it had been the policy of the Imperial Picture Gallery to concentrate on the art of the current era. Consequently, even at the time of the above-mentioned decision, its collection already contained key works of contemporary painting. Examples include *The Dead Saint Cecilia* by Johann Evangelist Scheffer von Leonhardshoff,[4] an important example of Romantic religious painting, and Peter Krafft's *The Militiaman's Departure*[5] (fig. 1), a combination of history and genre painting and a model for the figure painting of the next generation, as well as Joseph Fischer's *The Capital and Residential City of Vienna Seen from Nussdorf*[6] and the four views of Naples by Joseph Rebell,[7] which express a forward-looking understanding of nature. These new acquisitions were immediately placed in the showrooms on the second floor, where Heinrich Friedrich Füger (→ p. 369, fig. 4), the gallery director at the time, took great care to ensure a historical continuity between old and new art.[8]

From now on, however, the latest art was to be given even stronger emphasis. It may have been the Musée du Luxembourg in Paris, which since 1818 had only displayed works by living painters, that inspired Francis I's decision, or perhaps it was the frequent call for an institution that could illustrate the evolution of the arts and thus enable their state-organized promotion.[9] Naturally, he also wanted to bring together the newly acquired works in his museum "in their own dedicated rooms

1 Francis I on April 9, 1827, ÖStA/HHStA, OKäA-B, Zl. 715/1827.
2 See note 1; see also Albrecht Krafft in the foreword to the gallery guide of 1837: The "Modern School" "was started by the Imperial-Royal Gallery Director Joseph Rebell in 1825 [sic] at the order of His Majesty Emperor Francis I under the leadership and maintenance of His Excellency the Imperial-Royal Grand Chaplain Johann Rudolf Graf Czernin, continued by his successor in office (1829) Peter Krafft, and completed in 1836"; Krafft 1837, p. IV.
3 ÖStA/HHStA, OKäA-B, Zl. 1121/1828.
4 ÖStA/HHStA, OKäA-B, Zl. 178/822 and 281/822, now in the Belvedere, Vienna, inv. no. 2244.
5 ÖStA/HHStA, OKäA-B, Zl. 767/816. In 1820, its pendant, *The Militiaman's Return*, was also acquired; ÖStA/HHStA, OKäA-B, Zl. 848/820. Both now in the Belvedere, Vienna, inv. no. 2242 and 2243.
6 ÖStA/HHStA, OKäA, Zl. 990/822, now in the Belvedere, Vienna, inv. no. 2539.
7 *The Port of Granatello near Portici with Vesuvius in the Background*, *Sunset over the Campi Flegrei Looking toward the Islands Prócida and Ischia*, *Sea Storm near the Arco di Miseno near Miliscola, Looking toward Nisida*, and *The Town of Vietri with a View of the Gulf of Salerno*; ÖStA/HHStA, OKäA-B, Zl. 900/820. All four now in the Belvedere, Vienna, inv. nos. 2148, 4429, 2123, and 2369.
8 See Hoppe-Harnoncourt 2021.
9 Notably the landscape painter Albert Christoph Dies, who repeatedly called for a museum of modern art in several issues of the *Vaterländische Blätter*; Dies 1811, No. 9, p. 53.

in the Picture Gallery."[10] Thus, Joseph Rebell (→ p. 369, fig. 5), who had been appointed as its director, established the "Gallery of Living Artists on the ground floor of the Belvedere," as he reported himself.[11] Here he presented the new acquisitions from the Academy exhibition, including Josef Danhauser's *The Scholars' Room*,[12] works by Ferdinand Georg Waldmüller and Johann Nepomuk Schödlberger, landscapes by Josef Feid, the *Self Portrait* by Johann Baptist Lampi the Elder, and *Venus Sleeping on a Day Bed* by his son, Johann Baptist Lampi the Younger.[13] Recently acquired works by Carl Peter Goebel the Elder (*Jacob Blessing Joseph's Sons*), Marco Gozzi (*Monza Palace with Park*), and Johann Nepomuk Höchle (*The Allied Armies, Emperor Francis I of Austria and Crown Prince Ferdinand at the Head, Enter the Vosges in July 1815*) were probably also on display here,[14] and it is highly likely that the more recent works originally on the second floor were relocated to the ground floor, too.

Rebell's plans to establish the "Modern School" as a department in its own right on the ground floor of the Upper Belvedere, that is, to create an exhibition space for contemporary art on a par with the Old Masters on the upper floors, were brought to an abrupt end by his early death in December 1828. His successor Peter Krafft (→ p. 369, fig. 6) had little enthusiasm for the idea, and instead chose the four rooms on the western side of the second floor for the collection of contemporary art, even though this space offered no room for expansion to accommodate the ever-growing collection. The resultant constant rearranging and rehanging is reflected in the 1837 catalogue of the Imperial Picture Gallery, which, in contrast to the "Italian" and "Dutch School," gave no room description for the "Modern School," but merely an alphabetical list of names and artworks.[15] The pictures presumably covered the walls in multiple rows, as this was the only way to fit 141 artworks into 500 square meters of hanging space (approximately 120 running meters of wall area).[16] If these numbers alone are already impressive, the situation becomes even more incredible bearing in mind the many large-format paintings, which, in addition to those already mentioned, included similar "wall-filling" works, such as *The Traunfall Waterfall near Gmunden* by Johann Nepomuk Schödlberger,[17] Ludwig Ferdinand Schnorr von Carolsfeld's pendant pair *Faust and Mephisto in the Study Room* and *Faust and Gretchen in Prison*,[18] Anton Petter's *Entrance of Emperor Maximilian I in Ghent*,[19] and Hubert Maurer's *Let the Children Come to Me*.[20] The largest picture was Anton Hickel's *William Pitt Addressing the House of Commons on the French Declaration of War* of 1793.[21] Smaller formats were also represented, mostly works by younger artists acquired at the Academy exhibitions: Friedrich von Amerling's *Fisher Boy*[22] (fig. 2), Waldmüller's *A Beggar Boy on the Hohe Brücke*,[23] Matthias Rudolf Toma's *Cliffs near Schottwien*, and Rudolf von Alt's *St Stephen's Cathedral in Vienna*,[24] to name but a few.

10 Francis I on April 8, 1827, ÖStA/HHStA, OKäA-B, Zl. 715/1827.
11 Quote from the diary of Carl Christian Vogel von Vogelstein, in Grabner 2022d, p. 193.
12 Now in the Belvedere, Vienna, inv. no. 2109.
13 Both now in the Belvedere, Vienna, inv. nos. 3642 and 2519.
14 All three now in the Belvedere, Vienna, inv. nos. 3030, 7883, and 3099. For more on the circumstances surrounding the works' acquisition for the Imperial Picture Gallery, see Grabner 2022c, p. 151.
15 Krafft 1837, pp. 289–316 and addendum pp. 1–4. Unlike the "Modern School," which "does not form a cohesive whole, but is increased annually through the purchase of new works by living artists, each time necessitating a change in the arrangement," (Krafft 1837, p. 290) the gallery director considered the display of Old Masters on the first floor, in the eastern rooms of the second floor, and on the ground floor as complete and unchangeable. Indeed, no notable acquisitions were made for this section in the following decades that would have made a reorganization necessary.
16 With thanks to Patrick Ebner from the Belvedere Facilities Management for calculating the available wall space.
17 ÖStA/HHStA, OKäA-B, 1632/822, now in the Belvedere, Vienna, inv. no. 3735.
18 ÖStA/HHStA, OKäA-B, Zl. 1603/821 (*Faust and Mephisto in the Study Room*, the pendant to *Faust and Gretchen in Prison* was only finished in 1833). Both pictures are now held in the Belvedere, Vienna, inv. no. 3311a and 3311b.
19 ÖStA/HHStA, OKäA-B, Zl. 1633/822 and 990/822, now in the Belvedere, Vienna, inv. no. 3722.
20 Now in the Belvedere, Vienna, inv. no. 3256.

How and by which channels did the collection grow over the course of the nineteenth century?[25] The most significant source of acquisitions were the Academy exhibitions. Furthermore, from 1830, the exhibitions of the Society for the Promotion of the Fine Arts ("Old Art Society"); from 1850, the exhibitions of the Austrian Art Society; from 1868, the Künstlerhaus exhibitions; and, in 1873, the Vienna World's Fair (Hans Canon, *The Lodge of Saint John*[26]). The emperor also commissioned works directly from artists, which he transferred or donated to the museum on their completion. This gave rise, for instance, to a respectable collection of works from Northern Italy, commissioned by Emperor Ferdinand I on his coronation trip from Milan to Venice in 1838: from Francesco Hayez, Michelangelo Grigoletti, Andrea Appiani, Teodolinda Migliara, Luigi Bisi, and Domenico Induno, among others.[27] Emperor Franz Joseph I, meanwhile, commissioned the Czech artist Václav Brožik with a depiction of the 1515 double wedding, titled *Tu felix Austria nube*,[28] a history painting of enormous dimensions (fig. 3). A large part of the collection also consisted of the cartoons made by Carl Blaas between 1859 and 1871 for the painting of the Hall of Fame in the Arsenal. The art market and auctions were monitored as well, and then there were bequests from other art collectors. The collection grew significantly thanks to some generous donations, such as, in 1878, from the imperial-royal master builder Anton Ölzelt von Newin (Waldmüller's *Christmas Morning*, Josef Danhauser's *The Rich Glutton* and *The Monastery Soup*, Joseph von Führich's *Jacob Meets Rachel with Her Father's Herd*, and Franz Defregger's *The Last Contingent*[29]); in 1894, from the banker Georg Güterbock (Emil Jakob Schindler's *On the Dalmatian Coast Near Ragusa*[30]); in the years around 1900, from city architect Karl Rudolf Ritter von Wessely (Albin Egger-Lienz's *Good Friday*[31] [fig. 4]) and from Johann II, Prince of Liechtenstein (Waldmüller's *Brushwood Gatherers in the Vienna Woods*, Constant Troyon's *Chicken in Front of a Farmhouse*, Alexandre Calame's *View of Lake Geneva*[32]). In 1912, Ludwig von Reithoffer, founder of the Semperit rubber factory, donated key works from his collection, including Peter Fendi's *The Storm*, *Horses Drinking at a Trough in Hungary* by August von Pettenkofen, along with *The Ruin of Liechtenstein Castle near Mödling* (fig. 5) and *Poor Children are Given Winter Clothes by Spittelberg Parish at Michaelmas*, two notable paintings by Waldmüller.[33]

In 1891, after relocation of the Imperial Picture Gallery to the Kunsthistorisches Museum on Ringstrasse, the ever-growing collection was reorganized again. Works from the nineteenth century and the Old Masters were now placed together on the same floor, in three large glass-roofed rooms and four smaller rooms with side windows—taking up a quarter of the first floor.[34] The gallery guide produced for the occasion lists the 322 works displayed room by room[35] and a photo from 1910 pro-

21 The picture, with the dimensions 360 × 500 cm, is now at the National Portrait Gallery, London. Having caused a sensation from 1811 onward at the modern gallery established by the painter Anton Huglinger in Baden bei Wien, (Thausig 1909, p. XVII), it was acquired in 1817 for the Imperial Picture Gallery for 3000 guldens Viennese currency (= 1200 gulden C. M.) (ÖStA/HHStA, OKäA-B, Zl. 1498/816). In 1885, it was transferred, with consent from Emperor Franz Joseph I, to the collection of the National Portrait Gallery in London. See Thomasberger 1992/93, pp. 114–18.

22 Acquired at the Academy exhibition of 1830, now in the Belvedere, Vienna, inv. no. 2504.

23 Acquired at the Academy exhibition of 1830, now in an unknown private collection.

24 Both works were acquired at the Academy exhibition of 1832 and are now held at the Belvedere, Vienna, inv. nos. 3607 and 2081.

25 See also Grabner 2004.

26 Now in the Belvedere, Vienna, inv. no. 2083.

27 Grabner 2022a; Grabner 2022b.

28 Now in the Belvedere, Vienna, inv. no. 2768a–b.

29 All now in the Belvedere, Vienna, inv. nos. 2129, 2087, 2088, 2095, and 2551.

30 Now in the Belvedere, Vienna, inv. no. 3734.

31 Now in the Belvedere, Vienna, inv. no. 2919.

32 All now in the Belvedere, Vienna, inv. nos. 2106, 2119, and 2776.

33 All now in the Belvedere, Vienna, inv. nos. 1374, 1384, 1375, and 1385.

34 From 1891, the rooms of the "Modern School" were located in the area now occupied by the Italian school. On the second floor, drawings and prints from the nineteenth century were on display. This part of the collection, which had grown over the course of some thirty years, is not discussed in detail here due to lack of space.

35 Collection cat. Vienna 1891, pp. 341–54.

vides a glimpse inside one of the rooms (fig. 6). At the center of the two walls are two large history paintings: *Ferdinand II, Holy Roman Emperor, Refusing the Signing of the Religious Liberty Warrant Dossier* by Carl Wurzinger on the left and *Seizure of King Manfred's Family After the Battle of Benevento* by Eduard von Engerth on the right.[36] Placed alongside are smaller paintings, including Schnorr von Carolsfeld's *The Temptation of Christ*[37] and two Old Testament scenes by Joseph von Führich,[38] a *Still Life* by Josef Neugebauer, Danhauser's narrative paintings *The Rich Glutton* and *The Monastery Soup*, as well as *Reading the Will*, and the genre paintings *Christmas Morning* by Waldmüller and *The Lily of St Leonhard* by Wilhelm August Rieder.[39] As can be seen from the photo, the arrangement was not so much with an educational aim in mind as for decorative purposes, since the paintings were not organized by themes, nor chronologically or by genre.

By the time the Modern Gallery was established in the Lower Belvedere in 1903, the "Modern School" of the Imperial Picture Gallery had long lost the power of the new. Genre and portrait painting was increasingly following well-trodden paths, while history painting, formerly used to help consolidate the newly founded Austrian Empire, had also lost its luster. All in all, over the course of the second half of the century, the "Modern School" had acquired a reputation for being hopelessly behind the times.[40] An exception was a group of landscape painters, Emil Jakob Schindler, Robert Russ, Eugen Jettel, and Wilhelm Bernatzik, whose innovative portrayals of diverse weather conditions demonstrated a deep understanding of the natural world and keen powers of observation. Nevertheless, the imperial collection lacked the verve to compete with international art trends and the ambition to cultivate links with artists from outside the Austro-Hungarian Empire, as was by then commonplace elsewhere. On the other hand, in the years around 1900, the art of the first half of the nineteenth century was back in fashion. Even August Schaeffer, custodian at the Imperial Picture Gallery and himself a painter, suggested in his 1903 book *Moderne Meister*[41] that "the transformation in the general view of art that is occurring in our century actually took place in the 1830s."[42] Central for the evolution of the fine arts in the nineteenth century were therefore artists like Waldmüller, Danhauser, Amerling, Franz Steinfeld, Johann Baptist Reiter, Friedrich Gauermann, Rudolf von Alt, and many others of their generation. Their focus on the immediate present, on urban and rural life, their references to social injustice, and their depiction of nature as it was, set the tone for the choice of subjects of later generations of artists. Consequently, by the time the "Modern School" closed,[43] a number of pictures from this part of the collection were already on loan to the Austrian State Gallery, the successor of the Modern Gallery.[44]

36 Now in the Belvedere, Vienna, inv. no. 2321; the first-mentioned picture is now missing.

37 Now in the Belvedere, Vienna, inv. no. 3260.

38 *The Vision of Jerusalem's Inhabitants before the Conquest of the City by Antiochus IV* and *Jacob meets Rachel with her Father's Herd*, both now in the Belvedere, Vienna, inv. nos. 2541 and 2095.

39 All six now in the Belvedere, Vienna, inv. nos. 2544, 2087, 2088, 2086, and 3603.

40 See also the foreword by Franz Martin Haberditzl in collection cat. Vienna, 1924, pp. V–VIII.

41 Schaeffer 1903; see the essay on nineteenth century art by Ludwig von Hevesi, published in the same year (Hevesi 1903).

42 Schaeffer 1903, p. 1.

43 During the early years of the First World War, the "Modern School" was described in the contents page of the gallery guide as "currently being reorganized"; collection cat. Vienna 1917a.

44 Collection cat. Vienna 1917b. For the history of the Modern Gallery and its successor, the Austrian State Gallery, see the essay by Christian Huemer in this volume, pp. 178–91.

After the collapse of the Habsburg Empire and the resulting need to adjust the imperial collections to this new situation,[45] the establishment of a new museum in the Belvedere was proposed. The Austrian State Gallery and the modern section of the Kunsthistorisches Museum were combined to form the Austrian Gallery, and the various collections were reorganized. Subsequently, in 1923, the Baroque Museum was opened in the Lower Belvedere (→ p. 167).[46] The Gallery of the Nineteenth Century opened in the Upper Belvedere the following year, and, in 1929, the Modern Gallery, featuring the art of the "living generation since the nineties of the previous century" opened in the Orangery.[47] In the Upper Belvedere, works by international artists acquired by the State Gallery could thus be compared with the most significant works of nineteenth-century Austrian art from the imperial collections.[48] The "Modern School," founded by Emperor Francis I, with its well-rounded synopsis of artistic achievements in Austria and, above all, with its emphasis on the art of the Biedermeier era, thus proved formative for the identity of the Gallery of the Nineteenth Century in the Austrian Gallery.

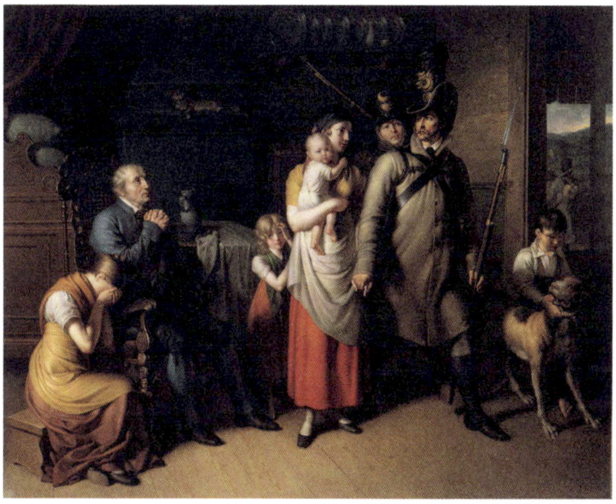

1

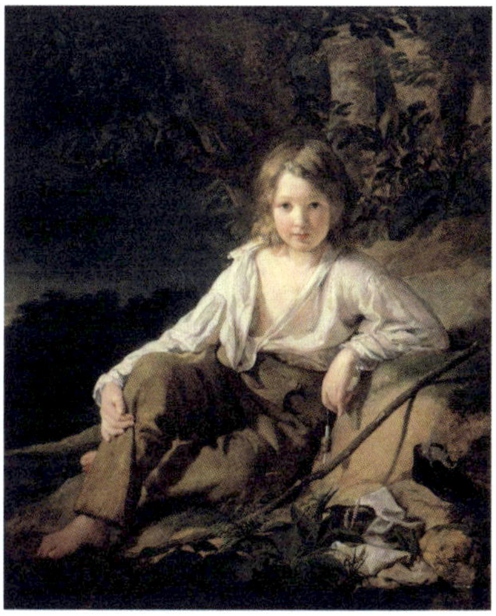

2

45 A comprehensive, concise summary of the museum program produced by Hans Tietze can be found in Krapf-Weiler 2004.
46 See the essay by Georg Lechner in this volume, pp. 202–09.
47 Collection cat. Vienna 1924, p. VIII.
48 Further loans came from the Albertina and the gallery of the Academy. The public collection was on show on both floors of the Upper Belvedere. The rooms on the ground floor were set aside for temporary exhibitions; collection cat. Vienna 1924, p. VIII.

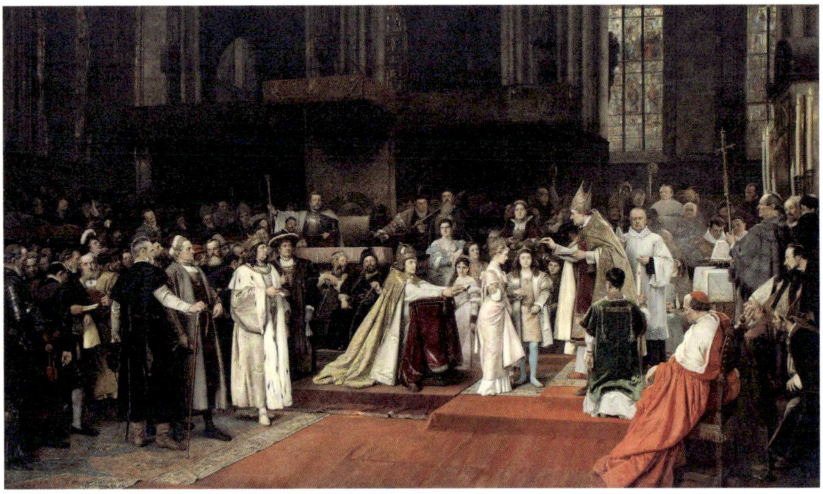

3

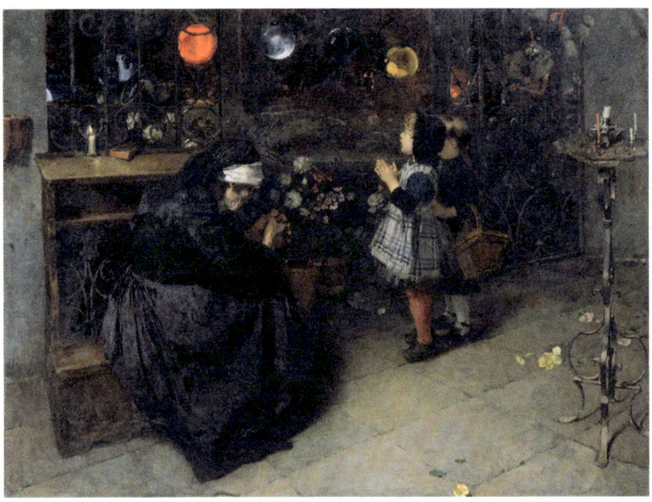

4

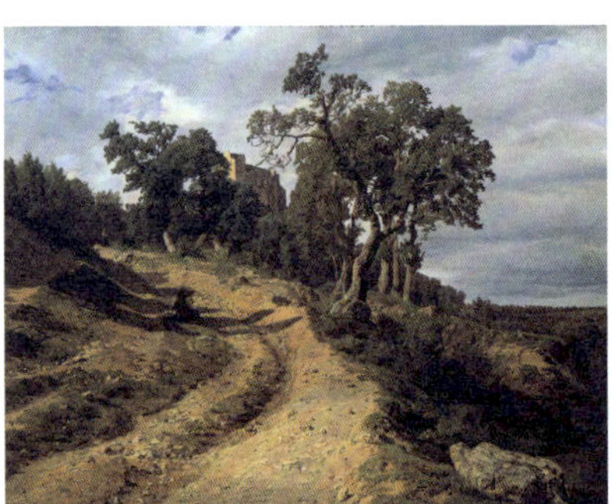

5

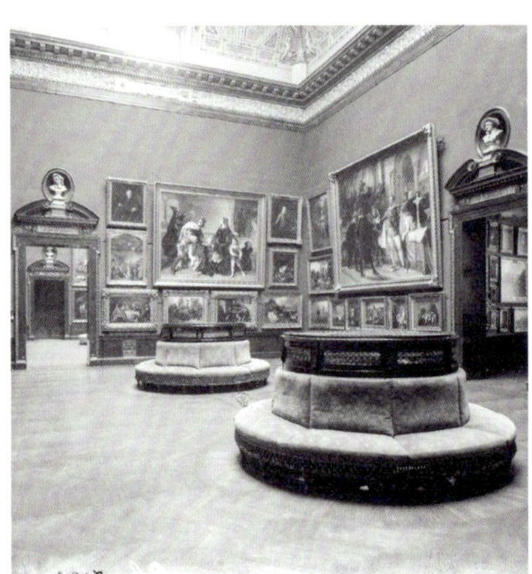

6

Fig. 1
Peter Krafft, *The Militiaman's Departure*, 1813, Belvedere, Vienna

Acquired for the Imperial Picture Gallery at the Academy exhibition, Vienna, in 1816.

Fig. 2
Friedrich von Amerling, *Fisher Boy*, 1830, Belvedere, Vienna

This depiction of Amerling's younger brother as a fisher boy was one of the Imperial Picture Gallery's first nineteenth-century genre paintings.

Fig. 3
Václav Brožík, *Tu felix Austria nube*, 1896, Belvedere, Vienna

Commissioned for the Imperial Picture Gallery by Emperor Franz Joseph I.

Fig. 4
Albin Egger-Lienz, *Good Friday*, 1892/93, Belvedere, Vienna

Donated to the Imperial Picture Gallery by Karl Rudolf Ritter von Wessely c. 1900.

Fig. 5
Ferdinand Georg Waldmüller, *The Ruin of Liechtenstein Castle near Mödling*, 1848, Belvedere, Vienna

Donated to the Imperial Picture Gallery by Ludwig von Reithoffer in 1912.

Fig. 6
A room of the "Modern School" in the Kunsthistorisches Hofmuseum, 1910, Austrian National Library, Vienna, Picture Archives

10

The Picture Gallery and the Academy of Fine Arts

Sabine Grabner

As imperial institutions, the Academy of Fine Arts and the Imperial Picture Gallery were closely linked. Only painters who had studied at the Academy could become directors or custodians of the Belvedere. Their selection was the responsibility of the curator of the Academy, while the final decision was made by the emperor. In the early 1820s, the idea was first mooted to appoint an art historian for the leading position, who, in contrast to a painter, would be able to appreciate all art genres, "to select and organize impartially, and instruct in their study."[1] Nevertheless, with the appointment of Joseph Rebell in 1824, a painter was again chosen for the post (→ p. 369, fig. 5). This tradition continued for the whole of the nineteenth century. Only with the appointment of Gustav Glück in 1911 did an art historian finally become director of the Imperial Picture Gallery.

According to article 55 of its 1812 statutes, the Imperial-Royal Academy of Fine Arts was the "supreme art authority of the nation," and was to be consulted, without exception, for "expert opinions in matters of art or public monuments."[2] This preeminence also had implications for the Imperial Picture Gallery. Consequently, the quality of a picture was determined by representatives from both institutions, and a purchase could only take place after a written evaluation by professors from the Academy. From at least 1828, Academy exhibitions were important sources for the acquisition of pictures.

On the other hand, the Imperial Gallery also played a major role in the academic development of young painters, for the emperor himself had determined in 1798 that students were to be given access to the gallery to expand their painterly skills by copying the artworks there. The custodians were required to provide instruction and support to the students. A modus vivendi formulated in the late 1820s was able to smooth out initial problems with student discipline. From now on, the aspiring artists were only allowed access to the Belvedere after introducing themselves to the director and with a reference from the Academy. Neatness, courtesy, and good manners were basic requirements, as was continuous attendance at the scheduled copying times. Failing that they risked losing their place. In the winter months, a room on the Italian side was designated for copying; in summer, the Marble Hall and the Gold Cabinet, later the so-called Carlone Hall on the ground floor.

Finally, it is worth mentioning that, for the duration of their tenure, the director and custodians with their families, and, in fact, all other staff working at the Belvedere, were living in the L-shaped building on the eastern side of the main courtyard in front of the Upper Belvedere, hence also known as the Directors' and Custodians' Wing.

1 Report by Klemens Wenzel Lothar von Metternich to Francis I on January 23, 1823, UAAbKW, Metternich-Registratur 1823, no. 5.
2 Lützow 1877, p. 165.

Chapter III

From the Modern Gallery to the Austrian Gallery

1903–1938

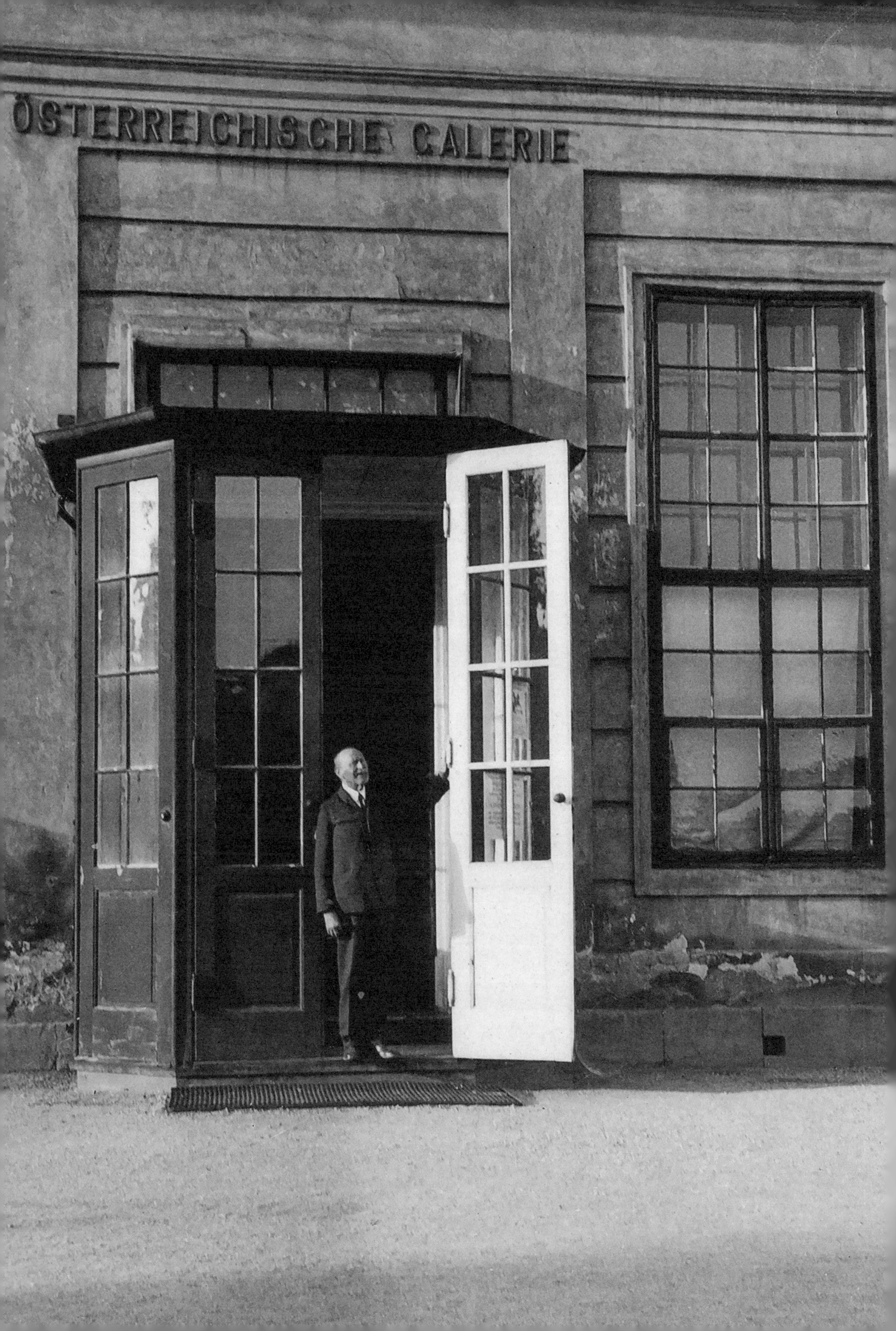
ÖSTERREICHISCHE GALERIE

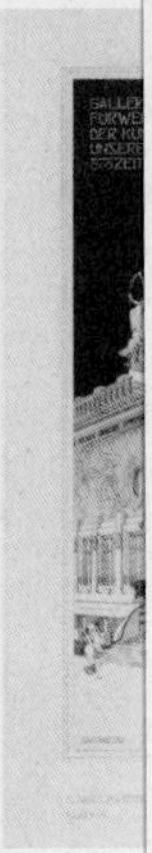

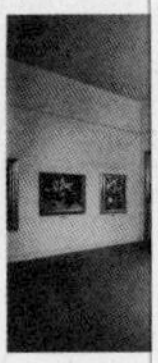

Chapter III
From the Modern Gallery to the Austrian Gallery

1903–1938

←
Entrance
Museum
Belveder
vedere A

To the Imperial-Royal Police Headquarters in Vienna. Repeated complaints have been received from tourists who, when inquiring about the location of the Modern Gallery, have been unable to obtain satisfactory information from the authorities, even those in the immediate vicinity.

The director would like to present the request that the police stations of the 1st, 3rd, and 4th districts be informed that the Imperial-Royal Modern Gallery in Vienna has been located in the 3rd district, Rennweg no. 6 (Lower Belvedere) since 1903.

—— Letter from director Dörnhöffer to the Imperial-Royal Police Headquarters in Vienna, AdB, Zl. 67/1910

The Belvedere has now become a veritable garden of the arts. One can move through the rooms without encountering many other visitors, both upstairs and downstairs. They are all tourists, for the Viennese stay away from their art treasures.

—— Hermann Menkes, "Garten der Kunst: Besuch im Belvedere," *Neues Wiener Journal*, July 6, 1930, p. 12.

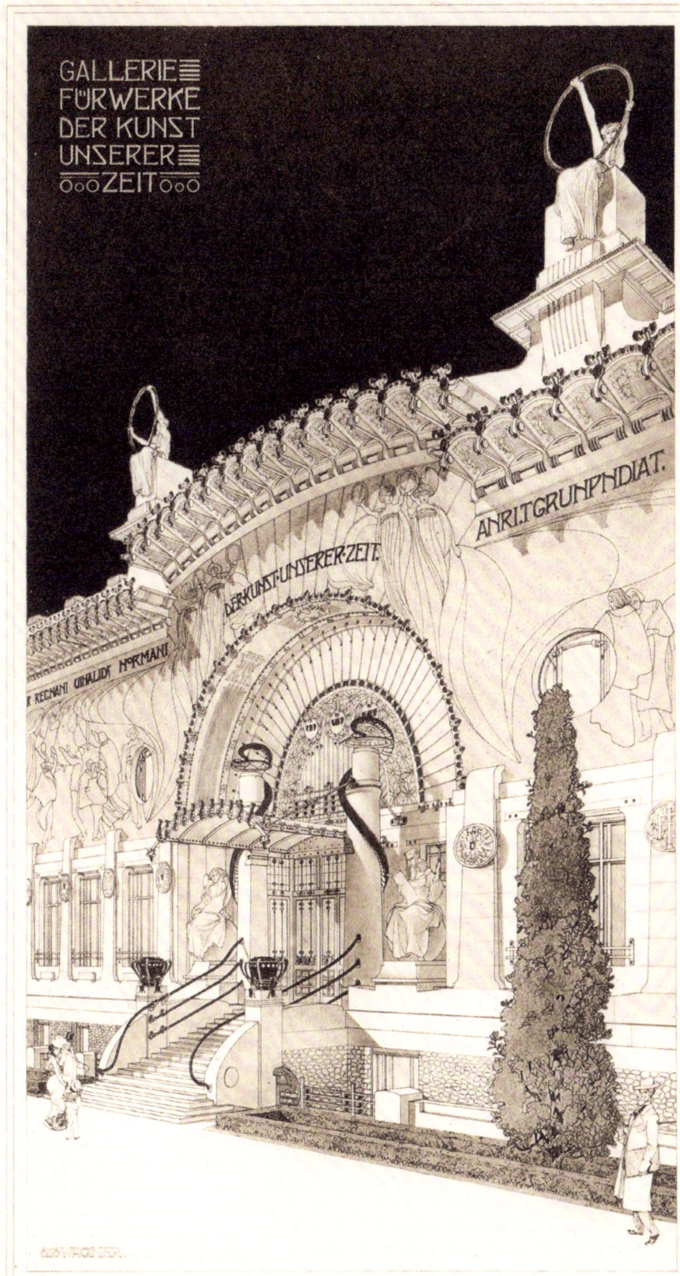

III. BAND. III. u. IV. HEFT Vervielfältigung vorbehalten

BLATT 25. Heliogravure des k. u. k. milit.-geogr. Inst. Wien, bei Ant. Schroll u. Co.

Otto Wagner, study for *Galerie für Werke der Kunst unserer Zeit*, 1906, Wien Museum

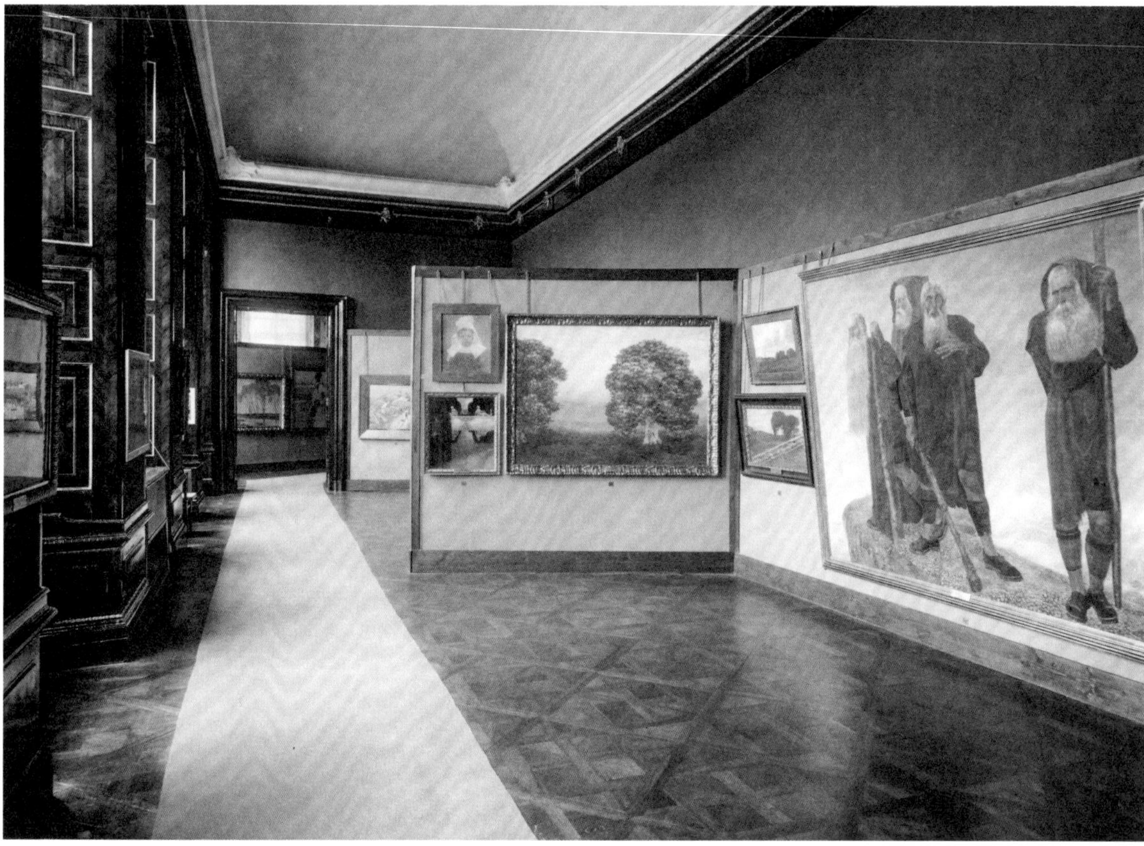

Modern Gallery in the Lower Belvedere with Karl Mediz's *The Ice Saints*, 1903

By and large, however, the collection still gives the strong impression of a provisional solution. The pictures appear quite out of place in these rooms, which stare at them with the splendor of bygone times. Has this perhaps been arranged thus with subtle intention? Is the intention of this by and large rather inharmonious provisional arrangement to stoke the longing for an artistically worthy permanent solution? Perhaps this wouldn't be a bad means to an end. For, at the moment, every visitor will be rapidly overcome by the desire to have these pictures brought to a better location as soon as possible.

—— "Die moderne Galerie," *Neue Freie Presse*, April 10, 1903, p. 5.

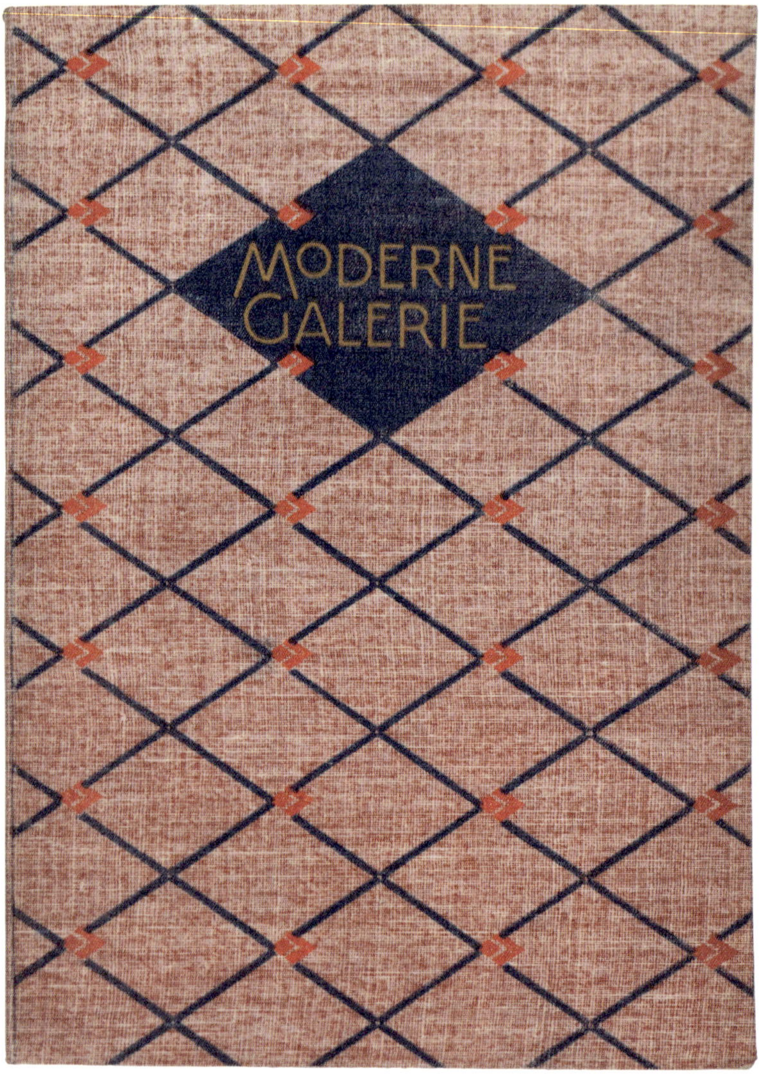

Catalogue of the Modern Gallery in Vienna, 1903, Belvedere Library, Vienna

I am raising the complaint that a visitor to the State Gallery, who, not being one of those foreign profiteers but having to save, makes use of the free-entry days, is then forced to pay the exorbitant sum of 50 kronen for a catalogue. Without this catalogue, a visit to the collection is quite impossible, as the pictures are only labeled with numbers. [...]

I have in front of me the June 1913 issue of the State Gallery gazette. This cost one krone at the time and contained pictures of significantly better quality. I know very well that paper and printing costs have increased dramatically since then; but that they should amount to fifty times the costs of 1917 seems quite unlikely to me. In any event, my income has not increased in tandem and, as I said, I find it very harsh that I should pay such an oppressive levy in order to meet my desire for further education, from which, of course, my students also benefit.

— Letter from Dr. Friedrich Gatscha, professor at the regional secondary school in Stockerau, AdB, Zl. 398/1921

He [says he is] unable [...] to tolerate being alone in the gallery rooms for long periods of time, even more since this feeling of solitude also deprives him of a good night's sleep.

—— Letter from Karl Cehak concerning the attendant Rudolf Reich, AdB, Building Inspectorate of the Imperial-Royal Technical University Vienna, Zl. 48/1904

On Saturday morning, my daughter Gertrud paid a visit to the Modern Gallery. While passing the gas heater in the Klinger Room, her dress caught fire. The attendant who came to help then revealed that the same heater had caused the same thing to happen with a lady's dress the previous year.

—— Letter from Dr. Anton Reitler to the office of the Modern Gallery, January 2, 1905, AdB, Building Inspectorate of the Imperial-Royal Technical University Vienna, Zl. 73/1905

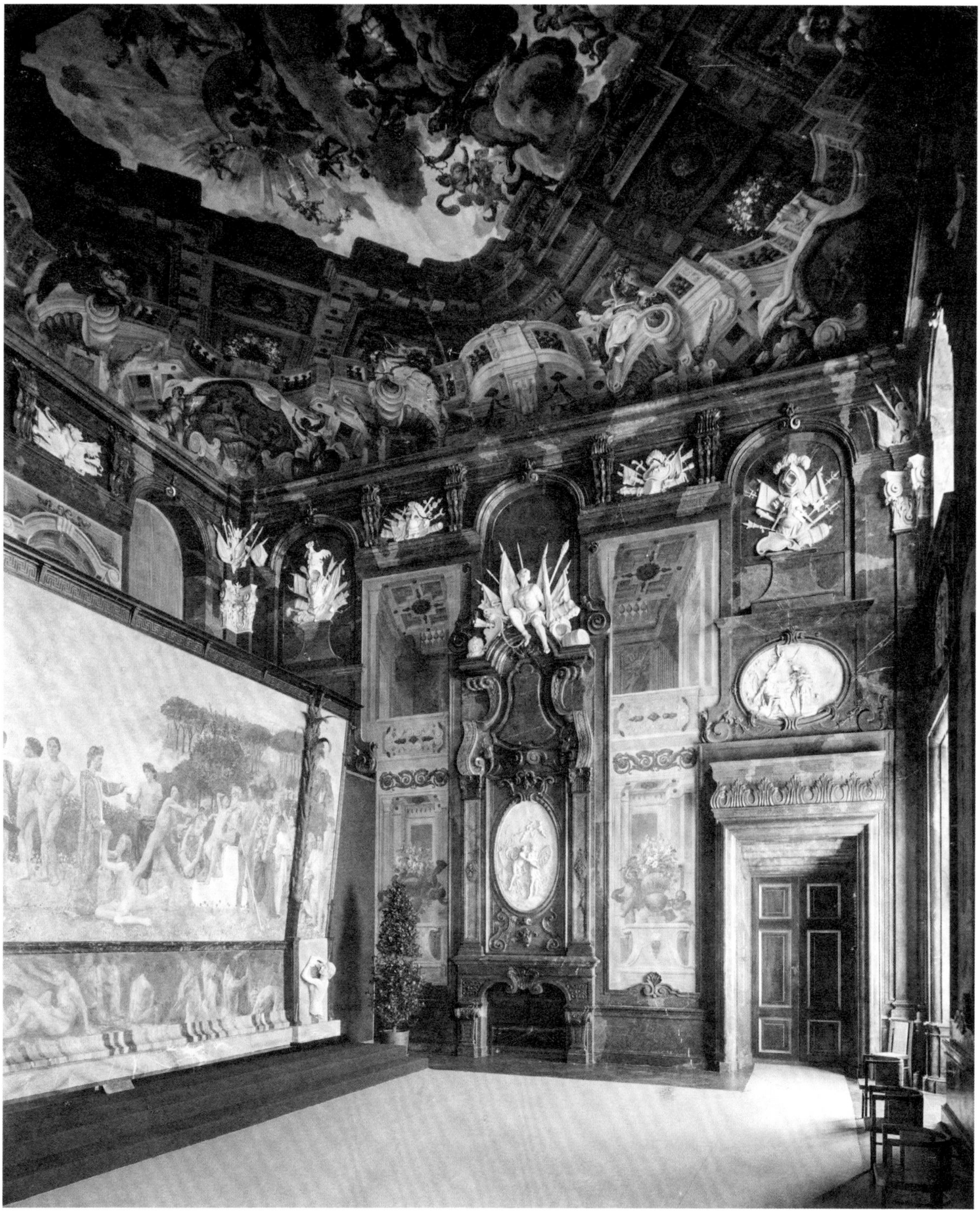

Modern Gallery in the Lower Belvedere with Max Klinger's *Christ on Olympus*, 1903

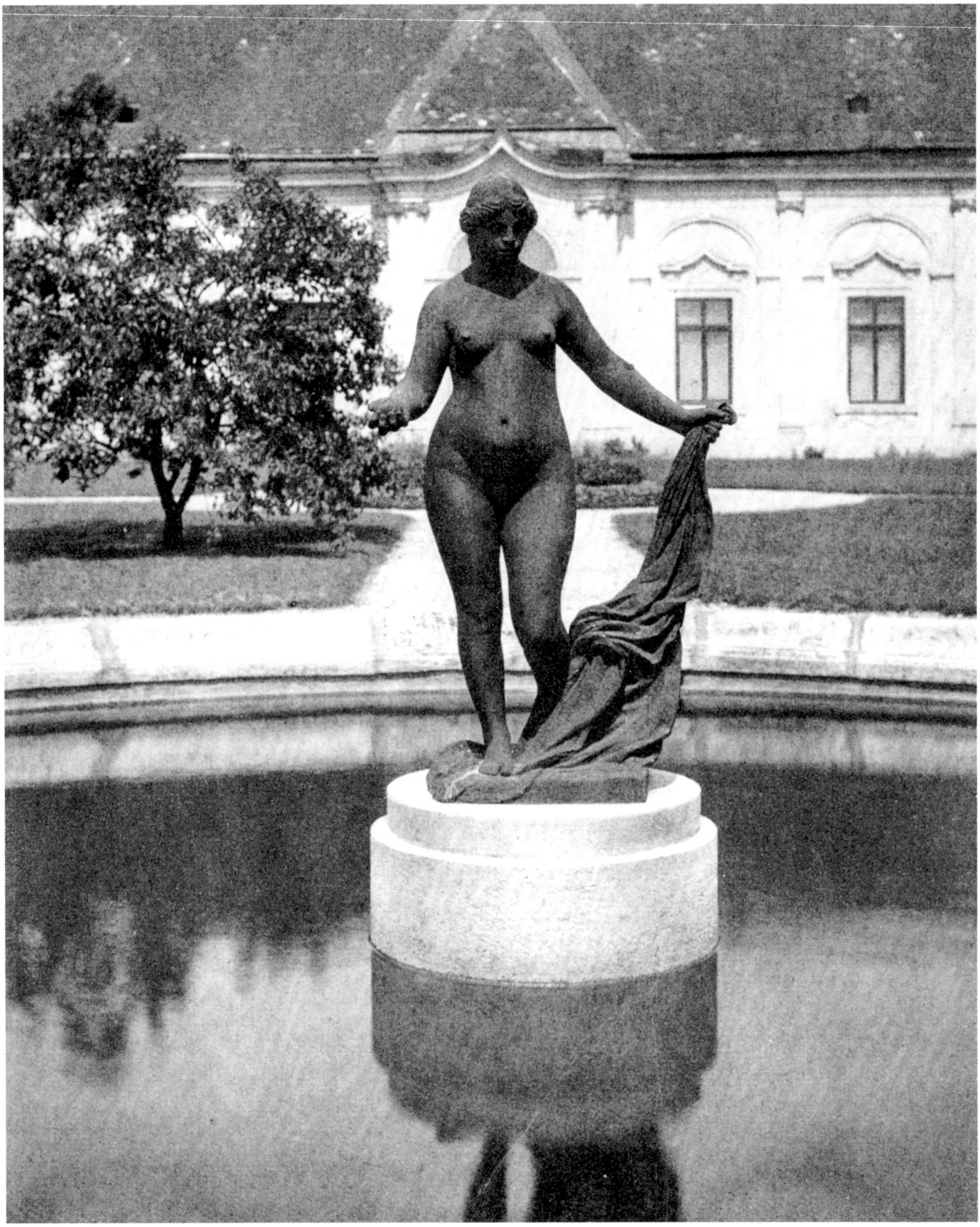

Venus Victorious (Venus Victrix) by Pierre-Auguste Renoir (1915/16) in the Privy Garden of the Lower Belvedere, 1929

(11)

A *Kiss* for the Modern Gallery

Stefan Lehner

"At last, the scarcely believable situation that, until now, Austria's 'Modern Gallery' has not owned a single representative work by Austria's greatest master has been rectified. It was left to Marchet's ministry to overcome the 'Klimt fear' that had for years prevailed in certain well-meaning bureaucratic circles."[1] With these words, Berta Zuckerkandl announced on August 4, 1908, in the *Wiener Allgemeine Zeitung* that Gustav Klimt's painting *Lovers* had been purchased for the recently founded Modern Gallery.

In 1908, on the site where the Konzerthaus and Akademietheater are now located, the so-called Klimt Group, led by Gustav Klimt, Josef Hoffmann, Koloman Moser, and Carl Moll, had a temporary exhibition building erected for the Kunstschau. Planned by Josef Hoffmann, the exhibition pavilion accommodated the works of 180 artists. Room 22 was designed by Koloman Moser and devoted entirely to Gustav Klimt. It featured sixteen paintings by Klimt, including the golden *Portrait of Adele Bloch-Bauer I* of 1907, *Three Ages of Woman*, *Danaë*, *Water Serpents*, and several landscapes. In a prominent position, opposite the entrance to this "Klimt church of new art,"[2] the now iconic painting *Lovers* was shown for the first time (fig. 1). Only ten days after the exhibition's opening on June 10, 1908, the committee of the Modern Gallery Vienna decided to purchase the painting. That same month, the art commission of the German department at the Modern Gallery in Prague also expressed an interest. In July, Norbert Wien, secretary of the

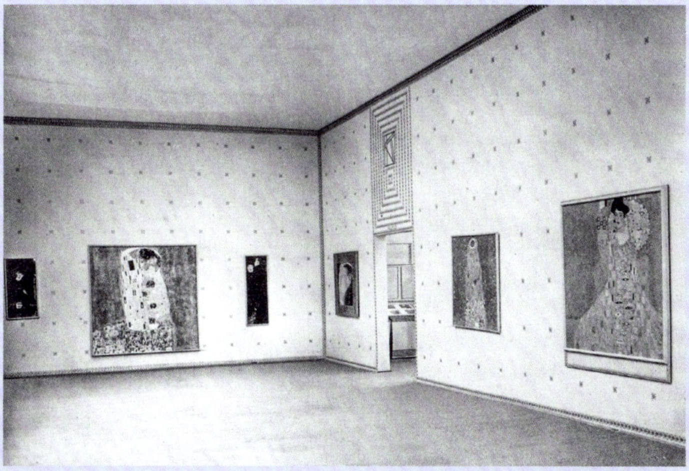

1

Fig. 1
Room 22 (Klimt Room) at the Vienna Kunstschau, 1908, in *Die Kunst*, vol. 18, 1908, p. 523, Belvedere Library, Vienna

Kunstschau, pressed the Ministry for Culture and Education in Vienna for a decision.[3] After official approval, the work was purchased for 25,000 kronen, payable in two installments of 12,500 kronen.[4] This was an exceptionally high price, as demonstrated by comparison with the sum of 5,000 kronen paid for *Interior of Prince Eugene of Savoy's Winter Palace on Himmelpfortgasse* by the well-established artist Carl Moll, another work acquired from the Kunstschau. On July 16, 1908, Klimt wrote a letter to the ministry stating:

"In response to the enquiry from Herr Sektionsrat Förster, I am pleased to reply that I will of course complete the not quite finished painting 'Lovers' immediately after the exhibition closes and will deliver it to the Imperial-Royal Ministry myself."[5]

An additional note also refers to the painting's unfinished state: "pro domo: the lower left-hand corner of Klimt's painting is not completely finished" (figs. 2, 3). On July 22, 1909, the museum eventually entered the painting in its collection with the inventory number 912 (fig. 4). It was put on display at the Lower Belvedere that same year. In a supplement to the Modern Gallery's catalogue, presumably published in autumn of 1909, the painting is listed in Room II with the catalogue number 322—already under the name by which it is now known around the world: *The Kiss*.

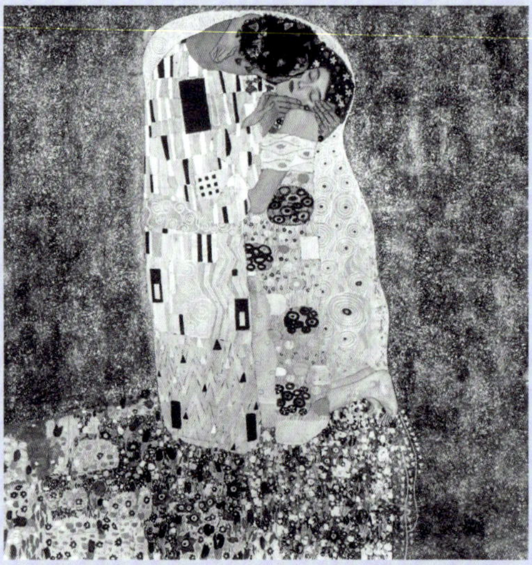

2

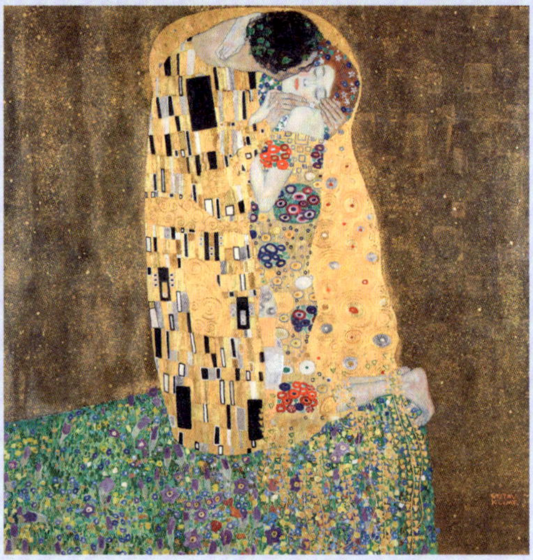

3

1 Berta Zuckerkandl, "Ankauf von Klimt-Werken durch Staat und Stadt," *Wiener Allgemeine Zeitung*, August, 4, 1908, p. 3.

2 Kunstschau 1908 in Vienna, *Wiener Allgemeine Zeitung*, June 9, 1908, p. 2.

3 ÖStA/AVA, FHKA, Zl. 32554/1908.

4 25,000 kronen in the year 1908 would have been the equivalent of 173,749.75 euros today; see https://www.eurologisch.at/docroot/waehrungsrechner/# (accessed on November 14, 2022).

5 ÖStA/AVA, FHKA, Zl. 32554/1908.

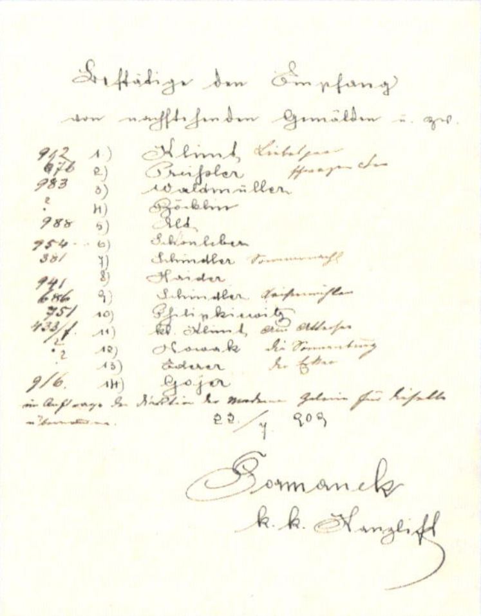

4

Fig. 2
The Kiss by Gustav Klimt, taken in Room 22 of the Vienna Kunstschau, 1908 (detail), photo: Moriz Nähr, Austrian National Library, Vienna, Picture Archives

Fig. 3
Gustav Klimt, *The Kiss*, 1908/09, Belvedere, Vienna

Fig. 4
Confirmation of the receipt of fourteen paintings for the Modern Gallery, including *The Kiss* by Gustav Klimt, July 22, 1909, Belvedere Archive, Vienna

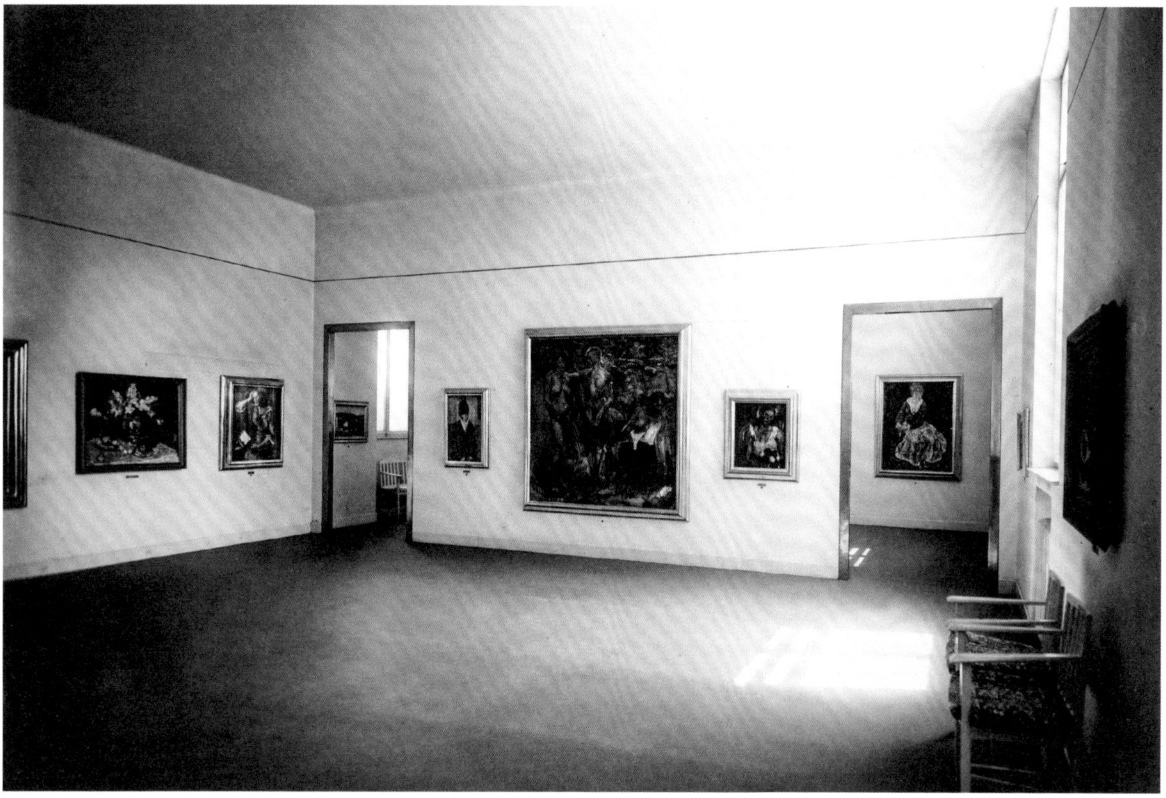

Modern Gallery in the Orangery of the Belvedere with Egon Schiele's *Portrait of the Artist's Wife, Edith Schiele* in the background, after 1931

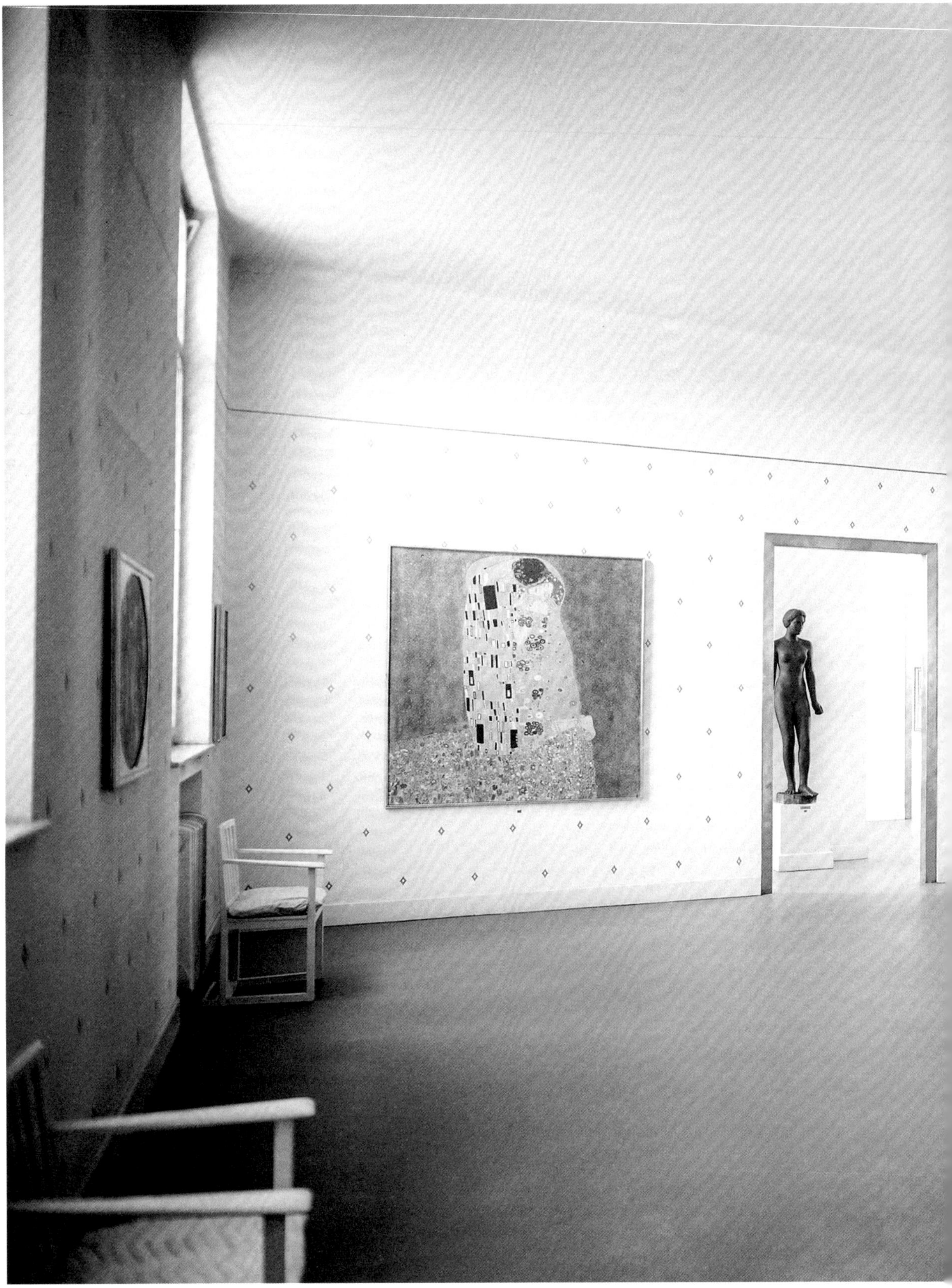

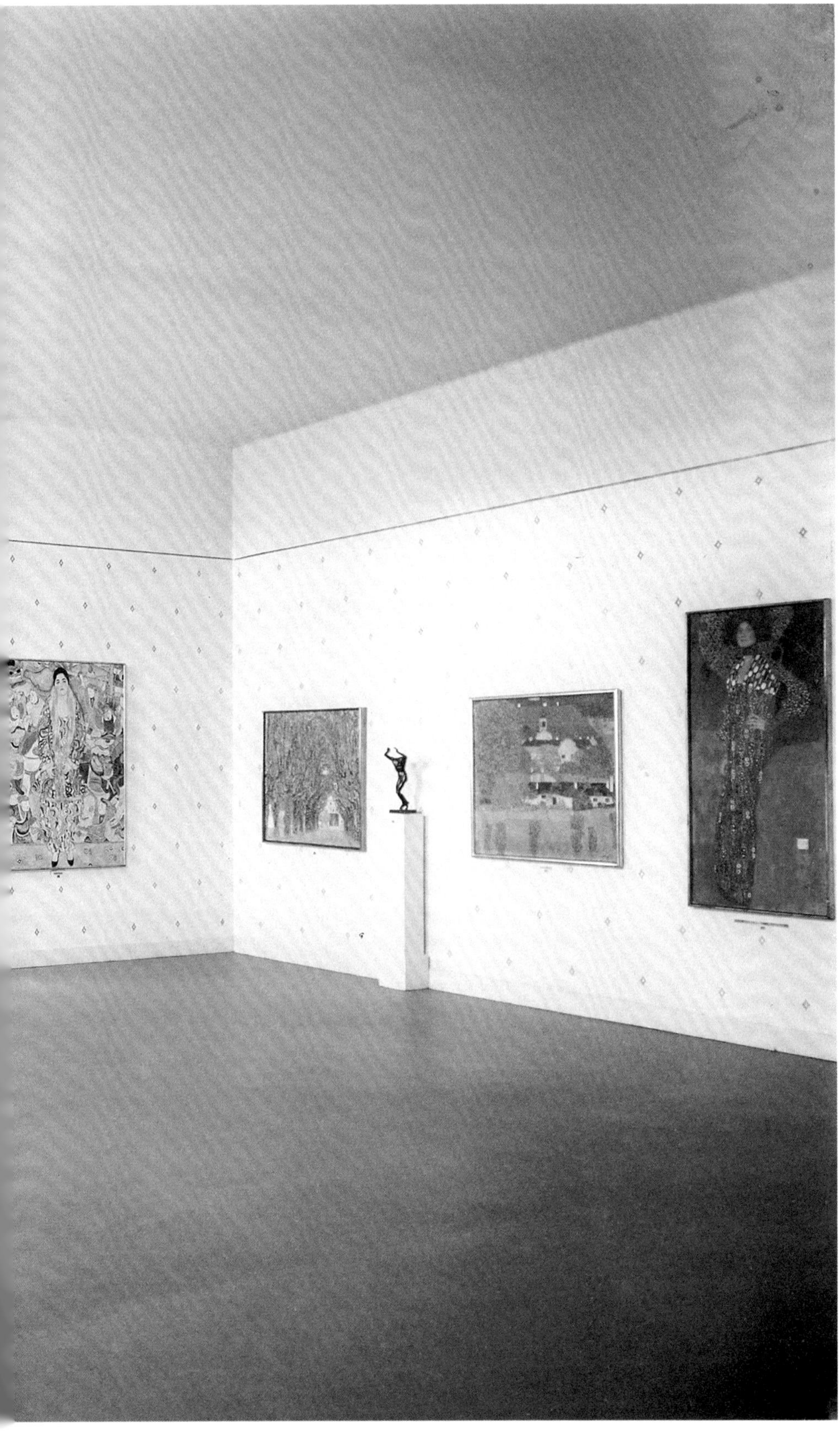

Klimt Room,
Modern Gallery in
the Orangery of
the Belvedere, 1929

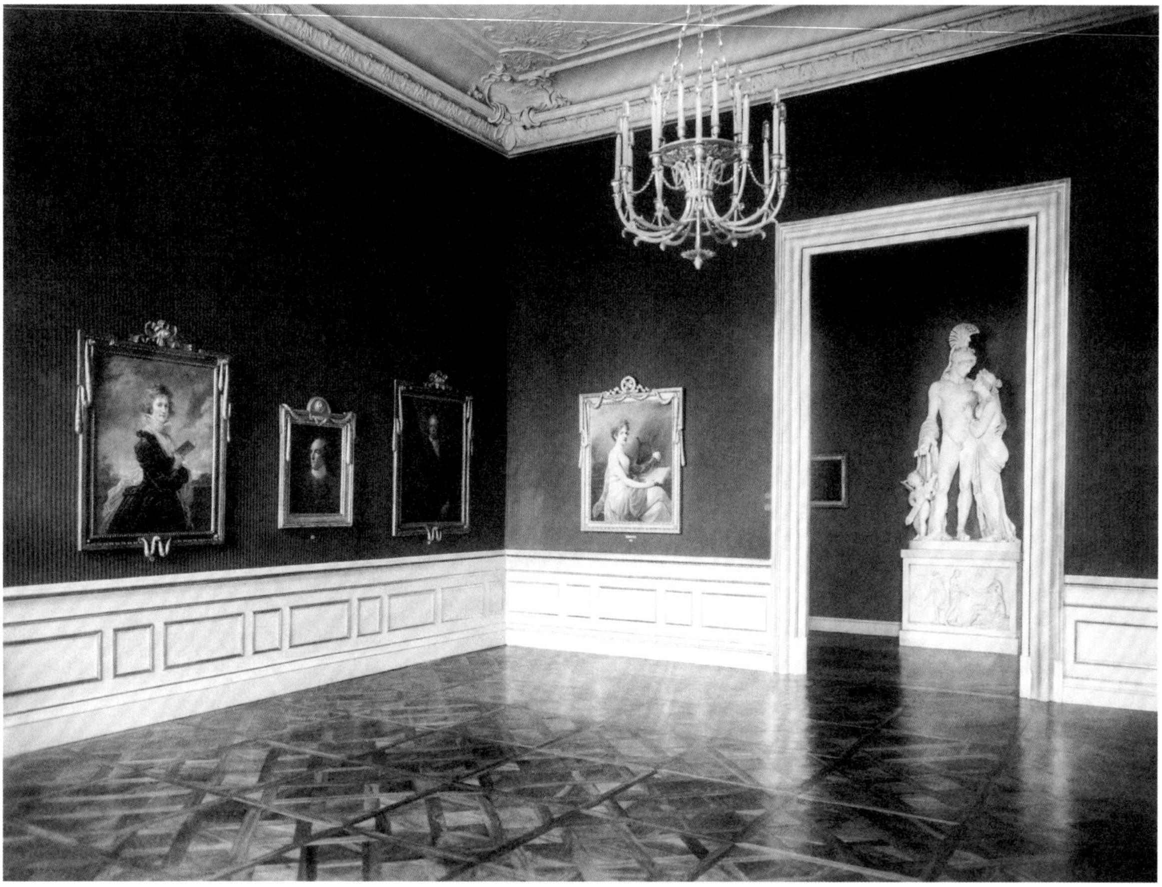

Gallery of the Nineteenth Century in the Upper Belvedere, 1925

Vienna—finally—has a gallery for new masters. Founded late, as a child of the Secession movement in the nineties, then burdened through the force of events with a series of older works going back as far as the Gothic period, purely because they were Austrian, rammed into an eternally provisional solution in the inadequate rooms of the Lower Belvedere, finally withdrawn from the public for years as a consequence of the necessary renovation works, it has hitherto been the wallflower of Vienna's art treasures. Now it is reborn in a splendid, worthy new setting, the most beautiful that Vienna has to offer; and the older members of the living generation, for whom the concept of the Belvedere is still associated with the exquisite enjoyment of art, will find this place of precious memories at the service of art once again.

—— Ernst Buschbeck, "Das neue Belvedere: Zur Eröffnung der Galerie des neunzehnten Jahrhunderts," *Neues Wiener Abendblatt*, October 15, 1924, p. 4.

Thank you very much for your kind letter. [...] For this reason, I would like to ask whether it would be convenient if I came to visit you tomorrow, Thursday, or the day after, on Friday, at around 12 o'clock.

We can talk then about your marvelous achievement. I was at the Baroque Museum yesterday and cannot even begin to express my enthusiasm.

—— Letter from Berta Zuckerkandl to director Franz Martin Haberditzl, May 23, 1923, AdB, Zl. 335/1923

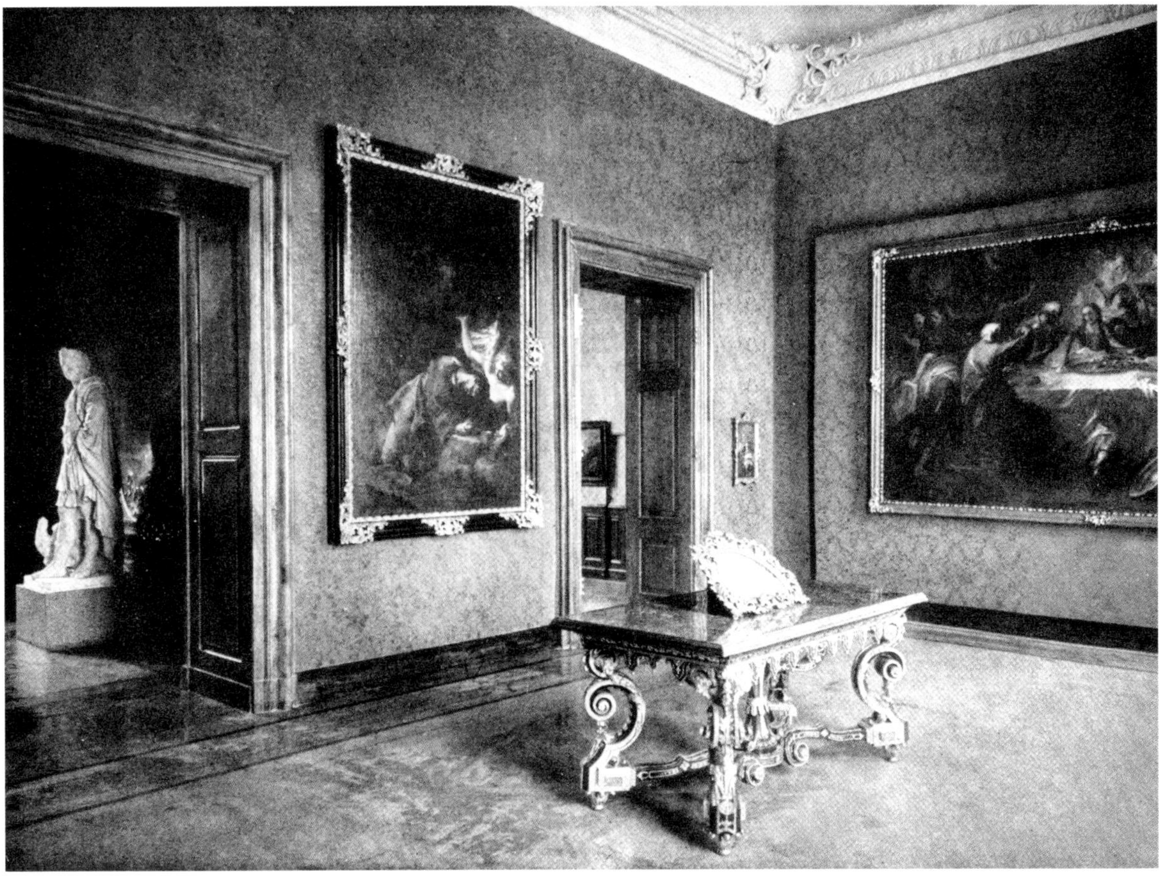

Green Room of
the Baroque Museum
in the Lower
Belvedere, 1923

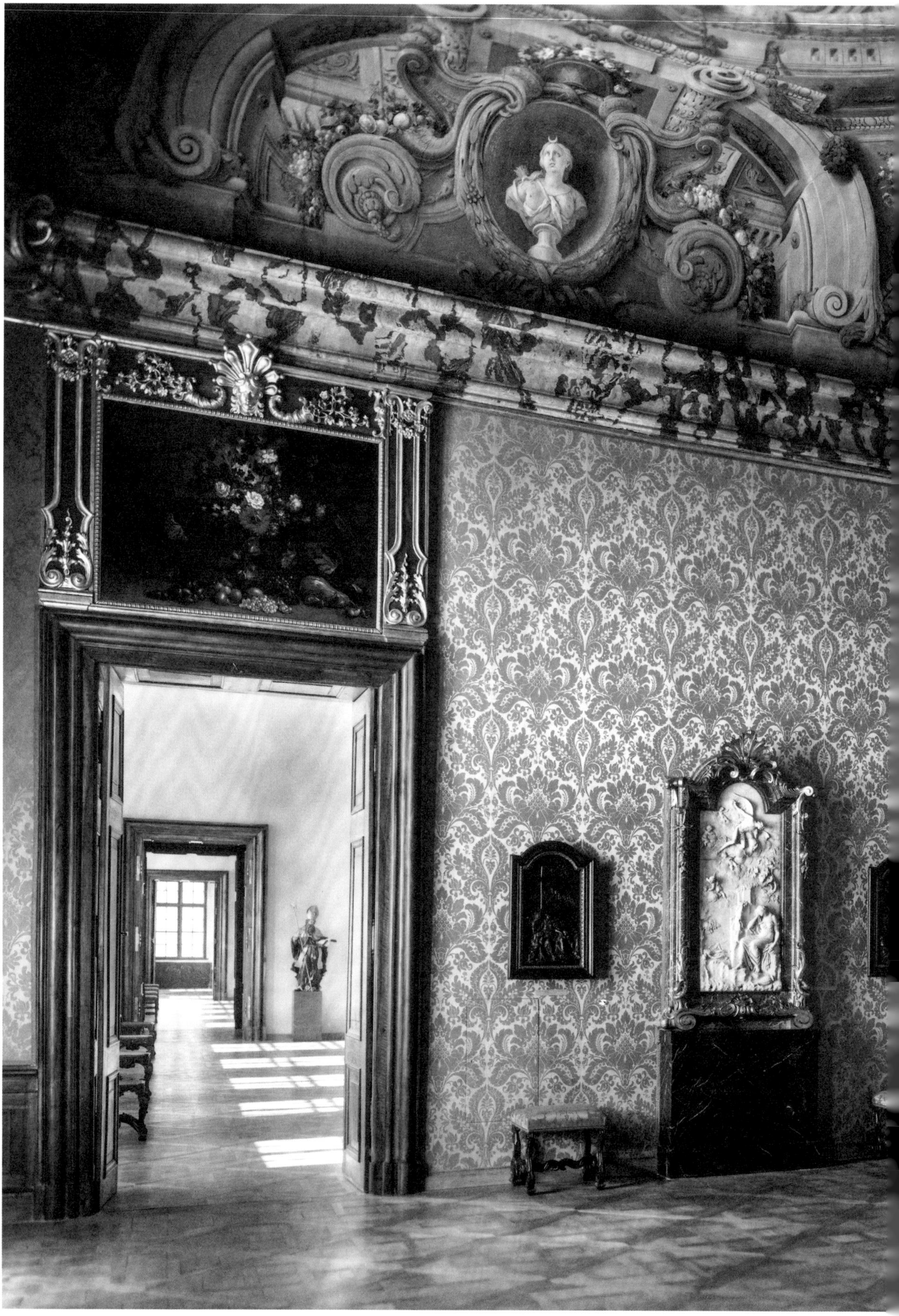

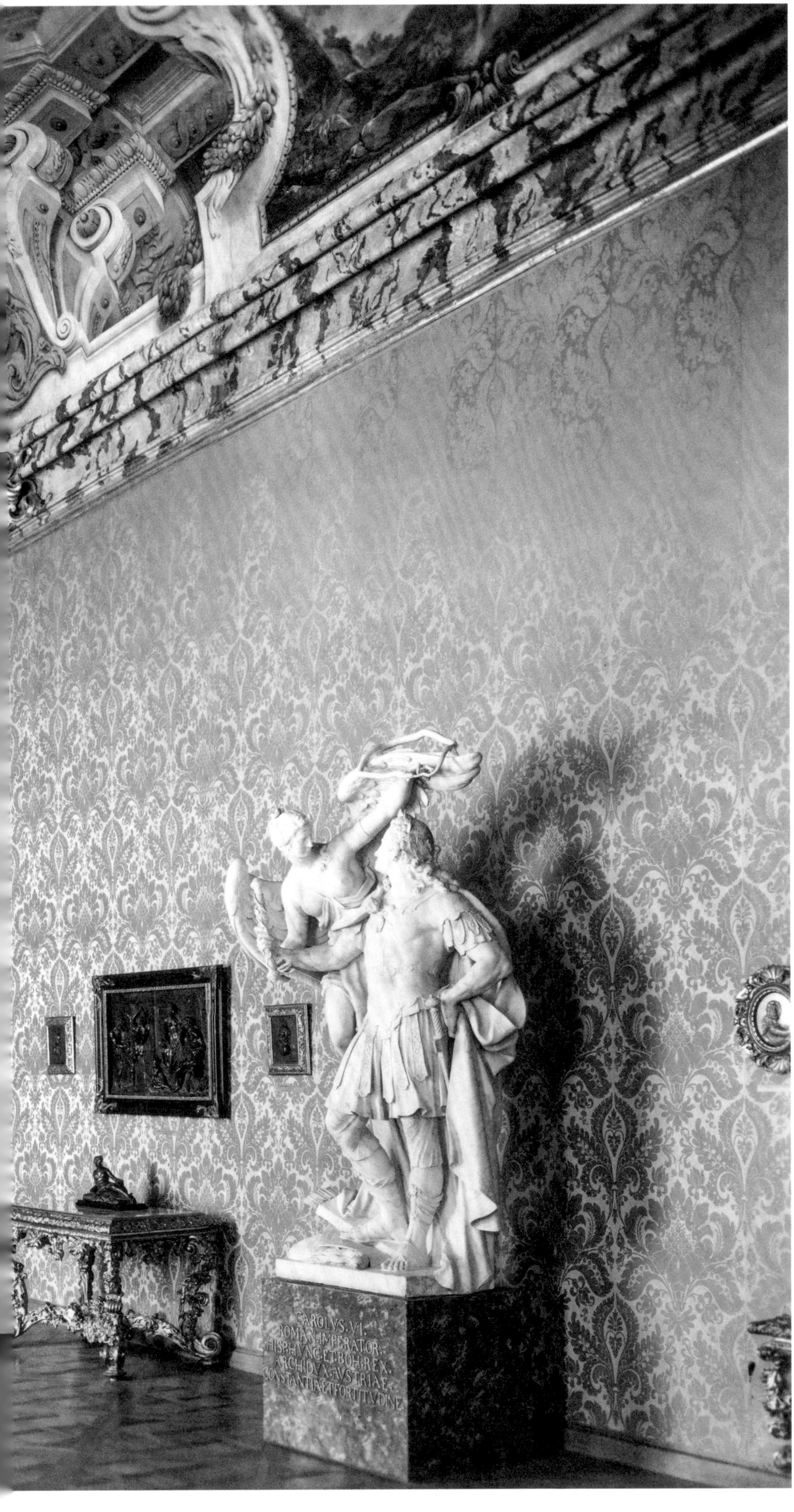

Yellow Room of
the Baroque Museum
in the Lower
Belvedere, 1934

P. 170

MATTHEW RAMPLEY — Museums of Modern Art in the Late Habsburg Empire

When, on May 7, 1903, the Modern Gallery formally opened its doors to visitors, it was the culmination of a campaign by leading figures of the Vienna art world to establish a showcase for recent and contemporary Austrian art. Yet, if we wish to understand its significance, we need to consider the wider art world of Austria-Hungary. For the Modern Gallery was a latecomer. As early as 1879, a National Museum was founded in Cracow. It did not bear the term "modern," but it had a similar scope to its counterpart in Vienna: to showcase recent and contemporary Polish art and to provide evidence of the accomplishments of the Polish nation.[1] The Modern Gallery of the Bohemian Kingdom had opened in Prague in 1902, while in 1905 a gallery of modern art was established in Zagreb. The Modern Gallery in Vienna was thus part of a wider pattern.

But what was a gallery of modern art? The answer was more complex than might at first seem to be the case. For there was a basic conflict between the ever-changing landscape of contemporary art and the idea of an institution devoted to housing a permanent collection of "modern" artworks for posterity. The Modern Gallery's location in a Baroque palace also seemed at odds with the idea of a "modern" gallery. A similar ambiguity beset its counterpart in Prague, which was initially accommodated in the Rudolfinum, a Renaissance-revival edifice containing the historic collections of the Society of Patriotic Friends of the Arts (fig. 1).

Contemporary commentators homed in on this issue. "So, we finally have a modern gallery! Do we have it? It is probably premature to celebrate," noted Franz Servaes, art critic of the *Neue Freie Presse* in April 1903.[2] The spaces in the Belvedere were inappropriate, he argued; the lighting was inadequate, its ornate Baroque decoration overshadowed the artworks (fig. 2). As if to support these comments, a substantial

1 Rampley 2021, pp. 31–32.

2 Franz Servaes, "Die Moderne Galerie," *Neue Freie Presse*, April 16, 1903, p. 1.

portion of the introduction to the official catalogue consisted of observations about the building and the interior décor, rather than about the artworks on display.[3]

The contents of the collection were also open to criticism. The gallery had works by, for example, Ferdinand Waldmüller, Friedrich von Amerling, and Ludwig Ferdinand Schnorr von Carolsfeld, all of them from the 1830s. When it came to more recent artists, its coverage was inconsistent. Gaps could be rectified in time, with adequate funds, but the collection stretched the meaning of the term "modern." It seemed to act merely to denote the last one hundred years, rather than a more specific aesthetic concept. Contemporaries criticized the confusion that could arise as a result. The musicologist Otto Deutsch complained about the lack of clarity over where one should draw the line between modern art, for: "The meaning of the modern keeps on shifting, even more so than that of historic art or contemporary art. Every year, every day. The 'modern' is free-moving, deceptive. Not only what is popular today, also, what is produced today, can become unmodern and out of date tomorrow. Consequently, the modern galleries are already contradicting themselves."[4]

The Modern Gallery in Prague did not suffer entirely the same flaws; its collections had a greater proportion of works by living or very recently deceased artists. Nevertheless, it had to face comparable questions as to how to define "modern" art and as to which artworks counted as significant examples. Toxic debates arose around the fact that the works collected did not represent the best current art and were thus not "modern." Numerous critics complained that it was parochial and outdated, a complaint that continued until the museum eventually closed in 1942.[5] Thus, in 1927, Vincenc Kramář, a friend of Picasso and Henri Kahnweiler (fig. 3), a major collector of Cubist art and director of the gallery of the Patriotic Friends of Art in Prague, proposed that the only solution was for the Modern Gallery to be integrated into a larger National Gallery of Art under his direction.[6] One particular point of criticism was the gallery's refusal in 1920 to purchase a group of works by the much-admired but recently deceased Cubist painter Bohumil Kubišta (fig. 4).[7] The problem was that, rather than collecting the most vibrant contemporary art, the Modern Gallery used as its touchstone the art of the late nineteenth century. Yet, even within a decade of its founding, this was already becoming problematic, so rapidly had artistic practice changed.

Such disputes highlight the fact that, although "modern" was an established term in art discourse, the concept of "modern art" was fluid and often contradictory. Arguably, it was only with the founding, in 1929, of the Museum of Modern Art (MoMA) in New York, that a canonical image of artistic Modernism began to emerge and take on institutionalized form.[8]

3 M. Sch-a, "Die moderne Galerie," *Illustrirtes Wiener Extrablatt*, May 5, 1903, p. 8; "Vorwort," anon. 1904.
4 Otto Erich Deutsch, "Die Unmoderne Galerie," *Die Zeit*, January 23, 1909, pp. 1–2, here p. 1.
5 See, for example, Matějček 1913; Čapek 1986.
6 Kramář 1927.
7 Vlnas 1994.
8 See Porter/Zalman 2020.

Alongside the problem of definition, the galleries of modern art illustrated how art institutions were caught up in conflicting ideas of identity in the late Habsburg Empire. "Austria" comprised an arc of lands from Polish Galicia in the east to Bohemia in the west and Dalmatia and Bosnia-Herzegovina in the south. Yet the Modern Gallery in Vienna only paid lip service to the idea that it was about anything other than art from the core German-speaking territories. Visitors looked in vain for more than a handful of works by Czech or Polish artists. Such absence revealed the prejudices of the Vienna elites, for whom Austro-German culture was the default norm of the empire. This assumption, however, was at odds with the cosmopolitan nature of much artistic practice. Secession exhibitions in Vienna often included works by members of the Sztuka art group from Cracow or the Mánes society in Prague, while one of the founding acts of Modernism in Prague was the publication, in 1895, of the "Manifesto of the Czech Modern," which repudiated cultural nationalism.[9]

Official indifference in Vienna towards artistic life elsewhere undoubtedly motivated the founding of "national" modern galleries beyond the core Austrian territories, where art circles felt neglected. The National Museum in Cracow exemplified this, as did the Modern Gallery in Prague. The latter was celebrated by the Czech-language press as redressing a historic imbalance and supporting "our national culture."[10] Indeed, the impulse behind its founding was a politically expedient concession to nationalist politicians. The imperial administration proposed it to gain support from the nationalist Young Czech political party for its legislative program in parliament. Although the Modern Gallery had separate German and Czech sections, the dominant figure for much of its existence was Karel Kramář, leader of the Young Czechs political party.[11]

This focus on national interests ran into criticism. The Vienna-based art historian Richard Muther argued that, while the Czech art world engaged with international contemporary art, the Modern Gallery had failed to do so; its collections were provincial and mediocre.[12] Although harsh, Muther's criticism was not entirely inaccurate, especially given complaints in Prague about the reluctance to embrace the most advanced modern art. Hence, the first catalogue of 1907 stated that the priority was the development of "local art" and its policy was to only collect artworks that had relevance to Bohemia.[13] This was anathema to artists whose gaze was directed towards Paris, Berlin, and Munich.

The modern galleries across the Habsburg Empire were thus driven by sometimes contradictory aims and were often out of touch with contemporary artistic life. For, while Modernism was an international phenomenon in which artists readily migrated and exchanged ideas across borders, the galleries of modern art were used as vehicles of national legitimation. The institutions in question may no longer exist, or have been

9 Josef Svatopluk Machar, F. X. Šalda et al., "Manifest české moderny," *Rozhledy*, no. 5.1, October 25, 1895, p. 1.

10 Anon., "Moderní galerie království českého," *Národní Listy*, August 26, 1902, p. 1.

11 Vlnas 1994, (see note 7).

12 Richard Muther, "Die Prager moderne Galerie," *Die Zeit*, June 22, 1905, pp. 1–3, here p. 2.

13 Anon. 1907, *Moderní galerie Království Českého*, n. p.

transformed beyond recognition, but in certain respects this latter feature still holds. The Belvedere and the concept of "Vienna 1900" (→ p. 293, ㉑) still play a crucial part in the external image of Austria, and the vibrant Modernist art of, for example, Poland, Croatia, and the Czech Republic still offers an important reference point in how the countries in question present themselves today.

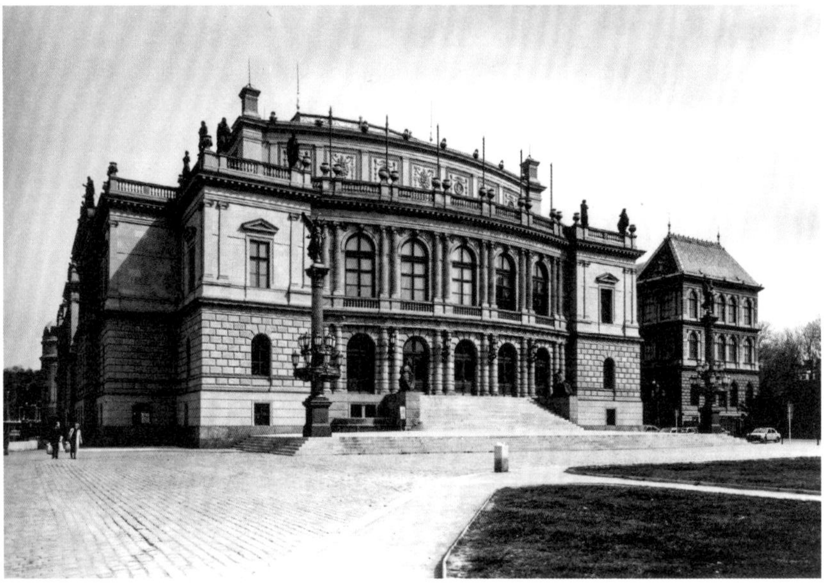

1

Fig. 1
Modern Gallery in the Rudolfinum in Prague, designed by Josef Zítek and Josef Schulz, 1884

⑫

The Imperial-Royal Traveling Museum

Christian Huemer

Around 1900, in parallel with the founding of the Modern Gallery, the arts council of the Imperial-Royal Ministry for Culture and Education was discussing the project of a "traveling museum." In both cases the objective was to counteract the "impoverishment of artistic sensibilities," specifically concerning the creations of the last one hundred years, on the premise that the Old Masters were more accessible to the general public than contemporary modern artists.[1] "We need to use the longing for pictures to stimulate the human capacity for learning," states an article in the *Wiener Zeitung* from October 25, 1903: "Especially at a time when even the smallest, most tranquil villages are reverberating with the sounds of the latest artistic controversy: 'Secession,' 'individual flair,' 'Modernism,' and other such phrases are now in common parlance at every coffeehouse and ladies' tea party. What art is and how it became what it is, however, on this common knowledge is more limited, for here we are dealing with concepts and not mere words."[2]

The traveling museum was a collection of high-quality black-and-white reproductions of some 220 paintings and sculptures from the late eighteenth century to the contemporary present. The original selection was made by Carl Moll (→ p. 189, fig. 1), who placed rather more emphasis on international Modernism from Joshua Reynolds to Auguste Rodin than on Austrian artists, who only made up about a quarter of the collection.[3] Boxed up and shipped in fifteen crates, the objective of the traveling museum was to take modern art from the imperial-royal capital and residence city of Vienna out into those regions of the crownlands whose towns and cities were as yet without a relevant public collection. The exhibitions, which ran for three to six weeks, were accompanied by a number of slideshow lectures, initially delivered by Moritz Dreger, curator at the Imperial Royal Museum of Art and Industry and author of the first catalogue of the Modern Gallery at the Belvedere. These lectures were described as "not a dry, art-historical treatise, not a list of dates and names, but they seek to illuminate the key problems facing the art of different eras, its relationship to life in general and to the overall development, and to bring it closer to the heart of the listener. The intention is also to establish a point of view for the contemplation of the museum itself."[4]

Of the more than twenty cities that applied to the ministry in Vienna to host an exhibition, the following shall be mentioned: Außig (Ústí nad Labem, now CZ, 1901), Teplitz-Schönau (Teplice, now CZ, 1902), Iglau (Jihlava, now CZ, 1903), Mährisch Ostrau (Ostrava, now CZ, 1903), Mährisch Schönberg (Šumperk, now CZ,

1903), Zwittau (Svitavy, now CZ, 1903), Salzburg (1904), Innsbruck (1904), Budweis (České Budějovice, now CZ, 1906), Villach (1909), Pola (Pula, now HR, 1907), and Trieste (now IT, 1907). At least 120 linear meters of well-lit walls were required, and the exhibition space had to be separate from the auditorium for the lectures. The cities in Moravia, where the exhibition was shown in spring 1903, recorded more than 14,000 visitors. Following his appointment as director of the Modern Gallery in 1910, Friedrich Dörnhöffer (→ p. 201, fig. 3) also signed responsible for the traveling museum.

1 AdB, Zl. 46/1909. See also van Heerde 1993, pp. 155–58; Henrichs 2021, pp. 188–91.
2 Julius Leisching, "Das k. k. Wandermuseum," *Wiener Zeitung*, October 25, 1903, p. 3.
3 See the catalogue of 1903 in van Heerde 1993, pp. 335–37.
4 AdB, Zl. 46/1909.

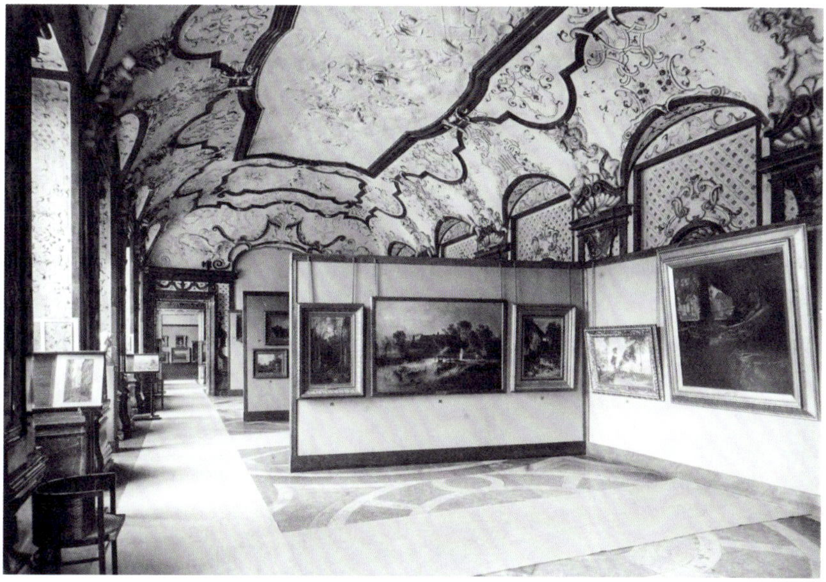

2

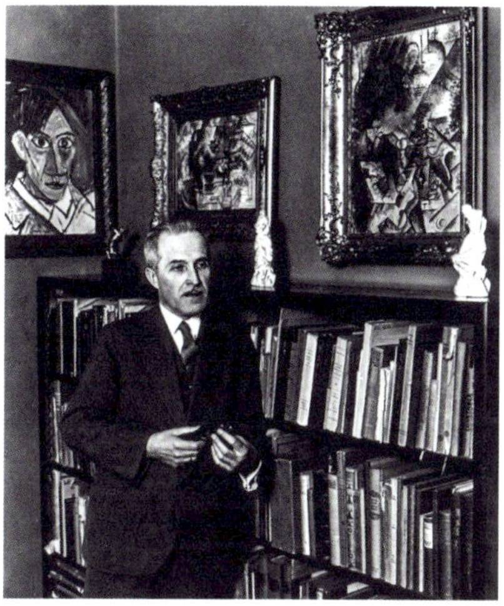

3

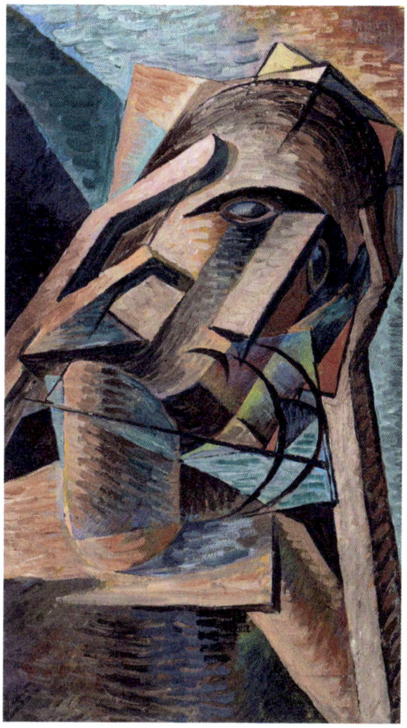

4

Fig. 2
Modern Gallery in the Lower Belvedere, 1903, photo: J. Löwy Kunst- und Verlags-anstalt Wien, Belvedere Image Archive, Vienna

Fig. 3
Vincenc Kramář in his study with works from his private art collection in the background, 1932

Fig. 4
Bohumil Kubišta, *Meditation*, 1915, National Gallery Prague

P. 178 CHRISTIAN HUEMER — A Palace as "Refuge" for Modernism

The establishment of the Modern Gallery in Vienna in 1903 resulted largely from a sense of inadequacy—particularly in the competition with other European cities.[1] The art historian Max Dvořák pointed out at the time that "only once the nationalist idea began to gain in significance for all public institutions" could a sense of unfairness develop about the fact that works "by old and foreign artists" quite naturally had "a permanent home" in magnificent palaces, while "the creations of artists embodying the new national spirit in art were homeless and not, like the old monuments, brought together in public collections for the present and future."[2] Paris had the Louvre and, since 1818, the Musée du Luxembourg for works by living artists. In the German-speaking world there was, above all, the National Gallery in Berlin, the Neue Pinakothek in Munich, and the Kunsthalle in Hamburg. After the Imperial Picture Gallery had found a worthy new home for its Old Masters with the completion in 1891 of its move from the Belvedere to the Kunsthistorisches Museum, attention now turned to finding a "refuge for the poor relations of the court," namely representatives of a modern Austrian school, which were inadequately and unsystematically represented at the imperial court.[3]

Initiatives for the founding of a state gallery for contemporary art had existed since the mid-nineteenth century. This was connected with the fact that directly after the revolution in 1848 and the accession to the throne of Emperor Franz Joseph I, promotion of the arts was seen increasingly as part of the state's responsibility toward society.[4] The establishment of an arts section within the recently created Ministry of Education signalled a gradual shift from dynastic to state patronage, in which the question of popular education was to acquire new significance

1 See the standard works on the subject: Henrichs 2021; Sauer 2008; Mlnarik 1996.
2 Dvořák 1915, pp. 2–3.
3 Tietze 1925, p. 22.
4 See van Heerde 1993; Gottsmann 2017.

(→ pp. 192–201). In 1866, Rudolf Eitelberger, first professor of art history at the University of Vienna, explicitly linked his call for a "historical gallery of modern pictures" with the state-forming role of the arts, pointing out that a "state is not created by brute force but through the inner conviction of its members."[5] The hope was that, especially in the multi-ethnic Austria-Hungary, art as a "soft power" could act as a counterbalance to particularistic forces. Moreover, artists hoped for additional resources to improve their economic situation, all the more so in the light of the long years of recession following the stock exchange crash of 1873. The artist community now became a driving force in the matter, with conservative representatives of the profession such as Adalbert Seligmann lobbying jointly with progressives like Theodor Hörmann.

The Genossenschaft der bildenden Künstler in Wien—Vienna's main artists' society of the time—had already discussed the subject of the Modern Gallery at a series of committee meetings before its first documented mention on February 21, 1894.[6] All of these documents stress the political will of the respective education minister but also the absence of the necessary premises and financial resources—which is why the support of a private association of wealthy art patrons was considered as well. Yet it was only with the founding of the Vienna Secession that the project started to take shape, mainly thanks to the "tireless initiator and implementer" Carl Moll (fig. 1).[7] On May 12, 1900, together with Johann Freiherr von Chlumetzky, Moll submitted an application to the arts council in the Ministry of Education. Having received the backing of Minister Wilhelm Ritter von Hartel, a subcommittee was set up to investigate the feasibility of establishing a Modern Gallery, and the project finally started to gather momentum. In a handwritten statement of support, Emperor Franz Joseph I confirmed that the creation of repositories for the arts was one of his most pleasant duties as a ruler.[8]

The purpose of the new institution—which, it was now being said, belonged to the present and future, not the past—was perhaps most clearly outlined in *Ver Sacrum*, the Secession's mouthpiece: "The public should no longer stand helplessly, grasping for points of reference, before creations that they can only see thanks to the happenstance of temporary art exhibitions, but instead should be empowered to enjoy one of the most momentous cultural phenomena of our time with open and seeing eyes, rather than reading about it, perhaps not until much later, in art history books."[9] To offer a comprehensible and concise presentation of the most recent developments, it was important not merely to establish a "collection of examples for an Austrian artists' lexicon," but to acquire only those works that "have the indelible imprint of the spirit of today's prevailing developments."[10] The author of these lines was no doubt aware that the noble desire to present the artistic intentions of the time would

5 Eitelberger 1879, p. 198.
6 Mlnarik 1996, p. 38.
7 Exh. cat. Vienna 1921, p. 9.
8 Van Heerde 1993, p. 182.
9 Alfred Roller, president of the Secession, to the Minister of Education Wilhelm Ritter von Hartel, in *Ver Sacrum*, no. 20, 1901, p. 342.
10 Ibid., p. 343.

not be fulfilled immediately, not least in view of the experimental nature of the undertaking, as he himself points out. The opportunity existed, he wrote, because a modern gallery of that nature had not yet been implemented fully and properly anywhere else.

The initial result was little more than a stopgap solution. For the time being, the works in state possession were to be put on display as soon as possible in the Lower Belvedere, since the presentation of existing works was seen as an essential duty toward the public. But then things suddenly became more urgent, in view of the desire to pre-empt the opening of the modern gallery in Prague (→ p. 174, fig. 1)—for which the emperor had made available two million kronen from his private purse. So as not to overburden the state budget, the committee established by the ministry sought to join forces with the City of Vienna and the province of Lower Austria. Under this agreement, the state would provide at least 60,000 kronen per year for new acquisitions and would bear all personnel costs and half of the operating costs; Lower Austria would contribute at least 20,000 kronen to enlarge the collection; and Vienna would pay the other half of the operating costs, contribute 30,000 kronen for the collection, and make available the premises and facilities.[11] This constellation proved increasingly complicated, however. After endless negotiations and numerous modifications, the decision of July 13, 1900, to build a new municipal museum on Karlsplatz—to be designed by the architect Otto Wagner, who had won a competition to that effect—turned out to be unworkable (fig. 2). The location of the Modern Gallery, which was to have been housed in the new museum, remained unresolved for years, and the whole project was left up in the air.

The handover to the public took place gradually—which is why art historians disagree whether May 7, 1903, can really be regarded as the official opening date. There seem to have been no major celebrations, and the whole affair was more of a "soft opening." Visitors entered the exhibition from the garden side; the rooms to the right of the entrance were dedicated to foreign artists, and those in the west wing, facing the Privy Garden, contained works by Austrian artists, progressing from the most recent to older ones. The exhibition comprised just under two hundred works—oil paintings, watercolors, drawings, woodcuts, sculptures—from the Romantic to the Modern era (→ p. 152), with overall numbers boosted by the many small-format works by artists such as Ferdinand Georg Waldmüller, Rudolf von Alt, and August von Pettenkofen. The room layout did not allow for "a strict system of arrangement," and the hanging committee was often guided by the "artistic mood" of individual rooms.[12] The Gold Cabinet thus featured ten colorful works by Hans Makart, including *The Five Senses*, set out in two rows like a stage set, and the suspended ceiling painting *The Four Parts of the World*. This theatrical

11 Anon., "Moderne Galerie und Städtisches Museum," in *Neue Freie Presse*, January 10, 1902, p. 6.

12 Coll. cat. Vienna 1903, pp. VIII–IX.

"Makart boudoir" or "Makart studio" was well received by critics. Ludwig Hevesi, for example, wrote that it could "not have been arranged more atmospherically."[13] Max Klinger's monumental painting *Christ on Olympus* (→ p. 157) was placed in the Marble Hall, its pendant *The Judgment of Paris* in Prince Eugene's former state bedroom (fig. 3). In other rooms, the exhibition architect Max Fabiani erected partition walls, so that smaller works could be hung without the need to cover up the magnificent stuccowork and frescos on the walls, as had originally been planned. Hevesi found this arrangement "quite pleasing. Cabinets have been created with the dividing walls, each containing roughly similar works; all light or all dark, shimmering ones here, heavier ones over there; so each section had its own mood."[14]

A start had been made, even if the impression of haphazardness could not be completely eliminated. Some critics expressed the hope that the temporary and incomplete nature of the exhibition would draw attention to the urgency of obtaining a new building and the need for more extensive subsidies. This first version of the Modern Gallery was essentially a colorful potpourri of state-owned works, supplemented by the assets of the province of Lower Austria and the City of Vienna. Further significant contributions were made in the form of donations from generous patrons of the arts, such as Johann II, Prince of Liechtenstein,, Count Karl von Lanckoroński-Brzezie, or the Trieste architect Alexander Hummel, who donated Klinger's *Judgment of Paris*. The Secession also made its mark on the Modern Gallery by acquiring major international Modernist works. In fact, the Secession's articles of association stipulated that the net profit from exhibitions (after deduction of one-third for the reserve fund) was to be used for donations. As a result, even before the Modern Gallery opened, paintings like *The Evil Mothers* by Giovanni Segantini, *Spring* by Akseli Gallén-Kallela, and *Plain near Auvers* by Vincent van Gogh (fig. 4) had already been acquired at Secession exhibitions. Such "crystallization points" of international Modernism were to form a blueprint for domestic art, and it is therefore all the more surprising that they were originally shown in separate rooms, rather than being arranged in fruitful dialogue with each other.[15]

The media response to the exhibition design, which was so far removed from the Secessionist spatial design ideals, was mixed.[16] However elegant the palace's Baroque rooms were in their own right, they were hardly in line with the contemporary vision of how an exhibition space should be. Franz Servaes in the *Neue Freie Presse* also criticized the lighting, "because the windows are in deep niches and the broken, tapering light is often unsatisfactory. Some parts of the walls are almost completely in darkness, others are exposed to an overly bright light that reflects off the pictures."[17] Moreover, the need for a logical histori-

13 Ludwig Hevesi, "Die Moderne Galerie in Wien," in *Kunstchronik: Wochenschrift für Kunst und Kunstgewerbe*, 14th year, no. 29, 1903, p. 458.
14 Ibid., p. 460.
15 At the end of this volume is a visualization illustrating the rapid growth of the collection in the years leading up to the opening of the Modern Gallery (→ p. 374).
16 Forsthuber 1991.
17 Franz Servaes, "Die Moderne Galerie," in *Neue Freie Presse*, April 16, 1903, p. 1.

cal order was highlighted, as demonstrated for Modernism at a Vienna Secession exhibition that had ended only a few weeks earlier. Entitled *Development of Impressionism in Painting and Sculpture*, it had attracted 16,000 visitors and received press coverage in "around one hundred articles [...] at home and abroad," making it the most significant artistic event of the year 1903 (fig. 5). It benefited from a large number of high-quality international loans and, across five sections, presented Impressionism in Europe for the first time as a cohesive and logically developing phenomenon. The media devoted particular attention to the evident process of historicization of the avant-garde, not least as works by precursors of the movement—Delacroix and Goya, Rubens and Vermeer, Tintoretto and El Greco—were also included in the exhibition. Servaes observed a "sudden change in the weather": Whereas the young art revolutionaries had until recently still aspired to be "original geniuses, who had created a new art based unconditionally on nature alone," they were now intent on setting up "ancestral halls" that proclaimed a direct link to the major movements of the past.[18] The selection and arrangement of the works in the Modern Gallery, the "Secession museum," lacked a comparable narrative, which, incidentally, was also the case for Ludwig Hevesi's *Geschichte der modernen Kunst III: Österreichische Kunst 1848–1900*, published in the same year.[19]

It took six years before the Ministry of Education finally decided, in 1909, to employ the gallery's first director. Until the appointment of Friedrich Dörnhöffer (→ p. 201, fig. 3), the gallery was run by a commission "composed of the most incompatible elements," which over time had become increasingly incapable of making decisions.[20] It consisted of ministry officials and representatives from three competing Viennese artists' associations, who were at pains, for example, to ensure that their members received equal treatment when it came to purchases. Carl Moll ultimately resigned from the commission in disgust, claiming that its sole purpose was to represent "the interests of the Gallery and not those of the associations."[21] Under these circumstances, additions to the collection were always compromise solutions that, while not upsetting anyone, were never completely satisfactory either. The infelicitous purchasing policy resulting from a lack of real expertise and good intuition was also criticized in the *Neue Freie Presse*.[22] Whereas in Germany directors with decision-making powers—such as Hugo von Tschudi in Berlin and Munich, or Alfred Lichtwark in Hamburg—were able to acquire major international Modernist works for their museums, Vienna had neither an organizational constitution nor a collection strategy.

This was to change rapidly under Friedrich Dörnhöffer, the former curator of the court library's collection of prints. As a proven expert who was respected by the different artistic camps, he proposed a new

18 Ibid., "Secession," in *Neue Freie Presse*, January 22, 1903, p. 1.
19 Hevesi 1903.
20 Adalbert Seligmann, "Die Moderne Galerie," in *Neue Freie Presse*, March 6, 1907, p. 2.
21 Carl Moll (as Karl Moll), "Die Oesterreichische Galerie," in *Neue Freie Presse*, July 8, 1929, p. 2.
22 Anon., "Verkauf eines Füger-Bildes ins Ausland," in *Neue Freie Presse*, April 30, 1906, p. 10.

strategy for the Modern Gallery within a few months of taking office. In view of the limited financial resources and the rapidly rising prices on the international art market, he deemed it a "futile undertaking for the state to embark on unrestrained collection activities in all directions."[23] Instead, he considered it important to fill the gaps and refine the museum's profile. As for Modernism, whose beginnings he shifted back from the mid-nineteenth to the late eighteenth century, strict attention should be paid to achieving a quality collection by acquiring only aesthetically outstanding works of pioneering significance. Regarding art from other countries, only "the most important works influencing the development of European art as a whole" should be considered.[24] Since the cooperation with the province of Lower Austria and the City of Vienna was now a dead letter, Dörnhöffer suggested extending the field to include all periods of Austrian art from the Middle Ages to the present. The logical consequence of this was the change of name from Modern Gallery to Austrian State Gallery. Seeing that most of the works in the Imperial Picture Gallery were by artists with a connection to the court, he argued that Vienna lacked a representative overview of the development of Austrian art through all time. Modernism itself "will not reveal its full impact unless it is presented within its historical foundation. It is only in this context that the inner coherence and the essential features that have remained constant over the years will come to the fore."[25]

Dörnhöffer's vision for the Modern Gallery can only be guessed at because in 1914 he moved to Munich to succeed Hugo von Tschudi as director of the Bavarian State Painting Collections. In 1911, he was responsible for the Austrian pavilion at the International Exhibition of Art in Rome. As in the Kunstschau exhibitions in Vienna in 1908 and 1909, the Secessionist architect Josef Hoffmann designed a temporary exhibition building based on the concept of the Gesamtkunstwerk. The design approach was that the outer frame of this strictly utilitarian building should not stand in competition with the works but should serve to underline their artistic quality.[26] In his foreword to the catalogue, Dörnhöffer described the profound change that had taken place in the design of exhibitions in the preceding few years. "On the one hand, the notion increasingly prevails that an artwork requires a particular environment to fully reveal its inherent power. On the other hand, there is a vibrant desire for the colorful mixture of an exhibition to be presented as a uniform whole, within which the impact of each object, by being part of the overall harmony, is not only retained but further elevated."[27] The character of the small and select collection presented in bright, light-flooded rooms, coupled with sculptures outdoors, was highly praised by the Italian press. Particular admiration was lavished on Klimt's major works, which were arranged neatly and reverently in an oval, apse-like room (fig. 6). A presentation

23 "Programm-Entwurf für M. G.," Vienna, May 25, 1910, AdB, Zl. 145/1910.
24 Ibid.
25 Ibid.
26 Miksovsky 2000.
27 Friedrich Dörnhöffer, in exh. cat. Rome 1911, n. p.

of this nature would have been simply impossible in the Baroque main buildings of the Belvedere. To that end, it was necessary to look at the possibilities presented by more neutral auxiliary buildings, such as the former guards' complex or the orangery.

After the downfall of the monarchy and the proclamation of the republic, the situation changed once again, and hitherto unheard-of possibilities suddenly presented themselves. Franz Martin Haberditzl (→ p. 201, fig. 4), who was appointed director in 1915, built on the idea of a state gallery with expanded remit as a means of overcoming the paradox of a permanent temporary solution. On November 19, 1918, only a few days after the end of the war, and knowing that under the circumstances a new building was increasingly unlikely, he sought permission from the Ministry of Education to requisition the Upper Belvedere for the project.[28] He also laid claim to the less architecturally prominent parts of the Lower Belvedere, specifically the guards' complex. These were purely utilitarian buildings and thus relatively easy to adapt: "For instance, a series of small intimate rooms can be created, which are absolutely necessary for Biedermeier art, which is made solely for small rooms. There are large rooms and halls with tall ceilings (stables and riding schools without any artistic décor), which can be modified and side-lit, making them ideal for displaying the large Klinger paintings, the Makart picture, and similar major nineteenth-century works. Medium-sized rooms with bright overhead lighting can be created for the Impressionist works."[29] Even though the "second" Modern Gallery in the Orangery did not open until years later (1929, → pp. 161–63), the departure from the Baroque rooms in the palace was an astute move. The project was financed by the Friends of Austrian Museums (→ p. 195, ⑭).

New opportunities also arose as a result of the nationalization of the imperial collections combined with Tietze's museum reform (→ p. 187, ⑬). Among other things, the consolidation of seventeenth- and eighteenth-century Austrian art led to the establishment of the Baroque Museum in the Lower Belvedere (1923, → pp. 202–09), which received all-round praise for the harmony between the exhibited objects and their setting. The Gallery of the Nineteenth Century in the Upper Belvedere (1924), meanwhile, included works that had formerly been part of the modern section of the imperial painting collection. Still under Emperor Franz Joseph, an extensive set of works on loan had been handed over to the State Gallery, fulfilling a claim that went back as far as the idea of the Modern Gallery. In spite of the perennial shortage of funds in the interwar years, Haberditzl was able to improve the collection quantitatively and qualitatively through his network of collectors, patrons, and art dealers. For example, Adele Bloch-Bauer promised to loan all six Klimt paintings in her possession, with the prospect of a later donation.[30]

28 "Inanspruchnahme des Oberen und Unteren Belvere für die Galerie," November 19, 1918, AdB, Zl. 573/1918.
29 Ibid.
30 Almost six hundred works by over 250 artists were acquired under Haberditzl's aegis; see Kugler 2004, p. 182.

By using the Belvedere complex in its entirety, it was possible for the first time to develop a coherent concept for the museum, now (since 1921) called the Austrian Gallery. Bruno Grimschitz (→ p. 255, fig. 1), long-standing member of staff to Haberditzl, explained it as follows: "Whereas the large rooms of the Baroque Museum with their exaggerated pomp reflect the aristocratic lifestyle of the feudalist eighteenth century, and the rooms in the Upper Belvedere clearly underscore the more intimate dimension of nineteenth-century bourgeois life and art, the Modern Gallery aims to create a space that matches the artistic creations of the most recent generation: a neutral, pragmatic setting, without ornamentation, without any particular mood, providing an anonymous background in the sense of a rarified exhibition hall that represents a contemporary passageway on the artwork's path from artist to owner."[31] The difference compared to the "first" Modern Gallery could not have been greater. The puritanical strictness of the exhibition set-up was striking—attributable, in addition to the neutral framework, to the widely spaced arrangement of the pictures. With almost the same number of rooms as the former gallery, the number of exhibits was reduced by more than a quarter, with eleven of the thirty-one sculptures being shown in the Privy Garden (→ p. 158 and fig. 7). Many of the works on paper from the original display had been transferred to the Albertina as part of the museum reform. The entrance hall featured the tapestry *Landscape with Herons* by Robin Christian Andersen (fig. 8). The walls were limewashed in strong, clear colors: white, sulfur yellow, glossy aluminum gray, dark blue, dark brown, and orange. Rubber instead of wood flooring emphasized modernity in the choice of materials. The only restrained highlights were the brightly polished brass doorframes. There were no explanatory wall texts either. Not even the Museum of Modern Art in New York, which opened in the same year, could offer a more radical exhibition design (fig. 9). The German art dealer Karl Haberstock wrote to the Belvedere: "I can assure you that I know of no modern gallery that feels so harmonious. The ideas you have employed here are sure to become era-defining for our museum landscape."[32]

31 Grimschitz 1929, pp. 482–83.

32 Karl Haberstock to the director of the Austrian State Gallery, September 19, 1929, AdB, Zl. 561/1929.

⑬

Hans Tietze's Museum Reform

Katinka Gratzer-Baumgärtner

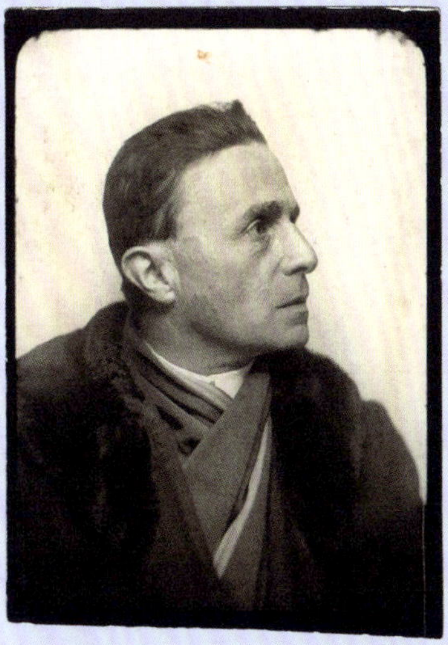

1

Fig. 1
Hans Tietze, c. 1930, Belvedere Archive, Vienna

The end of World War I saw the collapse of the Habsburg monarchy and the declaration in November 1918 of the Republic of German-Austria. Both the victorious powers and the successor states of the former monarchy demanded the appropriation of art objects owned by the house of Habsburg-Lorraine. A law was therefore hurriedly adopted prohibiting the export and sale of objects of historical, artistic, or cultural significance. One week after the abdication of Emperor Charles I, the former imperial museums came under state control. It was at this time that the art historian Hans Tietze (fig. 1), an official at the Central Commission for Monument Protection, began his campaign, expressed in numerous articles, for the preservation of Austria's art assets and a reorganization of state museums.[1] His protest was also aimed at the government itself, which had proposed to support the suffering populace, particularly in the starvation winters immediately after the war, by selling off art objects.

In 1919, in his position at the Ministry of Internal Affairs and Education as commissar responsible for the protection of German-Austrian science and art collections, Tietze began to draw up a concept for reforming the Austrian museum system with the aim of merging the imperial collections and the state-owned cultural assets. His concept also included educational aspects and proposals to refine the collection profiles. Tietze's objective was "to turn the cultural treasures of the privileged few into the property of everyone" and in this way to create a "most vibrant cultural factor."[2]

Tietze's ambitious proposal for restructuring was to make a clear demarcation between the different collections and to simplify their management. The museum reform required, for example, the systematic transfer of drawings from the Austrian Gallery to the Albertina, which would become a "central international repository of graphic art of all kinds."[3] Despite handing over its works on paper, however, the Austrian Gallery reserved the right to continue to collect watercolors. Medieval objects were transferred to the Kunsthistorisches Museum, which in return had to hand over its Baroque works for the Baroque Museum to be established in the Lower Belvedere.

Hans Tietze's museum reform was in line with the Social Democrats' educational policy, but his somewhat superficial art-historical approach of dividing the collections according to material was strongly criticized by some. There were equally strong objections to the legislation on the sale of state-owned art objects, which proposed the targeted sale of duplicate prints in order to purchase other art objects with the proceeds. The debate about the wisdom—or not—of the new collection profiles continued well into subsequent decades. Even as late as 1949, Albertina director Otto Benesch responded to requests from the Belvedere by citing the "unchanged validity" of the museum reform from the early 1920s.[4]

What remains is the fact that, from 1923 onward, many artworks were exchanged between museums and thus torn from their original collection context.

1 See Krapf-Weiler 2004; Perlhefter 2001; Haupt 1991.
2 Krapf-Weiler 2004, p. 169; Perlhefter 2001, p. 64.
3 Director of the Albertina Josef Meder to the Federal Ministry of Internal Affairs and Education, September 22, 1921, ÖStA/AVA, BMU, Zl. 20.617/1921.
4 Otto Benesch to Karl Garzarolli-Thurnlackh, December 19, 1949, AdB, Zl. 640/1949.

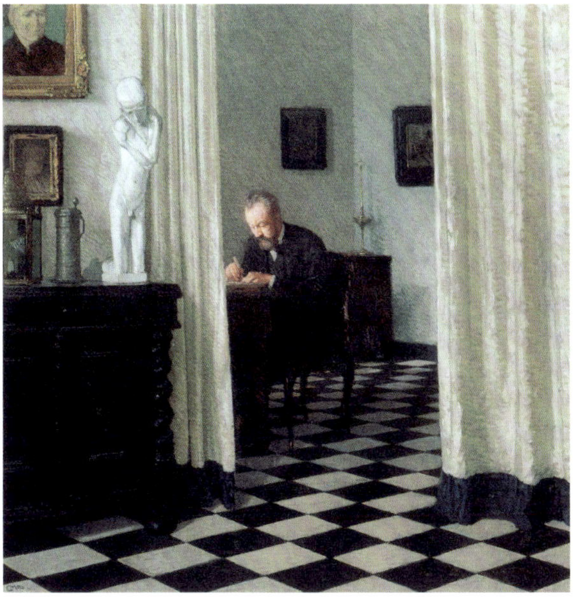

1

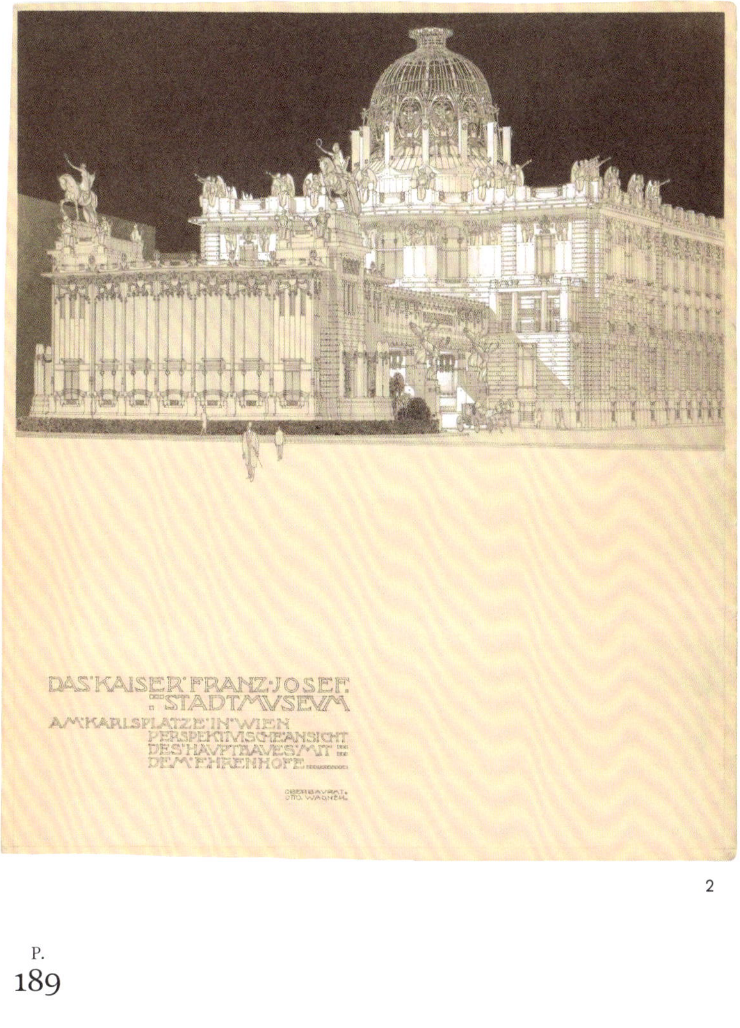

2

Fig. 1
Carl Moll, *My Studio*, 1906, Academy of Fine Arts, Vienna

Fig. 2
Otto Wagner, *Emperor Franz Joseph City Museum, Major Project, Perspective*, 1903, Wien Museum

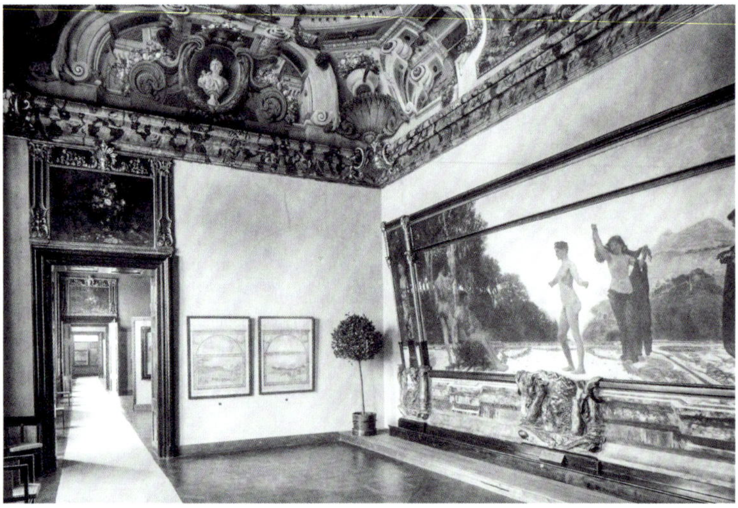

3

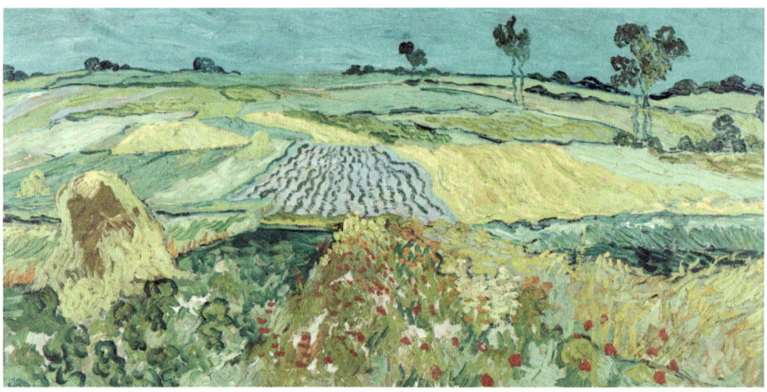

4

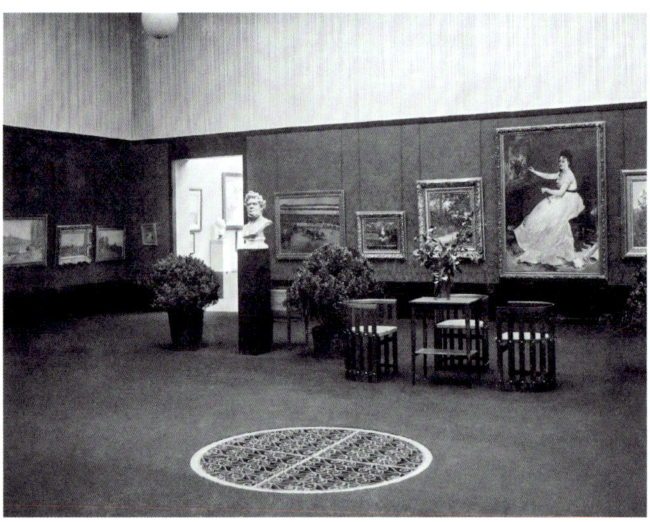

5

Fig. 3
Modern Gallery in the Lower Belvedere with Max Klinger's *The Judgment of Paris*, 1903, photo: J. Löwy Kunst- und Verlagsanstalt Wien, Belvedere Image Archive, Vienna

Fig. 4
Vincent van Gogh, *Plain near Auvers*, 1890, Belvedere, Vienna

Fig. 5
Development of Impressionism in Painting and Sculpture, exhibition at the Vienna Secession, 1903, Austrian National Library, Vienna

Fig. 6
View of the International Exhibition of Art in Rome, 1911, Belvedere Image Archive, Vienna

Fig. 7
Plan for the arrangement of sculptures in the Privy Garden of the Modern Gallery, 1929, Belvedere Image Archive, Vienna

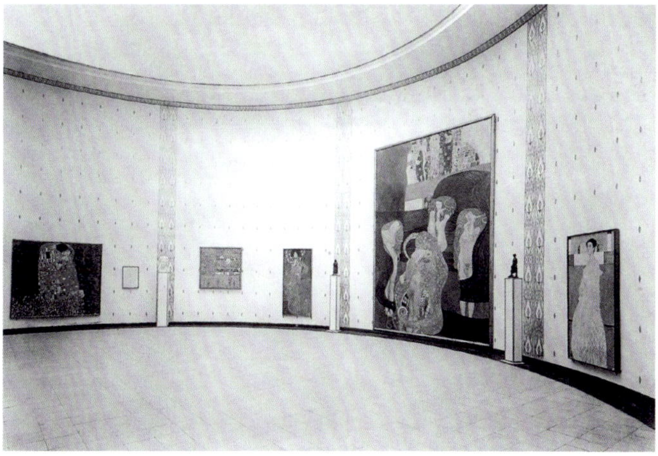

6

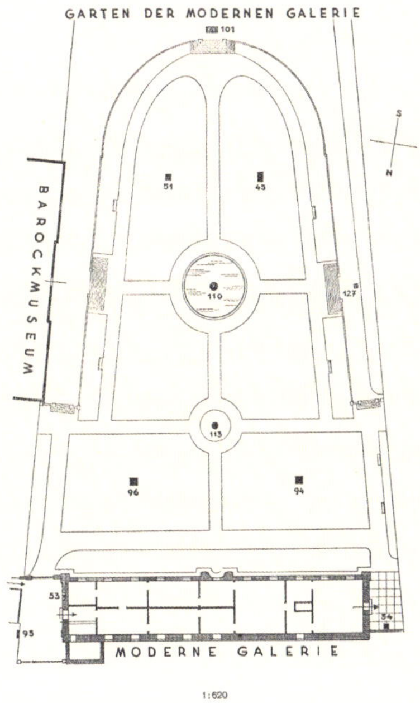

7

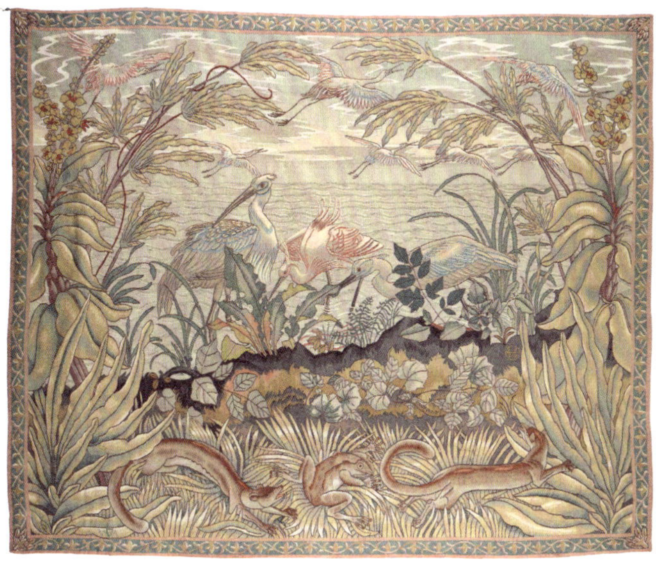

8

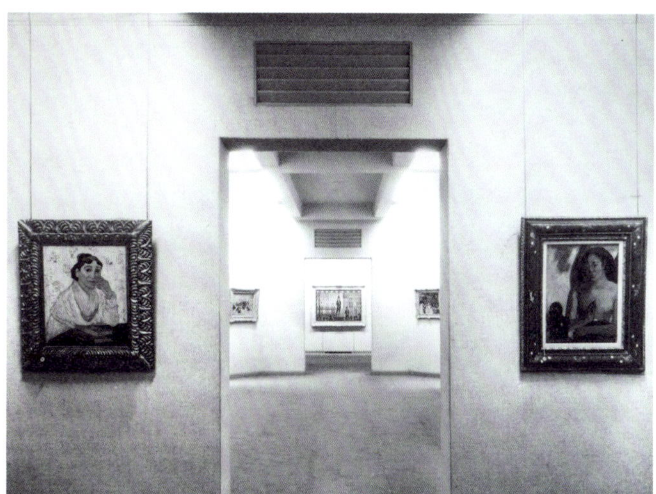

9

Fig. 8
Robin Christian Andersen, *Landscape with Herons*, 1923, Belvedere, Vienna

Fig. 9
Cézanne, Gauguin, Seurat, van Gogh, exhibition at the Museum of Modern Art, New York, 1929, Photographic Archive, The Museum of Modern Art Archives, New York

P. 192 CÄCILIA HENRICHS — Art for All? The Austrian State Gallery between Art Appreciation and Education

The establishment of the Modern Gallery, later renamed Austrian State Gallery, took place at a time of conflicting trends in art education. The opening of museums to a broader public had support not just from representatives of the *Volksbildungsbewegung* (popular education movement) but also, for example, from the Vienna Secession. In the manifesto accompanying the founding of the Modern Gallery, the following objective was formulated: "[...] to educate the great masses of the art-appreciating public so as to awaken their latent drive [...]. And here we address all of you, without distinction of class or wealth."[1] This noble ideal was based on an artist's perspective and attributed works of art with the ability to make an inherently strong impression on any kind of observer.

On the part of museum experts, who were then already in a process of professionalization, these notions were affirmed by some and rejected by others. The museum reformer Hans Tietze belonged to the first group and concluded in 1924, concerning the status of Vienna's museums and their approach to dealing with the public: "It was and remains vital to propagate an interest in their treasures beyond a circle of regular visitors and to replace the inferred rational impact with an immediate one of sentiment. One must also give thought to what one wishes to present to the public and how to present it."[2] Here, Tietze prioritizes emotion over reason and, thus, instruction. This was an important aspect in the opening of the museum, as it allowed it to be visited without preconditions. For Tietze, the experience of art was to be steered primarily through exhibition design.

The gulf between ideal and reality is demonstrated most strikingly in the initial design for the Modern Gallery in 1903. In the Baroque

1 Anon., "Weshalb wir eine Zeitschrift herausgeben?" in *Ver Sacrum*, yr. 1, no. 1, 1898, p. 6.
2 Tietze 1924a, no. 4, p. 122.

rooms of the Lower Belvedere, provisional partition walls were placed, on which the works of modern art had to compete for the visitors' attention with the opulent surroundings (fig. 1, → pp. 152–57). When, by contrast, in 1923, the Baroque collection of the State Gallery was exhibited in the same rooms, objects and space united into a harmonious whole. Only with the second Modern Gallery, established in the former Orangery in 1929, was modern art provided with a suitable setting for a comprehensive overall experience. In the remodeling of these rooms, modern materials were given preference that were still unusual for museums at the time. The floor was laid with rubber, the doors framed with brass, and the simple, uniform gold frames were hung against tinted, whitewashed walls.[3] The importance of the impact of these colors in combination with the exhibited works is highlighted in the catalogue of 1929, which, alongside the usual information on artworks and artists, includes views of the exhibition with a description of the colors used in each room (fig. 2, → pp. 158–63).

Aside from the exhibition design, which, while catering less to the public's prior knowledge, was undoubtedly aimed at visitors with an existing appreciation of art, further measures were taken to attract a wider audience. In the early years following the gallery's opening, interest primarily came from external parties, who applied for group permits and for free entry on paid entry days. The spectrum of visitors ranged from school children of all ages and genders[4] to smaller clubs and societies, such as the Verbindung für historische Kunst (Society for Historical Art)[5] or the Arbeiter-Abstinentenbund (Workers' Abstinence League).[6] A tour by qualified museum staff was not included.

This passive strategy changed after the First World War and the ensuing expansion of the collection's scope. After the Austrian State Gallery reinstated normal opening hours, which had been reduced during the war, a dedicated lecture room was set up in the Upper Belvedere. The aim of this endeavor was to "offer working people a much more involved experience of the true essence of the collection than could be achieved by merely extending visiting hours."[7] Benches were installed for an audience of sixty to one hundred, who, for a small fee, could attend one-hour lectures about three to four original works of art.[8] To fill these seats with the desired audience, workers' organizations were offered blocks of half-price tickets, as well as the opportunity to agree the dates of each lecture. All of these plans—from setting up the hall, to organizing the logistics, and agreeing lecture content with the Ministry of Education—fizzled out, however, as, in spite of placing adverts in all of Vienna's daily newspapers, nobody came to the first few lectures.[9] And even later on, the highest audience numbers came to fourteen, leading director Franz Martin Haberditzl to conclude that "this institution for the benefit of public education requires considerable time to achieve success."[10] There was no second

3 Grimschitz 1929, pp. 482–83.
4 AdB, Zl. 1085/1912 and 126/1918.
5 AdB, Zl. 131/1910.
6 AdB, Zl. 169/1916.
7 AdB, Zl. 387/1919.
8 AdB, Zl. 387/1919.
9 AdB, Zl. 473/1920.
10 AdB, Zl. 473/1920.

(14)

From the Austrian State Gallery Society to the Friends of Austrian Museums in Vienna, 1911/12–1938

Cäcilia Henrichs

On December 30, 1911, Emperor Franz Joseph I approved the renaming of the Modern Gallery, founded in 1903, to Austrian State Gallery. The aim of this gallery was to showcase a representative cross section of Austrian art from the Middle Ages to the present. To support this objective, the State Gallery Society, modeled on the Kaiser Friedrich Museumsverein, established in Berlin in 1897, was formed.[1] On December 30, 1911, director Friedrich Dörnhöffer (→ p. 201, fig. 3) wrote to Johann II, Prince of Liechtenstein, that the "project has now become a reality."[2] The twenty-six founding members included Baron Felix von Oppenheimer, Victor Zuckerkandl, Count Karol Lanckoroński, and Ferdinand Bloch, who, in return for a one-off contribution of five thousand kronen, were granted a lifetime membership (the regular membership fee was five hundred kronen). This provided a starting capital of thirty thousand kronen. To guarantee exclusivity, membership candidates required recommendations from two existing members. This process created a socially homogeneous group, united by a common taste in art. By 1924, the society had grown to five hundred members. "By purchasing works of fine art and lending them to the public collections free of charge," the society dedicated itself to "the cultivation of Austrian art appreciation."[3]

Yet, the State Gallery Society—as implied in its name—was most closely linked with the Austrian State Gallery. Up until 1918, the gallery benefited from the purchase of eleven high-caliber works, starting with *On Corpus Christi Morning* by Ferdinand Georg Waldmüller (fig. 1), acquired in 1912, the first year of the society's existence. A further four works, including Feuerbach's *Henriette Feuerbach, the Artist's Stepmother* and Manet's *The Old Musician* (fig. 2) were acquired jointly with the Austrian state.

1919 marked a significant turning point: with the incorporation of the imperial collections into state ownership, the Gallery Society broadened its scope. As a result, from 1921, the

1 See Mayer M. 2012.
2 AdB, Zl. 1044/1911.
3 Österreichischer Staatsgalerieverein in Wien, *Bericht über das 1. Vereinsjahr 1912*, Vienna 1913, Statuten, p. 7.

organization began to operate under the new name of Friends of Austrian Museums in Vienna. However, it still contributed to the major refurbishment works at the Austrian Gallery: both the Baroque Museum in the Lower Belvedere (→ pp. 167–69) and the Gallery of the Nineteenth Century in the Upper Belvedere (→ p. 164) received funding; thanks to this financial support, Prince Eugene's former orangery in the Lower Belvedere could be adapted for the reopening of the Modern Gallery in 1929 (→ pp. 161–63).

In the interwar period, the Friends of Austrian Museums expanded their activities and, from 1923, organized their own exhibitions, in addition to the lecture program already launched the previous year. As representative of a public collection, Franz Martin Haberditzl (→ p. 201, fig. 4) was a board member and adviser to the exhibition committee for the first exhibition at the Secession, *From Füger to Klimt*, in 1923. As the years progressed, however, his contribution became restricted to the loan of works from the Austrian Gallery. In 1933, an exhibition dedicated to Prince Eugene of Savoy was held in the rooms of the Upper Belvedere, but only in return for a generous compensation payment to the gallery. After the annexation of Austria in March 1938, all groups and organizations came under Nazi control. As a result of the "Aryan paragraph," which required the organization to exclude its Jewish members, the Friends of Austrian Museums lost a significant proportion of its then approximately 1,400 members; Felix von Oppenheimer was removed from his post as president and Franz Martin Haberditzl was replaced as a member of the board by Bruno Grimschitz (→ p. 255, fig. 1).

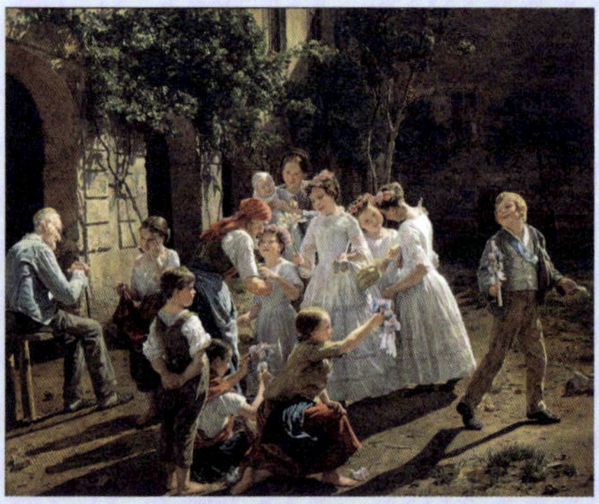

1

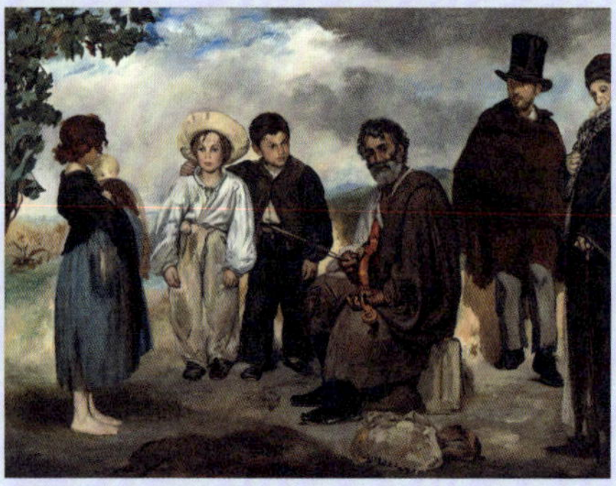

2

Fig. 1
Ferdinand Georg Waldmüller, *On Corpus Christi Morning*, 1857; 1912 permanent loan of the State Gallery Society (today Society of Friends of the Österreichische Galerie Belvedere), Vienna

Fig. 2
Édouard Manet, *The Old Musician*, 1862, National Gallery of Art, Washington; 1913 purchased from Galerie Arnot, Vienna, with support from the Austrian State Gallery Society. 1923 exchange with Galerie Barbazanges, Paris, for Camille Corot's *Madame Legois* and Pierre-Auguste Renoir's *Bather with blond, loose hair*

attempt, since the experience with workers' organizations had been very similar at the Kunsthistorisches Museum, too. Instead, a short lecture series was planned jointly by both museums, to be held in public education institutions in the outer districts of the city. The aim here was to meet the public where they lived and encourage them to visit the museum.[11]

The Volksbildungsamt (Office for Popular Education), which was part of the Department of Education, also became involved and wanted to install a working group at the Austrian State Gallery with the aim of "intensifying popular lecture activity."[12] The response from the gallery was negative, with no reason given. In subsequent years, however, academic tours of the collection continued to be offered, suggesting that it had been the popular nature of the planned tours that had met with disapproval. The high standard of these events was to be maintained by the gallery's academically qualified staff. Invigilators, on the other hand, were instructed "not to enter into longer conversation with visitors while on duty, nor to offer explanations of the objects on display. Questions of this nature are to be referred to the catalogue [...]."[13] Naturally, security concerns also played a role in this guidance, as it was undesirable for invigilators to be too easily distracted. Yet, it also reveals a certain elitism, which Hans Tietze polemicized against in a 1924 *Kunstblatt* article. About the generally adopted approach to museum education at the time, he wrote: "Just as art belonged to the art lovers, the museum belonged to the experts. [...] The general public, forced to bow to the superior judgment of the initiated, had to make do with the scraps from the table of the true owners of the house. As a genuine *Bildungspöbel* [cultural mob], it slavishly followed the ideals of those deemed to be the cultural authority."[14]

While the content conveyed in the gallery itself was dominated by the academic exploration of and interaction with the original artwork, the external popular education lectures continued as before. Lectures at the Urania and also at the Österreichische Radio-Verkehrs AG (RAVAG; the first Austrian radio station, founded in 1924) were relatively easy to organize for the gallery, who only had to provide the relevant members of staff. As early as June 23, 1911, gallery director Friedrich Dörnhöffer (fig. 3) was invited to give a lecture at the Vienna Urania. In the absence of a specific theme, this early attempt was not very successful.[15] Over the ensuing years, however, Dörnhöffer's successor Franz Martin Haberditzl (fig. 4) and his colleague Bruno Grimschitz regularly gave lectures at the Urania on various topics relating to Austrian art.[16]

Conversely, tours of the Austrian State Gallery were offered by lecturers from the Urania, perhaps taking a less scholarly but more didactically focused approach. The anticipated rush of visitors, however, never materialized. The new medium of radio was also employed.[17] Gallery staff were invited to speak on general questions of art, as well as on

11 AdB, Zl. 473/1920.
12 AdB, Zl. 448/1920.
13 AdB, Zl. 565/1911.
14 Tietze 1924a, no. 4, p. 121.
15 AdB, Zl. 612/1911.
16 Between 1924 and 1942, Grimschitz held a total of eighty-six courses at the Urania; his director Haberditzl held six between 1910 and 1913.
17 In Germany, radio was already being used as a means of public education as early as 1919, as it had a very broad reach, spatially as well as socially; Zeising 2013, p. 86.

individual exhibitions, at the RAVAG radio college.[18] As broad and effective as this spectrum of communication tools may sound, it is difficult to get a clear picture of its content. Reflecting back on this situation, Alfred Stix, then director of the Albertina's Graphic Art Collection, commented in 1930 that efforts at popularization were "mostly in the field of diluted art history" and had been unable to retain the interest of the public for long.[19] As in many museums, even today, a fine line was walked between oversimplification and overcomplexity in calibrating museum communications to suit different visitor groups. The criticism, expressed very publicly by Max Dvořak in the *Neue Freie Presse* in 1915, reveals the extreme prejudice of the academically trained art historian. He warned of "pernicious [...] popularization pedagogics that, as the academies once did with their technical rules, strip art of its inherent worth through reproductions, slide presentations, and picture magazines, debasing it to a commons for phony educated philistines."[20] The fear of an erosion of the noble arts and its resulting destruction, or at least desecration, was a significant obstacle in the opening of museums to a wider public.

All of this begs the question: how seriously was this idealistic aspiration to attract a truly broad audience actually pursued? The gallery rules from 1911, which remained largely unchanged in subsequent years, stipulated: "Visits are permitted for all respectably attired persons. Visitors carrying children in their arms will be denied entry."[21] This provision in itself already excluded a significant number of people from visiting the gallery. The same can be said of another aspect, noted by the popular educator and director of the Austrian Museum of Art and Industry, Eduard Leisching, for Vienna's museum landscape in general: "[...] the relatively high cost of tickets and exhibition catalogues is truly reason enough to prevent many, and especially those we are trying to reach, from visiting the exhibitions."[22] As was common at the time, works in the Austrian State Gallery were merely given a number and, to find out a picture's title and artist, visitors had to consult the gallery catalogue. There were a number of complaints about this, including one from a teacher who, wanting to prepare himself for a later visit with his pupils, was obliged to buy the catalogue from his meager wages (→ p. 155).[23] If these costs posed an obstacle even for a civil servant, how much more of an obstacle must they have presented for workers. Not to mention that, after a fourteen-hour day, they were more likely in the mood for lighter amusement than a visit to an art museum.

Nevertheless, at the State Gallery, a significant step was taken to facilitate evening visits of precisely this nature: since its opening in autumn 1924, the Gallery of the Nineteenth Century was fitted with electric lighting. This had the consequence of increasing the fire risk for the museum, as well as the costs of staff, who had to work longer hours. The asso-

18 AdB, Zl. 681/1925. No gallery staff were involved in the meeting itself. Afterwards, however, two dates were set: on January 27, 1926, Grimschitz spoke about the Baroque Museum and two days later Heinrich Schwarz about the Gallery of the Nineteenth Century.
19 Stix 1930, pp. 60–61.
20 Dvořak 1915, p. 4.
21 AdB, Zl. 565/1911.
22 Leisching 1927, p. 421.
23 AdB, Zl. 398/1921.

ciated expectations in terms of popular education, meanwhile, remained unfulfilled. Quite the opposite, the availability of artificial lighting opened up the possibility of using the Upper Belvedere for high-society events (fig. 5).[24] This example epitomizes the entire dilemma facing the Austrian State Gallery and its communications strategy: Although, in spite of all reservations, clear efforts were made to explain the museum to the general public and thus open it up to a wider audience, all too frequently these efforts continued to address those with an existing appreciation of art. The only new audience, largely drawn in by the Modern Gallery, were the newly wealthy middle classes, for whom a museum visit still formed part of the educated bourgeoisie curriculum. The State Gallery furthermore attracted art collectors, not least through its affiliated Gallery Society (→ p. 195, ⑭). When considered retrospectively, despite the constant strain on its finances, the Austrian State Gallery did much to open up the museum to the public and provide educational offerings for all strata of society. The limited success of these efforts was probably more a result of the situation of society as a whole.

24 In this context, Haberditzl said that "a social contact was made between the museum and the public," AdB, Zl. 798/1928.

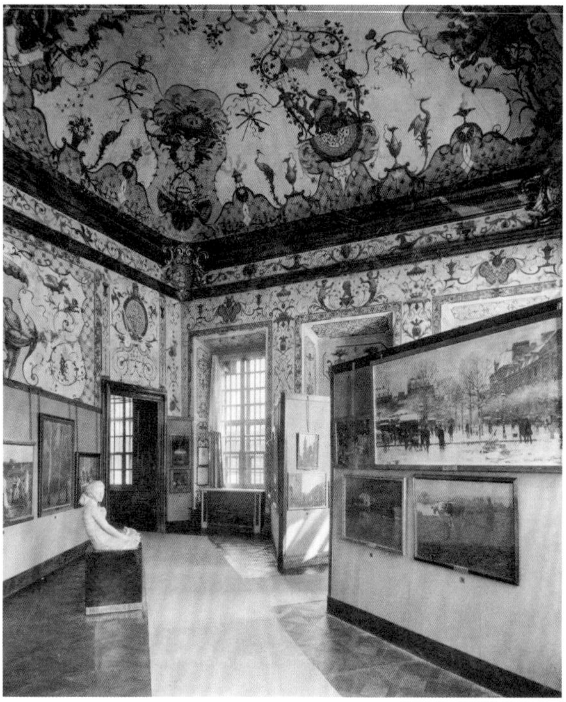

1

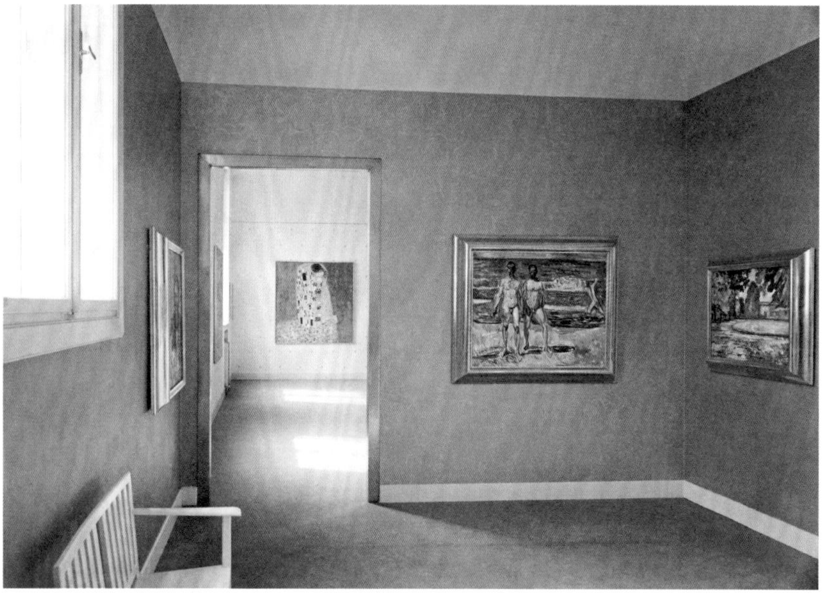

2

Fig. 1
Hall of Grotesques of the Modern Gallery in the Lower Belvedere, with Luigi Loir's *Place de la République*, c. 1903, photo: J. Löwy Kunst- und Verlagsanstalt Wien, Belvedere Image Archive, Vienna

Fig. 2
The Silver-Gray Room, Modern Gallery in the Orangery of the Belvedere, with paintings by Edvard Munch, 1929, photo: Hans Georg Balack, Belvedere Library, Vienna

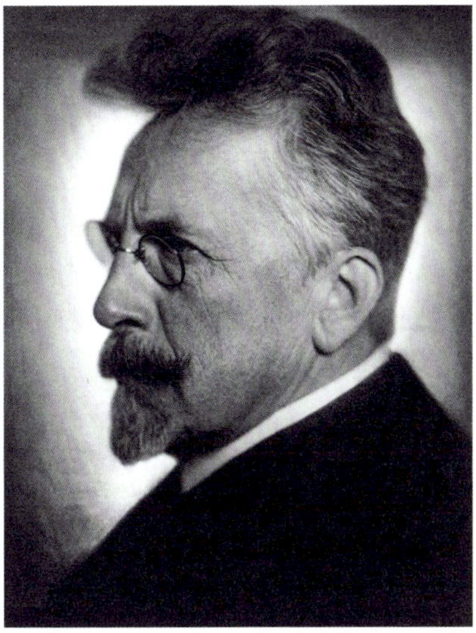

3

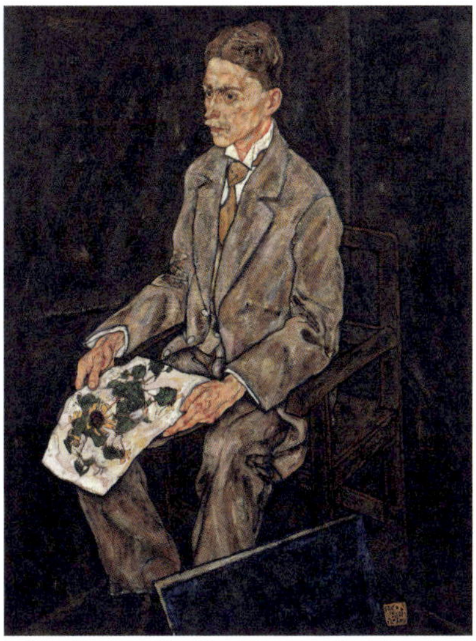

4

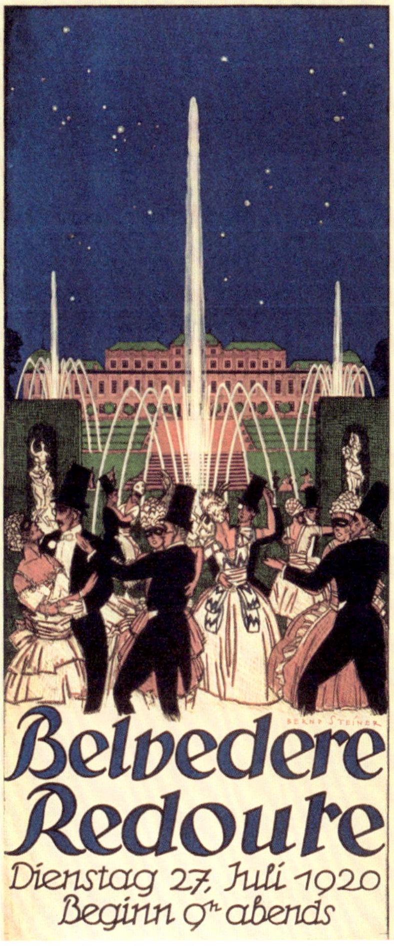

5

Fig. 3
Friedrich Dörnhöffer, c. 1910, Belvedere Image Archive, Vienna

Friedrich Dörnhöffer was director of the Modern Gallery, later the Imperial-Royal Austrian State Gallery, from 1909 to 1914.

Fig. 4
Egon Schiele, *Dr. Franz Martin Haberditzl*, 1917, Belvedere, Vienna

Franz Martin Haberditzl was director of the (Imperial-Royal) Austrian State Gallery (after 1921 the Austrian Gallery) from 1915 to 1938.

Fig. 5
Poster for the "Belvedere Redoute" ball, July 27, 1920, design: Bernd Steiner, Austrian National Library, Vienna, Picture Archives

GEORG LECHNER — The Foundation of the Baroque Museum in the Lower Belvedere

When the Austrian Baroque Museum opened on May 11, 1923, the interplay between its historical interior and the exhibited artworks garnered particular praise.[1] In his foreword to the catalogue published for the occasion, director Franz Martin Haberditzl, too, lauded the palace's release from later modifications and the introduction of Baroque artworks as a happy circumstance (→ p. 166).[2] And Hans Tietze, author of the reorganization of the state museums, saw it neither as a museum in the conventional sense nor as a palace, but as a place "in which setting and content form a true unity, mutually elevating each other to a higher level."[3] Furthermore, the ideational significance of this museum for the young Republic of Austria—now so small by comparison to the Habsburg Empire—must not be underestimated.[4] In the late nineteenth century, Austrian Baroque had already been established as specific to the country and was well on its way to being seen as a national style.[5] It is therefore not surprising that after World War I particular emphasis was given to the republic's Baroque aspect and that the Baroque Museum was created and promoted.

The establishment of the museum was certainly not a spontaneous idea, but reflects the contemporary academic interest in the art of this era.[6] Special mention should be given here to Albert Ilg, who, already in the late nineteenth century, had published works on the Baroque in Austria. With regard to the Belvedere, his writings about Franz Xaver Messerschmidt, Georg Raphael Donner, and Prince Eugene of Savoy as an art connoisseur are of great importance.[7] Martin Johann Schmidt, called Kremser Schmidt, was also honored early on in a monograph.[8]

Works of Austrian Baroque art had been purchased since the 1870s for the Imperial Picture Gallery, still housed in the Upper Belvedere at the time. In 1876, for instance, *The Holy Kinship* by Franz Anton Maulbertsch was acquired, an artist not represented in the collection until then.[9] After an interlude at the Kunsthistorisches Museum, opened in 1891, this painting and many others were returned to the Belvedere for the Baroque Museum's displays. In exchange, the medieval objects then housed at the

1 Cf. Adalbert Franz Seligmann, "Das Wiener Barockmuseum," *Neue Freie Presse*, May 12, 1923, p. 6.
2 Coll. cat. Vienna 1923, p. VII.
3 See note 1.
4 Cf. Tietze-Conrat 1923, p. 166.
5 Cf. Stachel 2007; Krapf 2008, p. 23.
6 Regarding the beginnings of research into Baroque art in Austria, see Schmidt 2013.
7 Ilg 1885; Ilg 1893; Ilg 1889.
8 Mayer 1879.
9 Further examples of these early acquisitions are the paintings *Christ on the Cross* from the workshop of Kremser Schmidt and the *Resurrection of Christ* by Franz Xaver Wagenschön, acquired in 1875 and 1877 respectively (Belvedere, Vienna, inv. nos. 4164 and 4073).

Belvedere were moved to the Kunsthistorisches Museum, although it is interesting to note that the transfers in both directions were merely recorded as loans at the time.[10] It was not until after World War II that these paintings and sculptures were included in the museum inventories.[11] Objects from the Austrian Museum of Art and Industry, now the Museum of Applied Arts, on the other hand, were treated differently, with a distinction made between works that had been permanently transferred and those on loan.[12] Thus, in 1922, five of Franz Xaver Messerschmidt's "Character Heads," together with other works, were accessioned into the collections of the Austrian Gallery at the Belvedere.[13]

These were two of the sources for the first presentation, as, before 1923, the Austrian Gallery's holdings of seventeenth- and eighteenth-century artworks were still fairly negligible, and certainly not sufficient to fill displays in the envisaged rooms. Despite the fact that after 1912—when the Modern Gallery was renamed as the Imperial-Royal Austrian State Gallery and its remit expanded—acquisitions of medieval and Baroque objects had increased, the number of works remained relatively modest. Support in the form of loans came from the Albertina, the Academy of Fine Arts, the Schottenstift monastery, and the Abbey of Saint Paul, among other institutions. Moreover, various private individuals contributed to the development of the collection with gifts.

The building and the artworks were there, but in the period of economic turmoil following World War I, finding the funds for the necessary renovations and refurbishment was no easy task. Assistance came from the industrialist Camillo Castiglioni, who, in 1922, donated two hundred million kronen for the promotion of the arts, seventy-five million of which was allocated to setting up the Baroque Museum.[14] This paid for redecorating the rooms, for picture frames, and much more besides. The financial records also list costs for paint removal and a cast of Messerschmidt's statue of Maria Theresa.[15] Previously, this and its pendant sculpture of Francis Stephen I had been at Franzensburg castle in Laxenburg, where it had been coated in white oil paint to match the surrounding marble sculptures by Paul Strudel. After its transferal to the Belvedere, it was replaced by a copy that is still at Laxenburg today.[16]

In 1923, the Lower Belvedere was not yet available in its entirety to accommodate the Baroque Museum, as some of the rooms to the east of the Marble Hall housed antiquities from Ephesus (→ p. 207, ⑮).[17] As a result, the entrance to the museum was via an added porch on the garden side, which disrupted the rhythm of the façade (fig. 1). Visitors stepped directly into the Blue Room, with exhibits focusing on portraiture and art from the early eighteenth century.[18] In the Hall of Grotesques, a considerable number of medals, small sculptures, drawings, and oil sketches were on display, while works by Franz Xaver Messerschmidt and Balthasar

10 AdB, Zl. 7/1922.
11 AdB, Zl. 472/1948.
12 AdB, Zl. 7/1922.
13 *Old Age*, *The Artist's Serious Countenance*, *An Intentional Wag*, *A Strong Worker*, and *An Old Cheerful Smiler* (Belvedere, Vienna, inv. nos. 2282–2286).
14 *Neues Wiener Journal*, November 22, 1922, p. 3.
15 AdB, Zl. 534/1922.
16 See Pötzl-Malikova 2015, pp. 216–19, no. 7.
17 Coll. guide Vienna 1919. The guide in the Belvedere library has a supplementary information sheet from a later date, revealing that some of the exhibits were still in the Lower Belvedere and were accessible via the Baroque Museum.
18 The description of the various rooms follows the catalogue of 1923 (coll. cat. Vienna 1923, pp. XV–CII).

Ferdinand Moll were presented in the adjoining Marble Gallery (fig. 2). Balthasar Permoser's *Apotheosis of Prince Eugene of Savoy* dominated the Mirror Room, as the Gold Cabinet was then called, and casts of Messerschmidt's "Character Heads" graced some of the wall brackets (fig. 3). The final small room was devoted to Franz Anton Maulbertsch. On the other side of the palace, the Blue Room was followed by the Red Room, containing two altarpieces originating from St. Ulrich's Church in Vienna. In the Yellow Room (fig. 4) and the Marble Hall, the focus was on Georg Raphael Donner's works, the highlight being the figures from the Mehlmarkt fountain. A cabinet of sketches, the Green Room with Paul Troger's *Agony in the Garden* and works by Kremser Schmidt, as well as a landscape room rounded off the tour.

In 1932, the Palace Stables provided a new home for the excavations from Ephesus.[19] This freed up space in the Lower Belvedere and further rooms could be adapted for the Baroque Museum. This time, the costs for this were covered by the Friends of Austrian Museums.[20] For visitors to this newly extended museum, one striking change was that the entrance was now via the passageway linking Rennweg and the Belvedere gardens. Three sculptures that had been acquired after 1923 were placed on display here, creating a more prominent entrance situation. These works—the *Apotheosis of Saint John of Nepomuk* (fig. 5) by Johann Jakob Schoy, and *Flora* and *Bacchus*, formerly attributed to Balthasar Permoser—are still in this location today, like the last relics of the no longer extant Baroque Museum.[21]

In examining the development of the Belvedere's Baroque collection, it is of interest, alongside analysis of documented acquisitions in the inventory, to compare the catalogues of the Baroque Museum from 1923 and 1934.[22] While in 1923 these already record 199 objects, in 1934 this number had increased to 286, in both cases including 54 medals. From 1934, the first room after the entrance contained Messerschmidt's "Character Heads" along with still lifes. The latter encompassed a work by Jan Anton van der Baren, a painting by Joannes de Cordua that had been acquired as recently as 1933, as well as four animal pieces by Philipp Ferdinand de Hamilton.[23] These three painters were Flemish artists who had worked for long periods in Vienna. This is noteworthy in that their works therefore did not represent the Austrian Baroque as such, but Baroque in Austria. Also notable is that the number of works by Maulbertsch had greatly increased, no longer merely filling a small room but now an entire hall. The holdings of sculptures had also grown significantly since the opening of the museum, which now presented a more complete picture of the Baroque.[24]

Following the evacuation of objects during World War II and the Lower Belvedere being hit by a bomb in February 1945, causing great

19 AdB, Zl. 386/1932.
20 AdB, Zl. 522/1932 and 339/1933.
21 Belvedere, Vienna, inv. nos. 2616 (Schoy), 3188 (*Bacchus*), and 3189 (*Flora*). Cf. coll. cat. Vienna 1934, pp. 9–11.
22 Coll. cat. Vienna 1923; coll. cat. Vienna 1934.
23 Coll. cat. Vienna 1934, pp. 12–14.
24 Cf. for example Wolfgang Born, "Barockmuseum erhält Zuwachs!," *Neues Wiener Journal*, March, 11, 1934, p. 13; A. Fr., "Das Wiener Barockmuseum," *Neues Wiener Abendblatt*, March 17, 1934, p. 4.

damage to the Hall of Grotesques in particular (→ p. 237), the building was reconstructed and restored, and the rehung Baroque Museum opened its doors again on February 4, 1953. Director Karl Garzarolli-Thurnlackh stressed that the maxim behind the reorganized museum had been "to emphasize even more clearly the specifically Austrian character and thus make this easier to understand."[25] Once again, loans were important to this end, most prominently a total of ten works by Kremser Schmidt from the Joanneum in Graz and Seitenstetten Abbey.[26]

Further redisplays took place in 1974 under director Hans Aurenhammer and in 1995, after the museum had been closed for refurbishment. In contrast to earlier displays, Michael Krapf, the curator in charge of the project, placed his focus on the finished work rather than the sketch, and gave particular attention to incorporating the rooms with preserved historical décor in his concept.[27]

This display existed until 2007, when the Baroque and the Medieval museums were closed in order to convert the Lower Belvedere and the Orangery into venues for special exhibitions. Both parts of the collection were later put on display at the Upper Belvedere, where it is now possible to explore Austrian art from the Middle Ages to the present day under one roof.

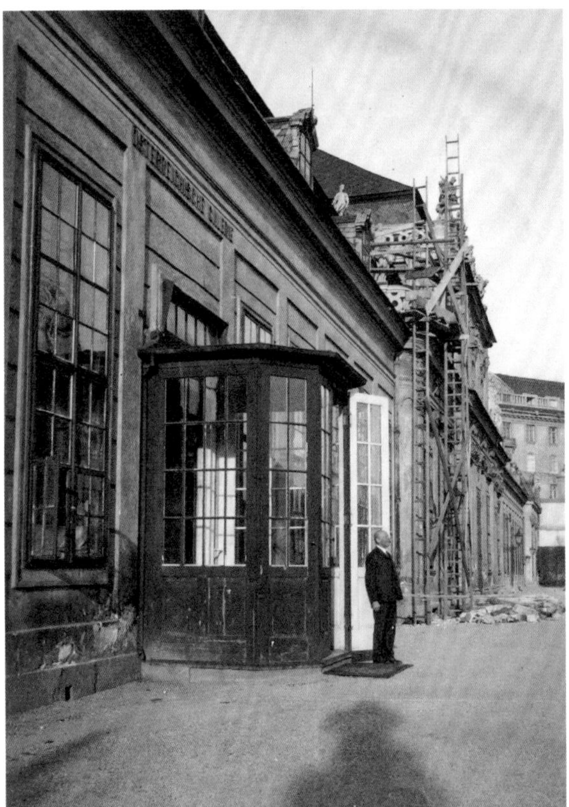

1

Fig. 1
Entrance to the Baroque Museum in the Lower Belvedere, c. 1933, Belvedere Image Archive, Vienna

25 Coll. cat. Vienna 1953, p. 3.
26 Coll. cat. Vienna 1953, p. 37.
27 Krapf 1995; Krapf 2008, pp. 25–26.

(15)

The Ephesos Museum Visits the Lower Belvedere

Georg Plattner

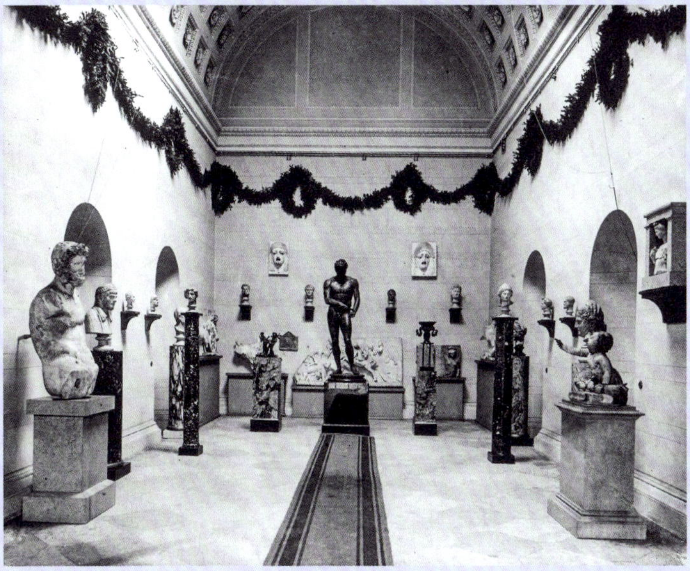

1

Fig. 1
Ephesus exhibition at the Theseus Temple in the Volksgarten, 1901

In 1895, Austria started excavations in Ephesus in Turkey. With his proposal for the project, Otto Benndorf, professor of classical archeology at the University of Vienna, had been able to convince the Ministry of Culture that excavations of this ancient metropolis would result in scientific insights and the discovery of rich finds. Sultan Abdul Hamid II consented to a portion of the finds being given to Emperor Franz Joseph and incorporated in the imperial collections in Vienna, on the basis of the diplomatic provisions applicable at the time.[1]

The Kunsthistorisches Museum Vienna had been open since 1891 and had no more room for the new discoveries. While plans for a stand-alone Ephesos Museum on Heldenplatz were still in their early stages, a provisional *Exhibition of Finds from Ephesus* was installed in 1901 at the Theseus Temple in the Volksgarten park (fig. 1).[2] The discovery, in 1903, of the spectacular reliefs from the Parthian Monument—an impressive state monument from the middle of the second century CE celebrating the size, significance, and foundations of the Roman Empire (fig. 2)[3] — called for additional exhibition space. In the early nineteenth century, objects from the imperial collections, including the antiquities collection, had already been exhibited in the Lower Belvedere, as documented in detail in the watercolors of Carl Goebel junior (→ p. 91). With the opening of an Ephesos exhibition on November 10, 1905, antiquity returned again to the Lower Belvedere.

The desire for more space is evident in this remark from collection director Robert von Schneider: "the […] promise of a coherent and systematic arrangement of all finds from Ephesus […] will only be fulfilled when the excavations on site are complete and a number of rooms now occupied by the 'Modern Gallery' are made available for this purpose."[4]

In 1906/07, Turkey's new antiquities law changed the parameters. The export of archaeological finds was now strictly forbidden, with the consequence that no new objects could be expected from Ephesus. Some items were even returned in order for excavations to be allowed to continue, and in 1911 the exhibition in the Belvedere was adapted accordingly.

With the establishment of the Austrian Baroque Museum in the Lower Belvedere in 1923 (→ pp. 167–69), the majority of the finds from Ephesus had to make way. The relief slabs from the Parthian Monument were "provisionally crammed together in a side room."[5] Eventually, in 1933, they were transferred to the Palace Stables to facilitate the expansion of the Baroque Museum. In 1943–44, the reliefs were brought into safe storage in the basement of St. Augustine's Church and in the substructures of Klosterneuburg Monastery,[6] which meant that the antiquities from the former imperial collections had now left the Belvedere once and for all. It was not until 1978 that the finds from Ephesus finally become fully accessible to the public in the newly established Ephesos Museum in the Neue Burg wing of the Hofburg.

1 Coll. cat. Vienna 1978, pp. 7–10 and 36–41.
2 Coll. cat. Vienna, 1901.
3 Oberleitner 2009.
4 Coll. cat. Vienna 1905, p. III.
5 Coll. cat. Vienna 1927, p. IV.
6 Oberleitner 2009, p. 41, note 27.

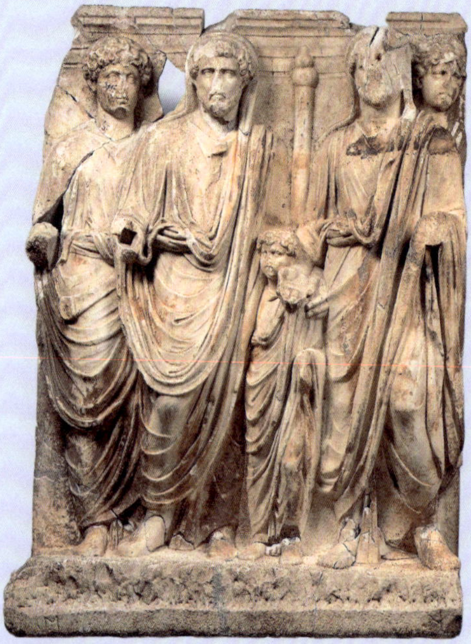

2

Fig. 2
The Roman emperors Hadrian, Antoninus Pius, Lucius Verus, and Marcus Aurelius from the Parthian Monument from Ephesus, middle of the 2nd century CE, Kunsthistorisches Museum Vienna, Collection of Greek and Roman Antiquities

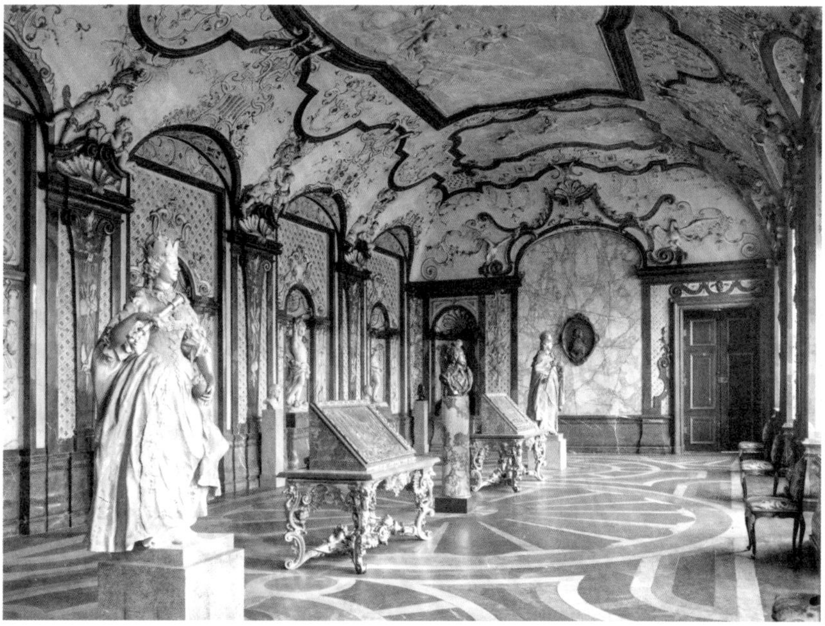

2

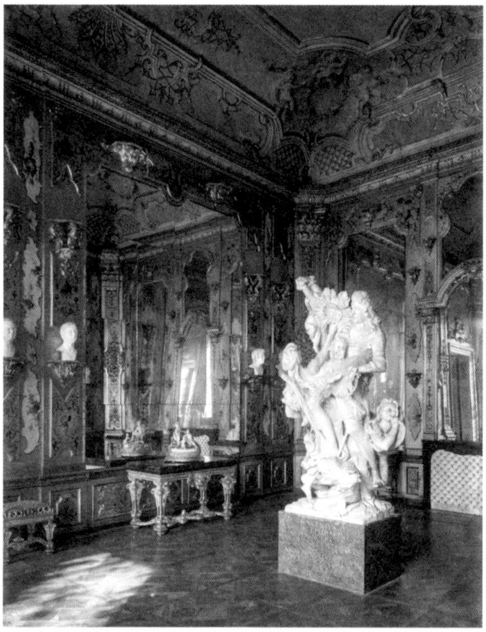

3

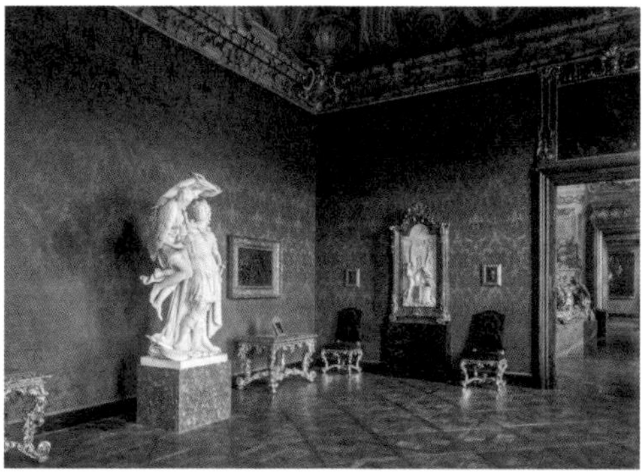

4

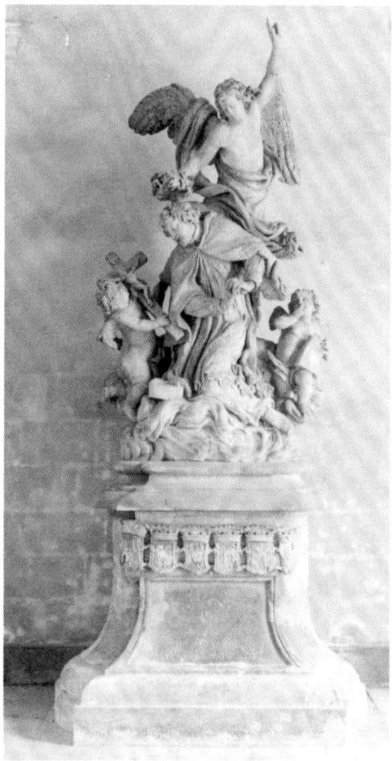

5

Fig. 2
Marble Gallery in the Lower Belvedere, 1923, Belvedere Image Archive, Vienna

Fig. 3
Mirror Room in the Lower Belvedere, 1923, Belvedere Image Archive, Vienna

Fig. 4
Yellow Room of the Baroque Museum in the Lower Belvedere, 1923, Belvedere Image Archive, Vienna

Fig. 5
Entrance to the Baroque Museum with the sculpture group by Johann Jakob Schoy, 1934, Belvedere Image Archive, Vienna

P. 210 BJÖRN BLAUENSTEINER — Origins of the Museum of Medieval Art

The Museum of Medieval Art in the Orangery of the Lower Belvedere opened on December 5, 1953, on the occasion of the fiftieth anniversary of the Austrian Gallery. But the idea of presenting medieval art in the Belvedere had quite a long prior history.

Friedrich Dörnhöffer (→ p. 370, fig. 9), the first director of the Modern Gallery, appointed in 1909, had already committed himself to the task of "presenting the development of Austrian art [...] in a museum setting without any chronological limitation."[1] Under Dörnhöffer, the Austrian State Gallery—as the museum was called after 1912 in reflection of this program—thus sought to acquire Austrian works of all eras and to lay the foundations for a medieval collection in this way. The first pre-Baroque purchase was *The Descent of the Holy Spirit* by the Master of Irrsdorf in 1910. This was followed in 1912 by Lucas Cranach's *Stigmatization of St. Francis* and in 1918 by fragments of Michael Pacher's *Salzburg Altarpiece*, which are still among the highlights of the collection.[2]

After World War I, the medieval holdings were transferred to the Kunsthistorisches Museum as part of Hans Tietze's reorganization of the federal museums. However, these new acquisitions from the recently renamed Austrian Gallery were not sufficient to establish the planned "department of early Austrian painting" there, as the former imperial painting collection had not contained many medieval Austrian works. The 1783 catalogue of its first public display in the Upper Belvedere lists only four works now part of today's medieval collection,[3] and, with the exception of the pictures brought to Vienna following the secularization of the Prince-Archbishopric of Salzburg in 1806/07,[4] no significant additions to the collection were made in the nineteenth century.

Gustav Glück, director of the Picture Gallery at the time, therefore added to the early Austrian holdings through systematic purchases.[5] The collection also benefited from the liquidation of court assets and the resulting incorporation of the pictures from Laxenburg, where Emperor Francis II/I had been collecting objects from all over Austria since 1799, particularly from dissolved monasteries,[6] in order to establish the "first—if only Romantic—collection of medieval Austrian art."[7] These acquisitions permitted the installation in 1934 of a "gallery of Austrian panel painting" in the Picture Gallery.[8] Between 1935 and 1942, the

1 Mitteilungen 1917, p. 2.
2 The Pacher panels had already been exhibited in the Vienna Künstlerhaus in 1918, together with other new acquisitions by the State Gallery; see Mitteilungen 1918, p. 16.
3 Swoboda 2013a, p. 241 (Urban Görtschacher, *Legend of Susanna*), p. 264 (Leonhard von Brixen, *Adoration of the Kings*; Master with the Barred Shield, *Adoration of the Kings*), and p. 267 (Passau painter, *St. Cyriacus*).
4 Pirckmayer 1872, p. 359 (no. 12: Conrad Laib, *Crucifixion of Christ*) and p. 360 (nos. 39–44: Master of Grossgmain, *Pretschlaipfer Triptych* and *Christ on the Cross*; Rueland Frueauf the Elder, *Salzburg Altarpiece*).
5 Deiters 2016, pp. 36–38, 57–58 and 79–82.
6 Hanzl 1998, pp. 35–47; the *Znaim Altarpiece* was also apparently sent to Laxenburg; see Gollinger 1828, pp. 103–04; Winkler/Kieslinger 1926/27, p. 398 (Ernst Winkler).
7 Coll. cat. Vienna 1971, p. 7 (Hans Aurenhammer).
8 Coll. cat. Vienna 1934b (quote p. 3).

museum also obtained a considerable number of Austrian sculptures through exchanges with the future Museum of Applied Arts, which formed the basis for a "collection of masterpieces of medieval Austrian sculpture" in the Kunsthistorisches Museum.[9]

After World War II, the young Austrian Republic sought to promote a new national identity, aiming in particular to dissociate itself from Germany and German nationalist ideology.[10] It is against this background that Karl Garzarolli-Thurnlackh, appointed director of the Austrian Gallery in 1947, was tasked by the Minister of Education with developing the Belvedere into a "museum of Austrian art."[11] Since the "extensive and very important art from medieval Austria [...] [had played] a significant and singular role" and called for "its own treatment by a museum," Garzarolli-Thurnlackh wrote several letters from 1951 onward, requesting the transfer of the medieval Austrian holdings from the Kunsthistorisches Museum to the Belvedere. He specifically asked for the "high art, in other words, painting and sculptures" from the Picture Gallery and the Collection of Sculpture, Arts and Crafts, but not for so-called "applied art." As a result, medieval glass painting and textiles remained at the Museum of Applied Arts. From a geographical point of view, "only works by artists whose œuvre was mainly created in or for Austria, who were born or lived in Austria, and, if no such information was available, whose works were made in Austria" were to be considered. Austria was defined as the present-day federal territory including Salzburg, along with certain adjacent territories formerly belonging and still closely linked to Austria, in particular South Tyrol and Carniola. Despite various objections by the collection curators at the Kunsthistorisches Museum, a decision by the Council of Ministers was made in January 1953 and an implementation decree passed.[12] In April of that year, Garzarolli-Thurnlackh reported to the minister that the Kunsthistorisches Museum would make available "all relevant works," with the exception of two Huber panels. The *Znaim Altarpiece* would also be transferred in place of the hotly disputed *Krumau Madonna*.[13]

The Museum of Medieval Art was officially opened in the Orangery in December 1953. The inaugural presentation consisted of just over one hundred works, chosen—with the exception of some permanent loans no longer in the collection[14]—from objects transferred from the Kunsthistorisches Museum (figs. 1–2).[15] These works still form the basis of the collection today, which focuses on paintings and sculptures created within the territory of present-day Austria and adjacent territories between 1200 and 1600.

In subsequent decades, the collection was enlarged through purchases and permanent loans (figs. 3–4),[16] catalogued,[17] and contextualized through dedicated special exhibitions.[18] In 2007, the medieval art was

9 Coll. cat. Vienna 1935 (quote p. 4).

10 On initiatives to develop an Austrian identity in the years after 1945, see Bruckmüller 1998, pp. 375–80.

11 Letter, Karl Garzarolli-Thurnlackh to BMU Ernst Kolb May 15, 1952; AdB, Zl. 719/1952. On the establishment of a Museum of Mediavel Austrian Art see also AdB, Zl. 512/1953; OeStA/AdR, UKW BMU, Kunstakten, SM 327.

12 Council of Ministers decision of January 13, 1953, Zl. 93.221-II/6/52; Federal Ministry of Education decree 1953 (letter to Karl Garzarolli-Thurnlackh) January 18, 1953, Zl. 22.312-II/6/53. see AdB, Zl. 512/1953.

13 Still in 1955, Garzarolli-Thurnlackh argued in a letter to the Kunsthistorisches Museum that the creator of the *Krumau Madonna* "emigrated from Bohemia as a German-speaking artist during the Hussite Wars" and then worked in Vienna or Salzburg; see AdB, Zl. 45/1955. The *Krumau Madonna* remained in the Kunsthistorisches Museum.

14 Coll. cat. Vienna 1953b, nos. 24, 33, 40, 61, 82, 101, and 103.

15 The list comprised 113 paintings, 71 sculptures, and the *Znaim* and *Obervellach Altarpieces*; AdB, Zl. 45/1955.

16 See esp. exh. cat. Vienna 1959, pp. 1–8; coll. cat. Vienna 1981, pp. 5–9; exh. cat. Vienna 1999, pp. 14–17.

17 Coll. cat. Vienna 1971; coll. cat. Vienna 1981.

18 See esp. exh. cat. Vienna 1969; exh. cat. Vienna 1970; exh. cat. Vienna 1973; exh. cat. Vienna 1983; exh. cat. Vienna 1997; exh. cat. Vienna 2013; exh. cat. Vienna 2017; exh. cat. Vienna 2021. In 1992, an exhibition series was inaugurated in collaboration with the Federal Monuments Authority, which until 2015 comprised a total of twenty-five presentations in the Belvedere of medieval artworks following their restoration.

removed from the Orangery in the course of restructuring to make room for special exhibitions. A selection of masterpieces from the collection is now on display in the west wing of the ground floor of the Upper Belvedere. The Palace Stables, where medieval art had already been presented in 1994 at a special exhibition devoted to the Master of Grosslobming, now houses a study collection, where most of the remaining works have been accessible since 2007 (fig. 5).[19]

After the sixteenth-century collection was significantly enhanced through the incorporation of the Maurer collection and re-examined in preparation for the *Age of Dürer* exhibition,[20] the "oldest" department in the Belvedere now bears the name Middle Ages and Renaissance. The octagonal room in the west wing of the ground floor of the Upper Belvedere is reserved today exclusively for art of the early modern period. The rearranged collection officially opened in 2023, a year in which a number of anniversaries are being celebrated, including the seventieth anniversary of the continuous presentation of medieval art in the Belvedere.

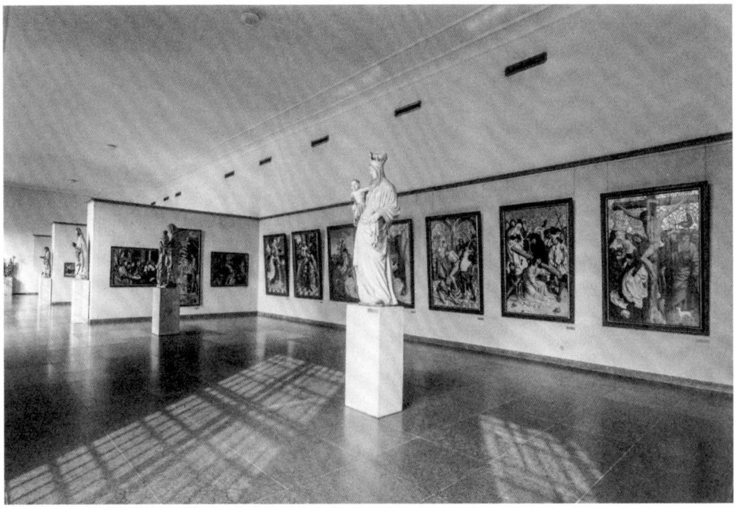

1

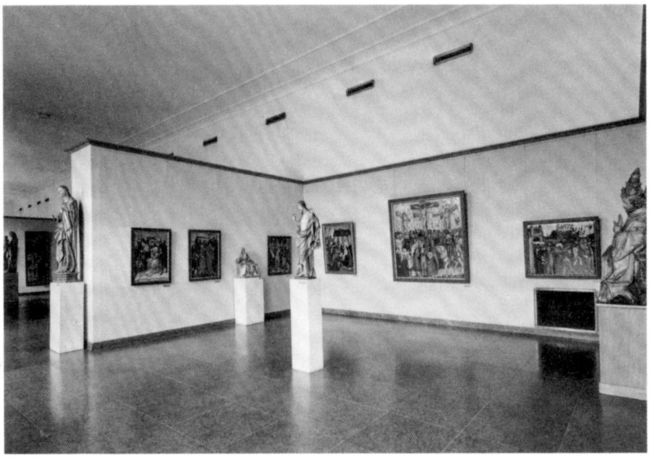

2

19 Exh. cat. Vienna 1994.
20 Exh. cat. Vienna 2021.

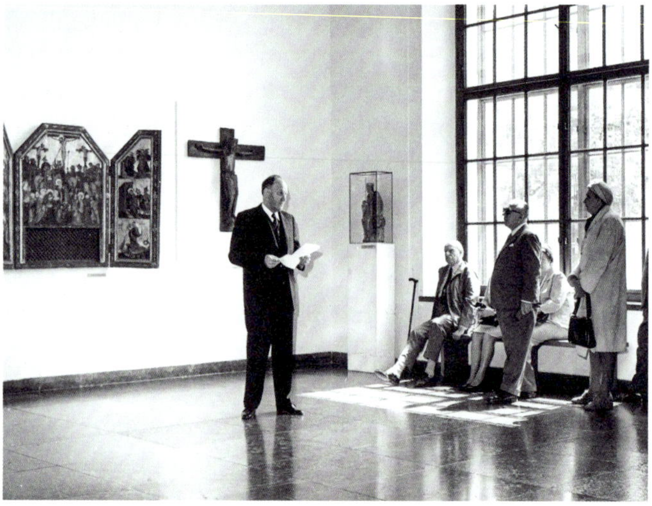

3

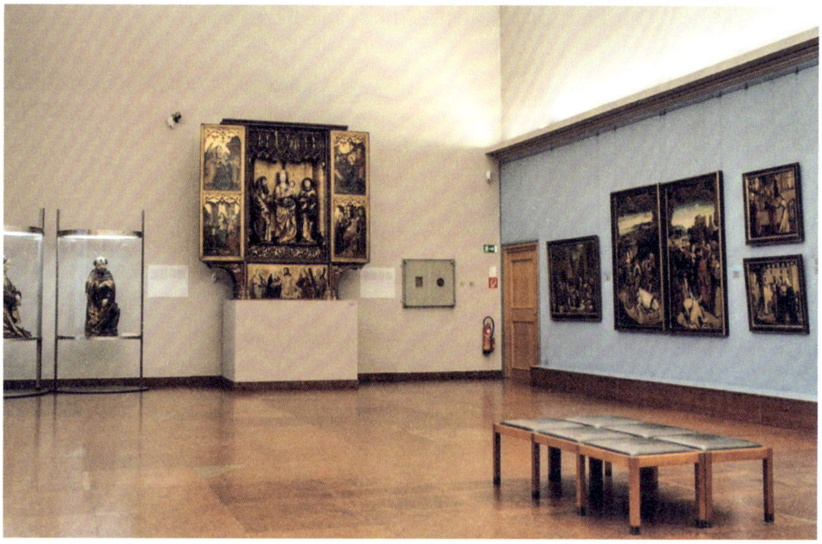

4

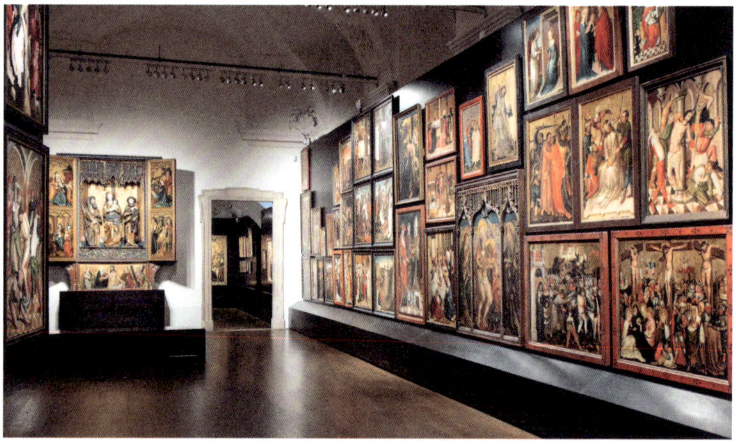

5

Fig. 1
Museum of Medieval Austrian Art in the Orangery of the Belvedere, 1960, photo: Julius Scherb, Belvedere Image Archive, Vienna

Fig. 2
Museum of Medieval Austrian Art in the Orangery of the Belvedere, 1960, photo: Julius Scherb, Belvedere Image Archive, Vienna

Fig. 3
Museum of Medieval Austrian Art in the Orangery of the Belvedere, presentation of the Roman crucifix, 1973, photo: Ekkehard Ritter, Belvedere Image Archive, Vienna

Fig. 4
Museum of Medieval Austrian Art in the Orangery of the Belvedere, with *Saint Joseph* by Hans Klocker, acquired through an exchange in 1987, and the Rogendorf altarpiece, since 1995 on permanent loan from the Kunsthistorisches Museum, after 1995/ before 2007, Belvedere Image Archive, Vienna

Fig. 5
Study Collection Middle Ages and Renaissance in the Palace Stables, 2023, Belvedere, Vienna

Chapter IV

The Museum during the Nazi Period

1938–1945

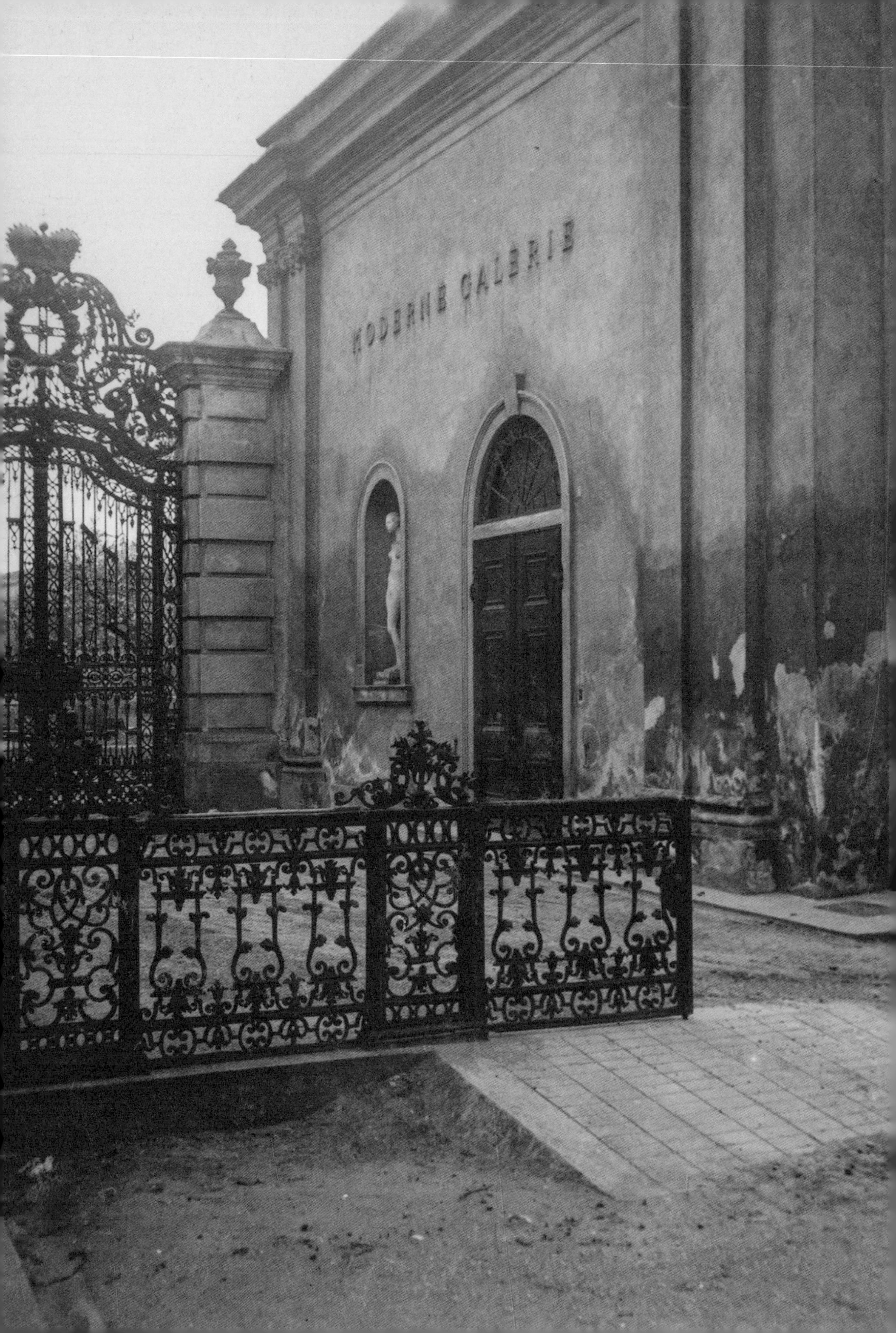
MODERNE GALERIE

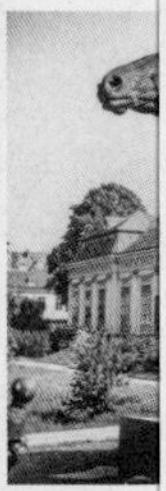

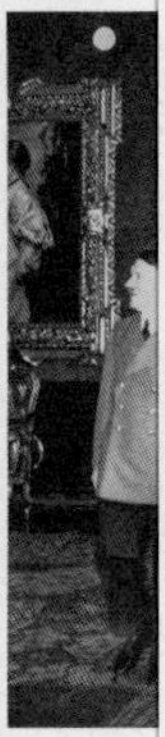

Chapter IV
The Museum during
the Nazi Period

1938–1945

←
Entrance
dern Gall
Orangery
Belveder
Austrian
Vienna

To avoid complaints by holders of annual season tickets, I shall remind you of my decree of January 10, 1941, Z/GK. 148-c of 1941. According to this, these tickets entitle their holders to visit museums, art exhibitions, and collections without restriction and free of charge during the calendar year 1941.

I request again that you instruct your attendants and ticketing staff [...] accordingly and impress upon them that the annual season tickets are also valid on Sundays, when museums, art exhibitions, and collections are open to everyone, and during guided tours, albeit without in this case entitling holders to take part in such tours free of charge.

— Reich governor in Vienna to the director's office of the Austrian Gallery, February 23, 1941, AdB, Zl. 82/1941

16

"Degenerate Art"

Christoph Zuschlag

"Degenerate art" was *the* central propaganda term used by the Nazis in their campaign against modern art.[1] It was the title of two traveling exhibitions (1933–1937 and 1937–1941) and was given as the reason for extensive seizures in German museums (1937). The fight against the Modernist aesthetic was an element of National Socialist art policy, which served exclusively to disseminate Nazi racial ideology. In reality, however, the intellectual and ideological background to this art policy dates back to the nineteenth century.

One of the "chamber of horrors" art exhibitions, shown in several German cities soon after the Nazis came to power, was the *Degenerate Art* traveling exhibition in September 1933, compiled from the holdings of the City Museum in Dresden. It was put together, among others, by the anti-Modernist Nazi artist Richard Müller, who became director of the Dresden Academy of Art in March 1933 and in this function dismissed Otto Dix as professor. Many of the artists pilloried in this exhibition, among them Oskar Kokoschka, were former students or teachers at the Dresden Academy. Between 1934 and 1937, the Dresden exhibition visited twelve other cities. In 1937 it was integrated in the Munich exhibition of the same name, which had been commissioned by the Ministry of Propaganda and opened on July 19, 1937, one day after the start of the *Grosse Deutsche Kunstausstellung*. It comprised some 750 works and was quite deliberately designed as a contrast to the exhibition of traditional German art. Even though the exhibition featured a wide range of modern art styles, the

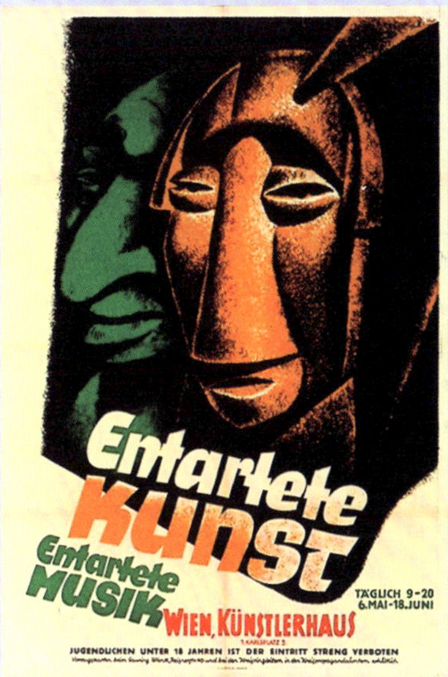

1

Fig. 1
Poster for the *Degenerate Art* exhibition, Künstlerhaus Vienna, May 6 to June 18, 1939, Austrian National Library, Vienna

Expressionists were targeted with particular vehemence.

After its opening show in Munich, the Ministry of Propaganda sent the exhibition on the road. Its content changed constantly as a result of the "disposal" of seized objects that began in 1938. By 1941 it had been shown in sixteen cities in the German Reich, including Salzburg (1938) and Vienna (1939), following Austria's annexation to Nazi Germany (fig. 1).

On March 22, 1938, Count Klaus von Baudissin, provisional director of the culture department in the Reich Ministry of Science, Education, and Culture, visited the Modern Gallery, the Austrian Gallery's collection of modern art, whose closure had been ordered the previous day. He noted in his report that it contained "only a few works of strikingly degenerate art," but recommended that works by Jewish artists, including Max Liebermann, be removed and placed in storage. He also anticipated seizures "as [...] in the previous year in Germany."[2] However, such seizures did not take place in Vienna, nor in other Austrian cities, presumably because the collections contained only relatively few works by supposedly "degenerate" artists.

1 Zuschlag 1995; Zuschlag 2022b.

2 Both quotes from Mayer M. 2005, p. 65; see also Mayer M. 2016.

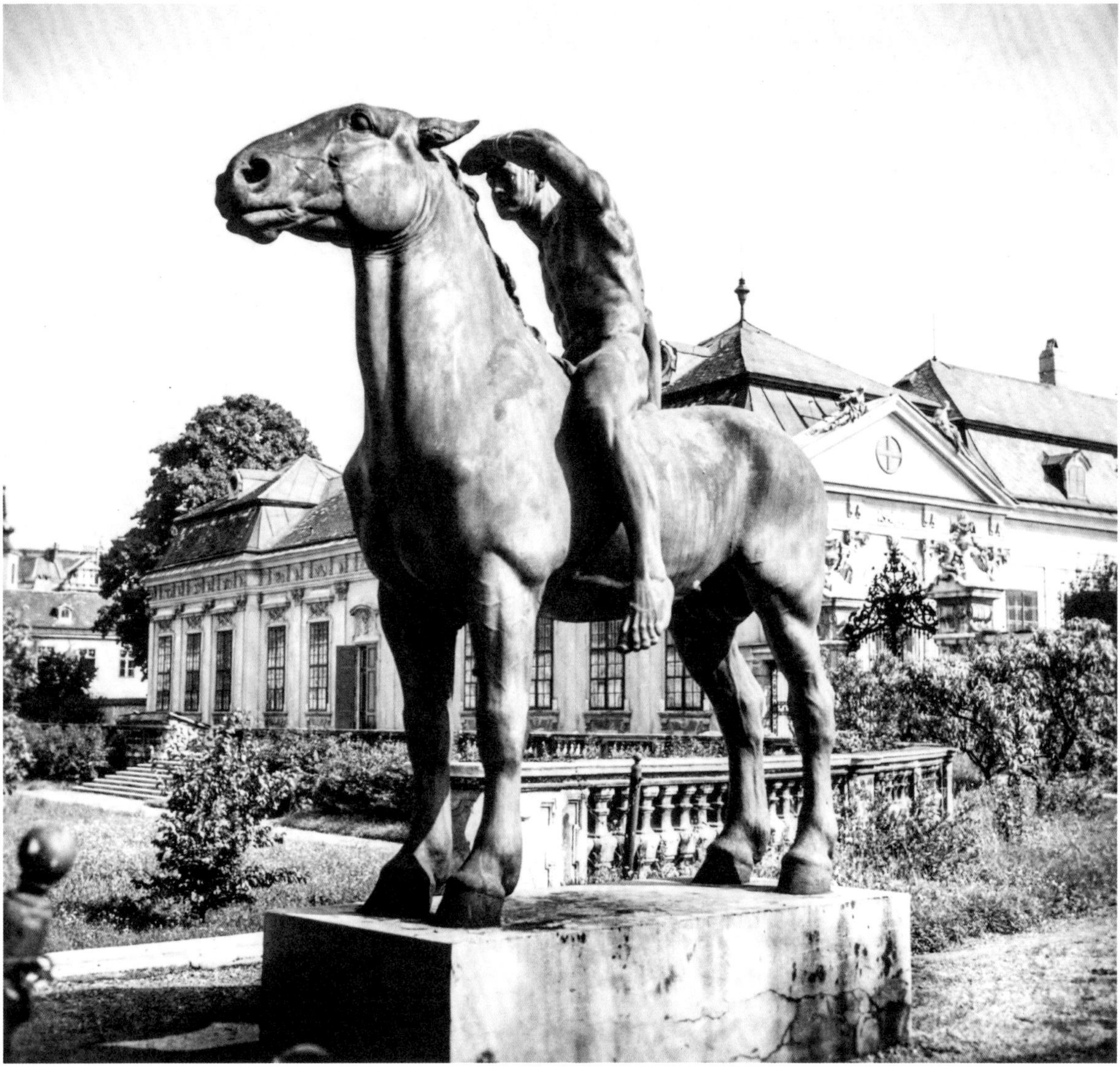

The Naked Rider (1908) by Josef Müllner in the Privy Garden of the Lower Belvedere, after 1936

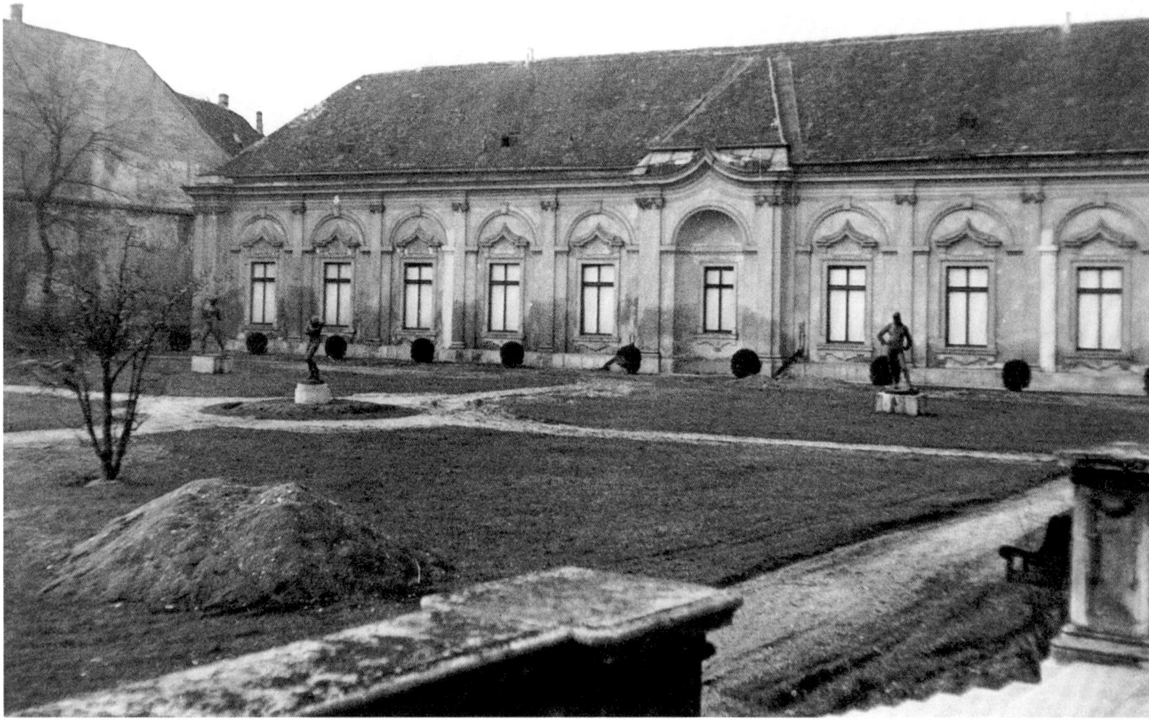

Privy Garden with the Orangery of the Lower Belvedere, 1938/39

Besuchsordnung der öffentlichen Sammlungen in Wien

Ganzjährig **Ganzjährig**

Name der Anstalt	Montag	Dienstag	Mittwoch	Donnerstag	Freitag	Samstag	Sonntag	Anmerkung
Kunsthistorisches Museum A. Hauptgebäude, I., Burgring 5 (B 37 4 37) a) Antikensammlung b) Ägyptische Sammlung c) Sammlung für Plastik u. Kunstgewerbe d) Gemäldegalerie e) Münzkabinett	Geschlossen	9–14 Eintritt 10 Rpf.	9–14 Eintritt 10 Rpf.	9–14 Eintritt 10 Rpf.	9–14 Eintritt 10 Rpf.	9–13 Eintritt 10 Rpf.	9–13 Eintritt 10 Rpf.	
		Amtliche Führungen im Hauptgebäude täglich 10 Uhr						
B. Neue Burg („Corps de Logis“) I., Heldenplatz (R 22 1 94) a) Waffensammlung	9–14 Eintritt 10 Rpf.	Geschlossen	9–14 Eintritt 10 Rpf.	Geschlossen	9–14 Eintritt 10 Rpf.	Geschlossen	9–13 Eintritt 10 Rpf.	
b) Sonderausstellungen (im Halbrund)								
C. Alte Burg Zugang vom Schweizerhof (R 23 9 42) Schatzkammern: (Wiedereröffnung, bzw. Eröffnung Herbst 1939) a) Weltliche u. geistliche Schatzkammern b) Sammlungen des Deutschen Ritterordens	9–14 Eintritt 10 Rpf.	9–14 Eintritt 10 Rpf.	9–14 Eintritt 10 Rpf.	9–14 Eintritt 10 Rpf.	Geschlossen	9–13 Eintritt 10 Rpf.	9–13 Eintritt 10 Rpf.	Besuchsstunden an Feiertagen wie an Sonntagen Am 1. Jänner, 13. März, 1. Mai, Oster- und Pfingstsonntag, 9. November, 24. und 25. Dezember geschlossen
D. Palais Pallavicini, I., Josefsplatz 5 Sammlung alter Musikinstrumente (Eröffnung Herbst 1939)	10–14 Eintritt 10 Rpf.	10–14 Eintritt 10 Rpf.	10–14 Eintritt 10 Rpf.	10–14 Eintritt 10 Rpf.	Geschlossen	10–13 Eintritt 10 Rpf.	10–13 Eintritt 10 Rpf.	
E. Unteres Belvedere, III., Rennweg 4 Reliefs aus Ephesos Prunkstall des Prinzen Eugen (Anmeldung beim Torwart)	9–18 Eintritt 10 Rpf.	9–18 Eintritt 10 Rpf.	9–18 Eintritt 10 Rpf.	9–18 Eintritt 10 Rpf.	9–18 Eintritt 10 Rpf.	9–18 Eintritt 10 Rpf.	9–13 Eintritt 10 Rpf.	
F. Theseustempel im Volksgarten Antike Skulpturen aus Ephesos	Geschlossen	Geschlossen	Geschlossen	Geschlossen	1. April bis 30. Sept. 14–17 Eintritt 10 Rpf.	Geschlossen	1. April bis 30. Sept. 10–13 Eintritt 10 Rpf.	
G. Schloß Schönbrunn, XIII. (A 45 7 17) Sammlung historischer Wagen (Wagenburg)	10–17 Eintritt 10 Rpf.	10–17 Eintritt 10 Rpf.	10–17 Eintritt 10 Rpf.	10–17 Eintritt 10 Rpf.	10–17 Eintritt 10 Rpf.	10–17 Eintritt 10 Rpf.	10–17 Eintritt 10 Rpf.	
H. Hauptmünzamt, III., Am Heumarkt 1 Sammlung historischer Prägestempel	Zugänglich nach Anmeldung im Münzkabinett (siehe A, e), Eintritt frei							
Österreichische Galerie (U 16 310) a) Barockmuseum, III., Rennweg 6 (Unteres Belvedere) b) Galerie des 19. Jahrhunderts, III., Prinz Eugen-Straße 27 (Oberes Belvedere)	Geschlossen	10–13 14–16 Eintritt 10 Rpf.	10–13 14–16 Eintritt 10 Rpf.	10–13 14–16 Eintritt 10 Rpf.	10–13 14–16 Eintritt 10 Rpf.	10–13 14–16 Eintritt 10 Rpf.	9–13 Eintritt 10 Rpf.	Feiertagsordnung wie oben
c) Moderne Galerie, III., Rennweg 6 (Orangerie)	Geschlossen	Geschlossen	Geschlossen	Geschlossen	Geschlossen	Geschlossen	Geschlossen	
Sammlungen der Akademie der bildenden Künste I., Schillerplatz 3 a) Bibliothek und Kupferstichsammlung	14–18 Eintritt frei	14–18 Eintritt frei	14–18 Eintritt frei	14–18 Eintritt frei	14–18 Eintritt frei	9–13 Eintritt frei	Geschlossen	
	An Schulferialtagen und im August geschlossen, im September 9–13							
b) Gemäldegalerie	9–13 Eintritt 10 Rpf.	Geschlossen	9–13 Eintritt 10 Rpf.	9–13 Eintritt 10 Rpf.	9–13 Eintritt 10 Rpf.	9–13 Eintritt 10 Rpf.	10–13 Eintritt 10 Rpf.	
c) Museum der Gipsabgüsse	Bis auf weiteres geschlossen. Zutritt nur gegen vorherige Anmeldung im Rektorat							
d) R. v. Albrecht-Hönigschmiedsche Kunstsammlung	Geschlossen	Geschlossen	Geschlossen	Geschlossen	Geschlossen	9–13 Eintritt 10 Rpf.	Geschlossen	
Naturhistorisches Museum I., Burgring 7 (B 37 203) A. Hauptgebäude a) Mineralogisch-petrographische Sammlung b) Geologisch-paläontologische Sammlung c) Prähistorische Sammlung d) Anthropologische Sammlung e) Zoologische Sammlung	9–14 Eintritt 10 Rpf.	Geschlossen	9–14 Eintritt 10 Rpf.	9–14 Eintritt 10 Rpf.	9–14 Eintritt 10 Rpf.	9–13 Eintritt 10 Rpf.	9–13 Eintritt 10 Rpf.	Feiertagsordnung wie oben
B. Museum für Völkerkunde I., Heldenpl., Neue Burg, Ringstraßenflügel (Zugang vom Heldenplatz)	9–14 Eintritt 10 Rpf.	Geschlossen	9–14 Eintritt 10 Rpf.	Geschlossen	9–14 Eintritt 10 Rpf.	Geschlossen	9–13 Eintritt 10 Rpf.	
Nationalbibliothek a) Druckschriften- und Zeitschriftenlesesaal I., Josefsplatz 1 b) Handschriftensammlung, I., Josefsplatz 1	9–19	9–19	9–19	9–19	9–19	9–19	Geschlossen	An Sonn- und Feiertagen ist die Nationalbibliothek für Leser geschlossen. Führungen (insbesondere größerer Gesellschaften und von Schulen) durch die Bibliothek über vorherige Anmeldung bei der Generaldirektion. Schüler und Studierende über Ansuchen Eintritt frei. Gruppenführungen an Sonntagen bei vorheriger Anmeldung gegen Sondergebühr. Vom 15. Juli bis 15. Sept. Besuchszeit 9–14
	Führungen im Prunksaale u. durch die ständige Ausstellung der Handschriftensammlung an Werktagen tägl. um 11 Uhr, Eintritt 10 Rpf.							
c) Musiksammlung, I., Augustinerbastei 6 (Albrechtsrampe) d) Kartensammlung, I., Josefsplatz 1 e) Papyrussammlung (griechische und orientalische Abteilung), I., Augustinerbastei 6 (Albrechtsrampe) f) Porträtsammlung (ehemalige Familien-Fideikommißbibliothek), I., Neue Burg g) Theatersammlung, I., Josefsplatz 1 *) (Goethe-Museum siehe unten)	9–15^{30}	9–15^{30}	9–15^{30}	9–15^{30}	9–15^{30}	9–13^{30}	Geschlossen	Führungen über Anmeldung beim Abteilungsvorstand (vom 15. Juli bis 15. Sept. keine Führungen) *) In der Theatersammlung auch Auskunft über Besuch des Museums der Staatstheater
Graphische Sammlung Albertina I., Augustinerbastei 6, Albrechtsrampe (R 23 0 69) Studiensaal	16–19 Eintritt 10 Rpf.	10–14 Eintritt 10 Rpf.	16–19 Eintritt 10 Rpf.	10–14 Eintritt 10 Rpf.	10–14 Eintritt 10 Rpf.	10–13 Eintritt 10 Rpf.	Geschlossen	An Feiertagen geschlossen. Vom 15. Juli bis 31. August ist der Studiensaal geschlossen. Die Ausstellung ist während dieser Zeit von 10 bis 13 Uhr geöffnet
Ausstellung	10-13 16-19 Eintritt 10 Rpf.	10–13 Eintritt 10 Rpf.	10-13 16-19 Eintritt 10 Rpf.	10–13 Eintritt 10 Rpf.	10–13 Eintritt 10 Rpf.	10-13 16-19 Eintritt 10 Rpf.	11 Uhr Führungsvortrag. Eintritt und Führung 70 Rpf.	
Staatliches Kunstgewerbemuseum (chem. Österreichisches Museum für Kunst und Industrie) I., Stubenring 5 (B 53 500)	Geschlossen Wenn ein Feiertag: 9–13 Eintritt 10 Rpf. Fällt der Montag auf einen Feiertag, so ist das Museum an dem darauffolgenden Dienstag geschlossen	9–14 Eintritt 10 Rpf.	9–14 Eintritt 10 Rpf.	9–14 Eintritt 10 Rpf.	9–14 Eintritt 10 Rpf.	9–14 Eintritt 10 Rpf.	9–13 Eintritt 10 Rpf.	Die Museumsbibliothek ist zu den gleichen Besuchsstunden bei freiem Eintritt geöffnet. Fachgelehrte, Künstler, Lehrkräfte und Studierende der kunstwissenschaftlichen und gewerblichen Lehranstalten haben gegen Vorweisung ihrer Legitimation, Schulen unter Führung von Lehrern an allen Besuchstagen freien Eintritt. Jeden Sonntag um 11 Uhr eine wissenschaftliche Führung
Ausstellung des Haus-, Hof- und Staatsarchivs I., Minoritenplatz 1	9–13 Eintritt 10 Rpf.	9–13 Eintritt 10 Rpf.	9–13 Eintritt 10 Rpf.	9–13 Eintritt 10 Rpf.	9–13 Eintritt 10 Rpf.	9–13 Eintritt 10 Rpf.	Sonn- u. Feiertag 10–13 Eintritt 10 Rpf.	Führungen an Werktagen für Gemeinschaftsbesuche nach vorheriger Anmeldung Schulen frei
Heeresmuseum X., Arsenal a) Heereskundliche Sammlung mit Ruhmeshalle b) Gemäldesammlung c) Heerestechnische Sammlung d) Österreich-Ungarns Heer im Weltkrieg	1. April bis 30. Sept. 9–17 1. Okt. bis 30. März 9–16 Eintritt 10 Rpf.	Ganzjährig 9–13 Eintritt 10 Rpf.	1. April bis 30. Sept. 9–17 1. Okt. bis 30. März 9–16 Eintritt 10 Rpf.	Ganzjährig 9–13 Eintritt 10 Rpf.	1. April bis 30. Sept. 9–17 1. Okt. bis 30. März 9–16 Eintritt 10 Rpf.	Geschlossen (ausgenommen Feiertage)	Ganzjährig 9–13 Eintritt 10 Rpf.	Am 1. Jänner, 13. März, Ostersonntag, 1. Mai, 9. November und 25. Dezember geschlossen
Spanische Reitschule I., Hofburg Reitstall	12–16 Eintritt 30 Rpf.	12–16 Eintritt 30 Rpf.	12–16 Eintritt 30 Rpf.	12–16 Eintritt 30 Rpf.	12–16 Eintritt 30 Rpf.	12–16 Eintritt 30 Rpf.	9–16 Eintritt 30 Rpf.	Auch an Feiertagen
Hoftafel- und Silberkammer I., Hofburg (Michaelertrakt)	Geschlossen	9–14 Eintritt 10 Rpf.	Geschlossen	9–14 Eintritt 10 Rpf.	Geschlossen	Geschlossen	9–13 Eintritt 10 Rpf.	
Schauräume der Hofburg	9-12 14-16 Eintritt 70 Rpf.	9-12 14-16 Eintritt 70 Rpf.	9-12 14-16 Eintritt 70 Rpf.	9-12 14-16 Eintritt 70 Rpf.	9-12 14-16 Eintritt 70 Rpf.	9–12 Eintritt 70 Rpf.	9–12 Eintritt 70 Rpf.	**Allgemeine Führung:** Kinder bis zu 14 Jahren in Begleitung Erwachsener 30 Rpf. Bei gemeinschaftl. Besichtigung und vorheriger Anmeldung zahlen Schulen mit Öffentlichkeitsrecht 10 Rpf., Vereine, Körperschaften und Wohltätigkeitsunternehmungen 30 Rpf., Reisegesellschaften mit mindestens 20 Teilnehmern 52 Rpf. für jeden Teilnehmer **Sonderführungen** (nur an Wochentagen) pro Person 1,33 RM. Kassaschluß eine halbe Stunde vor Ablauf der Besuchszeiten. Kinder unter 6 Jahren haben keinen Zutritt. Bei Naßwetter sind die Schauräume gesperrt
Schauräume des Schlosses Schönbrunn	1. Mai bis 30. Sept. 9–17 1. Okt. bis 30. April 9–16 Eintritt 70 Rpf.	1. Mai bis 30. Sept. 9–17 1. Okt. bis 30. April 9–16 Eintritt 70 Rpf.	1. Mai bis 30. Sept. 9–17 1. Okt. bis 30. April 9–16 Eintritt 70 Rpf.	1. Mai bis 30. Sept. 9–17 1. Okt. bis 30. April 9–16 Eintritt 70 Rpf.	1. Mai bis 30. Sept. 9–17 1. Okt. bis 30. April 9–16 Eintritt 70 Rpf.	1. Mai bis 30. Sept. 9–17 1. Okt. bis 30. April 9–16 Eintritt 70 Rpf.	1. Mai bis 30. Sept. 9–17 1. Okt. bis 30. April 9–16 Eintritt 70 Rpf.	
Schönbrunner Tiergarten	Ganzjährig geöffnet von 9 Uhr bis zur Zeit der Parksperre (Einbruch der Dunkelheit). Eintrittspreis 70 Rpf., Kinder bis zu 14 Jahren in Begleitung Erwachsener und Militär sowie Gliederungen der Partei in Uniform 30 Rpf. Bei gemeinschaftlicher Besichtigung zahlen Schulen mit Öffentlichkeitsrecht und Kindergärten 20 Rpf. Vereinsbesuche nach vorheriger Anmeldung 30 Rpf., Reisegesellschaften mit mindestens 20 Teilnehmern 50 Rpf. für jeden Teilnehmer, KdF-Mitglieder bei gruppenweisem Besuch 10 Rpf.							Führungen finden nicht statt. Kassaschluß eine halbe Stunde vor Ablauf der Besuchszeiten
Schönbrunner Palmenhaus	Ganzjährig geöffnet von 9 Uhr bis zum Eintritt der Dunkelheit. Eintrittspreis: Erwachsene 40 Rpf., Kinder bis zu 14 Jahren in Begleitung Erwachsener und Militär 20 Rpf., Vereine, Körperschaften, Wohltätigkeitsunternehmungen bei gemeinschaftlicher Besichtigung und vorheriger Anmeldung pro Person 20 Rpf., Schulen pro Person 10 Rpf., Herbergen 5 Rpf. KdF-Mitglieder bei Einzelbesuch 20 Rpf., bei gruppenweisem Besuch gegen vorherige Anmeldung 10 Rpf., bei Sonderschauen 50 Prozent Ermäßigung							
Schönbrunner Kammergarten	9–Einbruch der Dunkelheit Eintritt 15 Rpf.	9–Einbruch der Dunkelheit Eintritt 15 Rpf.	9–Einbruch der Dunkelheit Eintritt 15 Rpf.	9–Einbruch der Dunkelheit Eintritt 15 Rpf.	9–Einbruch der Dunkelheit Eintritt 15 Rpf.	9–Einbruch der Dunkelheit Eintritt 15 Rpf.	9–Einbruch der Dunkelheit Eintritt 15 Rpf.	Kinder in Begleitung von Erwachsenen 8 Rpf.

Visitor regulations for the public collections in Vienna, June 1939, MAK – Museum of Applied Arts, Library and Works on Paper Collection

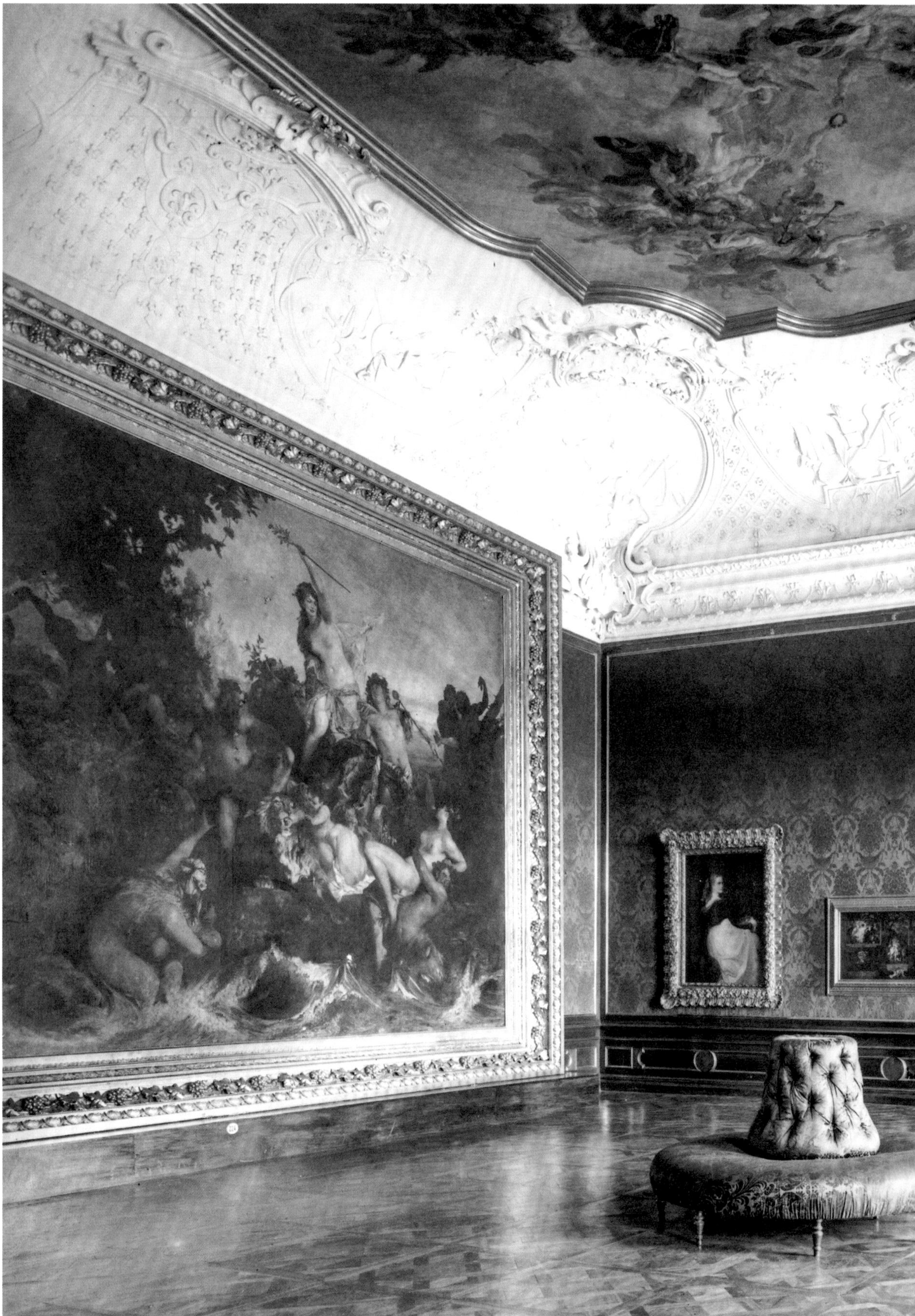

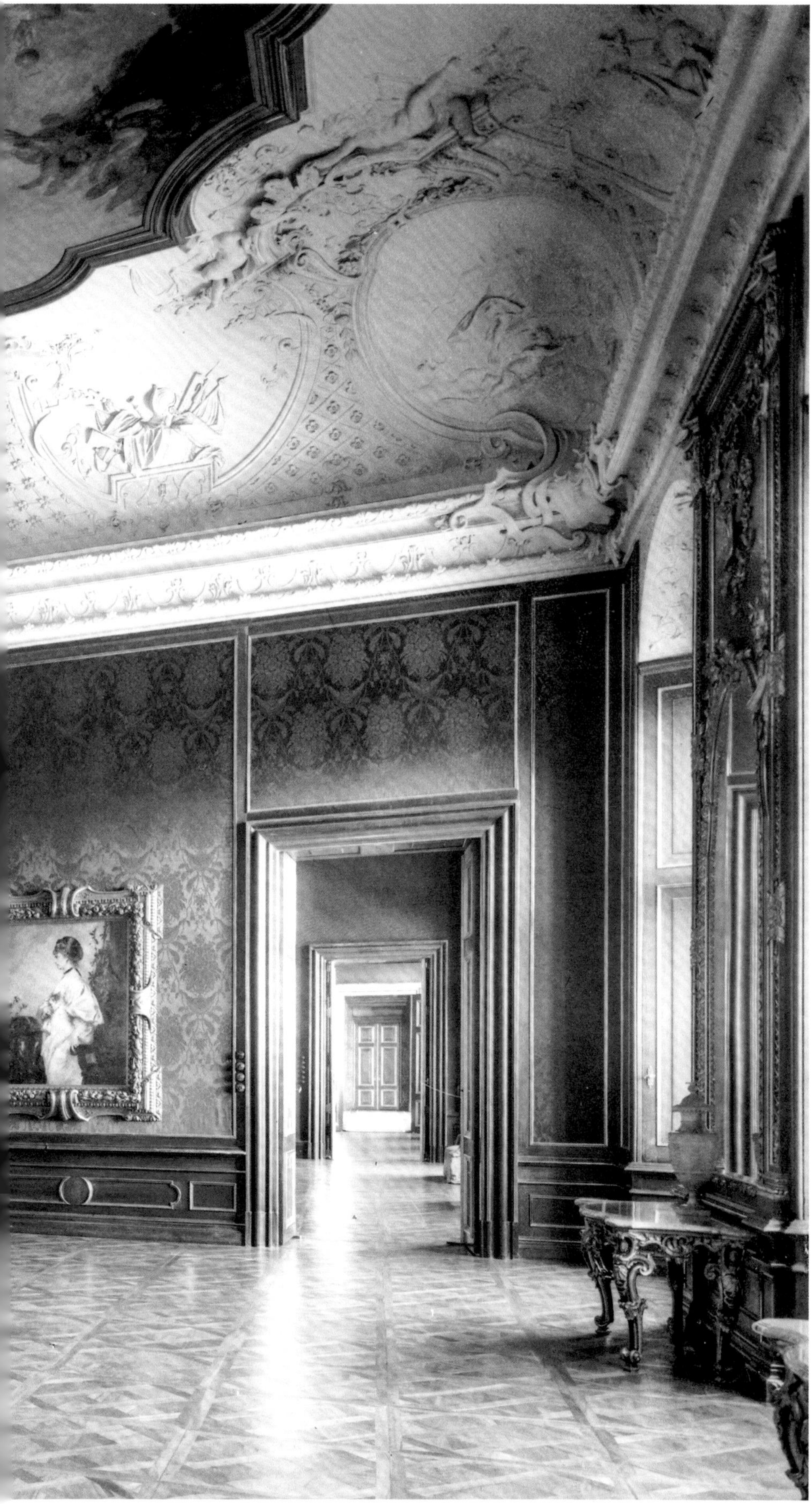

Makart Room in the Upper Belvedere with the painting *Triumph of Ariadne* and portraits by Hans Makart, before 1944

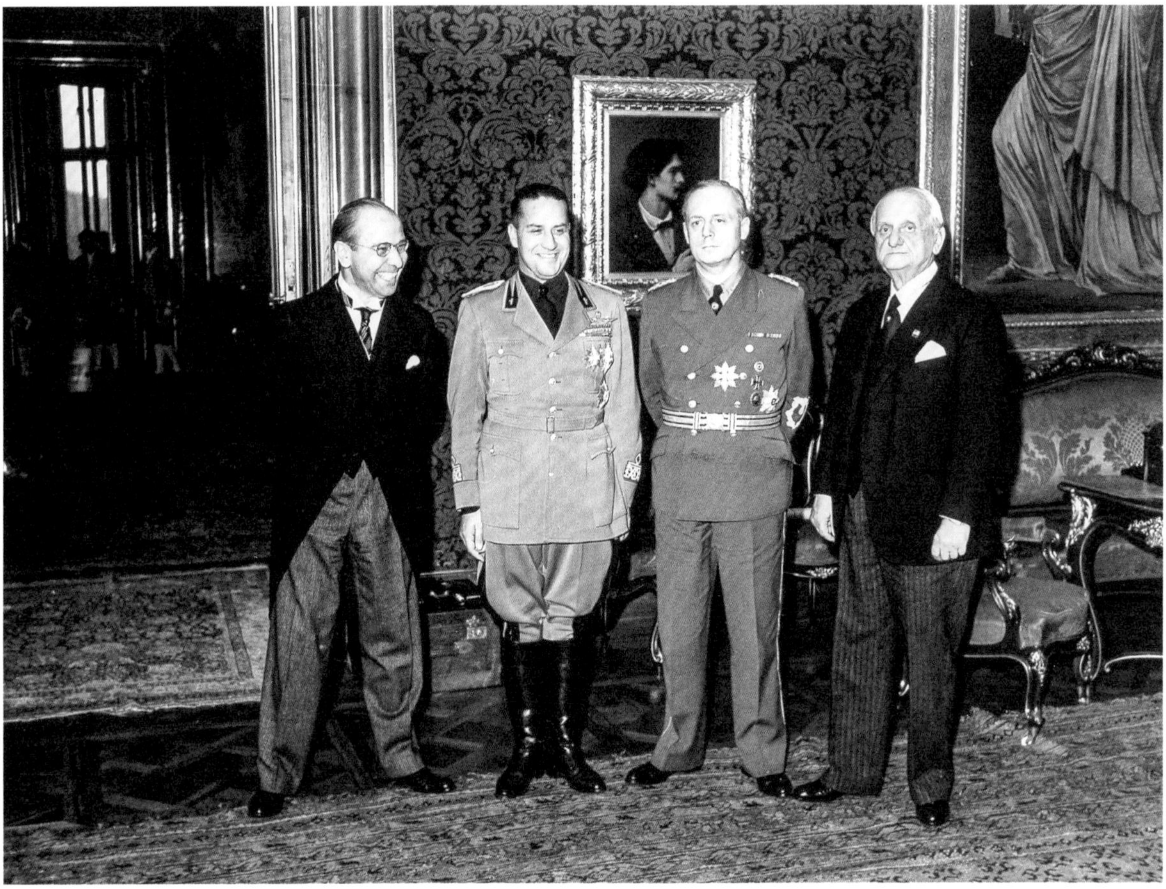

↑
First Vienna Arbitration Award in the Upper Belvedere; from l. to r., František Chvalkovský, Galeazzo Ciano, Joachim von Ribbentrop, and Koloman von Kánya, in the background *Self-Portrait with Cigarette* and *Orpheus and Eurydice* by Anselm Feuerbach, November 2, 1938

→ p. 231
From l. to r.: Adolf Hitler, Galeazzo Ciano, Saburō Kurusu, Pál Teleki von Szék, Stefan von Csáky, and Joachim von Ribbentrop at the reception in the Upper Belvedere on the occasion of Hungary's accession to the Tripartite Pact between the German Reich, Japan, and Italy, November 20, 1940

(17)

The Reich Chamber of Fine Arts, Vienna Office

Sabine Plakolm-Forsthuber

After the annexation of Austria to the German Reich in March 1938, the laws already existing in Germany were introduced in Austria. Among them was the Reich Chamber of Culture Law, which had defined cultural policy in Germany since 1933. The forced alignment of all artists with the National Socialist ideology marked the start of the Nazification and state control of German culture. The Reich Chamber of Fine Arts (RdbK) was one of the seven sections (literature, film, music, theater, press, and radio were the others) of the Reich Chamber of Culture, which was answerable to the Reich Minister of Public Enlightenment and Propaganda, Joseph Goebbels. The RdbK, headed between 1933 and 1945 by Eugen Hönig, Adolf Ziegler, and Wilhelm Kreis, was the central administrative body for artists in the Third Reich. Membership in it was a prerequisite for being allowed to practice art. Applicants were subject to a strict admission procedure that verified not only their artistic ability but also their "origin" and political reliability. Artists of Jewish origin, political opponents, and representatives of a modern-liberal approach to art had no chance of being admitted. Those whose applications had been rejected were banned from working, and compliance with this ban was enforced by the Gestapo. Exemptions were rare. In this way, the Nazi regime kept a tight control on the arts and was able to shape the nation's creative output in accordance with its ideology.

As in the German Reich, RdbK offices were established in the various Gaus (districts) in the "Ostmark" (the Nazi name for Austria). In April 1938, Gauleiter Josef Bürckel appointed the painter and Künstlerhaus president Leopold Blauensteiner (fig. 1) as "leader of all fine arts institutions." In August 1939, Blauensteiner was put in charge of the Vienna office of the RdbK. Its first director until 1944 was the architect and painter Marcel Kammerer, who was succeeded by the writer Franz Schlögel. Blauensteiner was assisted by representatives of the various disciplines, including the painter Igo Pötsch, the sculptor Ferdinand Opitz, and the architect Robert Örley. The office was initially located in the Künstlerhaus, but in 1939 moved to the premises of the Reich Propaganda Department in the "Aryanized" Palais Epstein (Reisnerstrasse 40, 3rd district) and then, shortly before the end of the war, to the Trattnerhof (Graben, 1st district).

Blauensteiner was one of the most powerful National Socialist culture functionaries in Vienna. His tasks included overseeing the admission procedure, which required close liaison with the Vienna Gau NSDAP administration, the Gestapo, and the RdbK in Berlin. Art exhibitions had to be approved by him, and he also intervened against "degenerate art" (→ p. 221, (16)), monitored prices on the art market, sat on competition juries, and approved travel, financial subsidies, and material allocations. He was tried after the war by a *Volksgericht* (people's court).

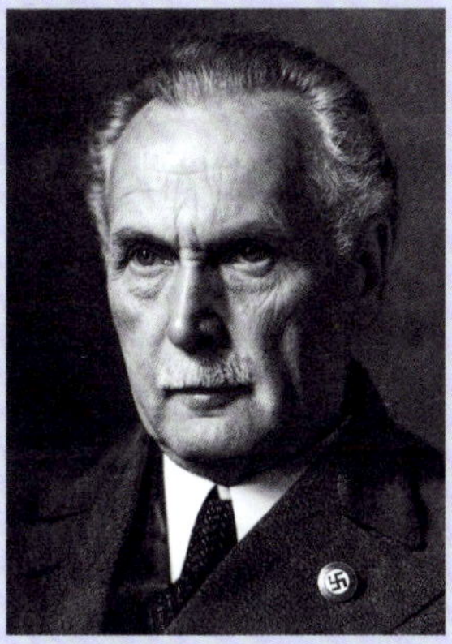

1

Fig. 1
Leopold Blauensteiner with Nazi party lapel badge, undated, photo: Otto Schmidt, Austrian National Library, Vienna

18

Deaccession

Christoph Zuschlag

Deaccession in museums refers to the disposal of objects, for example, through sale or exchange,[1] or any other means of dismantling a collection. During the Nazi period, museums lost works of modern art not only through the official seizure of "degenerate" art but also to a large extent through "voluntary" disposals not ordered by official bodies.[2] In an enthusiastic demonstration of their conformity, museum directors such as Hermann Voss in Wiesbaden or Count von Baudissin in Essen were more than willing to divest themselves of unwelcome works of modern art. As temporary director of the Staatsgalerie Stuttgart, Baudissin, member of the NSDAP since 1932 and the SS since 1935, organized the 1933 exhibition *Novembergeist—Kunst im Dienste der Zersetzung* (November Spirit—Art in the Service of Subversion). The following year he became director of Museum Folkwang in Essen, where, in July 1936, he sold Wassily Kandinsky's painting *Improvisation 28* to the Berlin art dealer Ferdinand Möller, who subsequently sold it in the USA. Today it is in the Solomon R. Guggenheim Museum in New York.

It is not only the actual deaccessions but also the attempted ones that are of interest, however. For example, documents in the archive of the Kunsthalle Mannheim show that the museum corresponded with various art dealers and private individuals between 1933 and 1937 in an attempt to dispose of a number of paintings. Among them were two pictures by the Jewish artists Marc Chagall and Jankel Adler, which had been at the center of the 1933 exhibition *Images of Cultural Bolshevism*. No deals were concluded, and the two works were seized in 1937 and included in the *Degenerate Art* exhibition.

Max Liebermann, deceased in 1935, was a special case.[3] In terms of style, his works were not necessarily among those stigmatized by the Nazis, and he was not represented in the *Degenerate Art* exhibition. Nevertheless, the Nazi state attempted to extinguish the memory of this famous but undesirable Jewish artist. At a conference of museum directors on August 2, 1937, Minister of Education Bernhard Rust ordered Liebermann's pictures to be taken down. Thereafter, museums in Breslau/Wrocław, Chemnitz, Cologne, Dortmund, Düsseldorf, Halle, Hamburg, Leipzig, Oldenburg, and Stuttgart disposed of at least thirty-five works by Liebermann, mostly through exchanges but also, in some cases, through sale.

The Modern Gallery in Vienna did not follow this pattern.[4] In reply to an inquiry by the Hamburg art dealer Hildebrand Gurlitt, the director of the Austrian Gallery wrote on June 24, 1941, that "the disposal of works by Liebermann is out of the question because of an order that the contents of the Modern Gallery are to remain intact." Bruno Grimschitz (→ p. 255, fig. 1) also declined an inquiry by an Oslo art dealer on September 24, 1941, regarding the sale or exchange of pictures by Munch, Matisse, van Gogh, Cézanne, Picasso, and other artists.

1 Gammon 2018.
2 Zuschlag 2016.
3 Zuschlag 2021.
4 Mayer M. 2005, p. 67.

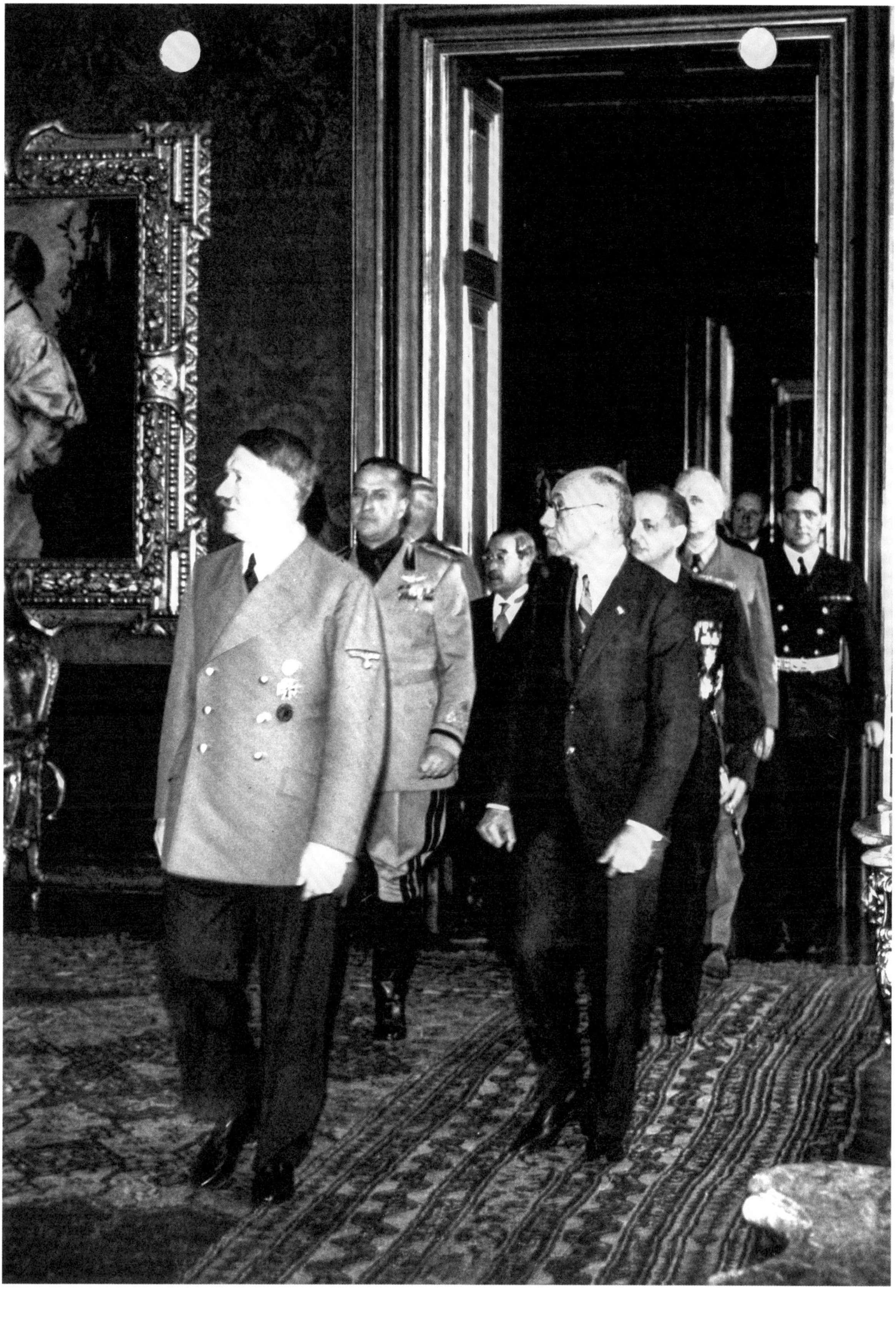

The undersigned director considers that the extensive use of the palace by the aforementioned police command post places this most important Baroque palace on Viennese soil in the most acute danger, [...] not least as the palace is close to two train stations and the Arsenal and has been at particular risk for some time through the installation of searchlights and the aforementioned air raid bunker.

—— Bruno Grimschitz to the general cultural adviser Hermann Stuppäck, October 2, 1944, AdB, Zl. 240/1944

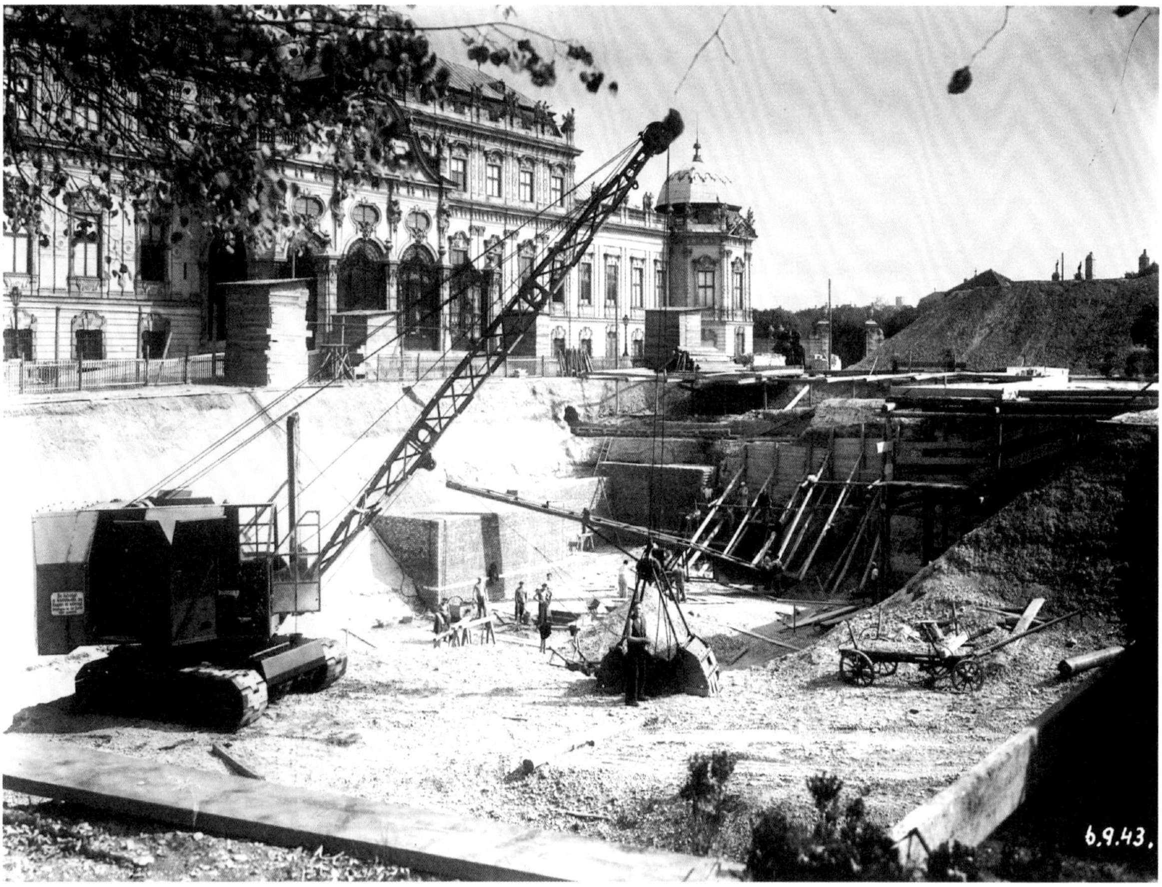

Construction of the bunker on the south side of the Upper Belvedere, September 6, 1943

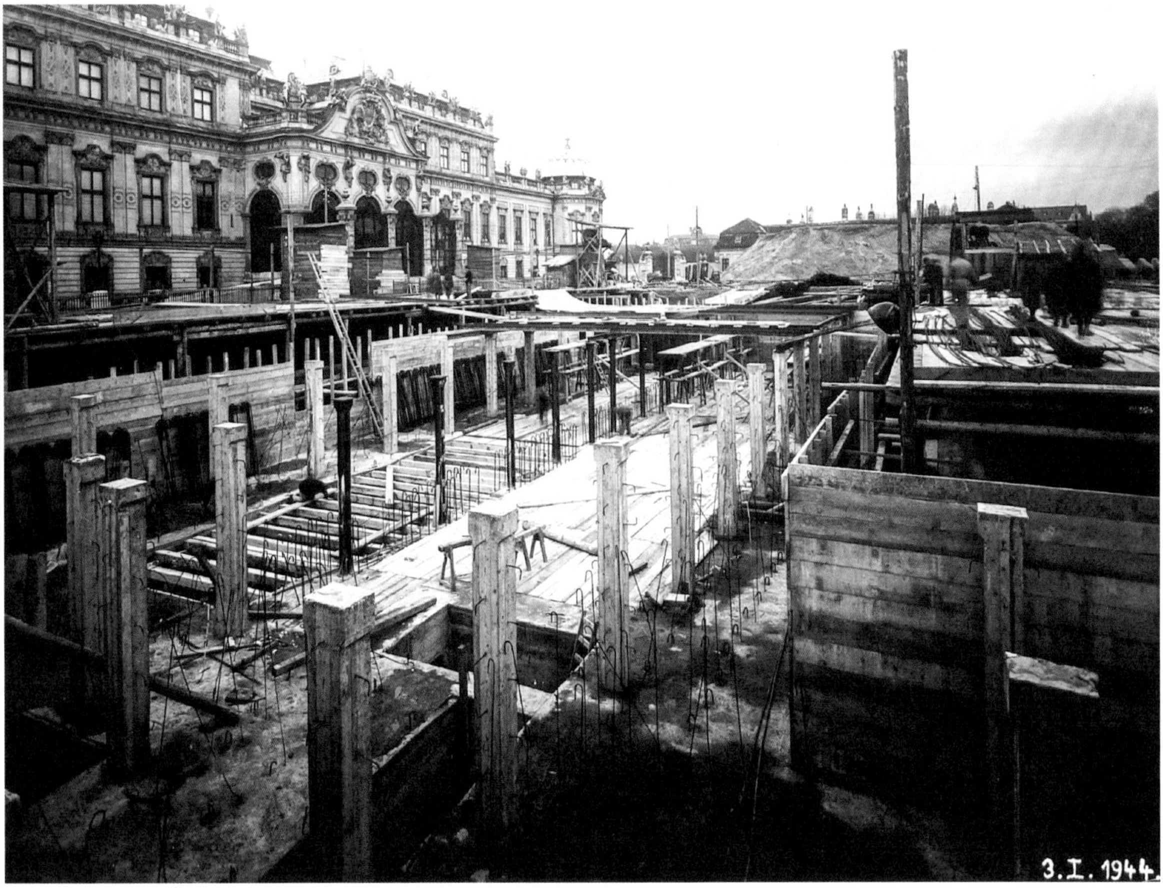

Construction of the bunker on the south side of the Upper Belvedere, January 3, 1944

The undersigned director also reports that there are 13 tonnes of coke, and with minimal heating of the Upper Belvedere palace the said exhibitions can remain open until the beginning of March. Even if it does close, it must be ensured that the temperature does not drop below +6 degrees, so as to protect the precious artworks of the gallery and Prussian palaces from damage.

—— Director of the Austrian Gallery to the Office of the State Theaters, Art Venues, and Museums, January 29, 1942, AdB, Zl. 87/1942

As the continued presence of the police command post in the bunker makes a new attack likely, the [...] director's office has already, over the past weeks, cleared the palace of all artworks, the library, and the archive of the Austrian Gallery. Furthermore, as it is not possible to continue working in the heavily damaged building, without light, telephone, and water, we are forced to move administrative operations to the Albertina. [It is also requested] that the police command post be transferred to another bunker in Vienna, so as to prevent the highly likely complete destruction of this masterpiece of German Baroque architecture.

— Bruno Grimschitz to the Office of the State Theaters, Art Venues, and Museums, November 21, 1944, AdB Zl. 240/1944

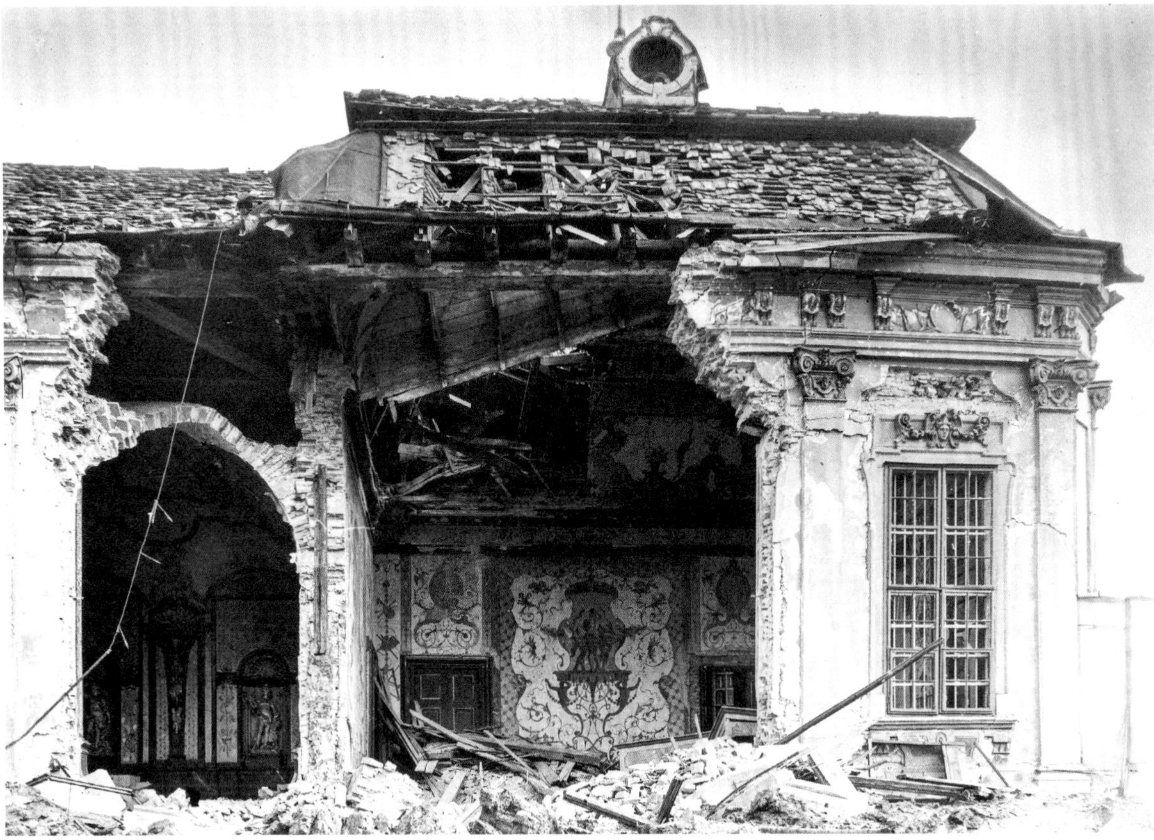

Lower Belvedere,
bomb damage in the
Hall of Grotesques,
1945

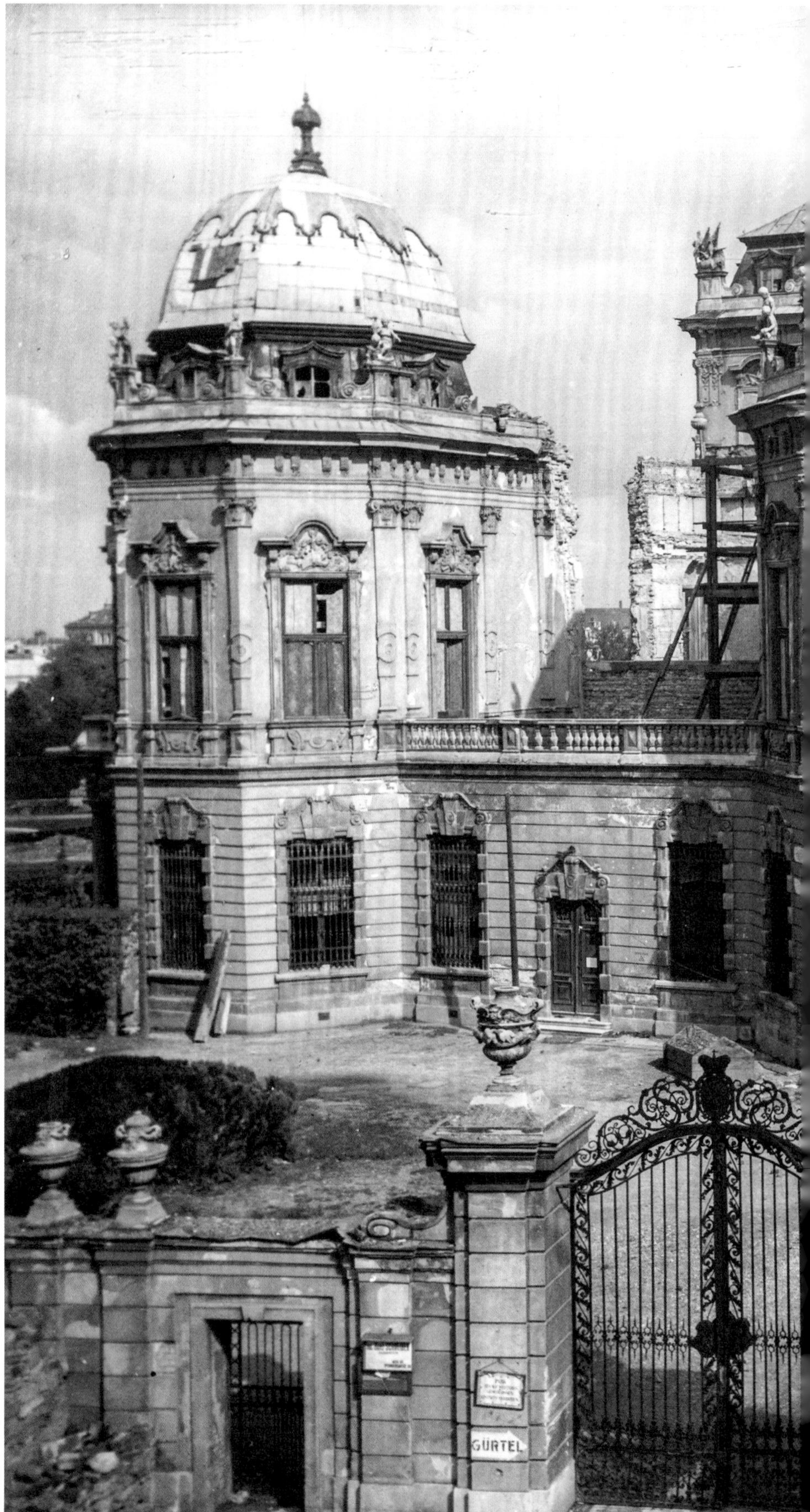

Upper Belvedere, war damage on the west side, July 1945

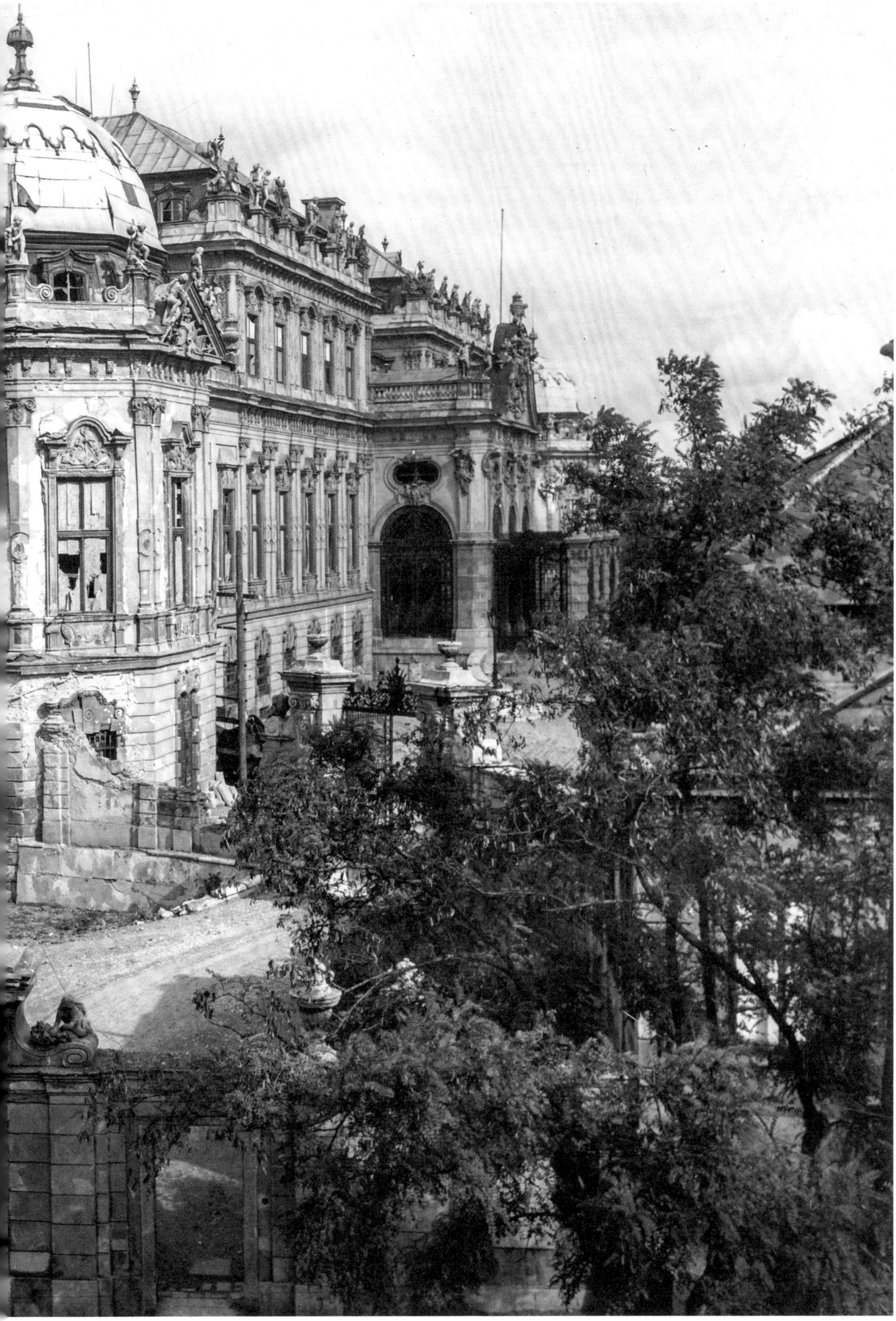

P. 240 CHRISTOPH ZUSCHLAG —

The Complicity of Museums in National Socialist Cultural Policy

How did the accession to power of the Nazis on January 30, 1933, affect museums and modern art collections in the German Reich? To what extent did these institutions support or oppose the National Socialist state? And what were the consequences for art acquisition strategies and exhibitions? These are the complex questions this essay aims to address in brief.

Soon after Adolf Hitler's appointment as Reich Chancellor on January 30, 1933, the National Socialist regime began to systematically expand and extend its reach into all areas of political and social life.[1] The Law on the Restoration of the Professional Civil Service of April 7, 1933, had serious consequences for museums, as it provided the basis for the dismissal of officials on "racial" or political grounds. Several dozen professors at art academies and universities lost their positions overnight, along with around thirty-five museum directors or department heads, including many supporters of modern art, such as Lilli Fischel (Karlsruhe), Ernst Gosebruch (Essen), Gustav F. Hartlaub (Mannheim), Carl Georg Heise (Lübeck), and Max Sauerlandt (Hamburg). They were replaced by supporters of the NSDAP and/or the Militant League for German Culture, an umbrella organization bringing together various *völkisch* (German ethnic) and conservative nationalist associations. It was these individuals for the most part who, from early 1933, organized special exhibitions in the different cities aimed at pillorying the modern art holdings of the respective museums. These exhibitions, described in the print media of the time as "chambers of horrors" or "exhibitions of shame," had titles such as *Images of Cultural Bolshevism* (Mannheim), *Government Art 1918–1933* (Karlsruhe), *November Spirit—Art in the Service of Subversion* (Stuttgart), or *Art of the Intellectuals 1918–1933* (Breslau/Wrocław). These titles are

1 See Zuschlag 1995; I am grateful to Monika Mayer for her invaluable assistance with my contributions to this volume.

illustrative of the underlying political motive: The works were shown to the public as symptoms of the degeneracy of the Weimar Republic, with the aim of discrediting it and celebrating the victory of the National Socialists. In terms of political function, ideology, and propaganda effect, these "chambers of horrors" anticipated at the local level the centrally organized *Degenerate Art* exhibition in Munich in 1937 (fig. 1), which was also shown in Vienna in 1939 (→ p. 221, ⑯). In this way, the museums were active participants in the dissemination of enemy stereotypes and Nazi propaganda.

While Modernism thus came under attack in many places from as early as 1933, the Kronprinzenpalais in Berlin, which housed the National Gallery's modern art collection, remained open until 1936, the year of the Berlin Olympics. On the top floor, visitors were still able to admire Expressionist works by artists such as Ernst Barlach, Käthe Kollwitz, and Franz Marc. This paradoxical situation was the result of ideological differences and rivalries within the Nazi leadership, which in the early years of the Nazi dictatorship prevented the development of a clear cultural policy. In fact, National Socialist cultural policy was characterized until the end by contradictions and arbitrariness.

Before and after the *Degenerate Art* exhibition opened in Munich, around 21,000 works by 1,476 artists were seized in German museums by order of the Ministry of Propaganda (around one-third of them paintings, sculptures, watercolors, and drawings, and two-thirds prints).[2] After 1938, these were "disposed of": 46 percent were sold or exchanged—mainly for nineteenth-century works—33 percent were destroyed, and the remaining 21 percent were unsold works either traded on commission by art dealers or used in the traveling *Degenerate Art* exhibition. In a few cases (1.5 percent), they were returned to their owners or lenders.[3] Apart from these confiscations by the state, which the museums were powerless to oppose, the "voluntary" surrender of modern artworks through sale or exchange was also widespread (→ p. 230, ⑱).

During the Berlin Olympics in 1936, the National Gallery staged an exhibition in the Kronprinzenpalais entitled *Great Germans in Portraits of Their Time*—a good example of the way museums now chose their exhibition themes to be in line with Nazi ideology. Other exhibitions, not only staged by museums but also by the Reich Chamber of Fine Arts[4] and other Nazi organizations, had titles such as *The Streets of Adolf Hitler in Art*, which was also shown in early 1938 at the Vienna Secession, *German Farmer—German Soil*, *The Beauty of Work*, *Germany's Greatness*, *A Hard-Working Nation*, *Blood and Soil*, *Woman and Mother—Life Source of the Nation*, and *Heroic Art*. Apart from exhibitions illustrating National Socialist ideology with its racial stereotypes and role models, or celebrating the supposed achievements of the Nazi regime, there were also

2 Database of confiscated "degenerate art," Degenerate Art Research Center, Department for Art History, FU Berlin, https://www.geschkult.fu-berlin.de/e/db_entart_kunst/datenbank/index.html (accessed on August 16, 2022).
3 Hüneke 2010, pp. 77–78.
4 Holzschuh/Plakolm-Forsthuber 2021; Kubowitsch 2016.

those explicitly designed to encourage polarization and the identification of a specific enemy, such as *Global Enemy No. 1—Bolshevism* and *The Eternal Jew*.[5] Sudeten German art exhibitions and *Art of the Ostmark* openly prepared the ground for the regime's annexation plans starting in 1938. From 1939, there were also exhibitions glorifying the war and demonizing the enemy: *Poland Campaign in Pictures and Portraits*, *Art of the Front*, *Artists View the War*, *Robber State England*. The focus on applied arts and crafts is also notable. The Kunstmuseum Moritzburg in Halle, for example, organized an exhibition in early 1937 entitled *Decorative Arts in the Gau Halle-Merseburg*, and the Städtische Kunsthalle Mannheim presented *Artists in Industry—Exemplary Design of Industrial Products* in 1941/42.

Acquisition strategies were also changing. In the first years of the Nazi rule, museums—notwithstanding the aforementioned "chambers of horrors"—were still able to purchase works, say, by Expressionists, sometimes in considerable quantities. In early 1935, for example, Folkwang Museum in Essen acquired almost the entire graphic œuvre of Emil Nolde (only for it to be confiscated two years later).[6] In 1937, the seizure of "degenerate art" and the Munich exhibition marked an intensification of the clamp-down on modern art, yet works by proscribed artists were still occasionally being purchased. At the same time, museums duly promoted art that was in line with Nazi ideology and acquired works, for example, at the annual *Great German Art Exhibition* in Munich. Others focused on "German" applied arts and crafts.

With the start of the war, museums were closed and their holdings gradually placed in storage to protect them from destruction. Despite this, a great number of artworks were lost in air raids and fires, but also through looting. After the war, the fate of the evacuated works depended on which occupying power reached the depots first. For example, in 1943, the Kunsthalle Bremen stored works in Karnzow Castle near Kyritz in Brandenburg. Shortly after the war, the castle was looted by locals and members of the Red Army. A total of 101 drawings and prints were taken to Moscow, where, in 1993, they were deposited anonymously in the German embassy. In 2000, Russia officially returned the works to the Kunsthalle Bremen.[7]

Much further research is still needed regarding the political and administrative background to museum activities in Nazi Germany, the protagonists and their scope for action, the curating of exhibitions, and the way they were received by the public.[8] The long-held one-sided view that all museums were merely victims of National Socialist cultural policy also needs to be revisited, including a critical analysis of the involvement of individual protagonists in Nazi art looting. Two German museum directors, Hans Posse and Hermann Voss, functioned as special consultants for Hitler's planned "Führermuseum" in Linz.[9] Viennese museum

5 For a detailed recent discussion of National Socialist enemy stereotype exhibitions, see Burgstaller 2022.
6 Fulda/Ring/Soika 2019.
7 Zuschlag 2022, p. 157.
8 For a *tour d'horizon* on the subject, see Baensch/Kratz-Kessemeier/Wimmer 2016.
9 Iselt 2010; Lupfer/Rudert 2015.

officials, too, such as Bruno Grimschitz (→ p. 255, fig. 1) —who, as a member of the NSDAP, became director of the Austrian Gallery after the annexation of Austria in March 1938—acted as art consultants on behalf of the Nazi authorities and appraised the seized Jewish art collections.

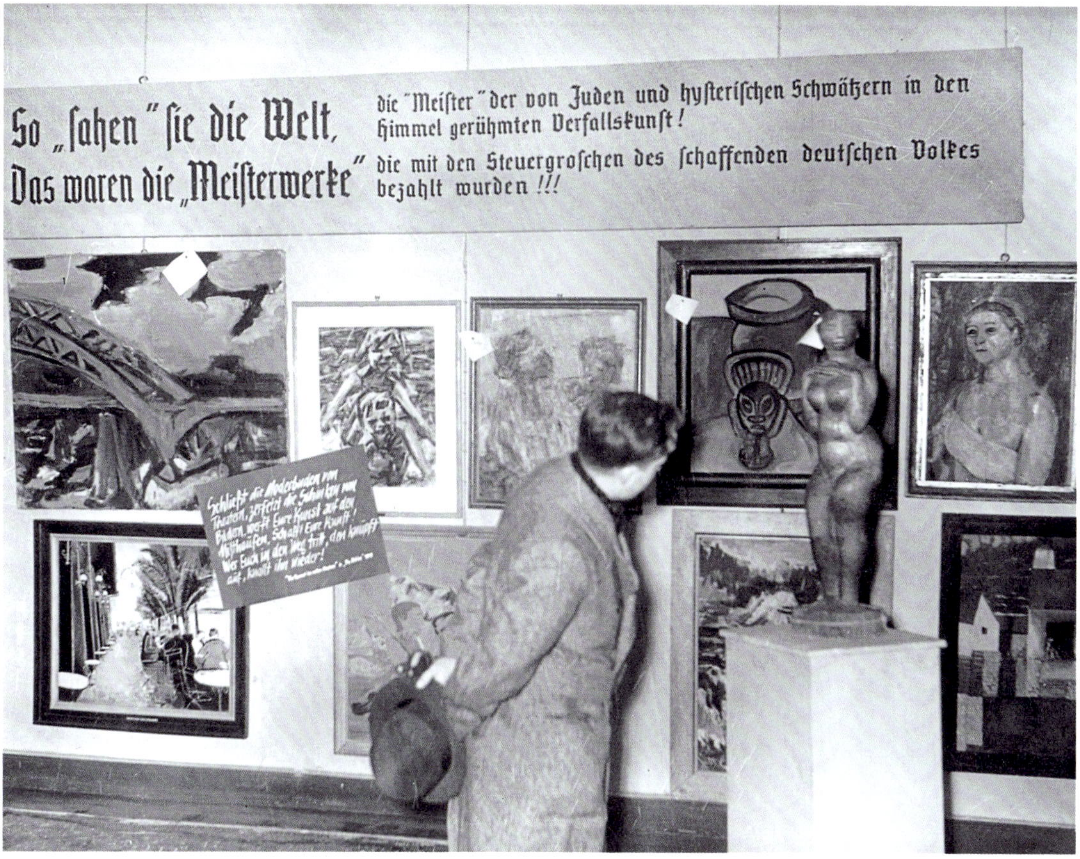

1

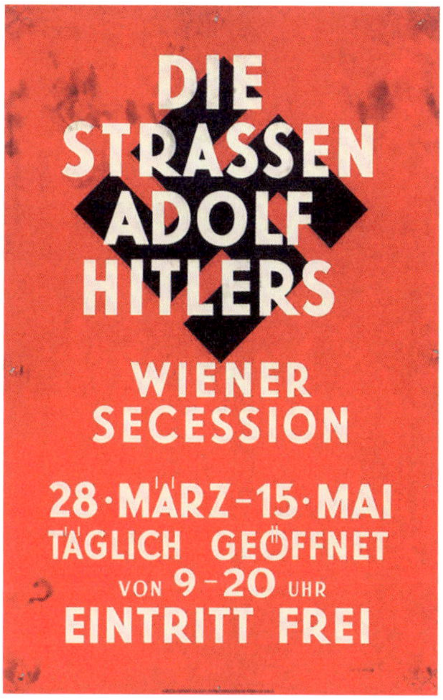

2

Fig. 1
Degenerate Art exhibition, Haus der Kunst, Berlin, 1938, photo: Scherl, SZ Photo/Historical Archive, Munich

Fig. 2
Poster for the exhibition *The Streets of Adolf Hitler*, Vienna Secession, March 28 to May 15, 1938, Bancroft Library, UC Berkeley

P. 246 MONIKA MAYER — The Austrian Gallery during the Nazi Period

An article entitled "Raub und Zerstörung an Wiener Kunstbesitz" (Theft and destruction of Viennese cultural assets) about the fate of museums during the Nazi period appeared on May 4, 1945, in the newspaper *Neues Österreich*. It claimed that "the representative core of Viennese art collections had suffered considerably" not only "through the war events" but also through salvaging measures and the "outright abduction" of works of art.[1]

In his response to this article, Bruno Grimschitz (fig. 1),[2] director of the Austrian Gallery, asserted that the museum had lost only "three paintings of inferior artistic value" and that "otherwise the Austrian Gallery did not lose any works of art." On the contrary, between 1938 and 1945, thanks to an "unusually rich acquisition policy, for the most part running completely contrary to National Socialist guidelines," the museum had been able to obtain "over two hundred prestigious artworks."[3] No mention was made of the looting and destruction of Jewish art collections[4] in Austria. As will be outlined here, the collection, acquisition, and personnel policies of Vienna's museums after the annexation of Austria to the German Reich in March 1938 exemplified the close connection at various levels between museums and the Nazi bureaucracy. This essay looks at questions of inclusion/exclusion in museum activities during the Nazi period as exemplified by the Austrian Gallery. Topics such as the "elimination" of employees and collectors on racial grounds, the closure of the Modern Gallery in 1938, acquisitions through looting and in line with National Socialist art policy, the evacuation and storage of artworks to protect them from air raids, but also the museum's attitude to "degenerate art" and Jewish artists will be discussed.

1 "Raub und Zerstörung an Wiener Kunstbesitz," *Neues Österreich: Unabhängiges Wiener Tagblatt*, May 5, 1945, p. 3.
2 For information about Bruno Grimschitz, member of staff at the Austrian Gallery since 1919, see Mayer, 2005; www.lexikon-provenienzforschung.org/en/grimschitz-bruno (accessed on September 25, 2022).
3 Letter, Bruno Grimschitz to the Office for State Theater, Art Institutions, and Museums, May 9, 1945, AdB, Zl. 36/1945.
4 See Lillie, 2003.

The Modern Gallery, established in 1929 in the Orangery of the Lower Belvedere to house the collection of twentieth-century art, was closed on March 22, 1938, a few days after the annexation. The Austrian Ministry of Education ordered that it should remain closed and its holdings placed in storage (fig. 2).[5] After visiting the gallery, Count Klaus von Baudissin, provisional director of the culture department in the Reich Ministry of Education, determined that there were only a few manifestly "decadent" works in the Modern Gallery and predicted that some of its holdings were likely to be seized, as had happened systematically the previous year in Germany.[6] He also suggested that pictures by Jewish artists should be removed. Indeed, during the salvaging operations in summer 1939, works by Lovis Corinth (fig. 3), Oskar Kokoschka, and Egon Schiele, which in the German Reich were considered "degenerate," but also paintings by Jewish artists such as Tina Blau and Max Liebermann, were moved to external storage locations, where they survived the war unscathed. In this context, the Hamburg art dealer Hildebrand Gurlitt was informed in June 1941 that the disposal of works by Liebermann was "out of the question because of an order that the holdings of the Modern Gallery are to remain intact."[7] In October 1939, the Modern Gallery premises were assigned to the Central Monument Protection Office to store secured artworks.[8]

On April 6, 1938, Grimschitz informed the Ministry of Education that he had taken over the provisional management of the Austrian Gallery (fig. 4), "since Director Hofrat Dr. Franz Martin Haberditzl has applied for indefinite leave."[9] At the same time, Grimschitz dismissed the curator Heinrich Schwarz[10] on racial grounds and announced the temporary appointment of the art historian Kurt Blauensteiner.[11] The required proof of Blauensteiner's "Aryan" pedigree was provided by the fact that his father, the painter and National Socialist culture functionary Leopold Blauensteiner (→ p. 229, fig. 1), was a member of the Reich Chamber of Culture.[12]

After Haberditzl's (→ p. 201, fig. 4) "permanent retirement" at the end of July 1938, Grimschitz was officially appointed acting director of the museum on August 20, 1938, and became its full director on December 28, 1939.

A member of the NSDAP since May 1938,[13] Grimschitz held numerous positions during the Nazi period and became one of the most influential persons in the art and culture sector of the "Ostmark." Apart from his undisputed expertise, the files in the Gau personnel department highlighted his political reliability and his nationalist attitude, even before 1938, when the NSDAP was banned.[14] From January 1940 to February 1941, he was also acting director of the Picture Gallery of the Kunsthistorisches Museum. In October 1941, Reich governor Baldur von Schirach appointed him as head of the Prince Eugene Museum, which was

5 Letter, Bruno Grimschitz to the Austrian Ministry of Education, May 6, 1938, AdB, Zl. 202/1938.

6 Count Klaus von Baudissin, expert opinion on the inventory of the Modern Gallery and Austrian Gallery, March 25, 1938, ÖStA/AVA, BMU, 15B1, Albertina, Zl. 9.349/1938; see also the essay by Christoph Zuschlag in this volume, p. 240.

7 Letter, Fritz Novotny to Hildebrand Gurlitt, June 24, 1941, AdB, Zl. 250/1941.

8 Letter, Ministry of Internal and Cultural Affairs to Bruno Grimschitz, October 10, 1939, AdB, Zl. 712/1939.

9 Letter, Bruno Grimschitz to the Austrian Ministry of Education, April 6, 1938, AdB, Zl. 196/1938.

10 For information on Heinrich Schwarz, expelled from Austria in 1938 as a "Jew," see Wendland, 1999, pp. 630–35.

11 Letter, Bruno Grimschitz to the Austrian Ministry of Education, April 6, 1938, AdB, Zl. 196/1938.

12 Letter, Bruno Grimschitz to the Ministry of Internal and Cultural Affairs, July 16, 1938, AdB, Zl. 608/1938.

13 Party member with membership number 6,228.429 since May 1, 1938, ÖStA/AdR, BMU, personnel file Bruno Grimschitz.

14 Letter, Gauleitung Vienna to the Gau personnel department, April 21, 1942, ÖStA/AdR, BMI, Gau file Bruno Grimschitz, Zl. 179.197.

to be established in the prince's Winter Palace on Himmelpfortgasse in Vienna (→ p. 49, ④).

In August 1941, Grimschitz was appointed as adviser to the Reich Chamber of Fine Arts cultural asset purchasing section, which dealt with the acquisition of art objects seized from Jews.[15] The unscrupulousness with which he exploited the knowledge acquired through these expert appraisals in order to obtain works of art is illustrated by the case of Vally Honig. In 1942, Grimschitz informed the Institute for Monument Preservation about Honig's deportation and requested an investigation of the whereabouts of the "very beautiful pictures" in Honig's collection.[16] In June 1944, he was appointed head of the Zweckverband Salzburger Museum (Salzburg Museum administration association), where he worked together with the art dealer Friedrich Welz.[17] Further evidence of the high opinion the official Nazi bureaucracy had of Grimschitz's competence as a museum director and art expert is the proposal by the Reich Ministry of Education in 1942 to appoint him director of the National Gallery in Berlin.[18]

Already in April 1938, Grimschitz had written to the Ministry of Education in Vienna requesting permission to develop the collections in terms of personnel, as well as its academic, artistic, and administrative aspects. He asked for "special subsidies so as to acquire artworks that are of essential significance for the representation of Austrian art in the Austrian Gallery and that under no circumstances should be removed from the country." He went on to point out that in view of the dismantling of collections and the far-reaching reorganization of Austrian private ownership as a consequence of the new political situation, the most precious examples of Austrian art, previously unavailable to the state, were now open for acquisition.[19] In June 1939, for example, Grimschitz, whom Hubertus Czernin describes as "one of the greatest beneficiaries of the expropriation of Jewish art collections,"[20] expressed his interest in thirteen paintings from Serena Lederer's[21] secured collection—including ten works by Gustav Klimt, among them the two Faculty paintings *Philosophy* and *Jurisprudence*, which the museum did indeed acquire in 1944 from Lederer's daughter Elisabeth Bachofen-Echt.[22]

Plans by the Nazi culture bureaucracy to remove "foreign artists" from the Austrian Gallery and thus turn it into a "purely national collection"[23] were vehemently and successfully opposed by Grimschitz: "Apart from the fact that the removal of French masterpieces would deprive the gallery of some of its most valuable assets, the transformation into an <u>Austrian</u> national gallery would necessarily also involve the removal of works by German artists."[24] Grimschitz also emphatically rejected the proposal to establish a "foreign gallery" in the Orangery of the Lower Belvedere. Instead, referring to the Austrian State Gallery's museum con-

15 Letter, Office of the Reich governor Vienna to Bruno Grimschitz, August 11, 1941, AdB, Zl. 349/1941.
16 Lillie 2003, pp. 521–23. After being arrested on October 5, 1942, Vally Honig-Roeren was deported to Maly Trostinec and murdered there. In 2006, the Art Restitution Advisory Board recommended the restitution of the "portrait of a man" by Waldmüller from the former Honig collection that had been acquired by Grimschitz in 1940, www.provenienzforschung.gv.at/beiratsbeschluesse/Honig-Roeren_Vally_2006-06-28.pdf (accessed on September 25, 2022).
17 Kerschbaumer 2000.
18 Transcript of a letter from the Reich Minister for Science, Education and Culture to the Reich governor in Vienna, May 28, 1942, ÖStA/AdR, BMU, personnel file Bruno Grimschitz.
19 Letter, Bruno Grimschitz to the Austrian Ministry of Education, April 15, 1938, AdB, Zl. 206/1938.
20 Czernin 1999, vol. 2, p. 310.
21 Letter, Austrian Gallery director to Hermann Berchthold, trustee custodian of the Lederer collection, June 30, 1939, AdB, Zl. 442/1939. Among the thirteen listed artworks by Klimt, Schiele, Maulbertsch, and Burne-Jones are the following ten works by Klimt: *Music*, *Golden Apple Tree*, *Philosophy* (and one study), *Jurisprudence*, *Beethoven Frieze*, *Danae*, *Portrait of a Lady*, and two landscapes.
22 AdB, Zl. 67/1944.
23 Letter, Austrian Ministry of Education to Bruno Grimschitz, April 1, 1938, AdB, Zl. 202/1938.
24 Letter, Bruno Grimschitz to the Austrian Ministry of Education, May 6, 1938, AdB, Zl. 202/1938.

cept implemented from 1912, he advocated the establishment of a museum of Austrian Gothic art with objects from the Kunsthistorisches Museum and the Museum of Applied Arts. Its planned location in the rooms of the Modern Gallery "should be seen as a temporary measure only, as the extensive side wings of the Lower Belvedere would offer sufficient space."[25]

On January 23, 1940, Bernhard Rust, Reich Minister for Science, Education and Culture, issued a decree once again allowing museums to officially acquire works by living artists: "In view of the current difficulties experienced by visual artists, I hereby agree to the acquisition by museums again of works by living artists. This is based on the assumption that there are no longer any museum directors who would purchase works that are not in line with the National Socialist conception of art."[26] In his report on the Austrian Gallery in February 1940, Grimschitz stated that an annual allocation of RM 50,000 to 70,000 would be necessary "to continue to enlarge the collections, to create the Gothic museum, and to represent modern art by purchasing works by living artists."[27]

With regard to the acquisitions by Grimschitz during the Nazi period, reference should also be made to the "Viennese" cultural policy under Reich governor Baldur von Schirach.[28] The former general cultural adviser Walter Thomas has highlighted the special assistance received by Vienna's museums during the Nazi period, pointing out that the Austrian Gallery also benefited from substantial hard-won subsidies obtained from Berlin to purchase new works for the state collections.[29]

Grimschitz himself always emphasized the exceptional support provided by von Schirach: "His energetic support and interest and his special financial subsidies enabled the museum to acquire a number of significant artworks of major importance for the gallery's collection program"[30] (fig. 5). He continues: "In 1941, it was above all works by German painters that framed the core of the gallery, namely Viennese painting, while this year [1942] the collection has been enriched through the addition of precious paintings by French masters. There are now four works by Corot, three each by Monet and Degas, and one each by Manet and Toulouse-Lautrec. [...] Thanks to the Reich governor particular interest in works by living artists, the museum has been able to acquire a large number of paintings and sculptures by contemporary Viennese and Rhenish artists."[31]

As a reflection of the National Socialist art agenda, between 1941 and 1944, the museum acquired works by Ferdinand Andri, Leopold Blauensteiner, Rudolf Hermann Eisenmenger (fig. 6), Fritz Behn, Oskar Laske, and Carl Moll, primarily from exhibitions at the Künstlerhaus in Vienna.[32]

One particular focus was the acquisition of works by living German sculptors. Grimschitz therefore requested that the premises of the Modern Gallery, which had been closed since March 1938, and the Privy

25 Letter, Bruno Grimschitz to General Advisory Office for Theater and Museums in the Reich Gau Vienna, February 15, 1940, AdB, Zl. 59/1940.

26 Letter, Reich Minister for Science, Education and Culture, January 23, 1940, AdB, Zl. 52/1940.

27 Letter, Bruno Grimschitz to General Advisory Office for Theater and Museums in the Reich Gau Vienna, February 15, 1940, AdB, Zl. 59/1940. In 1937, German museums were instructed "to purchase only works completed at least one generation ago. The current threshold is around 1910. This instruction follows from the decision by the Führer that the Ministry of Propaganda should be responsible for the promotion of living art and that living art is not made for museums." See letter, Austrian Ministry of Education to Bruno Grimschitz, April 1, 1938, AdB, Zl. 202/1938.

28 Rathkolb 1991, pp. 44–78; see essay by Sabine Plakolm-Forsthuber in this volume, p. 258.

29 Thomas 1947, pp. 140–41.

30 Bruno Grimschitz in exh. cat. Vienna, 1941, p. 3.

31 Bruno Grimschitz in exh. cat. Vienna, 1942, p. 3.

32 Mayer 2015.

Garden in front of it, where modern sculpture had been displayed since 1929, be restored to their original purpose.[33] In 1943, thanks to a special loan from the office of the Reich governor, sculptures by Karl Albiker, Georg Kolbe, Richard Scheibe, and Gerhard Marcks were added to the collection: "*Athena* [is] Albiker's only study in bronze for the war memorial in Karlsruhe; *Die Sinnenden* by Kolbe and *Flora* by Scheibe are currently on display in the Haus der deutschen Kunst in Munich, and the two works by Marcks (fig. 7) are the only bronzes by this exceptionally talented master among recent German sculptors."[34] The acquisition from Galerie Karl Buchholz in Berlin of the sculptures by Gerhard Marcks,[35] whose works had been labeled "degenerate" in the German Reich since 1937, is a good illustration of the inconsistency of Nazi art policy; yet it also shows the ambivalence of the collection policy under Grimschitz's management.

Although the Orangery was not used as a museum again until after the war, the Austrian Gallery remained open to the public, at least to a limited extent, until the "total war" was declared in August 1944. The Baroque Museum in the Lower Belvedere was closed completely from July 1939 to January 1940, and again from April 1941, on account of the air raid protection measures put in place. Even before the outbreak of World War II, in summer 1939, work started on the salvaging of objects from Viennese museums.[36] In a series of transports of the most valuable items, major works from the Gallery of the Nineteenth Century and the Baroque Museum were transferred to the charterhouse in Gaming, Lower Austria. The second batch, "valuable but not irreplaceable objects," remained in the Upper Belvedere, packed in crates and ready for transport if necessary.[37] With the exception of a few major paintings, including works by Klimt and Schiele, the holdings of the Modern Gallery were stored in a side wing of the Lower Belvedere. The large-format paintings by Hans Makart and Max Klinger, and also Baroque altarpieces, were not moved and remained in their allocated rooms. The protection of the monumental sculptures by Georg Raphael Donner, Franz Xaver Messerschmidt, and Balthasar Permoser (→ p. 209) in the Baroque Museum presented a serious problem, "because the Lower Belvedere palace consists only of ground floor rooms and the ceilings are mostly suspended from the roof structure, which is made extensively of wood."[38]

The office of the Reich governor called for increased air raid protection measures, in particular for the special exhibitions held until 1943 in the Upper Belvedere. Apart from three presentations of new acquisitions in 1940, 1941, and 1942, there were the commemorative exhibitions for Emil Jakob Schindler and Ferdinand Georg Waldmüller. The latter exhibition, which represented "a worthy continuation of the Austrian Gallery's greatly increased acquisition activity, despite the war,"[39] was

33 Letter, Bruno Grimschitz to the Office for State Theater, Art Institutions and Museums, March 31, 1942, AdB, Zl. 151/1942.

34 Letter, Bruno Grimschitz to the Office for State Theater, Art Institutions and Museums, August 6, 1943, AdB, Zl. 293/1943.

35 Gerhard Marcks was dismissed in 1933 as director of the Burg Giebichenstein Art School in Halle (Saale). In 1937, his works were removed from public collections as "degenerate." Two works by him were shown at the *Degenerate Art* exhibition in Munich. He was subsequently provisionally banned from exhibiting and repeatedly threatened with a ban from working; see Tiedemann, 2013.

36 See Mayer 2016.

37 Letter, Bruno Grimschitz to the Office for the Promotion of the Arts, State Theater, Museums and Public Education, April 7, 1941, AdB, Zl. 138/1941.

38 See note 37.

39 Walter Thomas, typescript of the opening speech, January 15, 1943, AdB, Zl. 7/1943.

extremely successful, running for just under two months in early 1943 and attracting around 40,000 visitors. In all, there were 119,154 visitors in 1943, almost twice the previous year's total.[40]

The temporary display of the Gallery of the Nineteenth Century in four rooms of the Upper Belvedere offered a selection of mostly "second-rate" works by Austrian, German, and French artists, including Friedrich von Amerling, Gustave Courbet, Theodor Hörmann, Anton Romako, Carl Schuch, Wilhelm Trübner, and Ferdinand Georg Waldmüller, but also two early works by Klimt, *After the Rain* and *Farmhouse with Birch Trees*. Grimschitz already complained in 1939 that, "through the removal of the evacuated and packed artworks," the Gallery of the Nineteenth Century had become "a useless torso."[41] The original paintings in the Makart Room in the Upper Belvedere, including the huge *Triumph of Ariadne*, and Max Klinger's *Judgment of Paris*, were left in place "to keep the rooms in which state ceremonies take place ready for use if required"[42] (→ pp. 226–31).

As the air raids became more intense, resulting in the need to step up the evacuation of works, hundreds of artworks, including the massive lead figures of Vienna's famous Donnerbrunnen, were transferred in 1943/44 to additional safe storage sites such as Immendorf Castle, Kirchstetten, and Schönborn Palace in Lower Austria, and from late 1944 onwards Lauffen salt mine near Bad Ischl.

In October 1944, Grimschitz expressed his concern at the risk to the Belvedere through the extensive use of the Upper Palace by the Central Air Raid Command Post for the Vienna Gau and the air raid bunker in front of the southern façade (→ p. 232). He pointed to the "immense danger" of air raids, "not least as the palace is close to two train stations and the Arsenal, and has been at particular risk for some time through the installation of searchlights and the aforementioned air raid bunker. [...] As far as the Gallery is concerned" the planned modifications to the collection rooms (light, telephone and bell cables, blackout facilities, installation of large stoves) "are also extremely worrying, as the palace interior's precious architectural features are likely to suffer."[43] The museum director's protests fell on deaf ears. On November 18, 1944, the Air Raid Command Post was attacked as an important military target, and the west wing of the Upper Belvedere (fig. 8) and the gardens suffered heavy damage. Thanks to the "total salvaging" of the gallery's holdings, no museum objects were affected.[44]

A further air raid in February 1945 ripped open the roof of the central pavilion and the ceiling of the Marble Hall in the Upper Palace and destroyed a corner pavilion of the Lower Belvedere (fig. 9). By the end of the war, the palace and grounds were completely devastated.

As a former member of the NSDAP, Bruno Grimschitz, under whose direction "the museum palace reached the zenith of its greatest

40 Letter, Bruno Grimschitz to the Office for State Theater, Art Institutions and Museums, May 16, 1944, AdB, Zl. 132/1944.

41 Letter, Bruno Grimschitz to the Ministry of Internal and Cultural Affairs, October 3, 1939, AdB, Zl. 597/1939.

42 Letter, Bruno Grimschitz to the Office for State Theater, Art Institutions and Museums, October 6, 1942, AdB, Zl. 326/1942.

43 Letter, Bruno Grimschitz to general cultural adviser Hermann Stuppäck, October 2, 1944, AdB, Zl. 240/1944.

44 Memo, Office of the Reich governor, December 3, 1944, ÖStA/AdR, BMU, 15B1, K. 150, Zl. 6.613/1944. In early May, the Klimt paintings from the Lederer collection stored at Immendorf Castle, Klimt's three Faculty paintings, and a painting by Karl Wurzinger from the Austrian Gallery, were destroyed by retreating SS troops; see Lehne 2007.

(19)

Art Market and Auctions in Vienna 1938–45

Leonhard Weidinger

Immediately after the annexation of Austria to the National Socialist German Reich in March 1938, the Jewish population began to suffer reprisals. Art collections were seized or secured and then taken over by the state. Many persecutees were forced to sell art objects to finance their escape and to pay the compulsory levies. Art dealerships profited from the large number of works that came onto the market as a result. In 1938, there were thirty-nine auctions in which household interiors were sold directly in the apartments (fig. 1), compared with twenty-three the previous year.[1]

More than forty Viennese art and antiques dealerships had Jewish owners or managers. They were placed under temporary administration and subsequently liquidated or "Aryanized," in other words, given new owners acceptable to the Nazi regime, all under the auspices of the Property Transaction Office and in the consultation with the Reich Chamber of Culture.

In 1937, six auction houses held auctions in Vienna: the Dorotheum, J. Fischer, Gilhofer & Ranschburg, Glückselig, Albert Kende, and S. Kende. After the annexation, J. Fischer and Glückselig were liquidated; Gilhofer & Ranschburg and Albert Kende—the latter renamed Auktionshaus Kärntnerstraße from 1940—were "Aryanized." From November 1938, S. Kende was run by Adolf Weinmüller as a branch of his auction house in Munich. Weinmüller's manager in Vienna was the art historian Franz Kieslinger, who also assisted Kajetan Mühlmann with art looting in Poland and the Netherlands.[2]

In March 1939, the Austrian Gallery acquired Amerling's portrait *Girl with a Straw Hat* (fig. 2) from Weinmüller in Vienna. It had previously belonged to the Jewish architect Ernst Gotthilf, who had been forced to leave Vienna, and was restituted to his legal successors in 2008.[3]

A special role was played by the Dorotheum. As a state-owned foundation, it was the ideal outlet for the tax authorities and Vugesta (Gestapo Office for the Disposal of the Property of Jewish Emigrants) to "liquidate" confiscated items, not least because it also auctioned furniture, books, stamps, and even automobiles, in addition to art.

Most Jewish art dealers were able to escape from Vienna. Some continued their work in exile. In the early 1940s, for example, Leopold Blumka, Max and Frederick Glückselig, Otto Kallir, Melanie and Herbert Kende, and Elkan and Abraham Silbermann all had art dealerships on 57th Street in New York City.

The development of the art market in Vienna was helped by the course of the war, as the city remained for a long time beyond the range of Allied bombers. The first air raid on Vienna was not until March 17, 1944. For that reason, art dealers from the "Altreich" transferred their businesses to Vienna. In October 1943, Hans W. Lange from Berlin held two auctions in the Dorotheum, the largest auction house in the German Reich. It bought paintings in France and the Netherlands and was one of the most important sources of works for the planned "Führermuseum" in Linz. The art market in general flourished until the last months of the war, with auctions taking place in Vienna as late as December 1944.

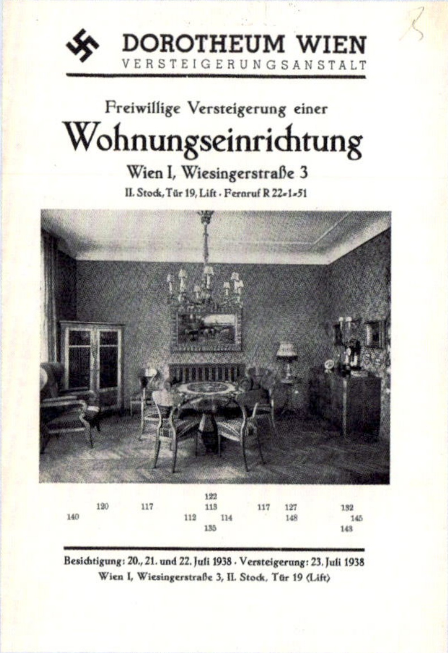
DOROTHEUM WIEN
VERSTEIGERUNGSANSTALT

Freiwillige Versteigerung einer
Wohnungseinrichtung
Wien I, Wiesingerstraße 3
II. Stock, Tür 19, Lift · Fernruf R 22-1-51

Besichtigung: 20., 21. und 22. Juli 1938 · Versteigerung: 23. Juli 1938
Wien I, Wiesingerstraße 3, II. Stock, Tür 19 (Lift)

1

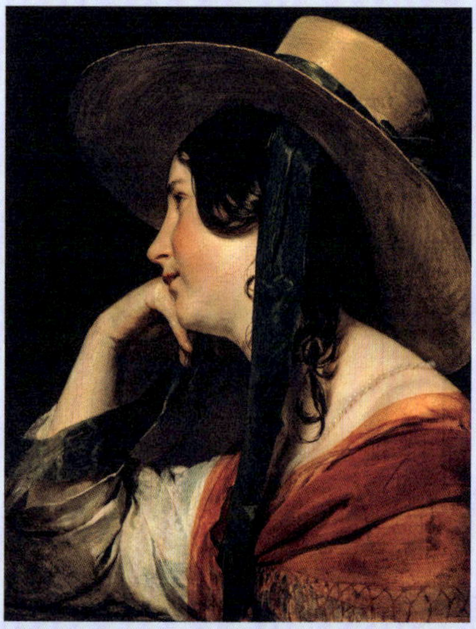

2

1 Weidinger 2017.
2 For details of art dealerships and persons involved in it, see the entries in the *Lexicon of Austrian Provenance Research*, https://www.lexikon-provenienzforschung.org/en (accessed on October 19, 2022).
3 www.provenienzforschung.gv.at/beiratsbeschluesse/Gotthilf_Ernst_2007-06-01.pdf (accessed on November 16, 2022).

Fig. 1
Dorotheum auction catalogue for a "voluntary auction of the contents of an apartment in Vienna I, Wiesingerstrasse 3," Vienna 1938

Fig. 2
Friedrich von Amerling, *Girl with a Straw Hat*, 1835, Liechtenstein, The Princely Collections, Vaduz–Vienna

abundance," as Hans Sedlmayr put it,[45] was removed from office in October 1945 and permanently retired with effect from October 31, 1947. The fact that this "greatest abundance" was also directly linked to the "Aryanization" of Jewish art collections[46] by the Nazi regime should not go unmentioned.

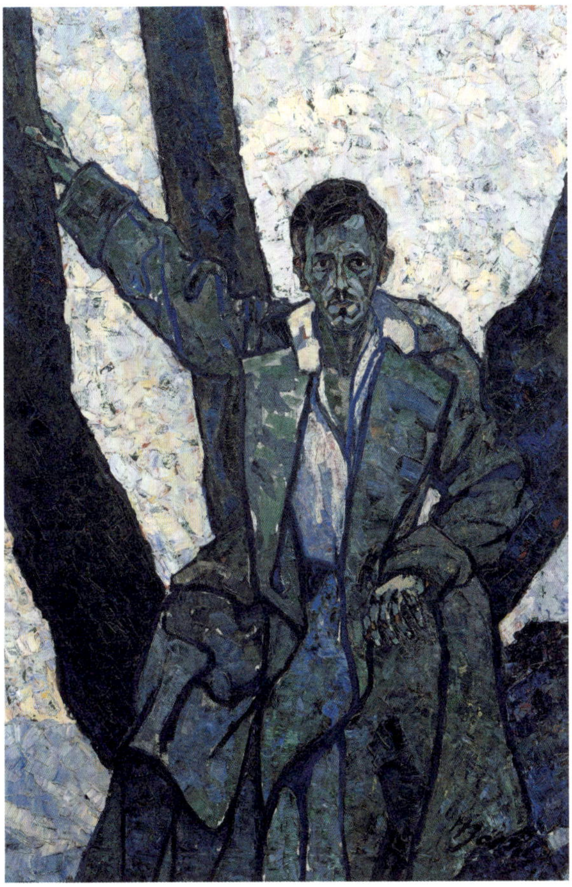

1

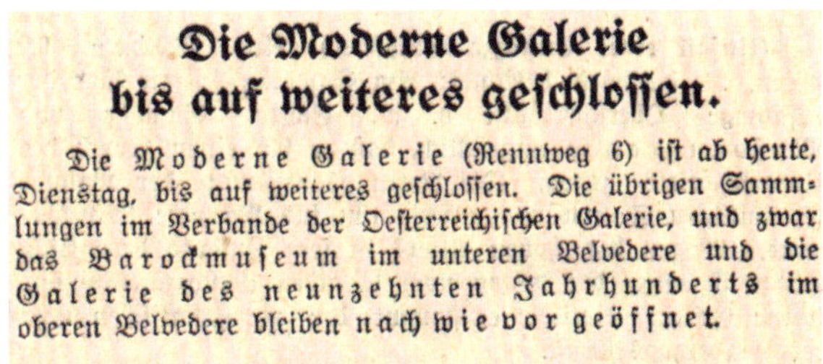

Die Moderne Galerie bis auf weiteres geschlossen.

Die Moderne Galerie (Rennweg 6) ist ab heute, Dienstag, bis auf weiteres geschlossen. Die übrigen Sammlungen im Verbande der Oesterreichischen Galerie, und zwar das Barockmuseum im unteren Belvedere und die Galerie des neunzehnten Jahrhunderts im oberen Belvedere bleiben nach wie vor geöffnet.

2

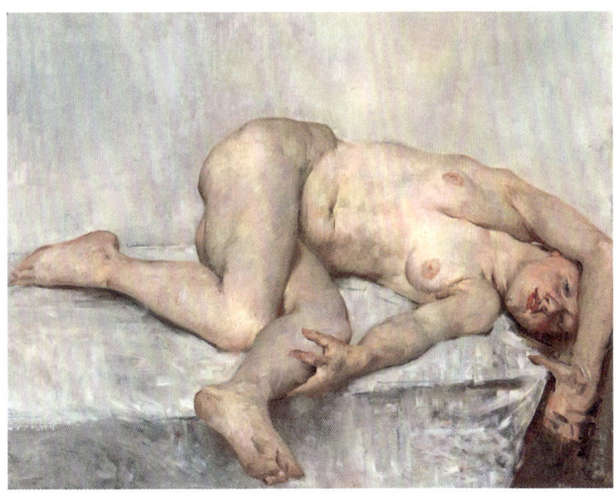

3

Fig. 1
Herbert Boeckl, *Bruno Grimschitz*, 1915, Belvedere, Vienna

Bruno Grimschitz was director of the Austrian Gallery from 1938 to 1945.

Fig. 2
Announcement of the closure of the Modern Gallery in the Orangery, *Neues Wiener Tagblatt*, March 22, 1938, Belvedere Archive, Vienna

Fig. 3
Lovis Corinth, *Reclining Female Nude*, 1907, Belvedere, Vienna

The painting was part of the art collection of Reich foreign minister and industrialist Walther Rathenau, a patron of modern German art, who was assassinated in Berlin in 1922. The Austrian Gallery acquired Corinth's nude and a double portrait by Edvard Munch from Rathenau's estate during the Nazi period.

45 Sedlmayr 1967.
46 Czernin 1999, vol. 2, p. 309.

1938

DIREKTION DER ÖSTERREICHISCHEN GALERIE

BAROCKMUSEUM IM UNTEREN BELVEDERE
GALERIE DES NEUNZEHNTEN JAHRHUNDERTS IM OBEREN BELVEDERE
MODERNE GALERIE IN DER ORANGERIE DES BELVEDERE

Original!

WIEN, 2. April 1938
III., PRINZ EUGENSTRASSE 27 / TELEPHON U 16-310

Sehr verehrter Herr Hofrat!

Ministerialrat Dr. Thomasberger rief mich telephonisch in meiner Wohnung an und gab mir den Auftrag, Ihnen mitzuteilen, dass das Ministerium Ihr Ansuchen um Beurlaubung aus Gesundheitsrücksichten erwartet. Welche Gründe das Ministerium veranlassen, mich mit diesem Auftrag zu betrauen, ist mir unbekannt. Über die Übergabe der Leitung hoffe ich, mich mit Ihnen im Laufe des heutigen Tages in der Galerie aussprechen zu können.

Mit herzlichen Empfehlungen bin ich
Ihr ergebener
Bruno Grimschitz

4

Fig. 4
Letter from Bruno Grimschitz to Franz Martin Haberditzl, April 2, 1938, private collection, Vienna

Fig. 5
Letter from the Reich governor's office Vienna to Bruno Grimschitz, April 30, 1942, AdB, Zl. 220/1942

220/42 3

Der Reichsstatthalter in Wien
Generalreferat für Kunstförderung, Staatstheater, Museen und Volksbildung
Wien, I., Reitschulgasse 2

Z/GK. 3484/b/42

Wien, den 30. April 1942

An den
Herrn Direktor der Österreichischen Galerie
in W i e n

Betrifft: Ankauf von Werken Monets und Corots.

Der Herr Reichsleiter hat das Gemälde von Claude Monet "Gartenweg" und die beiden Gemälde von Camille Corot "Waldlandschaft am Abend" und "Morgenlandschaft" angekauft und weist sie der Österreichischen Galerie ins inventarische Eigentum ein.

Die Gemälde befinden sich bereits in Ihrem Museum.

Im Auftrage:
T h o m a s .

Beglaubigt:

vom 7. ten Mai 1942
Direktion
... Galerie in Wien
Zl. 220 mit ... Beilagen

5

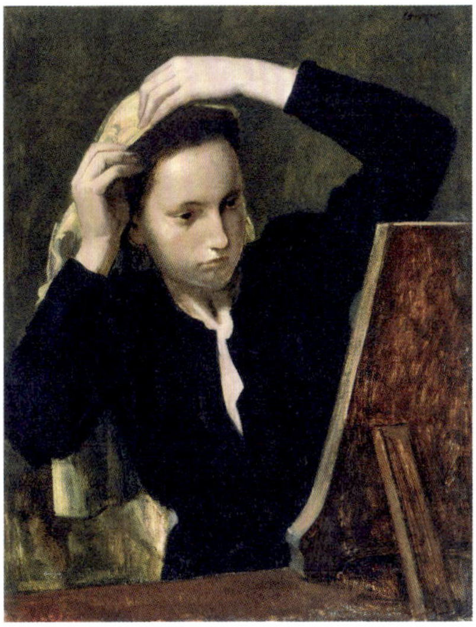

6

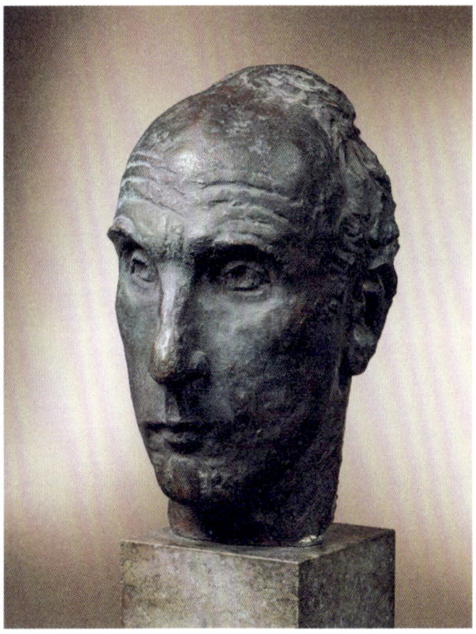

7

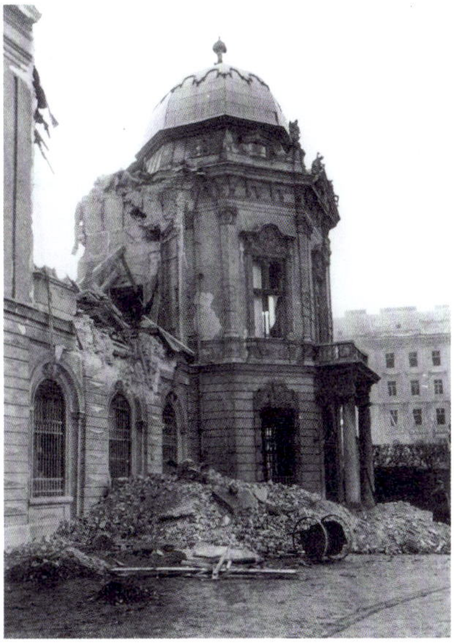

8

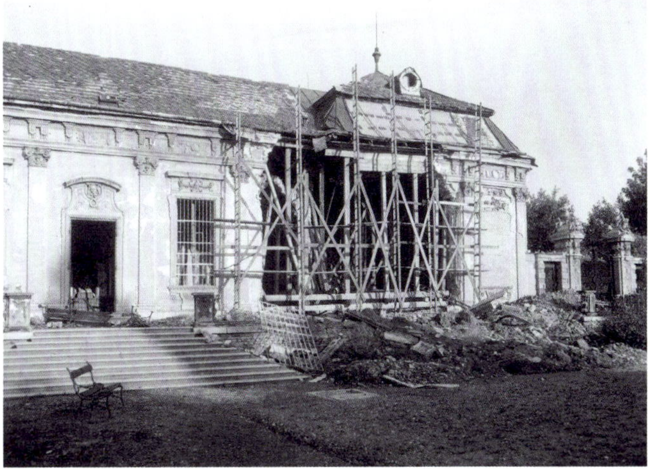

9

Fig. 6
Rudolf Hermann Eisenmenger, *Woman with Yellow Headscarf*, 1943, Belvedere, Vienna

The portrait by Rudolf Hermann Eisenmenger, purchased at the 1943 Künstlerhaus spring exhibition at the behest of Reich governor Baldur von Schirach, was allocated to the Austrian Gallery. The painter had been an illegal member of the Nazi Party since 1933 and, as president of the Künstlerhaus, was one of the most influential figures in Vienna's cultural scene during the Nazi period. In 1944, he was included in the Reich Propaganda Ministry's *Gottbegnadeten* list ("god-gifted" list).

Fig. 7
Gerhard Marcks, *Head of the Sculptor Toni Stadler*, 1935, Belvedere, Vienna

In 1933, the German sculptor Gerhard Marcks was dismissed as rector of the art school in Halle for political reasons. Two of his works were included in the Munich *Degenerate Art* exhibition in 1937. He was subsequently prohibited from exhibiting and was threatened repeatedly with a work ban. However, director Grimschitz argued in favor of the purchase of two of his sculptures in 1943, pointing to the outstanding quality of this "exceptionally talented master among recent German sculptors." This is an example of the inconsistency between Nazi cultural policy and the Austrian Gallery's collection strategy during this time.

Fig. 8
Upper Belvedere, war damage on the north side, 1945, Austrian National Library, Vienna

Fig. 9
Lower Belvedere, bomb damage in the Hall of Grotesques, 1945, Austrian National Library, Vienna

SABINE PLAKOLM-FORSTHUBER —
National Socialist Art Policy in the Gau City of Vienna

As everywhere among those parts of the population who supported the National Socialist idea, the cultural sector also welcomed and made preparations for the annexation of Austria to the German Reich in March 1938. Art and architecture played a major ideological role in National Socialism, and Vienna, as a recognized center for music, theater, and museums, therefore hoped that it would have a special status among the cities of the Third Reich. These expectations were further reinforced by the speech given by Adolf Hitler in Vienna City Hall on April 9, 1938—the eve of the "plebiscite"—in which he promised to create the "setting worthy of the pearl" that Vienna represented.[1] In reality, the plans the Nazis had for Vienna were quite the opposite of this propaganda. The city's political and cultural supremacy achieved during the Habsburg monarchy was to be diminished in favor of the Gaus (administrative regions) in the "Ostmark" (the name used in Nazi propaganda to describe the former independent state of Austria), and its cosmopolitan standing was to be downgraded so as to enhance the status of Linz, Hitler's favorite city. Unlike the "Führerstadt Linz," Vienna was only given the title of Gau city and had to content itself with a less prominent position in the shadow of the "Führerstädte" (Führer cities) and the Reich capital Berlin.[2]

The restructuring of the cultural sector took place in two phases. The first phase, which began with the annexation in March 1938, involved the complete reorganization of all cultural institutions and their alignment with the Nazi ideology. It was at this point that the hitherto illegal Nazi artists came into their own. Frictions arose on account of the unclear division of competence between the Reich, the regions, and the municipalities, which persisted in essence until the promulgation of the "Ostmark laws" in April 1939. The second phase, which was of greater relevance for National Socialist cultural policy in Vienna, began with the appointment of Baldur von Schirach as Gauleiter and Reich governor and the enterprising cultural program he envisaged for Vienna.[3]

There were precursors to the restructuring that took place after the annexation. After the NSDAP was banned on June 19, 1933, Nazi-minded

1 Anon., "'Auch diese Stadt wird eine neue Blüte erleben!' Des Führers Dank an Wien," in *Neues Wiener Journal*, April 10, 1938, p. 3.
2 Botz 2018, p. 371.
3 Rathkolb 2020.

artists organized themselves in an illegal "culture department," headed from 1935 by the writer Hermann Stuppäck.[4] After the annexation, he and his colleagues, including Leopold Blauensteiner (→ p. 229, fig. 1), Marcel Kammerer, Rudolf Hermann Eisenmenger, and Alexander Popp, demanded leading positions in Nazi cultural policymaking. The Bund deutscher Maler Österreichs (Association of German Painters of Austria) performed a similar role. From June 1937, its members included future elite Nazi artists. It was chaired by Leopold Blauensteiner, an illegal National Socialist, whose artistic career had begun around 1900 in the Vienna Secession and was to reach its high point with the powerful position he occupied under the Nazis.

The alignment of the art industry to the Nazi ideology began directly after the annexation. Politically undesirable artists and persons of Jewish origin were dismissed, provisional directors took over artists' associations, art colleges, museums, and theaters. The NSDAP member Bruno Grimschitz (→ p. 255, fig. 1) was appointed provisional director of the Austrian Gallery in the Belvedere. After the "plebiscite," Josef Bürckel became Reich Commissar for the Reunification of Austria with the German Reich. On May 17, 1938, he entrusted liquidation commissar Alfred Hoffmann with the task of incorporating societies, organizations, and associations.

The situation of the Jewish population deteriorated markedly with the entry into force of the Nuremberg race laws in the "Ostmark," as it was now officially called, on May 20, 1938. These laws also offered art institutions a legal instrument for getting rid of their Jewish members and employees. As early as April 6, 1938, Grimschitz announced the dismissal of the curator Heinrich Schwarz, who was expelled from Austria on racial grounds, and the temporary appointment of Kurt Blauensteiner, son of Leopold Blauensteiner, to the research department.

In June 1938, the regional office of the Reich Chamber of Fine Arts (→ p. 229, ⑰), established in Germany in 1933, began operating in the "Ostmark" under the leadership of Leopold Blauensteiner. Anyone wishing to work in the art sector was obliged to join this Nazi institution. Persons of Jewish origin, political opponents, and avant-garde artists were refused admission. The NSDAP Gau offices and the Gestapo played an important role in the admission procedure. The office collaborated closely with the headquarters in Berlin, which was under the control of Joseph Goebbels, president of the Reich Chamber of Culture.

The Künstlerhaus in Vienna was the center of National Socialist art propaganda, headed, after its merger with the Secession in 1939, by Rudolf Hermann Eisenmenger. It was the location of the most important exhibitions, starting with the major Alpine exhibition, which had been planned back in 1937 and now opened in ideologically modified form in

4 Holzschuh/Plakolm-Forsthuber 2021, p. 17.

March 1939, under the title *Mountains and People in the Ostmark*. With an added section on the economic situation, this exhibition was then shown, from May 1939, at the Messegelände exhibition grounds in Berlin. This was the first presentation in the Old Reich of artists from the "Ostmark," organized under the patronage of leading National Socialist cultural functionaries in Vienna, who were in charge of commissions, subsidies, and art purchases. The 107 objects bought by the Reich governor's office at the exhibition in Vienna were put up for sale again in Berlin, but sales were disappointing. Some of the pictures acquired by the Reich governor remained in storage for a long time in the Künstlerhaus and were handed over to the Federal Ministry of Finance in 1958.[5]

In charge of the promotion of the arts at a regional level was the art historian and erstwhile propaganda director of the Salzburg Festival, Kajetan Mühlmann, an illegal Nazi and member of the SS. As state secretary for art under Austrian Reich governor Arthur Seyss-Inquart, he was one of the persons responsible for the "Aryanization" of artworks from Jewish collections. One of his aims was to ensure that "the most important art treasures [should remain] in Austria and above all here in Vienna as part of the city's cultural heritage."[6] Mühlmann thwarted Hitler's art distribution plans and his preference for the "Führermuseum" in Linz.[7] He was, however, unable to prevent the removal of the Reich insignia to Nuremberg on September 6, 1938. On Mühlmann's instructions, Grimschitz turned down a request by the exhibition *The Eternal Jew* (Nordwestbahnhalle, 1938) to loan works by Jewish artists[8] and also rejected an inquiry concerning objects from Austrian collections for the Nazi propaganda exhibition *Degenerate Art* at the Künstlerhaus in 1939.[9] It should be pointed out that Austria did not have anything like the collection of avant-garde art that Germany had. Moreover, the museums in the German Reich affected by the seizures beginning in 1933 had a much larger inventory of "degenerate art" (→ p. 221, ⑯) than Vienna's museums. The Modern Gallery, the collection of contemporary art in the Orangery of the Lower Belvedere, was closed by Grimschitz in March 1938 by order of the Austrian Ministry of Education, its artworks initially placed in storage and then moved, from summer 1939, to depositories in Lower Austria. From October 1939, the premises were used by the Central Monument Protection Office to store secured artworks.[10]

Following the annexation, new plans were being hatched everywhere. Mühlmann, who lived in the garden parterre in the grounds of the Lower Belvedere, known as the "Kammerstöckl," looked immediately to refurbish the somewhat dilapidated section of the palace along Rennweg. In November 1938, he commissioned the architects Oswald Haerdtl and Helmut Sylvester Keidel to survey the site, with a view to using it for a museum of folk life and folk art. While Haerdtl's design from 1939

5 Confirmation of receipt by the Federal Ministry of Finance, July 17, 1958, Künstlerhaus archive, Vienna, file "Berge und Menschen der Ostmark."
6 https://www.lexikon-provenienzforschung.org/en/muehlmann-kajetan (accessed on August 8, 2022).
7 Schwarz 2004, p. 39.
8 Henrichs 2021, p. 152.
9 Gröning 2021, p. 83.
10 Mayer 2016, p. 177.

proposed installing the museum in the former stables around the five-sided courtyard, Keidel, who lived at Rennweg 6, suggested that part of the building on Rennweg 4 be demolished and a new building erected.[11] Neither of these projects was implemented. Mühlmann was dismissed by Bürckel in June 1939 on account of his "pro-Austrian tendencies."[12] In his function as "special representative for the protection of artworks," he continued his career as a Nazi art looter in occupied Poland and from 1940 in the Netherlands.

There were also some local efforts to foster an independent Viennese cultural policy. The most significant of these was the Kulturamt der Stadt Wien (Cultural Office of the City of Vienna), founded under deputy mayor Hanns Blaschke on September 28, 1938. Its aim was "the promotion and control of artistic life in Vienna."[13] Its various sections were organized essentially on the model of the Reich Chamber of Fine Arts. Apart from the fine arts, there were sections for architecture, applied arts, theater, and fashion, headed by deserving Nazi artists. The Cultural Office under Blaschke became one of the most important public sector commissioners of works by local artists. It invited tenders for monuments and art on buildings, renovated theaters, and established the Vienna Arts and Crafts Association and the Haus der Mode (House of Fashion), all in close collaboration with the Reich Chamber of Fine Arts.

After Seyss-Inquart left office in 1939, Bürckel, as Reich governor and Gauleiter, also took responsibility for cultural policy. The National Socialists' profoundly racist policy came to the fore in the new cultural agenda. At the opening of the *Degenerate Art* exhibition in the Künstlerhaus, Bürckel stressed its "educational task" of showing to "German Vienna" the extent of the "destructive forces that had worked to the detriment of German culture."[14] A similar sentiment was expressed in his speech at the Hofburg, given on March 3, 1940, entitled "Volk und Kultur," in which he announced the establishment of a department headed by him for the promotion of art, theater, museums, and culture.[15] His speeches also imply that Vienna's cultural policy was to be controlled from Berlin. It was this that led to the second phase.

Without going into further detail, it can be said that Gauleiter Bürckel's activities in Vienna were not well received—neither in general nor in terms of the Nazi propaganda agenda. He was dismissed and in 1940 became Reich governor of the Westmark in Saarbrücken. Hitler appointed the eloquent and talented Reich youth leader Baldur von Schirach as his successor and suggested that he take up residence in the Belvedere, but Schirach chose the "Aryanized" villa of the Jewish building inspector Arnold Spritzer at Hohe Warte 52–54, previously occupied by Bürckel.[16] He was assisted in cultural affairs by head dramaturge Walter Thomas from Bochum in his position as general cultural adviser. As Oliver Rath-

11 Letter, Oswald Haerdtl to Kajetan Mühlmann, November 26, 1938, ÖStA/AdR, ZNsZ RSthOe Abt. III – Büro Mühlmann, 1938–1940 (Teilbestand), Zl. 200.665/1938; letter from Helmut Sylvester Keidel to Kajetan Mühlmann, April 15, 1939, ibid., Zl. 79897/1939; Holzschuh/Platzer 2015, pp. 156–57.

12 Letter, Josef Bürckel to Kajetan Mühlmann, June 3, 1939, WStLA, Volksgericht-A1, Vg Vr Strafakten 105/52.

13 Blaschke 1943.

14 Anon., "Die Ausstellung 'Entartete Kunst' im Künstlerhaus," in *Völkischer Beobachter*, May 7, 1939, p. 16.

15 Bürckel 1939, p. 27.

16 Rathkolb 2020, p. 127.

kolb has pointed out, Schirach attempted to compensate for Vienna's loss of political influence by way of a cultural policy that emphasized traditional values.[17] He even envisaged a pioneering role for Viennese culture in the new fascist Europe and managed to obtain considerable funds to promote Viennese cultural institutions, including the Austrian Gallery. On August 14, 1941, he took control of the Künstlerhaus and allocated a large sum for its refurbishment. His activities were marked by regular awards, opera and theater visits, exhibition openings, and art prizes. He also enjoyed seeing himself as a patron of the arts. In line with Schirach's promotion of local culture, the Künstlerhaus focused increasingly on Viennese themes, with exhibitions such as *The Beautiful Women of Vienna* (1942), *The Vienna Cityscape* (1943), and *Pictures of Vienna in Art and Science 1900–1943* (1943/44), which were highly successful, in particular as they also helped distract from the progress of the war.

Interestingly, one exhibition initiated by Schirach almost brought his political career to an end. *Recent Art in the German Reich* (1943) harked back to the moderate figurative Modernism of the interwar years and as such was far removed from the Nazi art stereotypes (fig. 5). It is unlikely that Schirach realized that the 582 exhibits included a few works by artists such as Fritz Burmann, Josef Hegenbarth, and Milly Steger, whose art had been seized from German museums as "degenerate." After being tipped off by informers, Hitler and Goebbels sent experts to Vienna to take a look at the exhibition. In their reports, they described these exhibits as being examples of "degenerate" or "decadent" art.[18] Schirach was ordered to close the exhibition ahead of time. On June 24, 1943, he was summoned to the Obersalzberg, where Hitler is said to have referred to Schirach's activities and the exhibition as "cultural opposition" and ranted about "Viennese art liberalism."[19] The scandal was most likely instigated by Goebbels. The exhibition gave him the opportunity to oppose Schirach's high-handed cultural policy. In his diaries, he expresses his great satisfaction at the reprimand handed out to Schirach. The affair resulted in Vienna's cultural policy being put directly under Goebbels' control.[20] Schirach felt obliged to respond and, in 1943, dismissed his cultural adviser Thomas, who was succeeded by Hermann Stuppäck. The following year, as the war intensified, art and culture became of secondary importance and no longer offered much opportunity to further careers.

It can be said that most of the Nazi policymakers mentioned here knew how to exploit Vienna's tradition as a cultural center, not only to distance themselves from what they regarded as a "Prussian" influence, but also to serve their own interests. They did not want Vienna's special status to be lost and sought rather to ensure that it was given due recognition within National Socialist cultural policy. Eventually, cultural policy was reinterpreted during the war, and artists were put on a par with sol-

17 Rathkolb 2020, p. 203.
18 Holzschuh/Plakolm-Forsthuber 2021, pp. 300–04.
19 Thomas 1947, p. 218.
20 Fröhlich 1993, p. 580.

diers. For example, Hanns Blaschke announced in 1943: "The desire to remain true to one's race gives the artist the strength to create, the soldier the strength to make sacrifices, the worker the strength to keep working, and all of us enjoyment through art."[21] Cultural activities ended in 1944 with the closure of all cultural institutions as part of the "total war." The Austrian Gallery shut its doors in August 1944.

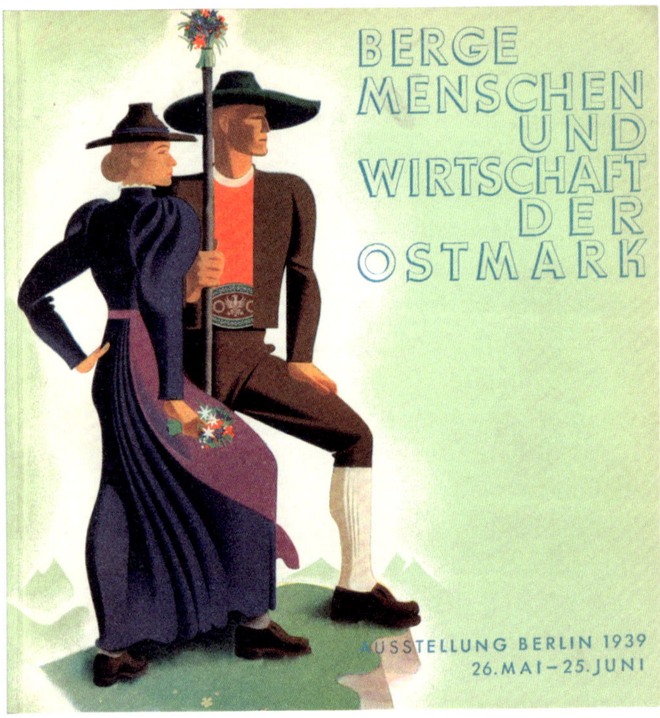

1

Fig. 1
Catalogue of the exhibition *Mountains, People and Economy of the Ostmark*, Berlin 1939, Vienna City Library

21 Quoted by anon., "Kulturbericht," in *Neues Wiener Tagblatt*, June 14, 1942, p. 3.

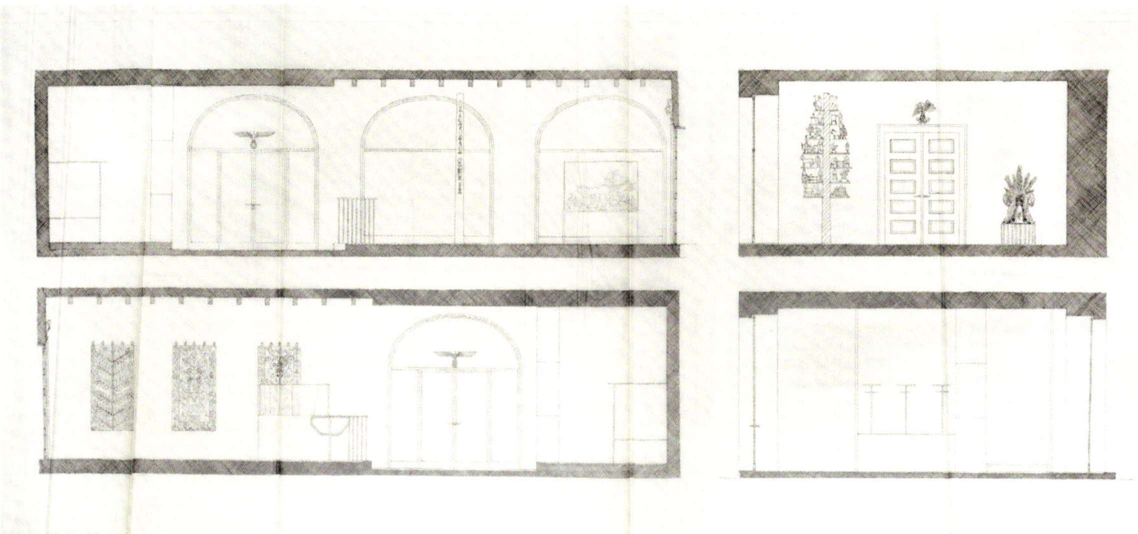

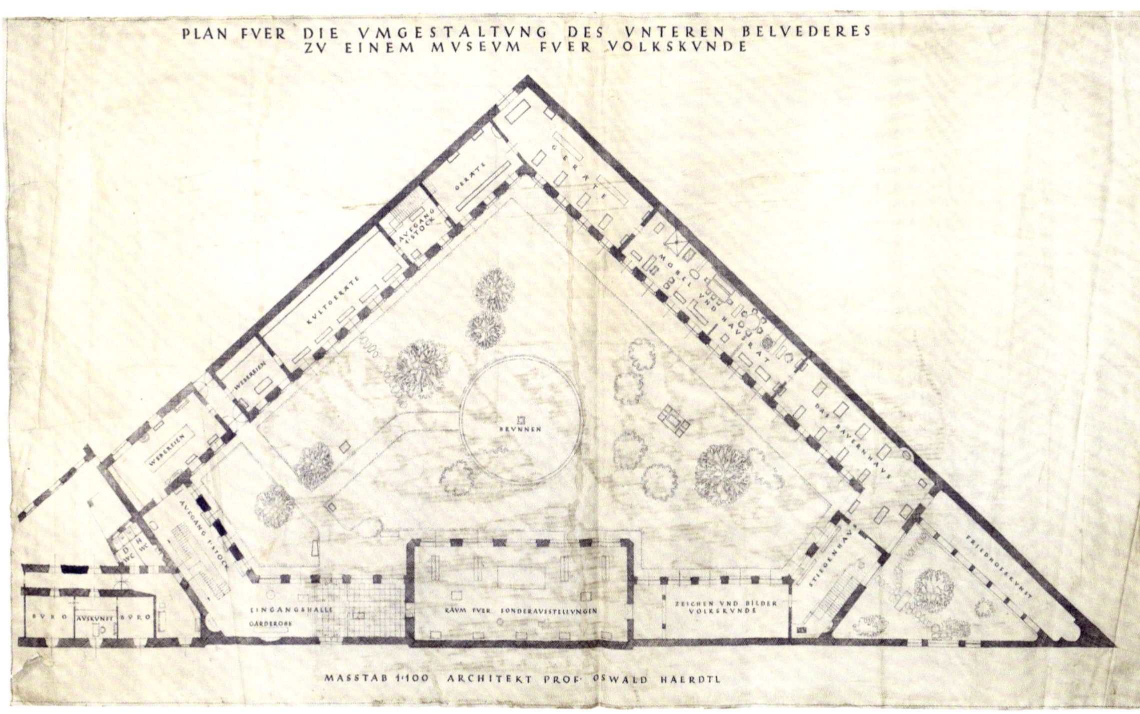

2

Fig. 2
Oswald Haerdtl, floor plan and room arrangement for the planned museum of ethnology in the Lower Belvedere, Architekturzentrum Wien, Collection

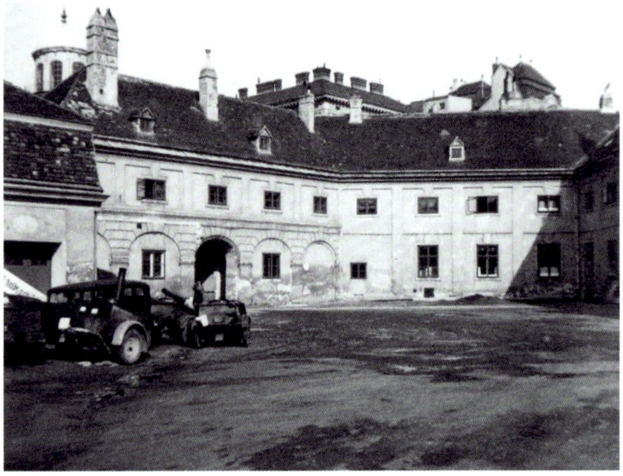

3

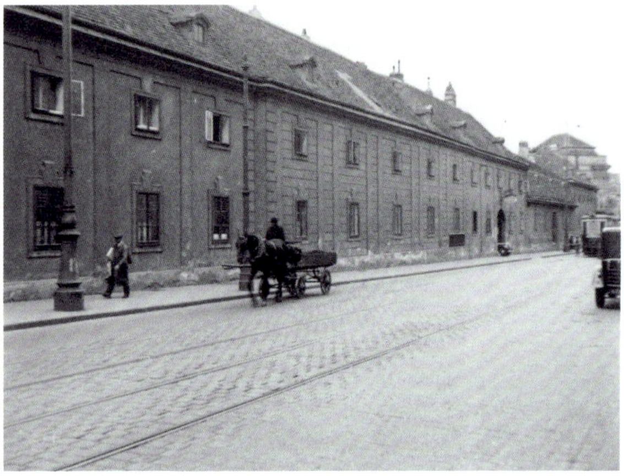

4

Fig. 3
Five-sided courtyard in the grounds of the Lower Belvedere, 1938/39, photo: Helmut Sylvester Keidel, Austrian State Archives, Vienna

Fig. 4
Building sections along Rennweg, 1938/39, photo: Helmut Sylvester Keidel, Austrian State Archives, Vienna

Fig. 5
Approval by Leopold Blauensteiner, director of the Vienna office of the Reich Chamber of Fine Arts, for the Gustav Klimt exhibition and for the exhibition *Recent Art in the German Reich*, January 20, 1943, Künstlerhaus Archive, Vienna

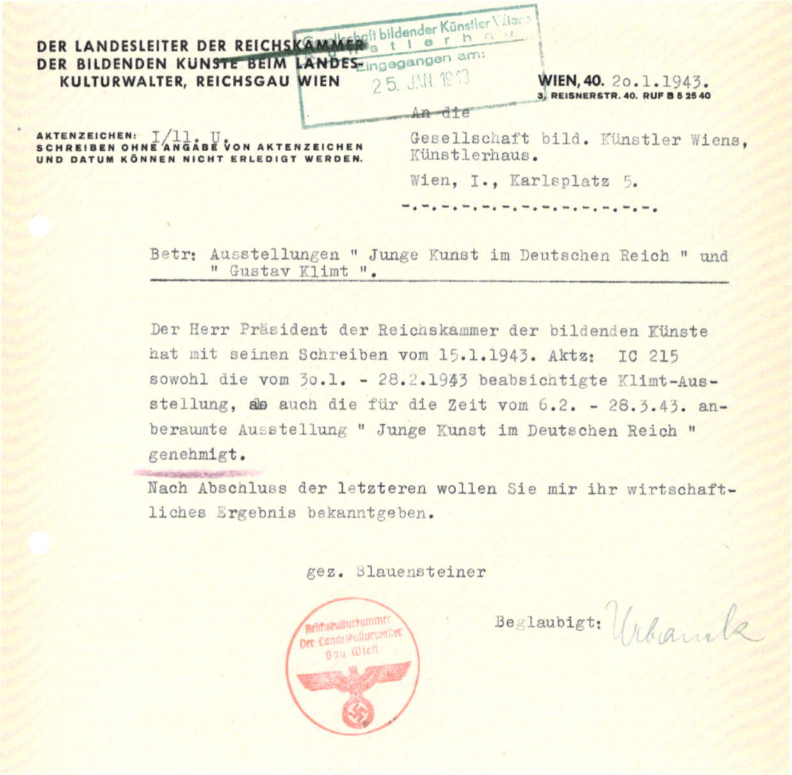

DER LANDESLEITER DER REICHSKAMMER
DER BILDENDEN KÜNSTE BEIM LANDES-
KULTURWALTER, REICHSGAU WIEN

Gesellschaft bildender Künstler Wiens
Künstlerhaus
Eingegangen am:
25. JAN. 1943

WIEN, 40. 2o.1.1943.
3, REISNERSTR. 40. RUF B 5 25 40

AKTENZEICHEN: I/11. U.
SCHREIBEN OHNE ANGABE VON AKTENZEICHEN UND DATUM KÖNNEN NICHT ERLEDIGT WERDEN.

An die
Gesellschaft bild. Künstler Wiens,
Künstlerhaus.
Wien, I., Karlsplatz 5.
-.-.-.-.-.-.-.-.-.-.-.-.-.-.

Betr: Ausstellungen " Junge Kunst im Deutschen Reich " und " Gustav Klimt ".

Der Herr Präsident der Reichskammer der bildenden Künste hat mit seinen Schreiben vom 15.1.1943. Aktz: IC 215 sowohl die vom 3o.1. - 28.2.1943 beabsichtigte Klimt-Ausstellung, als auch die für die Zeit vom 6.2. - 28.3.43. anberaumte Ausstellung " Junge Kunst im Deutschen Reich " genehmigt.

Nach Abschluss der letzteren wollen Sie mir ihr wirtschaftliches Ergebnis bekanntgeben.

gez. Blauensteiner

Beglaubigt: Urbanek

5

(20)

The Gustav Klimt Exhibition of 1943

Johanna Aufreiter

In early 1943, the Reich governor of Vienna Baldur von Schirach staged a retrospective[1] in the former Secession building to mark the twenty-fifth anniversary of the death and the eightieth anniversary of the birth of Gustav Klimt (fig. 1). After the merger of the Künstlerhaus and the Secession in 1939, the exhibition building on Friedrichstrasse was used as an outlet of the Vienna Künstlerhaus. Exactly one hundred works by Klimt— fifty oil paintings, forty-eight works on paper, and two sections of the *Beethoven Frieze*—were presented across six exhibition rooms (fig. 2).

Baldur von Schirach attached great importance to positioning Vienna alongside Berlin as a center of German culture in the Reich. For him, Klimt embodied everything Vienna stood for, an assessment he based on Emil Pirchan's book *Gustav Klimt: Ein Künstler aus Wien*, published the year before, in which the artist's biography had been "cleansed" of all undesirable and politically suspect traces and made "fertile" for National Socialism. On August 3, 1942, the general cultural adviser Walter Thomas from the central office of the Reich governor contacted Bruno Grimschitz, director of the Austrian Gallery (→ p. 255, fig. 1), and commissioned him to curate the commemorative exhibition, suggesting in addition that he might like to "avail himself of the services" of Emil Pirchan. He also gave him permission to return to Vienna any of Klimt's works that had perhaps been taken into safe storage and assured him of his full support for this endeavor.[2]

To align Klimt and his work with National Socialist ideology, the exhibition followed the practice of "cultural deletion." All references to the artist's Jewish circle of acquaintances and supporters—be they generous bourgeois patrons of the arts, Jewish collectors, or Jewish women portrayed by Klimt—were removed or anonymized. Any already "secured" works from collections (for example, from the Lederer and Bloch-Bauer families) were listed in the catalogue as privately owned, but without names. Portraits of Jewish women were given generic titles such as *Portrait of a Woman with Gold Background* (= *Adele Bloch-Bauer I*).[3] Around one-third of the paintings in the exhibition had been seized from Jewish collectors. The foreword to the catalogue (fig. 3) was written by Fritz Novotny, curator of the Austrian Gallery since 1939, "who is to be thanked for the design of this exhibition"[4] and who almost apologetically describes the sometimes "undue solidification [...] into ornamental patterns" in Klimt's painting. Only the pencil drawings were "unencumbered by this problem": "The most important feature of Klimt's art is his masterful drawing talent."[5]

The retrospective opened on February 7 and was scheduled to run until March 7, 1943. On March 6, an extension of the exhibition until Sunday, March 14, was announced in the *Kleine Volks-Zeitung* and elsewhere,[6] although it in fact closed on Friday, March 12. The show proved immensely popular, attracting 24,096 visitors to the Secession building. Media reports were also overwhelmingly positive. The *Völkischer Beobachter*, the NSDAP propaganda mouthpiece, devoted three articles to Klimt and the exhibition. On February 8, 1943, Thomas wrote a fulsome note of thanks to Grimschitz: "I must congratulate you on the really magnificent Klimt exhibition. It is one of the most impressive artistic undertakings I have seen in my time in

Vienna and provides an unprecedented insight into the creative work of the new style and the thinking of this time."[7]

After the exhibition closed, some of the works were removed for the duration of the war and taken for safe storage in Immenhof Castle in Lower Austria. As the Red Army approached, the retreating SS troops started a fire on May 8, 1945, and the castle burned to the ground. Alongside the three Faculty paintings *Medicine*, *Jurisprudence*, and *Philosophy*, the pictures lost included *Schubert at the Piano*, *Golden Apple Tree*, and *Wally*. The *Beethoven Frieze* had been moved in December 1943 to Thürnthal Castle near Fels am Wagram in Lower Austria and survived the war.

1 For details, see Lillie 2015; Lillie 2017, pp. 83–89
2 Walter Thomas to Bruno Grimschitz, August 3, 1942, AdB. Zl. 398/1942.
3 Natter 2000.
4 *Das kleine Volksblatt*, March 11, 1943, p. 6.
5 Novotny 1943.
6 *Kleine Volks-Zeitung*, March 6, 1943, p. 5.
7 Walter Thomas to Bruno Grimschitz, February 2, 1943, AdB. Zl. 398/1942.

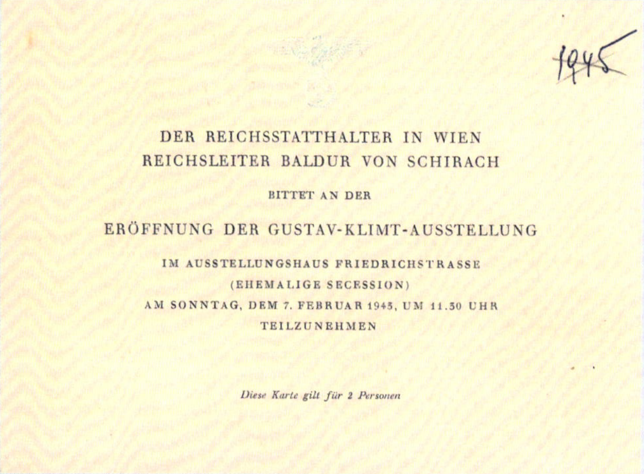
1945

DER REICHSSTATTHALTER IN WIEN
REICHSLEITER BALDUR VON SCHIRACH
BITTET AN DER
ERÖFFNUNG DER GUSTAV-KLIMT-AUSSTELLUNG
IM AUSSTELLUNGSHAUS FRIEDRICHSTRASSE
(EHEMALIGE SECESSION)
AM SONNTAG, DEM 7. FEBRUAR 1943, UM 11.30 UHR
TEILZUNEHMEN

Diese Karte gilt für 2 Personen

1

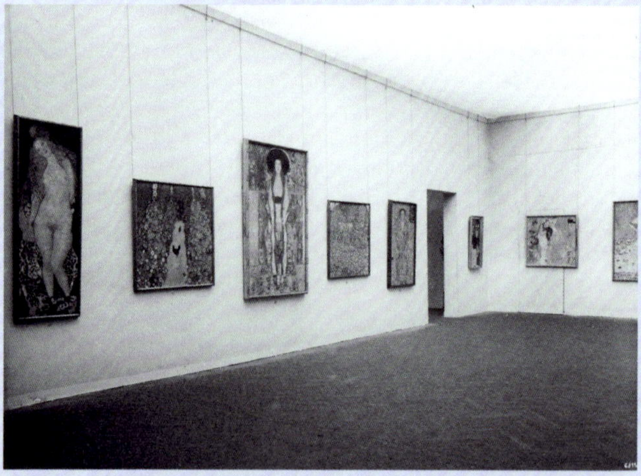

2

Fig. 1
Invitation to the opening of the Gustav Klimt exhibition, Ausstellungshaus Friedrichstraße, Vienna 1943, Künstlerhaus Archive, Vienna

Fig. 2
Gustav Klimt exhibition, in the center left of the picture the portrait *Adele Bloch-Bauer II*, listed in the catalogue as *Woman Standing*; Ausstellungshaus Friedrichstraße, Vienna 1943, Künstlerhaus Archive, Vienna

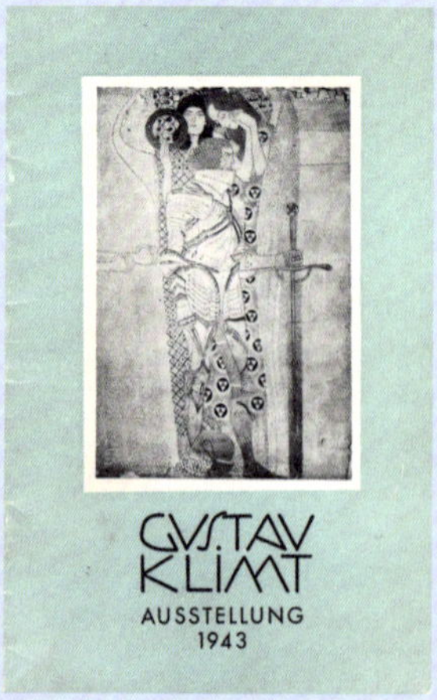

3

Fig. 3
Gustav Klimt exhibition catalogue, Ausstellungshaus Friedrichstraße, 1943, Belvedere Archive, Vienna

Chapter V

Changes and Continuities After 1945

1945–2023

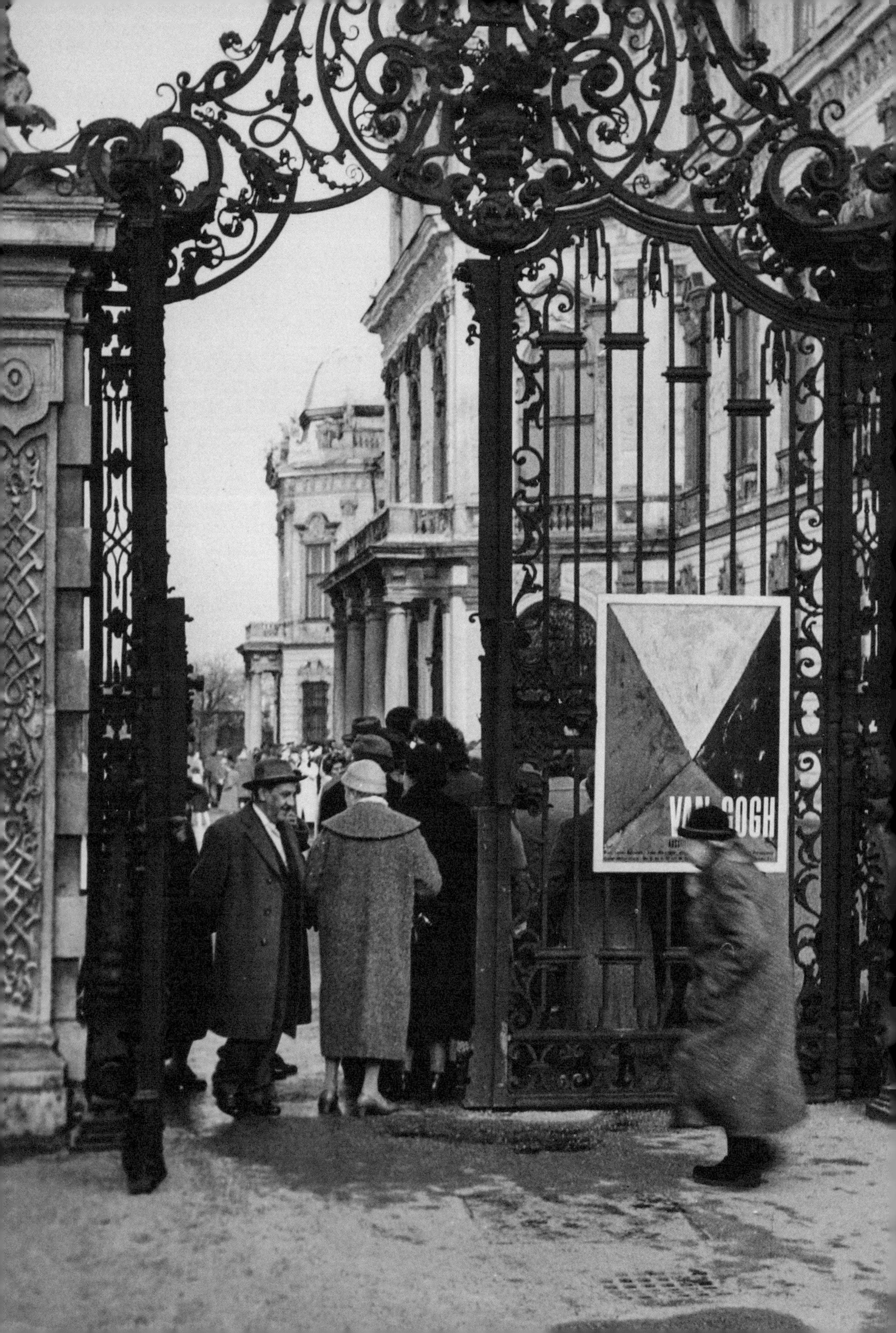
VAN GOGH

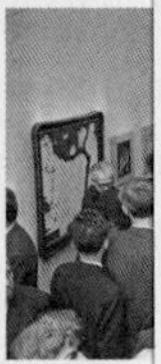

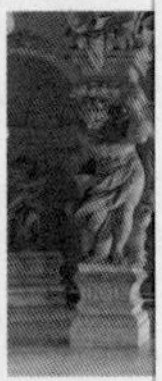

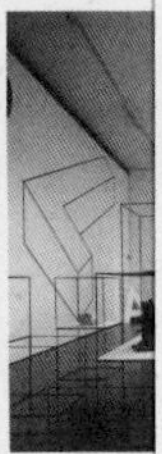

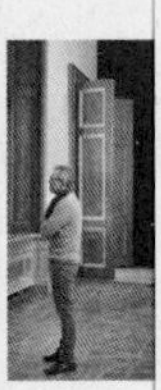

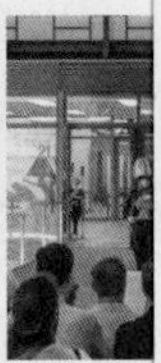

←
Queues o
the Uppe
for the V
exhibitio
vedere In
chive, Vi

Chapter V
Changes and Continuities
After 1945

In a letter dated November 10, 1955, the "Reichsbund der Arbeit-Schaffenden" in the 8th district of Vienna demanded the immediate removal of pictures by Egon Schiele (e.g. *Squatting Women*), stating "in their unsurpassable vulgarity these could perhaps serve as illustrations in a brothel; but their euphemistic description as 'art' is no more justified than the word 'love' is on the lips of a prostitute."

— Letter from the Federal Ministry for Education to the director of the Austrian Gallery, November 17, 1955; AdB, Zl. 696/1955

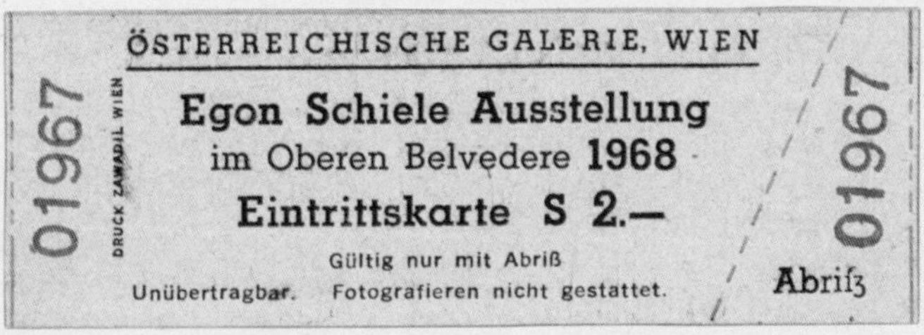

Entry ticket for the Egon Schiele exhibition, 1968, Belvedere Archive, Vienna

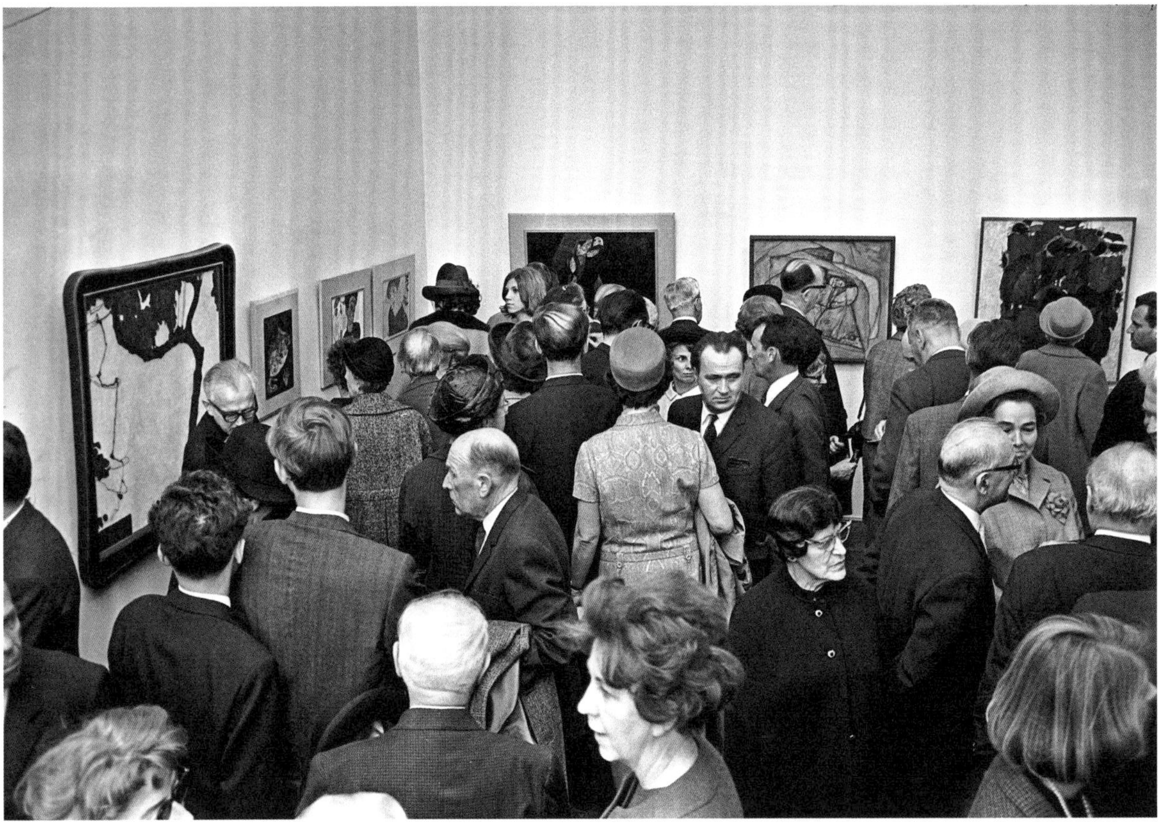

Opening of the first monographic Egon Schiele exhibition in the Upper Belvedere, April 8, 1968

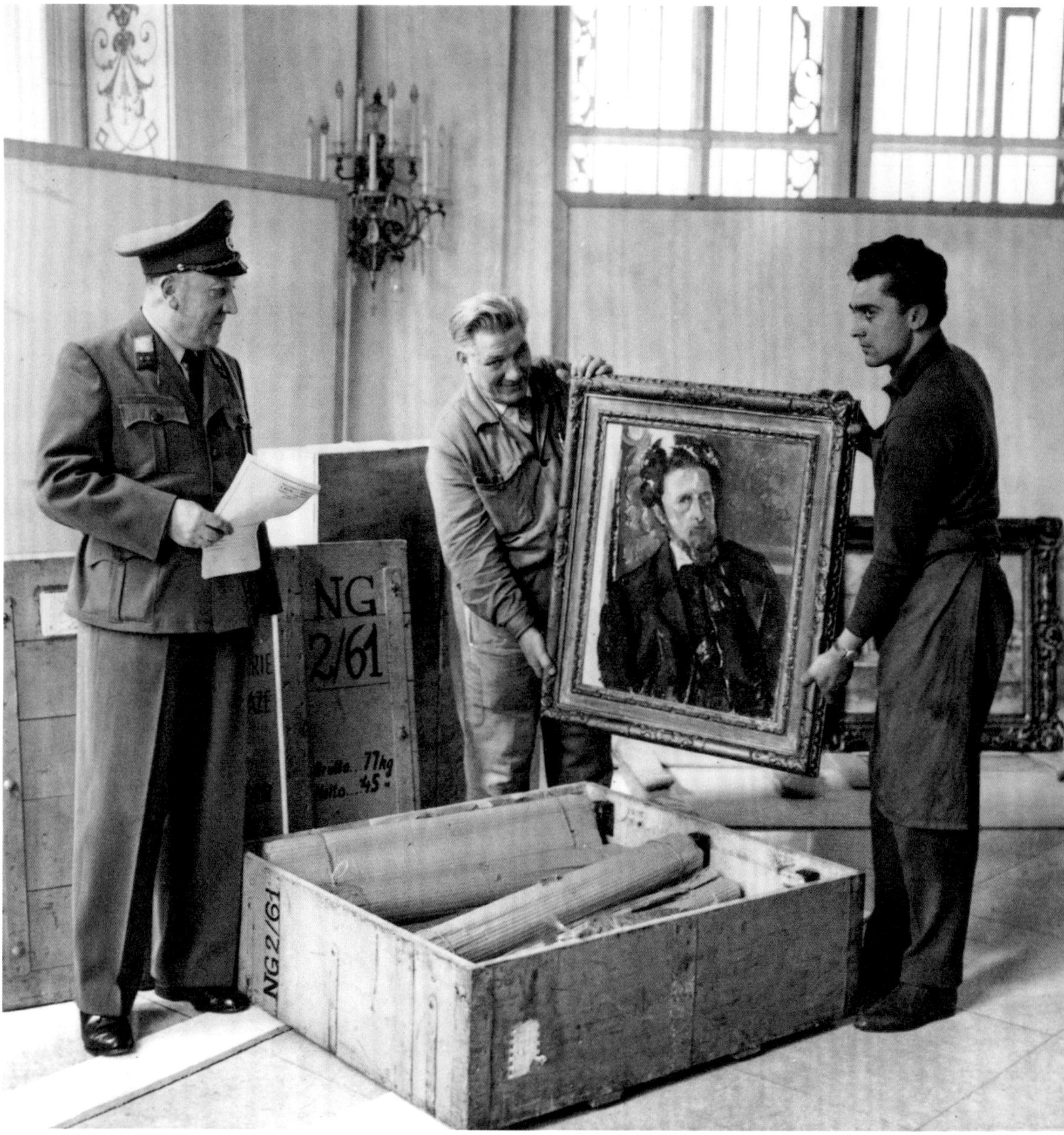

Unpacking of loans for the exhibition *Paul Cézanne 1839–1906* in the Upper Belvedere, April 5, 1961

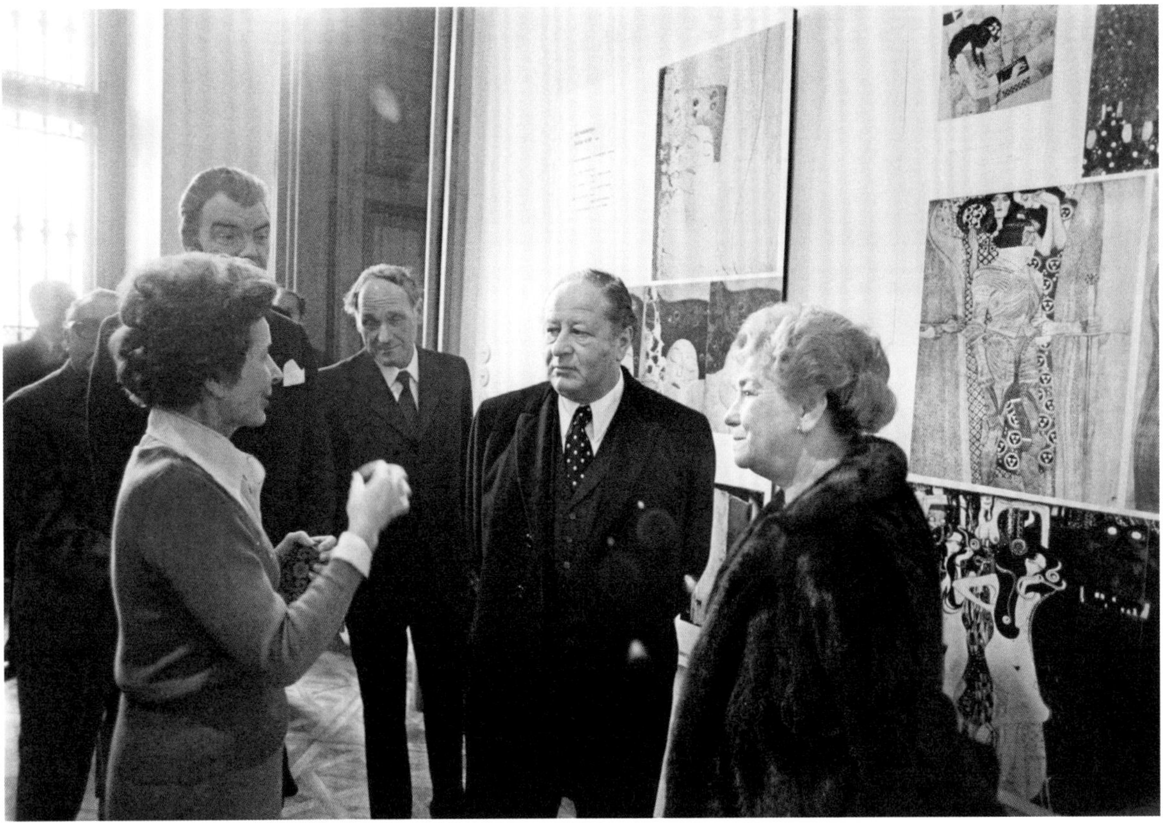

Federal Chancellor
Bruno Kreisky
and Minister of Science Hertha Firnberg
view the first restored piece of the
Beethoven Frieze
by Gustav Klimt in the
Upper Belvedere,
October 26, 1975

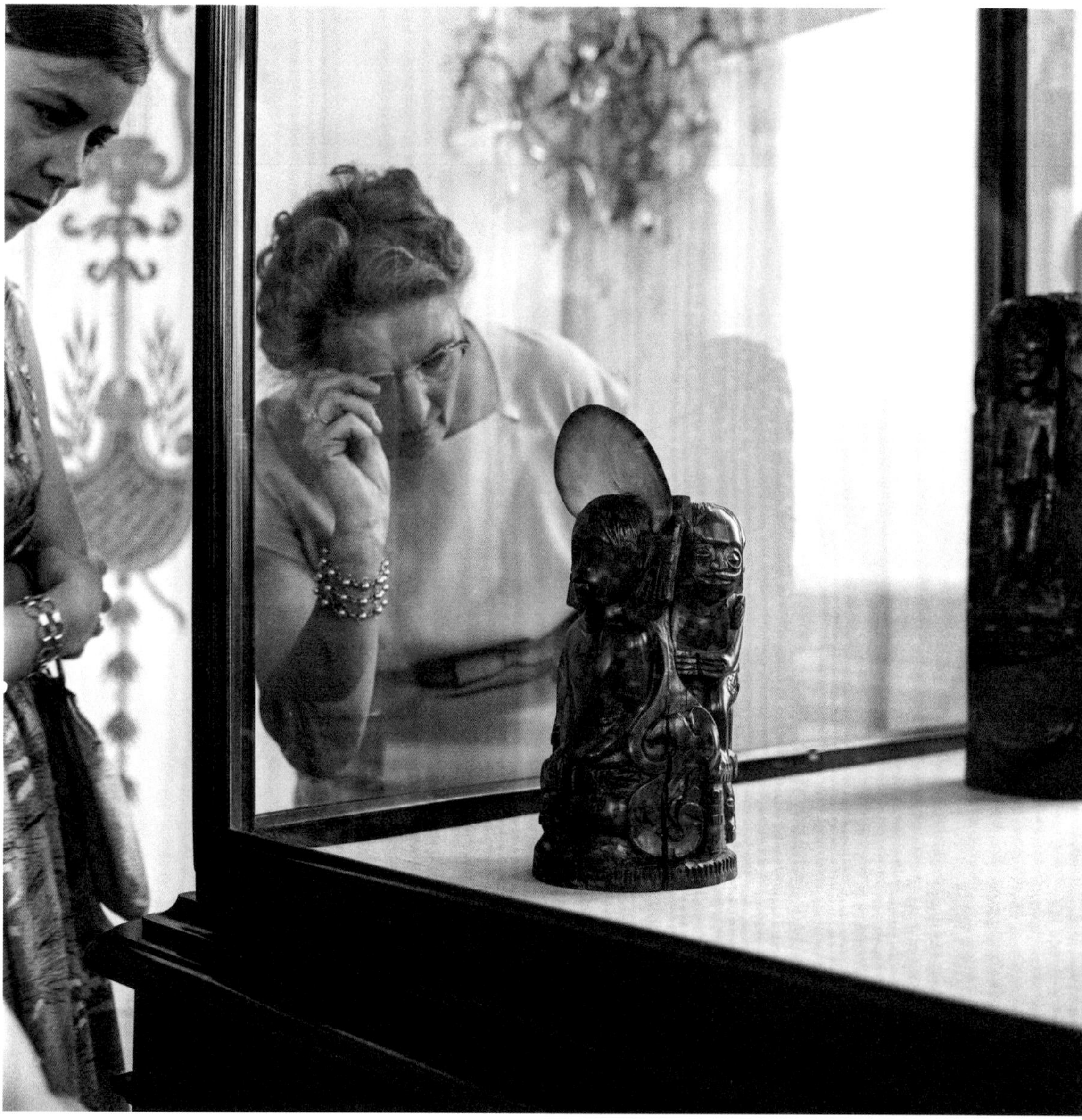

Visitors at the Paul Gauguin exhibition in the Upper Belvedere, 1960

I am more or less familiar with every gallery in Europe and would like to say that, even with less internationally renowned names than other galleries are able to sport, you are able to make a surprisingly good overall impression. [...] The plaques with the names of each painting and its painter, albeit coherent and attractive in themselves, are consistently positioned below the pictures and thus in some cases barely visible and very difficult to read.

—— Dr. H. Haegler to the director of the Belvedere, October 22, 1953, AdB, Zl. 224/1953

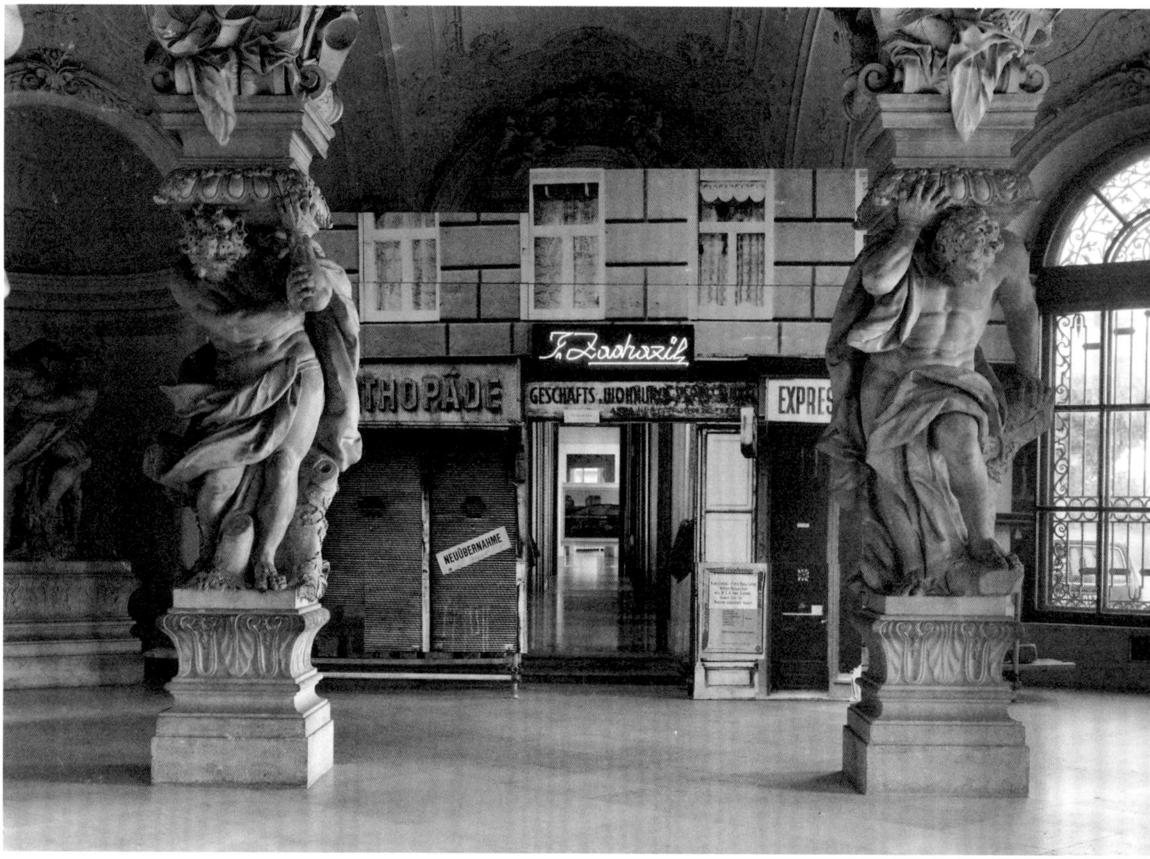

Solo exhibition of
Franz Zadrazil in
the Upper Belvedere,
1979

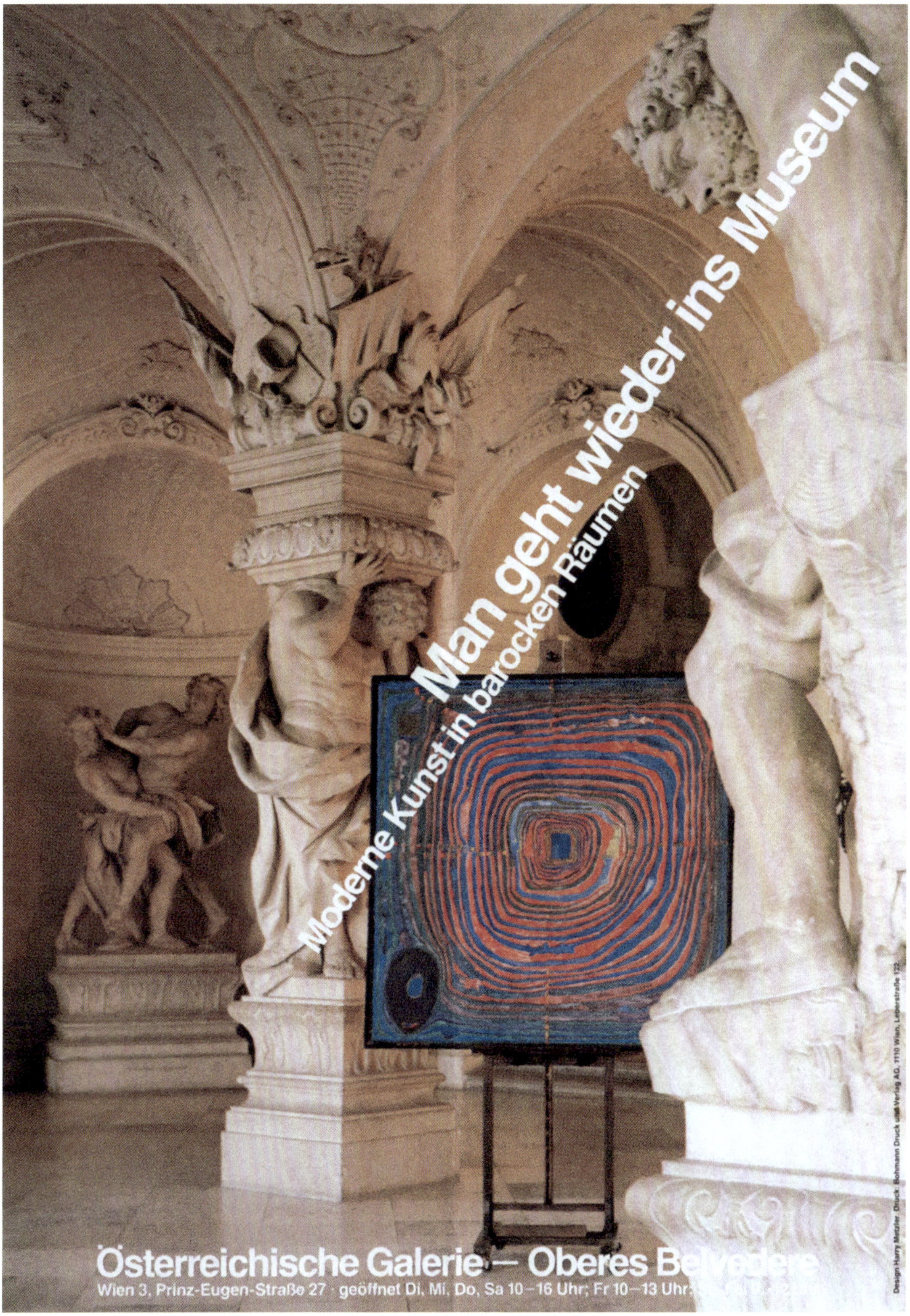

Poster *Man geht wieder ins Museum: Moderne Kunst in barocken Räumen*, 1982

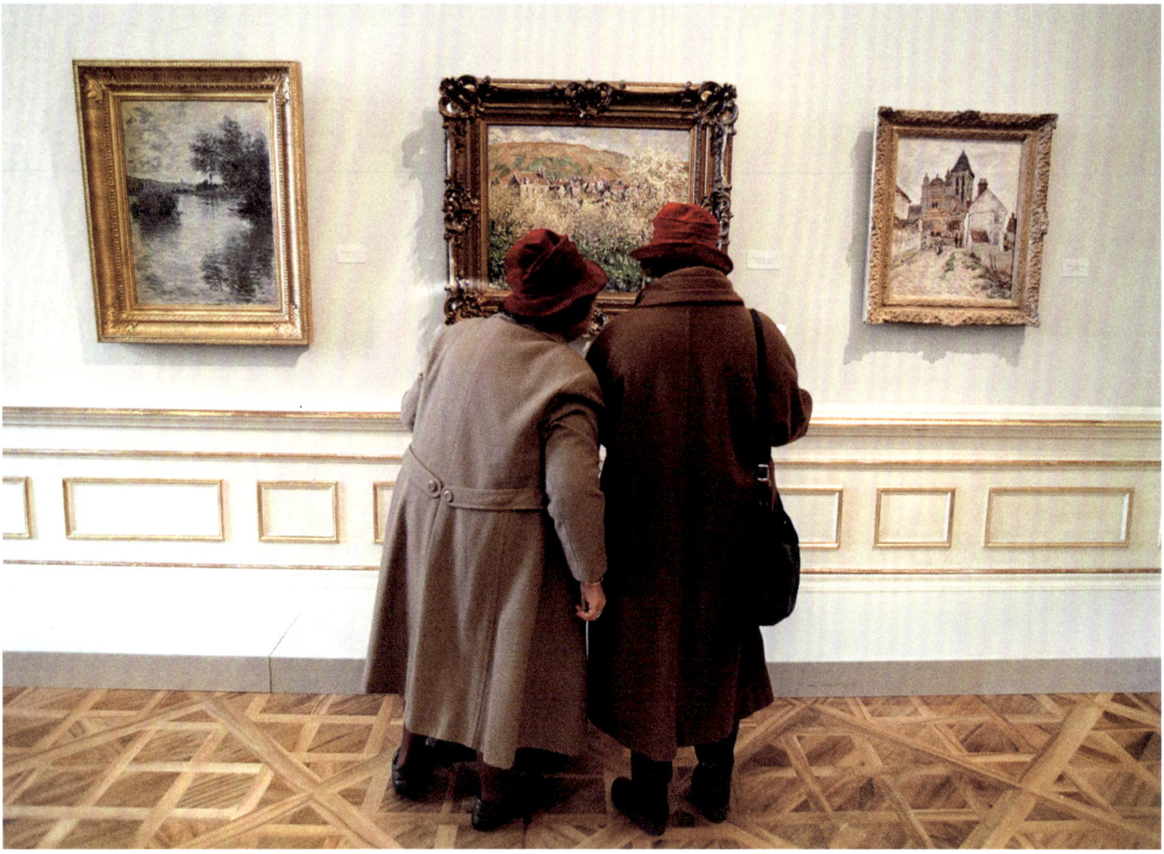

Visitors to the Claude Monet exhibition in the Upper Belvedere. With more than 300,000 tickets sold, it was an outstanding success. March 13, 1996

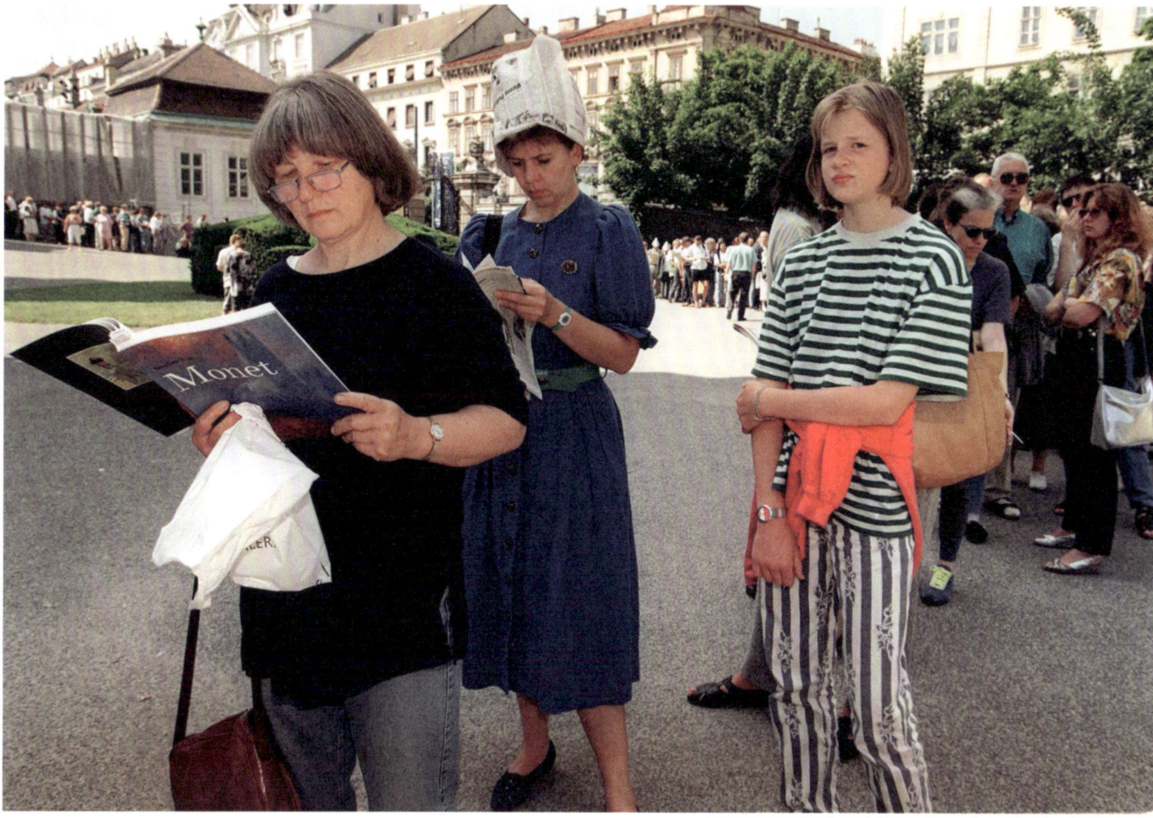

Even on the final day of the Claude Monet exhibition in the Upper Belvedere, art lovers still had to queue for hours. June 16, 1996

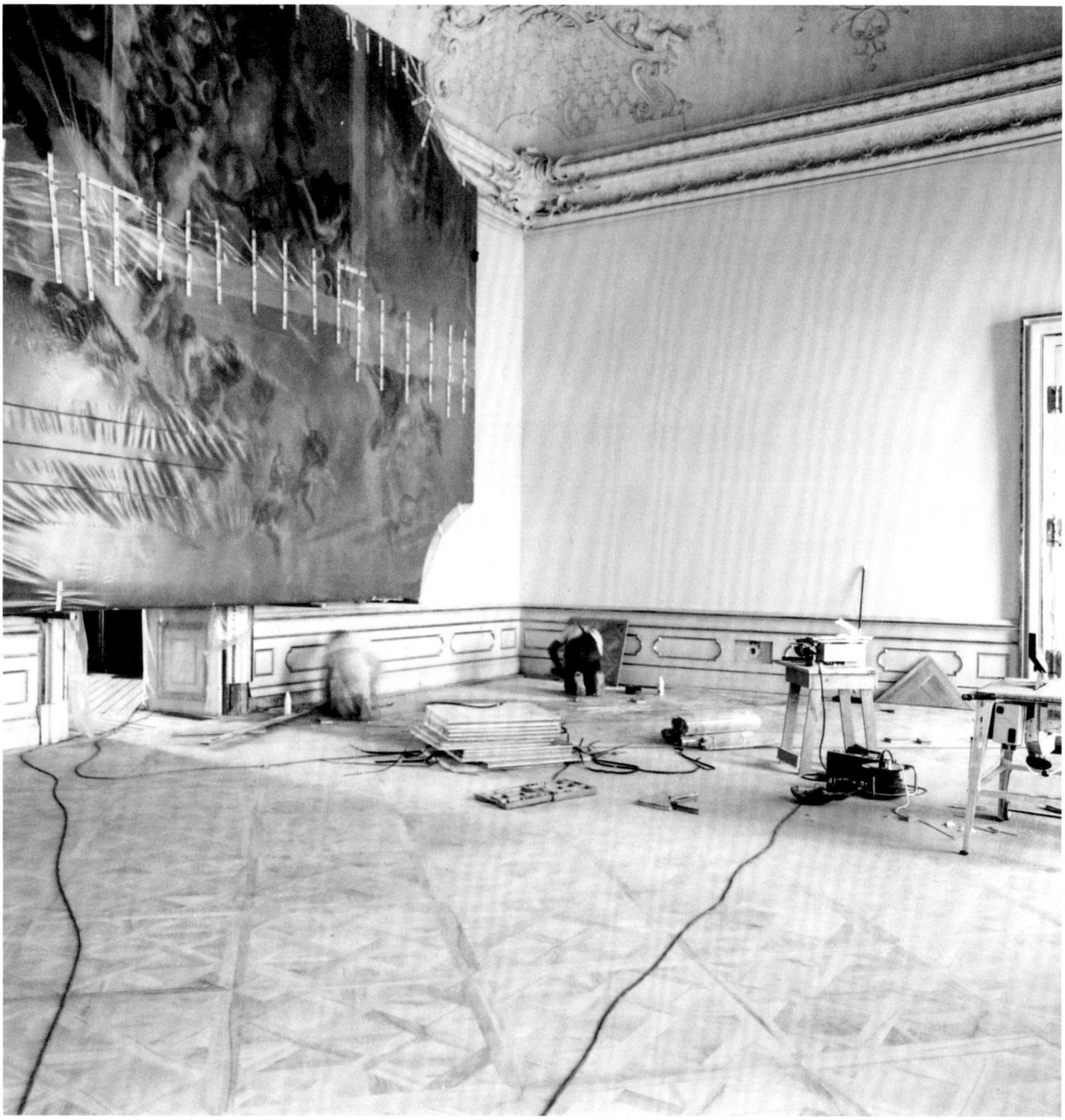

Remodeling and renovation works in the Upper Belvedere as part of the "A Billion for Our Museums" program, 1994

A month ago, some friends and I made a stop in Vienna. Our objective was to visit your city, and in particular the Upper and Lower Belvedere, which is world-famous for its extraordinary collections. To our great disappointment, we discovered that the Lower Belvedere was closed. [...] I understand that renovation works are necessary, but why do they all have to happen at the same time? My main criticism, though, is as follows: I find it particularly scandalous and deceitful that the entry price should stay the same, even though the majority of works cannot be viewed. Either close the museum in its entirety or open at least half of the Belvedere, otherwise I would call it having a laugh!

—— Letter from a visitor to the director of the Belvedere, June 22, 1995, AdB, Zl. 747/1995

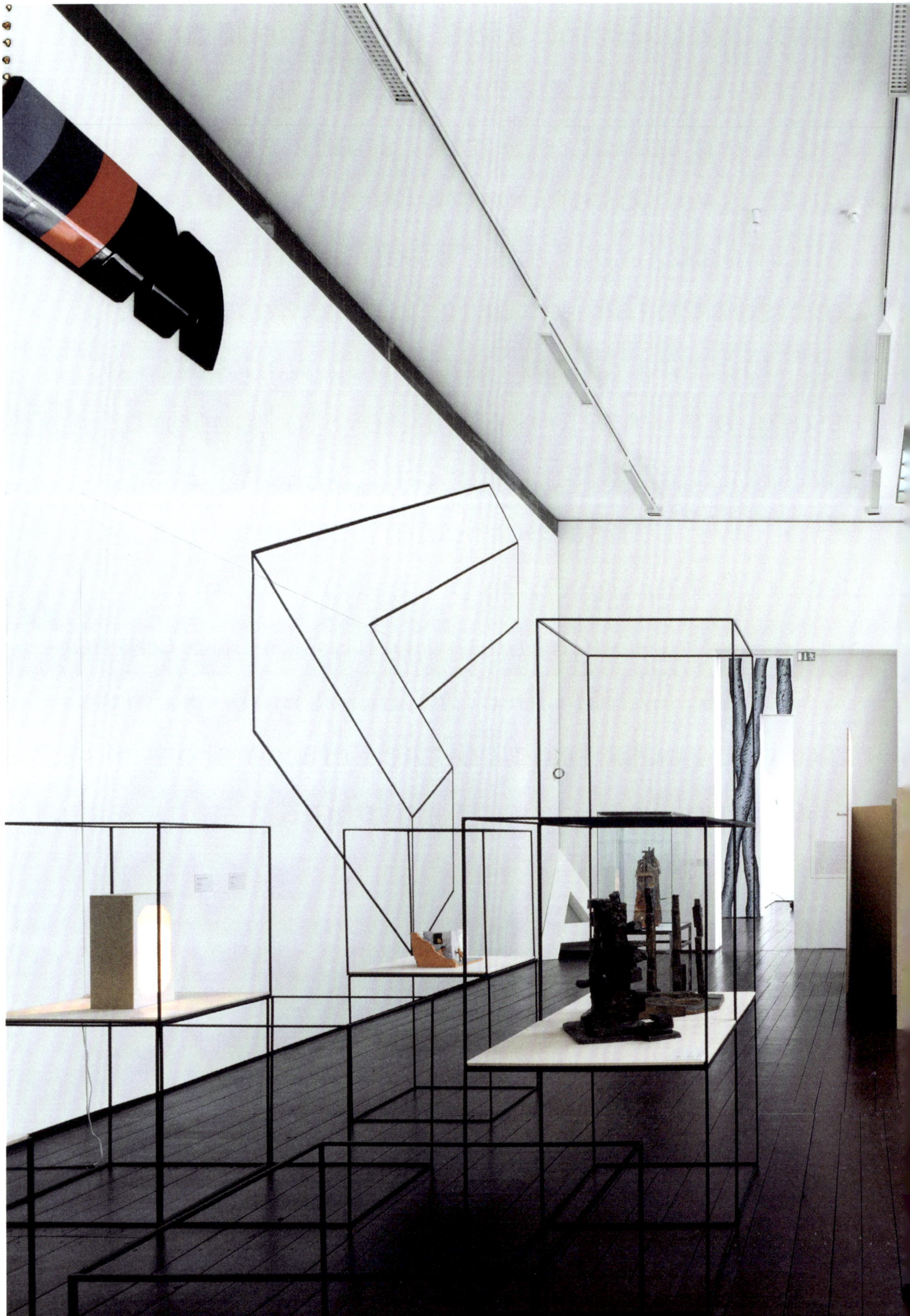

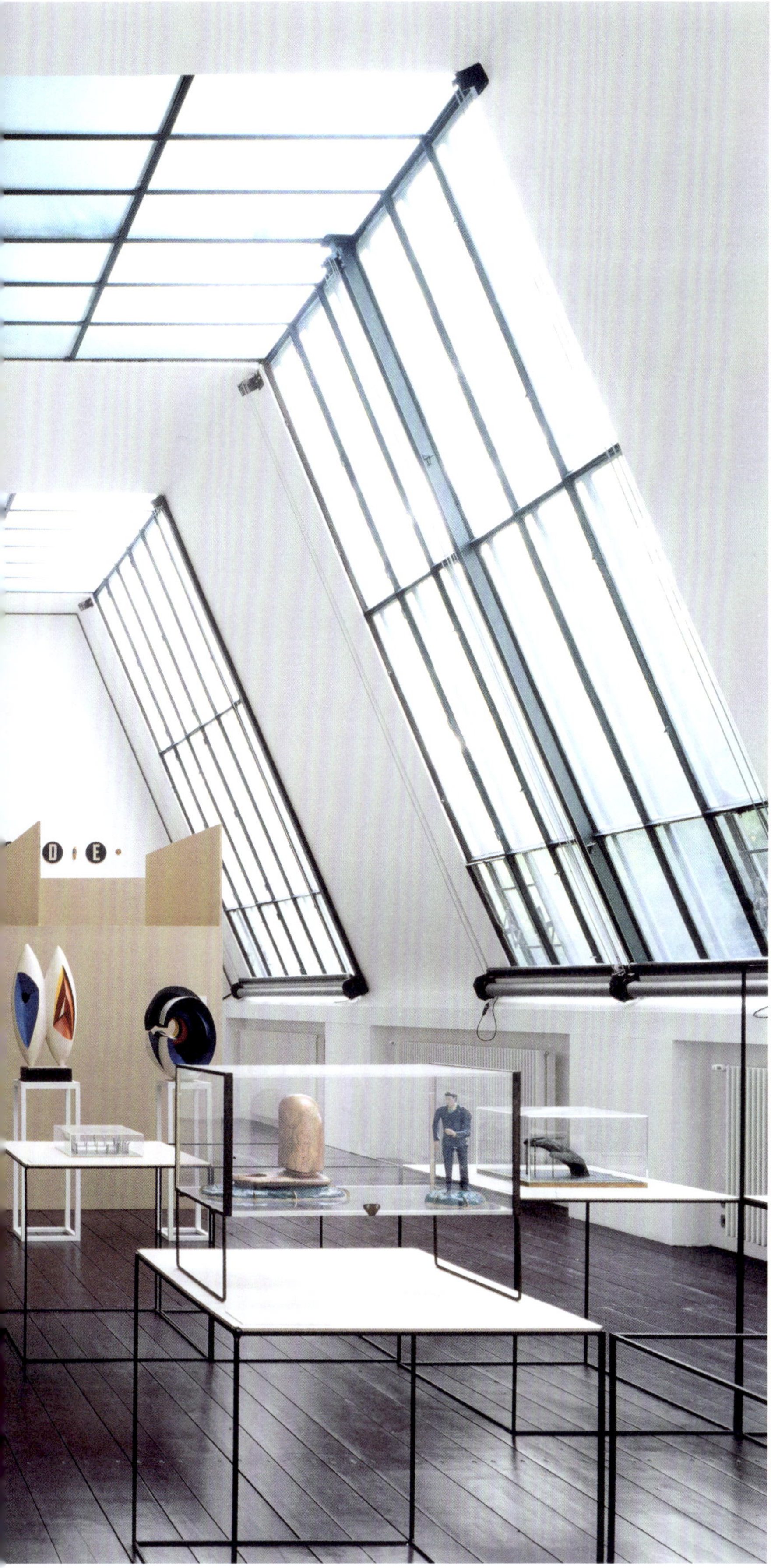

The opening exhibition *Objects: Sculpture in Austria after 1945* at Atelier Augarten, 2001

The Klimt exhibition with the juxtapositions of portraits by famous European artists is wonderful—on one condition: that no more than around five hundred visitors should be allowed into the exhibition spaces at once. Because of the crowds on New Year's Eve 2000, our visit was an absolute HORROR and not worth the entry charge. Every thermal spa, every cinema, concert hall, even ski pistes, show a reasonable level of restraint on the part of the organizers. So why not also in your gallery?

—— Letter from a visitor to the director of the Belvedere, January 4, 2001, AdB, Zl. 21/2001

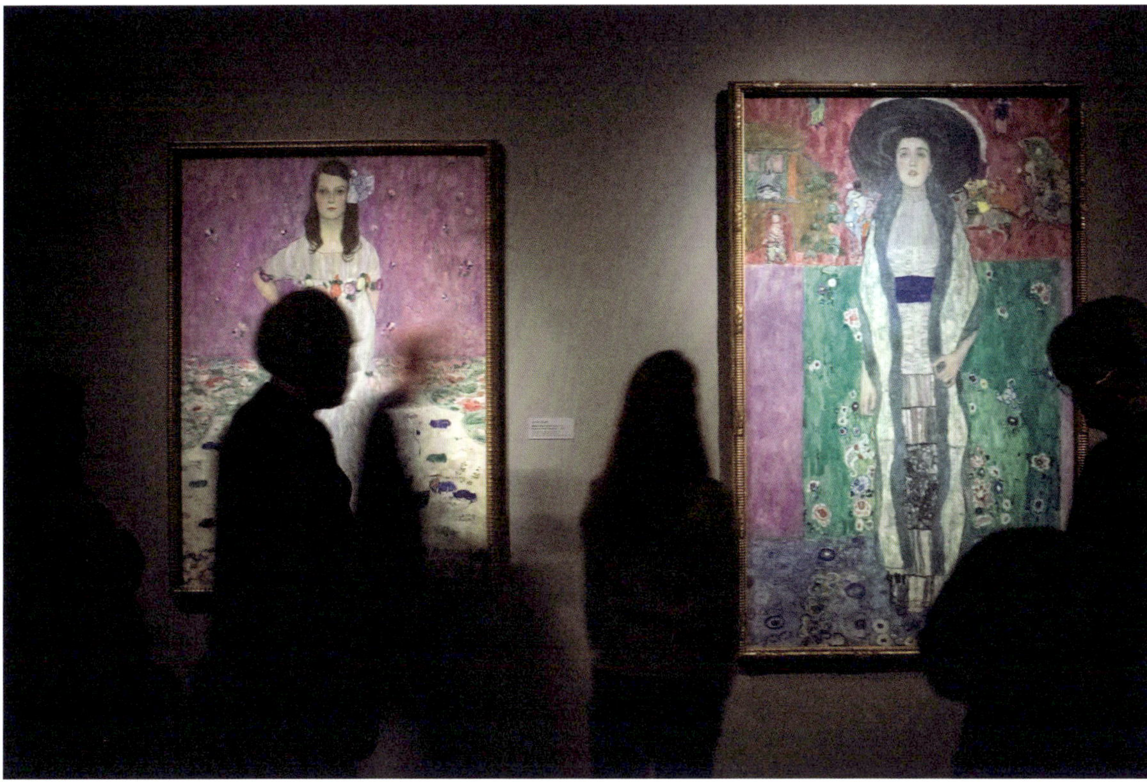

Klimt's Women exhibition in the Upper Belvedere, 2000/01

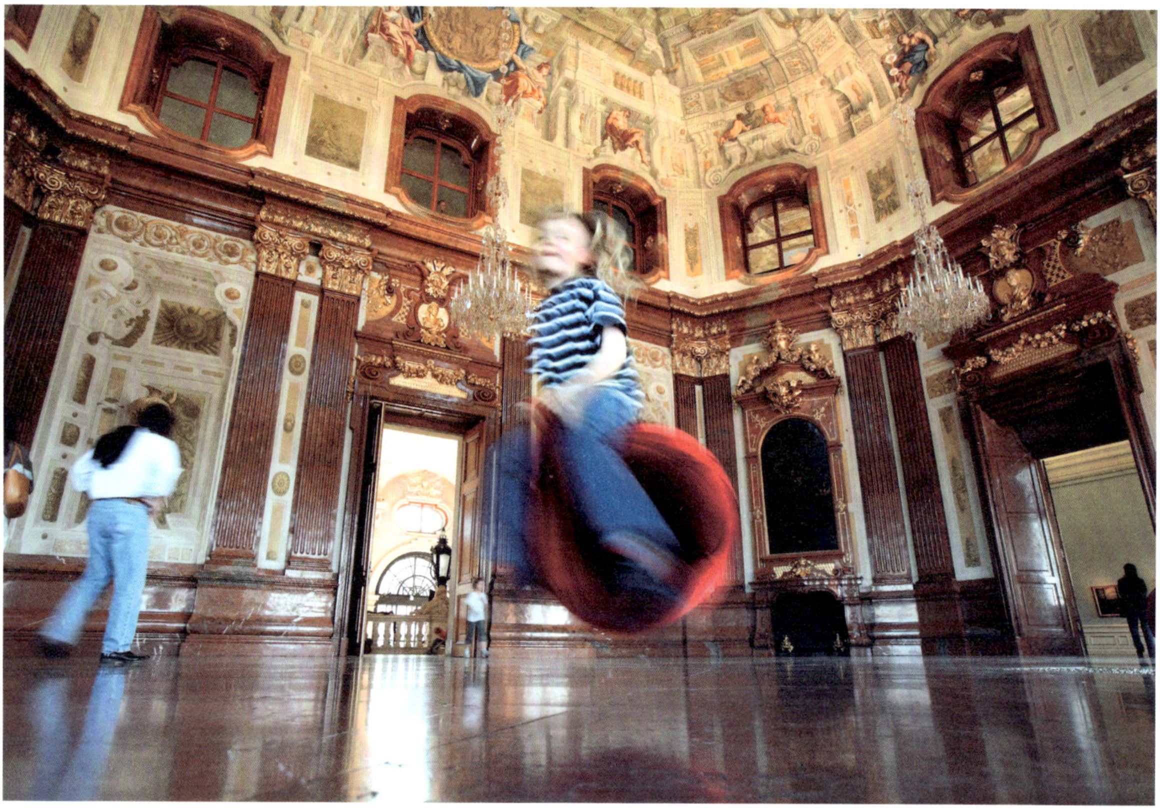

↑
Children bouncing through the Marble Hall of the Upper Belvedere on space hoppers made by the artist Gudrun Kampl, November 30, 2007

→ p. 291
Sculpture *Die Doppelgängerin (Scissors)* by VALIE EXPORT in the garden of the Belvedere, 2010

→ p. 292
Visitors of Gustav Klimt's works in the public collection of the Belvedere, 2016

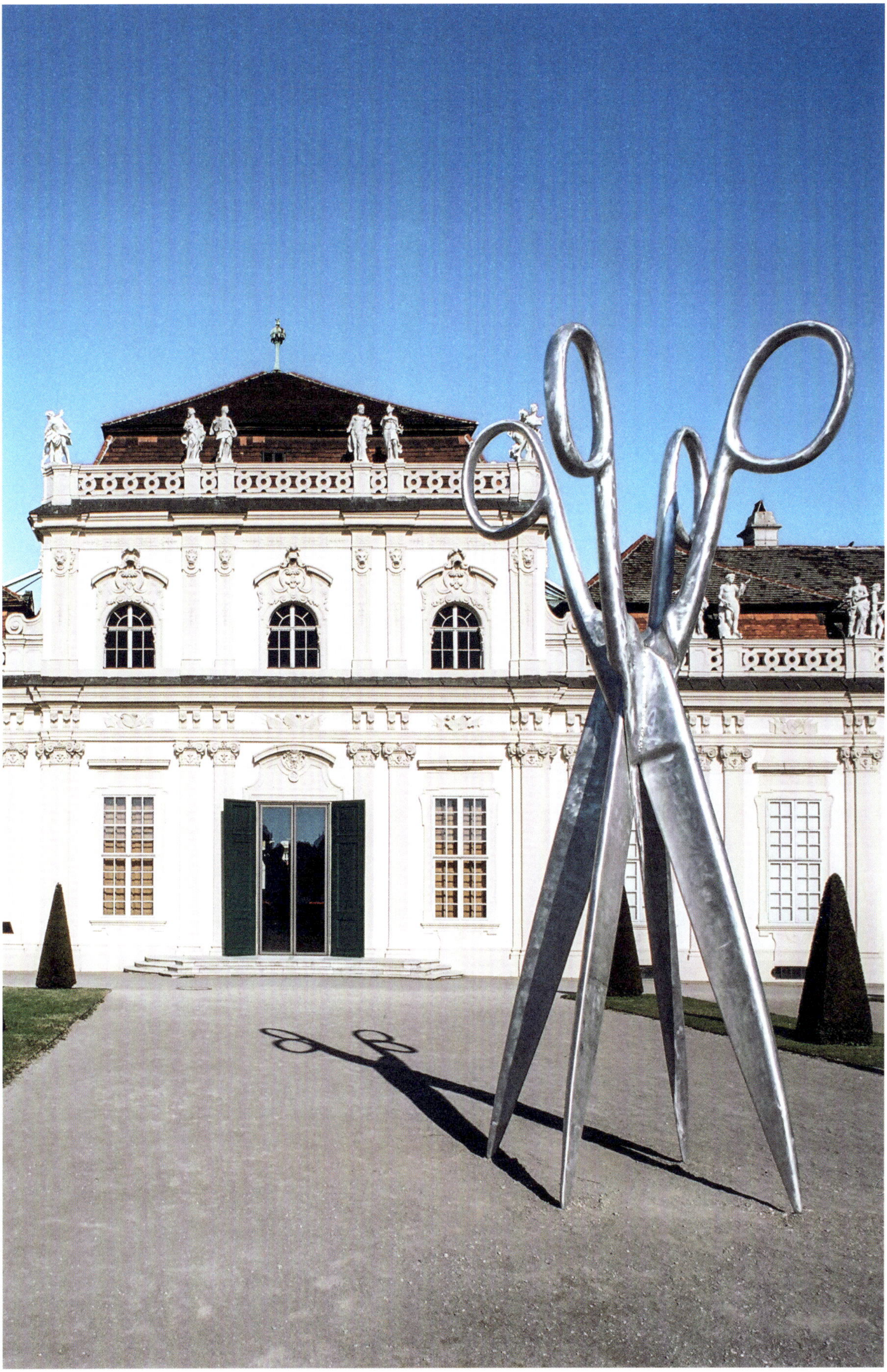

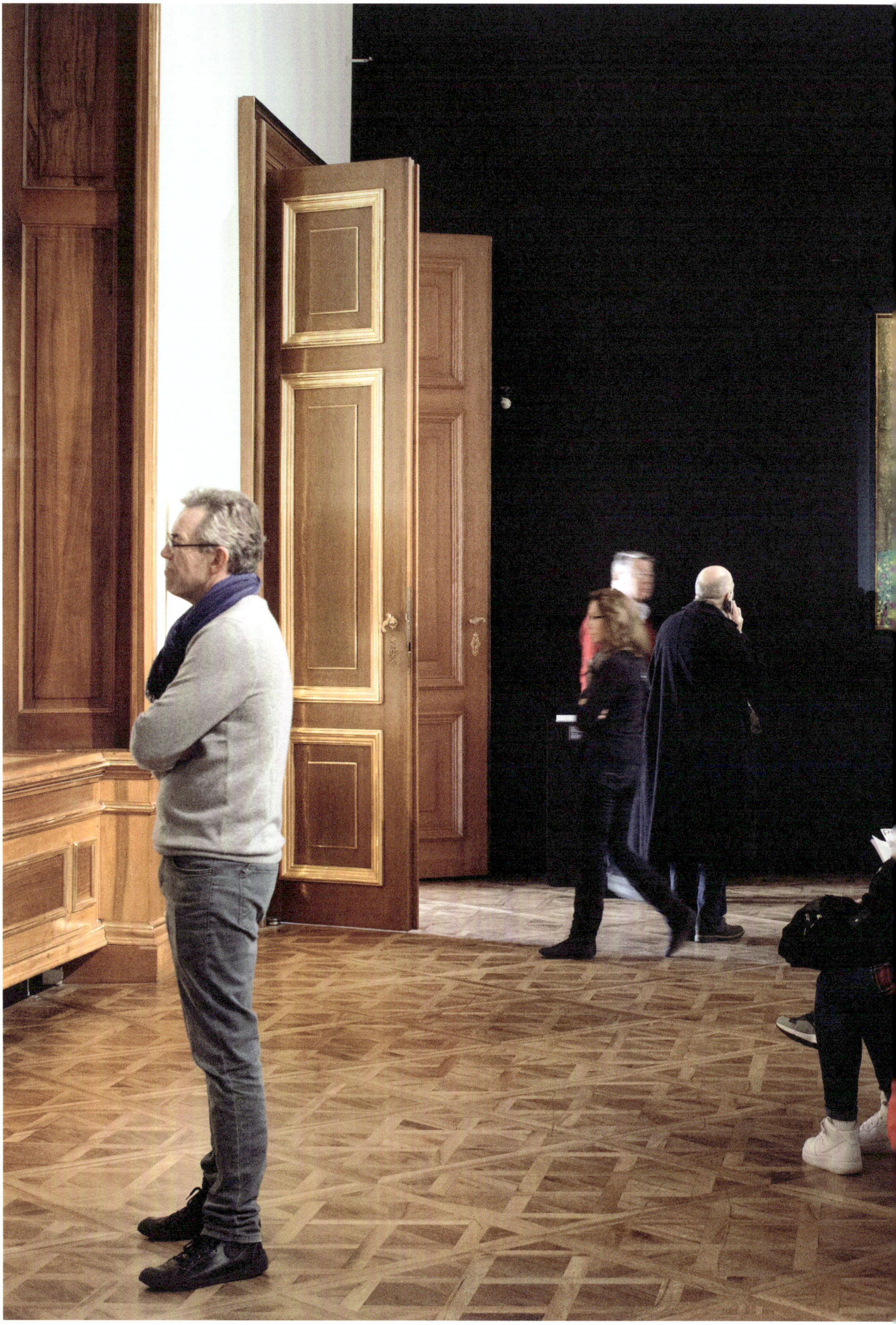

21

The "Vienna 1900" Brand

Franz Smola

The Belvedere today, along with the MAK, the Leopold Museum, the Wien Museum, and the Secession, are magnets for both locals and tourists wishing to immerse themselves in the world of "Vienna 1900." One of the stars of this era, who has enjoyed incredible popularity for several decades now, is Gustav Klimt. No other museum has as comprehensive a collection of his pictures as the Österreichische Galerie Belvedere. His most famous work, *The Kiss*, from 1908/09, has transformed the Upper Belvedere into a must-see for all visitors to Vienna (→ pp. 342–43).

Unsurprisingly, the City of Vienna itself played the leading role in the development of the "Vienna 1900" brand. In 1964, the municipal culture department organized an exhibition entitled *Wien um 1900* at the Historisches Museum der Stadt Wien on Karlsplatz (now Wien Museum), the Secession, and the Künstlerhaus, featuring key paintings, posters, and decorative art objects. Some twenty years later, in 1985, the Künstlerhaus was the venue of the exhibition *Dream and Reality: Vienna 1870–1930* organized by the Historisches Museum der Stadt Wien (fig. 1). The theoretical incentive for it had been provided a few years earlier by Carl Schorske with his pioneering work *Fin-de-Siècle Vienna*, published in German in 1981. With a considerably expanded timeframe, this major show also included sections on architecture, theater design, literature, music, and even psychiatry and young cinema. Once again, *The Kiss* was a main attraction, along with the *Beethoven Frieze*, on show again after restoration work that had taken nearly ten years. It had been acquired by the state in 1973 from Erich Lederer, and after its presentation at the exhibition was installed permanently on the lower floor of the Secession building.

However spectacular this show was for visitors to Vienna, not least thanks to the effective setting, designed by star architect Hans Hollein (fig. 2), it was also important to transport this theme beyond Austria's borders. This had already been done a year previously at the exhibition in Palazzo Grassi, *Le arti a Vienna: dalla Secessione alla caduta dell'impero Asburgico* (The arts in Vienna: from the Secession to the fall of the Habsburg Empire), curated by Maria Marchetti, Rossana Bossaglia, and Marco Pozzetto, during the 41st Biennale in Venice. An excellent copy of the *Beethoven Frieze* was prepared specially for this event and was to prove an attraction at all subsequent "Vienna 1900" exhibitions. In 1986, the theme was again celebrated at two prominent international art venues with the show *Vienne 1880–1938: L'apocalypse joyeuse*, curated by Jean Clair, at the Centre Pompidou in Paris from February to May 1986 (fig. 3), and

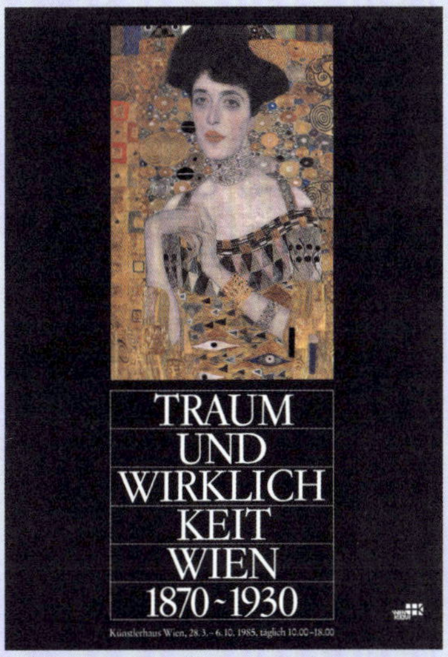

1

Fig. 1
Poster for the exhibition *Dream and Reality: Vienna 1870–1930* by the Historisches Museum der Stadt Wien, 1985, design by Tino Erben, Wien Museum

the exhibition *Vienna 1900: Art, Architecture and Design*, curated by Kirk Varnedoe and shown from July to October 1986 at the Museum of Modern Art in New York (fig. 4). Jean Clair's concept for Paris resembled the idea implemented by Werner Hofmann at the 1981 exhibition *Experiment Weltuntergang: Wien um 1900* at the Kunsthalle in Hamburg, but with an extended timeframe that also included the period until 1938. By linking the historical rupture of 1918 with the political catastrophe of Nazism, the exhibition in Paris diverged from the Vienna exhibition *Dream and Reality*, which only went as far as 1930. Klimt's *Kiss* was not shipped to Paris in 1986, but only to New York, and then, in 1989, to the Sezon Museum of Art in Tokyo for the exhibition *Vienna Around 1900: Klimt, Schiele and Their Time*. Since then, it has traveled abroad on only two more occasions, for the major Klimt retrospective in 1992 at the Kunsthaus Zurich, and in 1997 for a short interlude in Rome. After that, the painting has not left the Belvedere again. In subsequent years, other "Vienna 1900" exhibitions were shown in various cities, mostly curated by the Wien Museum—for example, in 1990 at the Pushkin Museum in Moscow, in 1991 at the Liljevalchs Konsthall in Stockholm, and in the same year at the Museum Louisiana in Humlebaek near Copenhagen. The Belvedere, too, has organized comparable projects, such as the *Viena 1900* exhibition in 1993 at the Museo Reina Sofía in Madrid, with over 430 objects.

Rising insurance premiums and the increasingly restricted availability of loan objects has made it more and more difficult to organize comprehensive exhibitions on this subject. Whenever they are held, however, they retain their popular fascination. This was demonstrated again, for example, at the exhibitions *Vienna: Art & Design—Klimt, Schiele, Hoffmann, Loos* at the National Gallery of Victoria in Melbourne, Australia, and *Wien 1900: Klimt, Schiele und ihre Zeit* at the Fondation Beyeler in Riehen, Switzerland, both held in 2011.

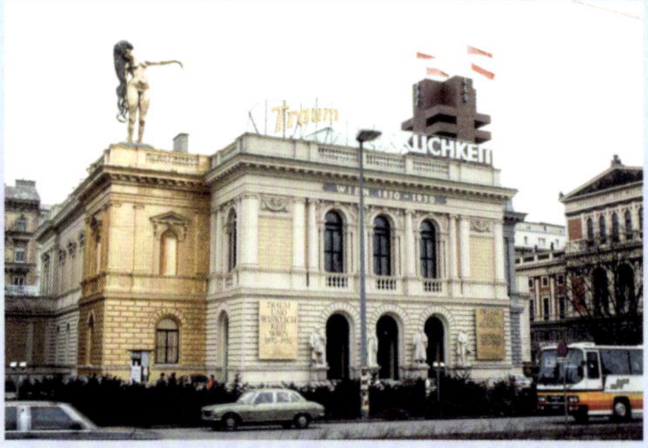

2

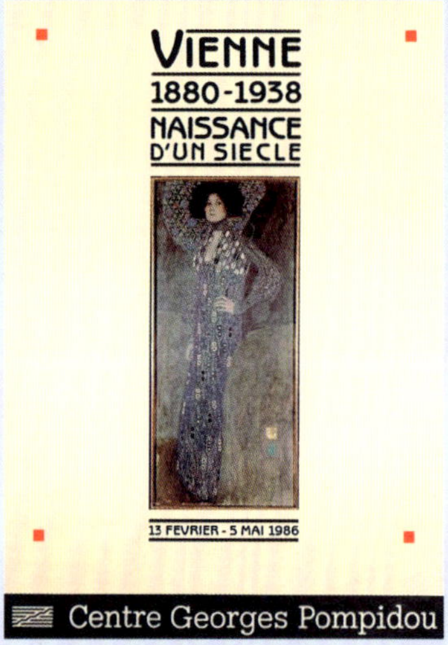

3

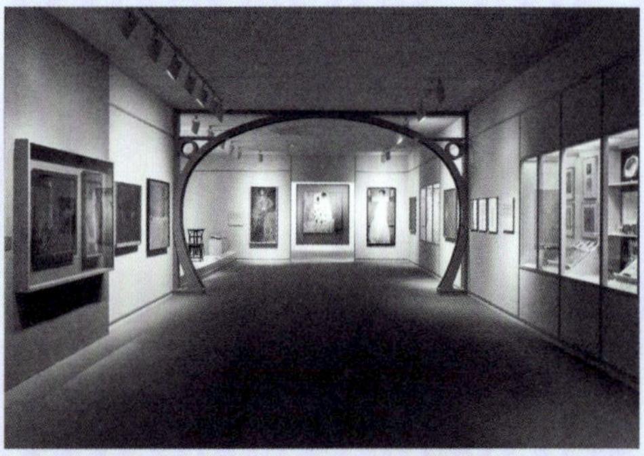

4

Fig. 2
Façade of the Vienna Künstlerhaus during the exhibition *Dream and Reality: Vienna 1870–1930*, 1985, photo: Votava

Fig. 3
Poster *Vienne 1880–1938: Naissance d'un siècle*, 1986, designed by Marc Walter

Fig. 4
Exhibition *Vienna 1900: Art, Architecture and Design*, 1986, Photographic Archive, Museum of Modern Art Archives, New York

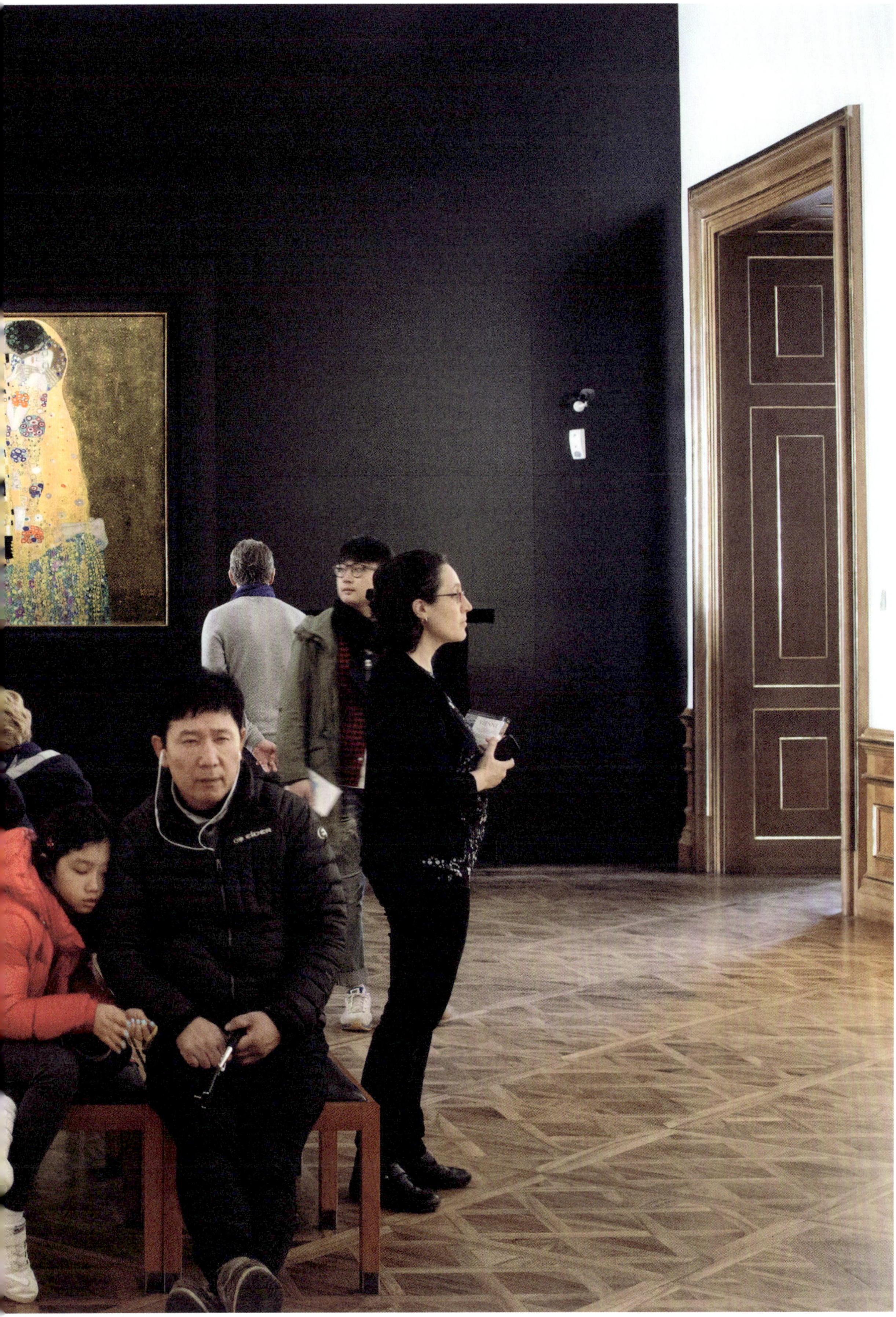

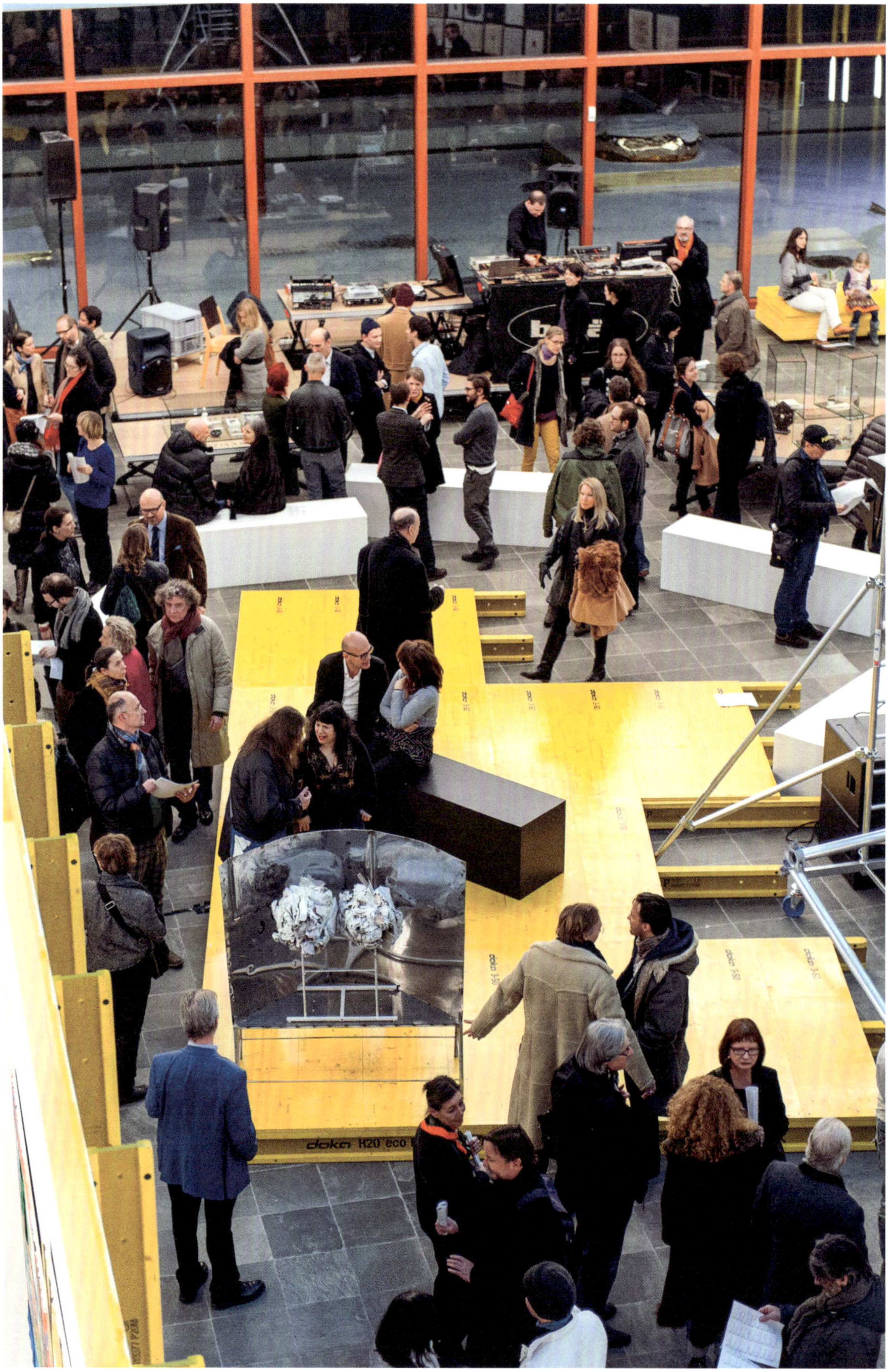
doka H20 eco

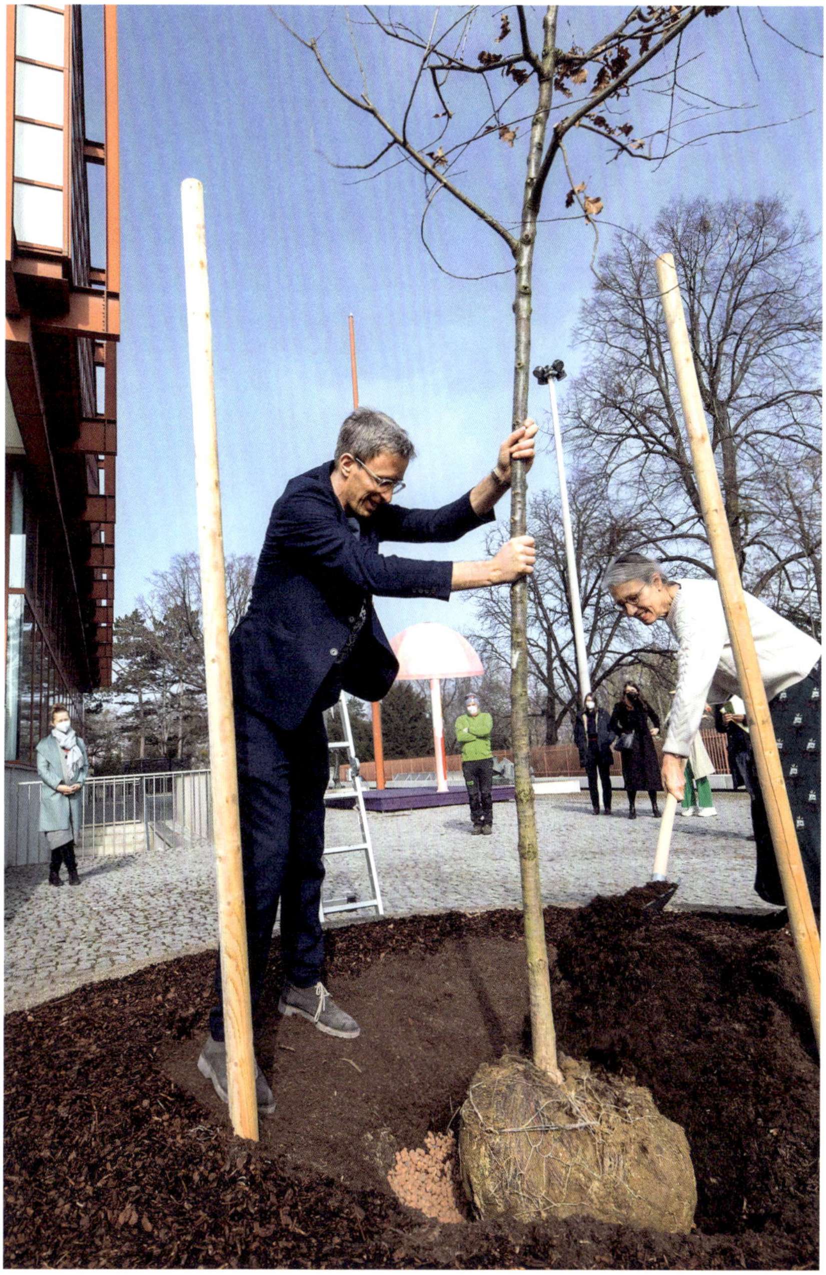

↑
Tree planting in the Belvedere 21 Sculpture Garden as part of the exhibition *Joseph Beuys — Think. Act. Convey.* With Harald Krejci and general director Stella Rollig, 2021

←
Opening of the exhibition *Franz Graf: See What Sees You*, 2014

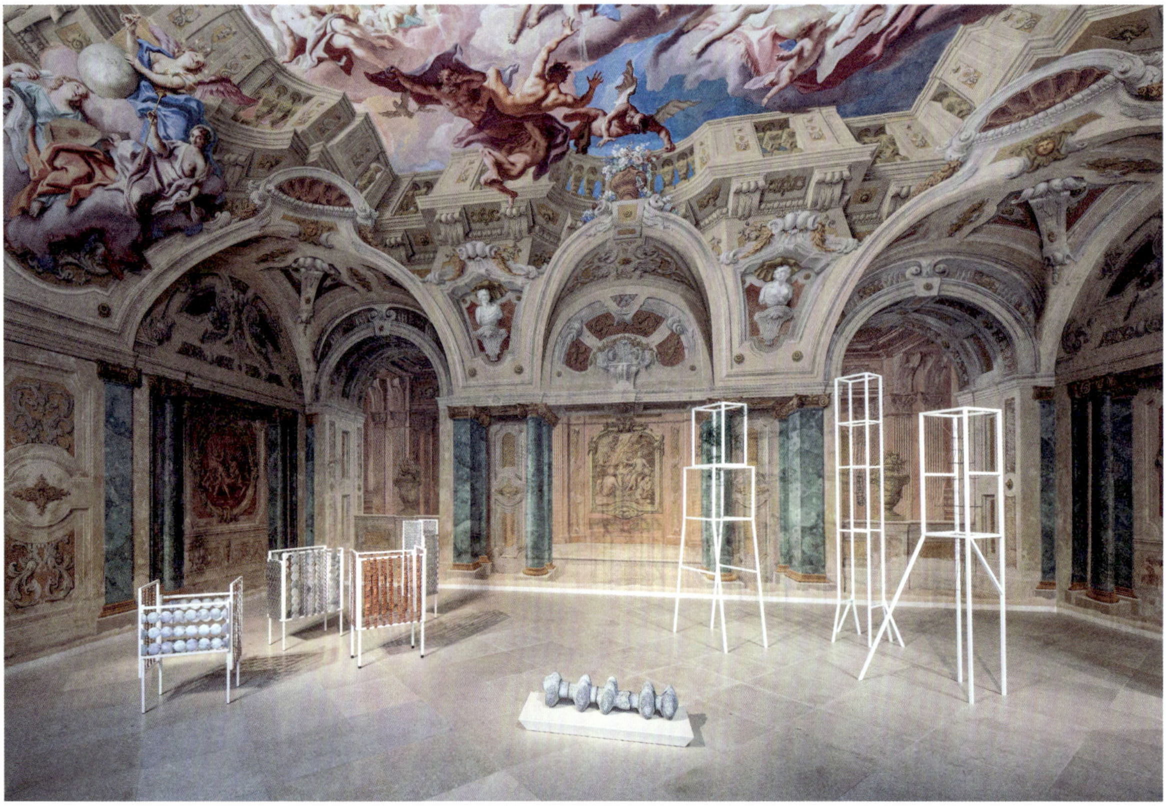

↑
Works by Christine and Irene Hohenbüchler at the CARLONE CONTEMPORARY exhibition series, 2021

→
The exhibition *Donna Huanca: Piedra Quemada* in the Lower Belvedere, 2018

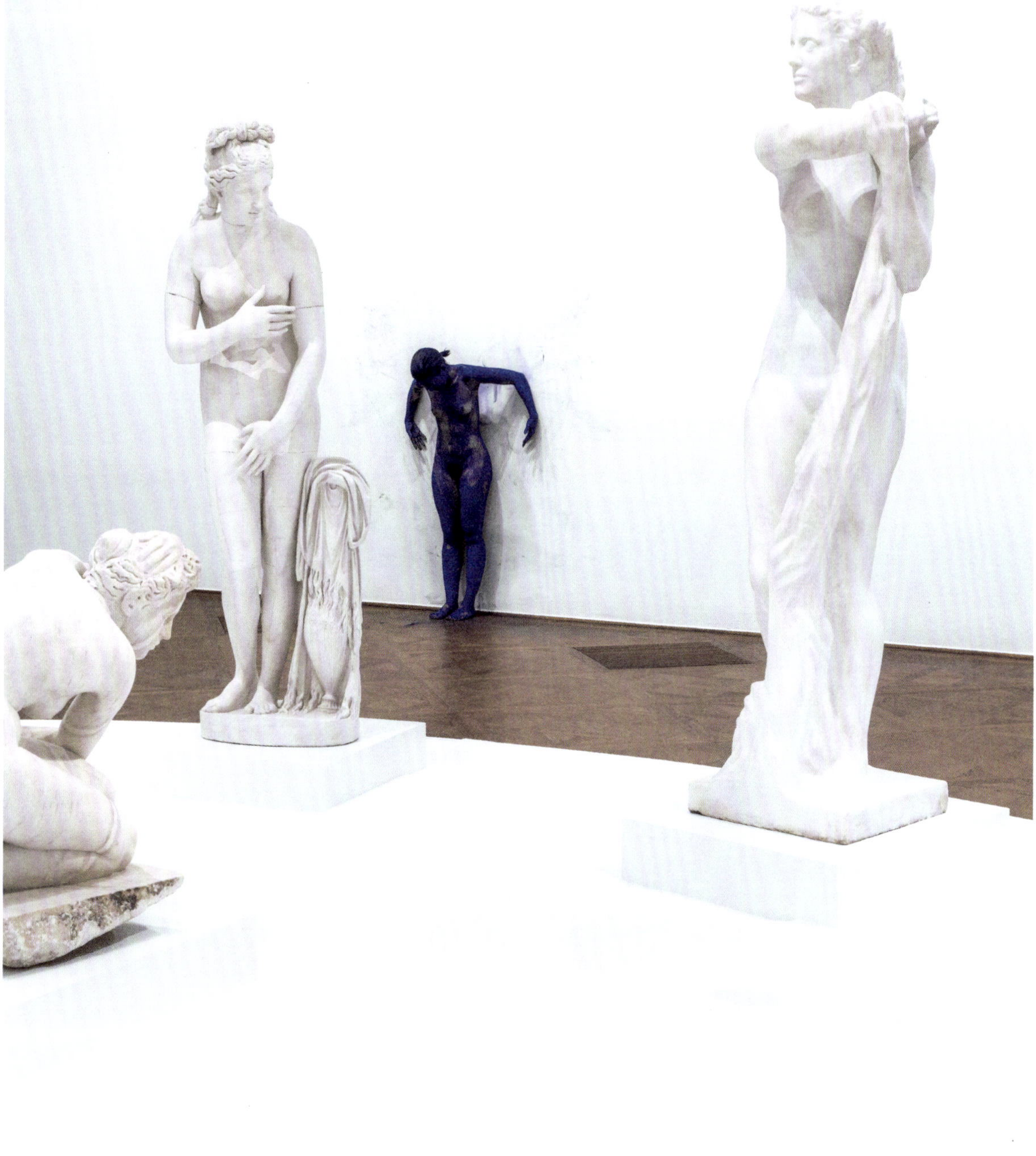

The *City of Women* exhibition is nice, but why is it that in 2019 we still need a separate exhibition dedicated to women like we did a hundred years ago?! Why can't we see these works all the time?

—— Feedback from a visitor, March 4, 2019, Belvedere, Vienna

The exhibition *City of Women: Female Artists in Vienna from 1900 to 1938* in the Lower Belvedere, 2019

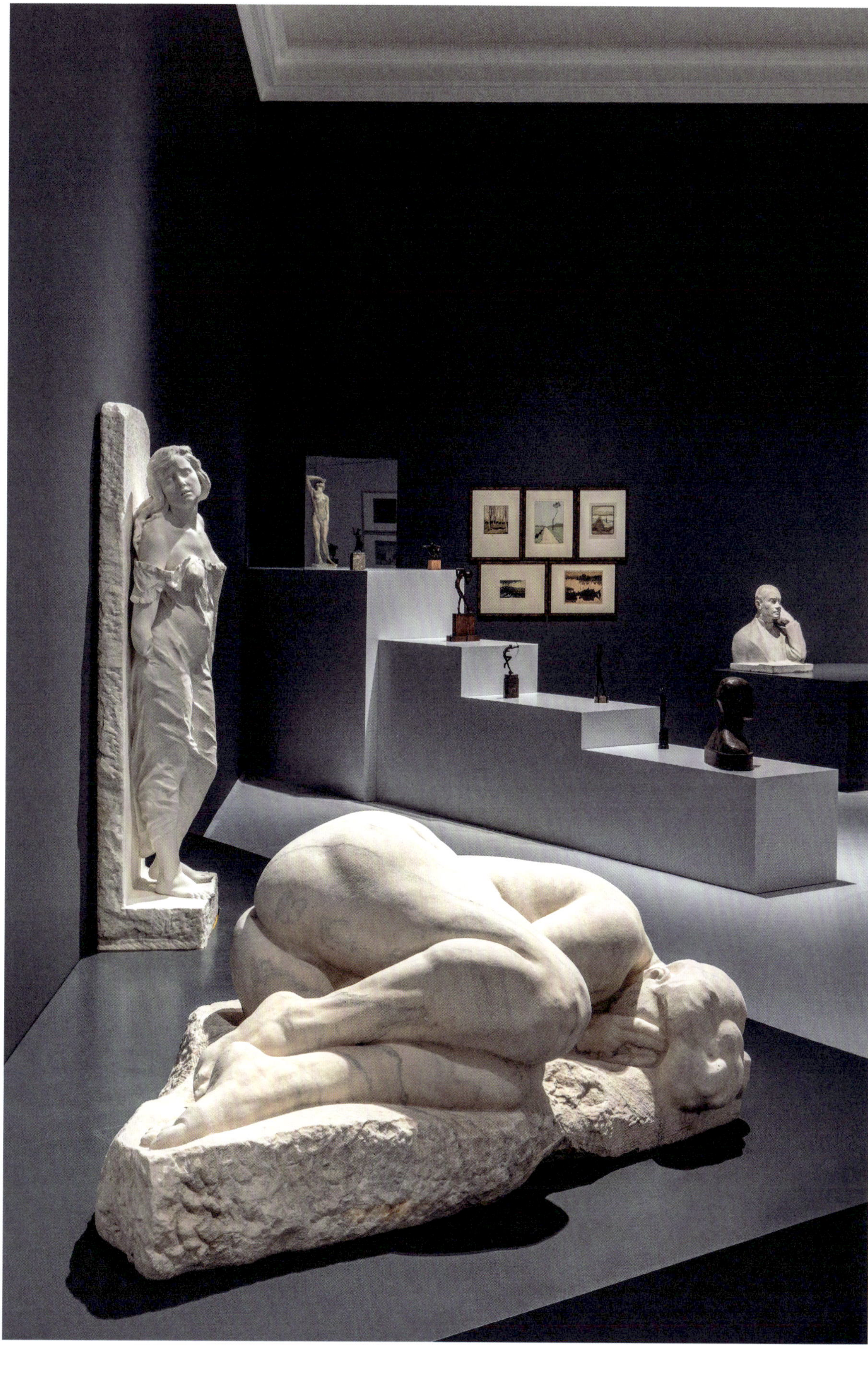

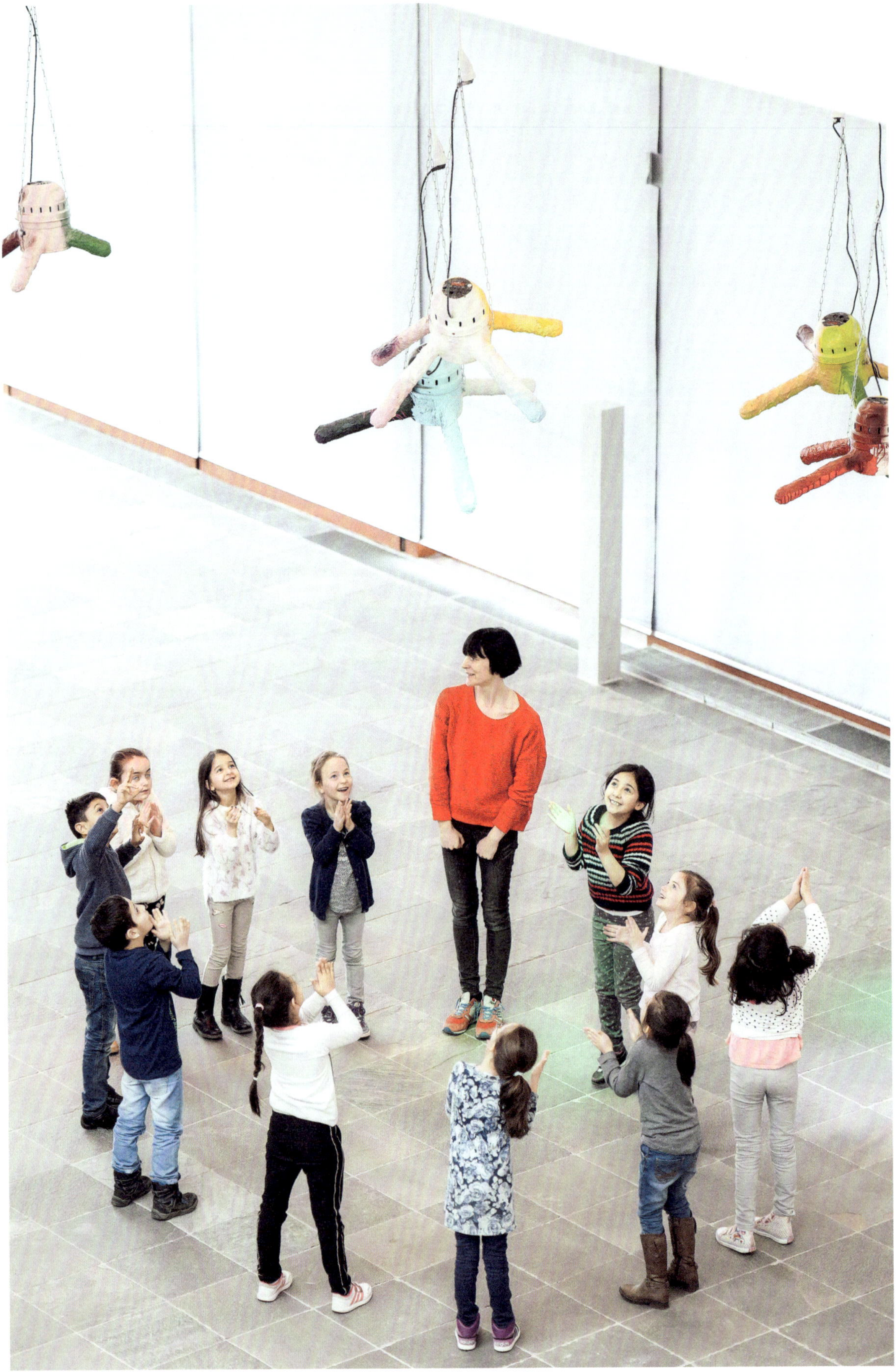

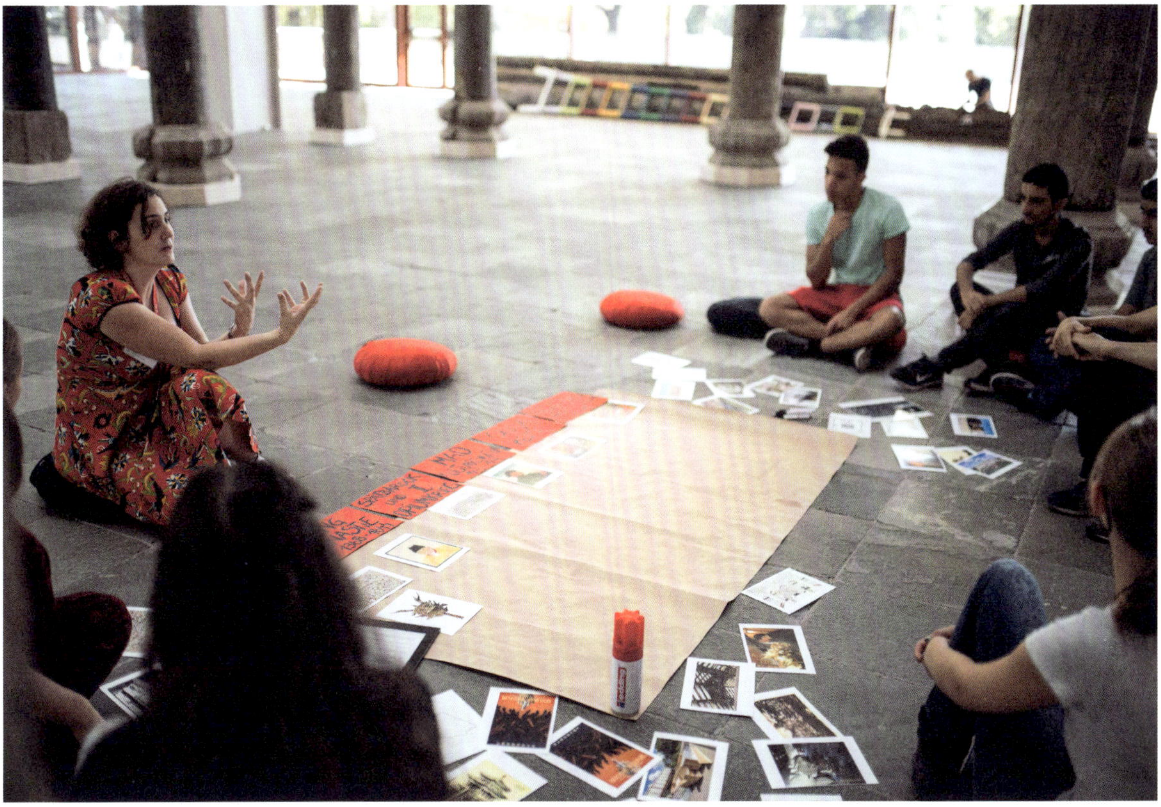

↑
As part of UNHCR Austria's "Long Day of Flight," the 21er Haus offered a free guided tour of the exhibition *AI WEIWEI translocation — transformation*, 2016

←
Children's program run by the Art Education Department at the exhibition *Franz West: Artistclub* at the 21er Haus, 2016

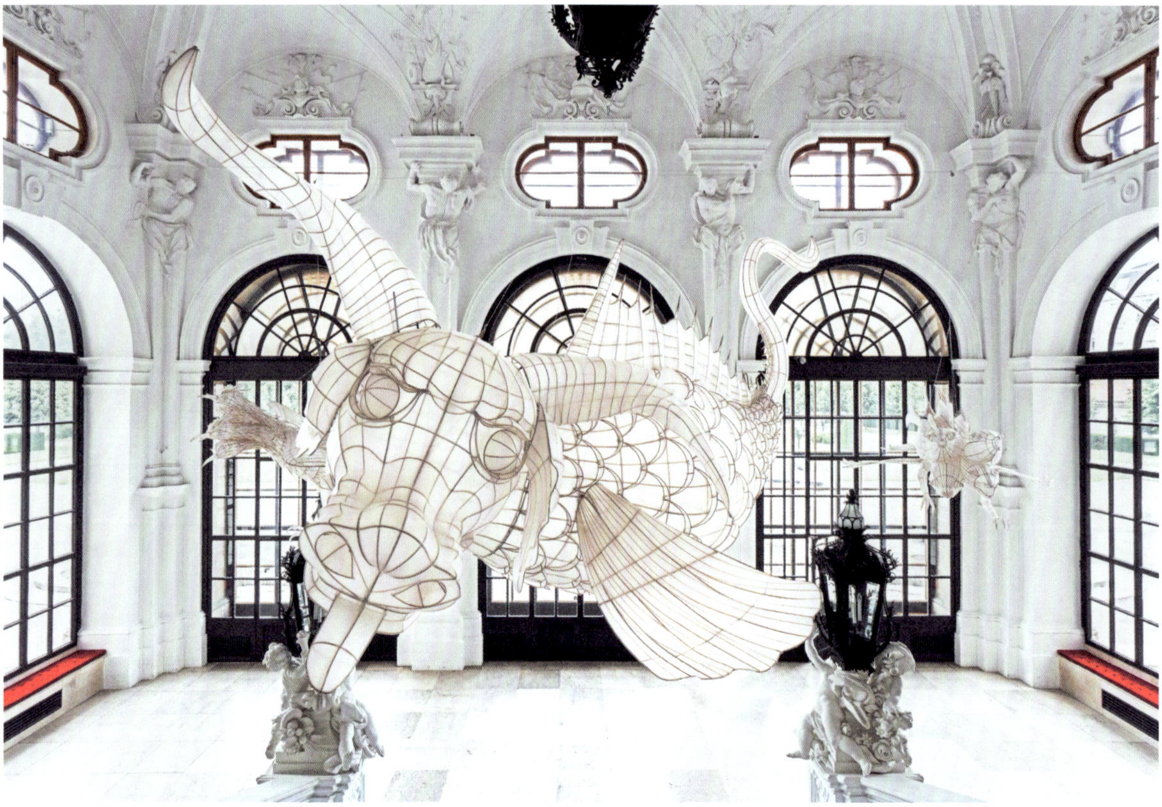

Installation by Ai Weiwei in the Upper Belvedere, 2016, Belvedere, Vienna

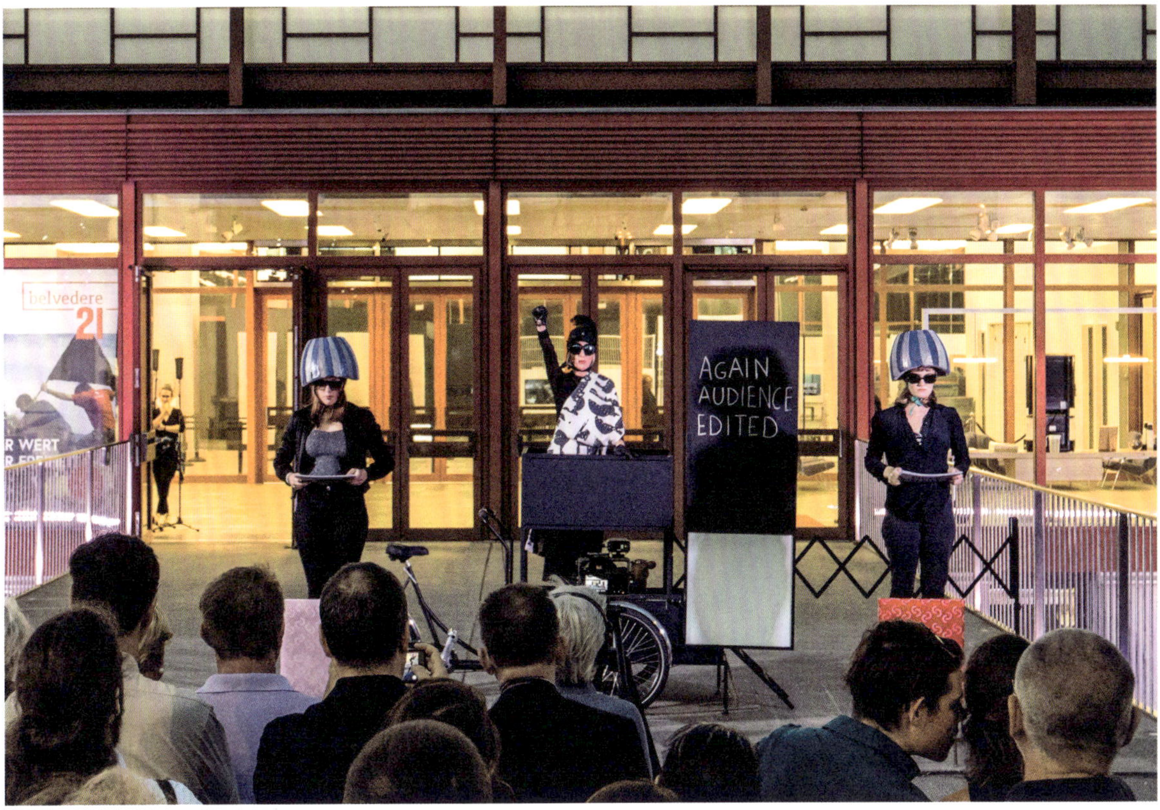

Carola Dertnig, *Again Audience*, performance as part of the opening of the exhibition *The Value of Freedom* in the Belvedere 21, 2018

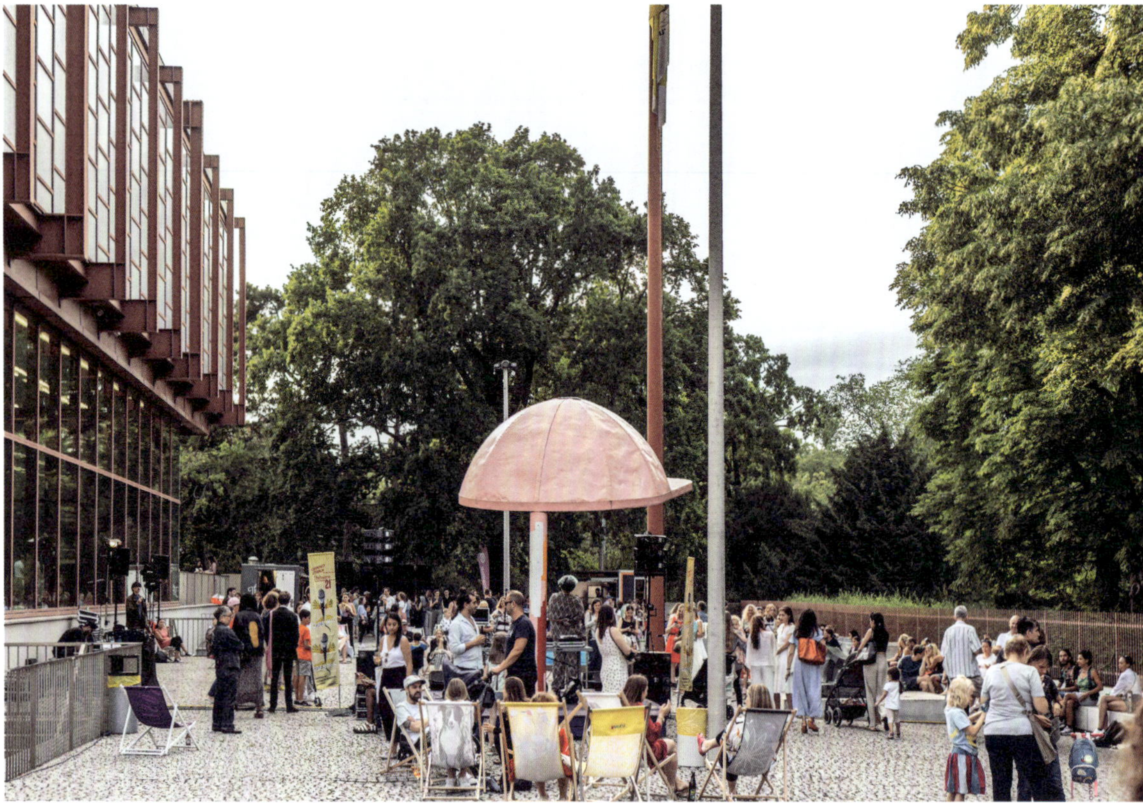

↑
The annual summer festival at the Belvedere with *Open Mic — The public microphone with Schudini The Sensitive*, July 15, 2022.

The oversized pink cap in the center belongs to the sculpture *B-Girls, Go!* by the artist Maruša Sagadin and forms a stage with a purple wooden deck.

→ p. 309
Rainbow flags outside the Belvedere 21 to mark the "Queering the Belvedere" public program, 2021, Belvedere, Vienna

(22)

Mapping the Hood: The Belvedere Quarter

Christiane Erharter

The neighborhood of the Belvedere 21—located between the Belvedere Palace, Schweizergarten, and the Arsenal (fig. 1)—is one of the largest inner-urban redevelopment areas in Vienna. In preparation for a construction project on a comparable scale to Berlin's Potsdamer Platz in the 1990s, the S-Bahn station Südbahnhof (South Station) was developed and renamed Quartier Belvedere in December 2012. In December 2019, public transport connections were improved when the D tram line was extended from the Hauptbahnhof (Central Station) via the Sonnwendviertel to Absberggasse in the 10th district. In the intervening period, the twenty-five-hectare site of the former Südbahnhof was redeveloped, including construction of the new Central Station—which opened in October 2014 and was fully operational by December 2015—and two new urban quarters: the Belvedere Quarter and the Sonnwendviertel (fig. 2).

The Vienna Südbahnhof has a long history as a hub connecting east and west, south and north. As far back as the nineteenth century, this area was associated with migration, when, during the construction of the Ringstrasse, laborers from Bohemia and Moravia arrived in the city to work in the brickworks on Wienerberg in the south of Vienna. From the early 1950s to the mid-1960s, workers from Turkey and the former Yugoslavia came to Austria through recruitment agreements. They often settled in Favoriten, Vienna's 10th district, which borders the station. In the 1990s, the Südbahnhof became associated with refugees fleeing the wars in the former Yugoslavia. While, during those years, refugees often disembarked at the bus terminal, by 2015, refugees from Syria were already arriving at the new Central Station and continuing their journey from there. These days, the station serves as a first port of call for refugees from Ukraine.

The Belvedere Quarter is a mixed-use development with office, business, and residential units. It includes the office buildings of Erste Group, Canetti Tower, The Icon Vienna, the Quartier Belvedere Central—spanning six building plots alone—and the apartment blocks Bel & Main Residences, BelView Apartments, and Parkapartments am Belvedere on Arsenalstrasse. The Sonnwendviertel, located behind this quarter, is a new neighborhood with five thousand apartments, providing homes for thirteen thousand people, equivalent to the population of a medium-sized Austrian town. Many partly self-organized housing and community projects have settled here, all of which have community spaces, including some that offer cultural activities—such as Gleis 21, Grätzelmixer, and CAPE 10—or, like Bikes and Rails, run a community café.

These changes to its urban environment have resulted in a repositioning of the Belvedere 21 in the city. Today it is situated at the heart of a cultural axis extending from the Wien Museum on Karlsplatz through the Belvedere Quarter and the Arsenal as far as the 10th district with the Brotfabrik cultural center. This new positioning was one of the reasons why, in 2018, the Belvedere was the first federal museum to establish the post of Curator for Community Outreach[1] at the Belvedere 21 as part of its new self-understanding as an integral participant in this ongoing urban transformation.

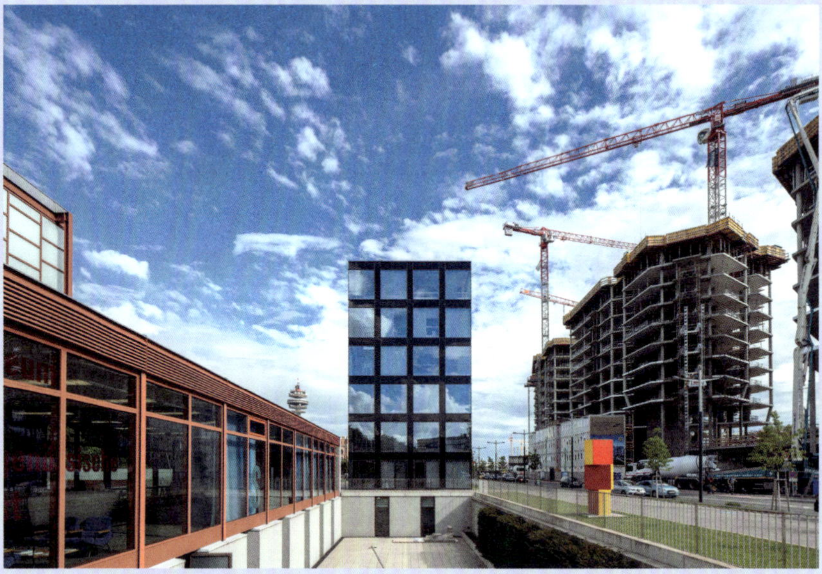

1

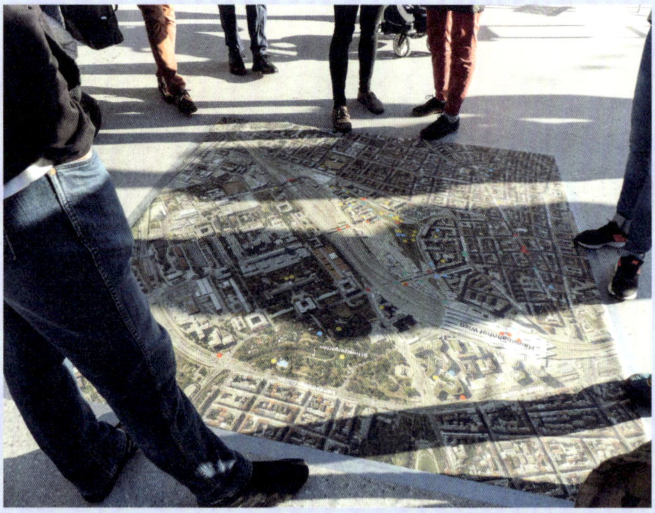

2

Fig. 1
The area around the Belvedere 21, 2017, Belvedere, Vienna

Fig. 2
Residents explore the Sonnwendviertel with the help of a large city map, 2019

1 Community outreach involves the museum reaching out to specific communities, which often entails leaving the museum space and organizing projects in public space. It seeks to actively include previously excluded, underrepresented, or marginalized communities in the museum.

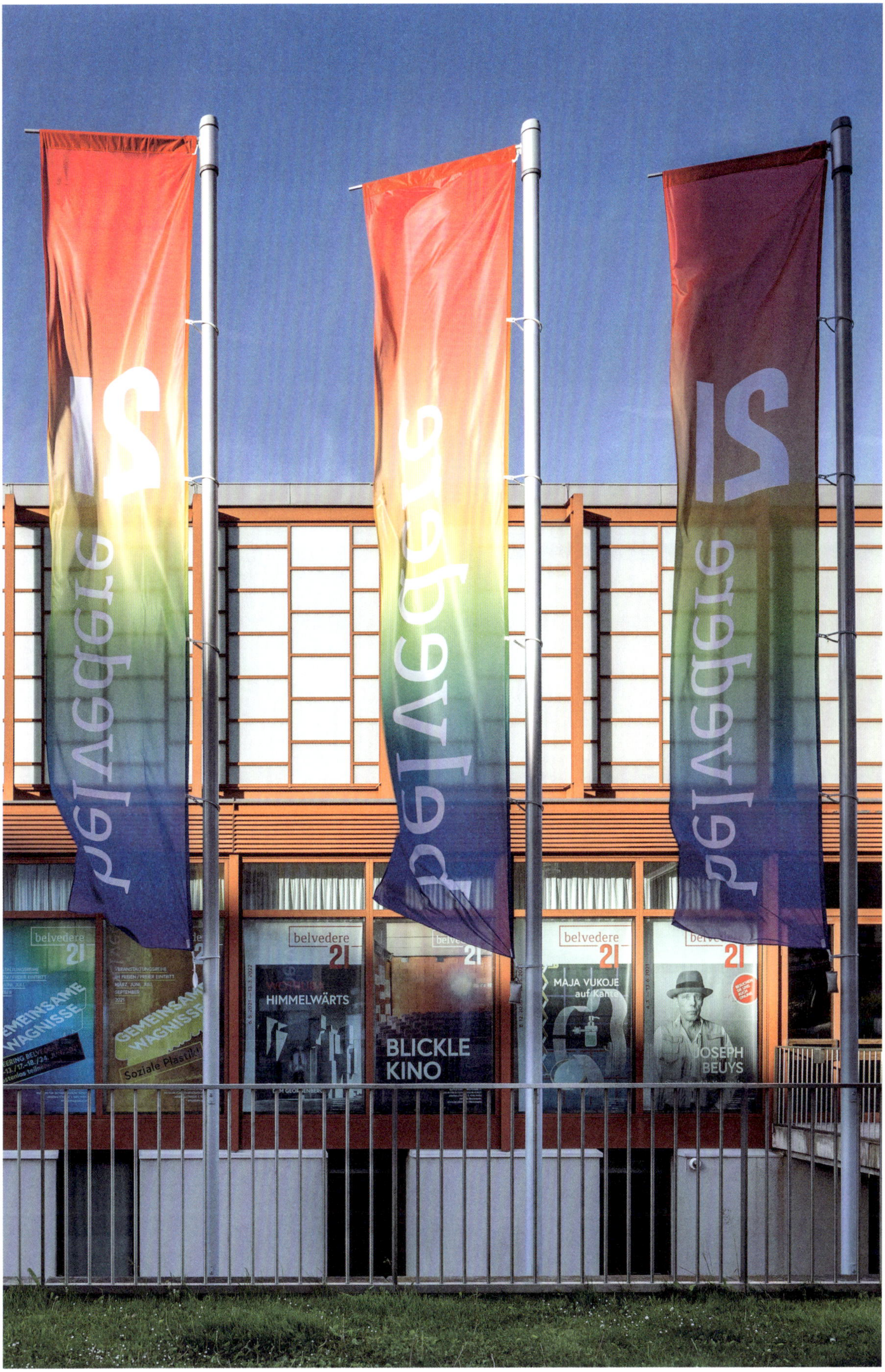
belvedere
21
GEMEINSAME WAGNISSE
Soziale Plastik
HIMMELWÄRTS
BLICKLE KINO
MAJA VUKOJE
auf Kante
JOSEPH BEUYS

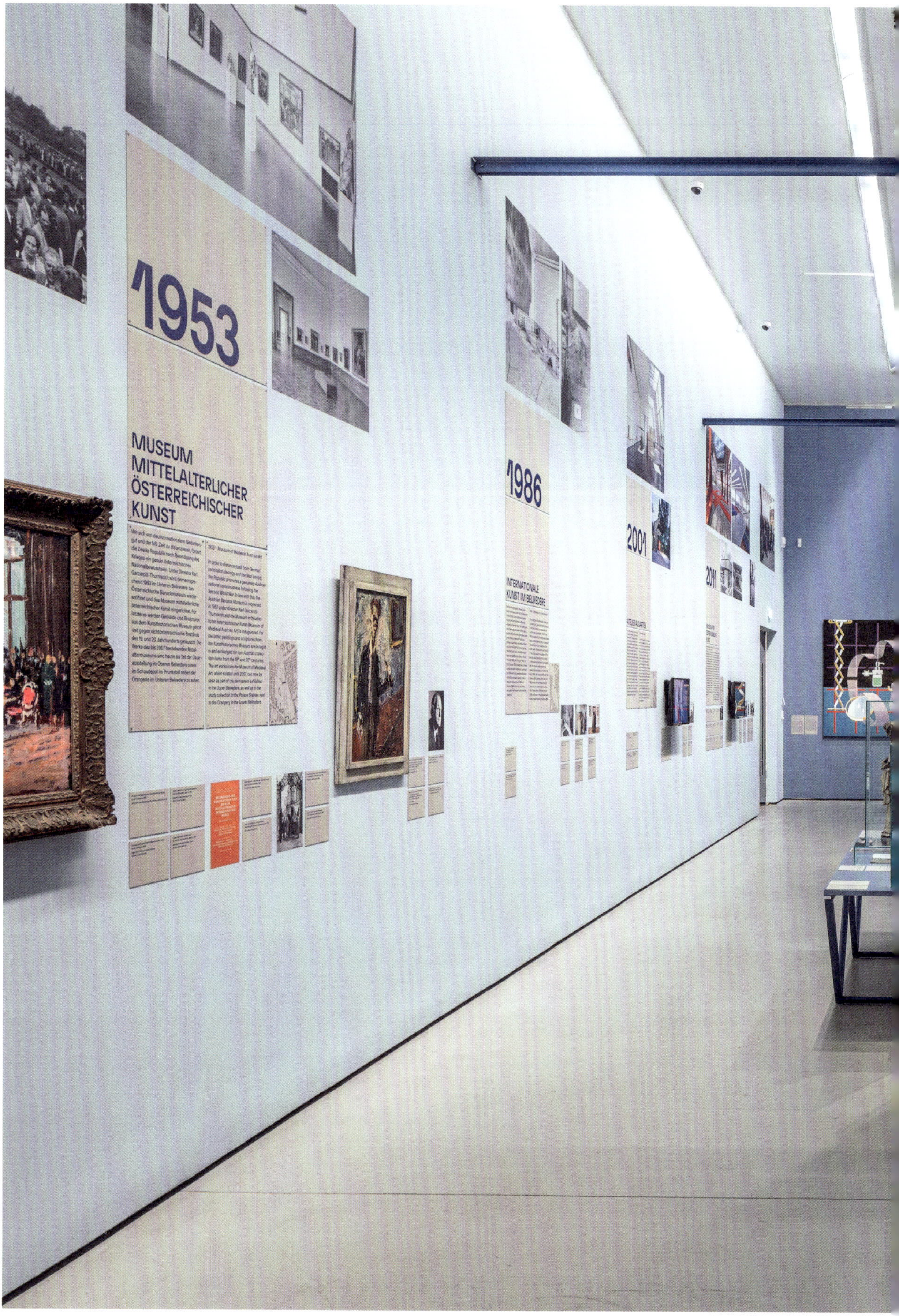
1953
MUSEUM MITTELALTERLICHER ÖSTERREICHISCHER KUNST
1986
INTERNATIONALE KUNST IM BELVEDERE
2001
2011

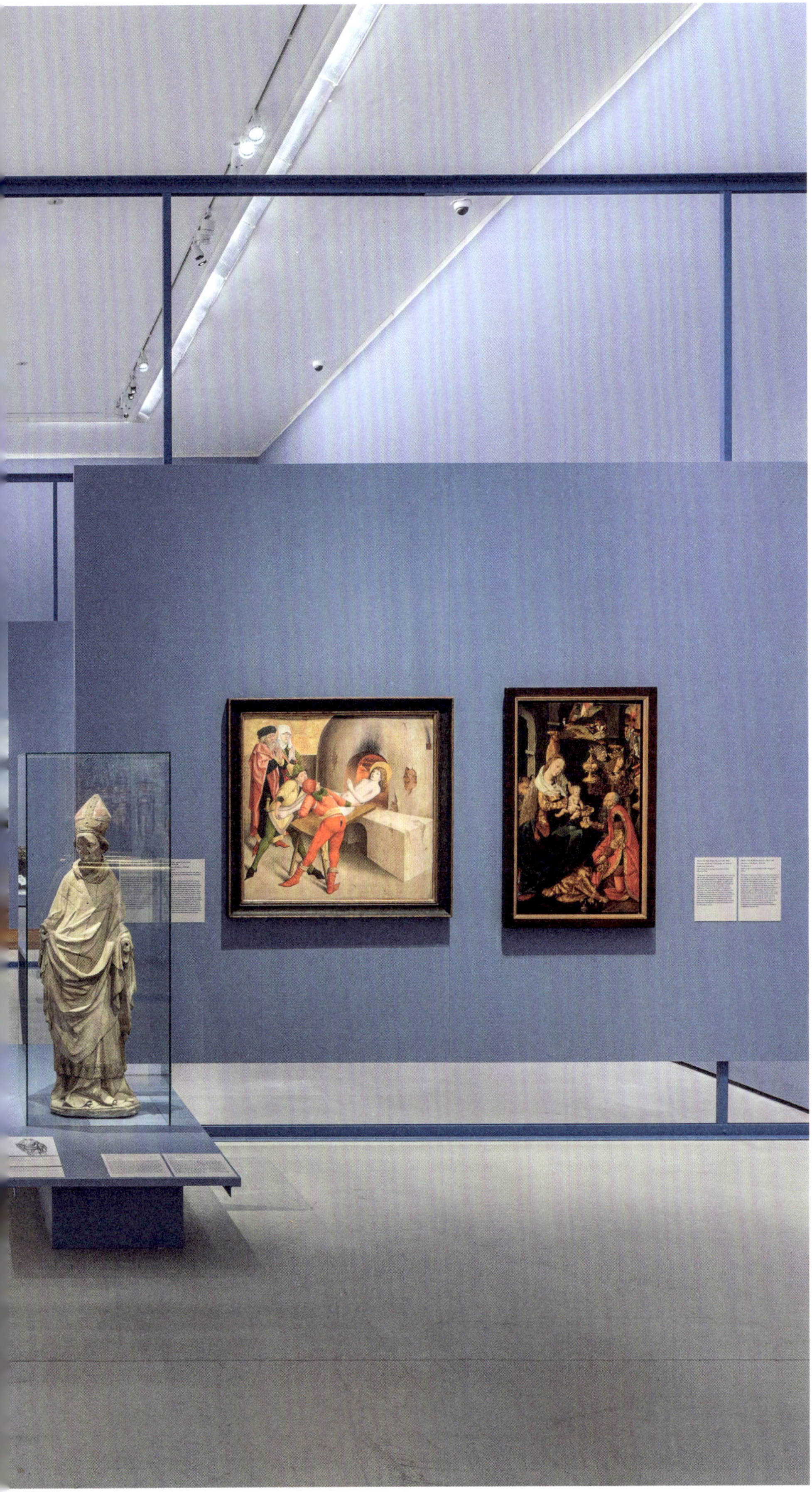

The exhibition *The Belvedere: 300 Years a Venue for Art* in the Orangery of the Belvedere, 2022, Belvedere, Vienna

P. 312 BRIGITTE BORCHHARDT-BIRBAUMER — "Our Modernism Is Homegrown!"

Austria's Delayed Reconnection with the International Avant-Garde after 1945

Austria's art policy after 1945 shows only fragmentary attempts to reconnect with the international avant-garde and to improve the public perception of contemporary art. At a 1950 exhibition in Vienna's Konzerthaus foyer, organized by the International Art Club founded in 1947, Rudolf Hausner's *Ark of Odysseus*, a painting in the Old Masters style with fantastic details, caused a scandal. There was even less public acceptance for the "2nd Literary Cabaret" performed in 1959 in the Porrhaus, the former Soviet cultural center near the Naschmarkt. The demolition of a piano there was an early example of Deconstructivism.[1] And it took four decades for the Viennese Actionists to be recognized and their works included in museums. Once the bomb-damaged museums had been rebuilt, some art historians, such as Fritz Novotny at the Belvedere and Otto Benesch at the Albertina, attempted to rehabilitate Classical Modernism after its defamation under the Nazis. The exhibitions from the late 1950s in the Upper Belvedere of works by Vincent van Gogh (1958, → p. 270), Paul Gauguin (1960, → p. 278), and Paul Cézanne (1961, → p. 276) were highly acclaimed by the public.[2] A similar trend could also be seen in Germany—for example with the program of the first Documenta in Kassel in 1955. It was not until documenta II in 1959 that the exhibition focused on contemporary art from the USA and the controversial history of abstraction.

Alongside the re-evaluation of Classical Modernism, the Allies, who remained in charge until 1955, endeavored in Vienna, Innsbruck, and Salzburg to improve the situation for the fledgling art scene and to overcome the inflexibility of the post-Nazi period with the help of innovative exhibitions, symposiums, and grants, and also the International University Weeks founded by Otto Molden and Simon Moser, which later became the European Forum Alpach. Their attempts at public education did not have much lasting success, despite exhibitions on Alexander Calder and the new French and American avant-garde. In 1946, the Künstlerhaus organized the exhibition *Never Forget!* (fig. 1), initiated by the Soviet occupying forces and supported by the communist Vienna City councilor Viktor Matejka.[3] In 1955, Sergius Pauser's moderate Expressionist painting of the signing of the State Treaty met with disapproval. Matejka continued to be a major supporter of contemporary art. As early as November 1945 he had published an appeal in New York émigré newspapers, encouraging Austrian artists and academics in the USA to return to Vienna. It was not until the 1970s that Bruno Kreisky's minister of science Hertha Firnberg (→ p. 277) renewed this call.

Until the 1960s, the Austrian avant-garde turned to Paris for inspiration, which it took not only from Surrealism but also from abstract

1 See the chronology compiled by the author in exh. cat. Vienna 2020, pp. 597–605.
2 These exhibitions were organized by the City of Vienna's culture department.
3 https://www.geschichtewiki.wien.gv.at/Niemals_vergessen!_Antifaschistische_Ausstellung,_Wiener_Künstlerhaus (accessed on March 13, 2023). Another exhibition on this subject was *Die uns verließen* in the Upper Belvedere, curated for the Wiener Festwochen 1980 by Elfriede Baum, curator at the Austrian Gallery, under the direction of Hans Aurenhammer.

Informalism. From 1949, the Paris studio of Greta Freist and Gottfried Goebel, as a French pendant of the Art Club, was the point of contact for Susanne Wenger, Maria Lassnig, Friedensreich Hundertwasser, Arnulf Rainer, and others.[4] New York had long replaced Paris as the art capital of the West, but abstract art, dramatically celebrated as the "international language" in reaction to the Realism of totalitarian states, did not arrive in Vienna until 1959 with Werner Hofmann's plans for the Museum of the Twentieth Century—although this domain should have been covered by the Austrian Gallery.[5] The museum, eventually named 20er Haus and opened in 1962, succeeded where Art Club artists like Curt Stenvert and Gerhard Rühm with their events at the Strohkoffer, the Art Club exhibition venue, had failed—namely to extend the definition of art to include experimental film, new music, and literature (→ p. 325, ㉓).

Oskar Kokoschka's 1949 portrait of mayor Theodor Körner, Alfred Hrdlicka's bust of Karl Renner in 1967, and even Pablo Picasso's "socially corrosive" paintings, were the target of violent protests by the Liga gegen entartete Kunst (League Against Degenerate Art, which had links to the FPÖ), accompanied by heated debates in the media.[6] In the "Vienna art war" of 1969, numerous artists, from Elias Canetti to Adolf Frohner, came out in support of Werner Hofmann (→ p. 326, fig. 4), art historian and founding director of the Museum of the Twentieth Century, who was accused of libel.[7] The Nazi legacy remained strong: For example, in 1955, former Nazi party member Rudolf Hermann Eisenmenger, president of the Künstlerhaus and one of the most influential figures in Vienna's cultural establishment during the Nazi period, was commissioned to design the fire curtain and tapestry for the newly reopened Opera House (fig. 2). The works of other former Nazi artists, too—Josef Thorak, for example—continued to be promoted and purchased by collectors. In 1968, the psychiatrist Heinrich Gross was summoned to provide an expert opinion in the court case against the artists involved in the "Art and Revolution" action in Lecture Hall 1 of the University of Vienna's New Institute Building. From 1938 to 1945, Gross had been in charge of the children's clinic Am Spiegelgrund, in which hundreds of young patients with "behavioral problems" had been tortured and murdered as part of the Nazi euthanasia program. Gross was never prosecuted for his crimes.[8]

A more international outlook, which Oskar Kokoschka achieved in Salzburg in 1953 with the founding of the International Summer Academy for Fine Arts as a "school of seeing," was also established in academia with the return of the "Ottos" from exile: Otto Benesch, Otto Demus, and also Otto Pächt, who in 1963 became ordinary professor of art history at the University of Vienna. Benesch was appointed director of the Albertina in 1947 and Demus president of the Federal Monuments Authority in 1946. Both of them also taught at the University of Vienna and were

4 Exh. cat. Krems 2021; exh. cat. Vienna 2007, esp. pp. 45–60.

5 Voggeneder/Borchhardt-Birbaumer 2019, esp. pp. 9–17.

6 Cf. attitudes to Egon Schiele's work in the postwar period; 1957 rejection of *Cardinal and Nun* ("not exhibited because of the subject matter"); Mayer M. 2014, pp. 317–18 (Reichsbund der Arbeit).

7 Exh. cat. Krems 2021, p. 15.

8 Borchhardt-Birbaumer 2020a, p. 72.

honorary members of the Art Club. In its statutes, the Art Club explicitly stated that members must not have been implicated in morally questionable political activities or associations—thereby stressing international connections as opposed to earlier collaboration with the Nazis.[9] On the other hand, Heinrich Schwarz, respected curator at the Belvedere from 1923 until his dismissal in 1938 and pioneering photography historian, who was forced to emigrate to the USA on racial grounds, was unable to return to the museum or the University of Vienna.

After the war, the painter and interim academy rector Herbert Boeckl summoned the sculptor Fritz Wotruba from Switzerland to the Academy on Schillerplatz, where Wotruba took over the masterclass in sculpture in 1946. The painter Albert Paris Gütersloh, who had been persecuted after 1938 and as such was politically untainted, was entrusted in 1945 with a masterclass in painting at the Vienna Academy. The first amnesty for former Nazi party members classified as "lesser offenders" was granted in 1948. By harking back to Franz Čižek's pioneering art classes for children, Kineticism, and Herbert Tasquil's Bauhaus theories, the University of Applied Arts once again became a place of innovation, attracting teachers like Helga Philipp, Peter Weibel, Adolf Frohner, Hans Hollein, and Oswald Oberhuber. As rector from 1979 the latter was instrumental in expanding the university's concept of art.[10] From 1980, it pioneered the Neue Geometrie, a response to the Neo-Expressionist painting style of the Neue Wilde.[11] It was here that, from 1962, the artistic confrontation with National Socialism began—with the first designs by Frohner, Hollein, Walter Pichler, and Bruno Gironcoli for a memorial to the victims of the Shoah. As yet, these sketches had no chance of being implemented in a public space. And after the installation in 1988 of Alfred Hrdlicka's *Memorial Against War and Fascism* on Albertinaplatz, it still took over a decade before Rachel Whiteread's memorial was unveiled on Judenplatz in 2000.[12]

In 1968, Otto Breicha's presentation of works by the Wirklichkeiten Group (members included Martha Jungwirth, Kurt Kocherscheidt, and Peter Pongratz) at the Secession offered an idiosyncratic version of Pop art in Austria (fig. 3), described ironically by the curator as "Alpine Pop." The group was associated with the future Nobel Prize winners for literature Elfriede Jelinek and Peter Handke through the activities in Graz, dubbed the "capital of culture," where, since the late 1950s, Wilfried Skreiner and others had shown themselves to be far ahead of their time with regard to contemporary art in Austria. This was well demonstrated by the organization of the steirischer herbst and the trigon biennale, the founding of forum stadtpark, and the establishment of the magazine *manuskripte*.[13]

The art historian Fritz Novotny, who had worked at the Austrian Gallery from 1939 and later became its director (1945–47, 1960–68, fig. 4),[14]

9 Borchhardt-Birbaumer 2015.
10 Exh. cat. Vienna 2001.
11 An initiative for Neue Geometrie was launched in 1946 by Leopold Wolfgang Rochowanski at Galerie Agathon in Vienna.
12 Hrdlicka's *Monument Against War and Fascism* gave rise to a major public debate lasting from 1988 to 1991, as did Rachel Whiteread's winning entry for the monument on Judenplatz, chosen by a jury headed by Hollein and unveiled on October 25, 2000.
13 Exh. cat. Graz 1992.
14 https://www.lexikon-provenienzforschung.org/en/novotny-fritz (accessed on March 13, 2023).

maintained contact for many years with expelled artists such as Gerhart Frankl and Trude Waehner, and was an acquaintance of the regime critic and gallery founder Monsignore Otto Mauer, who established Galerie (nächst) St. Stephan on the premises of Otto Kallir's Neue Galerie.[15] Novotny and the art historian couple Dora and Günther Heinz nevertheless criticized the proponents of contemporary art, such as Werner Hofmann, Nani, and Klaus Demus, who were friends of Paul Celan and his artist wife Gisèle Lestrange. Similarly, many people were later critical of Hermann Fillitz's friendship with the German collector Peter Ludwig. With the founding of the Austrian Ludwig Foundation in 1981, many objects from this collection became permanent loans to the Museum of Modern Art.[16] The creation in 1953 of the Museum of Medieval Art at the Austrian Gallery, along with the establishment of two tenured professorships at the Art History Institute of the University of Vienna, gave medieval research priority over contemporary painting. Although Gerhard Schmidt, assistant to Karl Maria Swoboda, head of the Art History Institute at the University of Vienna, published the first book on new painting in Austria in 1956, the overall attitude remained unchanged: "Our Modernism is homegrown."[17] And this despite the fact that, like Werner Hofmann, Schmidt had received a stipend for Paris in the postwar period. It was the Francophile Hofmann, however, who was the driving force behind the founding of the Museum of the Twentieth Century in Vienna, at the instigation of Heinrich Drimmel, minister responsible for art and science. Meanwhile, the decision to reuse Karl Schwanzer's pavilion for the 1958 World's Fair in Brussels instead of commissioning a new, purpose-built museum was a typically Austrian solution (→ p. 325, ㉓).[18]

There was no chance of a professorship for Hofmann at the Art History Institute of the University of Vienna, neither in the medieval section nor with Renate Wagner-Rieger, who, together with her assistants, was conducting a fundamental reassessment of Historicism. At the same time, however, Wagner-Rieger and her group prepared the ground for the rediscovery of Viennese Modernism from around 1900, which also attracted the attention of the art dealers Serge Sabarski and Otto Kallir in New York, both of whom had been forced to leave Vienna.[19] Thanks to numerous publications and exhibitions in the wake of Hans Hollein's Wiener Festwochen exhibition *Dream and Reality* in 1985, the popularity of fin-de-siècle Viennese Modernism remains undiminished to this day (→ p. 293, ㉑). One vocal supporter of contemporary art at the institute was Maria Buchsbaum, until 1990 art critic at the *Wiener Zeitung*. She was the first to highlight the innovative achievements of women artists such as Maria Szeni or Maria Lassnig. However, as with the first Vienna School of Art History, art criticism as a discipline was still seen as "non-scientific" and associated with the objectionable activities of the art market.[20]

15 Fleck 1982.
16 On Novotny's "failure" regarding restitution after 1945 and the unsuccessful bid to recall Gerhart Frankl from exile in London to a professorship at the Academy, see the essay by Luisa Ziaja in this volume, pp. 320–35.
17 Quote cited by Werner Hofmann in a telephone conversation with the author in 2002 on the rejection of his habilitation.
18 Hofmann 2011.
19 Mayer M. 2014, p. 309. I am grateful to Monika Mayer for pointing this out; Natter 2003.
20 Lachnit 2005, esp. pp. 22, 35–36.

Mention should also be made of Eva Frodl-Kraft, who worked at both the Federal Monuments Authority and the Art History Institute, and who critically examined the history of the discipline and also the work of professors Hans Sedlmayr and Josef Strzygowski, supporters of the Nazi doctrines. Frodl-Kraft, daughter of the philosopher and member of the Vienna Circle Victor Kraft, called for methodological pluralism instead of the formal style-critical approach of Alois Riegl and Heinrich Wölfflin. Günther Heinz and Gerhard Schmidt shared her view of methodological variety as opposed to the quasi-ideological positions of others. Despite the universal rejection of former Nazi party member Sedlmayr, who in his role as professor of art history had continued to preach the "Endsieg" until his dismissal in 1945, there was a general consensus that his book *Verlust der Mitte*, published in 1948 and reprinted several times, offered a good description of the critical (in the sense of pathological) state of Modernism.

Writing from today's perspective, the art historian Thomas Zaunschirm regards the abstract Informalism of the 1950s, even the painting of Georges Mathieu (fig. 5) and Markus Prachensky, as "fusty."[21] He talks of the "dour provinciality" of the Austrian art scene.[22] In retrospect, Art Brut offered an important contrast to the progress utopianism of the time, a counterbalance to the crisis of Modernism, seen not just by Sedlmayr as (psychoanalytically) pathological.[23]

Vienna's closeness to the Iron Curtain, placing it until 1989 right on the edge of the Western world, led Oswald Oberhuber, rector of the University of Applied Arts, to offer Peter Weibel and Bazon Brock guest professorships and later permanent professorial positions; he was unsuccessful, on the other hand, in his attempt to attract Joseph Beuys, considered one of the leading lights in the art world at the time, to the university. Before the appointment of Maria Lassnig in 1980, notable female teachers included Martha Jungwirth in Grete Rader-Soulek's class and Helga Philipp under Herbert Tasquil. Philipp showed an interest in the composer Josef Matthias Hauer and in Op art, and her forays into light art influenced not only the future professor Brigitte Kowanz, but also Heimo Zobernig, Franz Graf, and others. Aside from Weibel and VALIE EXPORT, the new media were especially important for female artists seeking to distance themselves from the dominance of a certain male swagger in painting, sculpture, and architecture. In 1977, a large group of female artists headed by Christa Hauer and supported by state secretary for women Johanna Dohnal founded the international artists association IntAkt (fig. 6).[24]

After some of the artists who had participated in the "Art and Revolution" action in 1968 had left Austria under threat of prosecution, the majority of the Viennese Actionists and members of the Wiener Gruppe

21 Zaunschirm 2001, pp. 31–47.
22 Zaunschirm 2001, p. 20.
23 The first Art Brut artist in Austria was Susanne Wenger, who depicted the 1944 air raids on Vienna in surreal and childlike-naïve color crayon drawings. See Borchhardt-Birbaumer 2020b, pp. 448–57. From 1970, Monsignore Otto Mauer exhibited works by the artists in the psychiatric clinic in Maria Gugging at his Galerie nächst St. Stephan.
24 Borchhardt-Birbaumer 2020c.

returned to Austria under chancellor Bruno Kreisky (1970–83). In the 1970s, there were over fifty contemporary art galleries in Vienna. From the late 1990s, the gallery owner Georg Kargl was an important supporter of female artists, including Elke Krystufek, Vera Frenkel, and Inés Lombardi. It was in this decade that the art scene became truly international, and contemporary art became a main focus. From 1992, arts minister Rudolf Scholten appointed federal art curators, and in 1998 the internationally applauded Art Restitution Act entered into force (→ p. 331, ㉔). This was also the time when Austrian tourism benefited from several major "Vienna 1900" retrospectives (→ p. 293, ㉑).

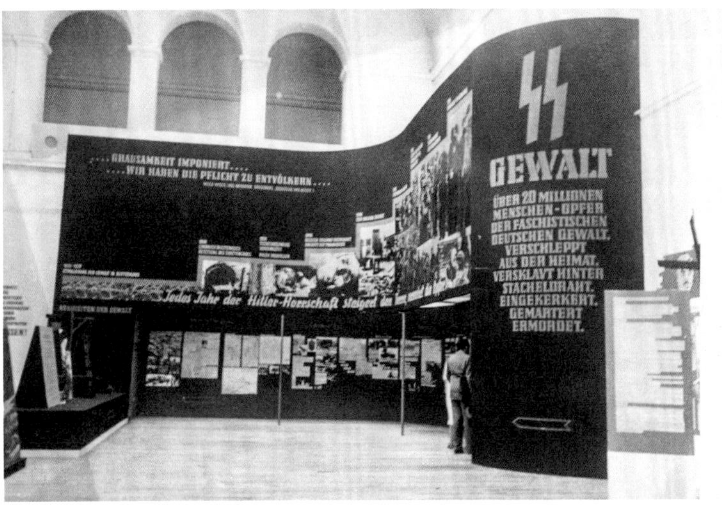

1

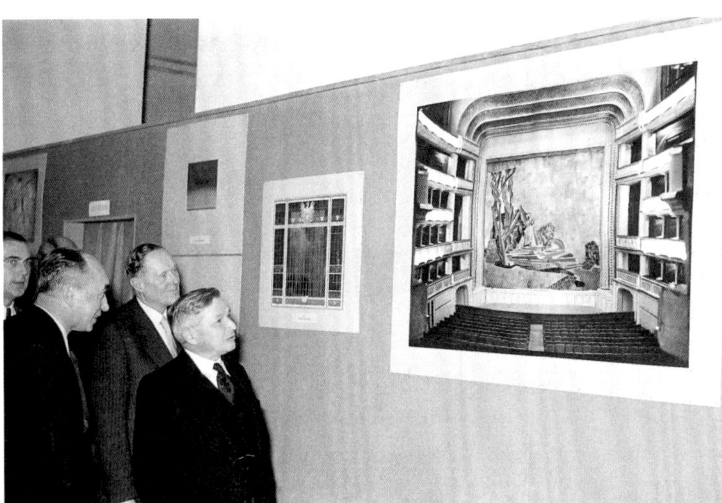

2

Fig. 1
Never Forget! exhibition in the Künstlerhaus, Vienna, September 14, 1946, photo: Franz Blaha, Austrian National Library, Vienna, Picture Archives

Fig. 2
Photo of *Orpheus and Eurydice* by Rudolf Hermann Eisenmenger, the winning design for the new fire curtain at the State Opera, 1954, Austrian National Library, Vienna, Picture Archives

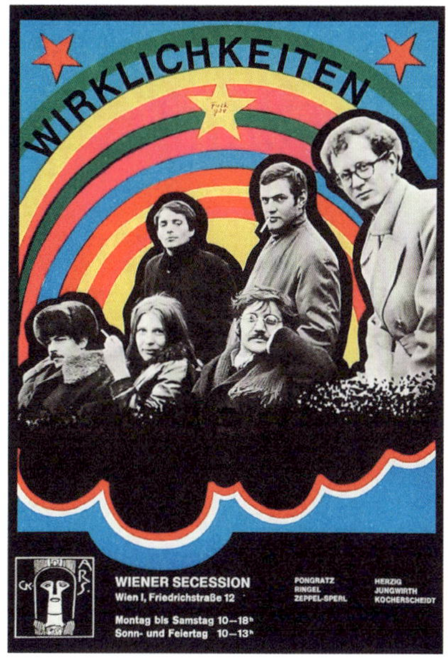

3

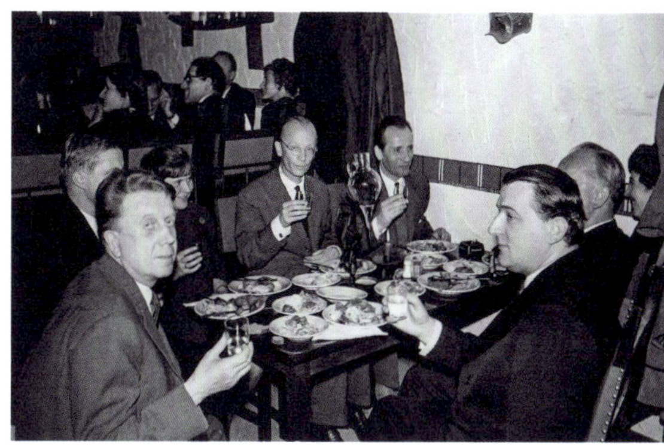

4

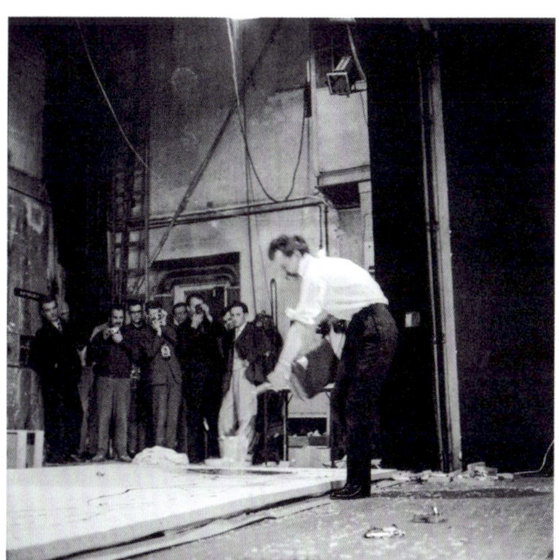

5

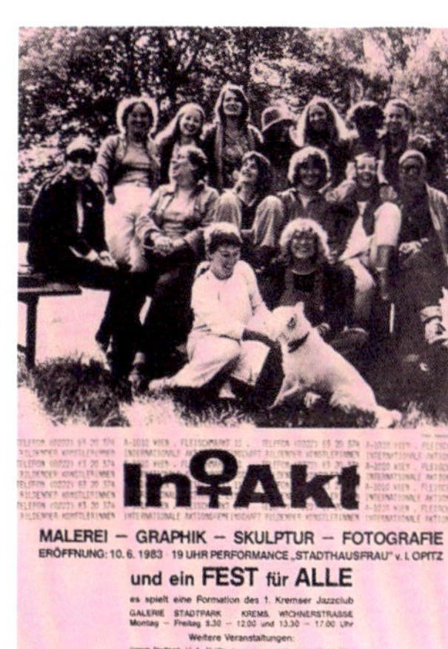

6

Fig. 3
Poster for the exhibition *Wirklichkeiten—Fuck you—Wiener Secession* in the Vienna Secession, 1968, Austrian National Library, Vienna, Picture Archives

Fig. 4
Meeting of art historians: Fritz Novotny, Günther Heinz, Gerhard Schmidt, and Dora Heinz, undated, private collection

Fig. 5
Georges Mathieu during his legendary painting action in the Theater am Fleischmarkt, 1959, photo: Barbara Pflaum

Fig. 6
Poster for an exhibition of the IntAkt artists group at Galerie Stadtpark in Krems, 1983, MAK—Museum of Applied Arts, Vienna

P. 320 LUISA ZIAJA — In Search of (a Place for) Contemporary Art

The Programmatic Development from 1945 to the Present

"Heavy sigh in view of the new acquisitions: 'What about the Modern Gallery?'"[1] is the headline introducing an article by artist Arnulf Neuwirth in the *Mitteilungen des Art Club Wien* in 1951, taking up an issue that runs through the history of this institution from its beginnings right up to the 2010s. It is as much about the search for a suitable location for contemporary art of the time as about its relevance in the institution's programmatic direction, and not least the question of whether—and how—to place this work in an international context. Contemporaneity and internationality—two key elements in the founding story of the Modern Gallery—serve as leitmotifs in this essay, putting into perspective the Austrian Gallery's programmatic development from 1945 to the present. In terms of substantive focus, associated identificatory potential, and identity-forming functions—and, not least, the actors involved and their decisions regarding institutional, collection, and exhibition policy—what transpires is a development characterized by contradictions, ambivalences, and ruptures, but also continuities.

Decisive junctures in the struggle for identity

Immediately after the war, and following the dismissal of Bruno Grimschitz, the custodian Fritz Novotny (→ pp. 371–72),[2] appointed interim director from 1945 to 1947, had very limited room for action. Due to the lack of construction materials, the roofs of both palaces, which had been badly damaged in the bombings of autumn 1944 and February 1945 (→ pp. 237–39), were only provisionally patched up with tarpaulins; at least the restoration of the ruined grounds could be tackled, however.[3] Although exhibitions in the buildings of the Belvedere remained out of the question for years, as soon as September 1945, Novotny, in collaboration with the general director of the Staatliche Kunstsammlungen Wiens (State Art

1 Neuwirth 1951.
2 For more on the role of Fritz Novotny as custodian and later director of the Austrian Gallery, see Katinka Gratzer-Baumgärtner, "Fritz Novotny," in *Lexikon der österreichischen Provenienzforschung*, July 2019, https://www.lexikon-provenienzforschung.org/novotny-fritz (accessed on January 16, 2023).
3 See Karl Garzarolli-Thurnlackh, speech for Minister Illig, opening of the Upper Belvedere, July 17, 1954, AdB, Zl. 281/1954.

Collections Vienna) Alfred Stix, managed to put together a presentation of drawings by Gustav Klimt, Egon Schiele, and Oskar Kokoschka at the Neue Galerie[4] and, in October 1946, curated the retrospective *Austrian Art from the Middle Ages to the Present* at the State Arts and Crafts Museum in Vienna (as the MAK was then still called) together with Karl Garzolli-Thurnlackh and Ignaz Schlosser.[5] In the years that followed, Novotny organized exhibitions from the Austrian Gallery's holdings at the Salzburg Residenz (*Austrian Baroque Art: Painting and Sculpture*, 1948[6]), at the Academy of Fine Arts in Vienna (*Anton Romako Memorial Exhibition*, 1950[7]), and at the Hofburg in Vienna (*European Painting in the Nineteenth Century*, 1951[8]). The collection was also moderately expanded: Thirteen paintings by artists including Oskar Kokoschka, Emil Jakob Schindler, and Herbert Boeckl were added to the inventory from the legacy of the artist and main initiator of the Modern Gallery Carl Moll (→ p. 189, fig. 1), after his suicide on April 13, 1945. Novotny also successfully acquired works by Richard Gerstl, Koloman Moser, and Alexej von Jawlensky, among others, as well as by the young painter Gerhild Diesner, an active figure in the Vienna Art Club after 1947.[9] Novotny's interest encompassed Austrian and international Modernism, as well as the contemporary production, in particular, of exiled artists such as Georg Ehrlich, Axl Leskoschek, Georg Merkel, and Gerhart Frankl, a long-standing friend, whom he tried to support upon Frankl's, ultimately only temporary, return to Vienna.[10] Moreover, as a result of Novotny's visit to her studio in Paris, Lilly Steiner donated a self-portrait to the Austrian Gallery and—possibly by way of admonishment—the painting *Composition baroque*, a nightmarish vision of Austria in flames in view of the annexation in 1938.[11] This focus on exiled artists was an exception in post-Nazi, post-war Austria. At the same time, with the enactment of the Ordinance on the Notification of Seized Property in 1946, Novotny's somewhat hesitant approach to the restitution of arts looted and acquired illegally during the Nazi period was very much in line with the general attitude of reluctance and ignorance on the part of the museums involved to actively confront this injustice, let alone not to prolong it in the post-war period by extorting "donations" in return for export licenses to émigrés.[12]

The appointment of Karl Garzarolli-Thurnlackh as director in 1947 (→ p. 371, fig. 12) was accompanied by far-reaching changes in the Austrian Gallery's thematic orientation, which would marginalize the role of international Modernism and contemporary art for decades. Garzarolli-Thurnlackh, who had been director of the paintings gallery and prints collection of the Landesmuseum Joanneum in Graz for many years and director of the Albertina in Vienna from 1946,[13] took on this task under the condition of being allowed to develop the Austrian Gallery into a "museum of Austrian art" or, in fact, an "Austrian National Gallery."[14] In

4 See Strobl 2004, p. 189.
5 Exh. cat. Vienna 1946. The groundbreaking nature of this exhibition was reflected in the new institutional profile a few years later.
6 Exh. cat. Salzburg 1948.
7 Exh. cat. Vienna 1950.
8 Exh. cat. Vienna 1951a.
9 The International Art Club, independent artists' association; the Austrian section was initiated in 1947 by Gustav Kurt Beck under the premise of "avant-garde of the new freedom." It pursued an anti-fascist orientation in a society permeated with post-Nazi continuities, and cultivated an international network assisted by exiles in the artistic centers of the time. Exhibitions in the Zedlitz Hall and the Strohkoffer provided fertile ground for the Austrian post-war avant-garde. See Breicha 1981; exh. cat. Krems 2021.
10 Gerhart and Christine Frankl fled to London in 1938 and returned to Vienna in September 1947, where they were confronted with numerous bureaucratic hurdles and financial challenges. At the intervention of Novotny and Garzolli-Thurnlackh, they found shelter for a year in the Lower Belvedere, where Frankl worked as a restorer. Disillusioned and without prospects, the couple decided in January 1949 to return to exile in London. See Jesse 2015.
11 See correspondence between Lilly Steiner and Karl Garzarolli-Thurnlackh, AdB, Zl. 165/1948.
12 See the text by Monika Mayer in this volume, pp. 331–32. See Blimlinger/Schödl 2018
13 For more on Garzarolli-Thurnlackh's involvement in the acquisition of looted arts, see Katinka Gratzer-Baumgärtner, "Karl Garzarolli-Thurnlackh," in *Lexikon der österreichischen Provenienzforschung*, February 2020, https://www.lexikon-provenienzforschung.org/garzarolli-thurnlackh-karl (accessed on January 16, 2023).
14 See letter from Karl Garzarolli-Thurnlackh to the Ministry of Education concerning the general director of the Staatliche Kunstsammlungen Karl Wisoko-Meytsky, Vienna, January 19, 1950, AdB, Zl. 20/1950.

the sense of "reclaiming Austria for the Austrians"[15] and "deepening the Austrian sense of belonging,"[16] the institutional self-understanding was to focus exclusively on the identity-building of the resurrected republic. Referring back to his letter of appointment dated April 1947, Garzarolli-Thurnlackh envisaged the museum's format as beginning with medieval art, stocked from the "picture and sculpture holdings of the Kunsthistorisches Museum" and housed in the Orangery of the Lower Belvedere, further encompassing the Baroque Museum in the Lower Belvedere and the Gallery of the Nineteenth Century in the Upper Belvedere. No space could be found in the existing rooms for twentieth-century art—even if of Austrian origin—which, depending on the various stages in the proposals, was variably to be presented in the orangery at Palais Schwarzenberg[17] or in a new building in the Horst'scher Garten[18] in the grounds of the Botanical Institute near the pond to the south of the Upper Palace. International holdings—a key part of the Modern Gallery's founding collection and therefore the nucleus of the institution—were to be disposed of and exhibited either in the Kunsthistorisches Museum (which, according to Garzarolli-Thurnlackh, rejected his redistribution proposals), the Academy of Fine Arts, or one of "Vienna's numerous unused palaces (Lobkowitz, Schwarzenberg, Kaunitz, etc.)."[19] Garzarolli-Thurnlackh considered the realization of a museum for Austrian art as "of prime importance to Vienna and Austria [...] not only for patriotic reasons, but also, undoubtedly, greatly in the interests of tourism."[20]

From 1947, in parallel with these programmatic deliberations, reconstruction work got underway, focusing initially on the Lower Belvedere and progressing to such an extent that by 1951 the first exhibitions could take place. The presentation *Masterpieces of Austrian Baroque Art*[21] served as a precursor to the reopening of the Baroque Museum, while *New Acquisitions 1947–1951*,[22] with exhibits "from the Austrian Middle Ages to the present, but also European art from the nineteenth and twentieth centuries," was presented as a kind of accountability report.[23] In contrast to the planned exclusive focus on Austria, works of German Expressionism, such as Max Beckmann's *Reclining Woman with Book and Irises*, purchased in 1948, were also included (fig. 1). The article by Arnulf Neuwirth, quoted at the beginning of this essay, was referring to this exhibition of new acquisitions, criticizing not only the envisaged concept of a "museum of Austrian art," as "the somewhat fusty idea, rooted in the chauvinistic spirit of the deepest nineteenth century, of an arrangement of art by country," but also the quality of "some of the third- and fourth-rate pictures by Austrian painters"[24]—a criticism that was to accompany the institution for a long time.[25]

The Lower Belvedere reopened fully to the public in 1953. On January 13, 1953, the Council of Ministers ratified the decision to dedicate the

15 Ibid.
16 See letter from Karl Garzarolli-Thurnlackh to Ministerial Secretary Alfred Weikert, July 29, 1949, AdB, Zl. 20/1950.
17 The orangery of Palais Schwarzenberg was at one point proposed to house medieval art and the Orangery of the Lower Belvedere the Modern Gallery. The construction of a single-story pavilion was also considered, as was the use of the former Liechtenstein Gallery. All of these plans were ultimately discarded for cost reasons. See Garzarolli-Thurnlackh 1957.
18 See "Planung und Kalkulation für die Errichtung eines Neubaus für die 'Moderne Galerie'," AdB, Zl. 20/1950.
19 See note 14.
20 Ibid.
21 Exh. cat. Vienna 1951b.
22 Exh. cat. Vienna 1951c.
23 Exh. cat. Vienna 1951c, p. 3.
24 Neuwirth 1951.
25 See, for example, Buschbeck/Csokor/Wotruba 1954.

Austrian Gallery exclusively to Austrian art. The Kunsthistorisches Museum transferred its significant collection of medieval Austrian paintings and sculpture, most of which had been acquired during the interwar period, to the Austrian Gallery, receiving its inventory of international art in return.[26] In February 1953, the Austrian Baroque Museum was reopened, and in December the Museum of Austrian Medieval Art was installed in the adapted Orangery—the roof had been raised and the façade altered by enlarging the south-facing windows (→ p. 213). In July the following year, the Gallery of the Nineteenth and Twentieth Century opened in the Upper Belvedere, presenting works of Neoclassicism, Romanticism, Historicism, and the Biedermeier period on the ground floor and across the whole of the first floor, while early twentieth-century art, from the Vienna Secession up to the 1950s, was shown on the second floor. "Recent" contemporary art, deemed by Garzarolli-Thurnlackh as unworthy of permanent display, was to be accommodated in temporary exhibitions in separate rooms on the ground floor, so that "ordinary visitors to the museum were not forced to engage with questions they had no desire to engage with."[27] The Ministry of Education responded emphatically, stating that it expected a "proper consideration of living art" and demanding a full list of participating contemporary artists.[28] The first temporary exhibition, *The Present*, in the summer of 1954, comprised around forty positions, many by artists who were active (at least occasionally) in the Art Club, including Gustav Kurt Beck, Maria Biljan-Bilger, Agnes Muthspiel, Hilde Polsterer, Wander Bertoni, Maria Lassnig, Arnulf Rainer, and Friedensreich Hundertwasser.[29] In spite of a few acquisitions and isolated exhibitions, such as, in 1957, *Six Austrian Artists of the Present*, curated by Klaus Demus and featuring Joannis Avramidis, Maria Lassnig, Erich Müller, Josef Pillhofer, Hedwig Wagner, and Traute Zemb,[30] the contemporary avant-garde was mostly ignored under Garzarolli-Thurnlackh. Nevertheless, even during the 1950s, works of contemporary art already entered the Austrian Gallery's collection by way of permanent loans from purchases made by the Artothek des Bundes, founded in 1948.

International Modernism as an audience magnet and the position of the post-war avant-garde

Contrary to the new, purely Austrian agenda, from the late 1950s, it was precisely the exhibitions of international Classical Modernism that brought the museum unprecedented public success. These "blockbuster exhibitions"—as they might be called in today's jargon—took place in the Upper Belvedere on the initiative of and in cooperation with the Cultural Office of the City of Vienna. Under the aegis of the Cézanne expert Fritz Novotny, director of the Belvedere from 1960 to 1968, exhibitions on *Vincent van Gogh* (1958, → p. 270),[31] *Paul Gauguin* (1960, → p. 278),[32] and *Paul*

26 Letter from the Ministry of Education to Karl Garzarolli-Thurnlackh, January 28, 1953, AdB, Zl. 512/1953.
27 Exhibition program of the Austrian Gallery of the Nineteenth and Twentieth Centuries in the Upper Belvedere, Karl Garzarolli-Thurnlackh to the Ministry of Education, Section II, February 2, 1954, AdB, Zl. 281/1954.
28 Letter from the Ministry of Education to the Austrian Gallery, March 3, 1954, AdB, Zl. 281/1954.
29 See list of participating artists in the letter from Karl Garzarolli-Thurnlackh to the Ministry of Education, July 9, 1954, AdB, Zl. 281/1954.
30 Exh. cat. Vienna 1957.
31 Exh. cat. Vienna 1958.
32 Exh. cat. Vienna 1960.

(23)

The History of the Museum of the Twentieth Century / 20er Haus

Claudia Slanar

"The intention to establish a 'gallery for artworks of our time'—the name of a museum project by Otto Wagner—in Vienna is as old as this century," Werner Hofmann, founding director of the Museum of the Twentieth Century, wrote in his foreword to the catalogue for its inaugural exhibition in September 1962.[1] The eventful story of the battle for a respectable collection of modern and contemporary art and a suitable venue for its presentation, had finally reached its conclusion.

The new building, which, at the initiative of the then Minister of Education Heinrich Drimmel, ultimately became a museum providing a "worthy setting for the discussion of the artistic questions of our time,"[2] was the Austrian Pavilion (fig. 1) designed by architect Karl Schwanzer for the 1958 World's Fair in Brussels. With a decree from the Council of Ministers, Drimmel had the building transported to Vienna and reconstructed, with a few architectural modifications, in the Schweizergarten.

The pavilion, which—owing to four steel supports carrying a cantilevered platform on a square floor plan—had the appearance of hovering above the ground, symbolized the Second Republic's departure toward a new future. For its conversion into a museum, however, the lower floor had to be glazed and a roof installed above the courtyard. The thus newly created space followed a museum ideal based on flexibility and transparency, but required a complicated (and costly) architectural redesign for (temporary) exhibitions.

Yet not just the exhibition spaces were infused with this new architectural spirit. The cinema on the ground floor (fig. 2), which had already been part of the World's Fair pavilion, also offered the possibility of presenting a medium closely tied to the history of twentieth-century art. Once again, it was Werner Hofmann who emphasized this special role of film and, in 1963, initiated the French film weeks at the 20er Haus cinema in collaboration with the Cinémathèque française.[3]

Exemplary of the museum's mission in its founding phase—international, dedicated to the historical avant-garde, and at the same time absolutely contemporary—was the aforementioned inaugural exhibition *Art from 1900 to the Present* (figs. 3–4). It is a testimony to Hofmann's concept for the museum, his aim of "recapitulating" important chapters of art history in the exhibitions, and of telling his own story of Modernism and its "multimateriality." It also illustrates the founding director's deft acquisitions policy, which sought to showcase the key trends in modern and contemporary art with multidisciplinary works by lesser-known artists. The aspiration to "establish a center for new and upcoming art on tradition-steeped cultural ground"[4] in its own building—with "a sixty-two-year delay,"[5] as the museum's second director Alfred Schmeller would later add wryly—was fulfilled for now.

1 Exh. cat. Vienna 1962, p. VII.
2 Heinrich Drimmel in exh. cat. Vienna 1962, p. V.
3 A booklet was published to accompany the film screenings: Bleier-Brody/Hofmann 1963.
4 Heinrich Drimmel in exh. cat. Vienna 1962, p. V.
5 Schmeller 1973, p. 37.

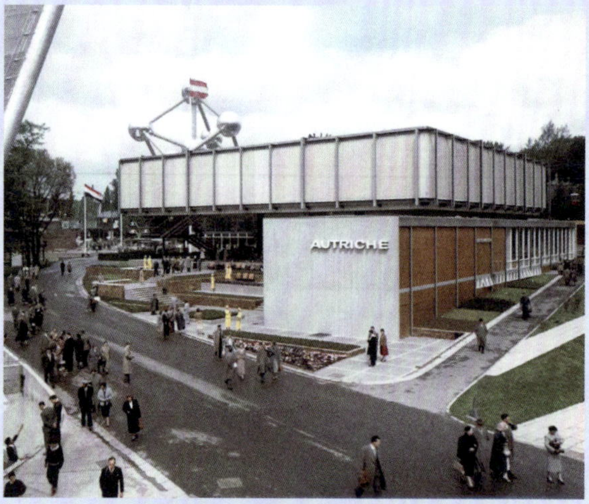

1

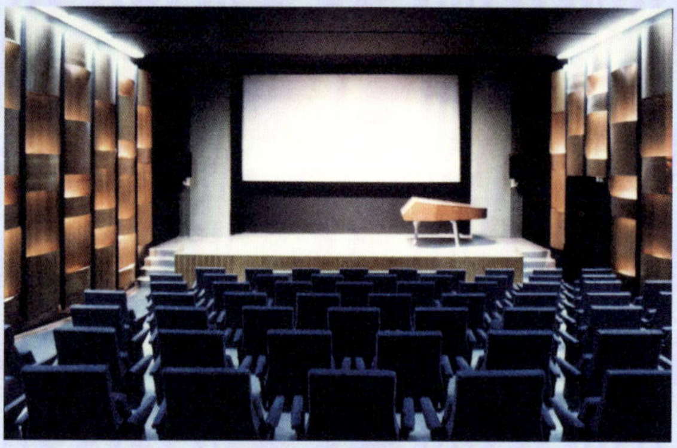

2

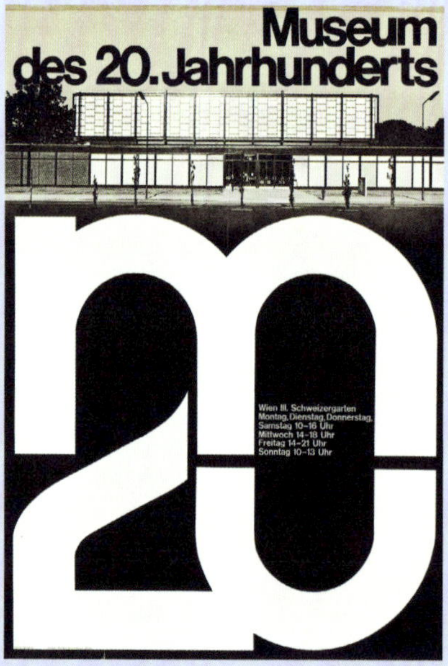

3

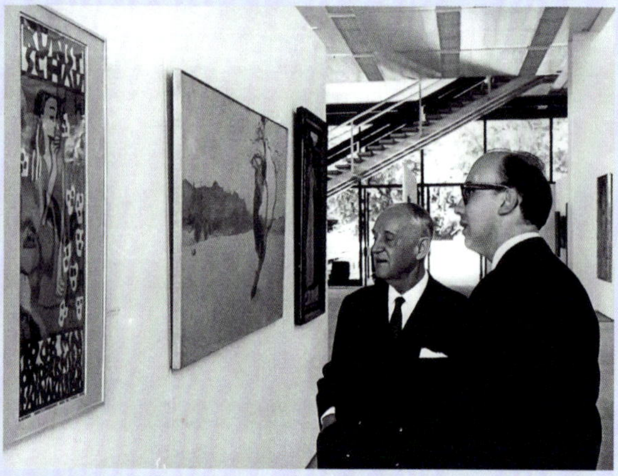

4

Fig. 1
The Austrian Pavilion at the World Expo in Brussels 1958, architect: Karl Schwanzer

Fig. 2
The cinema in the 20er Haus

Fig. 3
Poster for the Museum of the Twentieth Century, 1963, design: Georg Schmid, Austrian National Library, Vienna

Fig. 4
Federal President Adolf Schärf and Werner Hofmann at the opening of the exhibition *Art from 1900 to the Present*, 1962, Austrian National Library, Vienna, Picture Archives

Cézanne (1961, → p. 276)[33] were held, with the aim of promoting knowledge and appreciation of international trends, after the rupture caused by National Socialism. The exhibition series *Pioneers of Modern Painting*, which took place partly within the framework of the Wiener Festwochen, also included *Edvard Munch* (1959) at the Academy of Fine Arts in Vienna, *Ferdinand Hodler* (1962) at the Secession, *Wien um 1900* (1964) at the Historisches Museum der Stadt Wien, the Künstlerhaus, and the Secession, *Henri Toulouse-Lautrec* (1966) and *Pablo Picasso* (1968) at the Austrian Museum of Applied Arts, *Max Beckmann* (1967) at the Secession, and culminating in 1971 with *Oskar Kokoschka zum 85. Geburtstag*[34] at the Austrian Gallery.[35]

From 1967, almost thirty years after the closure of the Modern Gallery in 1938, the collection of international Modernism, now held by the Kunsthistorisches Museum, was exhibited as Neue Galerie in der Stallburg in Vienna's Hofburg.[36] Prior to this, masterpieces from this collection were shown only once in a special exhibition at the Academy of Fine Arts in 1956, and in 1962 at two exhibitions curated by Werner Hofmann, one in Zurich and one at the recently reopened Museum of the Twentieth Century in the Schweizergarten.[37] The founding of this museum in the Austrian Pavilion for the 1958 Brussels World's Fair, which had been moved to Vienna (→ p. 325, ㉓), was to have all manner of consequences for the future development of the Austrian Gallery at various points throughout its history. If the institution's attitude toward the post-war avant-garde had already been somewhat reticent—with occasional exceptions in the exhibition program and individual purchases[38]—it became increasingly so with the establishment of the 20er Haus (as the Museum of the Twentieth Century came to be known), which would thenceforth absorb a large proportion of the public funding available for contemporary art. At the same time, this agenda was to come under intense scrutiny as part of the Austrian Gallery's profile.[39]

Nevertheless, in 1969, the year of his appointment, Hans Aurenhammer, the Baroque expert who succeeded Novotny as director (→ p. 371, fig. 14)—a post he would hold until 1982—set out in search of a space for the Austrian Gallery of the Twentieth Century, his sights set on a wholesale flower market in Vienna's 5th district.[40] Yet again, however, the institution's plans for expansion came to nothing, leading the cultural journalist Harald Sterk to remark in the *Arbeiter-Zeitung* in 1975: "The imaginary museum for Austrian art post-1945: Modernism is still without a home."[41] In his article, he calls for a museum for the art of the present, as neither the Museum of the Twentieth Century nor the Austrian Gallery were able to fulfill the task of providing an adequate space for these positions. It was probably due to multiple factors that the tendency to ignore current artistic trends in favor of historical artefacts continued well into the 1980s.

33 Exh. cat. Vienna 1961.
34 Exh. cat. Vienna 1971.
35 In 1961, the Austrian Cultural Association, in cooperation with the British Council, showed *Henry Moore: Sculptures and Drawings* at the Academy of Fine Arts in Vienna and *Masterpieces of French Twentieth-Century Sculpture* in cooperation with the Institut Français de Vienne in the park of Palais Schwarzenberg.
36 Coll. cat. Vienna 1967.
37 Exh. cat. Vienna 1956; see Hammel-Haider 1992, p. 191.
38 An example is the first museum exhibition of the artists later known as the Vienna School of Fantastic Realism titled *Hausner Hutter Leherb Lehmden* in 1959. It is still notable for the absence of its key protagonists Ernst Fuchs and Arik Brauer. Exh. cat. Vienna 1959b.
39 See Smola 2006, p. 28.
40 See the letter from Hans Aurenhammer to the Ministry of Education, Vienna, September 8, 1969, and other related correspondence, AdB, Zl. 1043/1969. Other options were discussed over time, such as the Salesian Convent and the orangery of the Theresianium; see Haider 2004, p. 84.
41 See Harald Sterk, "Das imaginäre Museum für die österreichische Kunst nach 1945: Die Moderne ist noch immer obdachlos," in *Arbeiter-Zeitung*, July 11, 1975.

While the definition of art expanded considerably, especially during this period, pushing the boundaries of the traditional media of painting and sculpture, the Austrian Gallery was gripped by a persistent conservatism, compared, for instance, to the Museum of the Twentieth Century. Furthermore, approaches to historically charged topics and objects continued to be problematic and ambivalent. One of the many possible examples of this is in the simultaneity of an exhibition and an acquisition: In 1980, the museum dedicated an extensive show to artists who had been persecuted or driven out of Austria for racial or political reasons, euphemistically titled *The Ones Who Left Us: Austrian Painters and Sculptors of Emigration and Persecution* (fig. 2).[42] In the same year, the gallery purchased a bronze relief by Josef Thorak (fig. 3), an artist held in particular esteem by Adolf Hitler and who played a leading role under the Nazis. These contradictions are an expression of the reluctance to confront the Nazi continuities post-1945 that persisted into the 1980s and have only recently become the subject of increased discussion.[43]

Regarding the presence of the post-war avant-garde in the collection, the Artothek des Bundes emerged as an important source of permanent loans, most of which were early works by key protagonists such as Maria Lassnig, Arnulf Rainer, Wolfgang Hollegha, Josef Mikl, and Curt Stenvert. A degree of opening-up can be perceived from the mid-1980s, and, in 1984, under director Hubert Adolph, a "reading room for contemporary art" was established in the Upper Belvedere.[44] At Adolph's and Hermann Fillitz's instigation, and underpinned by developments in cultural policy, the decision was made in 1986 to transfer the collection of international Modernism (Neue Galerie in der Stallburg) back to the Austrian Gallery, thus enabling a renewed presentation of Austrian art in an international context. Under Adolph's directorship (1983–91, → p. 372, fig. 15), these works began to be integrated successively into the Gallery of the Nineteenth and Twentieth Century from mid-1989. In 1991, the German and French schools were given their own dedicated rooms,[45] and in 1996, under director Gerbert Frodl (1992–2006, → p. 372, fig. 16), the format of "blockbuster" exhibitions of Classical Modernism was taken up again with the show *Claude Monet*, curated by Stephan Koja (→ pp. 282–83).[46]

Reawakening and new perspectives

The international museum boom of the 1980s, with the establishment of major new museums across Europe and spectacular exhibitions—increasingly recognized as relevant factors in city and regional marketing—and the concept of a "new museology," which began to dismantle the elitist understanding of museums and called for a radical reevaluation of their role in society,[47] also triggered fundamental debates in Austria. Building maintenance had been neglected for years and investment was limited.[48]

42 Exh. cat. Vienna 1980.
43 See Gross/Brauneis 2021; Sommer/Sternfeld/Ziaja n. d.
44 See the report "Eröffnung eines 'Lesesaals für Gegenwartskunst' im Oberen Belvedere," *Mittagsjournal*, February 1, 1984, Österreichische Mediathek, https://www.mediathek.at/atom/0A4E30E7-351-00036-00000BA0-0A4D7CE5 (accessed on January 20, 2023).
45 See Adolph 1990/91, p. 139.
46 Exh. cat. Vienna 1996.
47 See Vergo 1989; Büchel 2022.
48 In 1986 the Baroque Palace Stables in the Lower Belvedere were renovated, while in 1984 Halbturn Palace in the Burgenland had been established as a summer venue for special exhibitions.

The direct subordination of museums to the Ministry of Education, with its restrictive regulations regarding organization, finance, and personnel, was seen as unwieldy and old-fashioned. This also, and in particular, applied to the Austrian Gallery, whose very existence in the given form was called into question.[49] With the "A Billion for Our Museums" program, adopted in 1986, a campaign of structural modernizations was introduced for federal museums, which at the Austrian Gallery was implemented in the form of extensive renovation works to all buildings and grounds, starting in September 1991 (→ p. 284).[50] At the same time, organizational reforms of federal museums from 1989 resulted initially in the granting of "partial legal capacity" and, later, with the outsourcing drive of 1999–2000, in "full legal capacity": federal museums became privately operating scientific institutions under public law.[51]

Gerbert Frodl, director of the Austrian Gallery from 1992, not only implemented a comprehensive reform of the institution, but also explicitly pushed the emphasis towards contemporary art, expressed through exhibitions and relevant acquisitions. Already in 1990, still under Frodl's predecessor Hubert Adolph, temporary exhibitions had started to take place at the Gustinus Ambrosi Museum in Vienna's Augarten.[52] The buildings, erected in the 1950s by the Republic of Austria for the sculptor Gustinus Ambrosi, comprising a workshop, domestic building, and museum, became part of the Austrian Gallery in 1978, since the institution was entrusted with Ambrosi's artistic and written estate after the artist's death.[53] The sculptor, deaf since childhood, was characterized by a political flexibility that enabled him to almost seamlessly—and for many years unquestioned—accept commissions from Emperor Franz Joseph I, the Austro-fascist corporatist state, the Nazi dictatorship, and the First as well as the Second Republic. The problematic and historically charged nature of this location was addressed for the first time in 1995 in the guest-curated, institution-critical *Spring Project*. Doris Guth and Matthias Michalka invited fourteen artists' groups to develop projects for this historically contaminated location, for which an ideological reappraisal was overdue. *The Spring Project* "sees itself as a demonstrative entry of the present into G. Ambrosi's studio and residential tracts, a further cracking-open of the associated hermetic structures; in short, as an artistic 'seizing' and a 'reoccupation' of the location."[54] The accompanying publication includes a critical examination of Ambrosi's place of activity, his biography and legacy, and of possible approaches to each. The relevance of this discussion was confirmed many years later, in 2011, in Nathalie Koger's film *Was ausgestellt wird (What Is Exhibited)*, which was acquired for the collection in the following year. Shot at the Gustinus Ambrosi Museum, where sculptures by the artist—such as busts of Engelbert Dollfuss, Benito Mussolini, and Karl Renner—are still exhibited without comment, the work reflects

49 In fact, there were heated debates at this time about dissolving the gallery in the Upper Belvedere and reducing it to the Baroque Museum as part of a new federal museum concept. See Haider 2004, pp. 84–85.
50 See Frodl 1992/93.
51 See the essay by Martin Fritz in this volume, pp. 336–43.
52 Exh. cat. Vienna 1990; exh. cat. Vienna 1991.
53 In a notarial deed dated May 20, 1957, the reason for the donation is recorded as death.
54 Exh. cat. Vienna 1995, n. p.

on images of the body, aesthetics, and conditions of exhibiting through the choreography of a Hula-Hoop dancer.

Although projects addressing the politics of history and memory remained the exception, over the course of the 1990s, the Augarten location (fig. 4) was increasingly experimenting with positions from the immediate present and current artistic strategies. After extensive renovation, it reopened in 2001 as Atelier Augarten: Center for Contemporary Art with the exhibition *Objects: Sculpture in Austria after 1945* curated by Thomas Trummer (→ p. 286). In subsequent years, Trummer's thematic presentations in particular were marked by an internationally oriented, theory- and topical discourse-informed curatorial practice that addressed the present with and through the vehicle of art. Within the framework of the contemporaneously established artist-in-residence program, artists from all over the world were invited to spend several months in Vienna and develop a project, often interrogating the institution or the collection. In this way, works by artists like Lisa Oppenheim, Silke Otto-Knapp, Ugo Rondinone, Gerard Byrne, and Marcin Maciejowski were added to the inventory, a response to the increasing importance of transnational collaboration and a revival of the motif of examining Austrian art in an international context. Fundamentally, since the 1990s, and even more so since 2000, contemporary art and relevant acquisitions enjoyed unprecedented attention. During this period, works of Austrian art since the 1960s were acquired, including key positions from protagonists of the different generations, such as Günter Brus, Marc Adrian, Cornelius Kolig, Bruno Gironcoli, H + H Joos, VALIE EXPORT, Heimo Zobernig, Lois Renner, Elke Krystufek, Lois Weinberger, Gelatin, Markus Schinwald, Mathias Poledna, Dorit Margreiter, and Hans Schabus.[55] In the words of Gerbert Frodl, these changes were made "in recognition and with the clear aim of understanding the Belvedere not only as a self-evidently historical location, but also as a productive center for Austrian art."[56] This became even more relevant with the incorporation of the former Museum of the Twentieth Century into the Österreichische Galerie Belvedere in 2002.

Renewal of the founding mission of contemporaneity and internationality

As early as October 1992, in the course of Frodl's appointment and in the context of plans for the new MuseumsQuartier, a cultural policy decision was announced that the 20er Haus was to become part of the Belvedere. Since 1962, the pavilion designed by Karl Schwanzer had been the most important place for modern and contemporary art in Vienna (→ p. 326, fig. 3).[57] Here, based on an expanded definition of art, current trends transgressing boundaries between the genres of visual art, literature, music, and film, were shown alongside traditional media. It was not only a place of

55 See, for example, exh. cat. Vienna 1999 and the annual reports of the Österreichische Galerie Belvedere from 1996 to 2005.

56 Frodl 2004, p. 50.

57 See the essay by Claudia Slanar in this volume, pp. 325–26.

Restitutions after 1945 and the 1998 Art Restitution Act

Monika Mayer

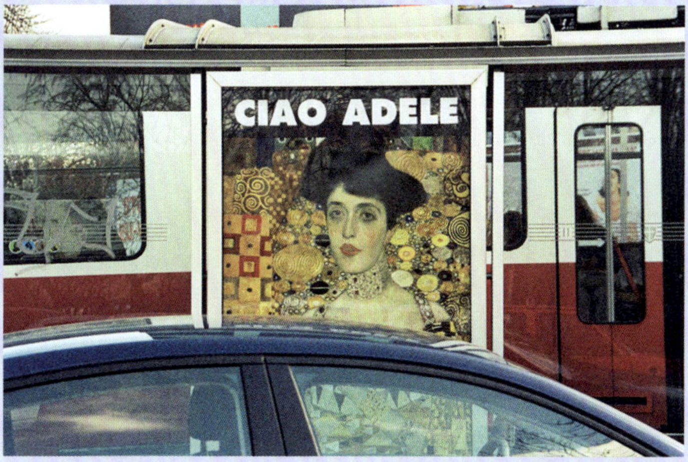

1

The Regulation on the Registration of Expropriated Assets, which entered into force on September 17, 1946, as a means of identifying "Aryanized" and other expropriated assets, served as the basis for restitution legislation in the liberated post-war Austria of the Second Republic. Under the regulation, the "owners"—and not the victims—were obliged to register suspicious assets. Accordingly, in autumn 1946, the interim director of the Austrian Gallery, Fritz Novotny, submitted a list to the district administrative office with twenty-six acquisitions from between 1938 and 1945 that were "probably or certainly originally owned by Jews."[1] In total, Grimschitz had in fact acquired over six hundred objects for the museum during the Nazi period. The artworks listed by Novotny came from eight named collections—including those of Viktor Ephrussi, Wilhelm Freund, and Leopold Weinstein—or were of unknown provenance, including purchases from the Dorotheum, the Vienna art market (→ p. 253, 19), and Vugesta (the Gestapo Office for the Disposal of the Property of Jewish Emigrants), and transfers from the Reich governor's office. Only ten of the registered objects were restituted to their rightful owners during the post-war period, and the museum made no effort to actively contact the victims of Nazi persecution. Nine further pictures from the collections of Josef Blauhorn, Gertrude Felsövanyi, and Robert von Mendelssohn were the objects of unsuccessful post-war restitution claims.

The decisive impulse for the establishment of official and systematic provenance research in Austria came in January 1998 with the seizure in New York of two paintings by Egon Schiele from the Leopold Collection. Under the Art Restitution Act promulgated on December 4, 1998, the Republic of Austria pledged to identify all artworks and cultural objects acquired unlawfully by the state since 1933 and to return them to their original owners or their legal successors.[2] This amounted to a paradigm shift in Austrian restitution policy. First, the collective compensation from the 1960s provided for in the 1955 State Treaty was abandoned in favor of the individual restitution of the immediate post-war years. Secondly, the principle of active restitution was invoked for the first time and without any deadlines for the assertion of claims. Heirless assets were to be given to the National Fund of the Republic of Austria for Victims of National Socialism. Since 1998, on the basis of the Art Restitution Act, over 60,000 objects from Austrian federal museums and collections have been restituted or their restitution recommended by the relevant federal ministers.[3] They include books, photographs, coins, furniture, decorative art objects, and technical appliances, but also major paintings and drawings from the Kunsthistorisches Museum, the Albertina, and the Österreichische Galerie Belvedere. By the end of December 2022, fifty-nine artworks and several books had been restituted by the Belvedere. Eleven further items recommended for restitution are still in the museum, subject to clarification of the legal succession.[4]

The restitution of five paintings by Gustav Klimt caused a worldwide sensation. After a legal battle lasting over six years, an arbitration court in 2006 finally ordered them to be returned to the descendants of Adele and Ferdinand Bloch-Bauer. The most famous of the five pictures, *Portrait of Adele Bloch-Bauer I* from 1907 (figs. 1–2), was purchased by Ronald Lauder for the Neue Galerie in New York for the record sum of 135 million US dollars. Thanks to provenance research in recent years, several art objects already registered in 1946 as having been expropriated have now also been returned. Alongside seven works by Feuerbach, Kupelwieser, Pettenkofen, Romako, Ludwig Ferdinand Schnorr von Carolsfeld, and Waldmüller from the collections of Josef Blauhorn, Wilhelm Freund, Gertrude Felsövanyi, and Gottlieb Kraus, Egon Schiele's late landscape *Four Trees* is worth highlighting here.[5] It was purchased in 1943 from the Vienna art dealer L. T. Neumann and listed after 1945 as "unknown owner." In fact, it was part of the Vienna collection of Josef Morgenstern, who was murdered in Auschwitz. Morgenstern's widow Alice survived the Nazi regime in hiding in Brussels, and in 2020 the picture was returned to her descendants.

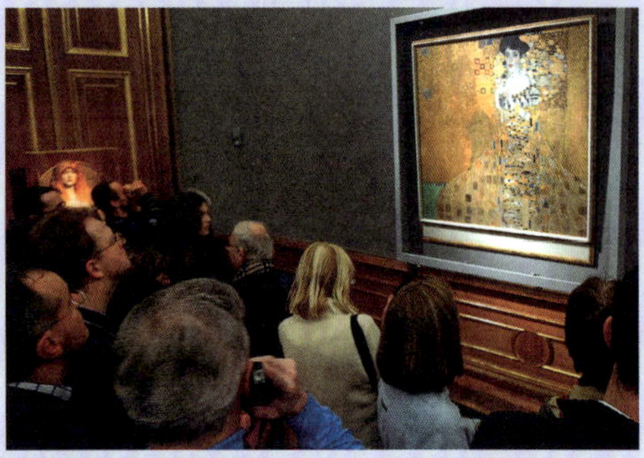

2

Fig. 1
Ciao Adele poster campaign by the advertising agency Gewista, following the decision to return Gustav Klimt's painting *Adele Bloch-Bauer I*; 2006, design by Rudi Strutzmann, photo: Manfred Werne

Fig. 2
Crowds of visitors at the Belvedere for the presentation of five paintings by Gustav Klimt shortly before their restitution to the descendants of Ferdinand Bloch-Bauer, 2006, photo: Herbert Pfarrhofer

1 AdB, Zl. 318/1946.
2 Federal Law on the Restitution of Works of Art and other Movable Cultural Assets from Austrian Federal Museums and Collections and Other Federal Property (BGBl. I No. 181/1998; BGBl. I No. 117/2009).
3 Blimlinger/Schödl 2018.
4 https://www.belvedere.at/en/discover/provenance-research (accessed on November 24, 2022).
5 https://provenienzforschung.gv.at/en/empfehlungen-des-beirats/beschluesse/beschluesse-alphabetisch (accessed on November 24, 2022).

(re)presentation, but often also a place of production for artistic and performance projects and—in keeping with its transparent shell—committed to the self-understanding of a democratic museum. With the construction of the new Museum of Modern Art in the MuseumsQuartier, the 20er Haus, by now also getting on in years, lost its purpose for a while. In spite of the early announcement to make it part of the Belvedere, the implementation of these plans took almost twenty years.[58]

From 2007, Agnes Husslein-Arco (→ p. 373, fig. 17), the first woman to become director of the Belvedere, further progressed the new emphasis on twentieth- and twenty-first-century art that had begun under Gerbert Frodl. Recognizing the historic opportunity for the institution to show an overview of Austrian art from the Middle Ages to the present in an international context and in rooms appropriate for the task, Husslein-Arco pressed ahead with plans to refurbish the 20er Haus. The architect Adolf Krischanitz, a student of Karl Schwanzer who had already collaborated with Frodl on a number of projects, including an exhibition for the project "20er Haus," emerged as the winner in a competition for the building's redesign (→ p. 342, fig. 2). To bring the 1950s pavilion up to date in terms of infrastructure, safety, security, and conservation standards, the open stairway was replaced with lateral staircases—possibly the most dramatic change to the listed building. The transparent design of the one-room museum was retained, however, as was the cinema with its remarkable aesthetic, which, after extensive renovation, has since been operating as Blickle Kino.[59] A new office tower was added to one side of the building, accommodating, among others, the Artothek des Bundes, the administration of which was integrated into the Österreichische Galerie Belvedere. This collection of modern and contemporary art, comprising more than 37,000 works, went some way to compensate for the omissions in the Austrian Gallery's acquisition policy regarding the post-war avant-garde. Furthermore, the estate of Fritz Wotruba entered the Belvedere, initially as a loan.[60] In November 2011, the former 20er Haus reopened as 21er Haus (fig. 5)—after more than one hundred years, the founding mission of the Modern Gallery was reaffirmed with a dedicated building for its contemporary art collection. Correspondingly, in the 2010s, under the aegis of Husslein-Arco (2007–16), this collection recorded the most comprehensive additions in the institution's history, which, alongside acquisitions and donations, also included a number of permanent loans. Husslein-Arco also initiated a reorganization of the Belvedere's different locations: The Baroque Museum and the Museum of Medieval Art in the Lower Belvedere were dissolved and their collections integrated into the presentation in the Upper Palace. The Lower Belvedere and the Orangery were now used for special exhibitions, and the former Palace Stables were adapted as a medieval show depot (→ p. 214, fig. 5).[61] While exhibitions at Atelier Augarten

58 See exh. cat. Vienna 2006; Husslein-Arco 2009; Husslein-Arco/Rainer/Steinbrügge 2011.

59 The Ursula Blickle Foundation supports maintenance and technical modernization, as well as the annual program. The Blickle Kino is a venue for the presentation of moving images at the interface of art and cinema and, increasingly in recent years, a platform for outreach aimed at opening the museum to different communities and their content programming.

60 With the dissolution of the Fritz Wotruba Private Foundation, his estate transferred into the ownership of the Österreichische Galerie Belvedere in 2021.

61 For more on the successful development of the institution from 2000, see the essay by Martin Fritz in this volume, pp. 336–43.

ended in 2011, the 21er Haus still hosted—often site-specific—projects by local and international artists, themed exhibitions, and regularly changing presentations from the collection across three floors. In terms of its program, the focus was on contemporary art made in Austria and its international contextualization. This orientation also continued after the appointment in 2017 of Stella Rollig as general director and Wolfgang Bergmann as chief financial officer (→ p. 373, fig. 18). In 2018, the 21er Haus was renamed the Belvedere 21, to leverage the recognition value of an umbrella brand. In recent years, the opening of the museum to different actors and communities has become an important focus, and today the Belvedere 21 is a vibrant place of artistic and curatorial experimentation, art communication, community, and social inquiry.[62]

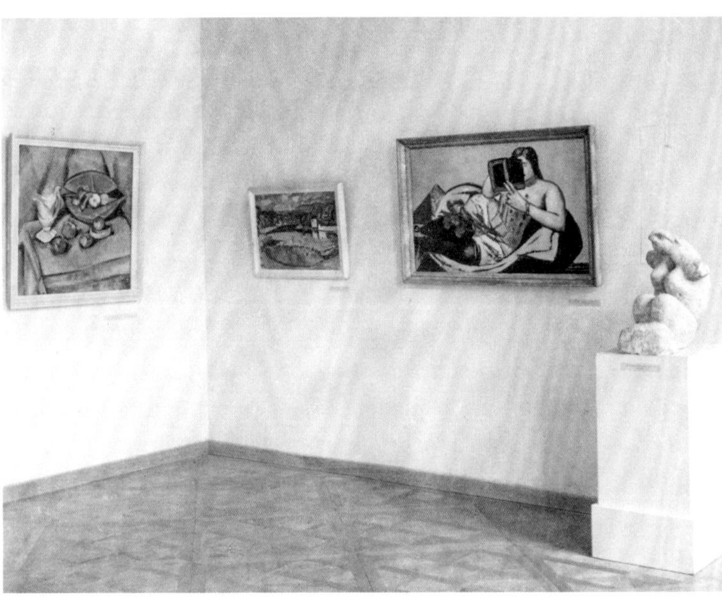

1

Fig. 1
View of the exhibition *New Acquisitions 1947–1951* in the Lower Belvedere, 1951, photo: Dr. Spiegelfeld, Belvedere Archive, Vienna

62 See the essays by Nora Sternfeld (pp. 344–52), Christiane Erharter (pp. 307–8), as well as Stella Rollig and Wolfgang Ullrich (pp. 356–65) in this volume.

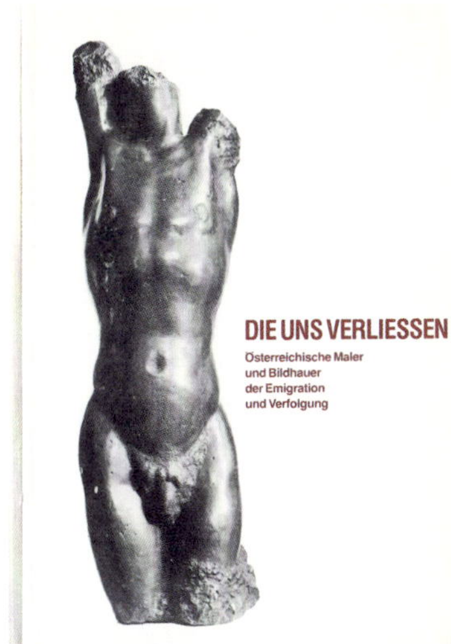

2

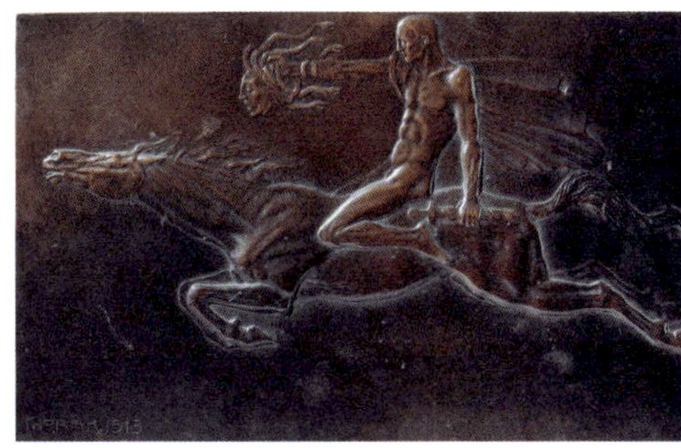

3

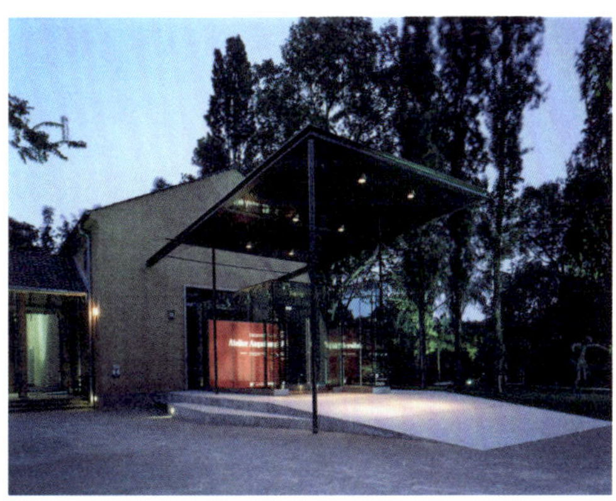

4

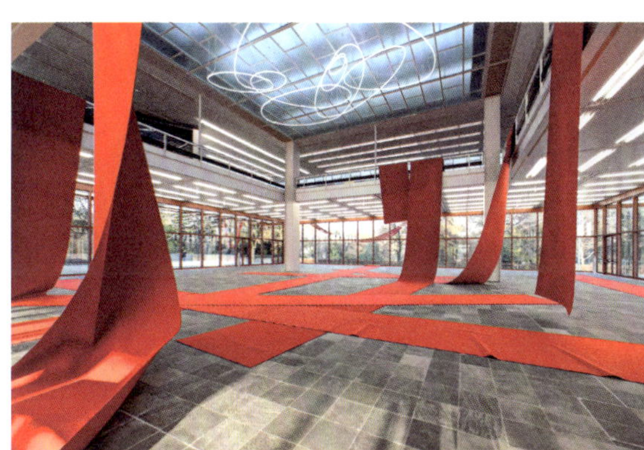

5

Fig. 2
Catalogue for the exhibition *The Ones Who Left Us*, 1980, Belvedere Library, Vienna

Fig. 3
Josef Thorak, *Perseus with the Head of Medusa*, 1913, Belvedere, Vienna

Fig. 4
View of the exterior of Atelier Augarten, 2001, photo: Margherita Spiluttini

Fig. 5
Schöne Aussichten (Great Prospects!), opening exhibition of the 21er Haus (now the Belvedere 21), 2011, photo: Wolfgang Thaler

MARTIN FRITZ — 2000 to 2020: Nineteen Years of Growth

The legal and financial history of the Österreichische Galerie Belvedere—from the entry into force of the Federal Museums Act in 2000 to the coronavirus lockdowns of 2020—reads like a heroic epic with a bitter punchline. But let's start at the beginning ...

Federal museums in Austria, including the Österreichische Galerie Belvedere, were under direct control of the state until the late 1990s. However, as early as during the reform-oriented political environment of the 1970s, the Ministry of Science already expressed criticism of this approach: "We must liberate ourselves from the constraints of state administration. Like the federal theaters, we need a 'top management team' organized according to private-sector principles," it says in a reform paper by undersecretary Dr. Carl Blaha.[1] Similarly, in the discussions about "New Public Management" during the 1980s, the embedding of museums directly into the ministerial bureaucracy was seen as an obstacle to progress. In particular, cameralistic budgeting rules, which funneled all revenue back to the state rather than to the respective institution, were seen as an impediment to innovation. Debates on the issue also stressed that the broad remit of a contemporary museum and the management requirements associated with this could not be adequately handled by a state administration.

Museum professionals at the time agreed that, alongside collecting, exhibiting, and research, the museum's remit also included the management of commercial services such as cafés and shops, professional marketing, and many other education and communication activities (fig. 1). Organizational forms modeled on private service providers were considered suitable for this purpose. Local discourse also highlighted the need to keep public sector enterprises free from political influence.

1 Untitled 104-page document. In other literature it is referred to as "Leitlinien für eine Museumsreform." Logged at the Ministry of Science under reference 31.682/1/32/75. Quoted copy: Archive of the Kunsthistorisches Museum, I–221. More on this attempt at reform in Fritz 2018.

Even though today—in view of a largely autonomous management on all levels—a discussion about greater opportunities for cultural-political influence would seem appropriate, it must be remembered that the unique historical development of Austria, with its succession of monarchic centralized bureaucracies, authoritarian regimes, and a party-political system of proportional representation, gave ample reasons for the outsourcing drive of the 1980s and '90s. A first step in the easing of cameralistic restrictions came with the institution of "partial legal capacity" in 1992.[2] This meant that museums were entitled to use the income from their now enhanced remit within their own institution. This increased financial freedom was expected to encourage development initiatives for federal museums, which were seen as in need of reform.[3]

This was followed by years of intensive lobbying for a new organizational format, conceptually linked at a cultural-political level with the development plans for the MuseumsQuartier. Negotiations regarding the location for the Museum moderner Kunst Stiftung Ludwig (mumok)—then situated in the Schweizergarten—had a direct impact on the future profile and remit of the Österreichische Galerie, since, following construction of a new building for today's mumok, the former 20er Haus[4] was to become part of the Belvedere (→ p. 325, ㉓).

Two years before completion of the MuseumsQuartier, the status quo in terms of museum policy was summarized in a short museum development plan, published as part of the 1998 culture report. An excerpt from this highlights another aspect of the development program, in the form of creating a new urban design accent through the Belvedere and its various associated buildings: "A further museum axis will be created with the incorporation of the 20er Haus into the Österreichische Galerie after the relocation of the Museum moderner Kunst Stiftung Ludwig to the new MuseumsQuartier."[5] Another paragraph elsewhere in the museum development plan reads as though it might have been written twenty-two years later, in the aftermath of the coronavirus crisis: "A further, closely related, fundamental task is the opening up of the museums to new visitor groups. This should, on the one hand, increase awareness among the local population of the museum as an institution, while, on the other hand, reducing the considerable reliance of some museums on unpredictable tourist flows."[6] The Belvedere's stance, formulated in its own contribution to the 1998 culture report, is more pragmatic: "In order to ensure that the tasks naturally expected of the museum can be fulfilled, both in terms of personnel and technology, the financial component is crucial. Already now and increasingly so in the future, funding and grants from various non-governmental sectors must also be leveraged to help the museum thrive. The fact that the state has to bear most of the burden will probably not change very much for the foreseeable future."[7]

2 Set down in section 31a of the Research Organizational Act (Forschungsorganisationsgesetz, FOG). Partial legal capacity made it possible to enter into sponsorship agreements and to generate and utilize profits.
3 For more on the discourse of the late 1980s, see, for example, Reininghaus 1987.
4 A reference to the "Museum of the 20th Century," the original name of today's mumok, when it was first established in 1962.
5 Culture Report 1998, Federal Ministry of Education and Cultural Affairs, Vienna 1999, pp. 13–14.
6 See note 5, p. 14.
7 See note 5, p. 59.

On January 1, 2000, the Federal Museums Act[8] came into force. With this, the structural reform generally referred to as "outsourcing" found its legal expression. The most significant changes were full financial autonomy and the establishment of a new supervisory body between the museum and the relevant ministry in the form of a board of trustees. In the initial phase of outsourcing, the current directors took over sole management of their museums, which had now been granted full legal capacity and were defined as "institutions under public law." In the following years, a four-eyes principle was gradually introduced at all federal museums, with the appointment of commercial managing directors alongside the existing directors, now titled "scientific" directors. With that, legislators also responded to cultural-political controversies regarding governance and compliance, which in 2016 would also reach the Belvedere.[9]

While the law defined uniform legal structures for all federal museums, individual museum regulations were enacted in parallel, in which "guidelines and specific purposes" were formulated for each museum. For the Österreichische Galerie Belvedere, these contain a specific intended purpose that reflects the perennial issue of locating "Austrian art movements within an international context,"[10] as well as the museum's connection with the Baroque palace complex: "As a whole, the ÖGBEL [Österreichische Galerie Belvedere] offers an overview of the visual arts from the Middle Ages up to the present day. Significant major works represent Austria's key art movements within an international context. Together with the Baroque palace complex, these major collections create an ensemble of European importance."[11] The close link between legal outsourcing as a means of managing the museum's expanded remit and the associated financial needs is made clear at the end of the same paragraph: "Through its own commercial activities and with support from patrons and sponsors, a continuous increase in equity contributions should be achieved to enable fulfillment of the objectives listed under section 3."[12] With this sentence the signal was given for a development that would define the Österreichische Galerie Belvedere for the next twenty years.

The expansion of services in the traditional areas of the museum is described in other essays in this volume.[13] A brief list should suffice here, from the development and operation of the Augarten Contemporary, to the incorporation and adaptation of the former 20er Haus (fig. 2), numerous renovation projects up to the foundation of the Belvedere Research Center, and the temporary use of Prince Eugene's former winter palace in the center of Vienna.

A description of the developments during these years would be incomplete, however, if we restricted our focus to museological core areas and exhibition history. If, in addition to the various statements on

8 Federal Museums Act, BGBl. I, no. 115/1998.
9 As part of her reapplication, the then director Agnes Husslein was confronted with allegations of non-compliance.
10 See also the essays by Brigitte Borchhardt-Birbaumer and Luisa Ziaja in this volume, p. 312 and p. 320.
11 Section 2 of the Museum Regulations for the Österreichische Galerie Belvedere, BGBl. II no. 397/2009.
12 See note 11.
13 See the essays by Brigitte Borchhardt-Birbaumer, Nora Sternfeld, and Luisa Ziaja in this volume, p. 312 and p. 320.

the "repositioning of the museum,"[14] one also analyzes the statistics published in the culture reports of the relevant ministries, it becomes clear that the success of the period between 2000 and 2020 is connected to an intensification in the operation of a top tourist attraction at a time when city tourism was experiencing constant growth (fig. 3).[15] By 2019, the proportion of the museum's independent commercial activities—at 53 percent already high even before outsourcing[16]—had increased to 70 percent. This was also made possible by an increase in visitor numbers from 496,649[17] in 2000 to 1,721,399[18] in 2019, combined with steady increases in ticket prices.[19] The 324 percent[20] increase in revenue over the course of twenty years facilitated an expansion of activities, although state funding in this period increased by a "mere" 95 percent.

The Belvedere's strategy was also in step with the international development of major urban museums with collection highlights and attractive buildings for tourism. Globally, museum and tourism marketing seeks to convey a unique selling proposition. In the case of the Belvedere this is the intertwining of Vienna's traditional "brands": the Baroque and the fin de siècle (→ p. 293, ㉑), represented in the Belvedere's marketing visuals by the palace and Gustav Klimt's *The Kiss*, as one of the collection highlights (fig. 4). Moreover, within Austria, the iconic images of the signing of the State Treaty in 1955 symbolically associate the Belvedere with the building of a national identity. Nevertheless, throughout the history of the Österreichische Galerie Belvedere, it was precisely this "Austrian" aspect that gave rise to major museological and cultural controversies. At the center of these was always the question of which art-historical, geographical, and/or chronological criteria should be used to demarcate the individual collections of the different federal museums.[21] Furthermore, the relatively late establishment of a museum of the twentieth century, that is, a museum of modern art, led to duplications in the treatment of twentieth-century and contemporary art at almost all federal museums.[22]

To clarify the position of each museum, short programmatic self-definitions have been included in the relevant ministry's annual reports since 2004 under the heading "Profile." For the Belvedere, it is interesting to note that, in the 2004 report, the connection between palace, Austrian identity, and art collection was made clear for the first time in a phrasing that had already disappeared in the following year's report: "As a historical location, a Baroque palace, and a significant art collection, the Belvedere is an indispensable part of Austrian identity."[23] The central role of the palace is emphasized in 2006—again, only for one year—with the following opening line: "The Belvedere, with its two palaces and historic grounds, is considered one of Austria's most beautiful surviving Baroque ensembles."[24] The reports from 2009 to 2016 consistently contain phrases taken from the new museum regulations issued in 2009, in which each

14 The title of an information paper covering the years 2007 to 2012.

15 Tourism statistics for Vienna show a 128 percent increase in overnight stays between 2000 and 2019.

16 This situation was due not least to a comparatively low level of federal funding. In 2000, for example, the amount of state funding available to the MAK amounted to 8.14 million euros, while the Belvedere received 4.59 million euros.

17 Culture Report 2000, Ministry of Education, Science, and Culture, Vienna 2001.

18 Art and Culture Report 2019, Federal Ministry for Arts, Culture, the Civil Service, and Sport, Vienna 2020.

19 What is remarkable here is that the average sales revenue per visit—at least according to a simple overall calculation—increased by only 2.30 euros in 19 years (from € 10.40 in 2000 to € 12.70 in 2019).

20 Comparison of the values for 2000 and 2019 in the Culture Report 2000 and the Art and Culture Report 2019.

21 More on this in the essay by Brigitte Borchhardt-Birbaumer in this volume.

22 In this context, it is notable that a curator for the twenty-first century at the Belvedere is already mentioned in the Culture Report 2000.

23 Culture Report 2004, Ministry of Education, Science, and Culture, Vienna 2005.

24 Culture Report 2006, Ministry of Education, Science, and Culture, Vienna 2007.

federal museum was assigned a "core competency" and a "complementary competency." For the Belvedere, the core competency was defined as "works of Austrian visual art in all media," complemented by "works of international art related to that core competency."[25] Since 2017, the emphasis of the opening paragraph has returned to the general cultural, historical, and—for the first time—touristic significance of the location: "The Belvedere is one of the world's oldest museums, and at the same time a place of contemporary art. It is a Baroque jewel and the site of the signing of the Austrian State Treaty. As one of the country's largest cultural institutions, it faces the challenge of balancing its own aspirations in terms of art and research with touristic needs."[26]

This challenge, here formulated by the Belvedere itself, was successfully mastered. The story since the outsourcings of the year 2000 can be described as a steady course of expansion and modernization—maintained despite changes in directorship—that was financed by an intensification of the institution's operation as a tourist destination. The broadening of the museum's scope thus made possible (and necessary) is reflected in the increase in full-time staff from one hundred[27] to 247 over the course of twenty years.[28]

However—to quote the introductory words of the foreword to the 2019 Art and Culture Report—"in March 2020, everything changed."[29] When, with the announcement on March 13, 2020, of the first coronavirus lockdown, all Austrian museums were closed and almost all private international travel came to a standstill, nobody could have anticipated the deep impact of these developments in the years to follow. In the context of this essay, two figures in particular are sufficient to illustrate this impact: After the record of 1.7 million visits in 2019, a mere 343,064 visitors were recorded in the first year of the pandemic. Hence revenue, which had been continually increasing for more than twenty years, dropped even below the level of the year 2000 (fig. 5). In the short term, operational cuts could be avoided with the help of public sector support, amendments to the exhibition schedule, and the release of reserves. However, at the point of writing this essay[30]—in 2022, a year of compounding crises—it is still unclear whether and when federal museums will be able to return to pre-Covid results. In the case of the Belvedere, the revival of city tourism plays the most significant role in achieving this aim. Thus, this essay ends where it began, with the 1998 museum development plan and its "unpredictable tourist flows,"[31] which had provided the main vehicle for the Belvedere's spectacular growth in the first fifth of the twenty-first century (fig. 6).

25 Section 13 of the Museum Regulations for the Österreichische Galerie Belvedere, BGBl. II no. 397/2009.

26 Culture Report 2017, Federal Chancellery, Arts and Culture Division, Vienna 2018.

27 Figure in 2000, Culture Report 2000, Ministry of Education, Science, and Culture, Vienna 2001, p. 48.

28 Figure in 2019, report by the Austrian Court of Audit: *Durchschnittliche Einkommen und zusätzliche Leistungen für Pensionen der öffentlichen Wirtschaft des Bundes 2019 und 2020*, p. 509.

29 Art and Culture Report 2019, Federal Ministry for Arts, Culture, the Civil Service, and Sport, Vienna 2020, p. 3 (note: the art and culture reports are published in the following year. The Art and Culture Report 2019 therefore already contained references to the coronavirus crisis).

30 The copy deadline for this text was September 1, 2022.

31 See note 6.

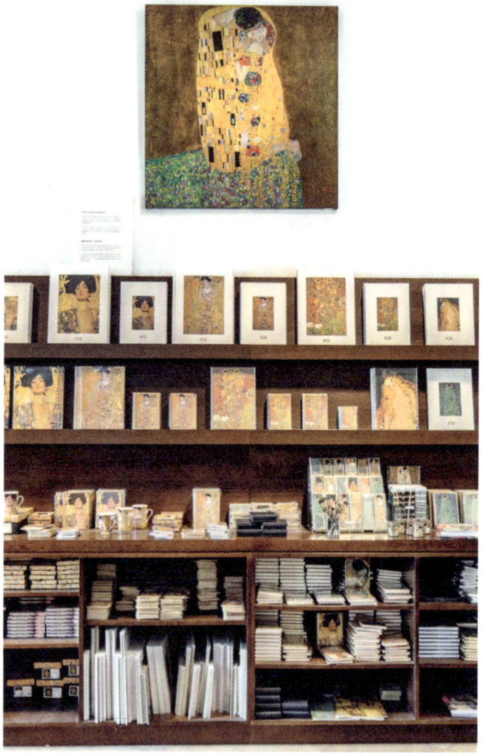

1

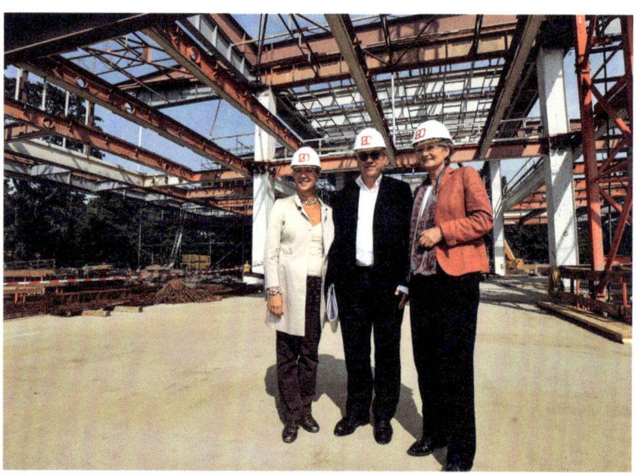

2

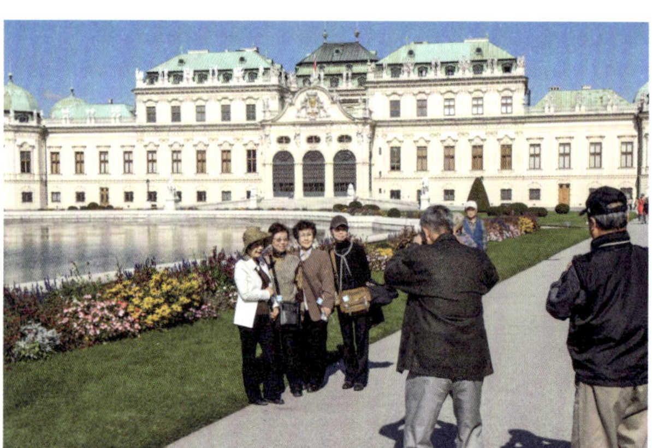

3

Fig. 1
Museum shop with Klimt merchandise in the Upper Belvedere, 2022, Belvedere, Vienna

Fig. 2
Remodeling of the 20er Haus: Minister of Culture Claudia Schmied, architect Adolf Krischanitz, and director Agnes Husslein-Arco posing for a press photo, September 10, 2009, photo: Niko Formanek

Fig. 3
International tourists in the gardens of the Belvedere, January 25, 2006, photo: Karl Thomas

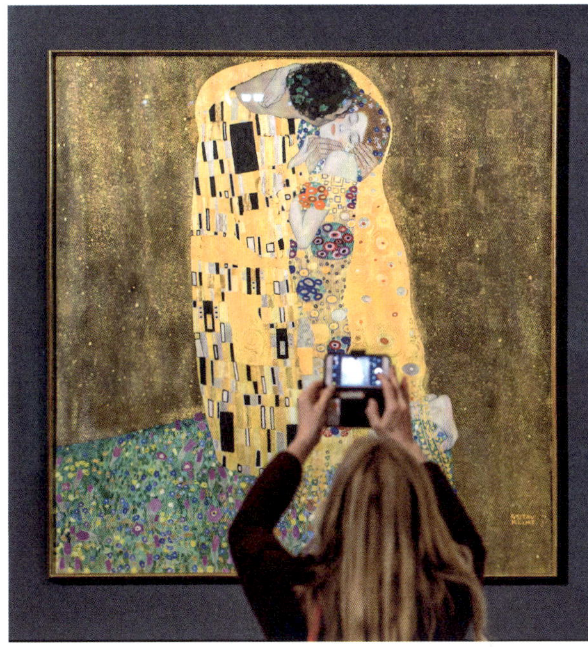

4

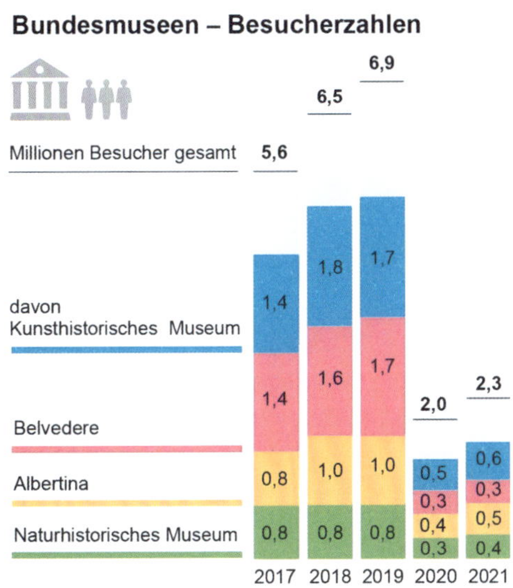

5

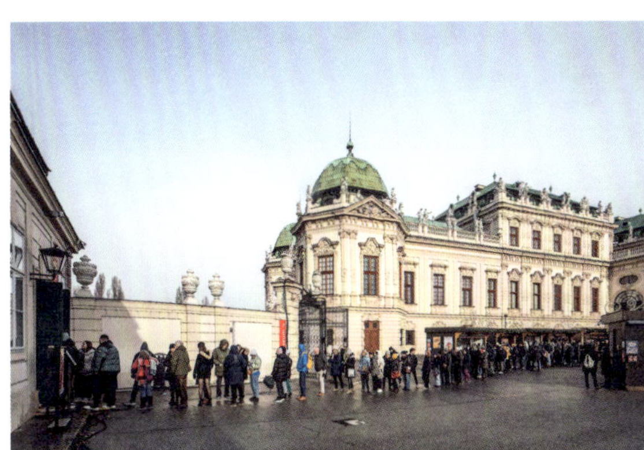

6

Fig. 4
The Kiss by Gustav Klimt, a key attraction for many tourists, 2018, Belvedere, Vienna

Fig. 5
Visitor numbers for Vienna's federal museums (Kunsthistorisches Museum, Natural History Museum, Belvedere, and Albertina) from 2017 to 2021

Fig. 6
Queues at the ticket office of the Upper Belvedere, December 15, 2022, Belvedere Image Archive, Vienna

P. 344

NORA STERNFELD — Critical Niches: Democratization Processes in the Belvedere's Recent History

Elites or the masses? Avant-garde or mainstream? Polarized questions such as these often dominate the public debate about the opening up of museums. And yet it is debatable whether these are really the right questions to ask, as in many cases they do not address the democratization but rather the managerialization of institutions. What, then, are the right questions? And what does all of this have to do with the Belvedere, whose three locations are situated between these poles?

A new international museum discourse has been emerging since the 2000s. There has been much talk in this context about "the museum of the future"[1] as an arena, platform, and contact zone. But however democratic these labels may sound, they are not always free of economic interests, nor do they have to do only with democratic institutional structures. In recent museum discourse, calls for democratization (with mantras such as openness, diversity, gender, or the environment) exist together with neoliberal imperatives (with calls for new management, a museum shop, a stylish café, for example).

In Austria, this first decade of the twenty-first century was a period of outsourcing, that is to say, of fundamental reforms in management structures to establish federal museums as legal entities and businesses in their own right. Since then, the Belvedere has experienced a boom in visitor numbers.[2] As far as the aforementioned "polarized questions" are concerned, the Belvedere's recent history as an institution could therefore serve as a good example for the aspect of visitor frequency. We could now argue, for example, that a focus on the marketing of an institution is not necessarily of benefit in terms of its democratization.[3] This is no doubt true, but—as I shall attempt to show in this essay—it also needs to be qualified.

1 See schnittpunkt/Baur 2020; Sternfeld 2018.
2 See essay by Martin Fritz in this volume, pp. 336–43.
3 For example, during the pandemic, when the opening of institutions for the local population, but in the absence of tourists, had to be fought for via the media.

The talk of opening up institutions and the call for a "museum of the future"—which, by the way, have been staples of museum discourse ever since the early days of modern museums—are thus perhaps a reflection of the oscillations between conservative, capitalist, and democratic trends. But turning specifically to democratization efforts in the recent history of the Belvedere, I am deliberately setting aside all of these contemporary buzzwords and will focus instead on three terms from the 1970s. For this, it is necessary to recall a largely forgotten museum history. In 1967, the art historian, critic, and curator Pierre Gaudibert[4] established a department at the Musée d'Art Moderne de la Ville de Paris (which opened in 1961), devoted to the democratization of the museum and of society. He gave the department the ambitious name "Animation, Recherche, Confrontation." Later on, in the 1990s, Hans-Ulrich Obrist was a curator there and had a marked influence on the department, referred to by the abbreviation ARC. While most people are unaware of what the abbreviation stands for—since the 1990s it has generally been assumed to refer to "art contemporain"—the department still exists to this day. The three underlying notions—animation, research, confrontation—which in the late 1960s epitomized the concept of a "museum of the future," have since been largely forgotten. As I still believe them to be relevant today, simultaneously rooted in the history of contemporary art museums and at risk of being forgotten, my question, in the context of the Belvedere, is to what extent they can be updated and applied to a description of democratization processes today.

Animation: public program and community outreach at the Belvedere 21

With the term "animation" Gaudibert refers to the "actualizing activation" that was to be part of the scope of his department. Around 1968, many artists, educators, activists, and those involved in museum work felt that institutions should not just offer spaces for contemplation but should also contribute to an "activation" of the public. This sounds highly topical again today. In fact, it was in the anniversary year "fifty years after 1968" that the Belvedere established a program[5] in which openness was seen in a political, democratizing context. The program itself was presented in seven installments from May to December 2018, starting with a series of screenings and discussions entitled "1968/2018: Where Has All the Spirit Gone?" This question is infused with a certain melancholy, because a nuanced consideration of the potential for democratization in a neoliberal context must take into account the fact that it is itself embedded in this same context. The new public program was therefore given a name that explicitly highlights this ambivalence: "Gemeinsame Wagnisse," a literal translation of the term "joint ventures," in other

4 *Pierre Gaudibert: Vers le musée du futur*, Musée d'Art Moderne de la Ville de Paris, May 19, 2021 to May 8, 2022.

5 During a meeting for the 2018 program, Luisa Ziaja, curator for contemporary art at the Belvedere, suggested that the theme "fifty years 1968" be dealt with not in an exhibition but in a public program.

words, corporate collaboration. The 1968 slogans implicit in this ambivalent name have long become corporate imperatives. The invitation to be ad*venturous* could, however, be reinterpreted and reappropriated in the sense of a counter-hegemonial, radical-democratic appeal: a convergence of struggles, "Reinventing Utopian Thinking" and "Reclaiming Democracy," as two further installments of the program were called. It proposes an *actualization* and *activation* within the existing conditions, rejecting 1968 nostalgia and asking what can be done jointly today, without leaving entrepreneurship wholly to market forces (figs. 1–2).

After the first year, the public program became an integral component of the events calendar. It has now been in place for five years, and events are organized regularly on different topics in the Sculpture Garden of the Belvedere 21. Over the years, it has acquired a curatorial perspective,[6] addressing the present and future of social struggles and, together with artists, theoreticians, and activists, asking questions about the good life for everyone or the coexistence of species from the perspectives of art, ecology, feminism, and activism. The month of June every year is devoted to the theme of "Queering the Belvedere." A further focus was a public debate about the Balkan war and the genocide in Srebrenica, under the heading "Retelling Stories."[7]

Furthermore, a community outreach program[8] was launched in 2018, which, together with groups and communities from the social and geographical context of the Belvedere 21, organizes collaborative interventions in the public realm. An associated events series is the *Open Mic* in the garden of the Belvedere 21 (fig. 3). Here, the program is determined by the public, consisting to date of presentations, debates, talks, spoken word, comedy, written contributions, and musical performances.[9]

Research: the Belvedere Research Center and the digital museum

While the institutional affirmation of democratization is most visible in public programs and outreach strategies, there have also been—and still are—other aspects that make a museum a democratic institution. For democratic openness is not just about being invited to participate in a predefined context, but also about opportunities to understand and critically appraise processes and history. The call for openness has historically included access to archive material, and hence to institutional decisions. Critical research and the examination of collections, archives, the provenance of objects and the associated stories of violence, of the gaps and discontinuities in the power narratives, are all part of the historical and present-day democratization of an institution. Since 2009, the Belvedere has had a research center, which devotes much energy and scrutiny to precisely this topic. Apart from documentation, cataloguing,

6 Headed by Christiane Erharter and Claudia Slanar.
7 "Gemeinsame Wagnisse," Public Program 2021, https://www.belvedere.at/sites/default/files/2021-06/Public%20Program%202021.pdf (accessed on November 10, 2022).
8 Also curated by Christiane Erharter.
9 https://www.belvedere.at/community-outreach#OpenMic (accessed on November 10, 2022).

and investigation of Austrian art history, it also pursues an unwavering open-content policy of making data accessible: archives, provenance research findings and dossiers, publications, and public domain works. Another important dimension of a democratic institution is digitality, a topic that is addressed at the Belvedere's annual online conference (fig. 4) "The Art Museum in the Digital Age." The question of the commons is given a new relevance with respect to common ownership of the museum in future and in the "digital condition."[10]

Confrontation: exhibitions that challenge the established canon

In Austria during the second half of the twentieth century, the Belvedere was not necessarily associated with progressiveness in art. If anywhere, this was to be encountered in the history of the 20er Haus, which opened in 1962 as the Museum of the Twentieth Century in the pavilion designed by Karl Schwanzer on the site of today's Belvedere 21.[11] At the Belvedere itself, it was the Augarten Contemporary—initially in Gustinus Ambrosi's studio in the Augarten—where projects questioning the established canon were shown in the 1990s.[12] *The Spring Project*[13] (1995), for example, which positioned itself at the heart of contemporary discourse and the then still young "new media," presented artists whose work was situation- rather than object-based. Another example was *tanzimat*[14] (2010), an exhibition that marked the Prince Eugene anniversary year with an alternative "Ottoman" perspective by artists from Turkey, Bulgaria, and Austria. In the Belvedere 21, monographic exhibitions such as *Monuments: Documents* by Simon Wachsmuth (2015/16) and *Das Reich* by Henrike Naumann (2020) examined the past and present as well as the danger of a future potentially marked by right-wing violence.

The collection exhibitions of the past ten years in particular—most recently *Avant-Garde and the Contemporary* (2021)—have featured a precise and subtle, yet no less clear-cut and necessary, questioning and redefinition of the canon. Judicious curating of works from the collection has also interrogated traditional historicizations and canonizations, the denial of continuities with National Socialist history, and colonial aspects. In this way, it has been possible to view the collection from ever new perspectives and to confront it with its gaps and discontinuities (fig. 5).

Conclusion: contemporary between numbers

With regard to the Belvedere as a whole, democratization is not very clearly in evidence, but it can be found in niche areas. Here it takes on a dimension that goes beyond the mere integration of fashionable marginalized positions and also encompasses the publication of research and a critical examination of history. Together with the public program

10 Stalder 2016.

11 In 2002, the building was taken over by the Belvedere and, following extensive refurbishment, reopened in 2011 as the 21er Haus.

12 Yet without further reflection on the locality of Gustinus Ambrosi's former studio, which has remained a memorial to this artist, who was celebrated during the Austrofascist period and also revered by Hitler, and where, along with other stone and plaster sculptures by the artist, busts of Hitler were still on display. The exhibition *The Spring Project* at least touched on this issue, without making a special point of it. See Guth/Michalka 1995, p. 6.

13 Curated by Doris Guth and Matthias Michalka.

14 *tanzimat*, curated by Eva Maria Stadler, Augarten Contemporary, January 21—May 16, 2010.

(25)

Expansions of the Museum into the Digital Space

Christian Huemer

The sight of a toddler walking up to a zoo aquarium and attempting to zoom in on a little fish, on what they assume is a tablet screen, clearly illustrates the extent to which our *Kulturtechniken* (cultural techniques) are influenced by the digital transformation. A generation has now reached adulthood for whom the internet has always been associated with sorting algorithms, reading with scrolling, and television with a series of autoplay videos. Correspondingly, the demands on museums are also changing radically, and not just since the onset of the coronavirus pandemic, when a digital presence suddenly became the sole way of reaching the public. As early as 1968, on the occasion of the "Computers and their Potential Applications in Museums" conference, a colossal IBM System/360 was rolled into the Metropolitan Museum of Art in New York as the "Trojan Horse of Technology."[1]

At the Belvedere, as in many other museums, the digital push began with the collection. According to the 2001 culture report, the museum's entire inventory was to be documented in digital photographs: "By linking the emerging image database with a collection database, a digital museum is being created that will in future be accessible to the public via the internet."[2] The project was the result of eFit Austria, an IT initiative backed by the Ministry of Education, Science, and Research (bm:bwk), with the aim of implementing the educational objectives of the eEurope 2002 Action Plan adopted at an EU summit in Feira, Portugal. Between November 2002 and October 2006, with the help of 1,240,000 euros kickstart funding, a substantial portion of the collection was digitized and systematically entered in the relational database TMS (The Museum System). The strength of the Belvedere's online collection lies in its high-quality (meta)data and comprehensive indexing of pictures using scientific classification systems such as ICONCLASS and MIDAS. This enables search inquiries by motif, such as Normandy, fog, or gray; by emotion, such as love, sadness, or loneliness; or by compositional device, such as *Rückenfigur*, deep horizon, or similar. Since 2018, the Belvedere has staked its claim as the first art museum in Austria to adopt an open content policy, whereby works from the collection that are in the public domain are available as free, high-quality downloads (fig. 1). The provision of free, open, and networked access to cultural heritage has since become a key objective, manifesting, for instance, in the launch of an open-access e-journal, the *Belvedere Research Journal*.

The process of digital transformation has brought fundamental changes to the role of the museum, since the primary focus is no longer the presentation of art objects, but the creation of art experiences, with the audience seeking active involvement as part of a "participatory turn." Under the banner of the "metaverse," worlds are now being created for social interaction, where people meet in real time as avatars to share their experiences. Although this utopia has not yet been realized in full anywhere, many cultural institutions are experimenting in this direction. For example, in 2020, the Belvedere made digital scans of the Palace Stables in the Lower Belvedere, generating an interactive 3D showroom for medieval art. Artificial intelligence is also increasingly being applied, in the form of automated transcription of handwritten sources from the archives, the ability to search the collection for pictures with formal or content similarities, or the reconstruction of lost artworks. As part of a collaboration with Google Arts & Culture, Gustav Klimt's Faculty Paintings, known only from black-and-white photos and contemporary descriptions, were digitally recolored with the help of machine learning (fig. 2). In February 2022, the Belvedere announced its "successful entry into the metaverse" with the release of ten thousand NFTs (non-fungible tokens) of Klimt's *The Kiss*, available for purchase as limited edition collectibles with a certificate of ownership and authenticity (→ p. 365, fig. 5). Since 2019, the Belvedere has been hosting its annual conference "The Art Museum in the Digital Age," held every January as a regular forum in which to explore and reflect on institutional parameters. In the Belvedere's anniversary year the online event welcomed more than one thousand delegates from fifty-six countries and five continents (→ p. 352, fig. 4).

1 Hoving 1968, p. VI.
2 Culture Report 2001, Ministry of Education, Science, and Culture, Vienna 2002, p. 69; Knickmeier 2008.

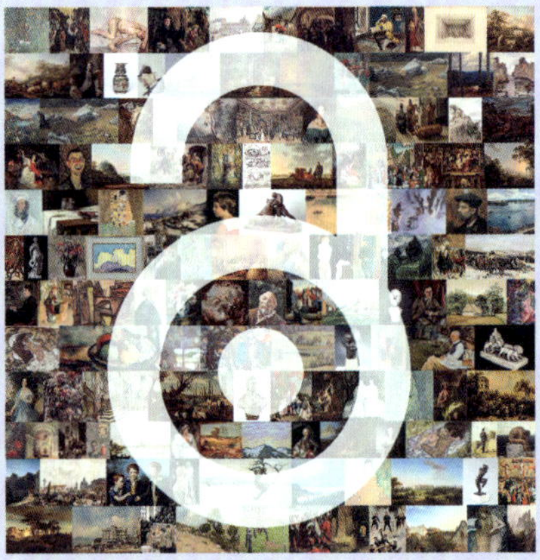

1

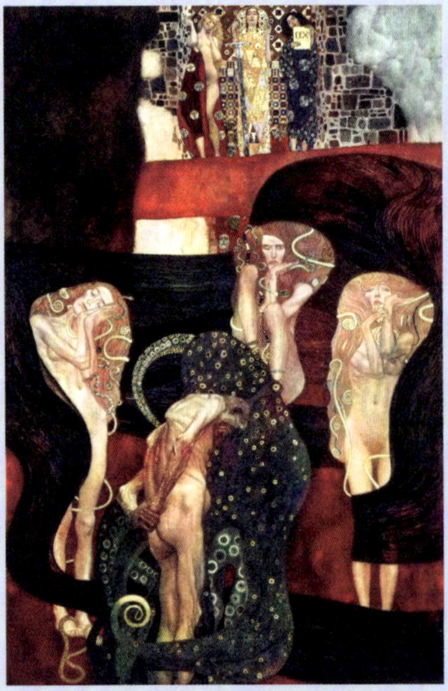

2

Fig. 1
Symbol for the online collection's open content policy, Belvedere, Vienna

Fig. 2
Black-and-white photograph of Gustav Klimt's painting *Jurisprudence* (1900–07), which was destroyed by fire in 1945, recolored with the help of Artificial Intelligence, Belvedere / Image by Google 2019

and sociocritical collaborations with local stakeholders, these research and curatorial approaches represent democratic elements of an institution that is not merely successful in marketing itself to the wider public but, especially in recent years, has also engaged in serious, often subtle, but no less important new and alternative perspectives, in many cases running counter to the marketing mainstream.

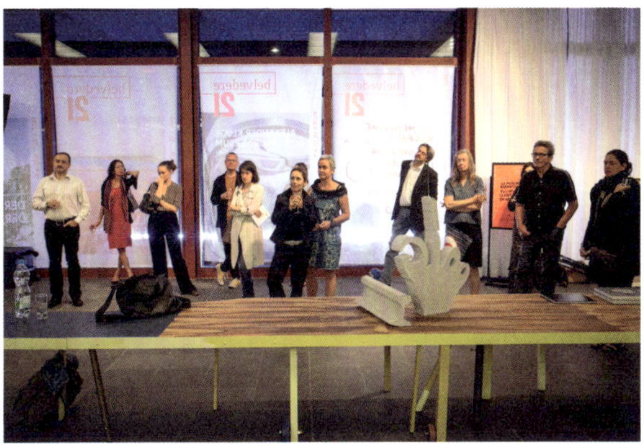

1

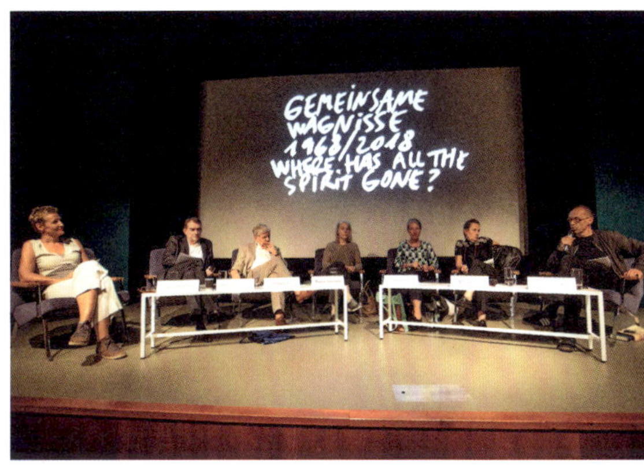

2

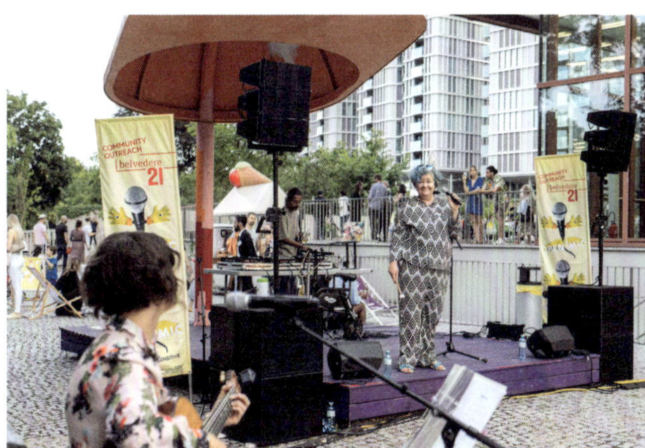

3

Fig. 1
Joint Ventures: A public program on the relevance of 1968 in the present day, September 21, 2018, Belvedere, Vienna

Fig. 2
Panel discussion during *Joint Ventures: A public program on the relevance of 1968 in the present day*, May 26, 2018, Belvedere, Vienna

Fig. 3
Open Mic — The public microphone with Schudini The Sensitive (musical accompaniment: Verena Dengler), a community outreach program during the Belvedere Summer Festival, July 15, 2022, Belvedere, Vienna

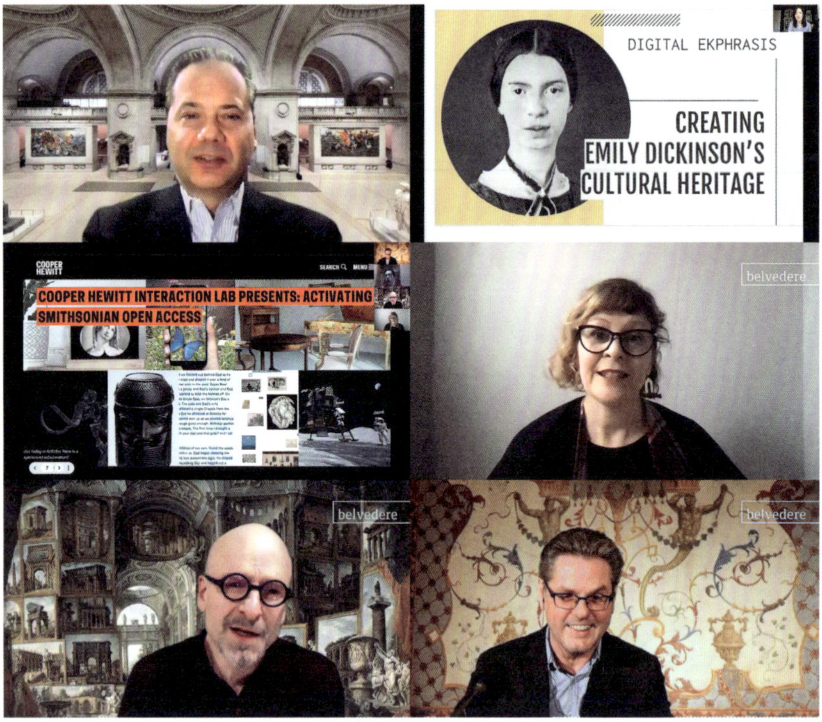

4

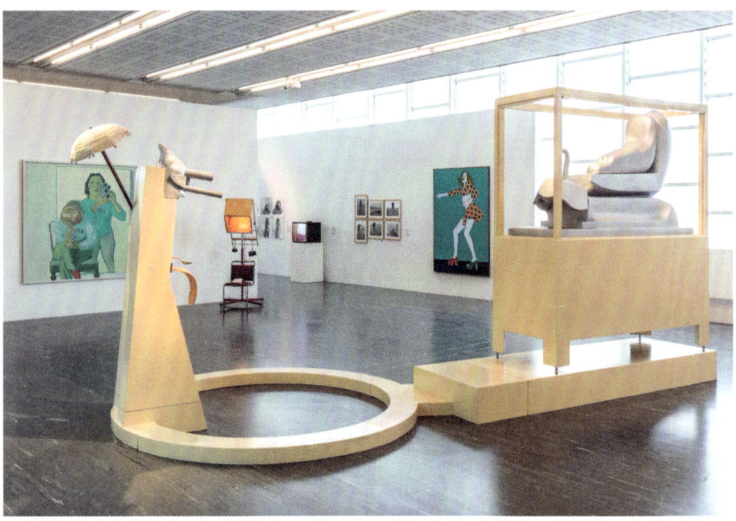

5

Fig. 4
"The Art Museum in the Digital Age" International Online Conference, January 17–21, 2022

Fig. 5
Avant-Garde and the Contemporary exhibition at the Belvedere 21, 2022, Belvedere, Vienna

(26)

Museum Self-Perceptions under the Microscope

Luise Reitstätter, Anna Frasca-Rath

A museum's self-image is manifested in "ego documents"[1]—from legal frameworks and directors' visions in annual reports and internal publications to contemporary mission statements. In the "Right to the Museum?" project, such written self-definitions relating to the museums' concepts of the public were at the center of an analysis carried out at five museums in Vienna.[2] While archival research into these documents sought to identify shifts in the discourse surrounding the relationship between the institutions and the public, the field research highlighted, among other things, how these documents were perceived by the public after visiting the permanent exhibition at these museums.[3] The following three short excerpts and the responses to them (in the form of percentage agreement rates and comments) offer an insight into how the Belvedere was conceived at different times and how it is experienced today.

"[The] main task [of the State Gallery] will be to demonstrate the general development of art from the end of the eighteenth century up to the present day in its essential […] phases by means of great, typical examples of the creative […] forces […]," states a memorandum on the collection program written by director Friedrich Dörnhöffer in 1911. The question "To what extent does this description correspond with your experience of the museum today?" generally received a positive response from respondents ("strongly agree" 28 percent and "somewhat agree" 46.4 percent). Additional comments on the intended objective of providing an effective historical display by means of great examples refer, on the one hand, to the concept—still considered valid today—of the museum as a representative model of a genealogy of art history. Dissonant responses, on the other hand, make it clear that the aspiration of such a comprehensive overview is difficult to achieve in a selective tour of a museum with additional locations, with a focus on Austrian greats such as Klimt and Schiele, and with only isolated works of contemporary art displayed in the Upper Belvedere. Furthermore, the reference to "creative forces"—in the sense of a "cult of genius"—is no longer considered up to date today.

"Today we therefore devote ourselves to […] the mission of researching and duly recognizing the great [works] by Austrian artists. This is implemented [among other things] through a multilayered exhibition offering, whereby a consistent effort is made to present domestic art in an international context." This museum mission statement was formulated by director Agnes Husslein-Arco in 2016/17 in the *Belvedere Magazine*, thereby, interestingly, continuing the theme of a (national) presentation of art through "great" examples more than one hundred years after the memorandum of 1911, with the addition of international contextualization. The increase in strong agreement with this statement by today's museum visitors ("strongly agree" 39.9 percent and "somewhat agree" 30.4 percent) may be due to its more contemporary wording. A review of the comments, however, also reveals disagreement in terms of the implementation of the research, due recognition, and international contextualization, in so far as visitors view the contextual information accompanying the exhibits as insufficient.

"Art is for everyone. [...] We communicate in a credible, understandable, and interactive way, addressing real-life topics and current issues. For our visitors, this opens new perspectives and broadens the scope of action. They leave the museum richer for having entered." This is a line from the Belvedere's current mission statement, which is available on its website. This quote achieves the highest correspondence with the perceptions of respondents after visiting the museum ("strongly agree" 41.1 percent and "somewhat agree" 29.8 percent). Upon closer analysis of the responses, however, clear differences emerge in terms of the reactions to individual elements of the statement. For example, in response to the inclusive intention of the phrase "art is for everyone," frequent mention is made of mechanisms of exclusion, such as high entry prices, the need for prior knowledge, and unconsidered groups. By contrast, "they leave the museum richer for having entered," in the sense of a transitory experience, receives predominantly positive responses, since, as one visitor noted, "to see significant works of art is always an enriching experience."

The ambition of addressing "real-life topics and current issues" turns out to be difficult to fulfill in an art museum with a conventionally reduced display, such as the Upper Belvedere. While visitors often claim to have learned something new (72 percent), it is much rarer for them to say they were inspired to think (57.7 percent), or even become more actively engaged and experiment themselves (11.9 percent). Instead, the Upper Belvedere is perceived as an art institution in the classical sense: "beautiful," "interesting," and "impressive" are the three adjectives used most frequently to describe the museum after a visit.

This brief overview of museum concepts and experiences paints the picture of an institution that can be characterized in the continuities and fault lines of polarities such as synoptic versus in-depth display and aesthetic education versus a focus on current issues. This discursive interweaving also highlights the identity-political challenges of diversity and democratization encountered by an art museum in the balancing act between classical vehicle for representation and the currently heightened desire for social relevance.

1 This is the term used in historical research to describe documents such as diaries, letters, and case files, in which a person locates themselves or is represented within their environment. When an institution is understood as an organism with an inscribed identity, the term can also be applied to written sources from museums pertaining to a specific, identifiable time and place.

2 Belvedere, the House of Austrian History, Kunsthistorisches Museum Vienna, Museum of Applied Arts, and the Austrian Museum of Folk Life and Folk Art.

3 For a concise summary of the project and an overview of its results, see Reitstätter/Galter 2023.

Perspectives

2023

P. 356
STELLA ROLLIG in Conversation with WOLFGANG ULLRICH

Wolfgang Ullrich: Sometimes I ask myself whether museums are currently undergoing the biggest transformation in their entire history. Or is that just an exaggerated perception from today's perspective? Someone like you, who heads an establishment going back three hundred years, is probably in a better position to judge. Museums have undoubtedly been confronted with a plethora of new tasks, challenges, and expectations in recent years and decades. A museum is now expected to reach as many people as possible, in fact, ideally to exclude no one at all. It is expected to be open to the most varied groups, rather than be defined merely through collecting, conservation, and research. A few years ago I wrote a text about recent museum buildings. For this, I looked at competition briefs and especially at architects' design statements. I noticed that all these texts talked about openness, usually in multiple ways: we will open up the building towards the city, open it to a wider public, open up our collections. Then I delved a bit further into this and discovered that openness was already a key word in many texts that were driving the agenda for museums as far back as the 1970s. So, this guiding principle has remained the same across the span of half a century—which permits the conclusion that perhaps not much has happened after all. Or has a lot happened, but the metaphor has remained the same purely out of convenience?

Stella Rollig: I would say, provocatively, that there are two areas of society in which you find the most rhetorical hocus-pocus: in politics and in the museum world. The metaphor of openness has indeed been making the rounds in museums for a very long time. The huge gap between aspiration and reality has become very apparent to me, especially in recent years. I'll mention two fairly new museums: the Whitney Museum in New York, built by Renzo Piano, and David Chipperfield's extension to the Kunsthaus Zurich. The architecture of both is not exactly inviting. In Chipperfield's outwardly harsh, almost unapproachable building, one has to climb a steep flight of stairs to reach the exhibition rooms. The foyer of the Whitney is noisy and chaotic. It only just about succeeds as a box office. The Whitney claims that it is part of its neighborhood, but the truth of the matter is that this neighborhood now consists solely of extended consumer spending opportunities for visitors to the museum—coffee shops and boutiques. Besides, the call to open museums has been around for much longer than the late bourgeois museum itself. When I think of Russian revolutionary art, with its call to storm the museums and palaces, you'll find these phrases are all already there. And you can go back even further in time—and think of the Belvedere, but also of other court museums. The Belvedere is one of the oldest museums in the world. It opened in the late 1770s, shortly before Maria Theresa's death, as an art gallery for everyone, including people from the lower classes.

WU: With no entrance fee?

SR: Yes, the gallery was free to visit on three days per week. A servant girl working for room and board would likely not have been able to pay an entrance fee. So, opening the museum for everyone has actually been around for about 250 years. Yet, at the same time, museums keep producing the same exclusion mechanisms. All our measures to prevent or counteract this are important and necessary, but have only limited success. It is a never-ending task for everyone working in a museum and striving to promote openness. For a few years now, we have been dealing with a constant stream of new challenges, coming from both within and without, which are becoming ever more complex and range from digital transformation to audience diversification. Doing justice to all of this and, for instance, even just starting to recognize the needs of minority groups, has been throwing up many new tasks.

WU: I find it interesting that you are skeptical about whether opening up museums can ever really be done successfully. What are the reasons for that?

SR: Let me start with the positive. It is succeeding—in small steps and in relatively small areas of activity. Let me illustrate this with our museum here. Like other museums, we have an intensive art education program. There is also a curator with a dedicated role in community outreach (→ p. 307, ㉒). We have a neighborhood forum. And we have, for instance, an annual program called "Queering the Belvedere" (fig. 1, → p. 309). This evolved out of the annual Pride Month in June, which is now celebrated internationally, and in which we have been actively and visibly involved for years. This program encompasses all our locations. Even in medieval art, for example, it is possible to look for traces of queerness. Another current program track is titled "30 years after Srebrenica," and with this we are addressing the Bosnian community in Vienna. Now in its second generation, this community plays an important role in Vienna's cultural life. And these things really create a kind of community spirit. Yet, we are talking about fifty to a hundred participants here. For an institution that, before Covid, had 1.7 million visitors annually, this level of outreach barely registers. This is what I mean when I say it succeeds in small steps and in small areas of activity.

WU: I would like to pick up on something here: It's not an easy task to track down something like queer traces in medieval art. To meet the expectations of different minorities, you either need more staff or you need staff with different training than before. But budgets are probably not increasing in step with these new challenges, so this must mean making cuts elsewhere. Or having to manage twice as many tasks with the same number of staff.

SR: We are really in the midst of a major sea change here. It's almost impossible, for example, to find art historians who are digitally savvy and can work with a database, or who understand what it means to translate art history research into the digital world. It shocks me to see how little attention is paid to this in university curricula. Ever since the 1990s, new courses for curators are being devised everywhere, often with very high theoretical standards. That's really important and wonderful. But the fact that the best art-history training does not really equip people with the requirements for working in a museum, because you also have to get this knowledge out there—and especially in digital form and via different channels—means that completely new curricula have to be developed. The entire higher education process needs to be reformed.

WU: You clearly see the digital transformation in museums as one of the most demanding current and future challenges. But I would make a distinction here. On the one hand, there are forms of working digitally that relate to the website. At the Belvedere, for instance, you have now made substantial parts of the collection digitally available (→ p. 349, ㉕). You can also deliver museum communication programs and other activities via the website. On the other hand, digitalization for museums is now also increasingly about making use of social media. This always throws up the question of which platforms to participate in and how intensively. What do you expect from your presence there? Is it just an extension of marketing activities, which then also take place on Instagram or TikTok, alongside other channels? Or are these platforms important for communicating something of substance? And how do the website and social media interact?

SR: It is impossible to do everything one would like to do, if one measures oneself against the Metropolitan Museum of Art, for instance, where Max Hollein and his team are offering every possible format, from education to gamified participative experiences. But the Met has over fifty people in their digital department, and we have five. In 2020, we put together a digital editorial team with colleagues who are all relatively young. We asked them: "What do you think is cool, what do you like, what would you get rid of, what would you do instead?" This then became a lengthy process. At its end, we decided which formats are right for us and which ones are not. One innovation, for example, has been the "Belvedere ABC," which has works of art at its center, but they are not its sole focus. The letter "J," for instance, stands for jogging, because the Belvedere Gardens are a popular jogging route for many people in Vienna (fig. 2). The intention is clear: we're trying to get people interested in the museum who, until now, may only have known it from the outside.

WU: Is it possible to find out what this is achieving? Does it really bring in new visitors? Does it generate a different kind of feedback? Are you learning lessons about new opportunities in art education? Or what kind of tool does it ultimately prove to be?

SR: It is a communication tool. The aim is to make the Belvedere better known and to attract new audiences from around the world. And also to provide new ways to access art. Ultimately, it leads to more people coming to the Belvedere. And to go into the Marble Hall with people who have perhaps never seen it before, and to hear them say: "This is amazing! It's beautiful!"—that is uplifting.

WU: Let me come back to the "J for jogging." Our attempts to convey the museum in different ways and from different angles relate, to a large extent, to the way we present the works of art themselves. It is no longer just about putting objects on display for their art-historical significance and because they belong to an established canon. We now give additional reasons why taking a deeper interest in them is worthwhile. The art is discussed, but there is always something else beyond it. To me, this also seems to be part of the paradigm shift of museums today embracing new objectives. A museum is no longer just a temple of art; it is expected to have relevance for society in many different ways. But this also leads to conflicts, because, the moment you say that it's not purely about the art, people come along and complain that an individual exhibit is racist or sexist or dubious on some other grounds and should really be removed. How do you respond when, all of a sudden, what is being shown is more open to criticism than it used to be, because it is no longer purely about its artistic value?

SR: Yes, that really is a wide field. It is no longer enough to say that a work of art is important because here the artist used central perspective for the first time, or because it was pioneering a new style. At university and also in museums I was taught what makes a work of art special in terms of style and art-historical development. But I'm more interested in the way it relates to the world beyond art! In what context was it created, and what were the artist's biographical circumstances at the time? My reputation among the art historians in our team has probably suffered, because I don't want to see texts about "impasto technique" in our exhibition captions. For me, it only gets interesting when a net is cast that relates to the rest of society, and ideally—just to make things a little more difficult—in no more than eight hundred characters.

Recently, I was in the Gemäldegalerie Alte Meister (Old Masters Picture Gallery) in Dresden. And I think what has been achieved there with short texts is an impressive example. They establish a connection to the time and the position of each respective artist in it: what was expected of them and how did they respond to that. This is something art historians need to start focusing on now. But writing texts in this way is not enough. We also need to select and arrange works of art accordingly. This means—and this is something I consider especially worthwhile—that museums no longer just show their "masterpieces," but also works that are perhaps not so perfect, or that were produced by artists who, for whatever reason, were important in their own time, but later fell into obscurity. Some works that in the past were considered only good for the museum depot may well be looked at differently today.

WU: When you think about new acquisitions or are planning a temporary exhibition, do you then consider not only the artistic value of a piece but also whether it can make an important contribution to a different public discourse?

SR: Yes, that is our ambition. And I admire art historians and curators who are able to deliver on this in their exhibitions. For example, we had an exhibition on the Viennese Biedermeier. The curator presented it as a period dominated by enormous social contrasts. The vibrancy and vividness of the paintings—Ferdinand Georg Waldmüller is perhaps the most famous exponent—has for a long time misled people into perceiving the Biedermeier period as idyllic and thinking of it as a feel-good era. The curator brushed this conception against the grain and succeeded in showing that the reality looked very different—that school children had no shoes to wear and were walking around in bare feet. Depicting the social inequalities of the *Vormärz* period in this way—I think that is very illuminating.

WU: In what area does the pressure from new expectations facing museums weigh most heavily on you personally? Is something like "Fridays for Future," that revolves around environmental issues, a stronger focus?

Are you having to do more to justify travel and transport now than even a few years ago? Or are minority issues more central?

SR: The environment is a huge topic. Museums are not inherently establishments with an eco focus (fig. 3). Our biggest energy use within the museum itself is climate control. We have two buildings that are three hundred years old. And we have a third building that was never intended to be a permanent art venue, but a pavilion for a temporary world exhibition. It's made of glass and steel, it's poorly insulated, but also a listed building, so it's never going to be green. The way the art market has developed—and not least as a result of the profit focus of many of the people involved—means that we now have exaggerated standards for climate control when transporting artworks. All those expensive climate-controlled crates, the elaborate transport operations, objects on loan being sent around the globe.... There is a lot that needs to change here.

But we are also under heavy pressure from stakeholder groups who feel underrepresented in the museum, especially people of color. It is a hugely fascinating debate and not always entirely harmonious (fig. 4). In this context we also have to highlight the classism that is so conspicuous in a museum. The members of the POC community who are asking questions of the museum are very well educated, usually with academic qualifications, they have international experience, multilingual backgrounds. With other groups we want to reach out to and invite in, by contrast, we often have to make them aware of our existence first.

Something we had to justify especially was the Belvedere's move into the NFT market. The fact that we were the first museum in Austria to release an NFT drop attracted not just international attention but also criticism (fig. 5).

WU: Because of the energy consumption?

SR: Yes, that especially. There was a whole host of reasons why the Belvedere entering the NFT market was considered objectionable. Some were ideological, claiming that we were participating in an immoral speculative financial market based on scarcity, private property, and exclusion. That can be debated. But it must be said that very few people have the rhetorical and intellectual armory to understand the global interdependencies of these systems and be able to criticize or to defend them. And this is why the environmental argument is often made. But we are also taking it seriously, and we are in the process of setting up a CO_2 compensation plan, because we don't want to leave that flank exposed. It is very fortunate that the minting process on the Ethereum blockchain has now switched from proof-of-work to proof-of-stake with "The Merge" in September 2022. It has been possible to reduce CO_2 emissions from minting NFTs drastically (by 99.9 per cent) as a result. But, basically, with the NFTs—and I really have to say it in such mundane terms—we have opened up a new line of business. And, bearing in mind that federal museums are required to generate their own income, that was a pretty good idea, really.

WU: So, the more money you can generate with NFTs, the more you're able to reduce your entrance fees?

SR: Unfortunately, that will never be possible. Our Klimt NFT did get off to a very successful start. Within a few weeks, we earned four and a half million euros. But that hasn't inflated our expectations. *The Kiss* is one of the most famous paintings in the world. Results like this will not be repeatable with every painting. Our admission fees, which are considered high by some, are simply part of applying market principles to federal museums since they were semi-privatized in around 2000. They now represent a significant part of our income.

WU: But the high entrance fees undo much of what is being achieved on the road to more openness. As museums have been increasing their outreach efforts in recent decades, their admission prices have increased in parallel. So, as intellectual barriers are being dismantled, new financial barriers are being installed at the same time.

SR: We have major internal discussions that repeatedly revolve around curators and art educators wanting to offer certain programs free of charge. For example, many events at the Belvedere 21 are offered at no charge, like the public program (→ p. 351) and the neighborhood forums (fig. 6). In these contexts, however, we also expect people to contribute their active participation. I personally would love for museums to be free of charge. That you could just walk in every so often, look at a few pictures, and walk out again—that would be my old-fashioned dream.

What we will really need to succeed in over the next few years, is to develop a well-thought-out approach to closing the huge chasm between our aspirations to be accessible, offer involvement, and foster diversity on the one hand, and the current status quo on the other. To achieve this and at the same time manage our traditional tasks—research, conservation, and expanding the collection, which I absolutely don't want to throw overboard—and to have each benefit from the others. I believe that art historians can learn a lot from engaging in an open-minded dialogue with their colleagues from art education and community outreach. There is a lot they can learn about questions, research questions, that can be asked of art. My wish is that all our activities can foster responsible and mature participation and that, beginning with the Belvedere and our artworks here, diverse and wide-ranging conversations can develop.

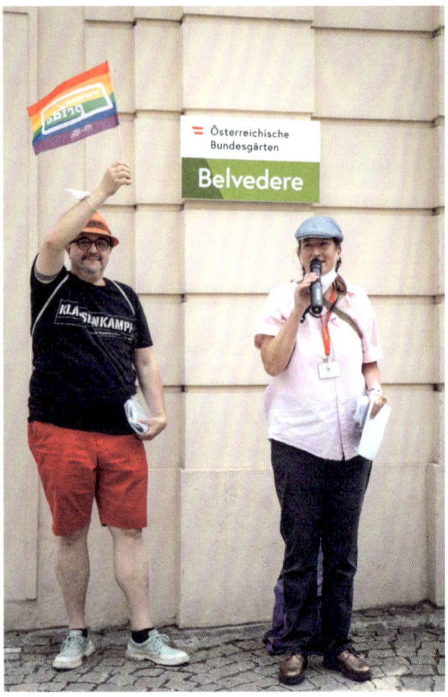

1

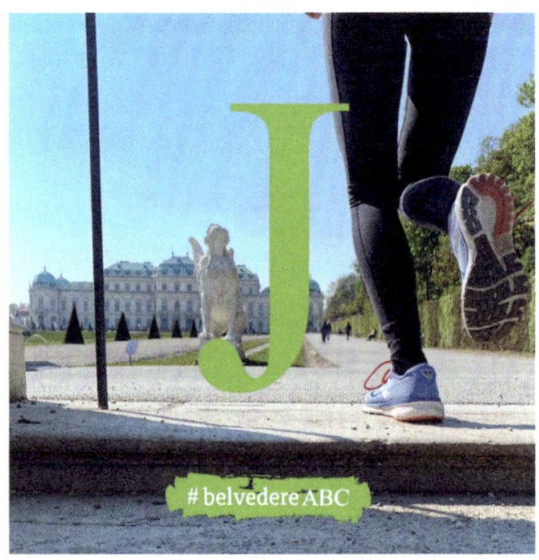

2

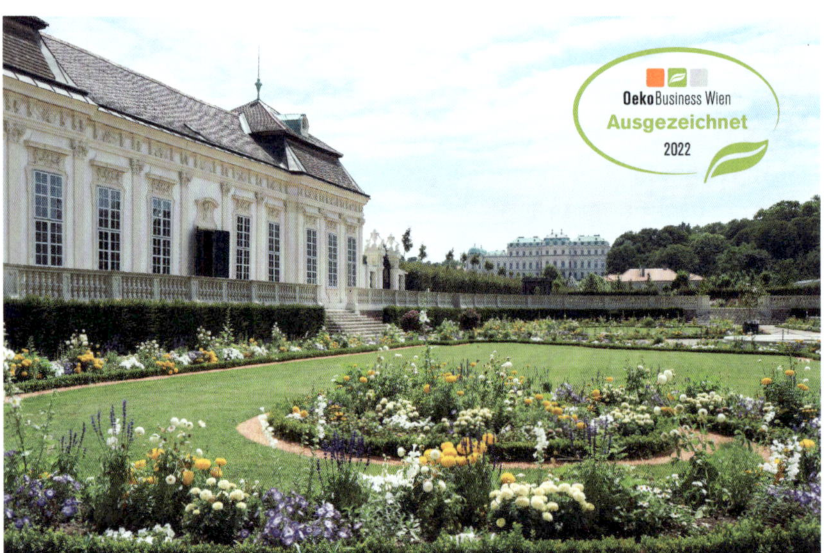

3

Fig. 1
The "Queering the Belvedere" public program; Queer History Tour with historian Andreas Brunner and curator Christiane Erharter, June 12, 2021, Belvedere, Vienna

Fig. 2
Facebook post for the "Belvedere ABC": "J for jogging: One of Vienna's most spectacular jogging routes! Intrepid runners regularly clock up 2,000 steps (that's 1.3 km) in one loop through the Belvedere Gardens," June, 22, 2022

Fig. 3
In 2021, the Belvedere obtained the Austrian Ecolabel, a seal of approval with which cultural institutions commit themselves to meeting environmental protection and quality standards.

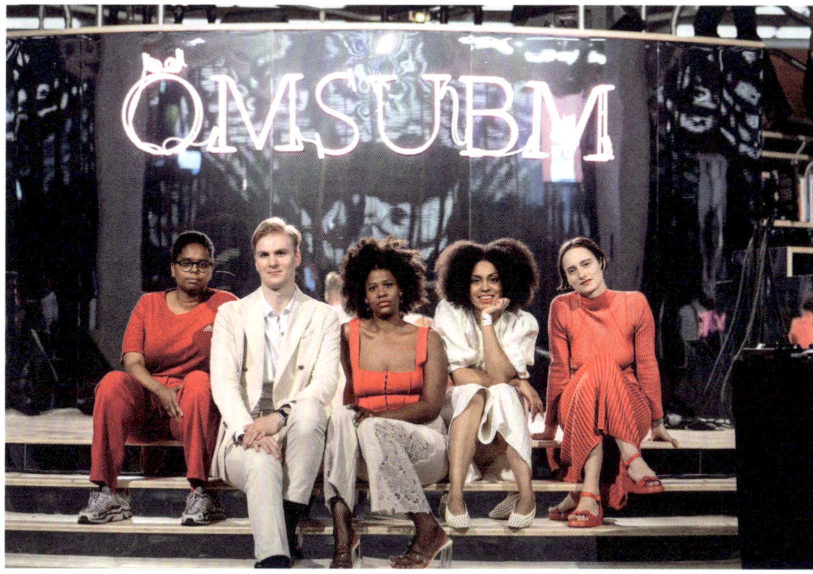

4

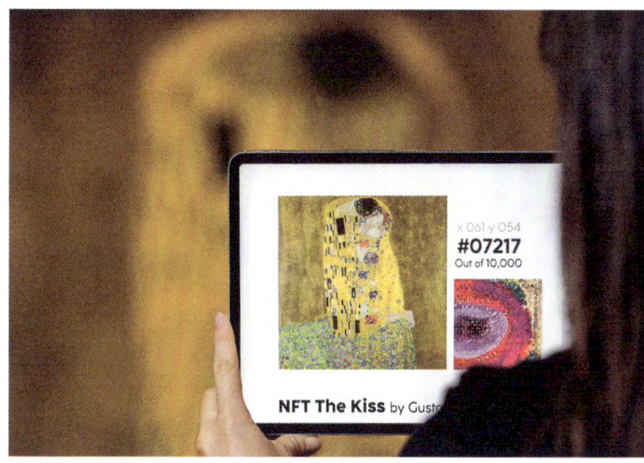

5

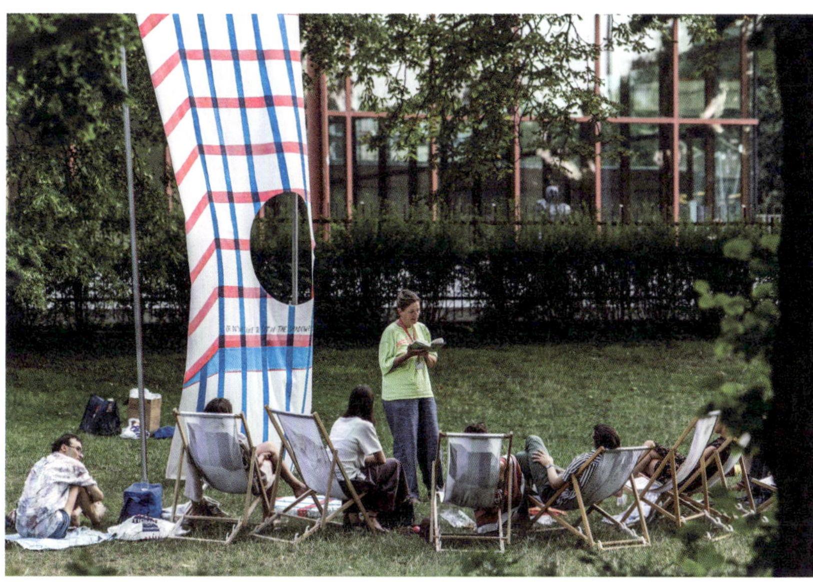

6

Fig. 4
The Belvedere 21 hosts *The Austrian Museum for Black Entertainment and Black Music (ÖMSUBM)*; from l. to r.: Dalia Ahmed, Frieder Blume, Anta Helena Reck, Joana Tischkau, Elisabeth Hampe, May 14, 2022

Fig. 5
On Valentine's Day 2022, the Belvedere launched a limited edition of ten thousand digital segments of Gustav Klimt's masterpiece *The Kiss* as NFTs, 2022, Belvedere, Vienna

Fig. 6
Community outreach in the Schweizergarten behind the Belvedere 21 with Marlene Hausegger's temporary mobile sculpture *Place in the Sun*, July 2020, Belvedere, Vienna

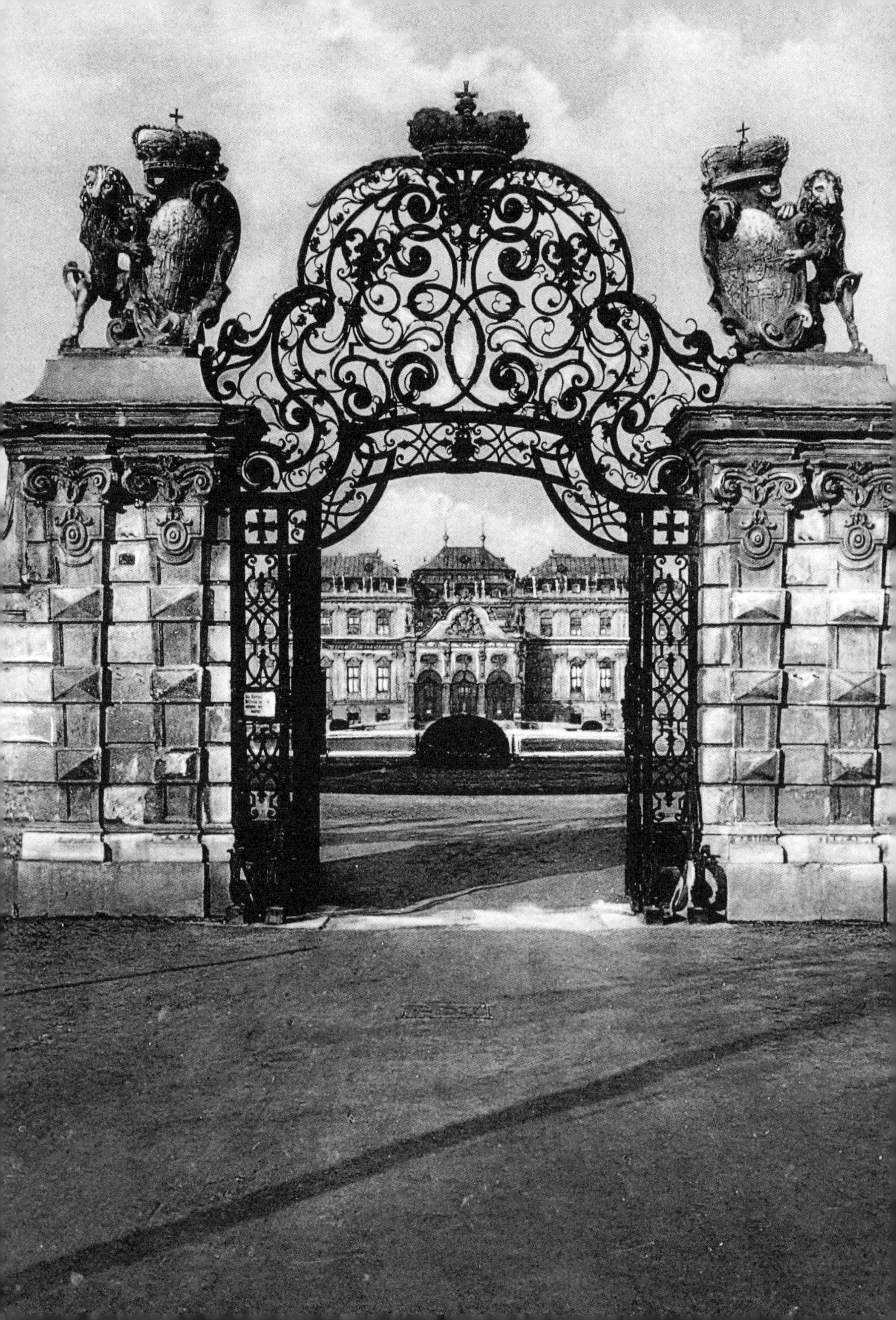

Appendices

←
Entrance to the Upper Belvedere, c. 1935, Wien Museum

P. 368 – 373 Chronology

From Summer Residence to Museum

The Belvedere was built at the instigation of Prince Eugene of Savoy (1663–1736). He arrived at the Habsburg court from Paris at the age of nineteen and enjoyed a successful career as a general under three emperors—Leopold I, Joseph I, and Charles VI. His main passions, however, were architecture, art, nature, and books. These interests are reflected in the plans for the Belvedere as an imposing summer residence with a menagerie, orangery, and picture gallery.

During the reign of Maria Theresa and her son Joseph II, the Upper Belvedere was used for the first time as a picture gallery, showing works from the imperial collections arranged by schools, as an important step towards the concept of a museum as a place of public enlightenment.

1

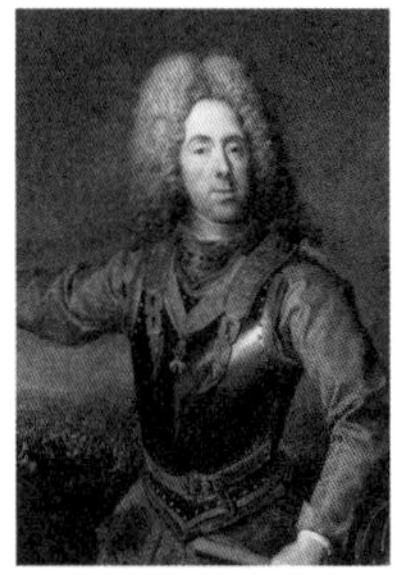

Jacob van Schuppen, *Prince Eugene of Savoy after the Battle of Belgrade on 16 August 1717*, 1718, Belvedere, Vienna, loan from the Rijksmuseum Amsterdam

2

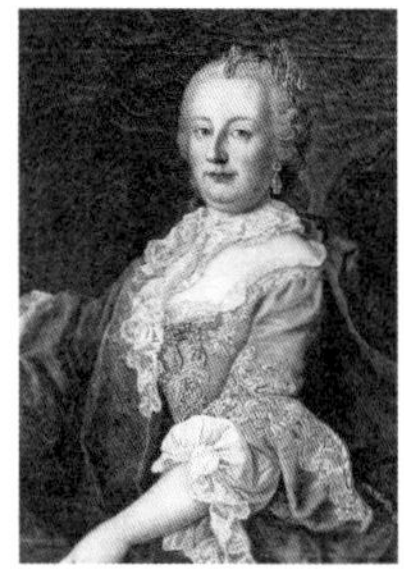

Martin van Meytens the Younger, *Maria Theresa as Queen of Hungary*, after 1759, Belvedere, Vienna, permanent loan from the Ministry of Education, Science, and Research

Prince Eugene

1663

Birth of Prince Eugene of Savoy in Paris.

1683

Prince Eugene's baptism of fire in the Battle of Vienna on September 12 at Kahlenberg Mountain, ending the Siege of Vienna and defeating the Ottomans.

Building of the Belvedere

1697

Prince Eugene (fig. 1) acquires a large plot of land on Rennweg, subsequent additions.

1708

Prince Eugene is made lieutenant-general and hence the most powerful man in the state after the emperor.

1712

Start of construction of the Lower Belvedere, architect Johann Lucas von Hildebrandt.

1717

Completion of the Lower Belvedere, start of construction of the Upper Belvedere.

1723

Completion of the Upper Belvedere.

from 1731

Publication of etchings of the Belvedere, based on drawings by Salomon Kleiner (→ p. 26, ②) as a documentation of his estate during Prince Eugene's lifetime.

1736

Death of Prince Eugene, leaving his niece Victoria of Savoy as his sole heir.

1752

Sale of the palace, henceforth known as the Belvedere, to Maria Theresa (fig. 2).

1770

Costume ball at the Belvedere to celebrate the marriage of Archduchess Marie Antoinette to the future King Louis XVI of France.

The Belvedere as a museum

1776

Decision to transfer the Imperial Picture Gallery from the Stallburg to the Upper Belvedere under the supervision of gallery director Joseph Rosa. From 1777, fixed opening hours and free admission.

1769–1805

Director Joseph Rosa (fig. 3).

1789

Start of the French Revolution, 1793 execution of Marie Antoinette.

1806–18

Director Heinrich Friedrich Füger (fig. 4).

3

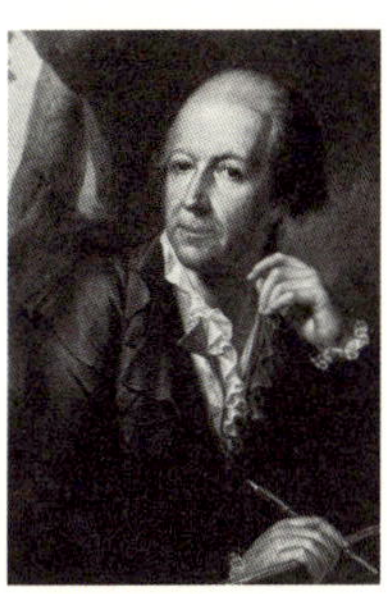

Martin Knoller, *Joseph Rosa*, 1791, Belvedere, Vienna

4

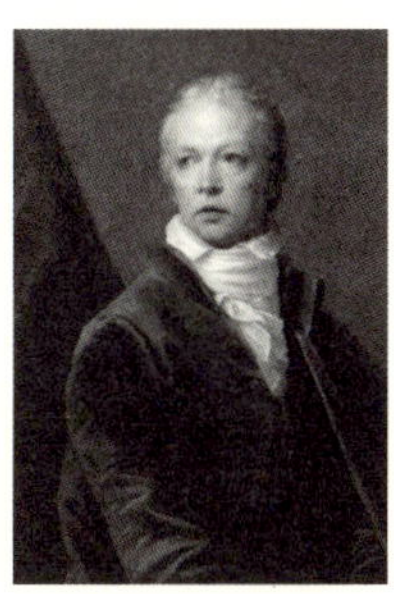

Heinrich Friedrich Füger, *Self-Portrait*, 1807, Paintings Gallery of the Academy of Fine Arts, Vienna

5

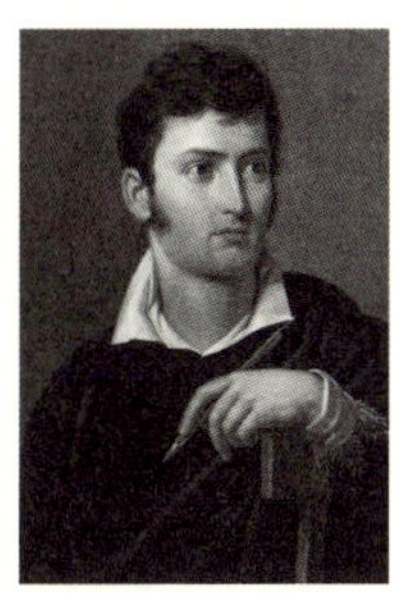

Joseph Rebell, *Self-Portrait*, 1824/25, Belvedere, Vienna

6

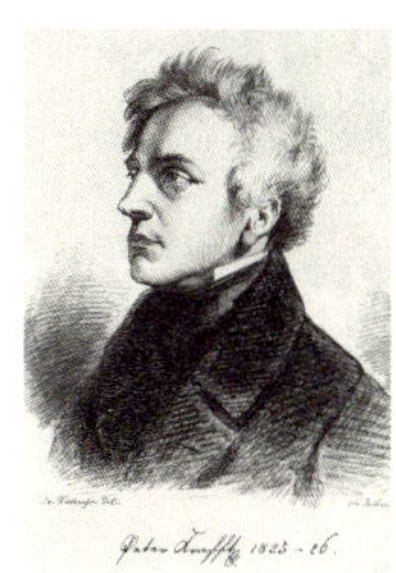

Franz Xaver Stöber after Josef Danhauser, *Peter Krafft*, 1825/26, Belvedere, Vienna

1809

Napoleonic Wars. Repeated evacuation of the imperial collections. Some four hundred paintings taken to France (later returned).

from 1813

Artifacts, curiosities, and armory (from the Ambras Collection), as well as antiques are put on display in the Lower Belvedere.

1824–28

Director Joseph Rebell (fig. 5).

1829–56

Director Peter Krafft (fig. 6).

1857–71

Director Erasmus von Engert (fig. 7).

1871–92

Director Eduard Ritter von Engerth (fig. 8).

1891

Opening of the Kunsthistorisches Museum; the Belvedere is intermittently vacant.

A Residence

from 1898

Conversion of the Upper Belvedere into a residence for the heir to the throne, Archduke Franz Ferdinand, and his family; architect Emil Ritter von Förster.

From 1903 to the present

The Modern Gallery, which opened in the Lower Belvedere in 1903, presented contemporary Austrian art in an international context. In 1911/12 it was enlarged and renamed Imperial-Royal Austrian State Gallery, with the extended remit of showing Austrian art from the Middle Ages to the present. After the collapse of the monarchy, the collections were restructured as part of the museum reform of 1919 and the works presented in both Belvedere palaces.

During World War II, some parts of the collection remained open until 1944, at which point holdings were taken into safe storage. War damage repairs took until 1953/54, when the museum was able to reopen. Today, the Belvedere sees itself as a place for discussion, collection, research, conservation, exhibition, and communication.

7

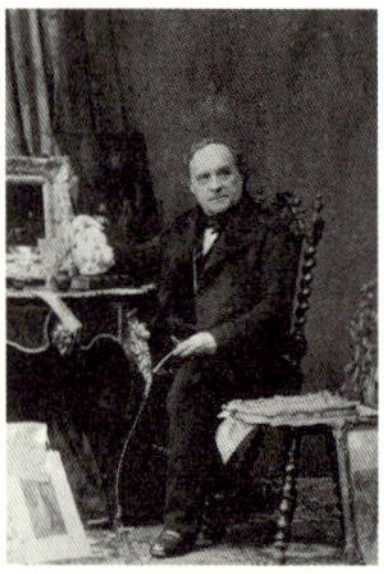

Erasmus von Engert, c. 1870, Belvedere, Vienna

8

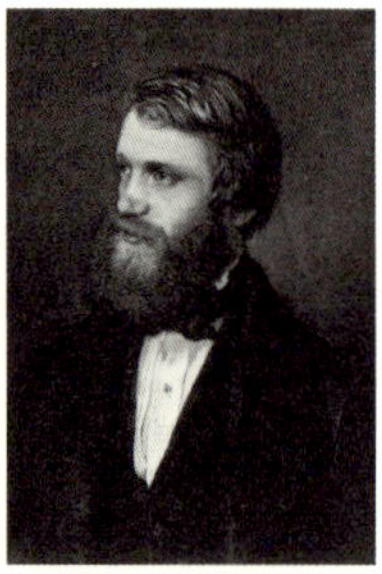

Eduard Ritter von Engerth, *Self-Portrait*, c. 1855, Belvedere, Vienna

9

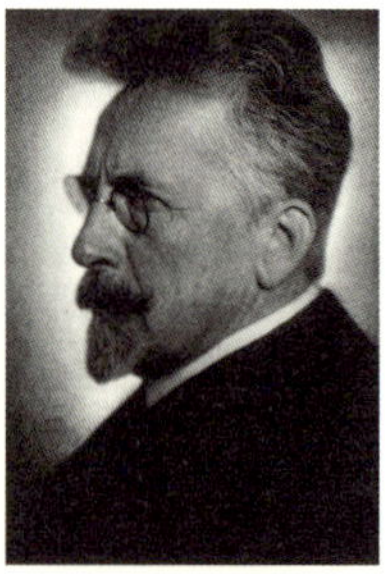

Friedrich Dörnhöffer, c. 1910, Belvedere, Vienna

10

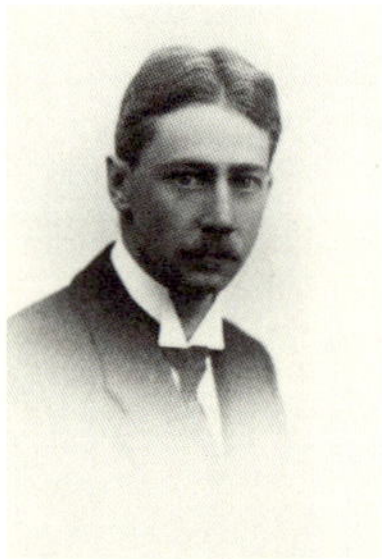

Franz Martin Haberditzl, c. 1915, private archive

1899

Architectural designs by Otto Wagner for a "gallery for works of art of our time."

1900

Founding of the Committee for the Establishment of a Modern Gallery, which includes the artists Edmund Hellmer, Carl Moll, and Otto Wagner.

1903

Opening of the Modern Gallery as a state museum with the objective of presenting Austrian art in an international context. Temporary premises in the Lower Belvedere.

1908

Gustav Klimt's painting *The Kiss (Lovers)* is acquired for the Modern Gallery (→ p. 159, ⑪).

1909

Friedrich Dörnhöffer (fig. 9), curator of the collection of prints at the Imperial Court Library, is appointed first director of the Modern Gallery.

1911/12

Renaming of the institution to Imperial-Royal Austrian State Gallery (k. k. Österreichische Staatsgalerie) and extension of its scope to presenting the development of Austrian art from the Middle Ages to the present. Founding of the Austrian State Gallery Society.

1913

Architectural designs by Otto Wagner for a new "Haus der Kunst" (House of Art).

1914

Assassination of Franz Ferdinand and his wife Sophie on June 28 in Sarajevo. Beginning of World War I.

1915

Franz Martin Haberditzl, head of the collection of prints at the Imperial Court Library, is appointed director of the Austrian State Gallery (fig. 10).

1917/18

Archduke Maximilian, brother of Charles I, the last emperor of Austria, resides with his family in the Upper Belvedere.

1918

End of World War I. Death of Gustav Klimt, Egon Schiele, Koloman Moser, Ferdinand Hodler, and Otto Wagner.

after 1918

Extended presentation of the collections in the Upper and Lower Belvedere as a result of Hans Tietze's museum reform (→ p. 187, ⑬).

1921

Renaming of the institution to Austrian Gallery.

1923

Opening of the Baroque Museum in the Lower Belvedere.

1924

Opening of the Gallery of the Nineteenth Century in the Upper Belvedere.

1929

The Modern Gallery as a collection of twentieth century art opens in the Orangery. Sculptures are presented in the Privy Garden.

11

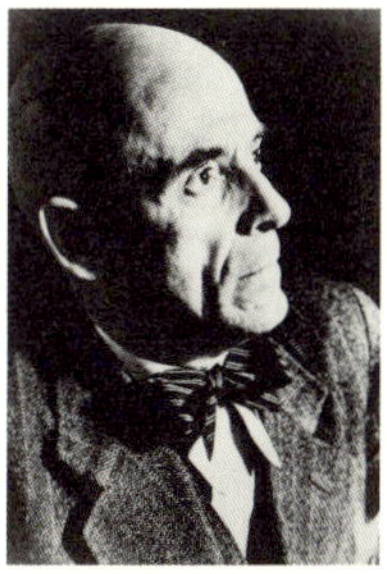

Bruno Grimschitz, n. d., Belvedere, Vienna

12

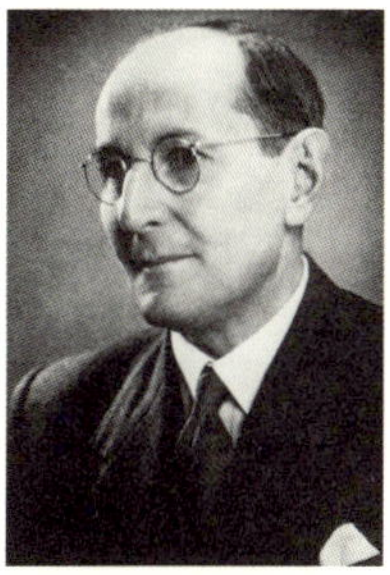

Karl Garzarolli-Thurnlackh, c. 1947, Belvedere, Vienna

13

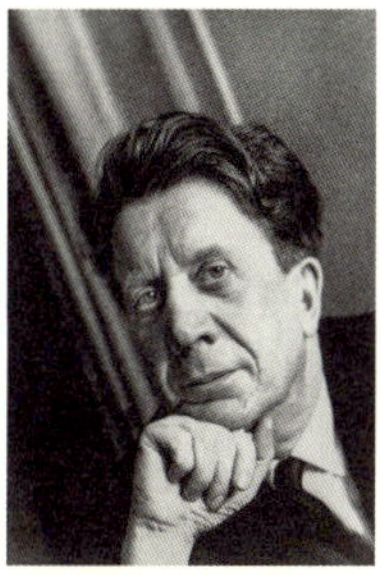

Fritz Novotny, n. d., photo: Olga J. Norbin, Belvedere, Vienna

14

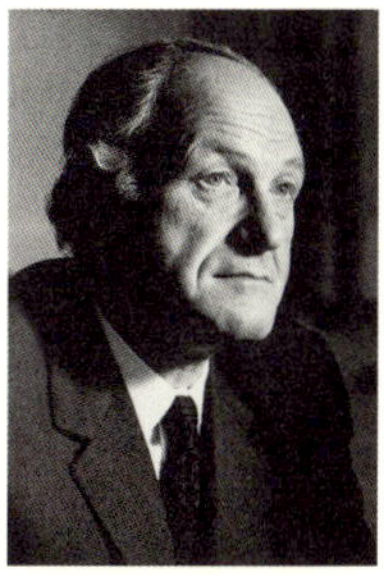

Hans Aurenhammer, 1982, photo: Elfriede Mejchar, Belvedere, Vienna

1938

Annexation of Austria to the Third Reich. Franz Martin Haberditzl is removed from office by the Nazis and replaced by his longstanding deputy Bruno Grimschitz, who remains director until 1945 (fig. 11). The Modern Gallery is closed.

1939

Start of World War II in Europe.

1939/40

Beginning of air raid protection measures and evacuation of artworks. The Baroque Museum is closed.

1943

An air raid bunker is built to the south of the Upper Belvedere (→ p. 233).

1944/45

Closure of the Austrian Gallery as "total war" is declared. Upper and Lower Belvedere are severely damaged in air raids.

1945

End of World War II.

Bruno Grimschitz, as a former member of the Nazi party, is removed from office. Fritz Novotny is appointed as interim director.

from 1945

Rebuilding and renovation of the Belvedere palaces.

1947

Karl Garzarolli-Thurnlackh becomes director of the Austrian Gallery (fig. 12).

1951

The first post-war museum presentation by the Austrian Gallery is the exhibition *New Acquisitions 1947–1951* in the Lower Belvedere.

1953

Reopening of the Baroque Museum in the Lower Belvedere and of the Museum of Medieval Art (→ p. 210) in the Orangery. Transfer of international holdings to the Kunsthistorisches Museum.

1954

The Gallery of the Nineteenth and Twentieth Century opens in the Upper Belvedere.

1955

Signing of the Austrian State Treaty in the Marble Hall of the Upper Belvedere.

1958–61

Major exhibitions of Classical Modernism in the Upper Belvedere: Vincent van Gogh, Paul Cézanne, Paul Gauguin (→ pp. 276–78).

1960–68

Director Fritz Novotny (fig. 13).

1968–82

Director Hans Aurenhammer (fig. 14).

1983–91

Director Hubert Adolph (fig. 15).

1986

Return of international nineteenth and twentieth century holdings from the Kunsthistorisches Museum.

15

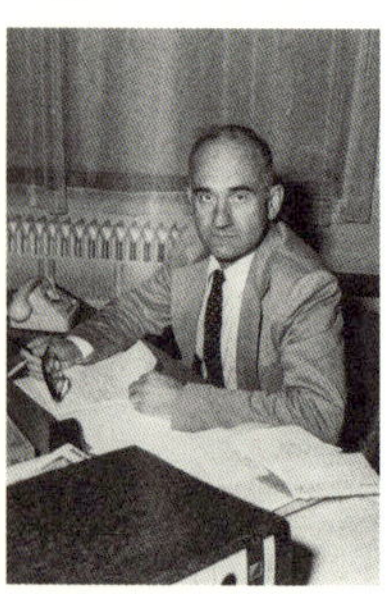

Hubert Adolph, 1980s, Belvedere, Vienna

16

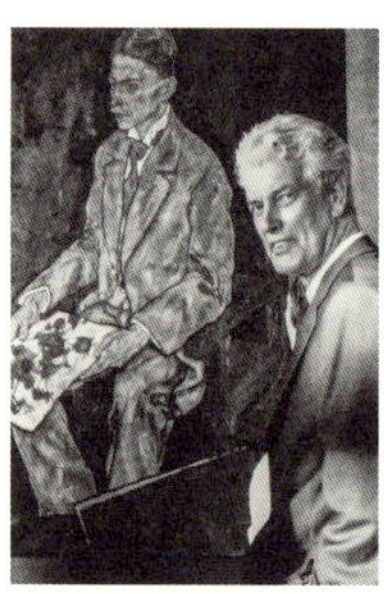

Gerbert Frodl, 2003, Belvedere, Vienna

1992–2006

Director Gerbert Frodl (fig. 16).

1994–97

Major refurbishment and redisplay of the collections as part of the "A Billion for our Museums" program (→ p. 284).

1998

Adoption of the Austrian Art Restitution Act and start of provenance research (→ S. 331, ㉔).

2000

Establishment of the Österreichische Galerie Belvedere as an independent legal entity.

2002

Incorporation of the 20er Haus (→ S. 325, ㉓) into the Österreichische Galerie Belvedere. The pavilion was originally designed by Karl Schwanzer for the World's Fair in Brussels in 1958.

2006

Restitution of five paintings by Gustav Klimt, including the portrait *The Lady in Gold*, to the heirs of Adele and Ferdinand Bloch-Bauer (→ S. 331, ㉔).

2007–16

Director Agnes Husslein-Arco (fig. 17).

2011

Opening of the 21er Haus (since 2017 Belvedere 21) as a new exhibition venue for Austrian contemporary art.

since 2017

Stella Rollig, General Director

Wolfgang Bergmann, Chief Financial Officer (fig. 18).

2023

300-year anniversary of the Upper Belvedere. A year of exhibitions and events to celebrate the palace's third centenary.

Compiled by Bettina Bosin, Dagmar Diernberger, Katinka Gratzer-Baumgärtner, Maike Hohn, Georg Lechner, and Stefan Lehner

17

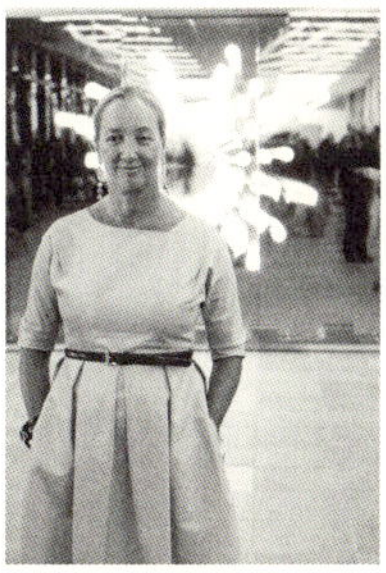

Agnes Husslein-Arco, 2013, photo: Natascha Unkart, Belvedere, Vienna

18

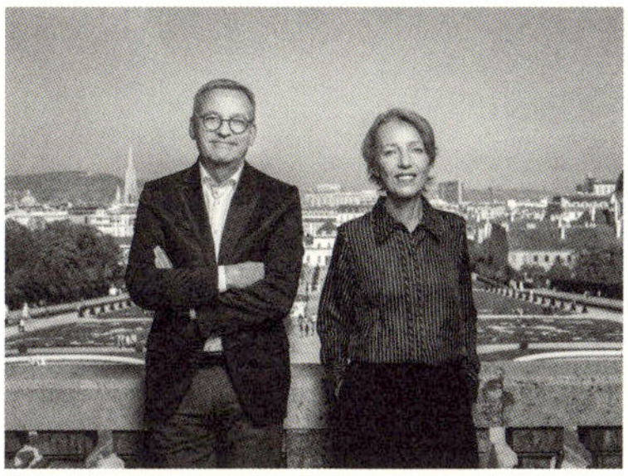

Wolfgang Bergmann and Stella Rollig, 2022, photo: Gianmaria Gava, Belvedere, Vienna

P.
374
–
377

Visualization of the Österreichische Galerie Belvedere's Collection Contents

The diagram illustrates the current contents and types of objects (as of December 2022) in the six curatorial departments of the Österreichische Galerie Belvedere. The size of the circles corresponds to the total number of objects in each collection. Each curatorial department is then subdivided by object type. The more objects of a particular type in the department, the larger the circle. Departments with a large variety of objects, such as the contemporary art collection, will therefore be shown as a greater number of smaller circles.

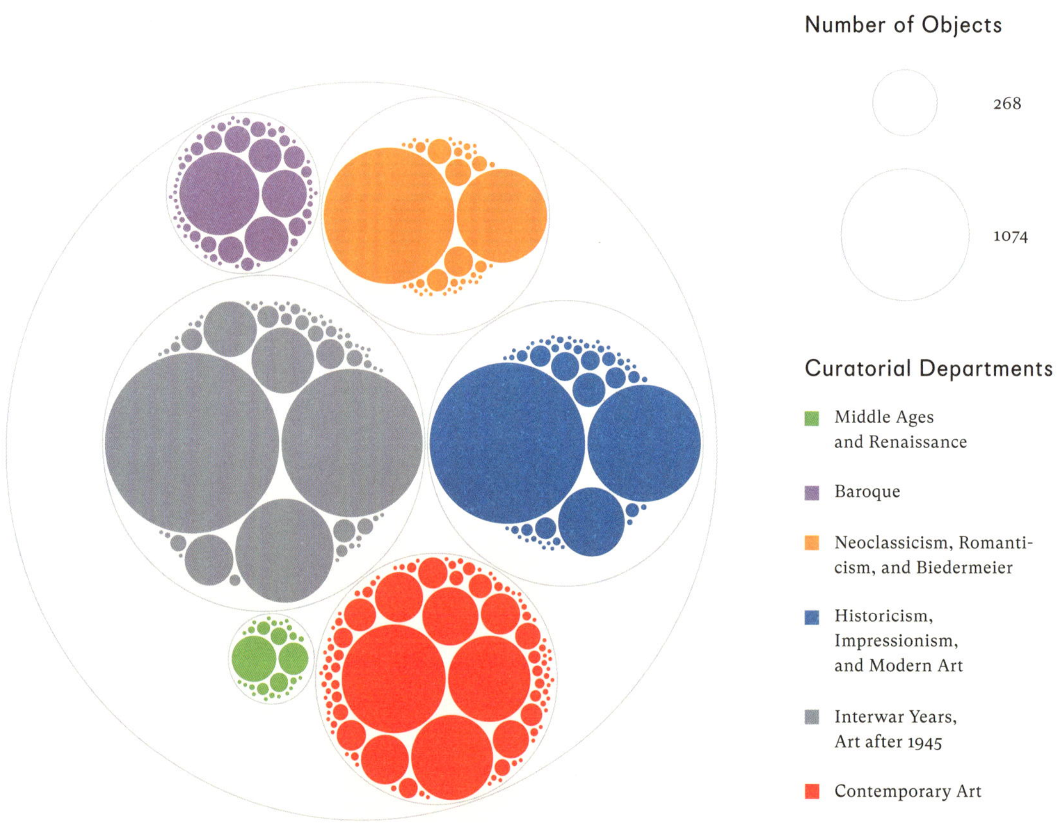

The bar charts show the ranking of object types within a curatorial department and in a comparison of the six curatorial departments. For the five most common object types within each collection—paintings, drawings, sculptures, photographs, and prints—the actual numbers are also given. Rare object types such as bookplates are summarized under the term miscellaneous.

Middle Ages and Renaissance

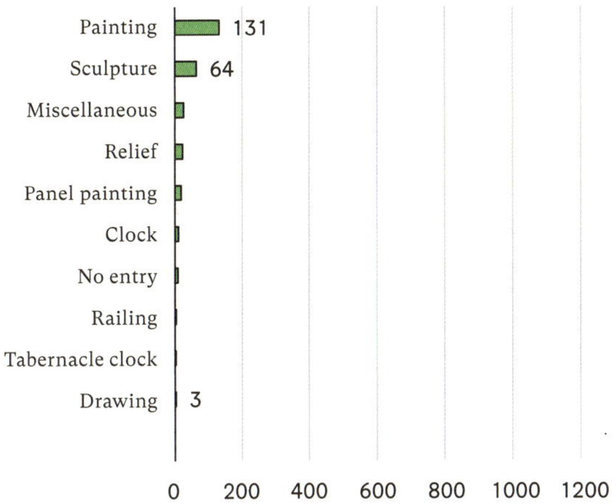

Historicism, Impressionism, and Modern Art

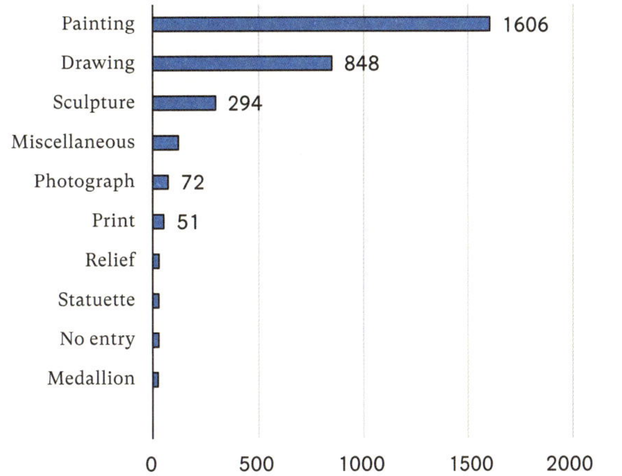

Baroque

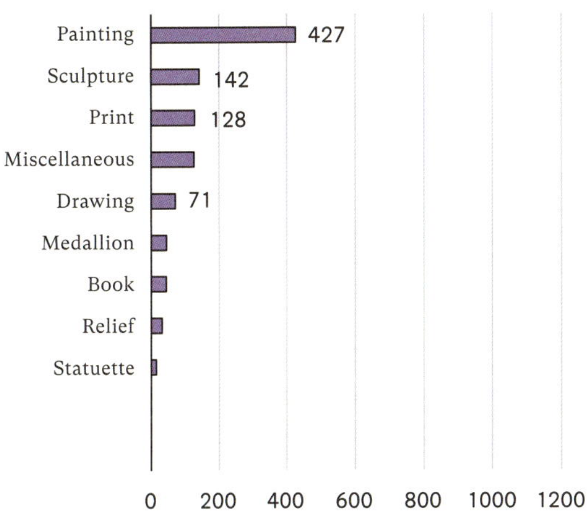

Interwar Years, Art after 1945

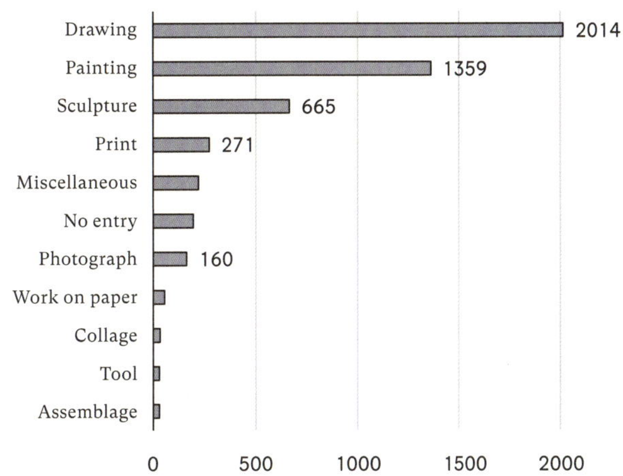

Neoclassicism, Romanticism, and Biedermeier

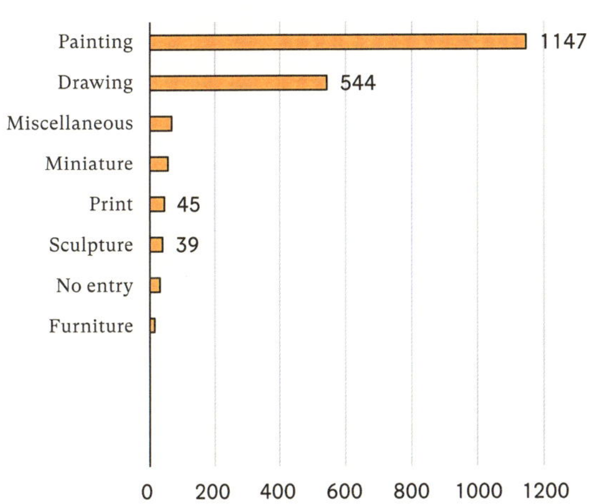

Contemporary Art

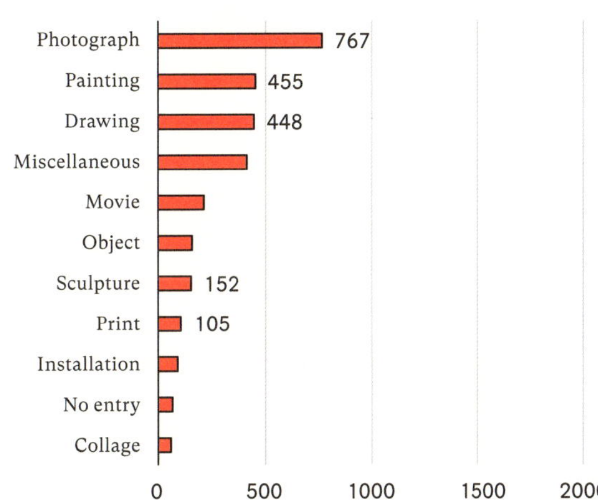

Contemporary Art Accessions (1811–1945)

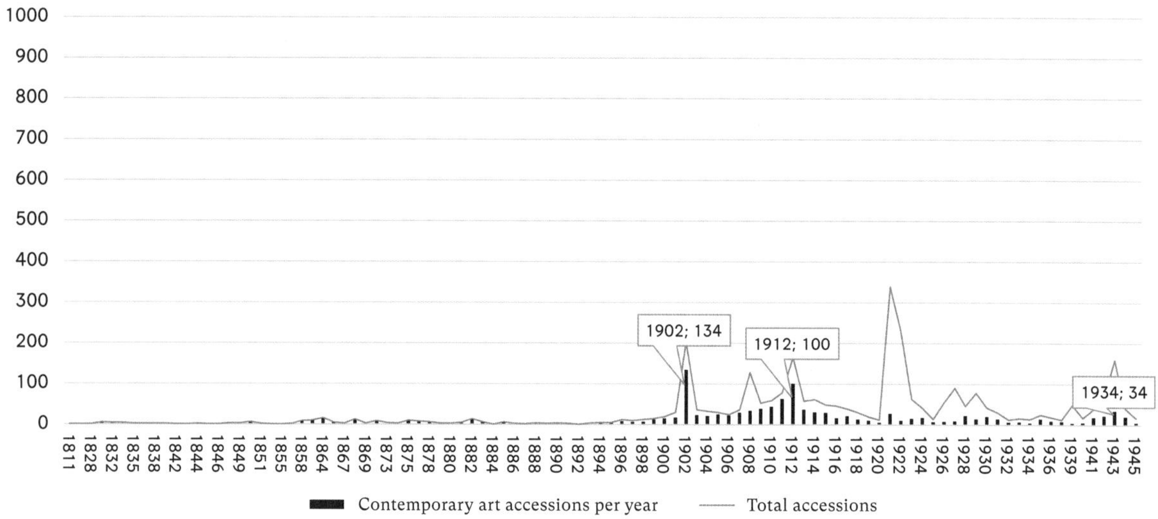

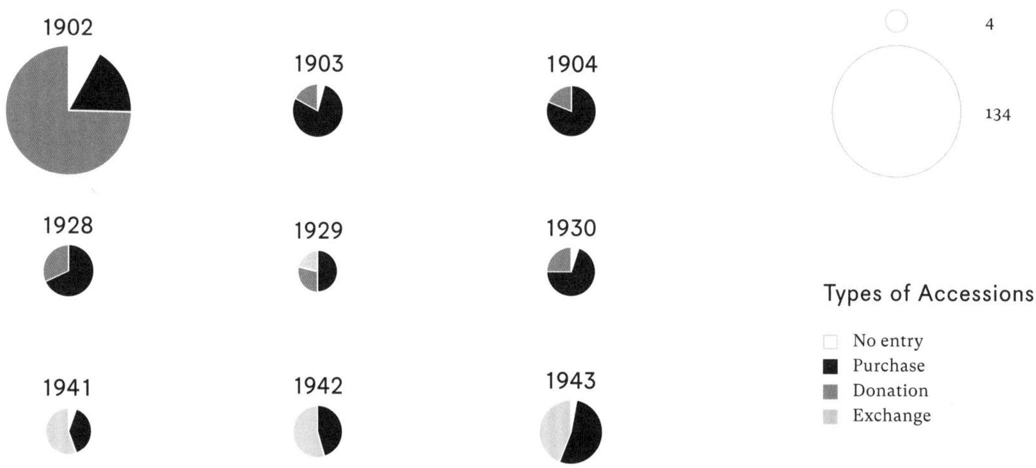

A museum database also serves as a digital inventory. The documented date of accession combined with the date of an artist's death makes it possible to determine whether a particular work was acquired during the artist's lifetime or later. It is possible in this way to reconstruct the history of the contemporary art acquisitions by the Österreichische Galerie Belvedere and its predecessors. The black bars in the two charts show the contemporary art accessions per year. The gray line above the bars shows the total accessions.

Contemporary Art Accessions (1946–2021)

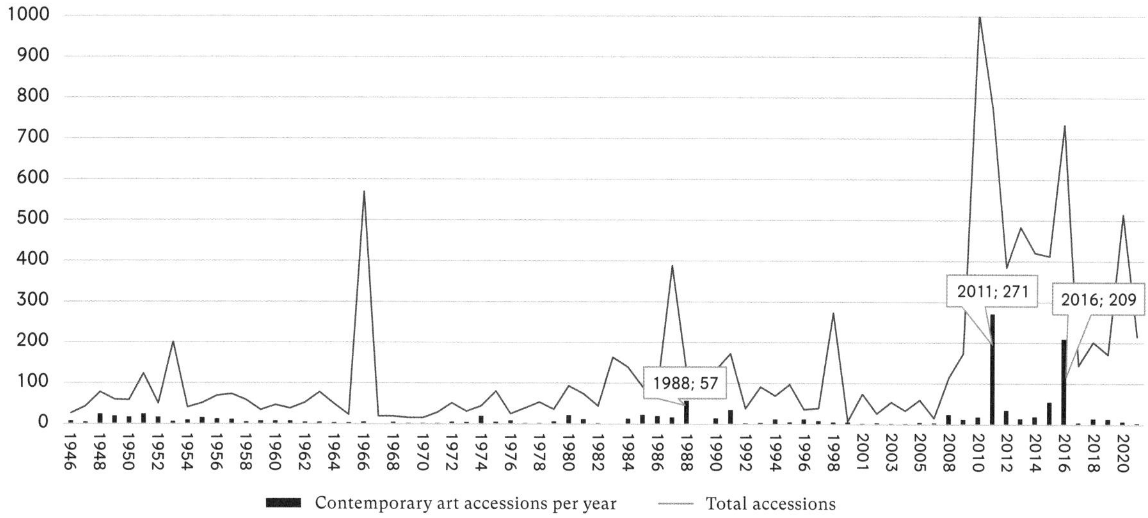

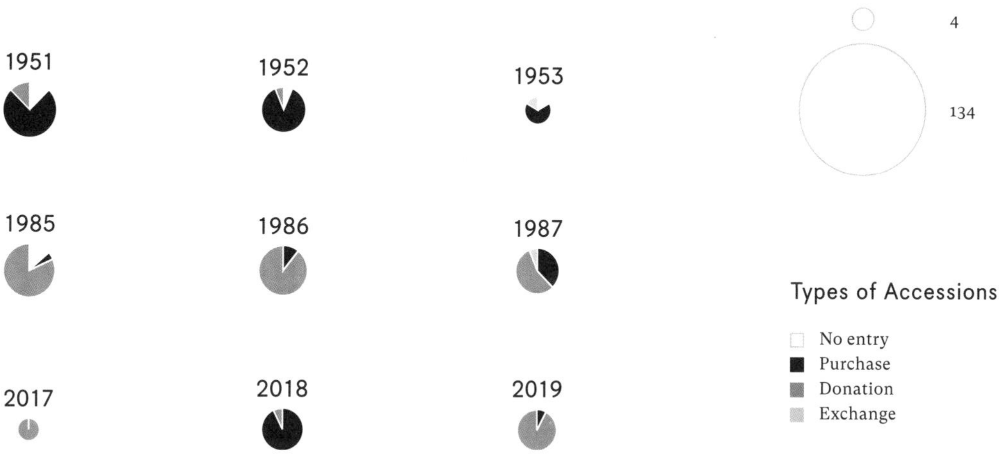

Of the 14,345 objects in the six curatorial departments, 2,508 (17.5 percent) were acquired during the artists' lifetimes. A further 7,747 objects (54 percent) were acquired after the death of the artists. For the remaining 4,090 objects (28.5 percent) the year of accession and/or the date of the artist's death are not known. It should be noted that this data visualization is to be understood as a merely quantitative analysis and does not make any kind of assessment about the quality of the annual collection growth.

Maximilian Kaiser.
Analysis carried out with the aid of The Museum System™, RAWgraphs 2.0 beta

P. 378 — 387

Bibliography

Adolph 1990/91
Hubert Adolph, "Jahresbericht 1991: Bautätigkeit und Einrichtung," *Mitteilungen der Österreichischen Galerie*, yr. 34/35 (1990/91), pp. 137–43.

Anon. 1739
Anon., *Des grossen Feld-Herrns Eugenii Herzogs von Savoyen Kayserl. und des Reichs General-Lieutenants Helden-Thaten [...] Sechster Theil* (Nuremberg, 1739).

Anon. 1898
Anon., "Ausstellungswesen," *Ver Sacrum*, yr. 1, no. 1 (1898), pp. 24–25.

Anon. 1904
Anon., "Vorwort," in *Katalog der modernen Galerie*, 2nd ed. (Vienna, 1904), pp. iii–xviii.

Anon. 1907
Anon., *Moderní galerie Království Českého* (Prague, 1907), n. p.

Apin 1728
Sigmund Jacob Apin, *Anleitung wie man die Bildnüsse berühmter und gelehrter Männer mit Nutzen sammlen und denen dagegen gemachten Einwendungen gründlich begegnen soll* (Nuremberg, 1728).

Auer/Black 1985
Leopold Auer and Jeremy Black, "Ein neu entdecktes Inventar der Gemäldesammlung Prinz Eugens," *Mitteilungen des Österreichischen Staatsarchivs*, vol. XXXVIII (1985), pp. 331–46.

Aurenhammer 1969
Gertrude Aurenhammer, "Geschichte des Belvederes seit dem Tode des Prinzen Eugen," *Mitteilungen der Österreichischen Galerie*, yr. 13, no. 57 (1969), pp. 41–183.

Baensch/Kratz-Kessemeier/Wimmer 2016
Tanja Baensch, Kristina Kratz-Kessemeier, and Dorothee Wimmer, eds., *Museen im Nationalsozialismus: Akteure—Orte—Politik* (Vienna/Cologne/Weimar, 2016).

Bartsch 1803–21
Adam Bartsch, *Le Peintre Graveur*, 21 vols. (Vienna, 1803–21).

Bartsch 1854
Friedrich von Bartsch, *Die Kupferstichsammlung der K. K. Hofbibliothek in Wien* (Vienna, 1854).

Baudi di Vesme 1886
Alessandro Baudi di Vesme, *Sull'acquisto fatto da Carlo Emanuele III re di Sardegna della quadreria del principe Eugenio di Savoia* (Turin, 1886).

Bayer/Corey 2020
Andrea Bayer and Laura D. Corey, eds., *Making the MET: 1870–2020* (New Haven, 2020).

Bickendorf 2007
Gabriele Bickendorf, "Schule des Sehens: Die künstlerischen Schulen und der kunsthistorische Blick," in *Kunstwerk—Abbild—Buch: Das illustrierte Kunstbuch von 1730 bis 1930*, eds. Katharina Krause and Klaus Niehr (Munich/Berlin, 2007), pp. 33–52.

Blaschke 1943
Hanns Blaschke, *Fünf Jahre Kulturamt der Stadt Wien* (Vienna, 1943).

Bleier-Brody/Hofmann 1963
Agnes Bleier-Brody and Werner Hofmann, *Französischer Film von 1900 bis heute: Museum des 20. Jahrhunderts, 4. November–4. Dezember 1963* (Vienna, 1963).

Blimlinger/Schödl 2018
Eva Blimlinger and Heinz Schödl, eds., *(k)ein Ende in Sicht. 20 Jahre Kunstrückgabegesetz in Österreich*, Schriftenreihe der Kommission für Provenienzforschung, vol. 8 (Vienna, 2018).

Borchhardt-Birbaumer 2015
Brigitte Borchhardt-Birbaumer, "Der Kunsthistoriker Gerhart Frankl oder die 'Quadratur des Zirkels'," in *Gerhardt Frankl: Rastlos*, eds. Agnes Husslein-Arco and Kerstin Jesse, exh. cat. Belvedere, Vienna (Vienna, 2015), pp. 61–71.

Borchhardt-Birbaumer 2020a
Brigitte Borchhardt-Birbaumer, "'Köpferl im Sand': Die Aufarbeitung des Nationalsozialismus in der Kunst," in exh. cat. Vienna 2020, pp. 60–72.

Borchhardt-Birbaumer 2020b
Brigitte Borchhardt-Birbaumer, "Großes Vorbild Art Brut," in exh. cat. Vienna 2020, pp. 448–57.

Borchhardt-Birbaumer 2020c
Brigitte Borchhardt-Birbaumer, "Feministischer Aktionismus in Wien 1967–1980," in exh. cat. Vienna 2020, pp. 528–71.

Botz 2018
Gerhard Botz, *Nationalsozialismus in Wien: Machtübernahme, Herrschaftssicherung, Radikalisierung, Kriegsvorbereitung 1938/39* (Vienna, 2018).

Bracht 2016
Christian Bracht, "'Unmaßgebliche Vorschläge, wie man seine Sammlung am besten anstellen soll.': Von historischen Bildnissammlungen zum Digitalen Portraitindex," in *Das Porträt als kulturelle Praxis*, eds. Eva-Bettina Krems and Sigrid Ruby (Berlin/Munich, 2016), pp. 300–17.

Brakensiek 2009
Stephan Brakensiek, "Kennerschaft aus Kassetten: Die Loseblatt-Sammlung als offenes Modell zur nutzbringenden Organisation einer Graphiksammlung in der Frühen Neuzeit," in *Graphik als Spiegel der Malerei: Meisterwerke der Reproduktionsgraphik 1500–1830*, eds. Stephan Brakensiek and Michel Polfer (Cinisello Balsamo/Milan, 2009), pp. 33–47.

Braubach 1963–65
Max Braubach, *Prinz Eugen von Savoyen: Eine Biographie*, 5 vols. (Vienna, 1963–65).

Braubach 1965
Max Braubach, "Die Gemäldesammlung des Prinzen Eugen von Savoyen," in *Festschrift für Herbert von Einem*, eds. Gert von der Osten and Georg Kauffmann (Berlin, 1965), pp. 27–43.

Breicha 1981
Otto Breicha, ed., *Der Art Club in Österreich: Zeugen und Zeugnisse eines Aufbruchs* (Vienna, 1981).

Bruckmüller 1998
Ernst Bruckmüller, "Die Entwicklung des Österreichbewusstseins," in *Österreichische Nationalgeschichte nach 1945. Die Spiegel der Erinnerung: Die Sicht von innen*, ed. Robert Kriechbaumer, vol. 1 (Vienna/Cologne/Weimar, 1998), pp. 369–96.

Büchel 2022
Julia Büchel, *Repräsentation—Partizipation—Zugänglichkeit: Theorie und Praxis gesellschaftlicher Einbindung in Museen und Ausstellungen* (Bielefeld, 2022).

Bürckel 1939
Josef Bürckel, *Volk und Kultur* (Vienna, 1939).

Burgstaller 2022
Rosemarie Burgstaller, *Inszenierung des Hasses: Feindbildausstellungen im Nationalsozialismus* (Frankfurt/New York, 2022).

Buschbeck/Csokor/Wotruba 1954
Ernst Buschbeck, Franz Theodor Csokor, and Fritz Wotruba, "'Belvedere' (ital.): Häßlicher Anblick. Kritik an der neuen 'Österreichischen Galerie'," *Forum. Österreichische Monatsblätter für kulturelle Freiheit*, yr. 1, no. 9 (September 1954), pp. 29–30.

Čapek 1986
Karel Čapek, "O modern galerii," *Spisy: O Umění a Kultuře III* (1926; Prague, 1986), pp. 29–31.

Cohn 1992
Marjorie B. Cohn, *A Noble Collection: The Spencer Albums of Old Master Prints* (Cambridge, MA, 1992).

Coll. guide Vienna 1919
Julius Banko, *Ausstellung von Fundstücken aus Ephesos im Unteren Belvedere*, 3rd ed. (Vienna, 1919).

Coll. cat. Vienna 1886
Eduard Ritter von Engerth, *Gemälde. Beschreibendes Verzeichnis: Kunsthistorische Sammlungen des allerhöchsten Kaiserhauses*, vol. 3: *Deutsche Schulen* (Vienna, 1886).

Coll. cat. Vienna 1891
Uebersicht der kunsthistorischen Sammlungen des Allerhöchsten Kaiserhauses (Vienna, 1891).

Coll. cat. Vienna 1901
Robert von Schneider, *Ausstellung von Fundstücken aus Ephesos im griechischen Tempel im Volksgarten* (Vienna, 1901).

Coll. cat. Vienna 1903
Katalog der Modernen Galerie in Wien: Herausgegeben im Auftrage des k. k. Ministeriums für Cultur und Unterricht (Vienna, 1903).

Coll. cat. Vienna 1905
Robert von Schneider, *Ausstellung von Fundstücken aus Ephesos im unteren Belvedere* (Vienna, 1905).

Coll. cat. Vienna 1907
August Schaeffer, *Führer durch die Gemäldegalerie*, part III, 2nd ed. (Vienna, 1907).

Coll. cat. Vienna 1917a
Übersicht der Kunsthistorischen Sammlungen des allerhöchsten Kaiserhauses (Vienna, 1917).

Coll. cat. Vienna 1917b
"Verzeichnis der Neuaufstellung 1917," *Mitteilungen aus der Österreichischen Staatsgalerie*, no. 1, 3rd ed. (Vienna, 1917).

Coll. cat. Vienna 1923
Das Barockmuseum im Unteren Belvedere (Vienna, 1923).

Coll. cat. Vienna 1924
Galerie des neunzehnten Jahrhunderts im Oberen Belvedere (Vienna, 1924).

Coll. cat. Vienna 1927
Robert von Schneider, *Ausstellung von Fundstücken aus Ephesos im unteren Belvedere*, 4th ed. (Vienna, 1927).

Coll. cat. Vienna 1934a
Das Barockmuseum im Unteren Belvedere, 2nd completely rev. ed. (Vienna, 1934).

Coll. cat. Vienna 1934b
Ludwig Baldass, *Österreichische Tafelmalerei der Spätgotik 1400–1525: Kunstgeschichtliche Übersicht und Katalog der Gemälde* (Vienna, 1934).

Coll. cat. Vienna 1935
Leone Planiscig and Ernst Kris, *Katalog der Sammlungen für Plastik und Kunstgewerbe* (Vienna, 1935).

Coll. cat. Vienna 1953a
Katalog der Neuaufstellung 1953: Österreichisches Barockmuseum in Wien (Vienna, 1953).

Coll. cat. Vienna 1953b
Karl Garzarolli-Thurnlackh, *Museum mittelalterlicher österreichischer Kunst in der Orangerie des Belvedere: Katalog 1953* (Vienna, 1953).

Coll. cat. Vienna 1967
Klaus Demus, ed., *Katalog der Neuen Galerie in der Stallburg* (Vienna, 1967).

Coll. cat. Vienna 1971
Elfriede Baum, *Katalog des Museums mittelalterlicher österreichischer Kunst* (Vienna, 1971).

Coll. cat. Vienna 1978
Wolfgang Oberleitner et al., *Katalog der Antikensammlung 2. Funde aus Ephesos und Samothrake* (Vienna, 1978).

Coll. cat. Vienna 1981
Elfriede Baum, *Supplement zum Katalog des Museums mittelalterlicher österreichischer Kunst* (Vienna/Munich, 1981).

Comoglio 2012
Sara Comoglio, "Principe Eugenio: corrispondenze ed inventari. Corrispondenza," in exh. cat. Turin 2012, pp. 280–90.

Comoglio 2022
Sara Comoglio, "Parodi ed Eugenio di Savoia: Il caso del Belvedere di Vienna," in *Domenico Parodi: L'Arcadia in giardino*, eds. Daniele Sanguineti and Laura Stagno, exh. cat. Palazzo Nicolosio Lomellino, Genoa (Genoa, 2022), pp. 83–92.

Czernin 1999
Hubertus Czernin, *Die Fälschung: Der Fall Bloch-Bauer und das Werk Gustav Klimts* (Vienna, 1999).

DaCosta Kaufmann 1995
Thomas DaCosta Kaufmann, *Court, Cloister and City: The Art and Culture of Central Europe 1450–1800* (London, 1995).

DaCosta Kaufmann 1999
Thomas DaCosta Kaufmann, "Das Theater der Pracht: Charlottenburg und die europäische Hofkultur um 1700," in *Sophie Charlotte und ihr Schloß: Ein Musenhof des Barock in Brandenburg-Preußen*, exh. cat. Stiftung Preußischer Kulturbesitz, Berlin (Munich/London/New York, 1999), pp. 43–56.

Daehner 2007
Jens Daehner, ed., *The Herculaneum Women: History, Context, Identities* (Los Angeles, 2007).

Deiters 2016
Wencke Deiters, *Die Wiener Gemäldegalerie unter Gustav Glück: Von der kaiserlichen Sammlung zum modernen Museum* (Munich, 2016).

Denis 1780
Michael Denis, *Die Merkwürdigkeiten der k. k. garellischen Bibliothek am Theresiano* (Vienna, 1780).

Dictionnaire 1694
Le Dictionnaire de l'Académie Françoise (Paris, 1694).

Diekamp 2005
Cornelia Diekamp, "Die Sammlung eines Prinzen: Zur Geschichte der Gemäldesammlung des Prinzen Eugen nach 1736 mit einer Rekonstruktion des 'Bilder-Saales' im Oberen Belvedere," *Belvedere. Zeitschrift für bildende Kunst*, no. 2 (2005), pp. 4–43.

Diekamp 2010
Cornelia Diekamp, "Die Galerie im Oberen Belvedere und die Bildersammlung Prinz Eugens im Belvedere und im Stadtpalais," in exh. cat. Vienna 2010a, pp. 127–31.

Diekamp 2012
Cornelia Diekamp, "La quadreria del principe Eugenio di Savoia ambientata nei suoi palazzi viennesi," in exh. cat. Turin 2012, pp. 51–75.

Dies 1811
Albert Christoph Dies, "Hingeworfene Bemerkungen über Kunst und deren Nothwendigkeit in Hinsicht auf Finanzwesen: Vorschlag zu einem Museum heutiger Kunst für die österreichischen Staaten," *Vaterländische Blätter für den österreichischen Kaiserstaat*, no. 6, January 19, 1811, pp. 33–35; no. 7, January 21, 1811, pp. 40–42, and no. 9, January 30, 1811, pp. 49–53.

Dvořák 1915
Max Dvořák (as Max Dworzak), "Die Aufgaben der österreichischen Staatsgalerie," *Neue Freie Presse*, June 18, 1915, pp. 1–4.

Egghardt 2007
Hanne Egghardt, *Prinz Eugen: Feldherr, Staatsmann, Mäzen* (Innsbruck/Vienna, 2007).

Eitelberger 1879
Rudolf Eitelberger von Edelberg, "Die Kunstbestrebungen Österreichs zur Zeit der Eröffnung des neuen Museums-Gebäudes (lecture on November 23, 1871)," in *Gesammelte Kunsthistorische Schriften. II. Band: Österreichische Kunst-Institute und kunstgewerbliche Zeitfragen* (Vienna, 1879), pp. 171–203.

Elias 1969
Norbert Elias, *Die höfische Gesellschaft* (Darmstadt, 1969).

Elias 1969/2002
Norbert Elias, *Die höfische Gesellschaft: Untersuchungen zur Soziologie des Königtums und der höfischen Aristokratie* (Frankfurt am Main, 2002).

Exh. cat. Bern 2016
Regula Berger, Matthias Frehner, and Rainer Lawicki, eds., *Liechtenstein: Die Fürstlichen Sammlungen*, exh. cat. Kunstmuseum Bern (Munich, 2016).

Exh. cat. Graz 1992
Peter Weibel and Christa Steinle, eds., *Identität: Differenz. Tribüne Trigon 1940–1990: Eine Topografie der Moderne*, exh. cat. steirischer herbst 92, Graz (Vienna/Cologne/Weimar, 1992).

Exh. cat. Krems 2021
Christian Bauer and Brigitte Borchhardt-Birbaumer, eds., *Aufbrüche: Künstlerinnen des Art Club*, exh. cat. Landesgalerie Krems (Cologne, 2021).

Exh. cat. Rome 1911
Internationale Kunstausstellung Rom 1911: Österreichischer Pavillon, exh. cat. Austrian Pavilion at the Esposizione Internazionale di Belle Arti, Rome (Vienna, 1911).

Exh. cat. Salzburg 1948
Karl Garzarolli-Thurnlackh, ed., *Österreichs Barockkunst: Malerei und Plastik*, exh. cat. Österreichische Galerie (Austrian Gallery), Vienna, in the state rooms of Salzburg Residenz (Salzburg, 1948).

Exh. cat. Turin 2012
Carla Enrica Spantigati, ed., *Le raccolte del principe Eugenio condottiero e intellettuale. Collezionismo tra Vienna, Parigi e Torino nel primo Settecento*, exh. cat. Reggia di Venaria,

Turin (Cinisello Balsamo, 2012).

Exh. cat. Vienna 1921
Carl Moll: Eine Auswahl aus seinem Werke anlässlich der Vollendung seines 60. Lebensjahres, exh. cat. Künstlerhaus, Vienna (Vienna, 1921).

Exh. cat. Vienna 1941
Neuerwerbungen der Österreichischen Galerie in Wien (Vienna, 1941).

Exh. cat. Vienna 1942
Neuerwerbungen der Österreichischen Galerie in Wien (Vienna, 1942).

Exh. cat. Vienna 1946
Alfred Stix, ed., *Österreichische Kunst vom Mittelalter bis zur Gegenwart*, exh. cat. Staatliches Kunstgewerbemuseum, Vienna (Vienna, 1946).

Exh. cat. Vienna 1950
Karl Garzarolli-Thurnlackh and Fritz Novotny, eds., *Katalog der Gedächtnisausstellung Anton Romako*, exh. cat. Österreichische Galerie (Austrian Gallery), Vienna, at the Akademie der bildenden Künste Wien (Academy of Fine Arts Vienna), (Vienna, 1950).

Exh. cat. Vienna 1951a
Karl Garzarolli-Thurnlackh, ed., *Europäische Malerei im 19. Jahrhundert: Ausstellung in der Wiener Hofburg*, exh. cat. Österreichische Galerie (Austrian Gallery), Vienna, at the Vienna Hofburg (Vienna, 1951).

Exh. cat. Vienna 1951b
Meisterwerke österreichischer Barockkunst, exh. cat. Lower Belvedere, Vienna (Vienna, 1951).

Exh. cat. Vienna 1951c
Neuerwerbungen 1947–1951, exh. cat. Lower Belvedere, Vienna (Vienna, 1951).

Exh. cat. Vienna 1956
Die Moderne Galerie des Kunsthistorischen Museums, exh. cat. Akademie der bildenden Künste Wien (Academy of Fine Arts Vienna), (Vienna, 1956).

Exh. cat. Vienna 1957
Klaus Demus, *Sechs österreichische Künstler der Gegenwart: XLIII. Wechselausstellung der Österreichischen Galerie*, exh. cat. Österreichische Galerie (Austrian Gallery), Vienna (Vienna, 1957).

Exh. cat. Vienna 1958
Kulturamt der Stadt Wien, ed., *Vincent van Gogh: 1853–1890*, exh. cat. Kulturamt der Stadt Wien at the Upper Belvedere, Vienna (Vienna, 1958).

Exh. cat. Vienna 1959a
Karl Garzarolli-Thurnlackh, ed., *Neuerwerbungen 1947–1959*, exh. cat. Österreichische Galerie (Austrian Gallery), Vienna (Vienna, 1959).

Exh. cat. Vienna 1959b
Hausner Hutter Leherb Lehmden. XLVII. Wechselausstellung im Oberen Belvedere, exh. cat. Österreichische Galerie (Austrian Gallery), Vienna (Vienna, 1959).

Exh. cat. Vienna 1960
Kulturamt der Stadt Wien, ed., *Paul Gauguin: 1848–1903*, exh. cat. Kulturamt der Stadt Wien at the Upper Belvedere, Vienna (Vienna, 1960).

Exh. cat. Vienna 1961
Kulturamt der Stadt Wien, ed., *Paul Cézanne: 1939–1906*, exh. cat. Kulturamt der Stadt Wien at the Upper Belvedere, Vienna (Vienna, 1961).

Exh. cat. Vienna 1962
Werner Hofmann et al., *Kunst von 1900 bis heute*, exh. cat. Museum des 20. Jahrhunderts, Vienna (Vienna, 1962).

Exh. cat. Vienna 1969
Hans Aurenhammer, ed., *Alltag und Fest im Mittelalter: Gotische Kunstwerke als Bilddokumente*, exh. cat. Österreichische Galerie (Austrian Gallery), Vienna (Vienna, 1969).

Exh. cat. Vienna 1970
Elfriede Baum, Dora Heinz, and Franz Windisch-Graetz, *Kärntner Kunst des Mittelalters aus dem Diözesanmuseum Klagenfurt*, exh. cat. Österreichische Galerie (Austrian Gallery), Vienna (Vienna, 1970).

Exh. cat. Vienna 1971
Kulturamt der Stadt Wien, ed., *Oskar Kokoschka zum 85. Geburtstag*, exh. cat. Kulturamt der Stadt Wien at the Österreichische Galerie (Austrian Gallery), Vienna (Vienna, 1971).

Exh. cat. Vienna 1973
Gert Ammann and Erich Egg, *Spätgotik in Tirol: Malerei und Plastik von 1450 bis 1530*, exh. cat. Österreichische Galerie (Austrian Gallery), Vienna (Vienna, 1973).

Exh. cat. Vienna 1980
Hans Aurenhammer, ed., *Die uns verließen: Österreichische Maler und Bildhauer der Emigration und Verfolgung*, exh. cat. Österreichische Galerie (Austrian Gallery), Vienna (Vienna, 1980).

Exh. cat. Vienna 1983
Ernst Bacher and Eva Frodl-Kraft, eds., *Glasmalerei des Mittelalters aus Österreich*, exh. cat. Österreichische Galerie (Austrian Gallery), Vienna (Vienna, 1983).

Exh. cat. Vienna 1986
Otto Mazal, ed., *Bibliotheca Eugeniana: Die Sammlungen des Prinzen Eugen von Savoyen*, exh. cat. Österreichische Nationalbibliothek und Graphische Sammlung Albertina, Vienna (Vienna, 1986).

Exh. cat. Vienna 1990
Hubert Adolph, ed., *Gustinus Ambrosi. Pläne und Entwürfe: 145. Wechselausstellung der Österreichischen Galerie*, exh. cat. Österreichische Galerie (Austrian Gallery), Vienna (Vienna, 1990).

Exh. cat. Vienna 1991
Hubert Adolph, ed., *Hans Pontiller 1887–1970: 159. Wechselausstellung der Österreichischen Galerie*, exh. cat. Österreichische Galerie (Austrian Gallery), Vienna (Vienna, 1991).

Exh. cat. Vienna 1994
Arthur Saliger, ed., *Der Meister von Großlobming*, exh. cat. Österreichische Galerie (Austrian Gallery), Vienna (Vienna, 1994).

Exh. cat. Vienna 1995
Doris Guth and Matthias Michalka, eds., *The Spring Project: 188. Wechselausstellung der Österreichischen Galerie*, exh. cat. Atelier Augarten, Österreichische Galerie (Austrian Gallery), Vienna (Vienna, 1995), n. p.

Exh. cat. Vienna 1996
Stephan Koja, ed., *Claude Monet: 196. Wechselausstellung der Österreichischen Galerie*, exh. cat. Österreichische Galerie (Austrian Gallery), Vienna (Vienna, 1996).

Exh. cat. Vienna 1997
Arthur Saliger, ed., *Conrad Laib*, exh. cat. Österreichische Galerie (Austrian Gallery), Vienna (Vienna, 1997).

Exh. cat. Vienna 1999
Michael Krapf and Almut Krapf-Weiler, eds., *Meister von Heiligenkreuz bis Elke Krystufek: Neuerwerbungen, Österreichische Galerie Belvedere, 1992–1999*, exh. cat. Österreichische Galerie (Austrian Gallery), Vienna (Vienna, 1999).

Exh. cat. Vienna 2001
Erika Patka and Gabriela Nagler, eds., *Farbenlust und Formgedanken: Abstrakte Wege in Österreich 1900–2000*, exh. cat. Frauenbad, Baden bei Wien; Alpen-Adria-Galerie, Klagenfurt; University of Applied Arts Vienna, Heiligenkreuzerhof (Vienna, 2001).

Exh. cat. Vienna 2006
Gerbert Frodl and Adolf Krischanitz, eds., *Kunst fürs 20er Haus. 20er Haus für die Kunst: Aus der Sammlung des 20. Jahrhunderts der Österreichischen Galerie Belvedere*, exh. cat. Österreichische Galerie Belvedere, Vienna (Vienna, 2006).

Exh. cat. Vienna 2007
Agnes Husslein-Arco, ed., *Wien—Paris: Van Gogh, Cézanne und Österreichs Moderne 1890–1960*, exh. cat. Belvedere, Vienna (Vienna, 2007).

Exh. cat. Vienna 2010a
Agnes Husslein-Arco and Marie-Luise von Plessen, eds., *Prince Eugene: General-Philosopher and Art Lover*, exh. cat. Belvedere, Vienna (Munich, 2010).

Exh. cat. Vienna 2010b
Sabine Haag and Gudrun Swoboda, eds., *Die Galerie Kaiser Karls VI. in Wien: Solimenas Widmungsbild und Storffers Inventar (1720–1733)*, exh. cat. Kunsthistorisches Museum Vienna (Vienna, 2010).

Exh. cat. Vienna 2013
Agnes Husslein-Arco and Veronika Pirker-Aurenhammer, eds., *Wien 1450: Der Meister von Schloss Lichtenstein und seine Zeit*, exh. cat. Belvedere, Vienna (Vienna, 2013).

Exh. cat. Vienna 2017
Björn Blauensteiner and Stella Rollig, eds., *Rueland Frueauf d. Ä. und sein Kreis*, exh. cat. Belvedere, Vienna (Vienna, 2017).

Exh. cat. Vienna 2020
Klaus Albrecht Schröder, ed., *The Beginning: Kunst in Österreich 1945 bis 1980*, exh. cat. Albertina modern, Vienna (Munich, 2020).

Exh. cat. Vienna 2021
Björn Blauensteiner and Stella Rollig, eds., *Dürerzeit: Österreich am Tor zur Renaissance*, exh. cat. Belvedere, Vienna (Vienna, 2021).

Exh. cat. Vienna/ Naples 1993
Wolfgang Prohaska and Nicola Spinosa, eds., *Barock in Neapel: Kunst zur Zeit der österreichischen Vizekönige*, exh. cat. Kunstforum der Bank Austria, Vienna; Castel Sant'Elmo, Naples (Milan, 1993).

Fischer 2013a
Nora Fischer, "Kunst nach Ordnung, Auswahl und System: Transformationen der kaiserlichen Gemäldegalerie in Wien im späten 18. Jahrhundert," in Swoboda 2013a, vol. 1, pp. 23–89 and 168–285.

Fischer 2013b
Nora Fischer, "Zwischen Ästhetik und Geschichte: Theoretische Positionen zur Systematik der kaiserlichen Gemäldesammlung in Wien im 18. und 19. Jahrhundert," doctoral thesis, University of Vienna, 2013.

Fischer 2021
Nora Fischer, "Von der 'Augenbelustigung' zur 'dem Auge sichtbaren Geschichte der Kunst': Wege der Ordnungsfindung in der kaiserlichen Galerie 1781," in *Schöne Wissenschaften: Sammeln, Ordnen und Präsentieren im josephinischen Wien*, eds. Nora Fischer and Anna Mader-Kratky (Vienna, 2021), pp. 77–94.

Fleck 1982
Robert Fleck, *Avantgarde in Wien: Die Geschichte der Galerie nächst St. Stephan Wien 1954–1982* (Vienna, 1982).

Forsthuber 1991
Sabine Forsthuber, *Moderne Raumkunst: Wiener Ausstellungsbauten von 1898 bis 1914* (Vienna, 1991).

Fortsetzung der Gedanken 1782
"Fortsetzung der Gedanken über den Zustand der Künste in Sachsen, bei Gelegenheit der Ausstellung vom Jahr 1781," *Deutsches Museum*, vol. 2 (1782), pp. 237–62.

Fossier 1997
François Fossier, *Les dessins du fonds Robert de Cotte de la Bibliothèque nationale de France: architecture et décor* (Paris/Rome, 1997).

Friedenthal 2008
Antoinette Friedenthal, "Aus der Werkstatt des Kenners: Adam Bartsch und sein Catalogue raisonné des Lucas van Leyden," in *Grammatik der Kunstgeschichte. Sprachproblem und Regelwerk im 'Bild-Diskurs': Oskar Bätschmann zum 65. Geburtstag*, eds. Hubert Locher and Peter J. Schneemann (Zurich, 2008), pp. 342–67.

Friedenthal 2017
Antoinette Friedenthal, "Marktwissen—Wissenschaft. Die Mariette, das Raffael-Œuvre für Prinz Eugen und Adam von Bartsch: Vergleichendes Sehen vom Pariser Graphikhandel zur Wiener Hofbibliothek," *Münchner Jahrbuch der bildenden Kunst*, 3rd series, vol. 68 (2017), pp. 47–84.

Friedenthal 2018
Antoinette Friedenthal, "Découverte d'un portrait de Pierre Ier Mariette/ A Newly Discovered Portrait of Pierre I Mariette," *Nouvelles de l'estampe*, no. 262 (2018), pp. 3–13.

Friedenthal 2022
Antoinette Friedenthal, "Prince Eugene of Savoy's Rembrandt Drawings: A Newly Discovered Provenance," *The Burlington Magazine*, vol. 164, no. 1430 (2022), pp. 450–61.

Friedenthal 2023a
Antoinette Friedenthal, "The Artist's Image as Overture to His Oeuvre: A Rediscovered Self-portrait by Pierre van Schuppen," *Master Drawings*, vol. 61 (2023), pp. 4–12.

Friedenthal 2023b
Antoinette Friedenthal, ed., *"La fureur de la curiosité m'emporte." Les Mariette et le prince Eugène de Savoie: Lettres d'un voyage à travers l'Europe, 1717–1719* (Paris, 2023, forthcoming).

Friedenthal 2023c
Antoinette Friedenthal, "Prinz Eugens Zeichnungen. Provenienzen und das Phänomen des bimedialen Klebebandes: Eine Typologie," in *Zeichnungssammlungen in Wien und Mitteleuropa*, eds. Christof Metzger, Stephanie Sailer, and Sebastian Schütze (Berlin, 2023, forthcoming).

Frimmel 1909
Theodor von Frimmel, "Aufzeichnungen Fügers vom Juni 1806 bis zum Oktober 1818," supplement to the *Blätter für Gemäldekunde*, ed. Theodor von Frimmel, installment III, May 1909, pp. 92–112.

Fritz 2018
Martin Fritz, "Museumsnutzungen im Großraum Hofburg und Museumsreformen von 1936 bis 1978 unter besonderer Berücksichtigung der Neuen Burg," in *Die Wiener Hofburg seit 1918: Von der Residenz zum Museumsquartier*, ed. Maria Welzig (Vienna, 2018), pp. 414–34.

Frodl 1992/93
Gerbert Frodl, "Jahresbericht 1992/1993," *Mitteilungen der Österreichischen Galerie*, yr. 36/37 (1992/93), pp. 153–225.

Frodl 2004
Gerbert Frodl, "Zwischenbilanz und 'Kritische Visionen'," in Frodl/Kräutler 2004, pp. 49–52.

Frodl/Kräutler 2004
Gerbert Frodl and Hadwig Kräutler, eds., *Das Museum. Spiegel und Motor kulturpolitischer Visionen. 1903–2003: 100 Jahre Österreichische Galerie Belvedere* (Vienna, 2004).

Fröhlich 1993
Elke Fröhlich, ed., *Die Tagebücher von Joseph Goebbels*, part II: *Diktate 1941–1945*, vol. 7: *Januar bis März 1943* (Munich, 1993).

Fuhrmann 1770
Mathias Fuhrmann, *Historische Beschreibung Und kurz gefaste Nachricht Von der Römisch. Kaiserl. und Königlichen Residenz-Stadt Wien [...]*, vol. 3 (Vienna, 1770).

Fulda/Ring/Soika 2019
Bernhard Fulda, Christian Ring, and Aya Soika, eds., *Emil Nolde. Eine deutsche Legende: Der Künstler im Nationalsozialismus*, 2 vols. (Munich/London/New York, 2019).

Furetière 1690
Antoine Furetière, *Dictionaire universel, contenant generalement tous les mots françois tant vieux que modernes, & les termes de toutes les sciences et des arts* (The Hague/Rotterdam, 1690).

Gaehtgens 2012
Thomas W. Gaehtgens, "Die Entstehung des Kunstmuseums in Deutschland in der Epoche der Aufklärung," in *Von mehr als einer Welt: Die Künste der Aufklärung*, eds. Moritz Wullen, Michael Lailach, and Jörg Völlnagel, exh. cat. Kunstbibliothek. Staatliche Museen zu Berlin (Petersberg, 2012), pp. 207–36.

Gammon 2018
Martin Gammon, *Deaccessioning and Its Discontents: A Critical History* (Cambridge/London, 2018).

Garzarolli-Thurnlackh 1957
Karl Garzarolli-Thurnlackh, "Zur Frage der Modernen Galerie," *Mitteilungen der Österreichischen Galerie*, yr. 1, no. 2 (1957), n. p.

Gauna 2011
Chiara Gauna, "M come Malvasia e Mariette: disegni, stampe e giudizi di stile tra Bologna, Parigi e Vienna," *Annali della Scuola Normale Superiore di Pisa. Classe di Lettere e Filosofia*, series 5, vol. 3, no. 1 (2011), pp. 159–203 and 285–92.

Gauna 2012
Chiara Gauna, "'La plus belle qu'il y eut au monde': la collezione di stampe del principe Eugenio," in exh. cat. Turin 2012, pp. 89–105.

van Gelder 1978
Jan Gerrit van Gelder, "Pastor Fido: Voorstellingen in de Nederlandse kunst van de zeventiende eeuw," *Oud Holland*, vol. 92 (1978), pp. 227–59.

Gilpin 1768
William Gilpin, *An Essay on Prints. [...] To which Are Added, some Cautions that May Be Useful in Collecting Prints* (London, 1768).

Ginhart 1948
Karl Ginhart, *Wiener Kunstgeschichte* (Vienna, 1948).

Gollinger 1828
Joseph Gollinger, "Die alte St. Wenzels-Kirche in Znaim," *Archiv für Geschichte*, vol. 19/20 (1828), pp. 101–04.

Gottsmann 2017
Andreas Gottsmann, *Staatskunst oder Kulturstaat? Staatliche Kunstpolitik in Österreich 1848–1914* (Vienna, 2017).

Grabner 2004
Sabine Grabner, "Die 'Moderne Schule' in der kaiserlichen Gemäldegalerie und andere Bestrebungen zur Förderung der zeitgenössischen Kunst im 19. Jahrhundert," in Frodl/Kräutler 2004, pp. 93–105.

Grabner 2013
Sabine Grabner, "Vom 'malenden' zum 'wissenschaftlichen' Galeriedirektor: Die Leitung der kaiserlichen Gemäldegalerie und die Installation der 'modernen Schule' durch die Direktoren Friedrich Heinrich

Füger, Josef Rebell und Johann Peter Krafft," in Swoboda 2013a, vol. 2, pp. 359–83.

Grabner 2018
Sabine Grabner, "Friedrich Heinrich Fügers Atelier beim Oberen Belvedere," *Studien zur Wiener Geschichte. Jahrbuch des Vereins für Geschichte der Stadt Wien*, yr. 74 (2018), pp. 33–48.

Grabner 2022a
Sabine Grabner, "Gemalt für Kaiser Ferdinand I. von Österreich: *I due Foscari* von Michelangelo Grigoletti," *Curator's Choice*, no. 1 (2022), https://doi.org/10.57836/erst-jq38 (accessed on January 4, 2023).

Grabner 2022b
Sabine Grabner, "Die künstlerischen Beziehungen zwischen Venedig und Wien zur Zeit des Königreichs Lombardo-Venetien," in *Viva Venezia! Die Erfindung Venedigs im 19. Jahrhundert*, eds. Stella Rollig and Franz Smola, exh. cat. Belvedere, Vienna (Vienna, 2022), pp. 73–83.

Grabner 2022c
Sabine Grabner, "Joseph Rebell als Direktor der kaiserlichen Gemäldegalerie," in *Joseph Rebell: Im Licht des Südens*, eds. Sabine Grabner and Stella Rollig, exh. cat. Belvedere, Vienna (Cologne, 2022), pp. 139–55.

Grabner 2022d
Sabine Grabner, "Joseph Rebells Leben," in *Joseph Rebell: Im Licht des Südens*, eds. Sabine Grabner and Stella Rollig, exh. cat. Belvedere, Vienna (Cologne, 2022), pp. 187–96.

Griffiths 1994
Antony Griffiths, "Print Collecting in Rome, Paris and London in the Early Eighteenth Century," *Harvard University Art Museums Bulletin* (1994), pp. 37–59.

Grimschitz 1929
Bruno Grimschitz, "Die Moderne Galerie in Wien," *Der Cicerone. Halbmonatsschrift für die Interessen des Kunstforschers und Sammlers*, yr. 21, no. 17 (1929), pp. 481–87.

Gröning 2021
Maren Gröning, "Fluchtpunkte der 'entarteten Kunst' in Wien," in *NS-Kunstraub in Österreich und die Folgen*, eds. Gabriele Anderl and Alexandra Caruso (Innsbruck/Vienna/Bolzano, 2021), pp. 80–89.

Gross/Brauneis 2021
Raphael Gross and Wolfgang Brauneis, eds., *Die Liste der "Gottbegnadeten": Künstler des Nationalsozialismus in der Bundesrepublik* (Munich, 2021).

Gruber 2008
Gerlinde Gruber, "'En un mot j'ai pensé à tout.' Das Engagement des Wenzel Anton von Kaunitz-Rietberg für die Neuaufstellung der Gemäldegalerie im Belvedere," *Jahrbuch des Kunsthistorischen Museums Wien*, vol. 10 (2008), pp. 190–205.

Guglia 1912
Eugen Guglia, *Das Theresianum in Wien: Vergangenheit und Gegenwart* (Vienna, 1912).

Gustavson 2012
Natalia Gustavson, "Gemälde zwischen Krieg und Frieden: Untersuchungen zur österreichisch-französischen Restauriergeschichte im Spannungsfeld des 'Napoleonischen' Kunstraubes," doctoral thesis, University of Applied Arts Vienna, 2012.

Guth/Michalka 1995
Doris Guth and Matthias Michalka, "Arbeitskonzept," in *The Spring Project: Materialsammlung* (Vienna, 1995), p. 6.

Gutkas 1985
Karl Gutkas, ed., *Prinz Eugen und das barocke Österreich* (Salzburg, 1985).

Haider 2004
Hans Haider, "Wandel und Image der Österreichischen Galerie Belvedere seit 1945," in Frodl/Kräutler 2004, pp. 79–86.

Hammel-Haider 1992
Gabriele Hammel-Haider, "'Moderne Galerie in Wien'—'Neue Galerie in der Stallburg'—Und nun?," in *Museumsraum Museumszeit: Zur Geschichte des österreichischen Museums- und Ausstellungswesens*, eds. Gottfried Fliedl, Roswitha Muttenthaler, and Herbert Posch (Vienna, 1992), pp. 189–93.

Hanzl 1998
Lieselotte Hanzl, "Die Franzensburg: 'Vollkommene Ritterburg' und 'Denkmal Franz' I'," in *Der Schloßpark Laxenburg: Ein Führer durch Geschichte und Gegenwart*, ed. Schloß Laxenburg Betriebsgesellschaft m. b. H. (Laxenburg, 1998), pp. 35–47.

Haskell 1963
Francis Haskell, *Patrons and Painters* (New York, 1963).

Hassmann 2013
Elisabeth Hassmann, "Quellen zur Geschichte der kaiserlichen Gemäldegalerie in Wien (1765–1787): Eine Chronologie zu den Aufstellungen unter Rosa und Mechel," in Swoboda 2013a, vol. 1, pp. 116–67.

Hassmann 2015
Elisabeth Hassmann, *Quellen und Regesten zur Schatzkammer, Gemäldegalerie und zu den drei Kabinetten aus dem Archivbestand des k. k. Oberstkämmereramtes: 1777 bis 1787 mit einem Nachtrag zu den Jahren 1748 bis 1776*, *Jahrbuch des Kunsthistorischen Museums Wien*, vol. 15/16 (Vienna/Cologne/Weimar, 2015).

Haupt 1991
Herbert Haupt, "Die Neuordnung des staatlichen Museumswesens," in *Das Kunsthistorische Museum: Die Geschichte des Hauses am Ring* (Vienna, 1991), pp. 73–76.

van Heerde 1993
Jeroen Bastiaan van Heerde, *Staat und Kunst: Staatliche Kunstförderung, 1895–1918* (Vienna, 1993).

Heineken 1771
Carl Heinrich von Heineken, *Idée générale d'une collection d'estampes* (Leipzig/Vienna, 1771).

Heineken 1778
Carl Heinrich von Heineken, *Dictionnaire des artistes dont nous avons des estampes*, vol. 1 (Leipzig, 1778).

Heineken 1786
Carl Heinrich von Heineken, *Neue Nachrichten von Künstlern und Kunstsachen* (Dresden/Leipzig, 1786).

Heinz 1963
Günther Heinz, "Die italienischen Maler im Dienste des Prinzen Eugen," in *Prinz Eugen und sein Belvedere* (Vienna, 1963), pp. 115–41.

Heinz 1967
Günther Heinz, "Zur Dekoration des Schlafzimmers des Prinzen Eugen in seinem Wiener Stadtpalast," *Mitteilungen der Österreichischen Galerie*, yr. 11, no. 55 (1967), pp. 69–79.

Henrichs 2021
Cäcilia Ute Regula Henrichs, "Die Moderne Galerie im Belvedere in Wien, 1903–1938," doctoral thesis, University of Vienna, 2021.

Hevesi 1903
Ludwig von Hevesi, *Österreichische Kunst im 19. Jahrhundert*, part 1: *1800–1848*, part 2: *1848–1900* (Leipzig, 1903).

Hilchenbach 1781
Carl Wilhelm Hilchenbach, *Kurze Nachricht von der kaiserl. königl. Bildergalerie zu Wien und ihrem Zustande im Jenner 1781* (Frankfurt am Main, 1781).

Hofmann 2011
Werner Hofmann, "Museen bieten Spielregeln für Deutungsspiele," in *21er Haus: Zurück in die Zukunft—Ein retrospektiver Blick auf ein Museum*, in Husslein-Arco/Rainer/Steinbrügge 2011, pp. 8–11.

Holzschuh/Plakolm-Forsthuber 2021
Ingrid Holzschuh and Sabine Plakolm-Forsthuber, *Auf Linie. NS-Kunstpolitik in Wien: Die Reichskammer der bildenden Künste* (Basel, 2021).

Holzschuh/Platzer 2015
Ingrid Holzschuh and Monika Platzer, eds., *"Wien. Die Perle des Reiches": Planen für Hitler*, exh. cat. Architekturzentrum Wien (Zurich, 2015).

Hoppe-Harnoncourt 2001
Alice Hoppe-Harnoncourt, "Geschichte der Restaurierung an der k. k. Gemäldegalerie. 1. Teil: 1772 bis 1828," *Jahrbuch des Kunsthistorischen Museums Wien*, vol. 2 (2001), pp. 135–206.

Hoppe-Harnoncourt 2012
Alice Hoppe-Harnoncourt, "The Restoration of Paintings at the Beginning of the Nineteenth Century in the Imperial Gallery," *CeROArt*, HS | 2012, https://doi.org/10.4000/ceroart.2336 (accessed on November 3, 2022).

Hoppe-Harnoncourt 2013
Alice Hoppe-Harnoncourt, "Eine ungewöhnliche Einrichtung wird zum fixen Bestandteil der kunsthistorischen Ordnung: Die Malereischule der 'Alten Deutschen Meister' von 1781 bis 1837," in Swoboda 2013a, vol. 1, pp. 91–114.

Hoppe-Harnoncourt 2021
Alice Hoppe-Harnoncourt, "Die Präsentation der 'alten' Malerei im Spiegel der

sich verändernden Kunstbetrachtung an der kaiserlichen Gemäldegalerie zwischen 1781 und 1837 am Beispiel der altdeutschen Schule und den Gemälden Pieter Bruegels d. Ä.," doctoral thesis, University of Vienna, 2021.

Hoving 1968
Thomas P. F. Hoving, "Foreword: Museums, Computers, and the Future," *Computers and Their Potential Applications in Museums* (New York, 1968), pp. V–XII.

Hüneke 2010
Andreas Hüneke, "Beschlagnahmte Kunstwerke im Atelier Ernst Barlachs: Böhmer als Händler der Aktion 'Entartete Kunst' und die Auslagerung von deren Restbeständen nach Güstrow," in *Ein Händler "entarteter" Kunst: Bernhard A. Böhmer und sein Nachlass*, ed. Meike Hoffmann, Schriften der Forschungsstelle "Entartete Kunst," vol. 3 (Berlin, 2010), pp. 73–88.

Husslein-Arco 2009
Agnes Husslein-Arco, ed., *20>21* (Vienna, 2009).

Husslein-Arco/Rainer/Steinbrügge 2011
Agnes Husslein-Arco, Cosima Rainer, and Bettina Steinbrügge, eds., *21er Haus: Zurück in die Zukunft—Ein retrospektiver Blick auf ein Museum* (Vienna, 2011).

Husslein-Arco/Schoeller 2011
Agnes Husslein-Arco and Katharina Schoeller, eds., *Das Belvedere: Genese eines Museums* (Weitra, 2011).

Ilg 1885
Albert Ilg, *Franz Xaver Messerschmidt's Leben und Werke: Mit urkundlichen Beiträgen von Johann Batka* (Leipzig/Vienna, 1885).

Ilg 1889
Albert Ilg, *Prinz Eugen von Savoyen als Kunstfreund* (Vienna, 1889).

Ilg 1893
Albert Ilg, *Georg Raphael Donner: Gedenkschrift zum 200. Jahrestage der Geburt des grossen österreichischen Bildhauers* (Vienna, 1893).

Iselt 2010
Kathrin Iselt, *"Sonderbeauftragter des Führers": Der Kunsthistoriker und Museumsmann Hermann Voss (1884–1969)*, (Vienna/Cologne/Weimar, 2010).

Jakubec 2019
Ondřej Jakubec, ed., *Karl von Lichtenstein-Castelcorno (1624–1695): Bishop of Olomouc and Central European Prince* (Olomouc, 2019).

Jesse 2015
Kerstin Jesse, "Ein Intermezzo in Wien 1947 bis 1949: Frankl und das Belvedere," in *Gerhard Frankl: Rastlos*, eds. Agnes Husslein-Arco and Kerstin Jesse, exh. cat. Belvedere, Vienna (Vienna, 2015), pp. 45–59.

Karner/Schütze/Telesko 2022
Herbert Karner, Sebastian Schütze, and Werner Telesko, eds., *Johann Bernhard Fischer von Erlach (1656–1723) und die Architektur des europäischen Barock* (Munich, 2022).

Keil 2009
Robert Keil, *Heinrich Friedrich Füger 1751–1818: Nur wenigen ist es vergönnt das Licht der Wahrheit zu sehen* (Vienna, 2009).

Kernbauer 2011
Eva Kernbauer, *Der Platz des Publikums: Modelle für Kunstöffentlichkeit im 18. Jahrhundert* (Cologne, 2011).

Kerschbaumer 2000
Gert Kerschbaumer, *Meister des Verwirrens: Die Geschäfte des Kunsthändlers Friedrich Welz* (Vienna, 2000).

Keyssler 1741a
Johann Georg Keyssler, *Travels through Germany, Bohemia, Hungary, Switzerland, Italy, and Lorraine* (London, 1757). (German original: *Neueste Reisen durch Deutschland, Böhmen, Ungarn, die Schweiz, Italien und Lothringen*, Hannover 1741).

Keyßler 1741b
Johann Georg Keyßler, *Fortsetzung Neuester Reisen, durch Teutschland, Böhmen, Ungarn, der Schweiz, Italien und Lothringen* (Hannover, 1741).

Kleiner 1731–40
Salomon Kleiner, *Residences Memorables De l'incomparable Heros de nôtre Siecle ou Representation exacte des Edifices et Jardins de Son Altesse Serenissime Monseigneur Le Prince Eugene Francois Duc de Savoye et de Piemont* (Augsburg, 1731–40).

Knickmeier 2008
Ralph Knickmeier, "Digitales Belvedere, Wien: The Museum System (Gallery Systems)," *Museum aktuell*, no. 5 (2008), *Anwendererfahrungsberichte zu Inventarisationsprogrammen* (additional download service), pp. 20–21.

Krafft 1837
Albrecht Krafft, *Verzeichniss der kais. kön. Gemälde-Gallerie im Belvedere zu Wien* (Vienna, 1837).

Krajewski 2017
Markus Krajewski, *Zettelwirtschaft: Die Geburt der Kartei aus dem Geiste der Bibliothek*, 2nd ext. rev. ed. (Berlin, 2017).

Kramář 1927
Vincenc Kramář, *Dnešní kulturní reakce a Moderní galerie* (Prague, 1927).

Krapf 1995
Michael Krapf, *Barockmuseum der Österreichischen Galerie im Unteren Belvedere. Neukonzeption der Sammlung*, leaflet (Vienna, 1995).

Krapf 2008
Michael Krapf, "Die Aufstellung der 'Sammlung Barock.' Eine Neupositionierung im Oberen Belvedere," in *Barock: Meisterwerke im Belvedere*, ed. Agnes Husslein-Arco (Vienna, 2008), pp. 17–27.

Krapf-Weiler 2004
Almut Krapf-Weiler, "Zur Neuorganisation der Wiener Museen 1919–1925 unter der Leitung von Hans Tietze," in Frodl/Kräutler 2004, pp. 159–78.

Krasa 1986
Selma Krasa, "'Imagines': Die Stich- und Zeichnungssammlung des Prinzen Eugen," in exh. cat. Vienna 1986, pp. 293–97 and 299–331.

Kubowitsch 2016
Nina Kubowitsch, "Nicht freiwilliger Entschluss, sondern gesetzlicher Zwang: Die Mitgliedschaft in der Reichskammer der bildenden Künste," in *Die Kammer schreibt schon wieder: Das Reglement für den Handel mit moderner Kunst im Nationalsozialismus*, ed. Anja Tiedemann, Schriften der Forschungsstelle "Entartete Kunst," vol. 10 (Berlin/Boston, 2016), pp. 69–81.

Küchelbecker 1730
Johann Basilius Küchelbecker, *Allerneueste Nachricht vom Römisch-Käyserl. Hofe* (Hannover, 1730).

Kugler 2004
Andreas Kugler, "Franz Martin Haberditzl—Ein Charakter prägt das Museum," in Frodl/Kräutler 2004, pp. 179–87.

Lachnit 2005
Edwin Lachnit, *Die Wiener Schule der Kunstgeschichte und die Kunst ihrer Zeit* (Vienna/Cologne/Weimar, 2005).

Le Brun 1992
Jean-Baptiste-Pierre Le Brun, *Réflexions sur le Museum national*, ed. Édouard Pommier (Paris, 1992).

Lechner 2011
Georg Lechner, "Die Anfänge der kaiserlichen Galerie im Belvedere 1776–1805," in Husslein-Arco/Schoeller 2011, pp. 68–91.

Lehne 2007
Andreas Lehne, "Die Katastrophe von Immendorf," *Belvedere. Zeitschrift für bildende Kunst*, special edition *Gustav Klimt* (2007), pp. 54–63.

Lehner 2021
Hanna Lehner, "Der montierte Künstler: Porträt-Arrangements in Klebebänden der (Frühen) Neuzeit," in *Pantheon und Boulevard: Künstler in Porträtserien des 19. Jahrhunderts. Druckgrafik und Fotografie*, eds. Annalena Brandt, Franz Hefele, Hanna Lehner, and Ulrich Pfisterer (Passau, 2021), pp. 39–65.

Lehr 1924
Fritz Herbert Lehr, *Die Blütezeit romantischer Bildkunst: Franz Pforr der Meister des Lukasbundes* (Marburg an der Lahn, 1924).

Leisching 1927
Eduard Leisching, "Gemeindepolitik und moderne Kunst: Eine Entgegnung," *Der Kampf. Sozialdemokratische Monatsschrift*, yr. 20, no. 9 (1927), pp. 418–25.

Letter from Vienna 1782
"Schreiben aus Wien über die Verdienste des Hrn. von Mechel um die K. K. Bildergalerie/Am 16. Nov. 1781," in *Miscellaneen artistischen Inhalts*, ed. J. G. Meusel, vol. 2, no. 11, contribution 4 (Erfurt, 1782), pp. 300–03.

Lhotsky 1941–45
Alphons Lhotsky, *Die Geschichte der Sammlungen. Zweite Hälfte: Von Maria Theresia bis zum Ende der Monarchie*, Festschrift des

Kunsthistorischen Museums zur Feier des fünfzigjährigen Bestandes, vol. 2 (Vienna, 1941–45).

Lillie 2003
Sophie Lillie, *Was einmal war: Handbuch der enteigneten Kunstsammlungen Wiens* (Vienna, 2003).

Lillie 2015
Sophie Lillie, "Die Gustav Klimt-Ausstellung 1943," in *Das Wiener Künstlerhaus: Kunst und Institution*, eds. Peter Bogner, Richard Kurdiovsky, and Johannes Stoll (Vienna, 2015), pp. 335–41.

Lillie 2017
Sophie Lillie, *Feindliche Gewalten: Das Ringen um Gustav Klimts Beethovenfries* (Vienna, 2017).

Lorenz 1985a
Hellmut Lorenz, "Vienna Gloriosa Habsburgica?" *Kunsthistoriker. Mitteilungen des österreichischen Kunsthistorikerverbandes*, yr. 2, nos. 4/5 (1985), pp. 44–49.

Lorenz 1985b
Hellmut Lorenz, "Barockarchitektur in Wien und im Umkreis der kaiserlichen Residenzstadt," in Gutkas 1985, pp. 235–48.

Lorenz 1987
Hellmut Lorenz, "Einige unbekannte Ansichten Salomon Kleiners aus dem Stadtpalast des Prinzen Eugen in Wien," *Wiener Jahrbuch für Kunstgeschichte*, vol. 40 (1987), pp. 223–34 and 383–86.

Lorenz 1993
Hellmut Lorenz, "Der habsburgische 'Reichsstil'—Mythos und Realität," in *Künstlerischer Austausch—Artistic Exchange: Akten des XXVII. Internationalen Kongresses für Kunstgeschichte*, ed. Thomas Gaehtgens, vol. 2 (Berlin, 1993), pp. 163–76.

Lorenz 1994
Hellmut Lorenz, "Architektur," in *Die Kunst des Barock in Österreich*, ed. Günther Brucher (Salzburg, 1994), pp. 11–96.

Lorenz 1999
Hellmut Lorenz, "Architektur," in *Barock*, Geschichte der bildenden Kunst in Österreich, vol. 4 (Munich/New York, 1999), pp. 219–302.

Lugt 1921
Frits Lugt, *Les marques de collections de dessins & d'estampes* (Amsterdam, 1921; reprint San Francisco, 1975).

Lupfer/Rudert 2015
Gilbert Lupfer and Thomas Rudert, eds., *Kennerschaft zwischen Macht und Moral: Annäherungen an Hans Posse (1879–1942)*, (Vienna/Cologne/Weimar, 2015).

Lützow 1877
Carl von Lützow, *Geschichte der kais. kön. Akademie der bildenden Künste: Festschrift zur Eröffnung des neuen Akademie-Gebäudes* (Vienna, 1877).

Mandroux-França/Préaud 2003
Marie-Thérèse Mandroux-França and Maxime Préaud, eds., *Catalogues de la collection d'estampes de Jean V, roi de Portugal par Pierre-Jean Mariette*, 3 vols. (Lisbon/Paris, 2003).

Matějček 1913
Antonin Matějček, "Moderní umění," in *Galerie v Rudolfině* (Prague, 1913), pp. 150–74.

Mayer A. 1879
Anton Mayer, *Der Maler Martin Johann Schmidt, genannt der "Kremser Schmidt"* (Vienna, 1879).

Mayer G. 2021a
Gernot Mayer, *Kulturpolitik der Aufklärung: Wenzel Anton von Kaunitz-Rietberg (1711–1794) und die Künste*, Stendaler Winckelmann-Forschungen, vol. 13 (Petersberg, 2021).

Mayer G. 2021b
Gernot Mayer, "Ursprungssuche und Identitätsfindung: Die Bilder der Burg Karlštejn und die Erfindung(en) der Kunstgeschichte im 18. Jahrhundert," in *Schöne Wissenschaften: Sammeln, Ordnen und Präsentieren im josephinischen Wien*, eds. Nora Fischer and Anna Mader-Kratky (Vienna, 2021), pp. 97–125.

Mayer M. 2005
Monika Mayer, "Bruno Grimschitz und die Österreichische Galerie 1938–1945: Eine biographische Annäherung im Kontext der aktuellen Provenienzforschung," in *NS-Kunstraub in Österreich und die Folgen*, eds. Gabriele Anderl and Alexandra Caruso (Innsbruck/Vienna/Bolzano, 2005), pp. 59–79.

Mayer M. 2012
Monika Mayer, "Museen und Mäzene: 'Jüdisches' Mäzenatentum und die Österreichische Galerie 1903 bis 1938," in *Kunst sammeln, Kunst handeln: Beiträge des internationalen Symposiums in Wien*, eds. Eva Blimlinger and Monika Mayer, Schriftenreihe der Kommission für Provenienzforschung, vol. 3 (Vienna/Cologne/Weimar, 2012), pp. 19–35.

Mayer M. 2014
Monika Mayer, "Egon Schiele und das Belvedere: Versuch einer Sammlungs- und Rezeptionsgeschichte 1912–2003," in *Die Praxis des Sammelns: Personen und Institutionen im Fokus der Provenienzforschung*, eds. Eva Blimlinger and Heinz Schödl, Schriftenreihe der Kommission für Provenienzforschung, vol. 5 (Vienna/Cologne/Weimar, 2014), pp. 299–318.

Mayer M. 2015
Monika Mayer, "'… auch die bildende Kunst muß einer neuen Blüte zugeführt werden.' NS-Kunstförderung in Wien am Beispiel des Künstlerhauses und der Österreichischen Galerie," in *Das Wiener Künstlerhaus: Kunst und Institution*, eds. Peter Bogner, Richard Kurdiovsky, and Johannes Stoll (Vienna, 2015), pp. 326–33.

Mayer M. 2016
Monika Mayer, "'Sonst verlor die Österreichische Galerie kein Kunstwerk …' Bergung, 'Entartete Kunst,' Fremddepot: Versuch einer 'anderen' Geschichte der Österreichischen Galerie 1938 bis 1945," in *Bergung von Kulturgut im Nationalsozialismus: Mythen—Hintergründe—Auswirkungen*, eds. Pia Schölnberger and Sabine Loitfellner, Schriftenreihe der Kommission für Provenienzforschung, vol. 6 (Vienna/Cologne/Weimar, 2016), pp. 175–95.

Mayer/Swoboda 2018
Gernot Mayer and Gudrun Swoboda, "Gemälde aus den Sammlungen Albani, Braschi und des Vatikans: Die Wiener Galerie als Profiteur des Napoleonischen Kunstraubs," *Jahrbuch des Kunsthistorischen Museums Wien*, vol. 19/20 (2017/18), pp. 93–133.

McKay 1977
Derek McKay, *Prince Eugene of Savoy* (London, 1977).

Mechel 1783
Christian von Mechel, *Verzeichniß der Gemälde der Kaiserlich Königlichen Bilder Gallerie in Wien, verfaßt von Christian von Mechel der Kaiserl. Königl. und anderer Akademien Mitglied nach der von ihm im Jahre 1781 gemachten neuen Einrichtung* (Vienna, 1783).

Mechel 1784
Christian von Mechel, *Catalogue des Tableaux de la Galerie Impériale et Royale de Vienne, composé par Chrétien de Mechel, Membre de diverses Académies, d'après l'arrangement qu'il a fait de cette Galerie en 1781* (Basel, 1784).

Meijers 1995a
Debora J. Meijers, "La classification comme principe: la transformation de la Galerie impériale de Vienne en 'l'histoire visible de l'art'," in *Les musées en Europe à la veille de l'ouverture du Louvre*, ed. Édouard Pommier (Paris, 1995), pp. 593–613.

Meijers 1995b
Debora J. Meijers, *Kunst als Natur: Die Habsburger Gemäldegalerie in Wien um 1780* (Milan, 1995).

Meijers 2007
Debora J. Meijers, "Christian von Mechel zwischen Kosmopolitismus und Patriotismus," in *Sammeln und Sammlungen im 18. Jahrhundert in der Schweiz*, eds. Benno Schubiger, Dorothea Schwinn Schürmann, and Cecilia Hurley (Geneva/Paris, 2007), pp. 28–46.

Meijers 2021
Debora J. Meijers, "Gnade, Vergünstigung oder Recht: Die Zugänglichkeit der k. k. Hofsammlungen in Wien und das Publikum," in *Schöne Wissenschaften: Sammeln, Ordnen und Präsentieren im josephinischen Wien*, eds. Nora Fischer and Anna Mader-Kratky (Vienna, 2021), pp. 215–29.

Meyer 2015
Véronique Meyer, "Collectors and Collecting Prints," in *A Kingdom of Images: French Prints in the Age of Louis XIV, 1660–1715*, eds. Peter Fuhring, Louis Marchesano, Rémi Mathis, and Vanessa Selbach, exh. cat. Getty Research Institute, Getty Center, Los Angeles (Los Angeles, 2015), pp. 36–44.

Miksovsky 2000
Katja Miksovsky, "Die Ausstellung als Gesamtkunstwerk: Der Österreichische

Pavillon auf der Internationalen Kunstausstellung 1911 in Rom," *Belvedere. Zeitschrift für bildende Kunst*, no. 1 (2000), pp. 64–75.

Mitteilungen 1917
Mitteilungen aus der k. k. Österreichischen Staatsgalerie, yr. 1 (1917).

Mitteilungen 1918
Mitteilungen aus der k. k. Österreichischen Staatsgalerie, yr. 2/3 (1918).

Mlnarik 1996
Heinz Mlnarik, "'Wien entbehrt dieser wichtigsten Grundlage für sein Kunstleben.' Von der Gründung einer Modernen Galerie zur Österreichischen Galerie," *Belvedere. Zeitschrift für bildende Kunst*, no. 2 (1996), pp. 38–53.

Müntz 1884
Eugène Müntz, "Lettres inédites de P. J. Mariette," *Courrier de l'Art*, yr. 4, no. 15 (1884), pp. 176–77.

Natter 2000
Tobias G. Natter, "Fürstinnen ohne Geschichte? Gustav Klimt und 'die Gemeinschaft aller Schaffenden und Genießenden'," in *Klimt und die Frauen*, eds. Gerbert Frodl and Tobias G. Natter, exh. cat. Belvedere, Vienna (Cologne, 2000), pp. 57–74.

Natter 2003
Tobias Natter, *Die Welt von Klimt, Schiele und Kokoschka: Sammler und Mäzene* (Cologne, 2003).

Neuwirth 1951
Arnulf Neuwirth, "Stosseufzer angesichts der Neuerwerbungen: 'Wo bleibt die Moderne Galerie?'," *Mitteilungen des Art Club Wien*, 1951, n. p.

Noll 1963
Rudolf Noll, "Die Antiken des Prinzen Eugen im Unteren Belvedere," in *Prinz Eugen und sein Belvedere* (Vienna, 1963), pp. 57–67.

Nossig 1893
Alfred Nossig, "Die Kunst unter den Kaisern Franz I. und Ferdinand I.," in *Kunstgeschichtliche Charakterbilder aus Österreich-Ungarn*, ed. Albert Ilg (Prague/Vienna/Leipzig, 1893), pp. 329–60.

Novotny 1943
Fritz Novotny, "Vorwort," in *Gustav Klimt: Ausstellung*, exh. cat. Ausstellungshaus Friedrichstrasse, Vienna (Vienna, 1943), n. p.

Oberleitner 2009
Wolfgang Oberleitner, *Das Partherdenkmal von Ephesos*, Schriften des Kunsthistorischen Museums, vol. 11 (Vienna, 2009).

Oberthaler 1996
Elke Oberthaler, "Zur Geschichte der Restaurierwerkstätte der 'k. k. Gemälde-Galerie'," in *Restaurierte Gemälde: Die Restaurierwerkstätte der Gemäldegalerie des Kunsthistorischen Museums 1986–1996*, eds. Wilfried Seipel and Hubert Dietrich, exh. cat. Kunsthistorisches Museum Vienna (Milan, 1996), pp. 26–33.

Passionei 1737
Domenico Passionei, *Orazione in morte di Eugenio Francesco principe di Savoja* (Padua, 1737).

Paul 2012
Carole Paul, ed., *The First Modern Museums of Art: The Birth of an Institution in 18th- and Early-19th-Century Europe* (Los Angeles, 2012).

Pénot 2009
Sabine Pénot, "Der napoleonische Kunstraub im Belvedere (1809) und seine Folgen," in *Napoleon: Feldherr, Kaiser und Genie*, ed. Matthias Pfaffenbichler, exh. cat. Schallaburg (Schallaburg, 2009), pp. 111–19.

Penzel 2007
Joachim Penzel, *Der Betrachter ist im Text: Konversations- und Lesekultur in deutschen Gemäldegalerien zwischen 1700 und 1914* (Münster/Hamburg/Berlin/London, 2007).

Perlhefter 2001
Verena Perlhefter, "Eine 'einleuchtende Einheitlichkeit'?—Hans Tietze und die Museumsreform von 1919," *Belvedere. Zeitschrift für bildende Kunst*, no. 1 (2001), pp. 60–73.

Pezzl 1787
Johann Pezzl, *Skizze von Wien: Ein Kultur- und Sittenbild aus der josefinischen Zeit* (Vienna, 1787).

Piles 1708
Roger de Piles, *Cours de peinture par principes* (Paris, 1708).

Pirckmayer 1872
Friedrich Pirckmayer, "Kunstschätze und Alterthümer," *Mittheilungen der Gesellschaft für Salzburger Landeskunde*, yr. 12 (1872), pp. 352–85.

Poch 2018
Patrick Poch, *Porträtgalerien auf Papier: Sammeln und Ordnen von druckgrafischen Porträts am Beispiel Kaiser Franz' I. von Österreich und anderer fürstlicher Sammler* (Vienna/Cologne/Weimar, 2018).

Pöllnitz 1735
Carl Ludwig von Pöllnitz, *The Memoirs of Charles-Lewis, Baron de Pollnitz. Being the Observations he made in his late Travels from Prussia thro' Germany, Italy, France, Flanders, Holland, England, etc. in Letters to his Friend* (London, 1739). (German original: Karl Ludwig von Pöllnitz, *Memoires*, 2nd ext. and rev. ed, vol. 1, Amsterdam 1735).

Porter/Zalman 2020
Austin Porter and Sandra Zalman, eds., *Modern in the Making: MoMA and the Modern Experiment, 1929–1949* (London, 2020).

Portús 2019
Javier Portús Pérez, ed., *Museo del Prado, 1819–2019: un lugar de memoria* (Madrid, 2019).

Pötzl-Malikova 2015
Maria Pötzl-Malikova, *Franz Xaver Messerschmidt. 1736–1783*, Belvedere Catalogues Raisonnés, vol. 4 (Vienna, 2015).

Prohaska 2001
Wolfgang Prohaska, "Die malerische Ausstattung des Palais unter Feldmarschall Daun," in *Palais Daun-Kinsky*, ed. Hellmut Lorenz (Vienna, 2001), pp. 125–57.

Rampley 2021
Matthew Rampley, "The Museological Landscape of Austria-Hungary," in *The Museum Age in Austria-Hungary: Art and Empire in the Long Nineteenth Century*, Matthew Rampley, Markian Prokopovych, and Nóra Veszprémi (University Park, PA, 2021), pp. 17–50.

Rampley/Prokopovych/Veszprémi 2020
Matthew Rampley, Markian Prokopovych, and Nóra Veszprémi, eds., *The Museum Age in Austria-Hungary: Art and Empire in the Long Nineteenth Century* (University Park, PA, 2020).

Rathkolb 1991
Oliver Rathkolb, *Führertreu und gottbegnadet: Künstlereliten im Dritten Reich* (Vienna, 1991).

Rathkolb 2020
Oliver Rathkolb, *Schirach: Eine Generation zwischen Goethe und Hitler* (Vienna/Graz, 2020).

Reininghaus 1987
Alexandra Reininghaus, "Kulturstaat Österreich: Die Museen verkommen," *ART. Das Kunstmagazin*, no. 6 (1987), p. 15.

Reitstätter/Galter 2023
Luise Reitstätter and Karolin Galter, eds., "Right to the Museum? 10 Insights into Museums' Concepts of the Public and Public Perceptions of Museums" (2023), https://archiv.ub.uni-heidelberg.de/artdok/7751 (accessed on October 21, 2022).

Rieger 2014
Rudolf Rieger, *Adam von Bartsch (1757–1821): Leben und Werk des Wiener Kunsthistorikers und Kupferstechers*, 2 vols. (Petersberg, 2014).

Rittershausen 1785
Joseph Sebastian von Rittershausen, *Betrachtungen über die Kaiserlich königliche Bildergalerie zu Wien* (Bregenz, 1785).

Rosa 1796a
Joseph Rosa, *Gemälde der k. k. Gallerie. Erste Abtheilung: Italienische Schulen* (Vienna, 1796).

Rosa 1796b
Joseph Rosa, *Gemälde der k. k. Gallerie. Zweyte Abtheilung: Niederländische Schulen* (Vienna, 1796).

Rosa 1804
Joseph Rosa, *Nachtrag zum Kataloge der k. k. Bildergallerie* (Vienna, 1804).

Sauer 2008
Barbara Sauer, "Der lange Weg zur Modernen Galerie in Wien," dissertation, University of Vienna, 2008.

Savoy 2006
Bénédicte Savoy, ed., *Tempel der Kunst: Die Geburt des öffentlichen Museums in Deutschland. 1701–1815* (Mainz, 2006).

Savoy 2011
Bénédicte Savoy, ed., *Kunstraub. Napoleons Konfiszierungen in Deutschland und die europäischen Folgen: Mit einem Katalog der Kunstwerke aus deutschen Sammlungen im Musée Napoléon* (Vienna/Cologne/Weimar, 2011).

Savoy 2015
Bénédicte Savoy, ed., *Tempel der Kunst: Die Geburt des öffentlichen Kunstmuseums*

in Deutschland 1701–1815 (Vienna/Cologne/Weimar, 2015).

Schaeffer 1903
August Schaeffer, *Moderne Meister* (Vienna, 1903).

Schlegel 1995
Friedrich Schlegel, *Gemälde alter Meister*, with commentary and afterword by Hans Eichner and Norma Lelless, 2nd improved ed. (Darmstadt, 1995).

Schmeller 1973
Alfred Schmeller, "Das Museum des 20. Jahrhunderts," in *Österreichs Museen stellen sich vor*, ed. Österreichisches Bundesministerium für Wissenschaft und Forschung, vol. 1 (Vienna/Berlin, 1973), pp. 36–41.

Schmidt J. 1933
Justus Schmidt, *Jahrbuch des Vereins für Geschichte der Stadt Wien*, 1933

Schmidt 2013
Birgit Schmidt [-Messner], "Die Wiener Schule der Kunstgeschichte und ihre Stellung zur Kunst des Barock," in *Barock since 1630*, eds. Agnes Husslein-Arco, Georg Lechner, and Alexander Klee, exh. cat. Belvedere, Vienna (Vienna, 2013), pp. 30–41.

Schnettger 2014
Matthias Schnettger, *Der Spanische Erbfolgekrieg: 1701–1713/14* (Munich, 2014).

schnittpunkt/Baur 2020
schnittpunkt and Joachim Baur, eds., *Das Museum der Zukunft: 43 neue Beiträge zur Diskussion über die Zukunft des Museums* (Bielefeld, 2020).

Schoeller 2011
Katharina Schoeller, "Von der Sommerresidenz zur kaiserlichen Gemäldegalerie: Das Belvedere in den Jahren 1752–1891," in Husslein-Arco/Schoeller 2011, pp. 150–63.

Schreiber 2004
Renate Schreiber, *"Ein Galeria nach meinem Humor": Erzherzog Leopold Wilhelm* (Vienna, 2004).

Schryen 2015
Annette Schryen, "Die K.-K. Bilder-Gallerie im Oberen Belvedere," in Savoy 2015, pp. 443–89.

Schütz 2009
Karl Schütz, "Joseph Rosa: Von Wien nach Dresden und zurück," in *Man könnt vom Paradies nicht angenehmer träumen*, eds. Andreas Henning, Uta Neidhardt, and Martin Roth, Festschrift für Harald Marx (Berlin, 2009), pp. 196–201.

Schütz 2011
Karl Schütz, "Gemäldegalerie und Kunstakademie in Wien im 18. Jahrhundert," in *Welt-Bild-Museum: Topographien der Kreativität*, eds. Andreas Blühm and Anja Ebert (Vienna/Cologne/Weimar, 2011), pp. 163–73.

Schwarz 2004
Birgit Schwarz, *Hitlers Museum. Die Fotoalben "Gemäldegalerie Linz": Dokumente zum "Führermuseum"* (Vienna, 2004).

Sedlmayr 1938
Hans Sedlmayr, "Die politische Bedeutung des deutschen Barock—der 'Reichsstil'," in *Gesamtdeutsche Vergangenheit: Festgabe für Heinrich Ritter von Srbik zum 60. Geburtstag* (Munich, 1938), pp. 126–40.

Sedlmayr 1967
Hans Sedlmayr, "Bruno Grimschitz," in *Gedenkbuch Bruno Grimschitz*, eds. Karl Ginhart and Gotbert Moro, Kärntner Museumsschriften, vol. 44 (Klagenfurt, 1967), pp. 175–77.

Seeger 2002
Ulrike Seeger, "Nuove ricerche sugli acquisti fatti da Carlo Emanuele III re di Sardegna nelle collezioni d'arte appartenute al principe Eugenio di Savoia," *Studi Piemontesi*, yr. XXXI, no. 2 (2002), pp. 321–39.

Seeger 2004
Ulrike Seeger, *Stadtpalais und Belvedere des Prinzen Eugen: Entstehung, Gestalt, Funktion und Bedeutung* (Vienna/Cologne/Weimar, 2004).

Sheehan 2002
James J. Sheehan, *Geschichte der deutschen Kunstmuseen: Von der fürstlichen Kunstkammer zur modernen Sammlung* (Munich, 2002).

Slavíček 1993a
Lubomír Slavíček, "Artis Pictoriae Amatores: Bohemian Baroque Art Collecting," in *Artis Pictoriae Amatores: Evropa v Zrcadle Pražskeho Sběratelství*, exh. cat. Národní Galerie, Prague (Prague, 1993), pp. 367–69.

Slavíček 1993b
Lubomír Slavíček, "Imagines Galleriae: The Černins as Collectors and Patrons of the Arts," in *Artis Pictoriae Amatores: Evropa v Zrcadle Pražskeho Sběratelství*, exh. cat. Národní Galerie, Prague (Prague, 1993), pp. 372–86.

Slavíček 1993c
Lubomír Slavíček, "Delitiae Imaginum: The Nostitzes as Collectors and Patrons of the Arts," in *Artis Pictoriae Amatores: Evropa v Zrcadle Pražskeho Sběratelství*, exh. cat. Národní Galerie, Prague (Prague, 1993), pp. 386–400.

Smentek 2014
Kristel Smentek, *Mariette and the Science of the Connoisseur in Eighteenth-Century Europe* (Farnham, 2014).

Smola 2006
Franz Smola, "Nach Klimt und Schiele: Kunst in der Österreichischen Galerie Belvedere von 1920 bis 2003," in exh. cat. Vienna 2006, pp. 26–29.

Sommer/Sternfeld/Ziaja n.d.
Monika Sommer, Nora Sternfeld, and Luisa Ziaja, eds., *Nicht einfach ausstellen. Kuratorische Formate und Strategien im Postnazismus* (in preparation).

Spantigati 1982
Carla Enrica Spantigati, "Vecchie e nuove precisazioni sulla quadreria del principe Eugenio," in *Conoscere la Galleria Sabauda: Documenti sulla storia delle sue collezioni* (Turin, 1982).

Spenlé 2004
Virginie Spenlé, "'Eine chronologische Historie der Mahlerey in Gemählden': Vorschläge aus dem Jahre 1771 zu einer Neuordnung der Dresdner Gemäldegalerie," *Zeitschrift für Kunstgeschichte*, vol. 67 (2004), pp. 461–78.

Stachel 2007
Peter Stachel, "Albert Ilg und die 'Erfindung' des Barocks als österreichischer 'Nationalstil'," in *Barock—ein Ort des Gedächtnisses: Interpretament der Moderne/Postmoderne*, eds. Moritz Csáky, Federico Celestini, and Ulrich Tragatschnig (Vienna/Cologne/Weimar, 2007), pp. 101–52.

Städel Museum 2015
Städel Museum, ed., *zum Besten hiesiger Stadt und Bürgerschaft: 200 Jahre Städel—eine Festschrift* (Munich, 2015).

Stalder 2016
Felix Stalder, *Kultur der Digitalität* (Berlin, 2016).

Sternfeld 2018
Nora Sternfeld, *Das radikaldemokratische Museum* (Berlin/Boston, 2018).

Stix 1930
Alfred Stix, "Die Entwicklung der Wiener Kunstsammlungen nach dem Umsturz," *Belvedere. Monatsschrift für Sammler und Kunstfreunde*, yr. 9, nos. 1–6 (1930), pp. 55–62.

Strebl 1968
Laurenz Strebl, "Die barocke Bibliothek (1663–1739)," in *Geschichte der Österreichischen Nationalbibliothek. Erster Teil: Die Hofbibliothek (1368–1922)*, ed. Josef Stummvoll (Vienna, 1968), pp. 163–217.

Strobl 2004
Alice Strobl, "Ausstellungsaktivitäten im besetzten Wien bis zur Gründung eines Museums österreichischer Kunst im Belvedere," in Frodl/Kräutler 2004, pp. 188–92.

Sugar 1994
Peter F. Sugar, ed., *A History of Hungary* (Bloomington/Indianapolis, IN 1994).

Sulzer 1771
Johann Georg Sulzer, *Allgemeine Theorie der Schönen Künste*, vol. 1 (Leipzig, 1771).

Švacha/Potůčková/Kroupa 2019
Rostislav Švacha, Martina Potůčková, and Jiří Kroupa, eds., *Karl von Lichtenstein-Castelcorno (1624–1695): Places of the Bishop's Memory* (Olomouc, 2019).

Swoboda 2013a
Gudrun Swoboda, ed., *Die kaiserliche Gemäldegalerie in Wien und die Anfänge des öffentlichen Kunstmuseums*, vol. 1: *Die kaiserliche Galerie im Wiener Belvedere (1776–1837)*, vol. 2: *Europäische Museumskulturen um 1800* (Vienna/Cologne/Weimar, 2013).

Swoboda 2013b
Gudrun Swoboda, "Al seguito di condottieri e marescialli: La pittura bolognese nelle collezioni viennese del Settecento," in *Bologna crocevia e capitale della migrazione artistica: Forestieri a Bologna e bolognesi nel mondo*, ed. Sabine Frommel (Bologna, 2013), pp. 129–41.

Swoboda/Prohaska 2010
Gudrun Swoboda and Wolfgang Prohaska, *Caravaggio und der internationale Caravaggismus*, Sammlungskataloge des Kunsthistorischen Museums, vol. 6 (Vienna, 2010).

Tammaro 2018
Silvia Tammaro, "Kunstagenten im Dienste Prinz Eugens von Savoyen: Ankäufe und Aufträge in Turin, Mailand, Bologna und Neapel," in *Travelling Objects: Botschafter des Kulturtransfers zwischen Italien und dem Habsburgerreich*, eds. Gernot Mayer and Silvia Tammaro (Vienna/Cologne/Weimar, 2018), pp. 89–114.

Tammaro 2022
Silvia Tammaro, "Anton Maria Zanetti and Antonio Daniele Bertoli as Agents in the Sale of Eugene of Savoy's Collection," in *Patrons, Intermediaries, Venetian Artists in Vienna & Imperial Domains (1650–1750)*, eds. Matej Klemenčič and Enrico Lucchese (Florence, 2022), pp. 125–34.

Terzoli 2021
Maria Antonietta Terzoli, "Fedeltà e emulazione: Una copia secentesca del Perseo e Andromeda di Tiziano," in *Close Reading: Kunsthistorische Interpretationen vom Mittelalter bis in die Moderne*, eds. Stefan Albl, Berthold Hub, and Anna Frasca-Rath (Berlin, 2021), pp. 308–25.

Thausig 1909
Paul Thausig, *Die erste moderne Galerie Österreichs in Baden bei Wien, 1811* (Vienna, 1909).

Thomas 1947
Walter Thomas, *Bis der Vorhang fiel: Berichtet nach den Aufzeichnungen aus den Jahren 1940 bis 1945 von W. Th. Anderman* (Stuttgart, 1947).

Thomasberger 1992/93
Edith Thomasberger, "Joseph und Anton Hickel—zwei josephinische Hofmaler," *Mitteilungen der Österreichischen Galerie*, yr. 36/37, nos. 80/81 (1992/93), pp. 5–133.

Tiedemann 2013
Anja Tiedemann, *Die "entartete" Moderne und ihr amerikanischer Markt: Karl Buchholz und Curt Valentin als Händler verfemter Kunst* (Berlin, 2013).

Tietze 1923
Hans Tietze, *Die Zukunft der Wiener Museen* (Vienna, 1923).

Tietze 1924a
Hans Tietze, "Die Umgestaltung der Wiener Museen," *Das Kunstblatt. Sonderheft Das Neue Wien*, no. 4 (April 1924), pp. 120–23, and *Das Kunstblatt*, no. 5 (May 1924), pp. 149–53.

Tietze 1924b
Hans Tietze, "Das Wiener Barockmuseum," *Kunst und Künstler*, vol. XXII (1924), pp. 66–72.

Tietze 1925
Hans Tietze, "Die Galerie des 19. Jahrhunderts in Wien," *Der Cicerone. Halbmonatsschrift für die Interessen des Kunstforschers und Sammlers*, yr. 17, no. 1 (1925), pp. 22–31.

Tietze-Conrat 1923
Erica Tietze-Conrat, "Das Österreichische Barockmuseum in Wien," *Belvedere. Illustrierte Zeitschrift für Kunstsammler*, vol. 3 (1923), pp. 166–71.

Trautwein 1997
Robert Trautwein, *Geschichte der Kunstbetrachtung: Von der Norm zur Freiheit des Blicks* (Cologne, 1997).

Urban/Rechberger 2011
Bettina Urban and Manuela Rechberger, "Die Anfänge der Restaurierwerkstätten im Belvedere 1781–1891," in Husslein-Arco/Schoeller 2011, pp. 139–47.

Vergo 1989
Peter Vergo, ed., *The New Museology* (London, 1989).

Vlnas 1994
Vít Vlnas, "Moderní galerie jako nedokončená diskuse," in *Moderní galerie tenkrát 1902–1942*, eds. Roman Musil et al. (Prague, 1994), pp. 7–13.

Voggeneder/Borchhardt-Birbaumer 2019
Elisabeth Voggeneder and Brigitte Borchhardt-Birbaumer, eds., *Werner Hofmann prospektiv* (Cologne, 2019).

Völkel 2007
Michaela Völkel, *Schloßbesichtigungen in der Frühen Neuzeit: Ein Beitrag zur Frage nach der Öffentlichkeit höfischer Repräsentation* (Munich/Berlin, 2007).

Walderdorff 2008
Imma Walderdorff, "Rekonstruktion der Gemäldesammlung des Erzstiftes Salzburg," in *Erzbischof Guidobald Graf von Thun 1654–1668: Ein Bauherr für die Zukunft*, ed. Roswitha Juffinger, exh. cat. Residenzgalerie Salzburg (Salzburg, 2008), pp. 327–439.

Weidinger n. d.
Leonhard Weidinger, "From Vienna to New York: On the Migration of Dealers, Collectors, and Artworks," in *20 Jahre Arbeitskreis Provenienzforschung* (in preparation).

Weidinger 2017
Leonhard Weidinger, "'... nicht allein mit Geschmack zusammengebrachte Einrichtungsstücke.' Wohnungsauktionen in Wien zwischen 1930 und 1940," in *Markt und Macht: Der Kunsthandel im "Dritten Reich,"* eds. Uwe Fleckner, Thomas W. Gaehtgens, and Christian Huemer, Schriften der Forschungsstelle "Entartete Kunst," vol. 12 (Berlin/Boston, 2017), pp. 253–90.

Wendland 1999
Ulrike Wendland, *Biographisches Handbuch deutschsprachiger Kunsthistoriker im Exil* (Munich, 1999), part 2, pp. 630–35.

Wezel 1783
Johann Karl Wezel, "Auszüge aus Briefen: Wien, den 15. Dez. 1782," *Deutsches Museum*, vol. 1 (1783), pp. 182–85.

Wieser 1968
Walter G. Wieser, "Die Hofbibliothek in der Epoche der beiden van Swieten (1739–1803)," in *Geschichte der Österreichischen Nationalbibliothek. Erster Teil: Die Hofbibliothek (1368–1922)*, ed. Josef Stummvoll (Vienna, 1968), pp. 219–323.

Wieser 1986
Walter G. Wieser, "Die Bildnissammlung des Prinzen Eugen," in exh. cat. Vienna 1986, pp. 273–75 and 277–90.

Winkler/Kieslinger 1926/27
Ernst Winkler and Franz Kieslinger, "Archa z kaple svatováclavské ve Znojmě," *Památky archeologické*, vol. 35 (1926/27), pp. 398–403.

Witt-Dörring 2006
Christian Witt-Dörring, "Materielle Zeugen auf dem Weg vom Barock zur Aufklärung," in *Mozart: Experiment Aufklärung im Wien des ausgehenden 18. Jahrhunderts*, ed. Herbert Lachmayer (Ostfildern-Ruit, 2006), pp. 87–93.

Wüthrich 1956
Lucas Heinrich Wüthrich, *Christian von Mechel: Leben und Werk eines Basler Kupferstechers und Kunsthändlers (1735–1817)*, (Basel/Stuttgart, 1956).

Zaunschirm 2001
Thomas Zaunschirm, "Die Krise der fünfziger Jahre," in *Sphingen, bunte Kühe und eine Ente* (Essen, 2001).

Zeising 2013
Andreas Zeising, "Rembrandt vor dem Mikrofon," in *Teilhabe am Schönen: Kunstgeschichte und Volksbildung*, eds. Joseph Imorde and Andreas Zeising (Weimar, 2013), pp. 85–114.

Zuschlag 1995
Christoph Zuschlag, *"Entartete Kunst": Ausstellungsstrategien im Nazi-Deutschland* (Worms, 1995) https://doi.org/10.11588/diglit.52006 (accessed on January 4, 2023).

Zuschlag 2016
Christoph Zuschlag, "'Freiwillige' Abgaben moderner Kunst durch deutsche Museen nach 1933," in Baensch/Kratz-Kessemeier/Wimmer 2016, pp. 223–34.

Zuschlag 2021
Christoph Zuschlag, "'Ballast, wertlos, entbehrlich.' Wie sich das Schlesische Museum der bildenden Künste in Breslau 1942 eines Bildes von Max Liebermann entledigte und wie sich dies in die Deakzessionen moderner Kunst in deutschen Museen während der NS-Zeit einfügt," in *"Entartete Kunst" in Breslau, Stettin und Königsberg*, eds. Meike Hoffmann and Andreas Hüneke (Paderborn, 2021), pp. 71–82 (English translation pp. 83–94).

Zuschlag 2022a
Christoph Zuschlag, *Einführung in die Provenienzforschung: Wie die Herkunft von Kulturgut entschlüsselt wird* (Munich, 2022).

Zuschlag 2022b
Christoph Zuschlag, "Die NS-Kampagne 'Entartete Kunst': Hintergründe, Begriffe, Stationen und Folgen," in *Zerrissene Moderne: Die Basler Ankäufe "entarteter" Kunst*, eds. Eva Reifert and Tessa Rosebrock, exh. cat. Kunstmuseum Basel (Ostfildern, 2022), pp. 29–54.

Index of Names

Page numbers in **bold** refer to figures and page numbers followed by "n" to the corresponding endnote.

Authors

Johanna Aufreiter
Johanna Aufreiter studied German philology and art history at the University of Graz and worked as a lecturer and university assistant at its Institute of Art History until 2013, when she transferred to the University of Vienna to lead the Laboratory for Cognitive Research in Art History (CReA). In 2017 she completed her doctorate on the topic of optical theories in the Middle Ages and, since 2018, has been working at the Belvedere Research Center and is a member of the committee for the Belvedere's annual conference "The Art Museum in the Digital Age." Her research focuses on optical theories, cognitive research, and digital art history, as well as medieval art. In addition to her work as a lecturer and author, she regularly speaks at exhibition openings.

Björn Blauensteiner
Björn Blauensteiner studied law and art history in Vienna, Utrecht, Berlin, and Frankfurt. From 2008 to 2010 he was a fellow at the IFK International Research Center for Cultural Studies and from 2010 to 2015 research assistant and curator at the Picture Gallery of the Kunsthistorisches Museum Vienna. Since 2016, he has been in charge of the Study Collection Middle Ages and Renaissance at the Belvedere, where he curated the exhibitions *Rueland Frueauf the Elder and his Circle* (2017) and *The Age of Dürer: Austria at the Gate of the Renaissance* (2021). His research focuses on northern Alpine art in the fifteenth and sixteenth centuries.

Brigitte Borchhardt-Birbaumer
Brigitte Borchhardt-Birbaumer studied painting and graphic design at the University of Applied Arts Vienna, and art history, archaeology, and Byzantine studies at the University of Vienna. She works as an art historian, journalist, and exhibition curator in Vienna, Munich, Passau, Ulm, St. Pölten, and Krems, as well as teaching at the University of Vienna, the Academy of Fine Arts Vienna, and the Max Reinhardt Seminar, Vienna. She lectures internationally and has produced numerous publications and contributions to exhibition catalogues. She received the Art Critic Award in 2007 and is a jury and advisory board member for several institutions and museums. Since 2009 she has been a member of the board of directors at the Kunsthistorisches Museum Vienna.

Thomas DaCosta Kaufmann
Thomas DaCosta Kaufmann is Frederick Marquand Professor of Art and Archeology at Princeton University and an internationally renowned expert in early modern Central European art. He researches European art between 1500 and 1800 in its global context and has made significant contributions to recent discussions on world art history. He has published over 250 essays and reviews, as well as fourteen books, and is the editor of five more. He has received numerous honorary doctorates and awards, including the Mitchell Prize for best art history publication. He was fellow of the American Academy in Rome and Berlin and the Netherlands Institute for Advanced Studies, and is a member of the Swedish, Polish, Latvian, and Flemish Academies of Science. He is currently working on a biography of Rudolph II.

Christiane Erharter
Christiane Erharter studied painting and graphic arts under Gunter Damisch at the Academy of Fine Arts Vienna and postgraduate critical studies at the Malmö Art Academy, Lund University. Since 2018, she has been curator for Community Outreach and Public Program at the Belvedere. She previously worked as a curator and project manager for the ERSTE Foundation in Vienna (2006–17), at the Office for Contemporary Art Norway in Oslo (2002–06), and as deputy director of the Galerie im Taxispalais in Innsbruck (2000–02). Publications include: *Extending the Dialogue: Essays by Igor Zabel Award Laureates, Grant Recipients, and Jury Members, 2008–2014* (2016); *Pink Labor on Golden Streets: Queer Art Practices* (2015).

Nora Fischer
Nora Fischer is an art historian based in Vienna. Before and after completing her doctoral thesis in 2013, she worked on a wide variety of research projects for the Da Ponte Institute Vienna, the Kunsthistorisches Museum, the Institute for Habsburg and Balkan Studies (IHB) at the Austrian Academy of Sciences, and the Austrian Centre for Digital Humanities, including "Bildertausch Florenz – Wien 1792–1821," "Zur Geburt der Kunstgeschichte aus dem Geist des Museums," and "Das Wien[n]erische Diarium: Digitaler Datenschatz für die geisteswissenschaftlichen Disziplinen." In 2021 she published (with Anna Mader-Kratky) the conference proceedings *Schöne Wissenschaften: Sammeln, Ordnen und Präsentieren im josephinischen Wien* for the IHB. Her research focuses on collections history, the organization and presentation of art in the early modern period, and the history of science.

Anna Frasca-Rath
Anna Frasca-Rath is an art historian with research interests in the European art history of the early modern and modern period, with particular focus on the social history of artists, transnational exchange processes in the arts, and discourses of materials and materiality. After studying cultural industries in Passau and Florence, she completed her doctorate in 2015 at the University of Vienna. Since then, she has curated several exhibitions, including at the Royal Academy of Arts in London. She is a research associate at the Institute of Art History of the University of Erlangen-Nuremberg. From 2020 to 2022 she was involved in the research project "Right to the Museum?" at the University of Vienna.

Antoinette Friedenthal
Antoinette Friedenthal is an independent art historian. After studying in Heidelberg, Berlin and London (Courtauld Institute of Art) and gaining professional experience at various institutions, including the Department of Prints and Drawings of the British Museum, she received her doctorate in 1999. She has worked as a research as-

sociate at the Bibliotheca Hertziana in Rome, and, having gained her doctorate at the Freie Universität (FU) Berlin in 1999 with a thesis titled "Selbstbildnis und Künstlerbild in der italienischen Renaissance," she worked as a research scholar at the Max Planck Institute for the History of Science in Berlin (1999–2002), and as a lecturer at the FU Berlin and Bern University of the Arts. She has published widely on artistic self-image, art-dealing and connoisseurship, and the historiography of art history and science. Her French edition of the correspondence between Jean and Pierre Jean Mariette, 1717–19, is due to be published in 2023. She is currently working on a book about the origin and function of the catalogue raisonné.

Martin Fritz

After a degree in law, Martin Fritz worked as an organizer, curator, and project manager in the visual arts, theater, and film in Vienna. He then became director of operations for the reopening (1996–98) of the P. S. 1 Contemporary Art Center in New York, managing director of the art project "In Between" at the Expo 2000 in Hannover (1998–2000), and overall coordinator of the Manifesta 4 in Frankfurt (2000–02). Since then, his activities as a curator, consultant, and publicist have focused on site-specific art and the city, institutional and contextual practice, and cultural management and policy. Martin Fritz was a board member of the International Foundation Manifesta from 2001 to 2007 and in charge of the Festival der Regionen from 2004 to 2009. From 2016 to 2020, he was rector of the Merz Akademie and chair of the Württembergischer Kunstverein Stuttgart. He currently works as associate professor at the University of Art and Design Linz and has been general secretary of the Austrian Commission for UNESCO since September 2022.

Thomas W. Gaehtgens

Thomas W. Gaehtgens was professor of art history at the FU Berlin from 1980 to 2007. In 1992 he organized the 16th International Conference of Art History in Berlin and was president of the Comité International d'Histoire de l'Art (CIHA) from 1992 to 1996. In 1995 he was visiting professor and in 1998/99 European Chair of the Collège de France in Paris. In 1997 he founded the German Center for Art History in Paris and was its director until 2007. From 2007 to 2018, he was director of the Getty Research Institute in Los Angeles. His research focuses on French art and architecture of the eighteenth and nineteenth centuries, American art, and the history of the museum.

Sabine Grabner

Sabine Grabner studied art history at the University of Graz and wrote her doctoral thesis on the painter Josef Danhauser. She has been curator of the nineteenth-century collections at the Belvedere since 1991. Her research focuses on Biedermeier and Neoclassicism. She has published widely on nineteenth-century art and has curated numerous exhibitions at the Belvedere, including on the works of Friedrich von Amerling, Josef Danhauser, Ferdinand Georg Waldmüller, Michael Neder, and the landscape painter Joseph Rebell. She is custodian of the Waldmüller Archive at the Belvedere and is currently working on the catalogue raisonné for Amerling.

Katinka Gratzer-Baumgärtner

Katinka Gratzer-Baumgärtner studied art history and restoration in Florence and Vienna. Since 2007 she has worked in a variety of roles in the Belvedere Archive and Research Center. As a member of the Commission for Provenance Research, she focuses on systematically researching the inventory of artworks; in her role as an archivist, she also works on cataloguing bequests as well as conducting research and writing articles for a wide range of exhibition and research projects.

Cäcilia Henrichs

Cäcilia Henrichs studied German, art history, and English language and literature at Heidelberg University from 2004 to 2010. After various roles, including as research associate for the "Material Text Cultures" series at the Collaborative Research Center 933 in Heidelberg, she completed an internship at the Staatsgalerie Stuttgart in 2018/19. In 2021 she completed her doctorate at the University of Vienna with a dissertation titled "Die Moderne Galerie im Belvedere in Wien von 1903 bis 1938." She now lectures at the State Academy of Fine Arts in Stuttgart and the Volkshochschule Heilbronn, and runs the Mediathek Schwaigern.

Alice Hoppe-Harnoncourt

Alice Hoppe-Harnoncourt works as an art historian in Vienna. After her degree in art history, she undertook a two-year internship at the Metropolitan Museum of Art in New York, focusing on the technical investigation of paintings. From 2003 to 2007 she worked as a curatorial assistant on exhibitions at the Albertina, Vienna, and as consultant on technical investigation at the Kunsthistorisches Museum Vienna. From 2007 to the present, she has been working on a variety of research projects for the Kunsthistorisches Museum Vienna, including "Katalog der deutschen Gemälde bis 1540" and "The Panels by Pieter Bruegel the Elder." In 2022 she completed her doctorate with a thesis on the Imperial Picture Gallery in the Belvedere around 1800.

Christian Huemer

Christian Huemer is director of the Belvedere Research Center. He studied art history in Vienna, Paris, and New York, where he gained his doctorate with a thesis titled "Paris—Vienna: Modern Art Markets and the Transmission of Culture (1873–1937)." Curatorial internships at the Solomon R. Guggenheim Museum and the Museum of Modern Art in New York were followed by teaching engagements at Hunter College in New York, Sotheby's Institute of Art in Los Angeles, and the University of Vienna. From 2008 to 2017 he was responsible for developing the Getty Provenance Index® databases. In this context, he organized research projects and their resulting publications, including *Markt und Macht: Der Kunsthandel im "Dritten Reich"* (2017) and *London and the Emergence of a European Art Market, 1780–1820* (2019). He is editor-in-chief for the book series *Studies in the History of Collecting & Art Markets* and managing editor of the *Belvedere Research Journal*.

Georg Lechner

Georg Lechner studied art history at the University of Vienna. Since 2009 he has been working in the Baroque Collection of the Belvedere, where he has curated the following exhibitions, among others: *Martin van Meytens the Younger* (2014–15), *Maria Theresa and the Arts* (2017), *Kremser Schmidt: On His 300th Birthday* (2018), and *Johann Jakob Hartmann* (2021). His research and publications focus on Austrian Baroque painting in general, portraiture, the reciprocity between paintings and prints, and the history of the Belvedere and its collections.

Stefan Lehner

Stefan Lehner originally trained as a kindergarten pedagogue, followed by studying history in Salzburg. He has been working at the Belvedere since 2005, since 2007 as a research assistant in the Belvedere Archive, where he is now responsible for the cataloguing of bequests. He has been involved in curating the exhibition *The Belvedere: 300 Years a Venue for Art* and has worked on numerous catalogues, including *Gustav Klimt and the Kunstschau 1908*, *Alfred Hrdlicka: Unsparing!*, *Klimt/Hoffmann—Pioneers of Modernism*, *Gustav Klimt & Emilie Flöge*, *Photographs*, and *150 Years Gustav Klimt*. In 2012/13 he studied at the Friedl Kubelka School for Artistic

Photography in Vienna under the direction of Anja Manfredi.

Gernot Mayer

Gernot Mayer is a research associate at the Department of Art History at Bonn University. He studied art history in Vienna and Venice. His research focuses on Italian and Central European art of the early modern period and the history of collecting, cultural transfer, and art patronage. His publications include the study *Kulturpolitik der Aufklärung: Wenzel Anton von Kaunitz-Rietberg (1711–1794) und die Künste* (2021) and the conference proceedings, coedited with Silvia Tammaro, *Travelling Objects: Botschafter des Kulturtransfers zwischen Italien und dem Habsburgerreich* (2018).

Monika Mayer

Monika Mayer studied history, art history, and European ethnology at the universities of Vienna and Innsbruck. She has been a research assistant at the Belvedere since 1992, and in charge of the Belvedere Archive and Provenance Research since 1998, as well as a member of the Commission for Provenance Research. She has worked as a curator and has published and lectured widely on the history of museums, provenance research, and arts policy under Austrofascism and National Socialism.

Sabine Plakolm-Forsthuber

Sabine Plakolm-Forsthuber studied art history and Romance studies at the universities of Vienna and Perugia. In 1986 she gained her doctorate at the University of Vienna and completed her habilitation in art history at the Vienna University of Technology (TU Wien) in 2000. She is extraordinary professor of art history at the TU Wien and also lectures at the University of Vienna. Her publications and research about Austrian art and architecture of the nineteenth and twentieth centuries focus in particular on women artists and architects, exhibition history and design, the architecture of the Otto Wagner Hospital in Steinhof and of Florentine convents from the Renaissance to the Counter-Reformation, the historical buildings of the Bank of Vienna and the Vienna Stock Exchange, and Nazi art policy in Vienna (together with Ingrid Holzschuh). She has been a member of the Art Restitution Advisory Board since 2022.

Georg Plattner

Georg Plattner is director of the Collection of Greek and Roman Antiquities and the Ephesos Museum at the Kunsthistorisches Museum Vienna. He studied classical archeology, ancient history, classical studies, epigraphy, and papyrology at the University of Vienna and gained his doctorate *sub auspiciis praesidentis* in Rome in 2003. His research focuses on Hellenistic and Roman Palmyra and, in particular, Roman Ephesus. He also lectures at the University of Vienna. At the Kunsthistorisches Museum he has curated exhibitions about Ephesus and Limyra, portraiture (*Talking Heads: Portrait(s) of the Kunsthistorisches Museum*, 2010), the cultural history of Vienna (*Art and Wine*, 2012), the works of the Austrian sculptor Joannis Avramidis, and, in 2014, the anniversary of his death, about the Roman emperor Augustus (*Europe's Fathers: Augustus and Charlemagne*).

Matthew Rampley

Matthew Rampley is extraordinary professor at the Department of Art History at Masaryk University in Brno. He studied German and Ancient Greek at Oxford University and in 1993 completed his PhD on German philosophy at the University of St. Andrews. From 2010 to 2019 he taught at the University of Birmingham. His research and teaching focuses above all on art and architecture in Central Europe between 1800 and 2000, contemporary art and art criticism, aesthetics, and the philosophy of art. His most important publications include *The Seductions of Darwin: Art, Evolution and Neuroscience* (2017), *The Vienna School of Art History: Empire and the Politics of Scholarship, 1847–1918* (2013), *Nietzsche, Aesthetics and Modernity* (2000). Matthew Rampley is also coeditor of the *Journal of Art Historiography.*

Luise Reitstätter

Luise Reitstätter is a cultural scientist. She teaches and conducts research on modern and contemporary art practices, museology and exhibition theory, and methods of empirical social research. After working as a curator in the international art scene, she completed her doctorate in 2013 with a study on the exhibition as a potential sphere of action in sociology and cultural studies. Since then, she has worked on numerous research projects, for instance, on rural images of longing and the updating of archive objects, language and inclusion in museums, digital art education, and commons movements. Since 2017 she has been a post-doc at the Department of Art History at the University of Vienna, where she heads the Laboratory for Cognitive Research in Art History (CReA). As part of her habilitation on contemporary and socially relevant museological practice, she is responsible for the research project "Right to the Museum?"

Stella Rollig

Stella Rollig has been CEO and artistic director of the Belvedere since January 2017. She studied German and art history at the University of Vienna and later worked as an arts journalist (for ORF, Der Standard, and others). From 1994 to 1996 she was the Austrian Federal Curator for the Fine Arts; during this time she also founded the discussion platform "Depot, Kunst und Diskussion" at MuseumsQuartier Wien. From 2004 to 2016 she was artistic director of the Lentos Kunstmuseum in Linz, and from 2011 also director of Nordico Stadtmuseum Linz. In addition to her curatorial roles, she has taught at numerous institutions.

Claudia Slanar

Claudia Slanar studied art history in Vienna as well as aesthetics and politics and creative writing at the California Institute of the Arts. Since 2014 she has been curator of the Ursula Blickle Video Archive and the Blickle Kino at the Belvedere 21, and since 2018 cocurator (together with Christiane Erharter) of the Belvedere's Public Program. She is author and coeditor of publications on contemporary art, film, and video, including monographs on the filmmaker James Benning and the artist Lukas Marxt. Recurring themes in her work include spatial theories, fictocriticism, feminist biography writing, and reenactment as an artistic-scientific practice. From 2024, she will be joint director with Dominik Kamalzadeh of the Diagonale Festival of Austrian Film.

Franz Smola

Franz Smola has been curator for late nineteenth- and early twentieth-century art at the Belvedere since 2017. From 2009 to 2017 he was collections curator at the Leopold Museum, Vienna, where he was also interim artistic director from 2013 to 2015. He regularly curates and cocurates exhibitions on international Classical Modernism, such as *Alberto Giacometti: Modernist Pioneer* (Leopold Museum, Vienna, 2014/15) and *Wolfgang Paalen: The Austrian Surrealist in Paris and Mexico* (Belvedere, Vienna, 2019/20), as well as on the subject of Vienna around 1900. He recently worked on the exhibition *Klimt: La Secessione e l'Italia* (Museo di Roma, 2021/22).

Nora Sternfeld

Nora Sternfeld is an art educator and curator. She is professor for art education at the HFBK Hamburg. From 2018 to 2020 she was documenta professor at the Kunsthochschule Kassel and from 2012 to 2018 professor in curating and mediating art at Aalto University in Helsinki. She is also co-director of the/ecm master's program in exhibition theory and practice at the University of Applied Arts Vienna, part of the core team of schnittpunkt: ausstellungstheorie & praxis and, since 2011, of the freethought platform for research, education, and production in London. In this role she was one of the artistic directors of the Bergen Assembly 2016 and has been a fellow at BAK, basis voor actuele kunst (Utrecht) since 2020. She publishes on contemporary art, educational theory, exhibitions, politics of history, and anti-racism.

Silvia Tammaro

Silvia Tammaro studied architecture and art history in Turin and Vienna. She gained her doctorate with a thesis on the emergence, transmission, and reception of the *Theatrum Sabaudiae* and the cultural exchange between Turin and Vienna. Since 2020 she has been in charge of a research project on the ambassadors from the Duchy of Savoy in Vienna, their patronage of the arts and activities as art collectors. Her other research interests include Italian art and architecture of the seventeenth and eighteenth centuries, the interconnections between literature and the visual arts, and artistic and cultural transfer between Italy and the Habsburg Empire.

Wolfgang Ullrich

Wolfgang Ullrich was professor of art studies and media theory at Karlsruhe University of Arts and Design from 2006 to 2015. Since then, he has been based in Leipzig, working as an art historian and freelance writer. He conducts research and publishes on the history and critique of the concept of art, pictorial sociology, and consumption theory. His most recent publications include *Selfies: Die Rückkehr des öffentlichen Lebens* (2019), *Feindbild werden: Ein Bericht* (2020), and *Die Kunst nach dem Ende ihrer Autonomie* (2022). He is coeditor of the book series *Digitale Bildkulturen*.

Leonhard Weidinger

Leonhard Weidinger is a historian. Since 2005 he has been provenance researcher for the Commission for Provenance Research at the MAK—Museum of Applied Arts in Vienna and has worked on a number of online projects. From 2011 to 2013 and in 2016/17 he was involved in the project "German Sales" by the Getty Research Institute, Los Angeles, and from 2017 to 2019 he worked on a number of projects for the Central Institute for Art History in Munich, where he was also a member of the board from 2014 to 2018. From 2017 to 2018 he was chair of the Arbeitskreis für Provenienzforschung e. V. (Research Association for Provenance Research). He has published widely in a variety of media and lectures at the University of Vienna. His research focus is on Austrian cultural history in the nineteenth and twentieth centuries, and digital media in the study of history.

Christian Witt-Dörring

Christian Witt-Dörring studied art history and archeology in Vienna. From 1979 to 2004 he was head of the furniture collection at the MAK—Museum of Applied Arts in Vienna, and from 1999 to 2018 curator at the Neue Galerie New York. His focus is the history of furniture and interiors, especially of the nineteenth and twentieth centuries. In addition to lecturing and teaching extensively on topics relating to art and art history, he has curated a number of major exhibitions, including *Dagobert Peche and the Wiener Werkstätte*, *Yearning for Beauty: 100 Years of the Wiener Werkstätte*, *Viennese Silver: Modern Design 1780–1918*, *Koloman Moser: Designing Modern Vienna*, *Ways to Modernism: Josef Hoffmann, Adolf Loos, and Their Impact*, and *Josef Hoffmann 1870–1956: Progress Through Beauty*.

Luisa Ziaja

Luisa Ziaja is an art historian, writer, and curator. She has been chief curator of the Österreichische Galerie Belvedere since December 2022, where she was curator of contemporary art since 2013. Since 2006, she has been co-director of the postgraduate master's program in exhibition theory and practice /ecm at the University of Applied Arts Vienna. From 2004 to 2012 she realized multi-year research and exhibition projects as a freelance curator; from 2000 to 2004 she worked at the Generali Foundation Vienna. She lectured at various universities and is the author and co-editor of numerous exhibition catalogues and anthologies, including the publication series *curating. ausstellungstheorie & praxis* in Edition Angewandte / De Gruyter. In her curatorial and discursive work, she engages, among others, with the relationship between contemporary art, society, and politics of history, as well as with the history and theories of exhibiting.

Christoph Zuschlag

Christoph Zuschlag studied art history, history, and archeology in Heidelberg and Vienna, gaining his doctorate in 1991. Thereafter he worked as assistant at the Institute of Art History at the University of Heidelberg until 1998. In 2002 he completed his post-doctoral degree (habilitation). From 2003 to 2006 he was research associate for the Degenerate Art Research Center at the Art History Department of the FU Berlin, and from 2007 to 2018 professor of art history and art education at the University of Koblenz in Landau. Since 2018 he has been Alfried Krupp von Bohlen and Halbach Professor of modern and contemporary art history at the Department of Art History at Bonn University, with a focus on provenance research and the history of collecting. His research interests include modern and contemporary art, art informel, the history of art institutions and art criticism, art and art policy under National Socialism, and provenance research.

Picture Credits

Albertina, Vienna: pp. 71 (figs. 5–7), 72 (fig. 9), 96;
Alice Hoppe-Harnoncourt: p. 135 (fig. 2);
Anna Blau: p. 291;
APA-Grafik/picturedesk.com: p. 343 (fig. 5);
Architekturzentrum Wien, Collection: p. 265;
Architekturzentrum Wien, Collection, photo: Margherita Spiluttini: p. 286, 335 (fig. 4);
Barbara Gindl/APA/picturedesk.com: p. 289;
Barbara Pflaum/brandstaetter images/picturedesk.com: p. 319 (fig. 5);
Birgit and Peter Kainz, Wien Museum: p. 293;
bpk | Bayerische Staatsbibliothek | Heinrich Hoffmann: pp. 228, 231;
Bundesdenkmalamt (Federal Monuments Authority), Vienna: pp. 73, 239;
Burghauptmannschaft Österreich, Vienna, Plan Archive: p. 99;
Centre Pompidou, 1986; Conception graphique: Marc Walter, Arbook: p. 294 (fig. 3);
Courtesy of National Gallery of Art, Washington: p. 196 (fig. 2);
Detroit Institute of Arts: p. 62 (fig. 8);
Digital image, The Museum of Modern Art, New York/Scala, Florence: p. 191 (fig. 9);
Digitized from a copy of the Dorotheum, Vienna: p. 254 (fig. 1);
Digitized from the Institute of Czech Literature, Czech Academy of Sciences: p. 177 (fig. 3);
eSeL (Lorenz Seidler): pp. 297, 351 (figs. 1 & 2), 364 (fig. 1);
Eva Würdinger: pp. 42, 364 (fig. 3);
From: *1810. La politique de l'amour: Napoléon I. et Marie-Louise à Compiègne*, exh. cat. Musée national du Palais impérial de Compiègne (Paris, 2010): pp. 25, 133;
From: *Acier Stahl Steel*, yr. 23 (March 1958)/Österreichisches Staatsarchiv, Archiv der Republik, Zl. 235624/1958: p. 326 (fig. 1);
Gebietsbetreuung Stadterneuerung, City of Vienna: p. 308 (fig. 2);
Gemäldegalerie der Akademie der bildenden Künste Wien (Paintings Gallery of the Academy of Fine Arts Vienna): pp. 189 (fig. 1), 369 (fig. 4);
Gerald Haenel/laif/picturedesk.com: p. 290;
Gianmaria Gava: p. 373 (fig. 18);
Herbert Pfarrhofer/APA/picturedesk.com: p. 332;
Historisches Museum Basel, Peter Portner: p. 116 (fig. 3);
Karl Thomas/Allover/picturedesk.com: p. 342 (fig. 3);
KHM-Museumsverband: pp. 98, 101, 117 (fig. 4), 134, 135 (fig. 3), 207, 208;
Künstlerhaus, Vienna, Archive: pp. 266 (fig. 5), 268 (fig. 1);
Kunst-Lichtbildanstalt Julius Scherb: p. 268 (fig. 2);
LIECHTENSTEIN. The Princely Collections, Vaduz–Vienna, online collections: p. 51 (fig. 3);
MAK—Museum of Applied Arts, Vienna: p. 319 (fig. 5);
MAK—Museum of Applied Arts, Vienna/Georg Mayer: p. 225;
MiC—Musei Reali, Galleria Sabauda: pp. 62 (figs. 5 & 6), 63 (fig. 10);
Michael Huey: p. 74;
Mirko Sirotek, Vienna: p. 319 (fig. 4);
mumok, Vienna: p. 326 (fig. 2);
Musée des Beaux-Arts de Dijon/Hugo Martens: p. 61 (fig. 3);
Natascha Unkart: pp. 296, 373 (fig. 17);
National Gallery in Prague: p. 177 (fig. 4);
Niko Formanek: p. 342 (fig. 2);
Nora Fischer: pp. 124 (figs. 2 & 3), 126;
ÖMSUBM: p. 365 (fig. 4);
ÖNB, Vienna: pp. 49, 70 (fig. 2), 71 (figs. 3 & 4), 85, 86, 127 (figs. 5 & 6), 142 (fig. 6), 160 (fig. 2), 162, 190 (fig. 5), 201 (fig. 5), 226, 237, 257 (figs. 8 & 9), 318 (fig. 2), 319 (fig. 3), 326 (figs. 3 & 4);
ÖNB, Vienna/Blaha: p. 318 (fig. 1);
ÖNB, Vienna/Otto Schmidt: p. 229;
ÖNB, Vienna/Rudolf Herrmann: p. 221;
ÖNB, Vienna: 397.456-A, title page: p. 72 (fig. 8);
Österreichisches Staatsarchiv (Austrian State Archives): pp. 100, 216, 224, 266 (figs. 3 & 4);
Ouriel Morgensztern: pp. 302, 306, 343 (fig. 4), 351 (fig. 3), 365 (figs. 5 & 6);
Photographic Archive, The Museum of Modern Art Archives, New York/Mali Olatunji: p. 294 (fig. 4);
Private archive/Watzek Photo: p. 370 (fig. 10);
Rijksmuseum Amsterdam, CC0 1.0: pp. 59, 117 (fig. 5);
Ritter, R 203; scan: Belvedere, Vienna: p. 214 (fig. 3);
RMN-Grand Palais (Musée du Louvre)/Adrien Didierjean: p. 62 (fig. 7);
Rudi Blaha/AP/picturedesk.com: p. 282;
Sächsisches Staatsarchiv Hauptstaatsarchiv Dresden (Saxon State Archives, Main State Archive): p. 107 (fig. 1);
Scherl/SZ-Photo/picturedesk.com: p. 245 (fig. 1);
Sculpture Collection, Staatliche Kunstsammlungen Dresden (Dresden State Art Collections)/Ingrid Geske: p. 41;
Silvia Tammaro's archive: p. 61 (fig. 4);
Techt Hans/APA/picturedesk.com: p. 283;
The Getty Research Institute, Special Collections, Los Angeles: pp. 107 (fig. 2), 108 (fig. 3);
The Trustees of the British Museum: pp. 51 (fig. 4), 109;
UC Berkeley, Bancroft Library: p. 245 (fig. 2);
UNHCR_Ina Aydogan: p. 303;
Votava/brandstaetter images/picturedesk.com: pp. 275, 277, 278, 294 (fig. 2);
Wien Museum, Vienna: p. 117 (fig. 6);
Wien Museum, Vienna, CC0: pp. 26, 70 (fig. 1), 76, 81, 151, 189 (fig. 2), 366;
Wienbibliothek im Rathaus (Vienna City Library), A-39548: p. 124 (fig. 1);
Wienbibliothek im Rathaus, A-92213: p. 264;
Wienbibliothek im Rathaus, Printed Works Collection: p. 88;
Wiener Stadt- und Landesarchiv (Vienna Municipal and Provincial Archives): pp. 233, 234;
Wiener Stadt- und Landesarchiv, Press and Information Services: p. 276;
Wikimedia, CC by 3.0: pp. 174, 331;
Wolfgang Thaler: pp. 292, 335 (fig. 4);

Unless otherwise stated: Belvedere, Vienna
Belvedere, Vienna/Image by Google 2019: p. 350 (fig. 2);
Belvedere, Vienna, photo: Carmen Müller: p. 214 (fig. 5);
Belvedere, Vienna, photo: Johannes Stoll: pp. 50, 51 (fig. 2), 91, 92, 94, 116 (fig. 1), 142 (fig. 5), 160 (fig. 3), 190 (fig. 4), 191 (fig. 8), 201 (fig. 4), 255 (fig. 3), 298, 299, 301, 304, 305, 308 (fig. 1), 309, 310, 342 (fig. 1), 343 (fig. 6), 352 (fig. 5), 368 (fig. 2);
Belvedere, Vienna, photo: Stefan Lehner/Johannes Stoll: p. 89;
Belvedere, Vienna, photo: Stefan Lehner: p. 154;
Belvedere, Vienna, photo: Valerie Weber: p. 364 (fig. 2);

P. 397 Abbreviations

Cover

Sources:
→ Architekt Krischanitz ZT GmbH, *Remodeling and Extension of the 21er Haus Vienna, SW View* (detail), 2011
→ Johann August Corvinus after Salomon Kleiner, *Elevation of the Garden Façade* (detail), 1736, Belvedere Library, Vienna
→ Johann August Corvinus after Salomon Kleiner, *Prospect of Prince Eugene's Gardens and the Adjoining Gardens of the Salesian Convent and Palais Schwarzenberg* (detail), 1731, Belvedere Library, Vienna

Archives / Institutions

→ AdB Archiv des Belvedere, Wien (Belvedere Archive)
→ BMF Bundesministerium für Finanzen (Austrian Ministry of Finance)
→ BMU Bundesministerium für Unterricht (Austrian Ministry of Education)
→ KHM Kunsthistorisches Museum Wien (Art History Museum)
→ ÖG Österreichische Galerie (Austrian Gallery)
→ ÖNB Österreichische Nationalbibliothek (Austrian National Library)
→ ÖStA Österreichisches Staatsarchiv (Austrian State Archives)
  · AdR Archiv der Republik (Archive of the Republic)
    ◦ BMI Bundesministerium für Inneres (Austrian Ministry of the Interior)
    ◦ BMU Bundesministerium für Unterricht
    ◦ ZNsZ RSthOe Zivilakten NS-Zeit, Reichsstatthalter Österreich (Nazi period civil documents, Reich Governor of Austria)
  · AVA Allgemeines Verwaltungsarchiv (archive relating to administrative matters of the Habsburg Monarchy)
    ◦ BMU Bundesministerium für Unterricht (Austrian Ministry of Education)
    ◦ FHKA Finanz- und Hofkammerarchiv (archive relating to the financial affairs of the Habsburg Monarchy)
  · HHStA Haus-, Hof- und Staatsarchiv (the House of Habsburg's main archive)
    ◦ HBA Hofbauamt (court construction office)
    ◦ OKäA Oberstkämmereramt (head chamberlain's office)
→ RdbK Reichskammer der bildenden Künste (Reich Chamber of Fine Arts)
→ UAAbKW Universitätsarchiv der Akademie der bildenden Künste Wien (University Archives of the Vienna Academy of Fine Arts)
→ WStLA Wiener Stadt- und Landesarchiv (Vienna Municipal and Provincial Archives)
→ Zl. Zahl (number)

Österreichische Galerie Belvedere
(name of the Austrian Gallery since 2000)
Short form: Belvedere

Former names:
→ Moderne Galerie (Modern Gallery, from 1903)
→ k. k. Österreichische Staatsgalerie (Imperial-Royal Austrian State Gallery, from 1911/12)
→ Österreichische Galerie (Austrian Gallery, from 1921)

Colophon

The Belvedere: 300 Years a Venue for Art

Publication

Editors:
Stella Rollig, Christian Huemer
Authors:
Johanna Aufreiter, Björn Blauensteiner, Brigitte Borchhardt-Birbaumer, Thomas DaCosta Kaufmann, Christiane Erharter, Nora Fischer, Anna Frasca-Rath, Antoinette Friedenthal, Martin Fritz, Thomas W. Gaehtgens, Sabine Grabner, Katinka Gratzer-Baumgärtner, Cäcilia Henrichs, Alice Hoppe-Harnoncourt, Christian Huemer, Georg Lechner, Stefan Lehner, Gernot Mayer, Monika Mayer, Sabine Plakolm-Forsthuber, Georg Plattner, Matthew Rampley, Luise Reitstätter, Stella Rollig, Claudia Slanar, Franz Smola, Nora Sternfeld, Silvia Tammaro, Wolfgang Ullrich, Leonhard Weidinger, Christian Witt-Dörring, Luisa Ziaja, Christoph Zuschlag
Conception:
Christian Huemer
Editing:
Christian Huemer, Eva Lahnsteiner
→ Chapter 1: Georg Lechner
→ Chapter 2: Georg Lechner, Sabine Grabner
→ Chapter 3: Stefan Lehner, Monika Mayer
→ Chapter 4: Monika Mayer
→ Chapter 5: Luisa Ziaja, Monika Mayer
Picture editing:
Eva Lahnsteiner, Stefan Lehner, Carmen Müller
Graphic design:
Marie Artaker
Design assistant and typesetting:
Kevin Mitrega, Schriftloesung
Translation (German – English):
Rebecca Law (pp. 25f., 41f., 49f., 52–63, 93f., 99f., 128–32, 135, 159f., 202–06, 209, 307f.)
Nick Somers (pp. 64–73, 118–27, 133f., 178–91, 210–14, 221–22, 229f., 240–68, 293f., 312–19, 331f., 344–48, 351f.)
Sarah Swift (pp. 356–65)
Jessica West (pp. 102–18, 136–43, 175f., 192–201, 207f., 320–30, 333–43, 349f., 353f.)
Copy-editing (English):
Betti Moser
Index:
Jutta Mühlenberg
Publication management and production:
Eva Lahnsteiner, Beba Pikall-Kotyza
Content and production editor on behalf of the publisher:
Katharina Holas, Birkhäuser Verlag, A-Vienna
Image editing:
Pixelstorm, Vienna
Printing and binding:
Gugler GmbH, Melk/Donau
Paper:
Wibalin Recycled Dusk, 120 g/m², Munken Lynx, 120 g/m², Pergraphica Timid Grey, 120 g/m²
Typefaces:
GT Super Text, Korpus Grotesk, Apoc, Lithops

This volume is published on the occasion of the exhibition *The Belvedere: 300 Years a Venue for Art*, December 2, 2022, to January 7, 2024, in the Orangery of the Belvedere, Vienna.

Curators of the exhibition:
Björn Blauensteiner, Sabine Grabner, Kerstin Jesse (contributed to the concept), Alexander Klee, Georg Lechner, Stefan Lehner, Monika Mayer and Luisa Ziaja

General and Artistic Director:
Stella Rollig
CFO:
Wolfgang Bergmann
Exhibition management and loans:
Stephan Pumberger
Exhibition production:
Sarah Kronschläger
Exhibition architecture:
studio-itzo, Vienna
Chief curator:
Luisa Ziaja
Education:
Michaela Höß
Communications and marketing:
Katharina Steinbrecher
Visitor services:
Margarete Stechl
Research Center:
Christian Huemer
Conservation department:
Stefanie Jahn

Belvedere
Prinz Eugen Strasse 27
1030 Vienna
www.belvedere.at

Printed in Austria

Library of Congress Control Number: 2023931783

Bibliographic information published by the German National Library
The German National Library lists this publication in the Deutsche Nationalbibliografie; detailed bibliographic data are available on the Internet at http://dnb.dnb.de.

ISBN 978-3-11-118631-3 (English retail edition)
e-ISBN (PDF) 978-3-11-118651-1
ISBN 978-3-11-118620-7 (German print retail edition)
ISBN 978-3-903327-46-7 (English museum edtion)
ISBN 978-3-903327-45-0 (German museum edtion)

www.degruyter.com